MATERIALISM AND MORALITY IN THE AMERICAN PAST:

Themes and Sources, 1600-1860

MATERIALISM AND MORALITY IN THE AMERICAN PAST:
Themes and Sources, 1600-1860

JOYCE O. APPLEBY
California State University
San Diego

**ADDISON-WESLEY
PUBLISHING COMPANY**
Reading, Massachusetts
Menlo Park, California · London · Don Mills, Ontario

This book is in the
ADDISON-WESLEY SERIES IN HISTORY

Consulting Editor:
Robin W. Winks

I would like to acknowledge my gratitude to my friend and colleague, Richard Steele, whose dogged criticism forced me to rethink and rewrite this book more times than I care to remember.

PREFACE

This book traces the development of a distinctive American culture through the writings of the men and women who participated in its creation. Its purpose is to provide readers—mainly college students trying to gain an insight into their own society—with the basic materials for a discussion course in American Civilization. The editor has brought two convictions to this work: that through discussion students can best re-create the issues of the past, and that to understand these issues discussions must center on the writings of the historical participants.

The development of a characteristic American outlook has been a fascinating process involving the interaction of old commitments and respected truths with the new experiences in the remarkably different environment of the New World. Often new assumptions went unrecognized until a public issue called for a statement of national policy or the definition of goals and values. Such times of decision usually provoked sermons, speeches, debates, pamphlets, essays, and books, and it is from this literature of the American experience that the following readings have been taken.

There are certain major themes in our history which form the structure for this study of American culture: the tension between liberty and equality, the conflicting demands of social goals and individual ambitions, the accommodation of dissent and diversity in democratic society, and the struggle for power between local and national governments. Important too, in giving focus to the material presented, is America's search for identity today with all of the poignant difficulties of a people seeking to reconcile their prejudices with their ideals of justice at home while trying to be both a powerful and a humane nation in the world.

These major themes are presented in chronological order so that the reader will be able to see how the decisions made at any given time were inexorably conditioned by the historical context. So too should those factors which have operated throughout the past and continue to exercise a profound influence upon the future become apparant through a careful examination of the roots of American culture.

San Diego   J.A.
January 1974

CONTENTS

INTRODUCTION

To study culture suggests that behind the reality of people living together there exists a network of ideas drawn from shared experiences which subtly weaves individual lives into one social fabric. In America this social fabric developed when the men and women who came both voluntarily and involuntarily to the New World were forced to adapt to the demands of a totally different environment. Responding to their new situation, they produced over the years a fresh reworking of the cultural heritage they had brought with them. Generation after generation confronting common human tasks with similar social skills produced the raw material of assumptions, reflections, attitudes and reactions preserved in letters, laws, sermons, diaries and polemical writings that forms the basis of this study. Our investigation of American culture from its beginning in the 17th century through the crisis of the Civil War falls naturally into two parts. The first deals with the emergence of modes of thought and behavior sufficiently different from those of England to lead to a war for independence; the second follows developments after the American Revolution when pressures arose to severely challenge the social and political arrangements of the new nation. We shall begin by looking at the historical forces which provided a unique context for the development of American culture. They are the time during which Englishmen established colonies in the New World, the absence of external controls during the initial period of settlement, and the abundance of productive resources at the disposal

1

of the colonists. Taken together, they mean that America was born modern, free, and rich.

Before the 16th century, Europe had a hierarchical social structure, a static economy, a single religious faith, and very limited knowledge of the physical world. The relations of the people to their land, their king, their master, their God and their station in life were pretty much fixed. Dominant ideas remained unchanged from one generation to the next, and the prevailing institutions reigned without serious challenge. The disruption of this ordered society constitutes the birth of the modern era. While it is not possible to say exactly what caused the transformation of medieval Christendom into modern Europe, a cluster of simultaneous developments signalled the change. In the middle decades of the 16th century, the one Christian church was fragmented into three major religious movements with many smaller splinterings. Throughout the century, men traveled beyond the known limits of the civilized world to explore the entire globe. Population growth put new pressures on existing social arrangements. A growing market for raw and manufactured goods stimulated economic enterprise. Ideas about God's creation, once believed to be eternally valid, were displaced in men's minds by explanations of the actual workings of the universe verifiable through a new scientific method. These events acted upon each other through several transitional centuries until what was medieval in European society had given way to what was modern.

By the early 17th century, when shiploads of colonists reached England's claimed latitudes in the Western hemisphere, this process of change had been going on for more than a century, and Europeans were well into their career of world domination. Sailing out from dozens of Atlantic and North Sea ports, they had turned the world into a vast resource for exploitation. When the peoples of Africa, Asia, or the continents of North and South America threatened to impede the European advance, they were subdued or enslaved. For those Europeans who stayed at home, the impact of these adventures was felt through the social dislocations caused by changes in prices, population, trade cycles, utilization of land resources, and the reorganization of labor. In order to take advantage of the new opportunities for creating wealth, men had to modify existing political and social forms to accommodate the new efforts to maximize productive resources. Bitter conflicts developed between the defenders of the old stable institutions and the champions of social change.

The English colonial empire was founded in the midst of such struggles. Those who emigrated to the colonies were intimately connected with these conflicts, but—unlike those who stayed at home where the forces for change were never able to completely erase the traces of the old—the colonists could bring only a personal memory of traditions that grew out of a venerable social order. The American colonies had no feudal past to be destroyed. Those responsible for building communities in the New World brought preferences and prejudices from Europe, but they could not bring with them the imposing monuments, the already-defined social relationships, or the vested interests to bind them—or even remind them—of long-established precedents. Born in the modern era and physically removed from its historic origins, American culture of necessity began as a new departure. The colonists tried to transplant a number of English institutions; without the supporting English environment, many of them could not survive.

America was also born free. There were, of course, governing bodies in the colonial settlements and social restraints much greater than those of the 20th century; compared to any other contemporary society, however, the English colonists enjoyed a remarkable freedom from internal control and outside interference. Preoccupied with internal problems and external rivalries, England proved to be the most lax of all the colonizing European nations. The only uniform regulations applied to the colonies were those detailed in the Navigation Acts, and these were only negligently enforced throughout most of the colonial period. This freedom from direction in most areas of community life meant that individual initiative and local government were given a free rein to shape colonial development.

Still another source of America's freedom was the diversity of ethnic and religious identities found in the colonies. While half the colonies adopted an orthodox religious position and compelled allegiance and support for it, English officials made no effort to secure a uniform establishment for the Church of England in the colonies. Indeed, religious toleration became one of the inducements for immigration, and the separate political status of the thirteen colonies permitted Protestants of various doctrinal persuasions to find or found a colony where they might live in peace. Even Catholics and Jews enjoyed a measure of toleration in certain colonies. This relaxed religious standard on the part of English authorities encouraged a variety of social experiments in the colonies. The various sectarian communities of Moravians, Mennonites, and Quakers come to mind, but there were also colonial communities built around fishing projects, the production of naval stores and—most ambitious of all—the rehabilitation of English debtors. All it took to put one of these settlements into operation were the concerted efforts of well-placed Englishmen and the opportune good will of an English monarch. Many of these colonial adventures confounded the expectations of their promoters, but even in failure their efforts contributed new elements to colonial society.

In the 18th century, ethnic diversity was added to religious variety. With a growing economy at home, influential Englishmen wanted to discourage the emigration of able-bodied men and women, so colonists seeking laborers turned more and more to the Continent for their servants. Immigrants continued to come from the British Isles, but active recruitment to relieve the colonial labor shortage was more successful in Holland, Switzerland, and the German principalities. Thus, in place of the orthodoxy and uniformity that characterized European societies, the American colonies developed a startling pluralism. Without intentionally setting out to prove new propositions about social organization, the colonists demonstrated that civil peace was possible without social homogeneity. American colonial freedom was circumstantial, but these new experiences forced the reworking of old values.

Lastly, we must consider the impact of American wealth on the colonists who were slowly developing a way of life different in significant ways from that of the mother country. Unlike the Spanish, the English found no El Dorado in their part of the New World. What they discovered instead was a means of creating wealth if they could meet certain conditions, principally the production of commodities in demand in the markets of Europe and the Caribbean. This meant that from the beginning America's economy was organized to function in the expanding trans-Atlantic commerce developed by the English, Dutch, and French. No English colony, regardless of the nature of its founding, escaped the influence of European commercial capitalism with its emphasis upon agricultural production and exchange. To participate profitably in this dynamic trade, the colonists had to respond to its incentives for enterprise, hard work, and businesslike practices. Without access to the international commerce of the Atlantic, these English outposts in the New World would have remained poor, rudimentary, and isolated. As an integral part of this growing complex of profitable exchange, the American colonies developed within a century from primitive settlements to thriving, populous colonies stretching 2,000 miles along the North American coastline.

Although America's potential wealth was turned into actual prosperity through the medium of European capitalism, there were significant differences in the two economies. In Europe, where land was scarce and people were plentiful, those few who possessed land enjoyed special social and political privileges. Even after the coming of age of European capitalism, the ownership of land continued to convey privileges and powers which no amount of success as a merchant or industrialist could match. Inheritance laws carefully preserved the land for the ruling classes; land supported the nobilities, the monarchies, and the churches of Europe. In the colonies, however, land was plentiful, and people were in short supply. Moreover, without workers the land itself was valueless. This shortage of labor kept wages high, stimulated immigration, and enhanced the status of the working man. The many possibilities for exploiting the land through the application of labor also created a demand in the colonies for slaves. White indentured servants supplied the colonial labor needs through most of the 17th century, but once England secured a dominant position in the slave trade, the greater profitability of slave labor and the increased availability of African slaves led to a rapid switchover to black labor in the colonies south of Pennsylvania. By 1750, one fifth of the colonial population was black, and the agricultural economy of Chesapeake Bay and the Carolinas was based upon slavery. Thus, given the European's willingness to enslave the African, the same colonial labor shortage which enhanced the position of the working white man led to the degradation in America of the involuntary black immigrants and their descendants.

The reversal of the traditional ratio of land to people had a profound effect upon all social relationships in the New World. Colonial land promoters—particularly the proprietors of Maryland, the Carolinas, and Pennsylvania—wishing to attract settlers, liberalized the terms of land-holding, promised religious toleration, and granted important guarantees of civil rights and political participation. Social mobility permitted the white man at the bottom to move up, but it also forced the man at the top to exert himself to retain his position. Aristocratic forms reflecting the fixed wealth of landed families could not survive in America where enterprise and dedication to work were important determinants of a man's success regardless of the social position he had inherited. The business of America was business long before President Coolidge made the comment; giving careful attention to one's affairs had become a cultural characteristic as early as the 18th century.

Colonial circumstances which rewarded independent effort destroyed the old values of an interdependent, stratified society. In European countries where wealth was controlled by a small portion of the population, the great mass of the people had neither incentive nor occasion for moving out of their servile positions. Personal ambition was confined to the men at the top of the social pyramid and those lucky and unusual few who managed to overcome class barriers. By contrast, America's many opportunities for making money led to the democratization of ambition. The acquisitive urge was liberated in America, and competition became an important force at all levels of the society. The American economy gained from the aggregate enterprise of its people, but the restless pursuit of profit that accompanied economic growth often created social instability and private anxieties. America's richness, like its modern origins and its freedom, operated in unexpected ways upon its people, but the net result was a steady differentiation from the cultural patterns of Europe.

The influence of these factors—the modern time of English colonization, the potential wealth, and the freedom from external control—can best be assessed from an historical perspective. The colonists themselves had to experience the differences in their American situation before they could form new values. This process went on unseen and undiscussed until some particular issue forced men and women to draw on their new experiences and make explicit their new beliefs. Such issues made the colonists aware that they were changing, but the freedom, abundance, and expanding opportunities of their situation muted the occasional discord with the mother country. It was only when the British government belatedly attempted to impose its full authority over the colonies in the 1760's that a crisis was precipitated which forced the colonists to come to terms with the inherent conflict between their political dependency and their growing sense of living in a distinct and independent society. Disentangling themselves from their loyalties to the mother country took time, all the more so because the colonists had always taken great pride in being English subjects. The fact that they had been unable to reproduce many English institutions and traditions did not mean that their English cultural heritage had played no part in determining colonial values. The concepts of political rights, rule of law, and representation had come to the colonies because of their English background. What the colonists had not realized until they opposed the English measures of the 1760's was that they had given these English concepts a far different emphasis.

The colonists' political vision had clearly been affected by their remarkable experiences in America. Local autonomy, social mobility, and widespread political participation were realities supporting American theories that could only find full expression in new institutions. The price to be paid for these new institutions turned out to be a war for independence. The ideas used to justify the resort to arms, although foreshadowed in Locke and current among contemporary European radicals, derived their real force from their widespread acceptance among all strata of American society. It was this unity of sentiment, ideals, and actual practices that made the Revolution possible.

Once independent, Americans were able to launch a remarkable social experiment. Explicitly rejecting the concept of society as being more important than its individual members, they began institutionalizing the liberal doctrines of political equality, popular sovereignty, and limited government. The economic opportunity and personal freedom which had been so marked a feature of life in the colonies now provided the undergirding for a new culture. In the ensuing decades, religion was deprived of all official support, government was limited to specific, enumerated powers, and the private goals of individual men and women were given a moral value far greater than that of the community. Social cohesion as it was known in older societies was abandoned in favor of personal fulfilment. The authority of institutions was displaced by the autonomy of the individual conscience.

The context of the American experiment had a tremendous influence upon these developments. In an action unique in the history of nations, three million people took possession of an immense, unoccupied domain. The acres which stretched behind the settled coastal valleys were among the most fertile in the world. Far from being overcrowded, the United States would have to attract a steady strem of immigrants to help develop this rich natural resource. Moreover, the unsettled land was owned by the government which itself was a creature of the people. In other countries freedom — when it was enjoyed at all — had been achieved by the careful balancing of rights. Restraint, respect for rules, and the careful definition of rights were essential for liberty under the law and required a strong investment of authority somewhere in the society to preserve this balance. But in America, freedom was much less a question of restraint and balance than it was of space and opportunity. Children, wives, servants, and ordinary citizens were indebted to abundance for their liberties. No strong authority was needed to constantly adjudicate competing claims for limited resources, and none was created. Thus Americans learned to enjoy freedom — even from powerful institutions. Mobility and opportunity took the place of authority as the principal devices for social control.

As the United States opened the door to a new kind of social organization, it inevitably closed the door to other human possibilities. The satisfaction of being a part of a corporate body joined by close community ties was given up for the freedom to be one's own person. The cohesion of a common faith and a common loyalty to a traditional way of life was lost.

The security of authority was traded for the opportunities of independence. Admirably suited for a nation of able, internally disciplined, and hard-working people, the system worked less well for those who were vulnerable and needed protection. The rapid extension of slavery in the early national period made a mockery of American pretentions to provide liberty and justice for all. Yet for the majority the success of their experiment in popular government was manifest everywhere in peace, prosperity, and growth. Implicit in the founding principles of the new nation was the controlling power of the majority. There compatibility between the experiences and expectations of the majority permitted the American ideals of limited government and individual freedom to sink deep roots into the national consciousness.

While this compatibility strengthened dominant American values, pressures from changing situations created new tensions. The French Revolution and the subsequent years of international warfare forced Americans to define their national purpose in relation to other people in revolt. European population growth and English industrialization led to a stepped-up demand for foodstuffs and cotton. While this encouraged the cultivation of the underdeveloped lands of the west and created a new center of power in the states which entered the nation without a colonial past, this rapid western expansion had less beneficial results. It involved the United States in a war for land conquest with her Mexican neighbor, and it promoted the spread of slavery. All of these developments called for explanations and justification of American actions which inevitably led to assessments of the "self-evident" American principles contained in the Declaration of Independence and implicit in the American faith in self-government. Most important of all, the underlying assumption that free individuals could order their lives humanely and justly without superintending institutions was put severely to the test by the Civil War crisis. Political idealism and economic opportunity which were the basis for a distinctive American society could obviously work at cross purposes, and as Americans searched for a way to resolve the conflicts between these two major cultural commitments, they were forced to grapple with the contradictions and ambiguities of their own cultural tradition.

THE FOUNDING
OF ENGLISH COLONIES
ON THE NORTH
AMERICAN CONTINENT

Chapter 1   1607-1640

The century in which England laid the foundation for her first colonial empire was one of strife and turmoil at home. Englishmen, eager to take advantage of opportunities in trade and agriculture, were insisting upon royal policies more compatible with economic enterprise. Parliamentary leaders were struggling for a share of the king's power, and the Puritan religious reformers were determined to return the Church of England to the pristine usages of the early Christian era. All of these reforming activities were part of an overall effort to remodel England. No longer could the traditional institutions of church and state contain these dynamic forces at work. At the same time those groups agitating for change were unable to prevent the severe dislocations caused by their pressure.

Both the opportunities to pursue new ventures and the upheaval that social change was causing helped promote English colonization. The one stimulated Englishmen with money to invest in New World ventures while the other set in motion a great migration of English men and women willing to make new homes across the Atlantic. The first successful English colonizing venture came from a group of investors who secured a charter from the king to establish a colony on the North American continent. In 1606, the Virginia Company of London sent out three shiploads of people and supplies under the command of Captain John Smith, and the following year these 108 men and boys founded England's first colony on a spit of land thrust into the Chesapeake Bay.

As the next twenty years of Jamestown's history was to prove, neither English entrepreneurs nor English statesmen knew much about what was involved in starting a self-sufficient colony. However, the flexibility which was to mark all English colonizing efforts eventually triumphed over the skimping and expediency of the Virginia Company's policies. The investors resident in London were agreeable to almost any program which promised to return a profit, and the men who managed the company's affairs were pragmatic in their approach. The original plan of maintaining a corporate venture was abandoned in favor of private farms. Political concessions were made to attract colonists, and a local consultive body was established. Even with these reforms, the company went bankrupt, and the king, upon advice from a special commission, revoked the Virginia Company's charter. Although establishing a self-sufficient settlement in the North American wilderness was far more of a task than the London investors had bargained for, when Virginia became a royal colony in 1626, the Virginia Company's experiments had been tested for their adequacy in the New World, and Virginia had a stable economic and social structure. Not having a strong sense of community, the colony fostered the assertive individualism associated with the frontier. Virginians, proud to live in a royal colony, were also susceptible to imitating English manners. They consciously patterned their political and religious establishments after those of the mother country, even as they improvised from day to day to wrest a comfortable living from their colonial outpost.

When George Calvert visited Virginia in 1629, the colony had several thousand people securely established along the banks of the James River. The tobacco they cultivated was the basis of their prosperity and the principal link between their primitive settlements and the mother country. Calvert, who soon became Lord Baltimore, liked what he saw in Virginia, but his Catholic affiliation made him unwelcome to the Church of England colonists of Virginia, so he returned home to solicit a charter to establish a new colony in the northern part of the Chesapeake Bay area. Successful in this effort, Lord Baltimore established in Maryland a different kind of colony, a proprietorship in which he, as overlord, exercised the powers associated with the traditional landholding forms of feudal England, his aim being to build an estate for himself and his heirs. Lord Baltimore was a Catholic and his offer of toleration to all who would settle in Maryland attracted settlers of different religious faiths and provided a refuge for any Catholics wishing to flee the increasingly militant Protestantism of England.

Maryland's first settlers profited immensely from Virginia's experience both in establishing a tobacco-based economy and in dealing with the Indians. Virginians were happy to acquire the English money Maryland colonists brought with them, and the Marylanders were fortunate to have a supply of food, building material and farm equipment available. Years later, Virginia's first native historian, Robert Beverley, bemoaned the fact that religious intolerance had forced Lord Baltimore to apply for a separate charter which thus divided the geographically unified Chesapeake Bay into two political units. The economy and society of Virginia and Maryland, as Beverley pointed out, were very much alike, but the feudal traditions Lord Baltimore tried to introduce and the problems created by a proprietorial government gave Maryland a separate identity. Like the distinctions between all of the separate backgrounds of the colonies, those between Virginia and Maryland led over the years to strong traditions of local autonomy which have remained an important part of American politics.

The colonial enterprises undertaken by the Virginia Company shareholders and Lord Baltimore and his associates were responses to new economic developments — the expansion in England's overseas trade and the growing market for commodities of the Western hemisphere. The planting of colonies in New England was the result of a different force — the irreconcilable religious differences among Englishmen. These New England colonies, however, were also affected by the general disruption of the old life patterns and profited too from the readiness of thousands of people to leave

England. Those indifferent to the great religious questions convulsing their society went to Virginia, Maryland, or the West Indian colonies of Barbados, St. Christopher, or Nevis, while English Puritans poured across the Atlantic to Massachusetts Bay and Connecticut. Different as the English colonies in the New World were, they all owed their establishment to the modern restructuring of English society which went on throughout the 17th century.

More than any other group of colonizers, the Puritans bent existing opportunities to their own goals. Most people think of these founders of New England as meek and mild people fleeing an unfriendly land where they sought only the right to worship as they pleased. This description is adequate enough for the small band of Pilgrims which settled at Plymouth in 1620, but it is far wide of the mark for the nearly 20,000 Puritans who emigrated to Massachusetts Bay during the 1630's. These outspoken critics charged the Church of England with preaching a sterile message, being indifferent to the moral laxity of its congregations, depending too much on sacraments in bringing men to God, and succumbing to the political influence of the king and his bishops. They left home not so much because they were persecuted as because they were frustrated in their efforts to reform and purify the national church of England. They did not want to be left alone to worship as they pleased. They wanted the power to tell other Englishmen what the true form of Christian worship was. They were not meek and mild, but courageous, capable, arrogant, and dedicated. Leaving England when hopes for reform were dim, they saw themselves as a kind of task force for Protestant Europe, and they expected their colony to be an example to all of Christendom. At first, the New World provided only the soil upon which they could build a community based strictly upon the Bible. It was only slowly and reluctantly, after events beyond their control isolated them, that New England's Puritans began to redefine their purpose and join their sense of mission to America and its future.

The Puritans had long nurtured the ideas they put into practice in Massachusetts Bay. They wanted above all to make men's dependence upon God the controlling fact of social and political institutions, infusing into every relationship a stern sense of God's justice and man's responsibility to him. Although like all Protestants, the Puritans fostered individualism with their emphasis on a one-to-one relationship with God, they valued the community more than the individual, for they believed that it was only through the covenanted community that God's goals could be realized. Following John Calvin, the 16th century French theologian, the Puritans believed that just a few men and women — the "elect" — would be saved from eternal damnation by God's choice, but these "visible saints" were not meant to withdraw from the world. Rather they were to be God's active agents in reforming society.

In their effort to build a covenanted Bible commonwealth, the Puritans were harking back to an older ideal, that of a corporate society which has a fundamental claim upon all its members. However, there were other, strikingly modern qualities which Puritanism imparted to its followers. The combativeness and confidence which Puritans displayed in their attacks upon the Church of England, for instance, could be useful in challenging other aspects of a traditional way of life. Their daily confrontations with God's enemies turned them into bold, disciplined activists. Puritans were free to follow the new scientific methods of inquiry and experimentation unencumbered by the forbidding dogmas of existing church establishments. Similarly, they could accept new attitudes toward trade and commerce when they were compatible with religious goals. Puritans bestowed a dignity upon work which aristocratic societies had long denied it. They considered gentlemanly leisure to be the devil's snare, whereas hard work, application to one's calling, industry, and resourcefulness were pre-eminent virtues. Obviously these qualities were well suited to a frontier life, but they were equally helpful to individuals adapting to modern capitalism with its emphasis on productivity and the rational pursuit of profit. Sanctioned by religion and reinforced by colonial experiences, the social values of Puritanism proved more enduring in the long run than the original Puritan goal of founding a Bible commonwealth.

The outbreak of civil war in England in 1642 profoundly effected the Puritan colonies. The flow of immigrants stopped, and New England was threatened by economic stagnation and physical isolation. Enterprising merchants then seized the initiative and developed an active role for New England in the intercontinental and island commerce of the Atlantic. Their success brought prosperity and a measure of independence to Massachusetts, but henceforth the churches had to compete with business for men's energies. Personal ambitions began to pull people from their commitment to Puritan goals. In succeeding decades the Puritan ideal of the covenanted community gave way, leaving behind a secularized ethos of hard work, inner discipline, and dedication to one's duty which took root in the American soil.

During the latter years of the 17th century, when the force of the Puritan movement had been spent, English efforts at colonization came from two new sources. The first source was that of English courtiers who used their influence at court to secure lucrative colonial charters. The Duke of York, King Charles II's brother and successor, acquired the vast area south of New England which had been wrested from the Dutch in 1667, while the area south of Virginia, known generally as the Carolinas, became a proprietary possession of a group of eight prominent courtiers. Like the promoters of the Virginia Company, these colonial sponsors were interested solely in finding the right formula for realizing a return from their princely estates. Their hopes for profit lay with the speedy cultivation of the land, from which they gathered quit rents, and from the sale of certain commercial privileges. Their colonial policies were directed toward attracting colonists and exploiting fully the possibilities of both trade and agriculture.

The second colonizing force of the late 17th century came from the Quakers. Like the Puritans before them, the Quakers were openly critical of English society, but unlike the Puritans they raised their voices at a time when Englishmen were sick of religious disputes. Their punishment for intruding upon the public consciousness was three decades of the severest persecution that Englishmen had ever known. The New World offered the Quakers an opportunity to put into practice the religious beliefs which were despised in England. First in New Jersey and then in Pennsylvania, through William Penn's proprietary colony, they were able to institutionalize their liberal political and social ideals. Penn himself had the peculiar distinction of being both a favored friend of the king and a dedicated Quaker. Both roles contributed to the success of Pennsylvania. Taking care to involve wealthy investors who could meet the initial costs of colonization, he also waged a vigorous promotional campaign for settlers. His close ties to the Quaker communities throughout the British Isles and Northern Europe stood him in good stead, and Pennsylvania became the fastest growing, most prosperous, and humanely conceived colony in the New World.

However, despite Penn's many virtues, the difference between the starving times in Virginia and the plenty in Pennsylvania was a measure of English colonial experience. The get-rich-quick dreams of English investors had been turned into the precious knowledge of what could and could not be done, and in the process the basis for a new departure from the old European culture had been laid three thousand miles away.

These first readings are from the records of the Virginia Company. They consist of letters to and from principal colonists and the company officers in London, along with a representative sampling of labor contracts, shipping orders, and memoranda from the King's Privy Council, covering the period between 1618 and 1626, which turned out to be critical for both the colony and its parent company.

The investors in the Virginia Company were sorely disappointed in their hopes for a return on their money. Instead of profits, the cost of establishing a few hundred Englishmen in the North American wilderness had involved more and more expenditures. Bad luck and bad planning accounted for some of the difficulties that plagued the settlers in Jamestown, but more than anything else there was a lack of experience. London share-holders optimistically expected the colonists to live off the fat of the land and devote their working time to producing marketable goods — hopefully gold and pearls taken from some English El Dorado. The fact that Spain a century earlier had happened on to the mines of Peru and Mexico whetted English appetites for a similar bonanza. Even if precious metals were not found, it was assumed that spices, sweetwoods, and tropical fruits could be prepared for speedy shipment home. Instead, the colonists found that they needed their full energies to survive, and survival itself proved too difficult for the great majority of them. Of the nearly 2,000 people sent out to Virginia after 1607, 400 remained in April of 1618. Many died en route in one particularly disastrous storm; others succumbed to the damps and diseases of the New World; many were picked off by Indians who lay in wait for the solitary hunter who ventured out of the palisaded settlement; and many died during the bleak winters of 1609 and 1610 when people actually starved to death. Dissension was the rule rather than the exception in the colony, and military discipline was

introduced. Reports of the severity of the colony's laws in turn discouraged prospective immigrants, and the colony seemed on the verge of stagnation if not actual destruction.

The most convincing reason for the company's failure was mismanagement, and with this explanation Sir Edwin Sandys, an energetic young Englishman, won control of the company. In 1618 he embarked upon an ambitious program to pump money and people into the colony to implement a variety of new projects. He also managed to secure a number of major reforms: secure title to property, opportunities to consolidate land-holdings in private farming communities, a consultive assembly for the colonists, and generous land dividends to attract new investors and immigrants. To enhance the profits of the company itself, Sandys sent out equipment and servants to make silk and wine and to manufacture iron, glass and salt. Sandys developed a new Indian policy and helped raise money for Virginia's growing population, which was spreading out along the broad, tidal rivers of the Bay.

People, supplies and equipment were poured into the colony during the next four years, only to be cut down in 1622 by a surprise Indian attack which took 357 lives in one day. Farm buildings and equipment were destroyed, leading to the death of 500 more colonists during the following winter. In faraway London, the distress cry from Virginia was badly misinterpreted, and instead of sending food, Sandys sent out more people. The massacre's survivors were strained to the utmost to keep themselves alive, and at home the company was bankrupt. After a thorough and bitter investigation, the King's advisors recommended the revocation of the Virginia Company charter, and Virginia became the first royal colony. Despite its failure, the company's legacy as a colonizing agent was sizeable. Sandy's assembly became the House of Burgesses; the private plantations of several hundred acres became the standard farming unit for another half century; land grants contingent upon the introduction of new colonists continued; and the tobacco strain developed by a company share-holder sustained the colony's economy for the next 150 years.

The selections from the *Virginia Company Records* which follow begin with the introduction of Sandys' reforms, which were announced to the colonists through the instructions to the new governor, George Yeardley. Subsequent selections follow developments in the next four years through the correspondence that went back and forth from Jamestown to London. The letters constitute a fascinating account of the evolution of Jamestown from a company town to a colonial settlement. The arrival of twenty Negroes on a Dutch ship is recorded; relations with the Indians who rimmed the fenced-in Jamestown is detailed, as is the controversy over tobacco growing. More than anything else, the exchange of letters reveals the poignant difference in perspective between the council chambers of the Virignia Company's London headquarters and the crude English outpost at Jamestown. While the officers of the Company toted up the number of farmers, vintners, ironworkers, boatwrights and brides sent out — no doubt envisioning them engaged in productive labor from the moment they arrived — those responsible for the colony's survival in Virginia desperately tried to communicate their true condition — hungry, sickened by new diseases and unfamiliar food, frightened by the Indians, overcrowded, fearful of dying, and discouraged beyond measure.

Instructions from the Virginia Company of London to the new Governor, George Yeardley, November, 1618

Our former cares and Endeavours have been chiefly bent to the procuring and sending people to plant in Virginia so to prepare a way and to lay a foundation whereon A flourishing State might in process of time by the blessing of Almighty God be raised. Now our trust being that under the Government of you Captain Yeardly with the advice and Assistance of the said Council of State such public provisions of Corn and

Susan Myra Kingsbury (ed.), *The Records of the Virginia Company of London*, Government Printing Office, Washington, D.C., 1933, III, 98-107, 153-68, 241-48, 393-94, 255-57, 262-64, 297-99, 494-95, 550-59, 622-23; IV, 174-82, 571-73.

Cattle will again be raised as may draw on those Multitudes who in great Abundance from diverse parts of the Realm were preparing to remove thither if by the late decay of the said public Store their hopes had not been made frustrate and their minds thereby clean discouraged. We have thought good to bend our present cares and Consultations according to the Authority granted unto us from his Majesty under his great Seal to the settling there of A laudable form of Government by Majestracy and just Laws for the happy guiding and governing of the people there inhabiting like as we have already done for the well ordering of our Courts here and of our Officers and actions for the behoof of that plantation. And because our intent is to Ease all the Inhabitants of Virginia forever of all taxes and public burthens as much as may be and to take away all occasion of oppression and corruption we have thought fit to begin (according to the laudable Example of the most famous Common Wealthes both past and present) to alot and lay out A Convenient portion of public lands for the maintenance and support as well of Magistracy and officers as of other public charges both here and there from time to time arising . . . And we will and ordain that all the said Tenants on the Governors and Company's Lands shall occupy the same to the half part of the profits of the said Lands so as the one half to be and belong to the said Tenants themselves and the other half respectively to the said Governor and to us the said Treasurer and Company and our Successors . . .

Our intent is to Establish . . .four Cities or Burroughs Namely the chief City called Jamestown, Charles City, Henrico, and the Burrough of Kiccowtan. And that in all these foresaid Cities or Burroughs the ancient Adventurers and Planters which [were] transported thither with intent to inhabit at their own costs and charges before the coming away of Sir Thomas Dale Knight and have so continued during the space of three years shall have upon a first division to be afterward by us augmented one hundred Acres of land for their personal Adventure and as much for every single share of twelve pound ten Shillings paid [for such share] allotted and set out to be held by them their heirs and assigns forever. And that for all such Planters as were brought thither at the Company's Charge to inhabit there before the coming away of the said

Sir Thomas Dale after the time of their Service to the Company on the common Land agreed shall be expired there be set out One hundred Acres of Land for each of their personal Adventurers to be held by them their heirs and Assigns for ever, paying for every fifty Acres the yearly free Rent of one Shilling . . . We do therefore herby ordain that all such persons as sithence the coming away of the said Sir Thomas Dale have at their own charges been transported thither to inhabit and so continued as aforesaid there be allotted and set out upon a first division fifty acres of land to them and their heirs for ever for their personal Adventure paying a free rent of one Shilling yearly in manner aforesaid . . .

And to the intent that godly learned and painful Ministers may be placed there for the service of Almighty God & for the spiritual benefit and comfort of the people, We further will and ordain that in every of those Cities or Burroughs the several quantity of one hundred Acres of Land be set out in quality of Glebe land toward the maintenance of the several Ministers of the parishes . . . and . . . there be raised a yearly standing and certain contribution out of the profits growing or renuing within the several farmes of the said parish and so as to make the living of every Minister two hundred pounds Sterling per annum . . .

And Whereas by a special Grant and licence from his Majesty a general Contribution over this Realm hath been made for the building and planting of a college for the training up of the Children of those Infidels in true Religion moral virtue and Civility and for other godly uses, We do therefore according to a former Grant and order hereby ratify confirm and ordain that a convenient place be chosen and set out for the planting of a University at the said Henrico in time to come and that in the meantime preparation be there made for the building of the said College for the Children of the Infidels according to such Instructions as we shall deliver . . .

Our Intent being according to the Rules of Justice and good government to alot unto every one his due yet so as neither to breed Disturbance to the Right of others nor to interrupt the good form of Government intended for the benefit of the people and strength of the Colony, We do therefore will and ordain that of the said particular plantations none be placed within

five Miles of the said former Cities and Boroughs . . . In like sort we ordain that no latter particular plantation shall at any time hereafter be seated within ten Miles of a former. We also will and ordain that no particular plantation be or shall be placed stragglingly in divers places to the weakening of them, but be united together in one seat and territory that so also they may be incorporated by us into one body corporate and live under Equal and like Law and orders with the rest of the Colony . . .

We do also hereby declare that heretofore in one of our said general and Quarter Courts we have ordained and enacted and in this present Court have ratified and Confirmed these orders and laws following: . . . That no patents or Indentures of Grants of Land in Virginia be made and sealed but in a full General and Quarter Court, . . . That for all persons not comprised in the order next before which during the next seven years after Midsummer day 1618 shall go into Virginia with intent there to Inhabit, If they continue there three years or die after they are shipped there, shall be a grant made of fifty acres for every person upon A first division and as many more upon a second division (the first being peopled), which grants to be made respectively to such persons and their heirs at whose charges the said persons going to Inhabit in Virginia shall be transported with reservation of twelve pence yearly Rent for every fifty acres to be answered to the said treasurer and Company and their Successors for ever after the first seven years of every such Grant . . .

Lastly we do hereby require and Authorize you the said Captain George Yeardley and the said Council of State, Associating with you such other as you shall there find meet, to Survey or cause to be Survey'd all the Lands and territories in Virginia above mentioned and the same to set out by bounds and metes especially so as that the territories of the said Several Cities and Boroughs and other particular plantations may be conveniently divided and known the one from the other, Each survey to be set down distinctly in writing and returned to us under your hands and seals. In Witness whereof we have hereunto set our Common Seal, Given in a great and general Court of the Council and Company of Adventurers of Virginia held the Eighteenth Day of November 1618, And in the years of the Reign of Our Sovereign Lord James by the grace of God King of England, Scotland, France, and Ireland, Defender of the Faith &c . . .

A report of the manner of proceeding in the General Assembly convened at James City in Virginia, consisting of the Governor, the Council of State and two Burgesses elected out of each Incorporation and Plantation, July 30th to August 4th, 1619

First. Sir George Yeardley, Knight, Governor and Captain general of Virginia, having sent his summons all over the Country, as well to invite those of the Council of State that were absent as also for the election of Burgesses, they were chosen and appeared . . .

The most convenient place we could find to sit in was the choir of the Church Where Sir George Yeardley, the Governor, being set down in his accustomed place, those of the Council of State sat next him on both hands except only the Secretary then appointed Speaker, who sat right before him, John Twine, clerk of the General assembly, being placed next the Speaker, and Thomas Pierse, the Sergeant, standing at the bar, to be ready for any service the Assembly should command him. But forasmuch as men's affairs do little prosper where God's service is neglected, all the Burgesses took their places in the choir, til a prayer was said by Mr. Bucke, the Minister, that it would please God to guide and sanctify all our proceedings to his own glory and the good of this Plantation. Prayer being ended, to the intent that as we had begun at God Almighty, so we might proceed with awful and due respect towards the Lieutenant, our most gracious and dread Sovereign, all the Burgesses were entreated to retire themselves into the body of the Church, which being done, before they were fully admitted, they were called in order and by name, and so every man (none staggering at it) took the oath of Supremacy, and entered the Assembly . . .

At the reading of the names of the Burgesses, Exception was taken against Captain Ward as having planted here in Virginia without any authority or commission from the Treasurer, Council and Company in England. But considering he had been at so great charge and pains to augment this Colony, and adventured his own person in the action, and since that time had brought home a good quantity of fish, to re-

lieve the Colony by way of trade, and above all, because the Commission for authorising the General Assembly admitteth of two Burgesses out of every plantation without restraint or exception, upon all these considerations, the Assembly was contented to admit of him and his Lieutenant (as members of their body and Burgesses) into their society . . .

After all the Burgesses had taken the oath of Supremacy and were admitted into the house and all set down in their places, a Copy of Captain Martin's Patent was produced by the Governor out of a Clause whereof it appeared that when the general assembly had made some kind of law requisite for the whole Colony, he and his Burgesses and people might deride the whole company and choose whether they would obey the same or no. It was therefore ordered in Court that the foresaid two Burgesses should withdraw themselves out of the assembly till such time as Captain Martin had made his personal appearance before them. At what time, if upon their motion, if he would be content to quit and give over that part of his Patent, and contrary thereunto would submit himself to the general form of government as all others did, that then his Burgesses should be readmitted, otherwise they were to be utterly excluded as being spies rather than loyal Burgesses, because they had offered themselves to be assistant at the making of laws which both themselves and those whom they represented might choose whether they would obey or not . . .

These obstacles removed, the Speaker, who for a long time has been extreme sickly, and therefore not able to pass through long harangues, delivered in brief to the whole Assembly the occasions of their meeting. Which done he read unto them the commission for establishing the Council of State and the General Assembly, wherein their duties were described to the life. Having thus prepared them he read over unto them the Great Charter, or commission of privileges, orders and laws, sent by Sir George Yeardley out of England. Which for the more ease of the Committees, having divided into four books, he read the former two the same forenoon for expeditions sake, a second time over, and so they were referred to the perusal of two Committees, which did reciprocally consider of either, and accordingly brought in their opinions. But some may here object to what end we should presume to refer that to the examination of Committees which the Council and Company in England had already resolved to be perfect, and did expect nothing but our assent thereunto. To this we answer, that we did it not to the end to correct or controll anything therein contained, but only in case we should find ought not perfectly squaring with the state of this Colony or any law which did press or bind too hard, that we might by way of humble petition, seek to have it redressed, especially because this great Charter is to bind us and our heirs forever . . .

The second petition of the General Assembly framed by the Committees out of the second book is. That the Treasurer and Company in England would be pleased with as much convenient speed as may be to send men hither to occupy their lands belonging to the four Incorporations . . . The third Petition humbly presented by this General Assembly to the Treasurer, Council and Company is . . . that they will be pleased to allow to the male children, of them and of all others begotten in Virginia being the only hope of a posterity, a single share a piece, and shares for their issues or for themselves, because that in a new plantation it is not known whether man or woman be more necessary . . .

The sixth and last is, they will be pleased to change the savage name of Kiccowtan, and to give that Incorporation a new name . . . These petitions thus concluded on, those two Comitties . . . could find nothing therein subject to exception, only the Governor's particular opinion . . . that in these doubtful times between us and the Indians, it would behoove us not to make as large distances between Plantation as ten miles, but for our more strength and security to draw nearer together. At the same time, there remaining no farther scruple in the minds of the Assembly touching the said great Charter of laws, orders and privileges, the Speaker put the same to the question, and so it had both the general assent and the applause of the whole Assembly, who, as they professed themselves in the first place most submissively thankful to almighty God, therefore so they commanded the Speaker to return (as now he doth) their due and humble thanks to the Treasurer, Council and Company for so many privileges and favours as well in their own names as in the names of the whole Colony whom they represented.

Here begin the laws drawn out of the Instructions given by his Majesty's Council of Virginia in England

By this present General Assembly be it enacted that no injury or oppression be wrought by the English against the Indians whereby the present peace might be disturbed and ancient quarrels might be revived. And further be it ordained that the Chicohomini are not to be excepted out of this law; until either that such order come out of England or that they do provoke us by some new injury.

Against Idleness, Gaming, drunkeness and excess in apparel the Assembly hath enacted as followeth:

First, in detestation of Idlenes be it enacted, that if any man be found to live as an Idler or renegade, though a freedman, it shall be lawful for that Incorporation or Plantation to which he belongeth to appoint him a Master to serve for wages, 'til he show apparent signs of amendment.

Against gaming at dice and Cards be it ordained by this present assembly that the winner or winners shall lose all his or their winnings and both winners and losers shall forfeit ten shillings a man, one ten shillings whereof to go to the discoverer, and the rest to charitable and pious uses in the Incorporation where the fault is committed.

Against drunkenness be it also decreed that if any private person be found culpable thereof, for the first time he is to be reproved privately by the Minister, the second time publicly, the third time to lie in bolts 12 hours in the house of the Provost Marshall and to pay his fee, and if he still continue in that vice, to undergo such severe punishment as the Governor and Council of State shall think fit to be inflicted on him.

Against excess in apparel that every man be assessed in the church for all public contributions, if he be unmarried according to his own apparel, if he be married, according to his own and his wives, or either of their apparel.

As touching the instruction of drawing some of the better disposed of the Indians to converse with our people and to live and labour amongst them, the Assembly who know well their dispositions think it fit to enjoin, least to counsel those of the Colony, neither utterly to reject them nor yet to draw them to come in. But in case they will of themselves come voluntarily to places well-peopled, there to do service in killing of Deer, fishing, beating of Corn and other works, that than five or six may be admitted into every such place, and no more, and that with the consent of the Governour. Provided that good guard in the night be kept upon them for generally (though some amongst many may prove good) they are a most treacherous people and quickly gone when they have done a villainy. And it were fit a house were built for them to lodge in apart by themselves, and lone inhabitants by no means to entertain them.

Be it enacted by this present Assembly that for laying a surer foundation of the conversion of the Indians to Christian Religion, each town, city, Borough, and particular plantation do obtain unto themselves by just means a certain number of the natives' children to be educated by them in true religion and civil course of life — of which children the most towardly boys in wit and graces of nature to be brought up by them in the first elements of literature, so to be fitted for the College intended for them that from thence they may be sent to that work of conversion.

As touching the business of planting corn, this present Assembly doth ordain that year by year all and every householder and householders have in store for every servant he or they shall keep, and also for his or their own persons, whether they have any Servants or no, one spare barrel of corn, to be delivered out yearly, either upon sale or exchange as need shall require. For the neglect of which duty he shall be subject to the censure of the Governor and Council of State, provided always that the first year of every new man this law shall not be of force.

About the plantation of Mulbery trees, be it enacted that every man as he is seated upon his division, do for seven years together, every year plant and maintain in growth six Mulberry trees at the least, and as many more as he shall think convenient and as his virtue and Industry shall move him to plant . . . Be it farther enacted as concerning Silk-flax, that those men that are upon their division or settled habitation do this next year plant and dress 100 plants, which being found a commodity, may farther be increased. And whosoever do fail in the performance of this shall be subject to the punishment of the Governour and Council of State. For hemp also both English and Indian and for English flax and Anise seeds, we do require and

enjoin all householders of this Colony that have any of those seeds to make trial thereof the next season. Moreover be it enacted by this present Assembly that every householder do yearly plant and maintain ten vines until they have attained to the art and experience of dressing a Vineyard either by their own industry or by the Instruction of some Vigneron . . .

All ministers shall duly read divine service, and exercise their ministerial function according to the Ecclesiastical laws and orders of the church of England, and every Sunday in the afternoon shall Catechize such as are not yet ripe to come to the Communion. And whosoever of them shall be found negligent or faulty in this kind shall be subject to the censure of the Governor and Council of State.

The Ministers and Churchwardens shall seek to present all ungodly disorders, the committers whereof if, upon good admonitions and mild reproof they will nor forbear the said scandalous offenses as suspicions of whoredoms, dishonest company, keeping with women and such like, they are to be presented and punished accordingly.

If any person after two warnings, do not amend his or her life in point of evident suspicion of Incontinency or of the commission of any other enormous sins, that then he or she be presented by the Churchwardens and suspended for a time from the church by the minister. In which Interim if the same person do not amend and humbly submit him or herself to the church, he is then fully to be excommunicate and soon after a writ or warrant to be sent from the Governor for the apprehending of his person and seizing on all his goods. Provided always, that all the ministers do meet once a quarter . . . to determine whom it is fit to excommunicate, and that they first present their opinion to the Governor ere they proceed to the act of excommunication . . .

No man shall trade into the bay, either in shallop, pinnace, or ship, without the Governor's license, and without putting in security that neither himself nor his Company shall force or wrong the Indians, upon pain that, doing otherwise, they shall be censured at their return by the Governor and Council of State . . .

No maid or woman servant, either now resident in the Colony or hereafter to come, shall contract herself in marriage without either the consent of her parents, or of her Master or Mistress, or of the magistrate and minister of the place both together . . .

The General Assembly doth humbly beseech the said Treasurer, Council and Company that, albeit it belongeth to them only to allow or to abrogate any laws which we shall here make, and that it is their right so to do, yet that it would please them not to take it in ill part if these laws which we have now brought to light, do pass current and be of force til such time as we may know their farther pleasure out of England; for otherwise this people . . . would in short time grow so insolent, as they would shake off all government, and there would be no living among them.

Their last humble suit is, that the said Council and Company would be pleased, so soon as they shall find it convenient, to make good their promise set down at the conclusion of their commission for establishing the Council of State and the General Assembly, namely, that they will give us power to allow or disallow of their orders of Court, as his Majesty hath given them power to allowe or to reject our lawes.

In sum Sir George Yeardley, the Governour, prorogued the said General Assembly til the first of March, which is to fall out this present year of 1619, and in the mean season dissolved the same.

John Rolfe: A letter from Rolfe in Virginia to Sir Edwin Sandys, Treasurer of the Virginia Company of London, January, 1620

Honored Sir
Studieng with myself what service I might do you, as a token of my grateful remembrance for your many favors and constant love showed me, as well in my absence as when I was present with you I could not at this time devise a better, then to give you notice of some particulars both of our present estate, and what happened since the departure of the Diana . . .

Presently after the Diana had her dispatch Sir George Yeardley (according to a Commission directed unto him and to the Council of State,) caused Burgesses to be chosen in all places who met at James City, where all matters therein contained were debated by several Committees and approved: and likewise such other laws enacted, as were held expedient & requisite for the welfare and peaceable goverment of this Common-weale . . .

The George was sent by the Cape Marchant (with the Governor's consent) to New-found-land to trade and buy fish for the better relief of the Colony and to make trial of that passage. One other reason (as I take it) was, for that the Magazine was well stored with goods, it was some what doubtful, whether a ship would be sent to carry home the crop so soon as the George might upon her return back. She departed hence about the 9th of July, and arrived here again about the 10 of September. She made her passage to Newfound-land in less than 3 weeks, and was at the bank amongst the French fishermen in 14 days. She came back hither again in 3 weeks, with bare winds, and brought so much fish as will make a saving voyage, which besides the great relief, giveth much content to the whole Colony.

The Sturgeon ship and the Trial departed hence together about the five of July. Mr. Pountys hath taken great pains in fishing, and toward Michelmas (the weather being somewhat temperate) made some good sturgeon. He hopeth by the spring to be better fitted, with Cellars and houses, and to do some good therein.

The Cattle in the Trial came exceeding well, and gave the Colony much joy and great encouragement. Both the horses and Mares will be very vendible here a long time, the Colony increasing with people as of late.

About the latter end of August, a Dutch man of War of the burden of a 160 tons arrived at Point-Comfort, the commander's name Capt Jope, his Pilot for the West Indies one Mr. Marmaduke, an Englishman. They met with the Trẽr in the West Indies, and determined to hold consort ship hitherward, but in their passage lost one the other. He brought not any thing but 20 and odd Negroes, which the Governor and Cape Marchant bought for victualls (whereof he was in great need as he pretended) at the best and easiest rate they could. He had a large and ample commission from his Excellency to range and to take purchase in the West Indies . . . He reported (whilst he stayed at Keqnoughton) that if we got not some Ordinance planted at Point Comfort, the Colony would be quite undone and that ere long: for that undoubtedly the Spaniard would be here in the next spring which he gathered (as was said)from some Spaniards in the West Indies. This being spred abroad doth much dishearten the people in general, for we have no place of strength to retreat unto, no shipping of certainty (which would be to us as the wooden walls of England), no sound and experienced soldiers to undertake, no Engineers and earthmen to erect works, few Ordinance, not a serviceable carriage to mount them on; not ammunition of powder, shot and lead, to fight 2 whole days . . .

The Governor hath bounded the limits of the 4 corporations: the Company's, the Governor's, the University and Glebe lands according to the commission. All the Ancient Planters being set free have chosen place for their dividends according to the Commission which giveth all great content, for now knowing their owne land, they strive and are prepared to build houses to clear their grounds ready to plant, which giveth the great encouragement and the greatest hope to make the Colony florrish that ever yet happened to them.

Upon the 4 of November the Bona Nova arrived at James City. All the passengers came lusty and in good health. They came by the west Indies, which passage at that season doth much refresh the people.

Lastly, I speak on my own experience for these 11 years, I never amongst so few, have seen so many falsehearted, envious and malicious people (yea amongst some who march in the better rank) nor shall you ever hear of any the justest Governor here, who shall live free from their scandal and shameless exclamations, if way be given to their reports. And so desiring your kind acceptance hereof, being unwilling to conceal anything from yourself (who now, to mine and many others' comforts, standeth at the helm to guide us, . . . I take my leave, and will ever rest At your service and command in all faithful duties

Broadside from the Virginia Company of London to the Governor and Council of Virginia, May 17, 1620

The Treasurer, Council and Company for Virginia, to the Governor of Virginia, and the Council of Estate there residing, Greeting . . . as it is apparent to all understanding minds, that the wealth, happinesse and stability of each particular Estate, is founded upon the strength and prosperity of the public, (the public having been of late years wholly decayed and ruined, to the inestimable loss and detriment of the whole Plantation . . . We [trust] that not only your selves, the Governor and Council, but the whole body of the Colony, and every member thereof, taking into due con-

sideration, how much the life and health of the public Tenants may import them all, as well for their ease of public burthens, as for support of public Justice, good order & government, will by all means apply themselves to the entertaining and providing for them so upon their first arrival, as that not only their lives and healths be not endangered as heretofore, but that also they may cheerfully set in hand, with the works and labours directed and prepared for them; [we] do earnestly pray and require both you, and them all, that all other business of less importance laid aside, they immediately afford all possible assistance, for the raising of houses and convenient lodgings for them, with other necessary relief and succour: Wherein whatsoever they shall do lovingly and freely of their own voluntary accord, we shall with due thanks accept it at their hands, (desiring that particular notice be given to us thereof) and for that which is to be done by them, above that proportion, there shall be recompence made of as many days work by those public Tenants, at the next possible opportunity; thinking it equal neither to refuse any help for the public, nor yet to charge the private above their contents and abilities. And, although we have absolute power derived from his Majesty, to establish and enjoy by order the performance hereof: yet seeing this aid is to be yielded but this once, (the public Tenants being henceforward to prepare for all new supplies) we have thought better by request, to try the love of the Colony, than their obedience by command.

Lastly, for as much as it is become very apparant (which we have often heretofore foreseen and forewarned) that the applying so altogether the planting of Tobacco, and the neglect of other more solid commodities, have not only redounded to the great disgrace of the Country, and detriment of the Colony; but doth also in point of profit, greatly deceive them which have trusted to it: We therefore endeavouring to reform this error, and to restore due reputation to that Land and people, have with great care and charge (assisted also with some particular Plantations) endeavoured to set up sundry real Commodities, and some other we have thought fit to recommend to your care to prosecute. First, Iron, being of most necessary use for the Colony. For the making whereof, we now furnish out 150 persons, to set up three Iron-works, with all Materials and other provisions thereunto belonging. Secondly, for

Cordage; we much commend the order taken by your selves, for the planting of Silk-grass there naturally growing, which we desire may be in the greatest abundance possible, as conceiving it to be of chief importance both for use and profit. Thirdly, for Pitch and Tarr, we advise and require, that the Polackers be returned in part to these their works, with such other assistance as shall be necessary. The like we shall desire for Pot-ashes and Soap-ashes, when there shall be fit store of hands to assist them, Requiring in the mean time, that care be generally taken, that Servants and Apprentices be so trained up in these works, as that the skill do not perish together with the Masters. The Fourth commodity recommended, is Timber of all sorts, with Masts, Planks, and Boards, for provisions of shipping, and sundry other Materials of much use and benefit. And to the ease and increase of divers of those works, provision is now sent, for the erecting of Sawing-Mills, which may fill the whole Colony also with Planks and Boards, to their great ease and help in setting up their Buildings. The fifth, is Silk, for which that Country is exceeding proper, having innumerable store of Mulberry trees of the best . . . The sixth is Vines, whereof the Country yieldeth naturally great store, and of divers sorts, which by culture will be brought to excellent perfection. For the effecting whereof, divers skilfull Vignerons heretofore, and some now are sent, with store also from hence of Vine-plants of the best sort. And here by the way we advise and desire, that Men of those Sciences, which are not natural to us, be extraordinarily cherished and encouraged in their workes: seeing if they should fail, it would be difficult to supply them. The last commodity, but not of least importance for health, is Salt: the works whereof having been lately suffered to decay; we now intending to restore in so great plenty, as not only to serve the Colony for the present, but as is hoped, in short time, the great fishings on those Coasts . . . These being the commodities (for Corn and Cattle we pass over, being only for sustenance of the people) which we desire to have set up with all care and diligence, as well for necessary use and profit, as for the honour and reputation of the Country and Colony; and for the advancing of which, we have spared neither care nor cost, which on our parts was requisite to our best understandings . . .

An indenture agreement between the owners of Berkeley's Hundred and Richard Smyth and his wife, September, 1620

This Indenture made the first day of September in the xvii[th] yeare of the reigne of our sovereign lord Kinge James of England &c. between Richard Berkeley, George Thorpe and Wm Tracy Esqs and John Smyth, gentleman on the one part And Richard Smyth of Wotton Underedge in the county of Gloucestershire; Joan, his wife, and Anthony and William, their sonns . . . Witnesseth that it is agreed between the said parties in manner following: first the said Richard Berkeley, George, William and John do hereby covenant with the said Richard Smyth, Joan, his wife, and Anthony and William, their sonns . . . to transport them (with God's assistance) into the land of Virginia with all convenient speed at their costs and charges in all things and there to maintain and keep them with convenient diet & lodging in their family there amongst their other servants from the day of their landing until one convenient house shall be for them erected & built in place convenient, and the same to be furnished with necessary implements (in supply of such as they want and have need of) and to allot unto them so much ground convenient and adjoining to the said house as they shall be able to clear, manure, order, dress, husband and use, either in orchards, gardens, vineyards or for Tobacco, corn, maize or Indian Wheat, oat, silk grass, flax or hemp, or for pasture and hay for cows & other cattle or for plantinge of olyves, sewing or plantinge of cotton wool, Aniseed, Wormseed and the like, the same house to be seated near the great river there, or some branch or creek thereof And the same house shall be so built and fitted for them to allow unto them convenient diet as the country can reasonably afford until one harvest be by them had and Inned which is supposed will be about the feast of St Bartholomew next, And also to deliver to them two cows of those which the said Richard, George, William, and John propose to send over in April next, and to each of them within the compas of one year next three suits of apparel . . . In Consideration whereof they the said Richard Smyth, Joan, his wife, Anthony & William, their sonns . . . do covenant & promise from time to time faithfully That they and their heirs will pay and deliver to them the said Richard, George, William and John & their heirs, one third part of all English corn & of maize or Indian wheat and the one half of all other profits, fruits, cattle seeds & increase whatsoever raised taken or had from the ground . . . and to be true and faithful tenants unto them the said Richard, George, William and John and their heirs, So likewise on their parts they promise to return all assistance, kindness, protection & defence wherein they shall justly have need of them, And that Indentures shall Enterchangeably be made and sealed to the effect of theis presents in convenient time after the patent of their land in Virginia shall be sealed to them the said Richard, George, William & John. Given Enterchangeably under their hands and seals the day and year first above written.

George Yeardley: A letter from Governor Yeardley in Virginia to Sir Edwin Sandys, June, 1620

Noble Sir

There lying at this present upon my shoulders so great a burden that I am not able to look into all particulars so suddenly as this Ship will depart, this great number of people also arriving Unexpected it hath not a little pusslled me to provide for the lodging of them, it being a thing of special consequence and necessity for theire health. Herein I must acknowledge your care and zeal for the hasty and speedy erecting this good work, in the sending so many people for sundry profitable employments in Each. I do here pass my promise unto you, and hold myself bound to do my best endeavor, and had not your zealous desires over hasted you and the passage at sea been So unfortunate to the duty, whereby I had no warning at all given to provide for these people, I should have been able to have done much better then now I can. Yet I beseech God to give a blessing to my endeavors; they are now all lodged within good houses as this Country doth afford not one but lyeth upon a bedstead high from the ground and have theire victuals well-dressed and it is also both amended and enlarged to their full content. Their provision which came with them out of England being nothing but meal is very harsh for them to feed upon being new comers . . . Indian-corn also of my own I feed them with whereof I thank the Lord and praised be his name, there is enough in the Country for all the people now Arrived . . . And had they arrived at a seasonable time of the yeare I would not

have doubted of their lives and healths, but this season is most unfit for people to arrive here. To tell you the very truth I doubt of much sickness for many of them to the number of 100. At least came some very weak and sick, some Crazey and tainted a shore, and now this great heat of weather striketh many more, but for Life I hope well. Yet the Company must be content to have little service done by new men the first year 'til they be seasoned.

The Cheif men for the Iron worke being dead at sea and upon theire present landing will give a great blow to the staging of that business. Little or nothing will be done therein this summer, it being a hot and heavy worke. If this summer with all the means I have to help them I can but build lodgings and transport their materials I shall think I have done well.

Your boatewryght died soon after his landing at James City whereby I have no means so speedily to set up the new shallop for transporting the people and their provisions. Yet had I not a shallop of my own to employ that way I know not what to do. I protest before God I run myself out of all the provision of Corn I have for the feeding of these people . . . Also for Clothes they come very short, wheresoever the fault is I know not. It behooves him to look to it the people are ready to mutiny for more affirming that more by him was promised. What shall I say? All I have or can make means for I am willing to offer for the performing and making good your promises there made, but Sir I beseech you be not offended if I deal plainly respecting the honor and reputation of my freinds. Suffer me I pray you to advise you that you do not run into so great matters in speedy and hasty sending so many people over hither and undertaking so great works, before you have acquainted me and have truly been informed by me of the state of the Plantation and what may be done here. If you do not observe this rule I shall and must fail in the executing of your projects . . . I have done what I can do and will do still to utmost power, but I pray, sir, give me both time to provide means and to build and settle before you lay one Load. If you will but take my advice hence, I will inform you truly and do to the utmost, and if I may not offend herein I will Challenge any man I may deal with upon terms for doing more then I have done and will do with God's permission considering the means

I have thus in these first beginings and where all things are to be forged out of the fier.

If you will but observe the season, and also to send men of such qualities and upon such conditions as I shall in my letters give you notice, no doubt then by God's grace but you shall advance the action which I know is your Cheif desire, and also gain to your self eternal honor and reputation. Except the Carpenters come for the Iron workes, there is now not one arrived, and never a boatwright, but that silly fellow which is dead and how do you think I should build without good and skilfull workmen. If you shall think fit to send any men before Christmas I pray send at least 6 months' victuals with them, at a bushel of meal a man per month at least. What you like of meal send in peas and oatmeall, but allow if of meal, peas, and oatmeal a pound of meal a day and a pint of peas or oatmeal per man. Pray think it not strange I should write thus to send victuals with your people for you may be pleased well to conceive that if such numbers of people come upon me unexpected, and that at an unhealthfull season and too late to set Corn, I can not then be able to feed them out of others' labors. What I can and am able to do if you will have patience, I will from time to time inform you, and doubt not but to give you full content but both you and I must give leave to time and so expect the blessing of God . . .

A letter to the Governor and Council in Virginia from the Virginia Company of London, August, 1621

We send you in this Ship one Widow and eleven Maids for Wives for the people in Virginia. There hath been especial care had in the choise of them, for there hath not any one of them been received but upon good Commendations, as by a note herewith sent, you may perceive. We pray you all therefore in general to take them into your care, and more especially we recommend them to you, Mr Pountis, that at their first landing they may be housed, lodged and provided for of diet til they be married: for such was the hast of sending them away, as that straightned with time we had no means to put provisions aboard: which defect shall be supplied by the Magazine Ship. And in case they cannot be presently Married we desire they may be put to several householders that have wives till they can be provided of husbands. There are neare fifty more

which are shortly to come, are sent by our most honorable Lord and Treasurer, the Earl of Southampton and certain worthy gentlemen who, taking into their consideration that the Plantation can never flourish 'til families be planted, and the respect of wives and Children fix the people on the Soil: therefore, have given this faire beginning, for the reimbursing of whose charges, it is ordered that every man that Marries them give 120 weight of the best leaf Tobbacco for each of them. In case any of them die that proportion must be advanced to make it up upon those that survive . . .

And though we are desirous that marriage be free according to the law of nature, yet would we not have these maids deceived and married to servants, but only to such freemen or tenants as have means to maintain them. We pray you therefore to be fathers to them in this business, not enforcing them to Marry against their wills. Neither send we them to be servants, save in case of extremity, for we would have their condition so much bettered as multitudes may be alured thereby to come unto you, and you may assure such men as marry those women that the first servants sent over by the Company, shall be consigned to them, it being our intent to preserve families, and to preferr married men before single persons . . .

The Adventurers of Martin's hundred intend to proceed in their Plantation. They have sent twelve lusty youths in this Ship which supply they will second with a greater of forty more in the Magazine Ship very suddenly to follow. Their governor, Mr Harwood, is enjoined to acquaint you with his Instructions, to whom we pray you accordingly give your best assistance.

We cannot but condemn the use that is made of our boats that are only employed in trading in the bay for Corn. Almost every letter tells of that trade which we only approve in case of necessity. For we conceive it would be much better for the Plantation and more honor for you and our nation, that the naturals should come for their provision to you, than you to beg your bread of them. We shall with a great deal more content hear of Store-houses full of corn of your own growth, then of a Shallopp laden with Corn from the Bay. We pray you therefore that a larger proportion of ground be assigned to every man to plant then formerly hath been, and that severest punishments be inflicted upon such as dare to break your constitutions herein, and that officers be not spared, nor their tenants nor servants dispenced with . . . And so desiring God to bless you and all your good endeavors tending to the advancement and establishing of your Colony, We bid you farewell.

A declaration of the state of the colony and affairs in Virginia with a relation of the barbarous massacre, 1622

The last May there came letters from Sir Francis Wyatt, Governor in Virginia, which did advertise that when in November last he arrived in Virginia and entered upon his government, he found the country settled in a peace, as all men there thought sure and inviolable, not only because it was solemnly ratified and sworn, and at the request of the Native King stamped in Brass, and fixed to one of his Oaks of note, but as being advantagious to both parts; to the Savages as the weaker, under which they were safely sheltered and defended; to us, as being the easiest way then thought to pursue and advance our projects of buildings, plantings, and effecting their conversion by peaceable and fair means. And such was the conceit of firm peace and amity, as that there was seldome or never a sword worn, and a Piece seldomer, except for a Deer or Fowl. By which assurance of security, the Plantations of particular Adventurers and Planters were placed scatteringly and stragglingly as a choice vein of rich ground invited them, and the further from neighbors held the better. The houses were generally set open to the Savages, who were always friendly entertained at the tables of the English, and commonly lodged in their bed-chambers. The old planters (as they thought now come to reap the benefit of their long travels) placed with wonderfull content upon their private dividents, and the planting of particular Hundreds and Colonies pursued with an hopeful alacrity, all our projects (saith he) in a fair way, and their familiarity with the Natives, seeming to open a fair gate for their conversion to Christianity . . .

As well on the Friday morning (the fatal day) the 22 of March, as also in the evening, as in other days before, they came unarmed into our houses, without Bows or arrows, or other weapons, with Deer, Turkies, Fish, Furs, and other provisions to sell, and trucke

with us for glass, beads, and other trifles. Yea, in some places, sat down at Breakfast with our people at their tables, whom immediately with their own tools and weapons, either laid down, or standing in their houses, they basely and barbarously murdered, not sparing either age or sex, man, woman or child; so sudden in their cruel execution that few or none discerned the weapon or blow that brought them to destruction. In which manner they also slew many of our people then at their several works and husbandries in the fields, and without their houses, some in planting Corn and Tobacco, some in gardening, some in making Brick, building, sawing, and other kinds of husbandry, they well knowing in what places and quarters each of our men were, in regard of their daily familiarity, and resort to us for trading and other negotiations, which the more willingly was by us continued and cherished for the desire we had of effecting that great master-piece of works, their conversion. And by this means that fatal Friday morning, there fell under the bloody and barbarous hands of that perfidious and inhumane people, contrary to all laws of God and men, of Nature & Nations, three hundred forty seven men, women, and children, most by their own weapons. Not being content with taking away life alone, they fell after again upon the dead, making as well as they could, a fresh murder, defacing, dragging, and mangling the dead carkasses into many pieces, and carrying some parts away in derision, with base and bruitish triumph.

Neither yet did these beasts spare those amongst the rest well known unto them, from whom they had daily received many benefits and favours, but spitefully also massacred them, without remorse or pity . . . One instance of it, amongst too many, shall serve for all. That worthy religious Gentleman, Master George Thorpe Esquire, Deputy of the College lands, sometimes one of his Majesty's Pentioners, and in one of the principal places of command in Virginia, did so truly and earnestly affect their conversion, and was so tender over them, that whosoever under his authority had given them but the least displeasure or discontent, he punished them severely. He thought nothing too dear for them, and as being desirous to bind them unto him by his many courtesies, he never denied them anything that they asked him . . . He was not only too kind and beneficial to the common sort, but also to their King, to whom he oft resorted, and gave many presents which he knew to be highly pleasing to him. And whereas this king before dwelt only in a cottage, or rather a den or hog-style, made with a few poles and sticks, and covered with mats after their wild manner, to civilize him, he first built him a fair house according to the English fashion, in which he took such joy, especially in his lock and key, which he so admired, as locking and unlocking his door an hundred times a day. He thought no device in all the world was comparable to it.

    Thus insinuating himself to this King for his religious purposes, he conferred after with him oft, and intimated to him matters of our Religion; and thus far the Pagan confessed, moved by natural Principles, that our God was a good God, and better much than theirs, in that he had with so many good things above them endowed us. He told him, if he would serve our God, he should be partaker of all those good things we had, and of far greater than sense or reason ever could imagine. He won upon him, as he thought in many things, so as he gave him fair hearing and good answer, and seemed to be much pleased with his discourse and in his company. And both he and his people for the daily courtesies this good Gentleman did to one or other of them, did profess such outward love and respect unto him, as nothing could seem more, but all was little regarded after by this Viperous brood, as the sequel showed, for they not only willfully murdered him, but cruelly and felly, out of devilish malice, did so many barbarous despights and foul scorns after to his dead corpse, as are unbefitting to be heard by any civil ear. One thing I cannot omit, that when this good Gentleman upon his fatal hour, was warned by his man (who perceived some treachery intended to them by these hell-hounds) to look to himself, and withal ran away for fear of the mischief he strongly apprehended, and so saved his owne life; yet his Master, out of the conscience of his own good meaning and fair deserts ever towards them, was so void of all suspicion, and so full of confidence, that they had sooner killed him, then he could or would believe they meant any ill against him. Thus the sins of these wicked Infidels, have made them unworthy of enjoying him, and the eternal good that he most zealously always intended to them . . .

That the slaughter had been universal, if God had not put it into the heart of an Indian belonging to one Perry to disclose it, who living in the house of one Pace, was urged by another Indian, his Brother (who came the night before and lay with him), to kill Pace, (so commanded by their King as he declared) as he would kill Perry, telling further that by such an hour in the morning a number would come from divers places to finish the Execution, who failed not at the time, Perry's Indian rose out of his bed and reveals it to Pace, that used him as a Son. And thus the rest of the Colony that had warning given them, by this means was saved. Such was (God be thanked for it) the good fruit of an Infidel converted to Christianity, for though three hundred and more of ours died by many of these Pagan Infidels, yet thousands of ours were saved by the means of one of them alone which was made a Christian . . .

    Thus have you seen the particulars of this massacre, out of Letters from thence written, wherein treachery and cruelty have done their worst to us, or rather to themselves, for whose understanding is so shallow, as not to perceive that this must needs be for the good of the Plantation after, and the loss of this blood to make the body more healthful, as by these reasons may be manifest:

    First, Because betraying of innocency never rests unpunished . . .

    Secondly, Because our hands which before were tied with gentleness and fair usage, are now set at liberty by the treacherous violence of the Savages, not untying the Knot, but cutting it; So that we, who hitherto have had possession of no more ground then their waste, and our purchase at a valuable consideration to their own contentment, gained, may now by right of War, and law of Nations, invade the Country, and destroy them who sought to destroy us, whereby we shall enjoy their cultivated places, turning the laborious Mattocke into the victorious Sword (wherein there is more both ease, benefit, and glory) and possessing the fruits of others' labours. Now their cleared grounds in all their villages (which are situate in the fruitfulest places of the land) shall be inhabited by us, whereas heretofore the grubbing of woods was the greatest labor . . .

    Fiftly, Because the Indians, who before were used as friends, may now most justly be compelled to servitude and drudgery and supply the room of men that labour, whereby even the meanest of the Plantation may imploy themselves more entirely in their Arts and Occupations, which are more generous, whilest Savages perform their inferiour works of digging in mines, and the like . . . Sixtly, This will for ever hereafter make us more cautious and circumspect, as never to be deceived more by any other treacheries, but will serve for a great instruction to all posterity there, to teach them that Trust is the mother of Deceipt, and to learn them that of the Italian, *Chi non fida, non s'ingamuu,* He that trusts not is not deceived, and make them know that kindnesses are misspent upon rude natures, so long as they continue rude, as also, that Savages and Pagans are above all other for matter of Justice ever to be suspected. Thus upon this Anvil shall we now beat out to ourselves an armour of proof, which shall for ever after defend us from barbarous Incursions, and from greater dangers that otherwise might happen. And so we may truly say according to the French Proverb, *A quel chose malheur est bon,* Ill luck is good for something.

A letter from the Treasurer and Council of the Virginia Company of London to the Governor and Council in Virginia, August, 1622

We have to our extreme grief understood of the great Massacre executed on our people in Virginia, and that in such a maner as is more miserable then the death itself; to fall by the hands of men so contemptible; to be surprised by treachery in a time of known danger; to be deaf to so plain a warning (as we now to late understand) was last year given; to be secure in an occasion of so great suspicion and jealousy as was Nenemathanewes death; not to perceive anything in so open and general conspiracy; but to be made in part instruments of contriving it, and almost guilty of the destruction by a blindfold and stupid entertaining of it; which the least wisdom or courage suffed to prevent even on the point of execution, are circumstances that do add much to our sorrow & make us to confess that it is the heavy hand of Allmighty God for the punishment of our and your transgressions, to the humble acknowledgment and perfect amendment whereof together with ourselves, we seriously advise and invite you; and in particular earnestly require the speedy re-

dress of those two enormous exesses of apparel and drinking, the cry whereof cannot but have gone up to heaven, since the infamy hath spread itself to all that have but heard the name of Virginia to the detestation of all good minds, the scorn of others, and our extreme grief and shame. In the strength of those faults, undoubtedly, and the neglect of the Divine worship, have the Indians prevailed, more then in your weaknes, whence the evil, therefore sprung the remedy must first begin, and an humble reconciliation be made with the divine Majesty by future conformity unto his most just and holy laws . . .

Apply all your thoughts and endeavors, and in especial, to the setting up of Staple Commodities, according to those often instructions, and reiterated advices that we have continually given you, the want whereof hath been the truest objection against the succeeding of this Plantation. We doubt not but by the *Abigail* to send you, and are further put in an assured hope to obtain the number 400 young men, well-furnished out of England and Wales at £20 a person, to repair with advantage the number that is lost, to set up the public revenues of the Company, and satisfy the deserts of worthy persons in the Colony. This supply we hope to procure, so as they may be with you before the Spring. The fear of your want of Corn doth much perplex us, seeing so little possibility to supply you, the public stock being utterly as you know exhausted, and the last years Adventures made by Private men not returned, as was promised, we have no hope of raising any valuable Magazine, but rather fear to see the effect of what we forwarned by the Warwick. Other ways and means are so uncertain, as we cannot wish you to rely upon anything, but yourselves. Yet shall there not be left any means unattempted on our part in this kind, and for other necessaries to supply you, hoping that the danger of this extremity will hence forward perswade you not to commit the certainty of your lives to the uncertainty of one harvest . . .

There come now over in this Ship, and are immediatly to follow in some others many hundreds of people to whom as we here think ourselves bound to give the best encouragment . . . There is no way left to increase the Plantation, but by abundance of private undertakers, so we think you obliged, to give all possible furtherance and assistance for the good entertaining, and well-settling of them, that they may both thrive & prosper and others by their welfare be drawn after them. This is the way that we conceive most effectual for the engaging of this State, and securing of Virginia, for, in the multitude of people is the strength of a Kingdom . . .

The people remaining of the Iron works, we desire may be committed unto the charge of Mr Maurice Barkley to be employed (since we cannot hope that the work should go forward) in such maner as may be most beneficial to themselves, and us, until such time as we may again renew that business, so many times unfortunately attempted, and yet so absolute necessary as we shall have no quiet until we see it perfected: to which purpose we desire there may by the first oportunity be sent us a particular list of the names and professions of the men, as also a note of the tools, and materials wanting for the executing of the work.

Of no lesse weight do we esteem the College affaires, which we pray you to take into your considerations not only as a public, but a sacred business; and in particuler we very earnestly request the care, and pains of Mr George Sandys for the settling and ordering of the tenants . . .

These are part of the remedies that are to be applied for the repairing of this late disaster. As for the Actors thereof, we cannot but with much grief proceed to the condemnation of their bodies, the saving of whose Souls, we have so zealously affected, but since the innocent blood of so many Christians, doth in justice cry out for revenge and your future security in wisdom require, we must advise you to root out from being any longer a people, so cursed a nation, ungratefull to all benefits, and incapable of all goodness, at least to the removal of them so far from you, as you may not only be out of danger, but out of fear of them, of whose faith and good meaning you can never be secure . . .

The improving of the Company's revenues, and recovery of their Debts is, of those things without which neither we nor you can subsist. Many other matters we have to write if time would give leave, for want whereof, we must reserve them til the departure of the *Abigail*. And now committing you and all your affaires, to the good guidance and protection of the Almighty, we bid you heartily farewell.

George Sandys: A letter from Sandys in Virginia to Sir Samuel Sandys in London, March, 1623

Sir

I humbly crave your parden if I have not written unto you so often as you expected . . . We found at our coming over the Country in peace, but in such a peace as presaged ruin: the people dispersed in small families far distant one from another, and, like the foolish Arcadians, exposed to the prey of whosoever would assail them. Yet could we not reform this mischief, they having patents granted from the Court in England to plant wheresoever they pleased, contrary to all order, discipline and example . . . Neither could the treachery of the Indians (although foreknown) have been but in part prevented who like violent lightning are gone as soon as perceived. Yet are we taxed with indiscretion and cowardice for drawing these miserable people to places of security, [we] who had neither victuals nor munitions (nor Could we help them with either) nor of strength to defend themselves, so that of necessity they must have perished either by the enemy or famine. But men that are ambitious to be counted wise will rather justify than acknowledge their errors and impute the fault to the execution when it is indeed in the project. We held not ourselves secure, said an ignoble nobleman, unless we had 1,000 soldiers to guard us. What a strict affinity is there between the devil and a liar! For my own part, I received not a man into my plantation although at one time I was so weak that I could not arm five able men. And for the Governor, the Councillors themselves were constrained to watch nightly by turns until the country allowed him a guard of 30 men. Sir Edwin writes that struck with a panic fear we proposed a removal of the colony to the Eastern shore. Indeed, I wrote home of such a proposition and named the proposer with his arguments which were hotly maintained by other . . . Yet these were refuted by us in points of reputation, being besides, as we alleged, an intolerable presumption for us to attempt such a change without your consents . . . We are much upbraided with Sir Thomas Dale. Yet (not to detract from the dead) what did he? Or what is extant of his endeavors? Or what Could not we do if we (as he) had 500 men at our own disposal, both fed and apparelled out of England? Whereas we have not one except we hire them with our private purses or take them injuriously from their masters. The tenants they sent on that so-absurd condition of halves are neither able to sustain themselves nor discharge their moiety, and are so dejected with their Scarce provisions and finding nothing to answer their expectation, that most give themselves over and die of Melancholy, the rest running so far in debt as keeps them still behind hand, and many (not seldom) losing their Crops whilst they hunt for their Bellies. Nor are their Commanders much better who, having little performed of what we promised, their means not worth the Collecting, converted their minds to other employments.

And now lest we should grow too rich, they have sent over (without any advice from us) a Captain of a ship, with extreme charges to the Country, to build a fort in the Sea (I might have said a Castle in the air) on a shoal of oyster shells, every tide overflown and at low water with every wind washed over by the surges, where when you have pierced the upper Crust, there is for many spears length no bottom to be found. The Captain died, to save his Credit, soon after. And I fear that their too much vain glory and presumption at home, together with our sins have drawn these afflictions upon us, the massacre being seconded with a general sickness, insomuch as we have lost, I believe, few less than 500, and not many of the rest that have not knocked at the doors of death.

Yet with our small and weak forces, we have chased the Indians from their abodes, burned their houses, taken their corn and slain not a few. The great King now sues for peace and offers a restitution of his prisoners, for whose sakes we seem to be inclineable thereunto and will try, if we can make them as secure as we were, that we may follow their Example in destroying them. We are now of ourselves about to erect a fort in as advantagious place as the other, but upon a solid foundation . . . I am ashamed, yet enforced to importune you once more for one year's Rent of my Annuity beforehand, this being a hard year, I having lost 23 men by sickness and received not one of those 25 which the Company Contracted to send me, having also paid almost £200 for my share in the hire of a ship without which both I and mine had famished, and discharged besides divers debts in England . . .

I humbly take my leave, your loving brother.

A letter from the Governor and Council of Virginia to the Privy Council of His Majesty Charles I, April 6, 1626

Right Honorables

The 23rd of March arrived the good ship, the Virgin, of Southhampton with letters from your Lordships of the 24th of October last, whereby we understand his Majesty's royal care of this Plantation, as well in present supply of our wants, as in taking order for the full and perfect settling of the affairs thereof. To the great encouragement of the whole Colony, She brings us an earnest of those larger supplies graciously promised by [his] Majesty, in Commodities though in proportion not answerable to our great wants, yet all very useful and well-conditioned, for which we must acknowledge our great bond to your Lordships and in particular to our singular good lord, The Lord High Treasurer. We must ever acknowledge it a singular favor from his Majesty that he hath been pleased to remit the imposition upon Tobacco in Consideration of supplying of the Colony. We humbly desire that your Lordships will be pleased to take order that it may be as well performed on their parts as promised . . .

Nothing hath been long more earnestly desired than the settling of the affairs of the Colony, as well as for the Government as other ways. Neither could there have been a greater Encouragement to the Planter, Then to understand it to be his Majesty's gracious pleasure that no person of whom they have heretofore justly complained should have any hand in the Government (either here or there). And we humbly desire your Lordships to solicit his Majesty (if it be not already done) for the speedy Accomplishment thereof . . .

His Majesty's gracious assurance that every man shall have his particular right preserved with addition of reasonable immunity will be a singular means of inviting many people hither and settling themselves here, who for the most heretofore, by reason of the many distractions and discouragements, have only endeavored a present crop and their hasty return, to the great hindrance of raising staple Commodities and all works of worth and continuance . . .

We humbly beseech his Majesty to continue his favor in prohibiting the importation and sale of all

Tobaccos except from this Colony and the Sommer Islands. And here we cannot but make remonstrance to your Lordships how prejudicial those petty Plantations of the English in the Salvage Islands in the West Indies must prove to this Colony . . .

Those great and important works of surprising the Indians, discoveries by sea and land, fortification against a foreign enemy, that they may be thorough and effectually performed will require no less numbers than five hundred soldiers to be yearly sent over for certain years with a full year's provision of victuals, apparel, arms, munitions, tools & all necessaries, To which worthy designs the Colony will be always ready to yield their best furtherance & assistance, as they have been very forward since the massacre, notwithstanding their great loss then sustained. And we conceive so great expence will have the better success if the ordering thereof be referred to the Governor and Council here residing with the advice (in special cases) of the General Assembly, both concerning this and all other things which may conduce to the settling of the Plantation . . .

We shall exactly observe his Majesty's Command that all judgments, Decrees, and important actions be given, determined and undertaken by the advice and voices of the greater part of the Council (which course also we heretofore observed in all our proceedings), and that all be done in his Majesty's name under whose royal Government and protection this Action (which hath hitherto labored under so many Difficulties) shall we doubt not receive the due perfection. And (as we never did) so we shall always forbear the Choosing of any Officers for longer time than during his Majesty's pleasure.

Thus beseeching your Lordships to Continue the Patronage of this Plantation that the beams of his Majesty's favor may, by your mediation and Counsels shine, and be derived upon us, to Cherish our Endeavors and quicken our new springing hopes that no Contrary gusts may nip them in the bud, nor envious cloud interpose itself between us and that comfortable light, we humbly take our leave.

The Puritan world view, like all cultural perspectives, rested upon assumptions which by their very nature are unprovable. First and most fundamental, the Puritans believed that there was one truth, that it was knowable, and that it should be defended against contrary opinions at all costs. They believed that man was corrupt and could be redeemed only through God's grace. Because of man's proneness to do evil, Puritans were certain that strong institutions of church and state were necessary to protect the individual from his sin and society from the sinner's wrong doing. Since God had clearly ordained governments and churches through his words in the Bible, man must seek to fulfill his obligations to God through these institutions and must subordinate his own will to that of the whole.

The Puritans — at least those spokesmen who have left a record of their intentions — were determined to turn Massachusetts Bay into a Bible commonwealth where both the church and civil governments were constructed from a Biblical blueprint. Thus, unlike the commercial projectors of Jamestown, the founders of Massachusetts Bay had a clear sense of the order they would establish in the New World. So clear was their purpose that rather than risk outside interference they arranged it so that only those men actually intending to emigrate could buy shares in the Massachusetts Bay Company. With all the shareholders leaving England as colonists, the charter itself was carried away, and English authorities succeeded in asserting their power over the Puritan colony only after years of conflict.

In the first reading, John Winthrop (1588–1648), who was the most distinguished man in the great Puritan migration from Old to New England, describes his vision of the Puritan mission in the New World. His speech was delivered to the America-bound passengers of the *Arbella*. Since Winthrop was elected governor repeatedly, his "Model of Christian Charity" can be considered an official picture of Puritan goals. Although like most of his contemporaries Winthrop accepted the idea of social inequality, he believed that through the different ranks of society each member became subordinate to the whole. His picture is

that of a corporate body where men's and women's differences and duties bind them together.

The cornerstone of the Puritan social structure was orthodoxy — that is, correct doctrines and practices based upon the Bible and enforced by appropriate authorities. To tolerate variety in religious opinions was not a virtue in Puritan eyes, but a damnable offense. They had been persecuted in England because of their noisy criticism of the Church of England. They persecuted others because dissent threatened their holy community. They had not made the hazardous trip to America for religious freedom. They had come to set an example of how God expected his children to live on earth. Nor were they hypocrites. Their spokesmen vigorously defended the punishment of those who offended the Lord with unorthodox opinions, nor did they bow before the new winds of religious liberty blowing through England. It was their descendents in the 18th century who became embarrassed about the intolerance of their forebears and circulated the notion that New England's founders were martyrs for religious freedom.

However, one of the fundamental weaknesses of Puritan thought was laid bare during the first few years of settlement in America. This was the contradiction between the Puritan assertion that there was one, knowable truth about God and the fact that within the Puritan fold equally committed men and women argued about what this truth was. First Roger Williams, then Anne Hutchinson, and then a succession of Baptists and Quakers arrived to disturb the peace of the Bible commonwealth with their highly inflammatory opinions. Williams maintained that the King of England had no right to grant lands which belonged to the Indians, that the Puritan churches should publicly scorn fellowship with the Church of England and that no government, however righteous, had the right to legislate in purely spiritual matters. Unwilling to keep silent, Williams was banished from Massachusetts Bay and took advantage of the endless space of the New World to make a home for his and other heresies in the area around Rhode Island.

Next Anne Hutchinson plunged the colony into turmoil with her belief in personal religious illumination which freed the individual from the authority of church, state, and the Bible. Again, after a characteristic period of argumentation and discussion, the Antinomians, as they were called, were banished. John Winthrop, however, was not content with getting rid of the local Antinomians. He wanted to protect the colony from any new arrivals from England, and so he persuaded the General Court to pass a law forbidding strangers to stay in Massachusetts Bay longer than three weeks without permission from a magistrate. Henry Vane, (1613–1662), a young Puritan gentleman who had served a term as governor of the colony, challenged this ordinance on grounds that it exceeded the magistrates' powers. The second reading is from this exchange between Winthrop and Vane. While the court order was obviously directed against the Antinomians, the more fundamental question was that of government power itself. The actual content of opinions thought to be dangerous can change, but the threat to ordered society remains — as does the essential conflict between corporate goals and individual rights. The issue has remained an enduring one, particularly in America, which from the outset has contained so many more variant opinions than traditional societies.

The last reading reveals yet another aspect of Puritan orthodoxy. This time the subject is the censuring of a Boston merchant for sharp business practices. Puritan ethics demanded that each person pursue a calling in life with industry and diligence, yet at no time were personal ambitions to take precedence over the common good as defined by the magistrates and clergy. This applied to all callings, be they in the professions or in the home-bound duties of the typical Puritan woman, but the tensions were most keenly felt by Puritan businessmen. Merchants who came to New England found that their dealings were closely watched. The same Puritan personal qualities of discipline and hard work which helped men prosper were also expected to keep in check the individualism associated with economic enterprise. God's grace might be inferred from worldly success, but success as a sign of righteousness worked both ways. The wealthy Puritan merchant who profited from the attention he gave to his own affairs was vulnerable to the charge that he

was laying up his treasures in this world. The inherent difficulty of maintaining a community ideal of just dealings in an economy relying upon personal initiative was brought out clearly when Robert Keayne (1595–1651) was called before the General Court for overcharging his customers. Winthrop described the case perfunctorily in his journal, but Keayne, deeply wounded, wrote an elaborate defense when he drew up a will over a decade later.

Despite the unlikeliness of a remote, religious colony like Massachusetts Bay being a place to make money, the New England economy developed rapidly. The business acumen of merchants like Keayne enabled the colony to thrive. Prosperity proved to be a mighty challenge to the fundamental principles of the Puritan Bible Commonwealth. Security, material well-being, even the astounding health of New Englanders, encouraged individual confidence and made the concept of total dependence upon God more a matter of doctrine than a felt reality. As the founders of Massachusetts Bay died off, the second generation began to lament the decline of piety, of community spirit, and of personal commitment. In time, with changing intellectual values from Europe and with increasing prosperity in the New World, the Puritan world view which had been shared by most of the other colonists, was replaced by the liberal propositions which underly modern culture. The colonists began to believe that man was not bathed in sin, that he need not be controlled by authoritarian institutions, and that truth as conceived by each individual was more important than the orthodox values set forth by the community.

Such a revolution in ideas took place over many years, but the roots of the change are discernible in the conflicts in which the Massachusetts colonists were embroiled in the 1630's. They are noticeable by the late 17th century, when William Penn and the proprietors of Carolina began advertising their colonies. The emphasis in these promotional tracts is upon the opportunity for private gain, the security of property, and the freedom from authority — particularly the authority of an orthodox church. The Quakers and Baptists who streamed into Pennsylvania in these decades had suffered from persecutions which attested to the strength of their religious convictions, but the English colonies in the New World appealed to the irreligious as well as the religious. Here there was the choice of living under authority or living free of it, living Godly lives according to one's particular persuasion or living where religious duties were carried lightly. The Old World offered no such choice.

John Winthrop: *A model of Christian charity (1630)*

God Almighty in His most holy and wise providence hath so disposed of the condition of mankind as in all times some must be rich, some poor; some high and eminent in power and dignity, others mean and in subjection.

The Reason hereof: First, to hold conformity with the rest of His world, being delighted to show forth the glory of His wisdom in the variety and difference of the creatures, and the glory of His power in ordering all these differences for the preservation and good of the whole, and the glory of His greatness: that as it is the glory of princes to have many officers, so this great king will have many stewards, counting Himself more honored in dispensing His gifts to man by man, than if He did it by His own immediate hand.

Secondly, that He might have the more occasion to manifest the work of His Spirit: first upon the wicked in moderating and restraining them, so that the rich and mighty should not eat up the poor, nor the poor and despised rise up against and shake off their yoke. Secondly, in the regenerate, in exercising His graces in them — as in the great ones, their love, mercy, gentleness, temperance, etc., in the poor and inferior sort, their faith, patience, obedience, etc.

Thirdly, that every man might have need of others, and from hence they might be all knit more nearly together in the bonds of brotherly affection. From hence it appears plainly that no man is made more honorable than another or more wealthy, etc., out of any particular and singular respect to himself, but for the glory of His creator and the common good of the creature, Man . . . All men being thus (by divine providence) ranked into two sorts, rich and poor. Under the first are comprehended all such as are able to live comfortably by their own means duly improved, and all others are poor according to the former distri-

---

Winthrop Papers, Massachusetts Historical Society, Boston, 1931, II, 315–18. Reprinted by permission.

bution. There are two rules whereby we are to walk one towards another: Justice and Mercy. These are always distinguished in their act and in their object, yet may they both concur in the same subject in each respect: as sometimes there may be an occasion of showing mercy to a rich man in some sudden danger or distress, and also doing of mere justice to a poor man in regard of some particular contract, etc. There is likewise a double law by which we are regulated in our conversation towards another: in both the former respects, the law of nature and the law of grace, or the moral law or the law of the Gospel . . .

This law of the Gospel propounds likewise a difference of seasons and occasions. There is a time when a Christian must sell all and give to the poor, as they did in the Apostles' times. There is a time also when Christians (though they give not all yet) must give beyond their ability, as they of Macedonia (Cor. 2,6). Likewise, community of perils calls for extraordinary liberality, and so doth community in some special service for the church. Lastly, when there is no other means whereby our Christian brother may be relieved in his distress, we must help him beyond our ability rather than tempt God in putting him upon help by miraculous or extraordinary means . . .

He that gives to the poor lends to the Lord, and He will repay him even in this life an hundredfold to him or his — *the righteous is ever merciful and lendeth and his seed enjoyeth the blessing.* And besides, we know what advantage it will be to us in the day of account when many such witnesses shall stand forth for us to witness the improvement of our talent. And I would know of those who plead so much for laying up for time to come, whether they hold that to be Gospel (Matt. 16.19)? *Lay not up for yourselves treasures upon earth*, etc. If they acknowledge it, what extent will they allow it? If only to those primitive times, let them consider the reason whereupon our Savior grounds it. The first is that they are subject to the moth, the rust, the thief. Secondly, they will steal away the heart: *where the treasure is, there will ye heart be also.* The reasons are of like force at all times. Therefore, the exhortation must be general and perpetual, withallways in respect of the love and affection to riches, and in regard of the things themselves when any special service for the church or particular distress of our brother calls for the use of them. Otherwise it is not only lawful but necessary to lay up, as Joseph did, to have ready upon such occasions as the Lord (whose stewards we are of them) shall call for them from us . . . All these teach us that the Lord looks that when He is pleased to call for His right in any thing we have, our own interest must stand aside til His turn be served. For the other, we need look no further than to that of John 1: *he who hath this world's goods and seeth his brother to need and shuts up his compassion from him, how dwelleth the love of God in him —* which comes punctually to this conclusion; if thy brother be in want and thou canst help him, thou needst not make doubt what thou shouldst do; if thou lovest God, thou must help him . . .

He that soweth sparingly shall reap sparingly. Having already set forth the practice of mercy according to the rule of God's law, it will be useful to lay open the grounds of it also. Being the other part of the commandment, and that is the affection from which this exercise of mercy must arise, the apostle tells us that this *love is the fulfilling of the law*, not that it is enough to love our brother and so no further; but in regard of the excellency of his parts giving any motion to the other, as the soul to the body and the power it hath to set all the faculties on work in the outward exercise of this duty: as when we bid one make the clock strike, he doth not lay hand on the hammer, which is the immediate instrument of the sound, but sets on work the first mover or main wheel, knowing that will certainly produce the sound which he intends. So the way to draw men to the works of mercy is not by force of argument from the goodness or necessity of the work, for though this cause may enforce a rational mind to some present act of mercy, as is frequent in experience, yet it cannot work such a habit in a soul as shall make it prompt upon all occasions to produce the same effect, but by framing these affections of love in the heart, which will as naturally bring forth the other as any cause doth produce the effect.

The definition which the Scripture gives us of love is this: *love is the bond of perfection.* First, it is a bond or ligament. Secondly, it makes the work perfect. There is no body but consists of parts, and that which knits these parts together gives the body its per-fection, because it makes each part so contiguous to others as thereby they do mutually participate with each other, both in strength and infirmity, in pleasure and pain. To instance in the most perfect of all bodies — Christ and His church make one body. The several parts of this body considered apart before they were united, were as disproportionate and as much disordering as so many contrary qualities or elements; but when Christ comes, and by His spirit and love knits all these parts to Himself and each to other, it is become the most perfect and best proportioned body in the world . . .

From hence we may frame these conclusions. First of all, true Christians are of one body in Christ (1 Cor. 12. 12. 13. 17). *Ye are the body of Christ and members of their part.* All the parts of this body being thus united are made so contiguous in a special relation as they must needs partake of each others strength and infirmity, joy and sorrow, weal and woe (1 Cor. 12. 26). *If one member suffers, all suffer with it, if one be in honor, all rejoice with it.* Secondly, the ligaments of this body which knit together, are love. Thirdly, no body can be perfect which wants its proper ligament. Fifthly, this sensibleness and sympathy of each other's conditions will necessarily infuse into each part a native desire and endeavor to strengthen, defend, preserve and comfort the other. To insist a little on this conclusion being the product of all the former, the truth hereof will appear both by precept and pattern . . . The like we shall find in the histories of the church in all ages: the sweet sympathy of affections which was in the members of this body one towards another, their cheerfulness in sorrowing and suffering together, how liberal they were without repining, harborers without grudging, and helpful without reproaching. And all from hence, because they had fervent love amongst them, which only makes the practice of mercy constant and easy.

The next consideration is how this love comes to be wrought. Adam in his first estate was a perfect model of mankind in all their generations, and in him this love was perfected in regard of the habit. But Adam rent himself from His creator, rent all his posterity also one from another, whence it comes that every man is born with this principle in him: to love and seek himself only. And thus a man continueth til Christ comes and takes possession of the soul and infuseth another principle: love to God and our brother. And this latter having continual supply from Christ, as the head and root by which he is united, gets the predominating in the soul, so by little and little expels the former . . . Nothing yields more pleasure and content to the soul than when it finds that which it may love fervently, for to love and live beloved is the soul's paradise both here and in heaven. In the state of wedlock there be many comforts to learn out of the troubles of that condition, but let such as have tried the most say if there be any sweetness in that condition comparable to the exercise of mutual love.

From the former considerations arise these conclusions: First, this love among Christians is a real thing, not imaginary. Secondly, this love is as absolutely necessary to the being of the body of Christ as the sinews and other ligaments of a natural body are to the being of that body. Thirdly, this love is a divine, spiritual nature: free, active, strong, couragious, permanent; undervaluing all things beneath its proper object, and, of all the graces, this makes us nearer to resemble the virtues of our heavenly Father. Fourthly, it rests in the love and welfare of its beloved . . .

It rests now to make some application of this discourse, by the present design, which gave the occasion of writing of it. Herein are 4 things to be propounded: first the persons, secondly the work, thirdly the end, fourthly the means. 1. For *the persons*. We are a company professing ourselves fellow members of Christ, in which respect, only though we were absent from each other many miles, and had our employments as far distant, yet we ought to account ourselves knit together by this bond of love, and live in the exercise of it if we would have comfort of our being in Christ . . . 2. For the *work* we have in hand. It is by a mutual consent, through a special overvaluing providence and a more than an ordinary approbation of the churches of Christ, to seek out a place of cohabitation and consorteeship under a due form of government, both civil and ecclesiastical. In such cases as this, the care of the public must oversway all private respects, by which not only conscience but mere civil policy, doth bind us. For it is a true rule that particular estates cannot subsist in the ruin of the public. 3. The *end* is to improve our lives to do more service to the Lord. The comfort and increase of the body of Christ, whereof we are members, that ourselves and posterity may be the better preserved from the common corruptions of this evil world, to serve the Lord and work out our salvation under the power and purity of His holy ordinances . . . Thus stands the cause between God and us. We are entered into covenant with Him for this work. We have taken out a commission. The Lord hath given us leave to draw our own articles. We have professed to enterprise these and those accounts, upon these and those ends. We have hereupon besought Him of favor and blessing. Now if the Lord shall please to hear us and bring us in peace to the place we desire, then hath He ratified this covenant and sealed our commission, and will expect a strict performance of the articles contained in it. But if we shall neglect the observation of these articles which are the ends we have propounded, and, dissembling with our God, shall fall to embrace this present world and prosecute our carnal intentions, seeking great things for ourselves and our posterity, the Lord will surely break out in wrath against us, be revenged of such a sinful people, and make us know the price of the breach of such a covenant.

Now the only way to avoid this shipwreck and to provide for our posterity, is to follow the counsel of Micah: *to do justly, to love mercy, to walk humbly with our God*. For this end we must be knit together in this work as one man. We must entertain each other in brotherly affection. We must be willing to abridge ourselves of our superfluities for the supply of others' necessities. We must uphold a familiar commerce together in all meekness, gentleness, patience, and liberality. We must delight in each other, make others' conditions our own, rejoice together, mourn together, labor and suffer together, always having before our eyes our commission and community in the work as members of the same body. So shall we keep the unity of the spirit in the bond of peace. The Lord will be our God, and delight to dwell among us as His own people, and will command a blessing upon us in all our ways, so that we shall see much more of his wisdom, power, goodness and truth than formerly we have been acquainted with. We shall find that the God of Israel is among us when ten of us shall be able to resist a thousand of our enemies, when he shall make us a praise and glory that men shall say of succeeding plantations:

"the Lord make it like that of New England." For we must consider that we shall be as a city upon a hill. The eyes of all people are upon us, so that if we shall deal falsely with our God in this work we have undertaken, as so cause Him to withdraw His present help from us, we shall be made a story and a byword through the world. We shall open the mouths of enemies to speak evil of the ways of God, and all professors for God's sake. We shall shame the faces of many of God's worthy servants, and cause their prayers to be turned into curses upon us til we be consumed out of the good land whither we are going.

John Winthrop: A declaration of the intent and equity of the order made at the last court, to this effect, that none should be received to inhabit within the jurisdiction but such as should be allowed by some of the magistrates (1637)

For clearing of such scruples as have arisen about this order, it is to be considered, first, what is the essential form of a commonwealth or body politic such as this is, which I conceive to be this — The consent of a certain company of people to cohabit together, under one government for their mutual safety and welfare.

In this description all these things do concur to the well being of such a body, 1 Persons, 2 Place, 3 Consent, 4 Government or Order, 5 Welfare.

It is clearly agreed, by all, that the care of safety and welfare was the original cause or occasion of common weales and of many families subjecting themselves to rulers and laws; for no man hath lawful power over another, but by birth or consent, so likewise, by the law of propriety, no man can have just interest in that which belongeth to another, without his consent. From these premises will arise these conclusions:

1. No commonwealth can be founded but by free consent.

2. The persons so incorporating have a public and relative interest each in other, and in the place of their co-habitation and goods, and laws &c. and in all the means of their welfare so as none other can claim privilege with them but by free consent.

3. The nature of such an incorporation ties every member thereof to seek out and entertain all means that may conduce to the welfare of the body, and to keep off whatsoever doth appear to tend to their damage.

4. The welfare of the whole is [not] to be put to apparent hazard for the advantage of any particular members.

From these conflusions I thus reason.

1. If we here be a corporation established by free consent, if the place of our co-habitation be our own, then no man hath right to come into us &c without our consent.

2. If no man hath right to our lands, our government privileges &c, but by our consent, then it is reason we should take notice of before we confer any such upon them.

3. If we are bound to keep off whatsoever appears to tend to our ruin or damage, then we may lawfully refuse to receive such whose dispositions suit not with ours and whose society (we know) will be hurtfull to us, and therefore it is lawful to take knowledge of all men before we receive them.

4. The churches take liberty (as lawfully they may) to receive or reject at their discretion; yea particular towns make orders to the like effect; why then should the commonwealth be denied the like liberty, and the whole more restrained than any part?

5. If it be sin in us to deny some men place &c amongst us, then it is because of some right they have to this place &c for to deny a man that which he hath no right unto, is neither sin nor injury.

6. If strangers have right to our houses or lands &c, then it is either of justice or of mercy; if of justice let them plead it, and we shall know what to answer: but if it be only in way of mercy, or by the rule of hospitality &c, then I answer 1st a man is not a fit object of mercy except he be in misery. 2d. We are not bound to exercise mercy to others to the ruin of ourselves. 3d. There are few that stand in need of mercy at their first coming hither. As for hospitality, that rule doth not bind further than for some present occasion, not for continual residence.

The following three selections are from Thomas Hutchinson (ed.), *A Collection of Original Papers Relative to the History of the Colony of Massachusetts Bay,* Thomas and John Heet, Boston, 1769, pp. 79-113.

7.   A family is a little commonwealth, and a commonwealth is a great family. Now as a family is not bound to entertain all comers, no not every good man (otherwise than by way of hospitality) no more is a commonwealth.

8.   It is a generall received rule, *turpius ejicitur quam non admittitur hospes,* it is worse to receive a man whom we must cast out again, than to deny him admittance.

9.   The rule of the Apostle, John 2. 10. is, that such as come and bring not the true doctrine with them should not be received to house, and by the same reason not into the commonwealth.

10.   Seeing it must be granted that there may come such persons (suppose Jesuits &c) which by consent of all ought to be reflected, it will follow that by this law (being only for notice to be taken of all that come to us, without which we cannot avoid such as indeed are to be kept out) is no other but just and needful, and if any should be rejected that ought to be received, that is not to be imputed to the law, but to those who are betrusted with the execution of it. And herein is to be considered, what the intent of the law is, and by consequence, by what rule they are to walk, who are betrusted with the keeping of it. The intent of the law is to preserve the welfare of the body; and for this end to have none received into any fellowship with it who are likely to disturb the fame, and this intent (I am sure) is lawful and good. Now then, if such to whom the keeping of this law is committed, be persuaded in their judgments that such a man is likely to disturb and hinder the public weale, but some others who are not in the same trust, judge otherwise, yet they are to follow their own judgments, rather than the judgments of others who are not alike interested: As in trial of an offender by jury; the twelve men are satisfied in their consciences, upon the evidence given, that the party deserves death: but there are 20 or 40 standers by, who conceive otherwise, yet is the jury bound to condemn him according to their own consciences, and not to acquit him upon the different opinion of other men, except their reasons can convince them of the error of their consciences, and this is according to the rule of the Apostle. Rom. 14.5. Let every man be fully persuaded in his own mind.

If it be objected, that some prophane persons are received and others who are religious are rejected, I answer 1st, It is not known that any such thing has as yet fallen out. 2. Such a practice may be justifiable as the case may be, for younger persons (even prophane ones) may be of less danger to the commonwealth (and to the churches also) than some older persons, though professors of religion: for our Saviour Christ when he conversed with publicans &c. sayeth that such were nearer the Kingdom of heaven than the religious pharisees, and one that is of large parts and confirmed in some erroneous way, is likely to do more harm to church and commonwealth, and is of less hope to be reclaimed, than 10 prophane persons, who have not yet become hardened, in the contempt of the meanes of grace.

Lastly, whereas it is objected that by this law, we reject good christians and so consequently Christ himself: I answer It is not known that any christian man hath been rejected . . . It is said that this law was made of purpose to keep away such as are of Mr. Wheelwright his judgment (admit it were so which yet I cannot confess) where is the evil of it? If we conceive and find by sad experience that his opinions are such, as by his own profession cannot stand with external peace, may we not provide for our peace, by keeping of such as would strengthen him and infect others with such dangerous tenets? and if we find his opinions such as will cause divisions, and make people look at their magistrates, ministers and brethren as enemies to Christ and Antichrists &c, is it not sin and unfaithfulness in us, to receive more of those opinions, which we already find the evil fruit of: Nay, why do not those who now complain join with us in keeping out of such, as well as formerly they did in expelling Mr Williams for the like, though less dangerous? Where this change of their judgments should arise I leave them to themselves to examine, and I earnestly entreat them so to do, and for this law let the equally minded judge, what evil they find in it, or in the practice of those who are betrusted with the execution of it.

Henry Vane: A brief answer to a certain declaration, made to the intent and equity of the order of court, that none should be received to inhabit within this jurisdiction, but such as should be allowed by some of the magistrates (1637)

The scope of the declaration is to defend and justify the order in question . . . The description which is set down in effect is this. A commonwealth is a certain company of people consenting to cohabit together under one government, for their mutual safety and welfare. In which description this main fault is found. At the best it is but a description of a commonwealth at large, and not of such a commonwealth as this (as is said) which is not only christian, but dependant upon the grant also of our Sovereign: for so are the express words of that order of Court to which the whole country was required to subscribe.

Now if you will define a christian commonwealth there must be put in, such a consent as is according to God: a subjecting to such a government as is according unto Christ. And if you will define a corporation, incorporated by virtue of the grant of our Sovereign, it must be such a consent as the grant requires and permits and in that manner and form as it prescribes, or else it will be defective. The commonwealth here described, may be a company of Turkish pirates as well as Christian professors, unless the consent and government be better limited than it is in this definition; for sure it is, all Pagans and Infidels, even the Indians here amongst us, may come within this compass. And is this such a body politic as ours, as you say? God forbid. Our commonwealth we fear would be twice miserable, if Christ and the King should be shut out so. Reasons taken from the nature of a commonwealth, not founded upon Christ, nor by his Majesty's charters, must needs fall to the ground . . . Members of a commonwealth may not seek out all means that may conduce to the welfare of the body, but all lawful and due means, according to the charter they hold by, either from God or the King, or from both: Nor may they keep out whatsoever doth appear to tend to their damage (for many things appear which are not) but such, as upon right and evident grounds, do so appear, and are so in truth. Thus far concerning that which hath been touched may for the present suffice.

The second thing is the reasons, which we shall set down and answer.

The first reason of the equity of the order is this, "If we be a corporation established by free consent, if the place of our habitation be our own, then no man hath right to come unto us without our consent."

Answer. We do not know how we that stand a corporation, by virtue of the King's charter, can thus argue; yet to avoid dispute, suppose the antecedent should be granted, the consequence does not follow. This is all that can be inferred, that our consent, regulated by the word and suitable to our patent, ought to be required, not this vast and illimited consent here spoken of, our consent is not our own when rightly limited, 1 Cor. 6. 19. 20. An unlawful dissent can hinder no man, though a lawful may.

The second reason runs thus, "If no man hath right to our lands, our government privileges, &c. but by our consent, then it is reason we should take notice of men before we confer any such upon them."

Answer. Beside the doubtfulness of the truth of the supposition, the question here is changed; for so most states do in taking the names of such as come to dwell among them, but the question is whether the admitting or rejecting of persons should depend upon such unlimited and unsafe a rule, as the will and discretion of men, suppose magistrates or others not regulated.

The third reason is thus framed, "If we are bound to keep off whatever appears to tend to our ruin and damage, then we may lawfully refuse to receive such whose dispositions suit not with ours, and whose society we know will be hurtful unto us, and therefore it is lawful to take knowledge of men before we do receive them."

Answer. This kind of reasoning is very confused and fallacious, for the question here is not only changed, but there is this further deceit of wrapping up many questions in one, and besides if it were put into a right form, the assumption would be false.

The question is not, as was said before, whether Knowledge may not be taken of men, before they be received, nor whether magistrates may refuse such as suit not with their dispositions, or such whose society they know will be hurtful to them; though the second of these is not nor cannot be proved; but whether persons may be rejected, or admitted, upon the illimited consent or dissent of magistrates. The assumption also would be false, for men are not to keep off whatever appears to tend to their ruin, but what really doth so . . . Let us then do unto our brethren at least as we would desire to be done unto by Barbarians, which is not to be rejected, because we do not suit with the disposition of their Sachem, nor because, by our coming, God takes them away and troubles them, and so, to their appearance, we ruin them.

The fourth argument stands thus: "The churches take liberty (as lawfully they may) to receive or reject at their discretion; yea particular towns make orders to such effect, why then should the commonwealth be denied the like liberty, and the whole more restrained than any part?"

Answer.   Though the question be here concluded, yet it is far from being soundly proved, yea, in truth, we much wonder that any member of a church should be ignorant of the falseness of the groundwork upon which this conclusion is built; for should churches have this power, as you say they have, to receive or reject at their discretion, they would quickly grow corrupt enough. Churches have no liberty to receive or reject, at their discretions, but at the discretion of Christ, whatsoever is done in word or deed, in church or commonwealth, must be done in the name of the Lord Jesus. Neither hath church nor commonwealth any other than ministeriall power from Christ, who is the head of the church, and the prince of the kings of the earth . . .

The fifth reason produced is, "If it be sin in us, to deny some men place amongst us, then it is because they have some right to our place."

Answer.   The question is here again changed, for it is not whether some may be denied, but whether any or all such as the magistrates illimited dissent shall rejecte. But besides this, we say, that the King's Christian subjects have right by his majesty's patent, to come over and plant in places not inhabited, for a double end, 1st. to enlarge his majesty's dominions; 2dly, for the conversion of the Pagans. And since his majesty hath given them right for these ends, we may not deny them, unless they forfeit it, either by denying the land which they inhabit to be an enlargement of his majesty's dominions, or becoming such dissolute and prophane persons as rather do harden the Indians than be a means of their conversion, for by so doing we shall exceed the limits of his majesty's grant, and forfeit the

privileges, government and lands which we challenge to be our own.

Moreover, we may not deny residence to any of his majesty's subjects without just grounds, except we will do injury both to the King and his subjects, who have adventured both their estates and lives to enjoy those privileges and liberties, which he hath granted them . . .

The seventh reason is this, "A family is a little commonwealth and a commonwealth is a great family, now a family is not bound to entertain all comers, no not every good man, otherwise than by way of hospitality, no more is a commonwealth."

Answer.   Here again the question is much changed, it should not have been proved that we are not bound to receive all comers nor all good men, but rather no comers at all, unless it be upon the unlimited consent of the magistrates. Although it be true, that there is some proportion between a family and a commonwealth, yet there is a great disparity in this matter. A master of a family hath another kind of right to his house and estate than this commonwealth hath to all the houses and lands within this patent. The master of a family may bequeath his whole estate to his wife and children, and so may not the body of this commonwealth to theirs . . .

The law is excused because it hath a good intent, but good intents do not make a law or action good, what was intended the execution doth declare. Now is it sufficient for those who are betrusted with the execution of this law to follow their persuasions, judgements, and consciences, except they be rightly ruled by the word of truth! . . .

These objections and answers being viewed, and what is unsound refuted, we come to the conclusion, wherein we are desired to judge what evil we find in the law, and this we will do faithfully by the help of Christ. This law we judge to be most wicked and sinful, and that for these reasons.

1.   Because this law doth leave these weighty matters of the commonwealth, of receiving or rejecting such as come over to the approbation of magistrates, and suspends these things upon the judgment of man, whereas the judgment is Gods, Deut. 1. 17. This is made a

ground work of gross popery. Priests and magistrates are to judge, but it must be according to the law of God, Deut. 17. 9, 10, 11. That law which gives that without limitation to man, which is proper to God, cannot be just.

2. Because here is liberty given by this law to expel and reject those which are most eminent christians, if they suit not with the disposition of the magistrates, whereby it will come to pass, that Christ and his members will find worse entertainment amongst us than the Israelites did amongst the Egyptians and Babilonians, than Abraham and Isaack did amongst the Philistines, than Jacob amongst the Shechemites, yea even than Lott amongst the Sodomites. These all gave leave to God's people, to sit down amongst them, though they could not claime such right as the King's subjects may. Now that law, the execution whereof may make us more cruel and tyranical over God's children than Pagans, yea than Sodomites, must needs be most wicked and sinful.

3. This law doth cross many laws of Christ, Christ would have us render unto Caesar the things that are Caesars, Math. 22. 21. But this law will not give unto the King's majesty his right of planting some of his subjects amongst us, except they please them, Christ bids us not to forget to entertain strangers, Heb. 13. 2. But here by this law we must not entertain, for any continuance of time, such stranger as the magistrates like not, though they be never so gracious, allowed by both God and good men, except we will forfeit unto them our whole estates, it may be and much more than our estates comes unto. Christ commands us to do good unto all, but especially to them of the household of faith. Many other laws there are of Christ, which this law dasheth against, and therefore is most wicked and sinful.

John Winthrop: A reply to an answer made to a declaration of the intent and equity of the order made at the court in May last, whereby none are to be received &c. but by allowance of the Magistrates (1637)

Contentions among brethren are sad spectacles, among the churches of Christ, especially when they come once to favour of bitternesse, which would have discourged me from publishing the former declaration, if I could have expected such an answer . . . Many faults doth the Answerer find in my declaration . . . I will join with him in the question, as he states it, viz.

Whether the admitting or rejecting of persons should depend upon the discretions of men, which he calls an unlimited and unsafe rule and their discretion not regulated, though they should be magistrates.

To this I reply, or rather answer, first, That which he takes for granted, and wherein lies the whole strength of his defence is untrue, viz. That the magistrates will and discretion in our case is not regulated, for first, the magistrates are members of the churches here and, by that covenant, are regulated to direct all their ways by the rule of the gospel, and if they fail in anything, they are subject to the churches correction. Secondly. As they are freemen, they are regulated by oath, to direct their aimes to the welfare of this civil body. Thirdly. As they are magistrates, they are sworn to do right to all, and regulated by their relation to the people, to seek their welfare in all things; so as here is no such irregulated discretion as is supposed, and it seems to me an improper speech and favouring of contradiction; for discretion always implies a rule for its guide. And herein I have occasion to take in his answer to my fourth reason drawn from the practice of our churches, and some towns where matters of admitting or rejecting are ordered by discretion . . . Did he ever hear, that our practise is, that none are propounded to the congregation, except they be first allowed by the elders, and is not this to admit or reject by discretion? Did he never hear of a christian man rejected by the church, or put off at least, because a brother hath professed want of satisfaction? Hath he never heard that the dissent of some few brethren may, by rule, (as hath been said) cause the rejection of a man, whom all the rest of the brethren shall approve of? And where is Christ's voice to be heard now, if he will have discretion shut out of the church. So says the instance of town matters (which he wisely declines and gives no answer to) he well knows that within the town of Boston it is an established order, that none should be received into cohabitation there, except they be allowed by certain men appointed to judge of their fitness for church-fellowship. And so, whereas the way of God hath always been to gather his churches out of the world; now, the world, or civil state, must be raised

raised out of the churches . . .

My fifth reason is, that it is no sin or injury to deny a man that which he hath no right unto, therefore we may deny some men place amongst us. In the answer, there is again complaint of changing the question, because I go about to prove that some men may be rejected, which he seemeth to grant, and if so then that which he maketh the main question will easily be cleared, for if we may reject some, then the care of this must be committed to some persons, for to speak of discerning Christ his authority in church or commonwealth, otherwise than as it is dispensed in the ministry of men, is a mere idea or fantasy. If then it must be committed to some persons, to whom may it more properly than to the fathers of the commonwealth? And if it cannot be foreseen who are to be received and who to be rejected, those persons must be trusted with the trial of them, and if no certain rule can be set down which may be sufficient to discern of every man, then must it be committed to their discretion, regulated by the work of God, and the duty of their place, which they are bound to observe. And whereas the Answerer cries out against this course as vast, illimited, sinful and injurious, and yet will not (and cannot) prescribe us a better, neither in his answer, nor at the court when he opposed the making of this law, may we not safely judge that such opposition and those reproachful termes as are cast from it, upon an ordinance of God, in the faces of those whom he would have to be had in honor for his sake, proceed rather from distemper of mind, than from any just cause of offence? . . .

It is apparent that the care of their welfare was the only occasion and ground (next the glory of God) of the making of this law: For, the court, taking notice how the hearts of the faithful were sadded by the spreading of diverse new and unfound opinions, and the uncharitable censures which they lay under by occasion of them, how brotherly love and communion decayed, how the ordinances of religion were neglected, and the faithful dispensers thereof (sometimes more precious than fine gold) slighted and reproached, throughout the whole countrey, they found it needful to provide remedy in time, that it might go well with the houshold of faith, and through the execution of this law should turn to the damage of some of this house-

hold, yet better it is some member should suffer the evil they bring upon themselves, than that, by indulgence towards them, the ehole family of God in this countrey should be scattered, if not destroyed . . .

John Winthrop: Journal (1639)

Mo. (November). At a general court holden at Boston, great complaint was made of the oppression used in the the country in sale of foreign commodities; and Mr. Robert Keaine, who kept a shop in Boston, was notoriously above others observed and complained of; and, being convented, he was charged with many particulars; in some, for taking above six-pence in the shilling profit; in some above eight-pence; and, in some small things, above two for one; and being hereof convict, (as appears by the records,) he was fined £200, which came thus to pass: The deputies considered, apart, of his fine, and set it at £200; the magistrates agreed but to £100. So, the court being divided, at length it was agreed, that his fine should be £200, but he should pay but £100, and the other should be respited to the further consideration of the next general court. By this means the magistrates and deputies were brought to an accord, which otherwise had not been likely, and so much trouble might have grown, and the offender escaped censure. For the cry of the country was so great against oppression, and some of the elders and magistrates had declared such detestation of the corrupt practice of this man (which was the more observable, because he was wealthy and sold dearer than most other tradesmen, and for that he was of ill report for the like covetous practice in England, that incensed the deputies very much against him). And sure the course was very evil, especial circumstances considered: 1. He being an ancient professor of the gospel: 2. A man of eminent parts: 3. Wealthy, and having but one child: 4. Having come over for conscience' sake, and for the advancement of the gospel here: 5. Having been formerly dealt with and admonished, both by private friends and also by some of the magistrates and elders, and having promised reformation; being a member of a church and commonwealth now in their infancy, and

John Winthrop, *The History of New England from 1630 to 1649*, James Savage (ed.), Phelps and Farham, Boston, 1825–26, I, 377–82.

under the curious observation of all churches and civil states in the world. These added much aggravation to his sin in the judgment of all men of understanding. Yet most of the magistrates (though they discerned of the offence clothed with all these circumstances) would have been more moderate in their censure: 1. Because there was no law in force to limit or direct men in point of profit in their trade. 2. Because it is the common practice, in all countries, for men to make use of advantages for raising the prices of their commodities. 3. Because (though he were chiefly aimed at, yet) he was not alone in this fault. 4. Because all men through the country, in sale of cattle, corn, labor, etc., were guilty of the like excess in prices. 5. Because a certain rule could not be found out for an equal rate between buyer and seller, though much labor had been bestowed in it, and divers laws had been made, which, upon experience, were repealed, as being neither safe nor equal. Lastly, and especially, because the law of God appoints no other punishment but double restitution; and, in some cases, as where the offender freely confesseth, and brings his offering, only half added to the principal. After the court had censured him, the church of Boston called him also in question, where (as before he had done in the court) he did, with tears, acknowledge and bewail his covetous and corrupt heart, yet making some excuse for many of the particulars, which were charged upon him, as partly by pretence of ignorance of the true price of some wares, and chiefly by being misled by some false principles, as 1. That, if a man lost in one commodity, he might help himself in the price of another. 2. That if, through want of skill or other occasion, his commodity cost him more than the price of the market in England, he might then sell it for more than the price of the market in New England, etc. These things gave occasion to Mr. Cotton, in his public exercise the next lecture day, to lay open the error of such false principles, and to give some rules of direction in the case.

Some false principles were these: —

1. That a man might sell as dear as he can, and buy as cheap as he can.

2. If a man lose by casualty of sea, etc., in some of his commodities, he may raise the price of the rest.

3. That he may sell as he bought, though he paid too dear, etc., and though the commodity be fallen, etc.

4. That, as a man may take the advantage of his own skill or ability, so he may of another's ignorance or necessity.

5. Where one gives time for payment, he is to take like recompense of one as of another.

The rules for trading were these: —

1. A man may not sell above the current price, i.e., such a price as is usual in the time and place, and as another (who knows the worth of the commodity) would give for it, if he had occasion to use it; as that is called current money, which every man will take, etc.

2. When a man loseth in his commodity for want of skill, etc., he must look at it as his own fault or cross, and therefore must not lay it upon another.

3. Where a man loseth by casualty of sea, or, etc., it is a loss cast upon himself by providence, and he may not ease himself of it by casting it upon another; for so a man should seem to provide against all providences, etc., that he should never lose; but where there is a scarcity of the commodity, there men may raise their price; for now it is a hand of God upon the commodity, and not the person.

4. A man may not ask any more for his commodity than his selling price, as Ephron to Abraham, the land is worth thus much.

The cause being debated by the church, some were earnest to have him excommunicated; but the most thought an admonition would be sufficient. Mr. Cotton opened the causes, which required excommunication, out of that in 1 Cor. 5. 11. The point now in question was, whether these actions did declare him to be such a covetous person, etc. Upon which he showed, that it is neither the habit of covetousness, (which is in every man in some degree,) nor simply the act, that declares a man to be such, but when it appears, that a man sins against his conscience, or the very light of nature, and when it appears in a man's whole conversation. But Mr. Keaine did not appear to be such, but rather upon an error in his judgment, being led by false principles; and beside, he is otherwise liberal, as in his hospitality, and in church communion, etc. So, in the end, the church consented to an admonition.

Robert Keayne: *Last will and testament (1653)*

I, Robert Keayne, citizen and merchant tailor of London by freedom and by the good providence of God now dwelling at Boston in New England in America, being at this time through the great goodness of my God both in health of body and of able and sufficient memory, yet considering that all flesh is as grass that must wither and will return to the dust and that my life may be taken away in a moment, therefore that I may be in the better readiness — freed from the distracting cares of the disposing of my outward estate . . . when the mind should be taken up with more serious and weighty considerations — I do therefore now in my health make, ordain, and declare this to be my last will and testament and to stand and to be as effectual as if I had made it in my sickness or in the day or hour of my death, which is in manner and form following.

First and before all things, I commend and commit my precious soul into the hands of Almighty God, who not only as a loving creator hath given it unto me when He might have made me a brute beast, but also as a most loving father and merciful saviour hath redeemed it with the precious blood of His own dear son and my sweet Jesus from that gulf of misery and ruin that I by original sin and actual transgressions had plunged it into. Therefore, I renounce all manner of known errors, all Popish and prelatical superstitions, all anabaptistical enthusiasms and familistical delusions, with all other feigned devices and all old and new upstart opinions, unsound and blasphemous errors, and other high imaginations that exalt themselves against the honor and trugh of God in the way of His worship and ordinances and against the dignity and scepter of the Lord Jesus Christ my Saviour.

I do further desire from my heart to renounce all

Bernard Bailyn (ed.), "The Apologia of Robert Keayne," *Publications of the Colonial Society of Massachusetts*, Colonial Society of Massachusetts, Boston, 1954, V, 249–50, 293–309. Reprinted by permission.

confidence or expectation of merit or desert in any of the best duties or services that ever I have, shall, or can be able to perform, acknowledging that all my righteousness, sanctification, and close walking with God, if it were or had been a thousand times more exact than ever yet I attained to, is all polluted and corrupt and falls short of commending me to God in point of my justification or helping forward my redemption or salvation. They deserve nothing at God's hand but hell and condemnation if He should enter into judgment with me for them. And though I believe that all my ways of holiness are of no use to me in point of justification, yet I believe they may not be neglected by me without great sin, but are ordained of God for me to walk in them carefully, in love to Him, in obedience to His commandments, as well as for many other good ends. They are good fruits and evidences of justification. Therefore, renouncing though not the acts yet all confidence in those acts of holiness and works of sanctification performed by me, I look for my acceptance with God and the salvation of my soul only from the merits or righteousness of the Lord Jesus Christ, and from the free, bountiful, and undeserved grace and love of God in Him.

It may be some . . . may marvel . . . that I should give away so much of my estate in private legacies and to private uses which might better have been spared and to give little or nothing to any public use for the general good of the country and commonwealth [except] what I have appropriated to our own town of Boston.

To answer this doubt or objection I must acknowledge that it hath been in my full purpose and resolution ever since God hath given me any comfortable estate to do good withal, not only before I came into New England but often since, to study and endeavor both in my life and at my death to do what I could do to help on any public, profitable, and general good here . . . My thoughts and intents have been about the castle for public defense, the college and schools for learning, the setting up of a bridewell or workhouse for prisoners, malefactors, and some sort of poor people, stubborn, idle, and undutiful youth, as children and servants, to have been kept at work in either for correction or to get their living, and some other things that I need not mention. In which things, though I could not have done so much as I desired, yet so much I should have done as might have proved an example and encouragement to others of greater estates and willing minds to have done more and to have helped to carry them on to more perfection. For I have held it a great degree of unthankfulness to God that when He hath bestowed many blessings and a large or comfortable outward estate upon a man that he should leave all to his wife and children to advance them only by making them great and rich in the world or to bestow it upon some friends or kindred that it may be hath no great need of it and to dispose none or very little of it to public charitable or good works such as may tend to His glory and the good of others in way of a thankful acknowledgment to Him for so great favors.

But the truth is that unkindness and ill requital of my former love, cost, and pains both in Old England and here which I have taken to promote the good of this place has been answered by divers here with unchristian, uncharitable, and unjust reproaches and slanders since I came hither, as if men had the liberty of their tongues to reproach any that were not beneficial to them. [These attacks came] together with that deep and sharp censure that was laid upon me in the country and carried on with so much bitterness and indignation of some, contrary both to law or any foregoing precedent if I mistake not, and, I am sure, contrary or beyond the quality and desert of the complaints that came against me, which indeed were rather shadows of offense . . . Yet by some it was carried on with such violence and pretended zeal as if they had had some of the greatest sins in the world to censure . . . Had it been in their power or could they have carried it they would not have corrected or reformed but utterly have ruined myself and all that I had, as if no punishment had been sufficient to expiate my offense [of] selling a good bridle for 2 s. that now worse are sold without offense for 3 s., 6 d. nails for 7 d., and 8 d. nails for 20 d. per hundred, which since and to this day are frequently sold by many for a great deal more. And so [it was] in all other things proportionably, as selling gold buttons for two shilling nine pence a dozen that cost above 2 in London and yet were never paid for by them that complained.

These were the great matters in which I had

offended, when myself have often seen and heard offenses, complaints, and crimes of a high nature against God and men, such as filthy uncleanness, fornications, drunkenness, fearful oaths, quarreling, mutinies, sabbath breakings, thefts, forgeries, and such like, which hath passed with fines or censures so small or easy as hath not been worth the naming or regarding. These [things] I cannot think upon but with sad thoughts of inequality of such proceedings, which hath been the very cause of tying up my heart and hands from doing such general and public good acts as in my heart I both desired and intended . . .

I know [that] the loud complaints of such persons before mentioned (though the most of them I had never dealt withal for a penny nor they with me) and others that had were drawn in against their own minds and intents that had no cause nor ground of dissatisfaction in themselves as themselves have acknowledged was the cause of that sharp and severe censure more than the true nature of the things complained of did deserve. This I must needs say if I should say no more, for I now speak the words of a man as if ready to die and leave the world, when there is no cause to daub with my own conscience to justify evil nor to extenuate my own faults, which will again be called to account, if not before washed away in the precious blood of Jesus Christ.

I did submit to the censure, I paid the fine to the uttermost, which is not nor hath been done by many (nor so earnestly required as mine was) though for certain and not supposed offenses of far higher nature, which I can make good not by hearsay only but in my own knowledge, yea offenses of the same kind. [My own offense] was so greatly aggravated and with such indignation pursued by some, as if no censure could be too great or too severe, as if I had not been worthy to have lived upon the earth. [Such offenses] are not only now common almost in every shop and warehouse but even then and ever since with a higher measure of excess, yea even by some of them that were most zealous and had their hands and tongues deepest in my censure. [At that time] they were buyers, [but since then] they are turned sellers and peddling merchants themselves, so that they are become no offenses now nor worthy questioning nor taking notice of in others. Yet [they cried] oppression and excessive gains, [when] considering the time that they kept the goods bought in their hands before they could or would pay and the quality or rather the business of their pay for kind, yea contrary to their own promises, instead of gains there was apparent loss without any gains to the seller.

The oppression lay justly and truly on the buyer's hand rather than on the seller; but then the country was all buyers and few sellers, though it would not be seen on that side then. For if the lion will say the lamb is a fox, it must be so, the lamb must be content to leave it. But now the country hath got better experience in merchandise, and they have soundly paid for their experience since, so that it is now and was many years ago become a common proverb amongst most buyers that knew those times that my goods and prices were cheap pennyworths in comparison of what hath been taken since and especially [in comparison with] the prices of these times. Yet I have borne this patiently and without disturbance or troubling the Court with any petitions for remission or abatement of the fine, though I have been advised by many friends, yea and some of the same Court, so to do, as if they would be willing to embrace such an occasion to undo what was then done in a hurry and in displeasure, or at least would lessen or mitigate it in a great measure. But I have not been persuaded to it because the more innocently that I suffer, the more patiently have I borne it, leaving my cause therein to the Lord.

Yet I dare not subscribe to the justness of that time's proceeding against me, nor did my conscience to the best of my remembrance ever yet convince me that that censure was either equal or deserved by me. I speak not this to grieve any godly heart or to lay any misinterpretation or scandal upon the whole Court or all the magistrates in general whom I have ever thought myself bound to honor and esteem and submit to in lawful things. And I am not ignorant of the great debates that was in the Court about this business and that the pretended zeal of some of the chief sticklers who drew what parties they could to their opinion was opposed by a considerable number both of the magistrates and deputies, and that there was no proof to witness nor no ground in law nor example to carry it as they did, and that there was more said by much in open Court in my defense than I speak here for my-

self, and that not [out of] respect or relation that they had to me, but from their own consciences and judgments and looked at it as most severe, though it may be they would not have wholly acquitted me. . . .

Therefore, I hope that what I have here writ out of the grief and trouble of my heart will be no offense to those whom I reverence in the Lord and intend to lay no blemish upon in the least kind, nor to no moderate or impartial man that was then either of the Court or out of it, for I intend not to give them just offense. If others shall and will misconstrue my true meaning, I must leave them to God, unto Whom I have and shall still commit my cause and cry to Him for right. And I have many testimonies in my spirit that He hath righted me therein, not only in the hearts and judgments of many men that knew and heard of those proceedings, but also in my very outward estate, that though some intended it for my great hurt, yet God hath been pleased to turn it to my good so that I have not since fared the worse nor lost by it but hath since carried me through many and great engagements with comfort.

But some that shall read or hear of the expressions in this my will will be ready to say [that] if I am and have been of this mind so long, how can it stand with that humble confession that I made both in the Court and in the church, when I endeavored in the one and did in the other give satisfaction, without carrying a great appearance of hypocrisy or at least of repenting my repentings.

I desire in this to clear my conscience both towards God and man and do not think that these things are improper to be mentioned in a will but very natural and suitable to it. Therefore I say, first, if my confession was humble and penetential, as is objected, [then] it did justly call for mercy and clemency and not for advantage and more severity, as some made use of it to that end (but with what equity I leave both them and it to the Lord, to Whom they must give an answer if some of them have not already done it, and to such a time wherein they may stand in need of mercy themselves and shall not find it; for there shall be judgment merciless to them that show no mercy). If my confession was not humble and penitent then the objection is needless. But I am glad the prevailing party at that time so took it, though they look upon it as an act of my guilt and use it as a weapon against me. But I think it will be a witness against them for their perverting of it.

I did not then nor dare not now go about to justify all my actions. I know God is righteous and doth all upon just grounds, though men may mistake in their grounds and proceedings, counsel have erred and courts may err and a faction may be too hard and outvote the better or more discerning part. I know the errors of my life. The failings in my trade and otherwise have been many. Therefore from God [the censure] was most just ... Yet I dare not say nor did I ever think (as far as I can call to mind) that the censure was just and righteous from men. Was the price of a bridle, not for taking but only asking, 2 s. for [what] cost here 20 d. such a heinous sin? [Such bridles] have since been commonly sold and still are for 2 s. 6 d. and 3 s. or more, though worse in kind. Was it such a heinous sin to sell 2 or 3 dozen of great gold buttons for 2 s. 10 d. per dozen that cost 2 s. 2 d. ready money in London, bought at the best hand, as I showed to many by my invoice (thought I could not find it at the instant when the Court desired to see it) and since was confirmed by special testimony from London? The buttons [were not even] paid for when the complaint was made, nor I think not yet; neither did the complaint come from him that bought and owed them nor with his knowledge or consent, as he hath since affirmed, but merely from the spleen and envy of another, whom it did nothing concern. Was this so great an offense? Indeed, that it might be made so, some out of their ignorance would needs say they were copper and not worth 9 d. per dozen. But these were weak grounds to pass heavy censures upon.

Was the selling of 6 d. nails for 8 d. per lb. and 8 d. nails for 10 d. per lb. such a crying and oppressing sin? And as I remember it was above two years before he that bought them paid me for them (and not paid for if I forget not) when he made that quarreling exception and unrighteous complaint in the Court against me, (he then being of the Court himself) that I had altered and corrupted my book in adding more to the price than I had set down for them at first delivery. If I had set down 8 d. after 2 years' forbearance for what I would have sold for 7 d. if he had paid me presently, I think it had been a more honest act in me than it was

in him that promised or at least pretended to pay me presently that he might get them at a lower price than a man could well live upon, and when he had got my goods into his hands to keep me 2 or 3 years without my money. All that while there was no fault found at the prices, but when he could for shame keep the money no longer, yet he will requite it with a censure in the Court. For my own part, as I did ever think it an ungodly act in him, so I do think in my conscience that it had been more just in the Court to have censured him than me for this thing, though this was the chiefest crime alleged and most powerfully carried against me ... To make the matter more odious he challenged me and my book of falsehood, supposing that because he had kept me so long from my money therefore by altering the figures I had made the price higher than at first I had charged them down, and that I required 10 d. per lb. for 6 d. nails. And so carried it in the Court (where he was the more easily believed because he was a magistrate and of esteem therein, though it was a most unjust and untrue charge, and only from his own imaginzation), till I cleared it by good testimony from an honest man in his own town whom he sent for the first nails and [who] brought them back and received the bigger nails for them. [This man] came to me of his own accord and told me he heard there was a difference between such a man and I, which he said he could clear, and related the matter fully to me which I was very glad to hear. [His words] brought all things to my mind, [especially] what was the ground of altering the figures in the book, which before I had forgot though I saw it was done with my own hand. And this was the very truth of the thing. I presently acquainted our honored governow Mr. John Winthrop and some others who were very glad that the truth of that reproach was so unexpectedly discovered and cleared. Many if not most of the Court was satisfied with it, and saw the thing to be very plain in my debt book. But the party himself would not be satisfied, [insisting that] they were 6 d. nails set down at 10 d. per lb., though [he] himself saw the figure of "8" as plain as the figure of "10." ...

Now I leave it to the world or to any impartial man or any that hath understanding in trade to judge whether this was a just offense or so crying a sin for which I had such cause to be so penitent (this being the chief [accusation] and pressed on with so great aggravation by my opposers) [or whether] my actions, innocent in themselves, were misconstrued. I knew not how to help myself, especially considering it was no oppressing price but usual with others at that time to sell the like so and since [then] frequently for almost half as much more, as I think all know, and yet both given and taken without exception, or at least without public complaint.

. . . I was much grieved and astonished to be complained of in Court and brought publicly to answer as a grievous malefactor only upon the displeasure of some that stirred in it more than properly did concern them and to be prosecuted so violently for such things as seemed to myself and others so trivial, and upon great outcries, as if the oppression had been unparalleled. And when all things were searched to the bottom nothing of moment was proved against me worthy of mention in a court but what I have here expressed. Yet no other way [was] left me for help, things being carried so highly against me by one party, as I had it by good informations, but by casting myself upon the favor or mercy of the court, as some had counseled me. Since, though, I think they have had cause to be grieved for as well as I because it had an effect contrary to expectation. The means which should have procured the more clemency was by some made an argument of my greater guilt. If this should convince me of the equity and honesty of such men's moderation who delight to turn things not to the best but worst sense, the Lord help me to see that which yet I have not done. This was not the way to bow and melt my heart, but rather to provoke it to cry more earnestly to God to do me right in such a case.

I confess still as I did then and as I have said before, that the newness and strangeness of the thing, to be brought forth into an open court as a public malefactor, was both a shame and an amazement to me. It was the grief of my soul (and I desire it may ever so be in a greater measure) that any act of mine (though not justly but by misconstruction) should be an occasion of scandal to the Gospel and profession of the Lord Jesus, or that myself should be looked at as one that had brought any just dishonor to God (which I have endeavored long and according to my weak ability desired to prevent), though God hath been pleased for

causes best known to Himself to deny me such a blessing. And if it had been in my own power I should rather have chosen to have perished in my cradle than to have lived to such a time. But the good pleasure of God is to keep me low in my own eyes as well as in the eyes of others, and also to make me humble and penitent, lest such mercies should have lifted me up above what is meet. Yet I do say still as I have often done be before, that those things for which I was questioned (in the best apprehension, guided by God's word, that I had then or have since attained to) did deserve no such proceedings as was carved out to me, though some blew up those sparks into a great flame . . .

But it may be some will reply to this that [though] my offenses might be looked at with the same eye in the church as it was in the court my penitency and godly or at least seeming sorrow might keep off the church's censure though it would not the Court's.

It is true that in anything wherein I might justly take shame or sorrow to myself God inclined my heart not to withstand it, for he that hides his sins shall not prosper, but he that confesseth and forsaketh them shall find mercy. In many [ways] we all sin in this. And who can say his heart is clean? Yet for the chief of the things that was most urged against me in Court and for which the sentence was passed against me, as the gold buttons, the bridle, the nails, the falsifying of my book, I did justify and stand to maintain that they was evident mistakes and that I was wronged about them: that they were 8 d. nails at 10 d. per lb. and not 6 d., that the buttons were gold and not copper, and that they cost 2 s. 2 d. per dozen in London, sold here at 2 s. 10 d. per dozen, and that there was no oppression in that price, that thought the figures in my book were altered, yet it was not for any such end as was pretended and urged against me, but upon that very cause that before I have related. Here I had no cause of penitency or confession of guilt [unless] it was for having been so used and reproached about them against all equity. But if they should have cast me out of the church 20 times for this I should have chosen it rather than to have confessed myself guilty for [anyone's] satisfaction wherein I knew myself (better than any else did) to be innocent . . .

I have been the longer and more particular in this

relation to ease my own oppressed spirit which hath
not been a little burdened about this thing and to leave
a testimony of my innocency, so far as I was innocent,
to the world behind me and [to show] how apprehen-,
sive I was and still am of the injury I then received
therein. Neither have I related nor left this testimony
behind me to censure or cast a reproach upon the
whole Court, either upon all the magistrates or all the
deputies . . . For I know it is not lawful to speak evil
of dignities nor to revile the rulers of the people nor to
curse them in our hearts though they should be evil or
do evil to us, but labor to leave it patiently and to comment all to God that judgeth righteously. This I have
endeavored to do. [For] I know that [since] pagans
and tyrants sometimes have admitted and mildly received and well interpreted and taken in good part the
just apologies that some who have been oppressed by
them have writ in their own defense, then those that
are godly and Christian will do it much more. Therefore, I hope none will misconstrue my true meaning
in this my will, nor draw my expression by any aggra-
vations contrary to what I have intended herein. And
for myself I desire patiently to bear the indignation of
the Lord, because I have sinned against Him . . .

SUGGESTIONS FOR FURTHER READING

Charles M. Andrews, *Our Earliest Colonial Settlements,* Cornell
University Press, Ithaca, N.Y., 1933.

Bernard Bailyn, *The New England Merchants in the Seventeenth
Century,* Harper, New York, 1955.

John Bakeless, *The Eyes of Discovery,* Dover, New York, 1961.

Wesley Frank Craven, *The Southern Colonies in the Seventeenth
Century, 1607–1689,* Louisiana State University Press, Baton
Rouge, 1949.

Sigmund Diamond, "From Organization to Society: Virginia
in the Seventeenth Century," *American Journal of Sociology,*
63 (1958).

Christopher Hill, *The Century of Revolution, 1603–1714,* W. W.
Norton, New York, 1961.

Howard Mumford Jones, "The Colonial Impulse: An Analysis
of the 'Promotion' Literature of Colonization," *Proceedings of
the American Philosophical Society,* **90** (1946).

Perry Miller, *Errand in the Wilderness,* Harper, New York, 1956.

———"Declension in a Bible Commonwealth," American Anti-
quarian Society *Proceedings,* LI (1941).

Edmund Morgan, *The Puritan Dilemma,* Little, Brown, Boston,
1958.

———"The First American Boom: Virginia, 1618 to 1630,"
William and Mary Quarterly, **18** (1971).

Gary Nash, *Quakers and Politics,* Princeton University Press,
Princeton, 1968.

Darrett B. Rutman, "God's Bridge Falling Down," *William and
Mary Quarterly,* **19** (1962).

James Morton Smith (ed.), *Seventeenth Century America,* University of North Carolina Press, Chapel, Hill, 1959.

AMERICAN CULTURE AND THE COLONIAL EXPERIENCE

Chapter 2   1696-1767

The English colonies established on the North American continent were distinct, separated from one another and different, yet during the course of the 18th century they produced a common culture which distinguished them from both the Mother Country and England's other western possessions. The colonists themselves had become Americanized through several generations of living in the New World, and as their colonies grew in size and complexity, their regular contacts with one another increased. Moreover, there were four cohesive forces working to overcome the particularities of New England, the Carolinas, Chesapeake Bay society, Georgia, New York, and Pennsylvania. These were the colonists' active participation in the trading economy of the Atlantic, the influence of new land and labor forces, common religious developments, and the problems of living under the domination of Great Britain.

Throughout the 17th century, when private individuals and trading companies laid the foundations of England's empire in the New World, political upheavals absorbed the attention of English statesmen. The outbreak of civil war had not stopped the flow of immigrants leaving the British Isles, but the consequent instability had prevented the formation of a colonial policy. During the Commonwealth period, when merchants assumed a larger share in the governing of England, Parliament passed its first comprehensive legislation regulating English commerce. The faraway colonial ports escaped rigorous enforcement of these first Navigation Acts, but their reprieve was only temporary. At the end of the century the English government was finally in a position to regulate trade, and Parliamentary statutes were passed in 1696 which codified and extended the principles of earlier policies. These statutes ensured England's continued monopolization of desired colonial staples, the restriction of all shipping to English and colonial bottoms, and the funneling of colonial imports through English port cities. Customs collectors, naval officers, admiralty judges, and royal solicitors became familiar figures in every major colonial port. While the colonies derived some benefits from this system, it unnecessarily restricted colonial trade in a dynamic commercial era when innovation and flexibility were the keys to prosperity.

In the closing years of the 17th century, English statesmen made an effort to introduce uniformity into the government of the colonies as well, bringing the proprietary and corporate colonies under royal rule. The Dominion of New England, incorporating the Puritan colonies into the Duke of York's great domain, was created. Efforts were made to revoke the proprietary charters of Pennsylvania and Maryland. Neither was completely successful. The Dominion of New England did not last three years, and Penn, at least, was able to fight off the attack on his proprietorship. The individual colonies retained their separate identities, but New Jersey, Delaware, Massachusetts, New York, Maryland, and the Carolinas became royal colonies with similar forms of government. Royal representatives from the crown-appointed governor to the smallest official acting in the name of the King were living links between the mother country and the colonies. Having influence in England assumed great importance for colonists as British control became more evident. This growth of British officialdom, however, was matched by the development of strong local political institutions — county courts, town meetings and colonial assemblies. The American colonies were too weak to survive as independent communities, but they were determined to work for as much autonomy as possible.

The differences in perspective between the mother country and the colonies further embarrassed their relations. The english thought of their New World possessions in terms of annual exports, revenue receipts, maintenance costs, and sources of staple commodities. Only rarely did they look across the Atlantic and see centers of human activity. The colonists could not help but operate under different assumptions. The colony was their home, the focal point of their civic life, their market place, and the first object of their loyalties. By mid-18th century, some colonial families had been in the New World for five generations. Twelve colonies stretched from Maine to South Carolina, each with its own political institutions and a sense of social identity. The thriving economy enabled American population and production to double every twenty-five years. Colonoial society was dynamic, but the English attitude toward it remained static.

The development of the colonial economy was paced by the expanding international commerce of the Atlantic. Chesapeake planters grew tobacco which was smoked, chewed, and sniffed throughout Europe. South Carolina plantations produced rice for Spain and Portugal. The grain-growing valleys of the middle colonies fed the island populations of the West Indies, and New Englanders spun a web of trade routes between Newfoundland, West Africa, Southern Europe, and the island colonies of the Caribbean. Where entrepreneurs in Europe were still struggling with vestiges of conservative economic structures, American capitalists — be they farmers or merchants — were unencumbered by the past in their pursuit of profit. The extent of free enterprise, of unfettered capitalism, and individual prosperity clearly worked to differentiate the society of the colonies from that of the mother country, even though it was England's aggressive leadership in this international economy that made colonial growth possible.

The profitability of labor in the colonies acted like a huge magnet pulling the displaced, the ambitious, and the cast out. English, Irish, Swiss, German Palatines, French Huguenots, and the twice-uprooted Scottish-Irish streamed across the Atlantic. Because so many of these sought-after workers could not pay for their passage to America, a system of labor contracts called indentures was developed which enabled immigrants to pledge their future labor to pay for the present cost of transportation. Once their term of years had been fulfilled, common men and women could lead lives unparalleled in the rest of the world. The free exercise of their religion was protected in most colonies, their wages were high, and their children's future rich with possibilities. The property qualifications which limited political participation to all but a few in England was easily met by the majority of free white men in the colonies. Social attitudes brought from the Old World died slowly, but circumstances in America were quietly working away at the static concepts of inherited gentility and permanent life stations.

The profitability of applying labor to land also encouraged the use of slave labor. The indigenous Indian population did not adapt to the demands of intensive labor, and white indentured servants, although used throughout the colonial period, were usually in short supply. Men and women stolen from the West Coast of Africa, alien in culture and absolutely vulnerable to their captors, could be pressed into lifetime bondage, thus reducing labor costs to an absolute minimum. At the close of the 17th century, England gained control of the African trade, ensuring a steady flow of slaves into the West Indian and southern continental colonies where agriculture was already devoted to the cultivation of a single crop. The reduction of labor costs to the level of just keeping slaves alive enabled planters to lower the prices of tobacco, rice, and sugar. Thus they greatly increased the size of their market as the luxuries of the previous century became the normal conveniences of a growing segment of European society. Even in the North slaves adapted to the demands of a mixed economy and accounted for nearly 6% of the population.

The economic role of the slave tells but half the story of the African in America. Slavery in the English colonies became inextricably bound up with race, and all questions of slavery had their social and legal as well as their economic sides. The colonists' ethnocentricity prevented their considering the possibility of living with black people on terms of parity, and between equality and slavery, there was no middle ground in the Anglo-American colonies. Unlike the Latin-American colonies, where slavery was a status that men and women could pass out of, in the English colonies manumission was made virtually impossible. Slave codes were developed by colonial legislatures to protect slaveowners' property and prevent slave revolts. Legislators found it expedient to restrict the liberty of all black men. Hence race and slave status were closely identified, making the position of the few free blacks very precarious. The legal records of the colonies, north and south, are filled with accounts of runaways, suspected slave uprisings, and brutal reprisals against those suspected of plotting against the white man. Some of the penalties prescribed in the slave codes were so hideous that the English Board of Trade disallowed the colonial statutes for prescribing punishments unknown to English law. At the same time English policy-makers were just as adamantly opposed to colonial laws which tried to limit the importation of slaves. Conscience, capitalism, and race prejudice pulled Englishmen in different directions while the colonists' fear of slave revolts acted as a powerful motive for continued repression.

For all its growth and prosperity, colonial society was far from stable. The black population remained an essentially hostile force within while Indians menaced outside, along the exposed frontier. In all the colonies there was a class of indentured servants whose crude behavior was a threat to ordered society, and in some colonies this class was further debased by regular shiploads of English convicts. Even within the great mass of hard-working colonial families the lack of clearly defined life stations introduced anxieties as well as opportunities. The constant need to adapt and innovate created additional pressures. Sliding into a rudimentary semi-civilized state was always a possibility made vivid by examples of people who had slipped the bonds of civilization altogether. Many lived isolated lives on the frontier, and even those in settled communities were thrown on their own resources more than in a traditional society. It is very difficult to assess the tensions generated by these conditions, just as it is difficult to measure the changes in outlook effected by ambition and opportunity, but the volatility of colonial society became apparent in the 1730's when communities from Massachusetts to South Carolina were convulsed by a wave of religious enthusiasms which fundamentally changed American religious patterns.

Clergymen in several different Protestant denominations were shocked by the fact that American prosperity had all but killed the religious fervor which had driven so many colonists to the New World. Seeking new ways to rekindle the faith of their congregations, they began to preach insistently about the decline of commitment. They attacked the self-reliance and self-centeredness that colonial society encouraged, viewing it as a denial of the sovereignty of God. These clergymen, all of them gifted preachers, had a remarkable and contagious success with their vivid descriptions of the uncompromising quality of God's law. Congregations responded with loud enthusiasm. So many men and women claimed to have experienced God's grace that the movement became known as the Great Awakening. Convinced that they were awakening more people to true Christianity in an afternoon of preaching than a lifetime of uninspired ministration would do, the leaders of the Great Awakening derided existing church life as sterile, and summoned clergy and congregation alike to a new spiritual standard. Despite the hope which this outpouring of religious zeal evoked, some churchmen were far from happy about the vigor of the attack against conventional church practices. Arguing that zeal evaporated and enthusiasm waned, these church conservatives maintained that a society of sin-prone men needed a stable, unified church led by sober, well-educated clergymen who could calmly minister to the long-term needs of their parishes. The very controversies stirred up by the revivals confirmed their suspicions, and when the Great Awakening finally subsided in 1742, they could point to the divided congregations as proof of their earlier fears.

Indisputably, American churches were never quite the same again. The Great Awakening caused a strengthening of personal piety, but this spiritual gain was accompanied by a weakening of church authority. The free-thinkers who had shifted their faith from the God of revelation to the God of nature gained a measure of freedom from the religious turmoil which accompanied the Great Awakening. Indifferent to the theological questions raised, the Deists or rationalists found that the disputes over grace, mortal sin, and salvation had made controversy itself respectable, and the choice of no church was now added to the rich variety of accepted religions in America.

The differences between English and American society that had developed over a century of separate existence were reflected also in a steady succession of political disputes between the aggressive leaders of the colonial legislatures and the royal governors. A majority of free white men in every colony could meet the property qualifications for voting which introduced Americans to a form of popular politics unknown to the rest of the world. Even though the political leadership in every colony was monopolized by the rich, well-born, and well-educated, the power of this elite was conditioned by the need to keep the support of the great majority of colonists of middling estate. Colonial leaders were effective in gaining autonomous political control to the extent that they could outwit the governor and his party and at the same time maintain good relations with their constituency. The task could not be done without developing a fresh set of political practices.

The destruction of traditional society was also going on throughout Europe, but nowhere was the process of accommodating modern changes more rapid or complete than in the Anglo-American colonies. From the time of their founding, the ideals of community life, authoritarian institutions, and aristocratic social theories had been forced to compete with the values fostered by the opportunities for the ordinary man to make his own personal goals the focal point of his life. During the first half of the 18th century, as the colonial frontier gave way to more complex societies, patterns of family life, political participation, business enterprise, and social control were formed to meet the specific needs of the American colonists.

Men and women continued to think of themselves as English — even foreign immigrants accepted the Englishness of their new home — but imperceptibly the colonists were shedding many of the attitudes that bound them to England and slowly replacing substantial parts of their inherited traditions with the forms of a new culture.

Although a Dutch ship visiting Jamestown in 1619 brought a score of slaves to the first English colony, slavery did not play an important part in the colonial economy until the end of the 17th century. Then a combination of factors led to the transformation of the Chesapeake area from one of small and medium-sized farms worked by free and indentured white labor to the large-scale plantation agriculture which we associate with the old South. The profitiability of using slave labor was demonstrated in the 1670's and 1680's, and after that the richer planters began expanding their operations by buying up the holdings of other farmers who moved out of the Tidewater area into the foothills or Piedmont area of Virginia and Maryland. The economic edge which the owner of a large, slave-worked plantation enjoyed proved decisive, and the society of Chesapeake Bay acquired a slave foundation. When, in the first decade of the 18th century, South Carolina planters found a profitable crop in rice, they too turned quickly to slave labor. In all a quarter of a million Africans were brought to the southern colonies in the first seventy-five years of the 18th century.

For the North, the small family farms proved effective units for raising cattle and wheat. Free labor was better suited to the fishing and lumbering industries, as well as to urban commerce and crafts. The cohesiveness of town settlements in New England and the middle colonies discouraged the emigration of people of alien culture, and religious scruples against slavery were more keenly felt. Still, the influx of slaves was noted in the North, and by the closing decade of the 17th century there were statutes passed in each colony taking cognizance of the black man's presence in America.

The colonists' religious and political ideals were at painful odds with their feelings of racial superiority, but the evil of slavery did not pass without comment, even as it was becoming firmly fixed in law and custom. In the following group of readings, slavery is discussed from four different perspectives. The first selection is an early anti-slavery tract, *The Selling of Joseph,* written by Samuel Sewall (1652–1730) in 1700. Sewall was a model of a Puritan magistrate throughout his long life. Wealthy, well-connected, honored with high political office, he never lost his keen sense of personal responsibility. He was one of the judges at the famous Salem witchcraft trials, but four years later, after deciding that the proceedings had been unjust, he made a public confession of his guilt. In a similar fashion, Sewall became troubled about slavery when he saw a marked increase in slave-holding in his beloved Massachusetts. Goaded by his conscience, Sewall wrote *The Selling of Joseph* and continued to press his privately printed copies upon friends and legislators until his death thirty years later.

Sewall's arguments against slavery, however, did not go unchallenged, and a fellow Superior Court judge, John Saffin (1632–1708) responded the following year with *A Brief and Candid Answer to a Late Printed Sheet entitled 'The Selling of Joseph.'* Although there is a personal side to the Sewall-Saffin clash, their public argument introduced themes which were to remain a part of the slavery debate in America for the next two centuries.

The most consistent and outspoken opponents of slavery in the New World were the Quakers. As early as 1696 their members were cautioned against importing slaves. By steady steps throughout the 18th century, the Society of Friends moved to an outright ban against slave-holding, largely because of the sustained efforts of Quaker abolitionists like Anthony Benezet. The third reading in this section is taken from Benezet's *A Caution and a Warning to Great Britain and Her Colonies.* Writing in 1766, Benezet used the full battery of anti-slavery arguments including accounts of the slave trade which vivified the horrors of the actual enslavement.

The last reading comes from Malachy Postlethwayt (1707–1767), a popular English commercial writer. Postlethwayt's discussion of the critical importance of the slave trade in the English economy points up one of the ironies of colonial slavery. While English law did not even recognize the status of slave — to step on English soil was to be free — English interests prevented any interference with slavery in the colonies. At various times, different colonial legislatures, usually prompted by fear of slave insurrections, attempted to limit the importation of blacks. The crown disallowed such laws as being inimical to the interests of Great Britain. In his earlier writings, Postlethwayt had inveighed against the inhumanity of the slave trade, but his later works reflected the official recognition of the importance of slavery to Britain's enormously profitable Atlantic commerce.

The spread of slavery in the colonies was not an accident or the result of impersonal forces of climate and economics. It began with the willingness of the colonists to use slave labor, and the form of American slavery was a consequence of the same individual freedom which was working to differentiate American society from that of the mother country. Only in this case the freedom was that of making significant choices unhampered by the injunctions of a traditional legal system or the binding authority of a strong church.

Samuel Sewall: The Selling of Joseph (1700)

Forasmuch as Liberty is in real value next unto Life: None ought to part with it themselves, or deprive others of it, but upon most mature Consideration.

The Numerousness of Slaves at this day in the Province, and the Uneasiness of them under their Slavery, hath put many upon thinking whether the Foundation of it be firmly and well laid; so as to sustain the Vast Weight that is built upon it. It is most certain that all Men, as they are the Sons of Adam, are Co-heirs; and have equal Right unto Liberty, and all other outward Comforts of Life. God hath given the Earth [with all its Commodities] unto the Sons of Adam, Psal 115. 16. And hath made of One Blood, all Nations of Men, for to dwell on all the face of the Earth, and hath determined the Times before appointed, and the bounds of their habitation: That they should seek the Lord. Forasmuch then as we are the Offspring of God &c. Act 17. 26, 27, 29. Now although the Title given by the last Adam, doth infinitely better Mens Estates, respecting God and themselves; and grants them a most beneficial and inviolable Lease under the Broad Seal of Heaven, who were before only Tenants at Will: Yet through the Indulgence of God to our First Parents after the Fall, the outward Estate of all and every of their Children, remains the same, as to one another. So that Originally, and Naturally, there

is no such thing as Slavery. Joseph was rightfully no more a Slave to his Brethren, than they were to him: and they had no more Authority to Sell him, than they had to Slay him. And if they had nothing to do to Sell him; the Ishmaelites bargaining with them, and paying down Twenty pieces of Silver, could not make a Title. Neither could Potiphar have any better Interest in him than the Ishmaelites had. Gen. 37. 20, 27, 28. For he that shall in this case plead Alteration of Property, seems to have forfeited a great part of his own claim to Humanity. There is no proportion between Twenty Pieces of Silver, and Liberty. The Commodity it self is the Claimer. If Arabian Gold be imported in any quantities, most are afraid to meddle with it, though they might have it at easy rates; lest if it should have been wrongfully taken from the Owners, it should kindle a fire to the Consumption of their whole Estate. 'Tis pity there should be more Caution used in buying a Horse, or a little lifeless dust; than there is in purchasing Men and Women: Whenas they are the Offspring of God, and their Liberty is,

. . . . *Auro pretiosior Omni.*

And seeing God hath said, He that Stealeth a Man and Selleth him, or if he be found in his hand, he shall surely be put to Death. Exod. 21. 16. This Law being of Everlasting Equity, wherein Man Stealing is ranked amongst the most atrocious of Capital Crimes: What louder Cry can there be made of that Celebrated Warning,

Caveat Emptor!

And all things considered, it would conduce more to the Welfare of the Province, to have White Servants for a Term of Years, than to have Slaves for Life. Few can endure to hear of a Negro's being made free; and indeed they can seldom use their freedom well; yet their continual aspiring after their forbidden Liberty, renders them Unwilling Servants. And there is such a disparity in their Conditions, Colour & Hair, that they can never embody with us, and grow up into orderly Families, to the Peopling of the Land: but still remain in our Body Politick as a kind of extravasat Blood. As many Negro men as there are among us, so many

Proceedings of the *Massachusetts Historical Society*, 1863–64, Boston, 1864, pp. 161–65.

empty places there are in our Train Bands, and the places taken up of Men that might make Husbands for our Daughters. And the Sons and Daughters of New England would become more like Jacob, and Rachel, if this Slavery were thrust quite out of doors. Moreover it is too well known what Temptations Masters are under, to connive at the Fornication of their Slaves; lest they should be obliged to find them Wives, or pay their Fines. It seems to be practically pleaded that they might be Lawless; 'tis thought much of, that the Law should have Satisfaction for their Thefts, and other Immoralities; by which means, Holiness to the Lord, is more rarely engraven upon this sort of Servitude. It is likewise most lamentable to think, how in taking Negros out of Africa, and Selling of them here, That which God ha's joyned together men do boldly rend asunder; Men from their Country, Husbands from their Wives, Parents from their Children. How horrible is the Uncleanness, Mortality, if not Murder, that the Ships are guilty of that bring great Crouds of these miserable Men, and Women. Methinks, when we are bemoaning the barbarous Usage of our Friends and Kinsfolk in Africa: it might not be unseasonable to enquire whether we are not culpable in forcing the Africans to become Slaves amongst our selves. And it may be a question whether all the Benefit received by Negro Slaves, will balance the Accompt of Cash laid out upon them; and for the Redemption of our own enslaved Friends out of Africa. Besides all the Persons and Estates that have perished there.

Objection 1. These Blackamores are of the Posterity of Cham, and therefore are under the Curse of Slavery. Gen. 9. 25, 26, 27.

Answer. Of all Offices, one would not begg this; viz. Uncall'd for, to be an Executioner of the Vindictive Wrath of God; the extent and duration of which is to us uncertain. If this ever was a Commission, How do we know but that it is long since out of Date? Many have found it to their Cost, that a Prophetical Denunciation of Judgment against a Person or People, would not warrant them to inflict that evil. If it would, Hazael might justify himself in all he did against his Master, and the Israelites, from 2 Kings 8. 10, 12.

But it is possible that by cursory reading, this Text may have been mistaken. For Canaan is the Person Cursed three times over, without the mentioning of Cham. Good Expositors suppose the Curse entaild on him, and that this Prophesie was accomplished in the Extirpation of the Canaanites, and in the Servitude of the Gibeonites. *Vide Pareum.* Whereas the Blackmores are not descended of Canaan, but of Cush. Psal. 68. 31. Princes shall come out of Egypt [Mizraim] Ethiopia [Cush] shall soon stretch out her hands unto God. Under which Names, all Africa may be comprehended; and their Promised Conversion ought to be prayed for. Jer. 13. 23. Can the Ethiopian change his skin? This shows that Black Men are the Posterity of Cush: Who time out of mind have been distinguished by their Colour. And for want of the true, Ovid assigns a fabulous cause of it.

Sanguine tum credunt in corpora summa vocato
AEthiopum populos nigrum traxisse colorem.
                                            Metamorph. lib. 2.

Objection 2. The Nigers are brought out of a Pagan Country, into places where the Gospel is Preached.

Answer. Evil must not be done, that good may come of it. The extraordinary and comprehensive Benefit accruing to the Church of God, and to Joseph personally, did not rectify his brethrens Sale of him.

Objection 3. The Africans have Wars one with another: Our Ships bring lawful Captives taken in those Wars.

Answer. For ought is known, their Wars are much such as were between Jacob's Sons and their Brother Joseph. If they be between Town and Town; Provincial, or National: Every War is upon one side Unjust. An Unlawful War can't make lawful Captives. And by Receiving, we are in danger to promote, and partake in their Barbarous Cruelties. I am sure, if some Gentlemen should go down to the Brewsters to take the Air, and Fish: And a stronger party from Hull should Surprise them, and Sell them for Slaves to a Ship outward bound: they would think themselves unjustly dealt with; both by Sellers and Buyers. And yet 'tis to be feared, we have no other kind of Title to our Nigers. Therefore all things whatsoever ye would that men should do to you, do ye even so to them: for this is the Law and the Prophets. Matt. 7. 12.

Objection 4.   Abraham had Servants bought with his Money, and born in his House.

Answer.   Until the Circumstances of Abraham's purchase be recorded, no Argument can be drawn from it. In the mean time, Charity obliges us to conclude, that He knew it was lawful and good.

It is Observable that the Israelites were strictly forbidden the buying, or selling one another for Slaves. Levit. 25. 39. 46. Jer. 34 8 . . . 22. And God gaged His blessing in lieu of any loss they might conceipt they suffered thereby. Deut. 15. 18. And since the partition Wall is broken down, inordinate Self love should likewise be demolished. God expects that Christians should be of a more Ingenuous and benign frame of spirit. Christians should carry it to all the World, as the Israelites were to carry it one towards another. And for men obstinately to persist in holding their Neighbours and Brethren under the Rigor of perpetual Bondage, seems to be no proper way of gaining Assurance that God ha's given them Spiritual Freedom. Our Blessed Saviour ha's altered the Measures of the ancient Love-Song, and set it to a most Excellent New Tune, which all ought to be ambitious of Learning. Matt. 5. 43, 44. John 13. 34. These Ethiopians, as black as they are; seeing they are the Sons and Daughters of the First Adam, the Brethren and Sisters of the Last Adam, and the Offspring of God; They ought to be treated with a Respect agreeable.

John Saffin: A brief and candid answer to a late printed sheet entitled "The Selling of Joseph" (1701)

That honorable and learned gentleman, the author of a sheet entitled "The Selling of Joseph," seems from thence to draw this conclusion, that because the sons of Jacob did very ill in selling their brother Joseph to the Ishmaelites, who were heathens, therefore it is utterly unlawful to buy and sell Negroes, though among Christians; which conclusion I presume is not well drawn from the premises, nor is the case parallel; for it was unlawful for the Israelites to sell their brethren upon any account or pretense whatsoever during life. But it was not unlawful for the seed of Abraham to

have bondmen and bondwomen either born in their house or bought with their money, as it is written of Abraham, Gen. 14. 14., and 21. 10., and Exod. 21. 16. and Levit. 25. 44. 45, 46v. After the giving of the law: And in Josh. 9.23. That famous example of the Gibeonites is a sufficient proof were there no other.

To speak a little to the gentleman's first assertion: "That none ought to part with their liberty themselves, or deprive others of it but upon mature consideration;" a prudent exception, in which he grants that upon some consideration a man may be deprived of his liberty. And then presently in his next position or assertion he denies it: "It is most certain, that all men as they are the sons of Adam are coheirs, and have equal right to liberty, and all other comforts of life," which he would prove out of Psal. 115. 16. "The earth hath he given to the children of men." True, but what is all this to the purpose, to prove that all men have equal right to liberty and all outward comforts of this life; which position seems to invert the order that God hath set in the world, who hath ordained different degrees and orders of men: some to be high and honorable, some to be low and despicable; some to be monarchs, kings, princes and governors, masters and commanders, others to be subjects, and to be commanded; servants of sundry sorts and degrees, bound to obey; yea, some to be born slaves, and so to remain during their lives, as hath been proved. Otherwise there would be a mere parity among men, contrary to that of the apostles, 1 Cor. 12 from the 13 to the 26 verse, where he sets forth (by way of comparison) the different sorts and offices of the members of the body, indicating that they are all of use, but not equal and of like dignity. So God hath set different orders and degrees of men in the world, both in church and commonweal. Now, if this position of parity should be true, it would then follow that the ordinary course of divine providence of God in the world should be wrong and unjust (which we must not dare to think, much less affirm), and all the sacred rules, precepts and commands of the Almighty which He hath given the son of men to observe and keep in their respective places, orders and degrees, would be to no purpose; which unaccountably derogates from the divine wisdom of the most High, who hath made nothing in vain but hath holy ends in all His dispensations to the children of men.

George H. Moore, *Notes on the History of Slavery in Massachusetts,* O. Appleton, New York, 1866, pp. 251–56.

In the next place, this worthy gentleman makes a large discourse concerning the utility and conveniency to keep the one, and inconvenience of the other; respecting white and black servants, which conduceth most to the welfare and benefit of this province: which he concludes to be white men, who are in many respects to be preferred before blacks. Who doubts that? Doth it therefore follow that it is altogether unlawful for Christians to buy and keep Negro servants (for this is the thesis), but that those that have them ought in conscience to set them free, and so lose all the money they cost (for we must not live in any known sin), this seems to be his opinion; but it is a question whether it ever was the gentleman's practise? But if he could persuade the General Assembly to make an Act that all that have Negroes and do set them free shall be reimbursed out of the public treasury, and that there shall be no more Negroes brought into the country; 'tis probable there would be more of his opinion, yet he would find it a hard task to bring the country to consent thereto, for then the Negroes must be all sent out of the country, or else the remedy would be worse than the disease; and it is to be feared that those Negroes that are free, if there be not some strict course taken with them by authority, they will be a plague to this country.

Again, if it should be unlawful to deprive them that are lawful captives or bondmen of their liberty for life being heathens; it [seems] to be more unlawful to deprive our brethren of our own or other Christian nations of the liberty (though but for a time) by sending them to serve some seven, ten, fifteen, and some twenty years, which oft times proves for their whole life, as many have been; which in effect is the same in nature, thought different in the time, yet this was allowed among the Jews by the Law of God; and is the constant practise of our own and other Christian nations in the world: the which our author by his dogmatical assertions doth condemn as irreligious; which is diametrically contrary to the rules and precepts which God hath given the diversity of men to observe in their respective stations, callings, and conditions of life, as hath been observed.

And to illustrate his assertion our author brings in by way of comparison the Law of God against man-stealing, on pain of death: intimating thereby that buying and selling of Negroes is a breach of that law, and so deserves death: a severe sentence. But herein he begs the question with a *caveat emptor*. For, in that very chapter there is a dispensation to the people of Israel to have bond men, women and children, even of their own nation in some cases, and rules given therein to be observed concerning them ...

In fine, the sum of this long harangue is no other than to compare the buying and selling of Negroes unto the stealing of men, and the selling of Joseph by his brethren, which bears no proportion therewith, nor is there any congruity therein, as appears by the foregoing texts.

Our author doth further proceed to answer some objections of his own framing, which he supposes some might raise.

Objection 1: That these blackamores are of the posterity Cham, and therefore under the curse of slavery. Gen. 9. 25, 26. The which the gentleman seems to deny, saying, they were the seed of Canaan that were cursed, etc.

Answer: Whether they were so or not, we shall not dispute: this may suffice, that not only the seed of Cham or Canaan, but any lawful captives of other heathen nations may be made bond men as hath been proved.

Objection 2: That the Negroes are brought out of pagan countries into places where the gospel is preached. To which he replied that we must not do evil that good may come of it.

Answer: To which we answer, that it is no evil thing to bring them out of their own heathenish country, where they may have ... knowledge of the true God, be converted and eternally saved.

Objection 3: The africans have wars one with another; our traders bring lawful captives taken in those wars. To which our author answers conjecturally and doubtfully ... He also compares the Negro wars, one nation with another, with the wars between Joseph and his brethren. But where doth he read of any such war? We read indeed of a domestic quarrel they had with him, they envied and hated Joseph; but by what is recorded he was merely passive and meek as a lamb. This gentleman further adds, that there is not any war but is unjust on one side, etc. Be it so, what doth that signify. We read of lawful captives taken in the wards, and lawful to be bought and sold without contracting the guilt of the aggressors; for which we have the example of Abraham before quoted; but if we must stay while both parties warring are in the right, there would be no lawful captives at all to be bought; which seems to be ridiculous to imagine, and contrary to the tenor of scripture, and all human histories on that subject.

Objection 4: Abraham had servants bought with his money, and born in his house. Gen. 14. 14. To which our worthy author answers, until the circumstances of Abraham's purchase be recorded no argument can be drawn from it.

Answer: To which we reply, this is also dogmatical, and proves nothing. He further adds, "In the mean time charity obliges us to conclude that he knew it was lawful and good." Here the gentleman yields the case; for if we are in charity bound to believe Abraham's practice in buying and keeping slaves in his house to be lawful and good, then it follows that our imitation of him in this his moral action is as warrantable as that of his faith; who is the Father of all them that believe. Rom. 4. 16.

In the close of all our author quotes two more places of scripture, viz. Levit. 25. 46, and Jer. 34, from the 8. to the 22. v. to prove that the people of Israel were strictly forbidden the buying and selling one another for slaves: who questions that? and what is that to the case in hand? What a strange piece of logic is this? Tis unlawful for Christians to buy and sell one another for slaves. Ergo, it is unlawful to buy and sell Negroes that are lawful captived heathens.

And after a serious exhortation to us all to love one another according to the command of Christ, Matt. 5, 43, 44, this worthy gentleman concludes with this assertion, "That these Ethiopians as black as they are, seeing they are the sons and daughters of the first Adam, the brethren and sisters of the second Adam, and the offspring of God, we ought to treat them with a respect agreeable."

Answer: We grant it for a certain and undeniable verity that all mankind are the sons and daughters of Adam, and the creatures of God. But it doth not therefore follow that we are bound to love and respect all

men alike; this under favor we must take leave to deny. We ought in charity, if we see our neighbor in want, to relieve them in a regular way, but we are not bound to give them so much of our estates as to make them equal with ourselves, because they are our brethren, the sons of Adam, no, not our own natural kinsmen. We are exhorted "to do good unto all, but especially to them who are of the household of Faith,", Gal. 6. 10. And we are to love, honor and respect all men according to the gift of God that is in them: I may love my servant well, but my son better. Charity begins at home, it would be a violation of common prudence and a breach of good manners to treat a prince like a peasant. And this worthy gentleman would deem himself much neglected if we should show him no more deference than to an ordinary porter. And therefore these florid expressions, the sons and daughters of the first Adam, the brethren and sisters of the second Adam, and the offspring of God, seem to be misapplied to import and insinuate that we ought to tender pagan Negroes with all love, kindness, and equal respect as to the best of men.

By all which it doth evidently appear both by scripture and reason the practice of the people of God in all ages, both before and after the giving of the Law, and in the times of the Gospel, that there were bond men, women and children commonly kept by holy and good men, and improved in service; and therefore by the command of God, Lev. 25, 44, and their venerable example, we may keep bond men and use them in our service still; yet with all candor, moderation and Christian prudence, according to their state and condition consonant to the Word of God.

The Negroes Character

Cowardly and cruel are those Blacks inate, Prone to revenge, imp of inveterate hate. He that exasperates them soon espies mischief and murder in their very eyes. Libidinous, deceitful, false and rude, the spume issue of ingratitude. The premises considered, all may tell, how near good Joseph they are parallel.

Anthony Benezet: A caution and a warning to Great Britain and her Colonies in a short representation of the calamitous state of the enslaved Negroes in the British Dominions* (1766)

At a time when the general rights and liberties of mankind, and the preservation of those valuable privileges

*Pp. 3-23, 30-32.

transmitted to us from our ancestors, are become so much the subjects of universal consideration; can it be an inquiry indifferent to any, how many of those who distinguish themselves as the Advocates of Liberty, remain insensible and inattentive to the treatment of thousands and tens of thousands of our fellow-men, who, from motives of avarice, and the inexorable degree of tyrant custom, are at this very time kept in the most deplorable state of slavery, in many parts of the British Dominions.

The intent of publishing the following sheets, is more fully to make known the aggravated iniquity attending the practice of ths Slave-Trade; whereby many thousands of our fellow-creatures, as free as ourselves by nature, and equally with us the subjects of Christ's redeeming grace, are yearly brought into inextricable and barbarous bondage; and many, very many, to miserable and untimely ends.

The truth of this lamentable complaint is so obvious to persons of candour, under whose notice it hath fallen, that several have lately published their sentiments thereon; as a matter which calls for the most serious consideration of all who are concerned for the civil or religious welfare of their country. How an evil of so deep a dye, hath so long, not only passed uninterrupted by those in power, but hath even had their countenance, is, indeed, surprising, and, charity would suppose, must, in a great measure, have arisen from this, that many persons in government, both of the Clergy and Laity, in whose power it hath been to put a stop to the Trade, have been unacquainted with the corrupt motives which gives life to it; and the groans, the dying groans, which daily ascend to God, the common Father of mankind, from the broken hearts of those his deeply oppressed creatures, otherwise the powers of the earth would not, I think I may venture to say, could not, have so long authorised a practice so inconsistent with every idea of liberty and justice . . .

Much might justly be said of the temporal evils which attend this practice, as it is destructive of the welfare of human society, and of the peace and prosperity of every country, in proportion as it prevails. It might be also shown, that it destroys the bonds of natural affection and interest, whereby mankind in general are united; that it introduces idleness, discourages

marriage, corrupts the youth, ruins and debauches morals, excites continual apprehensions of dangers, and frequent alarms, to which the Whites are necessarily exposed from so great an encrease of a people, that, by their bondage and oppressions, become natural enemies, yet, at the same time, are filling the places and eating the bread of those who would be the support and security of the country. But as these and many more reflections of the same kind, may occur to a considerate mind, I shall only endeavour to show, from the nature of the Trade, the plenty which Guinea affords its inhabitants, the barbarous treatment of the Negroes, and the observations made thereon by authors of note, that it is inconsistent with the plainest precepts of the gospel, the dictates of reason, and every common sentiment of humanity.

In an account of the European Settlements in America, printed in London, 1757, the author speaking on the subject, says: "The Negroes in our Colonies endure a slavery more complete and attended with far worse circumstances than what any people in their condition suffer in any other part of the world, or have suffered in any other period of time: proofs of this are not wanting. The prodigious waste which we experience in this unhappy part of our species, is a full and melancholy evidence of this truth. The Island of Barbados, (the Negroes upon which do not amount to eighty thousand) notwithstanding all the means which they use to increase them by propagation, and that the climate is in every respect (except that of being more wholesome) exactly resembling the climate from whence they come; notwithstanding all this, Barbados lies under a necessity of an annual recruit of five thousand slaves, to keep up the stock at the number I have mentioned. This prodigious failure, which is at least in the same proportion in all our Islands, shows demonstratively that some uncommon and unsupportable hardship lies upon the Negroes, which wears them down in such a surprising manner; and this, I imagine, is principally the excessive labour which they undergo." In an account of part of North America, published by Thomas Jeffery, printed in 1761, speaking of the usage the Negroes receive in the West-India Islands, thus expresses himself: "It's impossible for a human heart to reflect upon the servitude of these dregs of mankind, without in some measure feeling for their misery, which ends but with their lives. — Nothing can be more wretched than the condition of this people. One would imagine, they were framed to be the disgrace of the human species, banished from their country, and deprived of that blessing Liberty, on which all other nations set the greatest value, they are in a manner reduced to the condition of beasts of burden: In general a few roots, potatoes especially, are their food, and two rags, which neither screen them from the heat of the day, nor the extraordinary coolness of the night, all their covering; their sleep very short; their labour almost continual, they receive no wages, but have twenty lashes for the smallest fault." . . .

"The time that the Negroes work in the West-Indies, is from day-break till noon; then again from two o'clock till dusk: (during which time they are attended by overseers, who severely scourge those who appear to them dilatory) and before they are suffered to go to their quarters, they have still something to do, as collecting of herbage for the horses, gathering fuel for the boilers, &c. so that it is often half past twelve before they can get home, when they have scarce time to grind and boil their Indian corn; whereby it often happens that they are called again to labour before they can satisfy their hunger: and here no delay or excuse will avail, for if they are not in the field immediately upon the usual notice, they must expect to feel the overseers lash. In crop-time (which lasts many months) they are obliged (by turns) to work most of the night in the boiling-house." . . .

"It is a matter of astonishment, how a people who, as a nation, are looked upon as generous and humane, and so much value themselves for their uncommon sense of the benefit of Liberty, can live in the practice of such extreme oppression and inhumanity, without seeing the inconsistency of such conduct, and without feeling great remorse: Nor is it less amazing to hear these men calmly making calculations about the strength and lives of their fellow-men; in Jamaica, if six in ten, or the new imported Negroes survive the seasoning, it is looked upon as a gaining purchase: And in most of the other plantations, if the Negroes live eight or nine years, their labour is reckoned a sufficient compensation for their cost. — If calculations of this sort were made upon the strength and labour of beasts of burden it would not appear so strange, but even then a merciful man would certainly use his beast with more

mercy than is usually shown to the poor **Negroes**. — Will not the groans of this deeply afflicted and oppressed people reach heaven, and when the cup of iniquity is full, must not the inevitable consequence be pouring forth of the judgments of God upon their oppressors." . . .

The situation of the Negroes in our Southern provinces on the Continent, is also feelingly set forth by George Whitefield, in a letter from Georgia, to the inhabitants of Maryland, Virginia, North- and South-Carolina, printed in the year 1739, of which the following is an extract, "As I lately passed through your provinces, in my way hither, I was sensibly touched with a fellow-feeling of the miseries of the poor Negroes. Whether it be lawful for Christians to buy slaves, and thereby encourage the nations from whom they are bought, to be at perpetual war war with each other, I shall not take upon me to determine; sure I am, it is sinful, when bought, to use them as bad, nay worse, than as though they were brutes; and whatever particular exception there may be, (as I would charitably hope there are some) I fear the generality of you, that own Negroes, are liable to such a charge; for your slaves, I believe, work as hard, if not harder, than the horses whereon you ride. These, after they have done their work, are fed and taken proper care of; but many Negroes, when wearied with labour, in your plantations, have been obliged to grind their own corn, after they return home; your dogs are caressed and fondled at your tables; but your slaves, who are frequently stiled dogs or beasts, have not an equal privilege; they are scarce permitted to pick up the crumbs which fall from their master's table. — Not to mention what numbers have been given up to the inhuman usage of cruel task-masters, who, by their unrelenting scourges, have ploughed their backs, and made long furrows, and at length brought them even to death. When passing along, I have viewed your plantations cleared and cultivated, many spacious houses built, and the owners of them faring sumptuously every day, my blood has frequently almost run cold within me, to consider how many of your slaves had neither convenient food to eat, or proper raiment to put on, notwithstanding most of the comforts you enjoy were solely owing to their indefatigable labours. — The Scripture says, Thou shalt not muzzle the ox that treadeth out the corn. Does

God take care for oxen; and will he not take care of the Negroes also?" . . .

Some who have only seen Negroes in an abject state of slavery, broken-spirited and dejected, knowing nothing of their situation in their native country, may apprehend, that they are naturally unsensible of the benefits of Liberty, being destitute and miserable in every respect, and that our suffering them to live amongst us (as the Gibeonites of old were permitted to live with the Israelites) tho' even on more oppressive terms, is to them a favour; but these are certainly erroneous opinions, with respect to far the greatest part of them: Altho' it is highly probable that in a country which is more than three thousand miles in extent from north to south, and as much from east to west, there will be barren parts, and many inhabitants more uncivilized and barbarous than others; as is the case in all other countries: Yet, from the most authentic accounts, the inhabitants of Guinea appear, generally speaking, to be an industrious, humane, sociable people, whose capacities are naturally as enlarged, and as open to improvement, as those of the Europeans; and that their Country is fruitful, and in many places well improved, abounding in cattle, grain, and fruits: And as the earth yields all the year round a fresh supply of food, and but little clothing is requisite, by reason of the continual warmth of the climate; the necessaries of life are much easier procured in most parts of Africa, than in our more northern climes. This is confirmed by many authors of note, who have resided there; among others M. Adanson, in his account of Gorée and Senegal, in the year 1754, says, "Which way soever I turned my eyes on this pleasant spot, I beheld a perfect image of pure nature; an agreeable solitude, bounded on every side by charming landscapes, the rural situation of cottages in the midst of trees; the ease and indolence of the Negroes reclined under the shade of their spreading foliage; the simplicity of their dress and manners; the whole revived in my mind the idea of our first parents, and I seemed to contemplate the world in its primitive state: they are, generally speaking, very good-natured, sociable and obliging. I was not a little pleased with this my first reception; it convinced me, that there ought to be a considerable abatement made in the accounts I had read and heard everywhere of the savage character of the Africans. I observed, both in

Negroes and Moors, great humanity and sociableness, which gave me strong hopes, that I should be very safe amongst them, and meet with the success I desired, in my inquiries after the curiosities of the country."

William Bosman, a principal factor for the Dutch, who resided sixteen years in Guinea, speaking of the natives of that part, where he then was, says, "They are generally a good sort of people honest in their dealings;" others he describes as "being generally friendly to strangers, of a mild conversation, affable and easy to be overcome with reason . . . "

William Smith, who was sent by the African Company to visit their settlements on the coast of Guinea, in the year 1726, gives much the same account of the country of Delmina and Cape Corse, &c. for beauty and goodness, and adds, "The more you come downward towards that part, called Slave-Coast, the more delightful and rich the soil appears." Speaking of their disposition, he says, "They were a civil, good-natured people, industrious to the last degree. It is easy to perceive what happy memories they are blessed with, and how great progress they would make in the sciences, in case their genius was cultivated with study." He adds, from the information he received of one of the Factors, who had resided ten years in that country, "That the discerning natives account it their greatest unhappiness, that they were ever visited by the Europeans. — That the Christians introduced the Traffic of Salves; and that before our coming they lived in peace."

Andrew Brue, a principal man in the French Factory, in the account he gives of the great river Senegal, which runs many hundred miles up the country, tells his readers, "The farther you go from the sea, the country on the river seems more fruitful and well improved. It abounds in Guinea and Indian corn, rice, pulse, tobacco, and indigo. Here are vast meadows, which feed large herds of great and small cattle; poultry are numerous, as well as wild fowl." The same author, in his travels to the south of the river Gambia, expresses his surprise, "to see the land so well cultivated; scarce a spot lay unimproved; the low grounds, divided by small canals, were all sowed with rice; the higher ground planted with Indian corn, millet, and peas of different sorts, beef, and mutton very cheap, as well as all other necessaries of Life." The account this author gives of the disposition of the natives, is, "That they are generally good-natured and civil, and may be brought to any thing by fair and soft means." Artus, speaking of the same people, says, "They are a sincere, inoffensive people, and do no injustice either to one another or strangers."

From these accounts, both of the good disposition of the natives, and the fruitfulness of most parts of Guinea, which are confirmed by many other authors, it may well be concluded, that their acquaintance with the Europeans would have been a happiness to them, had those last not only bore the name, but indeed been influenced by the spirit of Christianity; but, alas! how hath the conduct of the Whites contradicted the precepts and example of Christ? Instead of promoting the end of his coming, by preaching the gospel of peace and good-will to man, they have, by their practices, contributed to enflame every noxious passion of corrupt nature in the Negroes; they have incited them to make war one upon another, and for this purpose have furnished them with prodigious quantities of ammunition and arms, whereby they have been hurried into confusion, bloodshed, and all the extremities of temporal misery, which must necessarily beget in their minds such a general detestation and scorn of the Christian name, as may deeply affect, if not wholly preclude their belief of the great truths of our holy religion. Thus an insatiable desire of gain hath become the principal and moving cause of the most abominable and dreadful scene, that was perhaps ever acted upon the face of the earth; even the power of their kings hath been made subservient to answer this wicked purpose, instead of being protectors of their people, these rulers, allured by the tempting bait laid before them by the European Factors, &c. have invaded the Liberties of their unhappy subjects, and are become their oppressors . . .

The misery and bloodshed, consequent of the Slave-Trade, is amply set forth by the following extracts of two voyages to the Coast of Guinea for slaves. The first in a vessel from Liverpool, taken verbatim from the original manuscript of the Surgeon's journal, viz.

"Sestro, December the 29th, 1724. No trade today, tho' many Traders come on board, they inform us, that the people are gone to war within land, and will bring prisoners enough in two or three days; in hopes of which we stay.

"The 30th. No trade yet, but our Traders came on board today, and informed us, the people had burnt four towns of their enemies, so that tomorrow we expext slaves off. Another large ship is come in: yesterday came in a large Londoner.

"The 31st. Fair weather, but no trade yet; we see each night towns burning; but we hear the Sestro men are many of them killed by the inland Negroes, so that we fear this war will be unsuccessful . . ."

Those, who are acquainted with the Trade, agree, that many Negroes on the sea-coast, who have been corrupted by their intercourse and converse with the European Factors, have learnt to stick at no act of cruelty for gain. These make it a practice to steal abundance of little Blacks of both sexes, when found on the roads or in the fields, where their parents keep them all day to watch the corn, &c. Some authors say, the Negro Factors go six or seven hundred miles up the country with goods, bought from the Europeans, where markets of men are kept in the same manner as those of beasts with us; when the poor slaves, whether brought from far or near, come to the sea-shore, they are stripped naked, and strictly examined by the European Surgeons, both men and women, without the least distinction or modesty; those which are approved as good, are marked with a red-hot iron with the ship's mark, after which they are put on board the vessels, the men being shackled with irons two and two together. Reader bring the matter home, and consider whether any situation in life can be more completely miserable than that of those distressed captives . . ."

Under these complicated distresses they are often reduced to a state of desperation, wherein many have leaped into the sea, and have kept themselves under water, till they were drowned; others have starved themselves to death, for the prevention whereof some masters of vessels have cut off the legs and arms of a number of those poor desperate creatures, to terrify the rest. Great numbers have also frequently been killed, and some deliberately put to death under the greatest torture, when they have attempted to rise, in order to free themselves from their present misery, and the slavery designed them . . .

As detestable and shocking as this may appear to such, whose hearts are not yet hardened by the practice of that cruelty, which the love of wealth, by degrees, introduceth into the human mind; it will not be strange to those who have been concerned or employed in the Trade. Now here arises a necessary query to those who hold the ballance and sword of justice; and who must account to God for the use they have made of it. Since our English law is so truly valuable for its justice, how can they overlook these barbarous deaths of the unhappy Africans without trial, or due proof of their being guilty, of crimes adequate to their punishment? Why are those masters of vessels . . . thus suffered to be the sovereign arbiters of the lives of the miserable Negroes; and allowed, with impunity, thus to destroy, may I not say, murder their fellow-creatures, and that by means so cruel as cannot be even related but with shame and horror?

When the vessels arrive at their destined port in the Colonies, the poor Negroes are to be disposed of to the planters, and here they are again exposed naked, without any distinction of sexes, to the brutal examination of their purchasers; and this, it may well be judged is to many of them another occasion of deep distress, especially to the females: Add to this, that near connections must now again be separated, to go with their several purchasers: In this melancholy scene mothers are seen hanging over their daughters, bedewing their naked breasts with tears, and daughters clinging to their parents; not knowing what new stage of distress must follow their separation; or if ever they shall meet again; and here what sympathy, what commiseration are they to expect; why indeed, if they will not separate as readily as their owners think proper, the whipper is called for, and the lash exercised upon their naked bodies, till obliged to part.

Can any human heart, that retains a fellow-feeling for the sufferings of mankind, be unconcerned at relations of such grievous affliction, to which this oppressed part of our species are subjected: God gave to man dominion over the fish of the sea, and over the fowls of the air, and over the cattle, &c. but imposed no involuntary subjection of one man to another.

The truth of this position, has of late been clearly set forth by persons of reputation and ability, particularly George Wallis, in his System of the Laws of Scotland, " . . . no man has a right to acquire or to purchase them; men and their Liberty are not either saleable or purchasable, one therefore has no body but himself to blame, in case he shall find himself deprived

of a man, whom he thought he had, by buying for a price, made his own; for he dealt in a trade which was illicit, and was prohibited by the most obvious dictates of humanity. For these reasons, every one of those unfortunate men, who are pretended to be slaves, has a right to be declared to be free, for he never lost his Liberty, he could not lose it; his Prince had no power to dispose of him: of course the sale was void. This right he carries about with him, and is entitled every where to get it declared. As soon, therefore, as he comes into a country, in which the judges are not forgetful of their own humanity, it is their duty to remember that he is a man, and to declare him to be free. — This is the law of nature which is obligatory on all men, at all times, and in all places." . . .

How dreadful then is this Slave-Trade, whereby so many thousands of our fellow-creatures, free by nature, endued with the same rational faculties, and called to be heirs of the same salvation with us, lose their lives, and are truly, and properly speaking, murdered every year. For it is not necessary, in order to convict a man of murder, to make it appear, that he had an intention to commit murder. Whoever does, by unjust force or violence, deprive another of his Liberty; and, while he has him in his power, reduces him, by cruel treatment, to such a condition as evidently endangers his life; and the event occasions his death, is actually guilty of murder . . .

Britons boast themselves to be a generous, humane people, who have a true sense of the importance of Liberty; but is this a true character, whilst that barbarous, Savage Slave-Trade, with all its attendant horrors, receives countenance and protection from the Legislature, whereby so many thousand lives are yearly sacrificed. Do we indeed believe the truths declared in the gospel? Are we persuaded that the threatnings, as well as the promises therein contained, will have their accomplishment? If indeed we do, must we not tremble to think what a load of guilt lies upon our Nation generally and individually, so far as we in any degree abet or countenance this aggravated iniquity . . .

Malachy Postlethwayt: The national and private advantages of the African trade considered (1772)

The most approved judges of the commercial interests of these kingdoms have ever been of opinion that our West India and African trades are the most nationally beneficial of any we carry on. It is also allowed on all hands that the trade to Africa is the branch which renders our American colonies and plantations so advantageous to Great Britain, that traffic only affording our planters a constant supply of Negro servants for the culture of their lands in the produce of sugars, tobacco, rice, rum, cotton, fustick, pimento, and all other our plantation produce, so that the extensive employment of our shipping in, to and from America, the great brood of seamen consequent thereupon, and the daily bread of the most considerable part of our British manufacturers are owing primarily to the labor of Negroes who, as they were the first happy instruments of raising our plantations, so their labor only can support and preserve them and render them still more and more profitable to their Mother kingdom.

The Negro trade, therefore, and the natural consequences resulting from it, may be justly esteemed an inexhaustible fund of wealth and naval power to this nation. And by the overplus of Negroes above what have served our own plantations, we have drawn likewise no inconsiderable quantities of treasure from the Spaniards who are settled on the continent of America, not only for Negroes furnished them from Jamaica, but by the last Assiento contract with the crown of Spain which may probably again be revived upon a peace being concluded with that kingdom.

What renders the Negro trade still more estimable and important is that near nine-tenths of those Negroes are paid for in Africa with British produce and manufactures only, and the remainder with East India commodities. We send no specie or bullion to pay for the products of Africa, but 'tis certain we bring from thence very large quantities of gold and not only that but wax and ivory; the one serves for a foreign export without the least detriment of our own product, the other is manufactured at home and afterwards carried to foreign markets to no little advantage both to the

nation and the traders. From which facts the trade to Africa may very truly be said to be, as it were, all profit to the nation . . .

And it may be worth consideration that while our plantations depend only on planting by Negro servants, they will neither depopulate our own country, become independent of her dominion, or anyway interfere with the interests of the British manufacturer, merchant or landed gentleman. Whereas were we under the necessity of supplying our colonies with white men instead of blacks, they could not fail being in a capacity to interfere with the manufactures of this nation — in time to shake off their dependency thereon and prove as injurious to the landed and trading interests as ever they have hitherto been beneficial.

Many are prepossessed against this trade, thinking it a barbarous, inhuman, and unlawful traffic for a Christian country to trade in blacks, to which I would beg leave to observe that though the odious appellation is annexed to this trade, it being called by some the slave trade, yet it does not appear from the best inquiry I have been able to make that the state of those people is changed for the worse by being servants to our British planters in America. They are certainly treated with great leniency and humanity, and as the improvement of the planter's estates depends upon due care being taken of their healths and lives, I can not but think their condition is much bettered to what it was in their own country.

Besides, the Negro princes in Africa, 'tis well known, are in perpetual war with each other. Since before they had this method of disposing of their prisoners of war to Christian merchants, they were wont not only to be applied to inhuman sacrifices, but to extreme torture and barbarity, their transplantation must certainly be a melioration of their condition, provided living in a civilized Christian country is better than living among savages. Nay, if life be preferable to torment and cruel death, their state can not, with any color of reason, be presumed to be worsted.

But I never heard it said that the lives of Negroes in servitude of our planters were less tolerable than those of colliers and miners in all Christian countries. However, while our rivals in trade receive great national emolument by the labor of these people, this objection will be of little weight with those who have

W. Otridge, London, 1772, pp. 427, 462–63; D. Browne, London, 1757, pp. 1–8.

the interest of their country at heart, or indeed the welfare of the Negroes.

But to resume the subject. As the present prosperity and splendor of the British colonies have been owing to Negro labor, so not only their future advancement, but even their very being depends upon our pursuing the same measures in this respect as our competitors do.

That our colonies are capable of very great improvements by the proper application of the labor of blacks has been urged by the most experienced judges of commerce. And if it be good policy to purchase as little from, and sell as much to, foreign nations of our own produce and manufactures, 'tis certainly very unwise and impolitic in us not to encourage our plantations to the extent they are capable of, in order to supply ourselves at least from thence with what we can't do without and take from other nations such essentials only as neither our own country or our plantations will afford us.

From these considerations it has been wisely proposed to extend the planting of coffee, cocoa, indigo, cochineal, logwood, hemp, flax, naval stores, and making of potash, and variety of other products which those lands admit of. Whereby, instead of being under the disadvantageous necessity of purchasing such valuable and useful merchandise from other nations, we might easily become capable not only of supplying ourselves, but exporting to others considerable quantities of our plantation produce. This would turn the balance of trade in our favor with countries where 'tis now against us and enable our colonies to increase their demand for British manufactures in proportion to our demand for their produce.

But all improvements proposed to be made in our plantations have always presupposed the well-being and prosperity of our African trade, to the end that they might not be destitute of a constant supply of Negroes for those purposes. Without which, instead of improvement, nothing but distress and poverty could ensue in all the British colonies while France, by wiser measures, would render their colonies still more opulent and, consequently, a more formidable nursery of naval power.

And however mean an idea some may entertain of the advantages arising from the direct trade to Africa, it can proceed from nothing but want of being duly acquainted therewith. Was all the gold that has, or easily might have been brought from thence, coined at the Tower with some impression to distinguish it from all other gold — as was formerly done — we should soon be sensible that we need be little beholding to any other nation for that valuable metal. Were we to extend our commerce into Africa to the pitch it will admit of, we must certainly export thither of the British produce and manufacture considerably more than we do to any one country in the whole world.

The continent of Africa is of great magnitude, the country extremely populous and the trade and navigation now well-known, easy, and not hazardous. As the natives in general stand in great need of European commodities so they have valuable returns to make us and such too that do in no respect interfere either with the produce and manufactures of those kingdoms or her American plantations which ought never to be forgot.

Central to Puritan thought of the 17th century, and to Presbyterian and Baptist doctrines as well, had been the belief that the individual Christian could not hope for salvation without knowing himself to have been converted. Religion from this perspective was more than correct behaviour and faithful subscription to official dogma; it was an experience deeply felt. The Puritans of Massachusetts Bay had actually tried to restrict their church membership to those who could convincingly describe their conversion experience. Succeeding generations were less sure of their ground, and demonstrations of saving grace were dropped as standards of church membership. Still the hope of a genuine religious conversion remained, and it was to this expectation that the men who sparked the remarkable outpouring of religious enthusiasm known as the Great Awakening drew attention. Their message was a sternly uncompromising one. Man is corrupt; God is sovereign. Only those who have truly experienced God's saving grace should consider themselves Christians.

Despite the remarkable successes of the Great Awakening preachers in rekindling religious concerns among the people, angry controversies broke out between them and their critics. In the Southern colonies where the Church of England was established by law, conflicts developed when itinerant preachers carried the message of the Great Awakening into Anglican parishes. According to the English Act of Toleration, those who were not members of the Church of England had the right to worship separately, but they had to seek written permission for nonconforming services, and their ministers needed licenses to preach. The Great Awakening fervor was particularly strong in the neglected frontier communities of Western Virginia and the Carolinas, and the officials of the church looked askance at these outbursts of religious enthusiasm that followed in the wake of itinerant preachers. Their efforts to silence them were rarely successful, but their attempt was bitterly resented and pushed to the fore the question of dissenters' rights.

In the middle colonies, the Great Awakening provoked a bitter dispute over the necessary qualifications for ministers. The revival leaders in the Presbyterian church insisted that most clergy had no saving grace and hence were helpless to bring their congregations to a knowledge of God's will. This insistence upon a personal religious experience was challenged by the more conservative clergy who were skeptical of emotional displays and felt that the church was more likely to endure by adhering to more objective qualifications like learning and behavior.

Controversy in New England turned on the question of the nature of the revivals themselves and the means preachers took to reach their congregations. Critics said that they deliberately stirred up their listeners, encouraging them to confuse emotional outbursts with genuine spiritual experiences; the revivalists defended their work by its fruits, a new absorption with religious matters in hundreds of communities. Our first two readings deal with the Great Awakening in New England. In the first, Jonathan Parsons (1705–1776), writing for a pro-revival journal, tells how the Great Awakening affected his congregation at Lyme, Connecticut. As he describes the background to his ministry, Parsons explains how he was first an Arminian, a term that refers to the doctrine that people can win their own salvation through good works. Calvinists considered Arminianism to be a pernicious doctrine, for it denied the sovereignty of God and the total dependence of man upon him. Yet the good life in America encouraged the spread of Arminianism, and it is this fatal attitude that Parsons blames for the spiritual deadness of New England.

Although few of the conventional clergymen were willing to acknowledge that they had departed from the stern Calvinism of their forebears, much of the tension created by the Great Awakening was a reflection of the larger struggle between an old ethos and a new morality. Charles Chauncey (1705–1787), one of the pillars of Boston's Congregational establishment, demonstrates this conflict in his answer to fellow clergymen like Parsons. Chauncey's sermon, *Enthusiasm Described and Cautioned Against*, was delivered at the commencement exercises at Harvard University in 1742, when the floodtide of the Great Awakening was finally ebbing. In making his case for reason, sobriety, and the sane practice of Christian virtues, Chauncey reveals how much 18th century rationalism had crept into orthodox New England thinking. For others, less learned and less devout than Chauncey, rationalism and Arminianism had blended into a kind of moral pragmatism with personal satisfaction and reasonableness taking the place of the uncompromising faith of the previous century. The Great Awakeners in fact were fighting the tides of the times, for increasingly the disposition of people was to be confident about human resources, have faith in man, and love God at a distance.

In the last reading Benjamin Franklin (1706–1790) attacks the official spokesman for the Presbyterian Synod of Philadelphia for dismissing a minister. Franklin's position is representative of the growing number of American colonists for whom rationalism had altogether replaced the religion of a personal God. These Deists, as they were often called, rejected the Bible's claim to be the revealed word of God and tended to treat Christian dogma as valuable only insofar as it promoted good morals. Franklin, who had fled the stern perspective of Puritan New England when he left Boston for Philadelphia, was hostile to religious orthodoxy and completely dead to the metaphysical questions of human purpose which lay at the base of the religious impulse. He was not free of combativeness towards formal religion, however, and when a young Presbyterian minister, Samuel Hamphill, was censured by his superiors for the doctrines he was preaching, Franklin jumped into the fray with an anonymously published defense of Hemphill.

The legacy of the Great Awakening was complex and contradictory. The harvest of Christian converts was impressive, but the religious homogeneity in most communities had been shattered. Many former one-church towns now had two warring congregations. Everywhere the frozen orthodoxy of the earlier period had thawed under the heat of doctrinal disputes. Baptist, Presbyterian, and Methodist ministers who carried the Great Awakening into the south made permanent inroads into the Anglican establishments there, and the revival meeting itself became a distinctive feature of religion on the frontier. In the cities the defense of man's reasoning capacity from church leaders like Chauncey and Deists like Franklin made it easier for people to endorse the new scientific approach to philosophical questions. Although the Great Awakening increased the number of separate congregations, it also represented the first religious movement common to all of the colonies. The ground had been laid for a religious outlook which was distinctively American.

Jonathan Parsons: An account of the revival of religion in the west parish of Lyme in Connecticut (1744)

There have been so many Prejudices in the Minds of People, against the late glorious Effusion of the Holy Spirit; and so many Misrepresentations of it respecting this Place in particular, that I have been long doubtful in my own Mind, whether it wou'd be conducive to the Interest of Christ's Kingdom, for me to give the Publick any Account of the very gracious Revival of Religion among us; or whether it was best to be silent, lest Men should reproach and mock yet more and more . . .

The Summer following my Ordination there was a great Effusion of the Holy Spirit upon the People. There appear'd to be an uncommon Attention to the Preaching of the Word, and a disposition to hearken to Advice; and a remarkable Concern about Salvation. 'Twas a general Inquiry among the Middle-aged and Youth, What must I do to be saved? Great Numbers came to my Study, some almost every Day for several Months together, under manifest Concern about their Souls. I seldom went into a House among my Neighbours, but they had some free Discourse about Religion, or were searching after the Meaning of some Texts of Scripture. I urg'd them very much to Works, and gave it as my Opinion (perhaps too hastily) that such awakened Souls ought to attend upon the Lord's-Supper: and in less than ten Months fifty-two Persons were added to the Church. There were several whole Families baptiz'd. Many of the young People were greatly reformed: they turned their Meetings for vain Mirth into Meetings for Prayer, Conference and reading Books of Piety . . . In that Day I was greatly in Love with Arminian Principles, and especially I abhor'd the

The Christian History, Kneeland and Green, Boston, 1744, pp. 118–27, 132–39, 146–47, 150–51.

Doctrine of God's absolute Sovereignty; and that might be one Reason why awaken'd Souls fell short of a saving Change, and settled down upon the Righteousness of the Law. The Doctrines that are natural for a Man of such Principles to preach, you know, are calculated to gratify the Pride of Men, to give them exalted Thoughts of their own Duties. I was exceedingly pleased with Dr. Tillotson's Notions about the Power of Man to perform the Conditions of the Gospel; or to do that to which God has join'd the Promise of special Grace; and some other Sermons of his that seem to be calculated to uphold such an Opinion. Dr. Clark also, and others of the like Stamp, that have calculated a Scheme of Religion suited to the corrupt Views of an haughty Heart, were my beloved Authors. I had a Zeal of God, but not a laudable one, because it was not according to Knowledge. Being ignorant of God's Righteousness, I endeavour'd to get others to establish their own Righteousness, and to keep them from submitting unto the Righteousness of God . . .

But God knows with how little Success I insisted upon the Things which I had learned and been assured of. Nothing seem'd to make any deep and lasting Impressions for good upon the Minds of People in general: it look'd to me, they liv'd easy without Christ, and without God in the World. Our young People took unwarrantable Liberties; Night-walking, Frolicking, and leud Practices, some grew bold in, and encourag'd and corrupted others thereby: Others fell into Party-Quarrels, and grew uneasy with the Plainness of the Preaching, and were pleas'd sometimes, to call it Censoriousness; especially if I told them, "that I could not, upon our Practice, reckon Conversions by the Number of those that had joined to the Church; or that I feared very few had been converted since my Ministry among them; and when I insisted upon it that an external Profession of the true Religion, join'd with a good Degree of doctrinal Knowledge, external Devotion, negative Blamelesness, and the like, were not good Evidences that a Person was a real Christian; but insisted upon it that all were spiritually dead by Nature, must have a Principle of spiritual Life implanted, must be converted to God, have sensible Communion with Christ, and live a life of Faith, as they would entertain well grounded Hopes of Heaven." These were hard Sayings, and many wou'd not receive them. Thus it was with us for

several Years, until I was awfully deserted of God, and got into a very dull, legal Frame my self, and then some were better pleas'd.

'Tis now almost four years since it pleased God to strengthen and enlarge my desires after the increase of Christ's Kingdom, and to stir me up to more ardent endeavours after the eternal Welfare of immortal Souls. Christ and his Cause grew exceeding precious; and one Soul appear'd of more Worth than a Thousand worlds; the Souls that were committed to my Charge lay with vast Weight and Tenderness upon my mind. The State of Religion look'd dismal: But few instances of Persons that I could meet with among them, that seem'd to be suitably affected with the Miseries of a perishing World, and the decaying State of Religion. The News of Mr. Whitefield's rising up with great Zeal for Holiness and Souls, had great Influence upon my Mind: God made Use of frequent Accounts about him to awaken my Attention, to humble me for past Deadness, and rouse me up to see my own Standing, and found an Alarm in some poor Sort, to a drowsy, careless People. When he came to Boston the venerable Dr. Colman wrote me an Account of his Zeal and Success in his daily Ministrations among them; which I freely communicated to one and another as I had Opportunity; hoping that such accounts from a father of the Country, so justly esteem'd, might have an happy Effect: and doubtless it was made Use of, by a gracious God, to draw the Attention of many among us, and stir up their Diligence in hearing the Word preached . . . But before I give a particular Account of these Effects, and other Things that have more lately fallen under my Observation respecting Religion, either at Home or Abroad, I beg your Patience a little . . .

If Persons, in great Numbers, are, in their general Course, turned from a careless vain and carnal to a careful and religious Conversation; from an immoral and loose, to a moral and strict Life; if they discover by all reasonable Evidence that they have a deep Sense of Sin and the Wrath of God, or afterwards, the Consolations of God; if they are apparently changed from worldly Pursuits to things of everlasting Importance; if from resting in Self-righteousness and Blamelesness they are made sensible of the Necessity of Faith and Holiness, and can't rest until they have what appears to us a good Evidence of resting in Christ; if they are turned from an apparent Irreverence and wandering in the House of God, and other Places of divine Worship, to an apparent devout and reverend Attendance on the Institutions of the Lord; if from spending Sabbaths in Idleness, or much of their Time in worldly Conversation, or Disputes, which gender Strife, they are turn'd to spend Sabbaths in publick and private Exercises of Worship with evident Care and Devotion, and in Christian Conferences about the Things of God; if there is, added to these Things, a manifest Reformation in relative Duties, and Persons apparently grow in Christian Knowledge at an unusual Rate, and really appear to have frequent and sensible Communion with Christ, if it makes Men better Husbands, Women better Wives, Fathers and Mothers better Parents, Children more careful in their Stations, People more prayerful for and loving to their Ministers (such as they think properly their Ministers:) If this in general is true of any People, all in a few Weeks or Months; I think we must conclude that such are under divine Influence, and God has graciously pour'd out his Spirit upon them, even tho' they precipitate into many imprudent Measures, or thro' wrong Judgment, they differ from us in many Things that are not fundamental. What if they cry out, faint, speak aloud in a public Assembly at an improper Time, happen to think they should tell their Neighbours their Fears that they are Strangers to Christ; what if they think themselves called to stay as long from their Families in the Night to pray to and praise God, as they have heretofore tarried to revel and drink, and to make themselves merry with vain Companions; what if in these and some other Things they believe differently from others; and in some other Things theyhave, for want of due Consideration, run into some Indecencies, but upon serious Reflection see the Mistake and reform; I can't think these Things any good Argument against their being under the Influences of the Holy Spirit, either convincing or sanctifying.

But I have exceeded my Design in hinting at Preliminaries, tho' I hope, you will forgive me, and carry these Things in your Mind, while you read on in the subsequent Part of my Account.

The Effects of that Sermon I spake of, preached on the 29th of March were then surprising. Indeed there were no Out-Cries; but a deep and general Concern upon the Minds of the Assembly discovered itself at that Time in plentiful Weeping, Sighs and Sobs. And what appear'd hopeful then, I found, upon conversing with many afterwards, to be true, as far as I could judge. Many told me that they never had such an awaken'd Sense of the Danger of putting off the grand Concern of their Souls to a future Season before, as God gave them under that Sermon: They were surprised at their own past Carelesness, and astonished that God had born with them so long. Several told me that tho' they had liv'd thirty forty or fifty Years under the Preaching of the Gospel, they had never felt the Power of the Word upon their Hearts, so as to be long affected thereby, at any Time as they did then. Before it was the Cry of their Hearts, 'When will the Sermon be over, and the Sabbath be ended'; but now the Minister always left off too soon, and the Time between Sermons was too long: they long for frequently returning Opportunities to hear. Before, they did not love Soul-searching Discourses, but now never cou'd hear too much of that Nature, together with many other Things of the like Import. . .

After this I observed that our Assemblies were greater and more attentive at Times of publick Worship than before. Sabbaths alone wou'd not suffice for hearing Sermons, but greater Numbers still urg'd for frequent Lectures. I was well pleas'd to observe such a flocking to the Windows, and a hearing Ear become general; and therefore I readily consented, upon the Request of the People, to preach as often as I cou'd, besides the stated Exercises of the Sabbath. Once every Week I carried on a publick Lecture, besides several private ones in various Parts of the Parish. And I could not but observe about this Time, that an Evening Lecture I had set up the Winter before in a private House, for the sake of a young Man that was a Cripple, tho' at first exceeding thin (but seven Persons, as I remember, besides the Family) was now greatly increas'd, and in about a Month grew up to several Hundreds, so that I was oblig'd to turn it into a publick Evening Lecture.

Now it pleas'd God to encourage my Heart, give me unusual Freedom, and such a firm State of bodily Health, that I could go thro' three Times the Service I had been able to endure at other Times; so that I was able to study and write three Sermons a Week, and preach several others of my old Notes (for I seldom in all the Time preach'd without Writing.) Sometime in this Month Mr. Griswold invited me to preach a Lecture for him, and I consented. While I was preaching from Psalm 119, 59, 60, I observ'd many of the Assembly in Tears, and heard many crying out in very great Bitterness of Soul, as it seem'd then by the Sound of Voices. When Sermon was over I cou'd better take Notice of the Cause; and the Language was to this Purpose, viz. Alas! I'm undone; I'm undone! O my Sins! How they prey upon my Vitals! What will become of me? How shall I escape the Damnation of Hell, who have spent away a golden Opportunity under Gospel Light, in Vanity? — And much more of the like Import — 'Tis true, Outcries were new and surprising at that Time: but knowing the Terrors of the Lord, I was satisfy'd that they were but what might be reasonably accounted for; if Sinners were under a true Sense of their Sins, and the Wrath of a Sin-hating God: And therefore I did not use any Endeavours to restrain them at that Time; but the greater Number cried out of themselves and their Vileness, the more I rejoyced in Hope of the good Issue. As I was satisfied that it was the Truth they had been hearing, so, by their Complaints, it appeard to be the Force of Truth that made them cry out, and threw many of them into Hysterick-Fits: And, if I mistake not, every one that were so violently seiz'd that Night, have since given good Evidence of their Conversion; but that, their Reverend Pastor can give the best Account of.

The visible Success of my Ministry in that and some other Lectures abroad, (tho' I rejoyc'd in the happy Prospect of the Advancement of the Kingdom of our divine Lord) was far from being a Means to damp my Hopes or slacken my Endeavours at Home. My heart burned with Love to and Pity for the People of my peculiar Charge: I had constant Supplies of Argument flowing into my Mind, and Zeal to urge a speedy Answer.

By the latter End of April our young People were generally sick of that vain Mirth, and those foolish Amusements that had been their Delight, and were form'd into several religious Societies for Prayer and reading Books of Piety under my Direction: Many of them were frequently in my Study for Advice; the Bent of their Souls was evidently towards the Things of another World: Whenever they fell into Companies, the great Salvation was the subject of their Conversation. They were so generally displeas'd with themselves for past Carelesness, and spending Time in Revels and Frolicks, that several, at the Desire of others, came to me, and desir'd me to preach them a Lecture upon the 14th of May (the Day of our Election in this Colony) which they had for many Years, accustomed themselves to spend in Feasting, Musick, Dancing, Gaming, and the like. . .

Some run back upon the Sins of riper Years (for there were several Persons upwards of 40 and some of more than 50 Years old, that discover'd great Concern by their pale Countenances and Tears, and trembling too.) Some cried out of the Hardness of their Hearts, others of their Unbelief: some were crying, God be merciful to me a Sinner; and others intreated Christians to pray for them. Thus they continued, at my House, for several Hours; and after I had taken what Pains with them, I tho't necessary for that Evening, and pray'd with them, they were advised to repair to their own Places of Abode; and accordingly all that were able went Home.

Now I tho't the People in great Danger, and especially those that were most deeply wounded. I knew, in all Probability, that Hell was in an Uproar; the Prince of Darkness see his Kingdom shaking, and he was in great Danger of losing many of his obedient Subjects: many threatned Rebellion, and were in Danger of being accused of Treason against his Crown; and therefore if possible, he would allure them back to former Fidelity; perswade them to settle down upon the Foundation of their own Works, or drive them to utter Despair of Mercy: And therefore I dare not sit in my Study the next Day (tho' that loudly call'd for me to be there,) but spent my Time abroad among distressed Souls, and others that fell in my Way that were more lightly touch'd. . . I continu'd to preach and exhort publickly and from House to House, about six Times a Week thro' this Month at Home, besides attending upon distressed Souls upon certain appointed Days in my Study. And tho' I spake to them with unusual Moderation, in my Study, (as well as in Sermons about this Time,) that I might have greater Advantage to instruct their Minds, yet I was commonly obliged to make several Stops of considerable Length, and intreat them, if possible, to restrain the Flood of Affection, that so they might attend to further Truths which were to be offer'd, and others might not be disaffected. Some would after a while recover themselves, and others, I'm satisfy'd could not. I have tho't since, whither I did not do wrong in endeavouring to restrain them: the Pains they took with themselves to keep from out-breakings was a greater Hindrance to their hearing, than their Out-cries were: and it was so far from satisfying others, that it was improv'd as an Argument against the Reality of their Concern, if, upon the utmost Violence used with them they could after some Time hold in. I find no such Restraints laid upon distressed Souls in the Apostles Days, tho', we must allow that they were as good Judges of what is Right in such a Case as other Men: and indeed, why might we not expect some Direction from the inspired Writers if it was our Duty to restrain them, and put them upon the Torture to keep Silence? If the Lord is pleas'd to make this open Shew of the Victories of his Grace, his Will be done: let him take his own Way: I think, upon Trial, the wondering Multitude are not the more likely to receive Conviction, for our prescribing to Him. . .

The Conversation of the People in general, was religious. If at any Time Neighbours met, the great Affairs of Salvation were the Subject of Discourse. In the Streets, in the Fields and in private Houses the Discourse was instructive: some enquiring the Way to Life, others in their proper Sphere, endeavouring to help the Distressed by their humble Advice and Counsel: some that knew the Terrors of the Lord, would persuade the careless, and modestly recommend the Grace of God to their Acceptance, from their own Experience of its Sweetness. — And as there were frequent Enquiries about the Things of infinite Concern, so there was a great Increase of Knowledge in religious Matters. According to the best Observation I could make, I believe, the People advanc'd more in their Acquaintance with the Scriptures, and a true doctrinal Understanding of the Operations of the holy Spirit in Conviction, Regeneration, and Sanctification, in six Months Time, than they had done in the whole of my Ministry before, which was nine Years. — Nor was this all, but many evidently look'd upon Sin with Abhorrence: they appeared to be renew'd in the Spirit of their Minds: Bitterness, and Wrath, and Anger, and Clamour, and Evil-speaking seem'd to be put away

from them, with all Malice: Their Fruit was unto Holiness: Love to God and Man, with their genuine Fruits were increasing. Rough and haughty Minds, became peaceful, gentle and easy to be intreated. . .

Many that were greatly affected and concern'd for a while are grown easy and careless as formerly; tho' there is a Number unto this Day remaining under Convictions. — I don't remember any two Instances among us that ever gave me Satisfaction of their Conversion, but what still manifest comfortable Signs of the Truth and Reality of it. — 'Tis possible that some may think me fond of Numbers; and wonder at it the rather since I have met with so much Difficulty, and have had so many ill Reports spread abroad concerning the Doctrines, it has been said that I have taught, as well as some other most abusive Representations of my Character. Yet, leaving such Things to him who will shortly bring into open Light all the hidden Things of Darkness; I think I am call'd of God to say, that if we may give credit to the Accounts Persons give of a clear Law-Work, and a Work of effectual Grace wrought upon their Hearts; after it has been strengthened by frequent repeated Accounts of their Communion with God, and a spiritual Conversation and good Life, in a general Course, for several Years together, I have Reason to hope about one Hundres and eighty Souls belonging to this Congregation, have met with a saving Change, since the Beginning of the late glorious Effusion of the holp Spirit among us; besides the frequent, and more than common Quicknings and Refreshings of others that were, hopefully, in Christ Years before. And, perhaps, we have a confirming Testimony of the Truth of the Work, above what some others have had, in the visible Meekness, Forbearance, Love, Forgiveness, and the like, with which they have generally behav'd themselves in the Time of injurious Calumnies; when the Work of God, and their personal Conduct have been misrepresented.

Charles Chauncey: Enthusiasm described and cautioned against (1742)

If any Man among you think himself to be a Prophet, or Spiritual, let him acknowledge that the Things that I write unto you are the Commandments of the Lord. 1 Cor. xiv. xxxvii.

Many things were amiss in the Church of Corinth when Paul wrote this Epistle to them. There were envyings, strife and divisions among them on account of their ministers. Some cried up one, others another; one said, "I am of Appollos." They had formed themselves into parties, and each party so admired the teacher they followed as to reflect unjust contempt on the other.

Nor was this their only fault. A spirit of pride prevailed exceedingly among them. They were conceited of their gifts and too generally disposed to make an ostentatious show of them. From this vainglorious temper proceeded the forwardness of those that had "the gift of tongues," to speak in languages which others did not understand, to the disturbance, rather than edification of the church. And from the same principle it arose that they spake not by turns, but several at once in the same place of worship to the introducing such confusion that they were in danger of being thought mad.

Nor were they without some pretence to justify these disorders. Their great plea was that in these things they were guided by the Spirit, acted under his immediate influence and direction. This seems plainly insinuated in the words I have read to you: "If any man think himself to be a prophet, or spiritual, let him acknowledge that the things that I write unto you are the commandments of the Lord." As if the Apostle had said, "you may imagine yourselves to be spiritual men, to be under a divine inspiration in what you do, but 'tis all imagination, mere pretence, unless you pay a due regard to the commandments I have here wrote to you, receiving them not as the word of man, but of God." Make trial of your spiritual pretences by this rule: if you can submit to it, and will order your conduct by it, well; otherwise you only cheat yourselves while you think yourself to be spiritual men, or prophets. You are nothing better than Enthusiasts. Your being acted by the Spirit, immediately guided and influenced by him, is mere pretence. You have no good reason to believe any such thing.

From the words thus explained, I shall take occasion to discourse to you upon the following particulars:

1. I shall give you some account of Enthusiasm in its nature and influence.

2. Point you a rule by which you may judge of persons whether they are under the influence of Enthusiasm.

3. Say what may be proper to guard you against this unhappy turn of mind . . .

The Enthusiast is one who has a conceit of himself as a person favored with extraordinary presence of the Deity. He mistakes the workings of his own passions for divine communication and fancies himself immediately inspired by the Spirit of God when all the while he is under no other influence than that of an overheated imagination.

The cause of this Enthusiasm is a bad temperament of the blood and spirits; 'tis properly a disease, a sort of madness, and there are few — perhaps none at all — but are subject to it . . . And various are the ways in which their Enthusiasm discovers itself. Sometimes it may be seen in their countenance. A certain wildness is discernible in their general look and air, especially when their imaginations are moved and fired. Sometimes, it strangely loosens their tongues and gives them such an energy as well as fluency and volubility in speaking as they themselves, by their utmost efforts, can't so much as imitate when they are not under the enthusiastic influence. Sometimes, it affects their bodies, throws them into convulsions and distortions, into quakings and tremblings. This was formerly common among the people called Quakers. I was myself, when a lad, an eye-witness to such violent agitations and foamings in a boisterous female speaker as I could not behold but with surprise and wonder . . .

And what extravagances in this temper of mind are they not capable of, and under the specious pretext too of paying obedience to the authority of God? Many have fancied themselves acting by immediate warrant from heaven while they have been committing the most undoubted wickedness. There is indeed scarce anything so wild, either in speculation or practice, but they have given into it. They have in many instances been blasphemers of God and open disturbers of the peace of the world.

But in nothing does the Enthusiasm of these persons discover itself more than in the disregard they express to the dictates of reason. They are above the force of argument, beyond conviction from a calm and sober address to their understandings. As for them, they are distinguished persons. God himself speaks inwardly and immediately to their souls. They see the light infused into their understandings and cannot be mistaken. 'Tis clear and visible there, like the light of bright sunshine, shows itself and needs no other proof but its own evidence. They feel the hand of God moving them within and the impulses of his Spirit and cannot be mistaken in what they feel. Thus they support themselves and are sure reason has nothing to do with what they see and feel. What they have sensible experience of admits no doubt, needs no probation. And in vain will you endeavor to convince such persons of any mistakes they are fallen into. They are certainly in the right and know themselves to be so. They have the Spirit opening their understandings and revealing the truth to them. They believe only as he has taught them, and to suspect they are in the wrong is to do dishonor to the Spirit . . .

And as the natural consequence of their being thus sure of everything, they are not only infinitely stiff and tenacious, but impatient of contradiction, censorious, and uncharitable. They encourage a good opinion of none but such as are in their way of thinking and speaking. Those, to be sure, who venture to debate with them about their errors and mistakes, their weaknesses and indiscretions run the hazard of being stigmatized by them as poor unconverted wretches without the Spirit, under the government of carnal reason, enemies to God and religion and in the broad way to hell . . .

This is the nature of Enthusiasm, and this its operation in a less or greater degree in all who are under the influence of it. 'Tis a kind of religious frenzy and evidently discovers itself to be so whenever it rises to any great height . . .

'Tis true, it won't certainly follow that a man, pretending to be a Prophet, or Spiritual, really is so if he owns the Bible and receives the truths therein revealed as the mind of God, but the conclusion, on the other hand, is clear and certain. If he pretends to be conducted by the Spirit and disregards the Scripture, pays no due reverence to the things there delivered as the commandments of God, he is a mere pretender, be his pretences ever so bold and confident or made with ever so much seeming seriousness, gravity, or solemnity.

And the reason of this is obvious; viz. that the things contained in the Scripture were wrote by holy men as they were moved by the Holy Ghost. They were received from God and committed to writing under his immediate, extraordinary influence and guidance. And the divine, ever-blessed Spirit is consistent with himself. He cannot be supposed to be the author of any private revelations that are contradictory to the public standing ones which he has preserved in the world to this day . . .

'Tis not, therefore, the pretence of being moved by the Spirit that will justify private Christians in quitting their own proper station to act in that which belongs to another. Such a practice as this naturally tends to destroy that order God has constituted in the church and may be followed with mischiefs greater than we may be aware of.

'Tis indeed a powerful argument with many in favor of these persons their pretending to impulses and a call from God, together with their insatiable thirst to do good to soul. And 'tis owing to such pretences as these that encouragement has been given to the rise of such numbers of lay-exhorters and teachers in one place and another all over the land. But 'tis one of the things wrote by the Apostle as the commandment of God, that there should be officers in the church, an order of men to whom it should belong, as their proper, stated work, to exhort and teach. This cannot be the business of others. And, if any who think themselves to be spiritual are under impressions to take upon them this ministry, they may have reason to suspect whether their impulses are any other than the workings of their own imaginations. And, instead of being under any divine extraordinary influence, there are just grounds of fear whether they are not acted from the vanity of their minds — especially if they are but beginners in religion, men of weak minds, babes in understanding as is most commonly the case . . .

And it deserves particular consideration whether the suffering, much more the encouraging, women, yea girls, to speak in the assemblies for religious worship is not a plain breach of that commandment of the Lord wherein it is said, "Let your women keep silence in the churches, for it is not permitted to them to speak." It is a shame for women to speak in the church. After such an express constitution, designedly made to restrain women from speaking in the church, with what face can such a practice be pleaded for? They may pretend they are moved by the Spirit and such a thought of themselves may be encouraged by others, but if the Apostle spake by the Spirit when he delivered this commandment, they can't act by the Spirit when they break it. 'Tis a plain case, these female exhorters are condemned by the Apostle, and if 'tis the commandment of the Lord that they should not speak, they are spiritual only in their own thoughts while they attempt to do so.

The last thing I shall mention as written by the Apostle is that which obliges to a just decorum in speaking in the house of God. It was an extravagance these Corinthians had fallen into, their speaking many of them together and upon different things while in the same place of worship. "How is it, brethren," says the Apostle, "when ye come together, everyone hath a psalm, hath a doctrine, hath a tongue, hath a revelation, hath an interpretation." It was this that introduced the confusion and noise upon which the Apostle declares if any unbeliever should come in among them, he would take them to be mad. And the commandment he gives them to put a stop to this disorder is that they should speak in course, one by one, and so as that things might be done to edifying . . .

In these and all other instances, let us compare men's pretences to the Spirit by the Scripture. And if their conduct is such as can't be reconciled with an acknowledgment of the things therein revealed as the commandments of God, their pretences are vain. They are prophets and spiritual, only in their own proud imaginations . . . But as the most suitable guard against the first tendencies towards Enthusiasm, let me recommend to you the following words of counsel.

1. Get a true understanding of the proper work of the Spirit and don't place it in those things wherein the Gospel does not make it consist . . .

Herein, in general, consists the work of the Spirit. It does not lie in giving men private revelations, but in opening their minds to understand the public ones contained in the Scripture. It does not lie in sudden impulses and impressions, in immediate calls and extraordinary missions. Men mistake the business of the Spirit if they understand by it such things as these. And 'tis probably from such unhappy mistakes that

they are at first betrayed into Enthusiasm. Having a wrong notion of the work of the Spirit 'tis no wonder if they take the uncommon sallies of their own minds for his influence . . .

2. Keep close to the Scripture and admit of nothing for an impression of the Spirit, but what agrees with that unerring rule. Fix it in your minds as a truth you will invariably abide by, that the Bible is the grand text by which everything in religion is to be tried, and that you can, at no time, nor in any instance, be under the guidance of the Spirit of God, much less his extraordinary guidance if what you are led to is inconsistent with the things there revealed either in point of faith or practice.

3. Make use of the Reason and Understanding God has given you. This may be thought an ill-advised direction, but 'tis as necessary as either of the former. Next to the Scripture, there is no greater enemy to Enthusiasm than Reason. 'Tis indeed impossible a man should be an Enthusiast who is in the just exercise of his understanding and 'tis because men don't pay a due regard to the sober dictates of a well-informed mind that they are led aside by the delusions of a vain imagination. Be advised then to show yourself men, to make use of your reasonable powers and not act as the horse or mule, as though you had no understanding.

'Tis true, you must not go about to set up your own Reason in opposition to revelation. Nor may you entertain a thought of making Reason your rule instead of Scripture. The Bible, as I said before, is the great rule of religion, the grand test in matters of salvation, but then you must use your reason in order to understand the Bible. Nor is there any other possible way in which as a reasonable creature, you should come to an understanding of.

You are, it must be acknowledged, in a corrupt state. The Fall has introduced great weakness into your reasonable nature. You can't be too sensible of this, nor of the danger you are in of making a wrong judgment through prejudice, carelessness, and the undue influence of sin and lust. And to prevent this, you can't be too solicitous to get your nature sanctified; nor can you depend too strongly upon the divine grace to assist you in your search after truth. And 'tis in the way of due dependence on God and the influences of his Spirit that I advise you to the use of your reason.

And in this way you must make use of it. How else will you know what is a revelation from God? What should hinder your entertaining the same thought of a pretended revelation as of a real one, but your reason discovering the falsehood of the one and the truth of the other? . . .

But it may be you will say you have committed yourselves to the guidance of the Spirit which is the best preservative. Herein you have done well; nothing can be objected against this method of conduct. Only take heed of mistakes touching the Spirit's guidance. Let me enquire of you, how is it the Spirit preserves from delusion? Is it not by opening the understanding and enabling the man in the due of his reason to perceive the truth of the things of God and religion? Most certainly. And, if you think of being led by the Spirit without understanding or in opposition to it, you deceive yourselves. The Spirit of God deals with men as reasonable creatures, and they ought to deal with themselves in like manner . . .

There is such a thing as real religion, let the conduct of men be what it will and 'tis, in its nature, a sober, calm, reasonable thing. Nor is it an objection of any weight against the sobriety or reasonableness of it that there have been Enthusiasts who have acted as though it was a wild, imaginary business. We should not make our estimate of religion as exhibited in the behavior of men of a fanciful mind . . .

Let us esteem those as friends to religion, and not enemies, who warn us of the danger of Enthusiasm and would put us upon our guard that we be not led aside by it. As the times are, they run the hazard of being called enemies to the holy Spirit and may expect to be ill-spoken of by many and loaded with names of reproach, but, they are notwithstanding, the best friends to religion, and it may be it will more and more appear that they have all along been so. They have been stigmatized as Opposers of the work of God, but 'tis a great mercy of God there have been such Opposers. This land had, in all probability, been overrun with confusion and distraction if they had acted under the influence of the same heat and zeal which some others have been famous for.

'Tis really best people should know there is such a thing as Enthusiasm and that it has been, in all ages, one of the most dangerous enemies to the church of God and has done a world of mischief. And 'tis a kindness to them to be warned against it and directed to the proper method to be preserved from it. 'Tis indeed one of the best ways of doing service to real religion, to distinguish it from that which is imaginary. Nor should ministers be discouraged from endeavoring this though they should be ill-thought or evil-spoken of. They should beware of being too much under the influence of that "fear of man which bringeth a snare," which is evidently the case where they are either silent or dare not speak out faithfully and plainly lest they should be called Pharisees or Hypocrites and charged with leading souls to the devil. 'Tis a small matter to be thus judged and reviled, and we should be above being affrighted from duty by this which is nothing more than the breath of poor, ignorant, frail man . . .

Thus it has been in other parts of the world. Enthusiasm, in all the wildness and fury and extravagance of it, has been among them and sometimes had a most dreadfully extensive spread. Ten thousand wild Enthusiasts have appeared in arms at the same time and this too in defense of gross opinions as well as enormous actions. The first discovery, therefore, of such a spirit, unless due care is taken to give check to its growth and progress, is much to be feared, for there is no knowing how high it may rise, nor what it may end in.

The good Lord give us all wisdom and courage and conduct in such a day as this! And may both ministers and people behave after such a manner as that religion may not suffer, but in the end, gain advantage and be still more universally established.

Benjamin Franklin: A defence of the Rev. Mr. Hemphill's observations (1735)

When I first read the Rev. Commission's Vindication, I was in doubt with my self, whether I should take any publick Notice of it. I had reason to believe this Part of the World was troubled with Impertinence enough already, and that a Reply would be only affording our Authors a new Occasion from more of it by another Publication. Besides, I had little Reason to hope, that the most obvious Refutation of what our Reverend Authors have said to flatter and deceive their unthinking Readers into an Opinion of their honest Zeal and inflexible Justice, should ever gain one Proselyte from the Dominion of Bigotry and Prejudice . . .

Tho' I believe no body will deny their undoubted Right to declare their Opinions, yet 'tis certain that to go farther, and deprive him as far as they can of Liberty to declare his; to deprive him of the Exercise of his Ministerial Function, and of a Livelihood as far as it depends on it, because his Principles were thought contrary to theirs, gave him a just Occasion to represent them as Men fir'd with a persecuting Spirit, since this was Persecution, as far as they could carry it. They farther add "Has not the Commission that Liberty which is common to all Societies, of Judging of the Qualifications of their own Members? Mr. Hemphill is possess'd with the same Right, and may declare Non-Communion with us, if he sees Reason for it." If, by judging of their Members Qualifications, they mean, that they have a Right to censure them, as they have done him, and expel 'em their Society; I think it is clear they have no such Right; for, according to this way of Reasoning, the Spanish Inquisitors may say to a Person they imagine heretical, You, 'tis true, have a Right to judge for your self, to quit our Communion, and declare yourself Protestant; but we have likewise the common and natural Right of Societies, to expel you our civil and ecclesiastical Society, destroy your Reputation, deprive you of your Estate, nay your Life, or in other Words do you all the Mischief we please, notwithstanding your Right of declaring Non-Communion with us. How so? Because we have the Power, and Inclination to do it. Are not these Reasons by which they vindicate themselves every whit as good to justify the Practice of the Inquisition? . . .

How then must we act, say they; have we no Power to suppress Error and advance Truth? Yes, all the Power that any Set of calm, reasonable, just Men can wish for. They may consider his Assertions and Doctrines expose their evil Tendency, if such they have, and combat the Falshood they find in them with Truth, which will ever be the most effectual Way to suppress them and to attempt any other Method of doing it, is much more likely to propagate such suppos'd Errors or false Doctrines, than suppress them: In this free Country where the Understandings of Men are under no civil Restraint, and their Liberties sound and untouch'd, there is nothing more easy than to shew that a Doctrine is false, and of ill Consequence, if it really be so; but if not, no Man, or Set of Men can

make it so, by peremptorily declaring it unsound or dangerous, without vouchsafing to shew how or where, as the Commission did at the Beginning of this Affair, and indeed have yet done no better . . .

Whether Hemphill's Notions of Christianity be or be not inconsistent with the darling Confession of Faith, he is not at all concern'd to enquire; whatever Notions he might have formerly entertain'd of this Idol Confession, he now declares it to be no more his Confession, &c. That his Description of Christianity is not inconsistent with, or subversive of the Gospel of Christ, is already prov'd. But our Authors attempt to prove the contrary; and indeed in such a manner as every Man of Common Sense laughs at. Hemphill has said in his Observations, "That what he means in his Account of Christianity, is, that our Saviour's Design in coming into the World, was to restore Mankind to that State of Perfection, in which Adam was at first created; and that all those Laws that he has given us, are agreeable to that original Law, as having such a natural Tendency to our own Ease and Quiet, that they carry their own Reward, &c." That is, that our Saviour's Design in Coming into the World, was to publish such a System of Laws, as have a natural Tendency to restore Mankind to that State of Perfection, in which Adam was at first created, &c. Hemphill's Meaning being thus in a few Words explain'd, it is altogether needless to say any thing about the Observations of these incomprehensible Writers upon this part of Hemphill's Doctrine. The Scriptures they have adduc'd to prove it false, and every thing they say about it are altogether impertinent and foreign to the Purpose, as every common Reader (our Authors excepted) will easily apprehend. And indeed if they (our Authors) had purposely endeavour'd to give the World an Idea of their impenetrable Stupidity they cou'd hardly have fallen upon more effectual Methods to do it, than they have (I'll not say in this Part of their Performance only, but) thro' the whole of it . . .

But lest they shou'd imagine that one of their strongest Objections hinted at here, and elsewhere, is designedly overlook'd, as being unanswerable, viz. our lost and undone State by Nature, as it is commonly call'd, proceeding undoubtedly from the Imputation of old Father Adam's first Guilt. To this I answer once for all, that I look upon this Opinion every whit as ridiculous as that of Imputed Righteousness. 'Tis a Notion invented, a Bugbear set up by Priests (whether Popish or Presbyterian I know not) to fright and scare an unthinking Populace out of their Senses, and inspire them with Terror, to answer the little selfish Ends of the Inventors and Propagators. 'Tis absurd in it self, and therefore cannot be father'd upon the Christian Religion as deliver'd in the Gospel. Moral Guilt is so personal a Thing, that it cannot possibly in the Nature of Things be transferr'd from one Man to Myriads of others, that were no way accessary to it. And to suppose a Man liable to Punishment upon account of the Guilt of another, is unreasonable; and actually to punish him for it, is unjust and cruel.

Our Adversaries will perhaps alledge some Passages of the sacred Scriptures to prove this their Opinion; What! will they pretend to prove from Scripture a Notion that is absurd in itself, and has no Foundation in Nature? And if there was such a Text of Scripture, for my own Part, I should not in the least hesitate to say, that it could not be genuine, being so evidently contrary to Reason and the Nature of Things. But is it alledg'd, that there are some Passages in Scripture, which do, at least, insinuate the Notion here contradicted? In answer to this, I observe, that these Passages are intricate and obscure. And granting that I could not explain them after a manner more agreeable to the Nature of God and Reason, than the Maintainers of this monstrous System do, yet I could not help thinking that they must be understood in a Sense consistent with them, tho' I could not find it out; and I would ingeniously confess I did not understand them, sooner than admit of a Sense contrary to Reason and to the Nature and Perfections of the Almighty God, and which Sense has no other Tendency than to represent the great Father of Mercy, the beneficent Creator and Preserver of universal Nature, as arbitrary, unjust and cruel; which is contrary to a thousand other Declarations of the same holy Scriptures. If the teaching of this Notion, pursued in its natural Consequences, be not teaching of Demonism, I know not what is . . .

'Twould be a needless Trouble (and the Reader would hardly forgive the doing it) to follow these dark Authors Step by Step, thro' all their incoherent Starts and Hints. I shall therefore only take Notice of one Thing more under this Article. Hemphill is condemn'd

for advancing this Piece of Heresy, viz. They who have no other Knowledge of God and their Duty, but what the Light of Nature teaches them; no Law for the Government of their Actions, but the Law of Reason and Conscience; will be accepted, if they live up to the Light which they have, and govern their Actions accordingly. To this our stern Authors answer, Will the Heathen be accepted of God, by living up to the Light which they have, and governing their Actions accordingly? then, say they, there is no need of Christ's Merits and Satisfaction, in order to our Acceptance with God. Well concluded! Pray, how came these Rev. Gentlemen to know that the Heathen, living up to the Light of Nature, may not have an Interest in the Merits and Satisfaction of Christ, or that they may not be accepted of God upon account thereof. The Merits of Christ's Death and Sufferings may be so great as to extend to the Heathen World, they may reap the Advantages of it, tho' they never had an Opportunity of hearing of him, provided they make a good Use of their Reason, and other Principles of Action within them. And to say otherwise is actually to lessen and diminish the Merits of the Redeemer of Mankind: The Holy Scriptures represent his Mission as a general Benefit, a Benefit which Regards all Men, and in Fact, tell us that Christ died for all. And can any imagine that our good God, as is here suppos'd, will eternally damn the Heathen World for not obeying a Law they never heard of; that is, damn them for not doing an Impossibility. Surely none can imagine such a thing; except such as form their Ideas of the great Governor of the Universe, by reflecting upon their own cruel, unjust and barbarous Tempers, as our Authors seem to do. If God requir'd Obedience to an unknown Law, Obedience to the Gospel from those that never heard of it, or who never were in a Capacity or Circumstances of being reasonably convinc'd of it, it would be in the first Place manifest Injustice; for surely, Promulgation or Publishing of a Law must be allow'd necessary, before Disobedience to it can be accounted criminal. It is utterly impossible to reconcile the contrary Notion with the Idea of a good and just God; and is a most dreadful and shocking Reflection upon the Almighty. In the next Place, we should find the Mission of our Saviour so far from being a general Benefit, as the Scripture teaches, that on the contrary it would be but a particular one, distributed only to the smallest Part of Mankind: But, which is more, this Mission of our Saviour wou'd be a very great Misfortune and Unhappiness to the greatest Part (three Fourths) of Mankind . . . Reason clearly teaches the Truth of such or such a Proposition, and that we find in the holy Scriptures some Passage that seems to contradict the clear Decisions of Reason, we ought not, for we really cannot, admit that Sense of the Passage that does so, altho' it shou'd be receiv'd by all the Divines, that call themselves orthodox, upon Earth; So that any Man must be altogether in the right to look out for another Sense of the Passage in Question, which will not contradict the clear Decisions of Reason.

This Principle is to be extended only to Propositions, which evidently contradict the clear and manifestly well-founded Decisions of Reason in general (as in the Case before us;) and I say that such Propositions, such Doctrines cannot be contain'd in divine Revelation; so that we must look for another Sense of the Passages, by which they wou'd pretend to establish these Propositions or Doctrines; we must, I say, look for a Sense agreeable to Reason and the known Perfections of God; and it is absolutely impossible to reconcile the Opinion here contradicted to either; and if this Notion be not to represent the Almighty, as stern, arbitrary, inexorable, & c. pray what is?

As for those Passages of Scripture, which are often adduc'd to prove the absolute Necessity of all Men's believing in Jesus Christ without Distinction, in order to Salvation; Reason, common Sense, Equity and Goodness oblige us to understand and apply them only to those to whom infinite Wisdom has thought proper to send the Gospel.

These Gentlemen can hardly take it amiss to be advis'd to take the utmost Care of saying any thing, or interpreting Scripture after a Manner injurious to the infinite Justice, Goodness and Mercy of God, and contradictory to Reason. If the christian Scheme of Religion be not a reasonable one, they wou'd make but a dull Piece of Work on't in attempting to vindicate the Truth of it . . .

One of the most significant developments in colonial America was the new style of politics which emerged from the repeated struggles between local legislators and royal officials. Superficially, colonial political institutions resembled English parliamentary politics, but there were substantial differences. The property qualification which was so easily met in the colonies eliminated all but a small percentage from political participation in England. Parliament and its constituency formed a society within a society, an elite whose shared English values were cemented further by the ties of wealth and status. Jealous of their position, ambitious and determined to remain on top, the men who ruled England were likely to view all challenges to the existing social order as personal threats. A whole set of accompanying political habits went along with their political perspective from the top. Conflicts within the ruling class were contained within orderly limits. Debates were confined to a small, educated audience, all of whom believed that social order was far too fragile a thing to expose to the rough and tumble of vulgar public discourse. Responsibility was given to those who had proved their ability to work within the status quo. With half the population of England living on the thin edge of subsistence, English upper class agreement on the need for tight social control is not remarkable, but it did produce a set of unspoken regulations which were stronger than the formal political arrangements.

By contrast in America, a majority of free white men in all of the colonies could vote and in many the eligible percentage went as high as 80%. This did not mean that political office was open to all comers. The society was in fact quite deferential, and a man's estate, his education, his family, and his ability to command others were recognized qualifications for office, but the well-born leaders in colonial politics had to accommodate the interests of the great middling class of farmers, mechanics, and merchants if they were to retain political responsibility. With such a large constituency, there could be no keeping issues quiet. Inevitably legislative policies became public topics, and winning over this large and often rambunctious public became critically important. Local leaders needed the support of numbers to pit against the prestige and authority of the governor and his party of close-knit appointees. They developed a different style of politics and — more importantly — different political values. The skills needed to persuade a few highly placed personages were altogether dissimilar from those effective with a large group of friends and neighbors. Where an elite class esteems loyalty, discretion, and a certain elegance in the performance of duties, colonial voters wanted a demonstration of honesty, candidness, and concern for the public good.

Thus it was that clashes between local parties and royal appointees were more than struggles over who should control the purse or how royal instructions should be interpreted. They became a contest between two orders of political organization — the one an incipient democracy and the other a misplaced aristocracy. In such a context it is not surprising that the two sides often disagreed on the rules of the game. Such an instance was the trial of John Peter Zenger, an obscure New York printer. In English law, any publication or speech designed to bring the government into disrepute was a crime called seditious libel. Although the English were famous for their freedom of the press, this freedom in the 18th century — in America as well as the mother country — meant freedom from prior restraint. Prevailing opinion still held that social order could not be maintained if those entrusted with preserving it were exposed to public ridicule or criticism.

Zenger was arrested for seditious libel because his press had been hired to print a new newspaper, designed solely to publicly expose the conduct of Governor William Cosby. Cosby's enemies were powerful men in New York, eminent lawyers from landed families who probably thought their control of colonial offices would prevent their being prosecuted. Cosby did have difficulty getting an indictment issued, but once it was issued, he pushed the prosecution of Zenger with his full powers. The opposition deftly turned the trial itself into an attack upon Cosby. They engaged a distinguished Philadelphia lawyer, Andrew Hamilton (1676–1741), to handle Zenger's defense. Hamilton, ignoring all the precedents of English law, which surely would have convicted his client, made a direct appeal to the jury's reasoning and experience. Rather than save his client from the charge of seditious libel, he attacked the idea of considering public exposure of official irresponsibility as a crime at all. The first reading in this section is taken from Hamilton's address to the jury.

Having won an acquittal with his unorthodox arguing of the case, Hamilton became the hero of the hour, and the jubilant New Yorkers published an account of the trial which was widely distributed. Jonathan Blenman, a prominent lawyer from the British West Indian colony of Barbados read the account and rushed into print with a rebuttal which is the second reading in this section. Blenman took issue with Hamilton's legal reasoning and in the process of exposing Hamilton's errors he reveals the different purposes of English common law and American politics. Although Hamilton won the case by convincing the jury that if a defendant could prove the truth of his published statements he should be acquitted, this principle was not widely accepted for another fifty years. In fact, colonial assemblies were readier than royal governors to act against printers so foolish as to attack their proceedings. However, the kernel of a new attitude towards the rights of the governed and the responsibilities of the governors had been planted.

The third reading presents another element which worked to change colonial politics. This was the assertiveness of the lower classes. The reading is a remonstrance from a group of South Carolina back country settlers who were driven to advertise their grievances because the government in Charleston had neglected them. Political participation by a city's poor or by the isolated families scratching out a thin existence on the frontier was rare, but when these people did rouse themselves they were always angry and often violent. Without the police resources to maintain order against mobs, royal and colonial leaders had to be receptive to their demands. In the case of the South Carolina frontiersmen, when they organized the Regulators to maintain order, the South Carolina legislature finally took

action and established circuit courts throughout the colony. Charles Woodmason, who actually composed the Remonstrance, was the Church of England clergyman for the South Carolina Back Country Parish. His position in the established church no doubt explains his antipathy to the itinerant preachers whose proselytizing he derided.

Andrew Hamilton: Speech to the Zenger trial jury (1735)

Mr. Hamilton. May it please Your Honour; I agree with Mr. Attorney, that Government is a sacred Thing, but I differ very widely from him when he would insinuate, that the just Complaints of a Number of Men, who suffer under a bad Administration, is libelling that Administration. Had I believed that to be Law, I should not have given the Court the Trouble of hearing any Thing that I could say in this cause . . .

Is it not surprising to see a Subject, upon his receiving a Commission from the King to be a Governor of a Colony in America, immediately imagining himself to be vested with all the Prerogatives belonging to the sacred Person of his Prince? And which is yet more astonishing, to see that a People can be so wild as to allow of, and acknowledge those Prerogatives and Exemptions, even to their own Destruction? Is it so hard a Matter to distinguish between the Majesty of our Sovereign, and the Power of a Governor of the Plantations? Is not this making very free with our Prince, to apply that Regard, Obedience and Allegiance to a Subject which is due only to Our Sovereign? And yet in all the Cases which Mr. Attorney has cited, to show the Duty and Obedience we owe to the Supreme Magistrate, it is the King that is there meant and understood, tho' Mr. Attorney is pleased to urge them as Authorities to prove the Heinousness of Mr. Zenger's offence against the Governor of New-York. The several Plantations are compared to so many large corporations, and perhaps not improperly; and can any one give an Instance, that the Mayor or Head of a Corporation, ever put in a Claim to the sacred Rights of Majesty? Let us not (while we are pretending to pay a great Regard to our Prince and His Peace) make bold

Livingston Rutherfurd, *John Peter Zenger,* New York, 1904, pp. 74–123.

to transfer that Allegiance to a Subject, which we owe
to our King only. What strange Doctrine is it, to press
every Thing for Law here which is so in England? I believe we should not think it a Favour, at present at
least, to establish this Practice. In England so great a
Regard and Reverence is had to the Judges, that if any
man strike another in Westminster Hall, while the
Judges are sitting, he shall lose his Right Hand, and
forfeit his Land and Goods, for so doing. And tho' the
Judges here claim all the Powers and Authorities within this Government, that a Court of King's Bench has
in England, yet I believe Mr. Attorney will scarcely
say, that such a Punishment could be legally inflicted
on a Man for committing such an Offence, in the presence of the Judges sitting in any Court within the Province of New-York. The Reason is obvious; a Quarrel
or Riot in New-York cannot possibly be attended with
those dangerous Consequences that it might in Westminster Hall; nor (I hope) will it be alledged, than any
Misbehaviour to a Governor in the Plantations will, or
ought to be, judged of or punished, as a like Unduti-
fulness would be, to Our Sovereign. From all which, I
hope Mr. Attorney will not think it proper to apply his
Law-Cases (to support the Cause of his Governor)
which have only been judged, where the King's Safety
or Honour was concerned . . .

Mr. Attorney. . . . The Case before the Court is,
whether Mr. Zenger is guilty of Libelling His Excellency the Governor of New-York, and indeed the whole
Administration of the Government? Mr. Hamilton has
confessed the Printing and Publishing, and I think nothing is plainer, than that the Words in the Information
are scandalous, and tend to sedition, and to disquiet
the Minds of the People of this Province. And if such
Papers are not Libels, I think it may be said, there can
be no such Thing as a Libel.

Mr. Hamilton. May it please Your Honour; I cannot
agree with Mr. Attorney: For tho' I freely acknowledge, that there are such Things as Libels, yet I must
insist at the same Time, that what my Client is charged
with, is not a Libel; and I observed just now, that Mr.
Attorney in defining a Libel, made use of the Words,
scandalous, seditious, and tend to disquiet the People;
but (whether with Design or not I will not say) he
omitted the Word false.

Mr. Attorney. I think I did not omit the Word false:
But it has been said already, that it may be a Libel,
notwithstanding it may be true.

Mr. Hamilton. In this I must still differ with Mr.
Attorney; for I depend upon it, we are to be tried upon this Information now before the Court and Jury,
and to which we have pleaded Not Guilty, and by it
we are charged with Printing and publishing a certain
false, malicious, seditious and scandalous Libel. This
Word *false* must have some Meaning, or else how came
it there? I hope Mr. Attorney will not say, he put it
there by Chance, and I am of Opinion his Information
would not be good without it. But to shew that it is
the principal Thing which, in my Opinion, makes a
Libel, I put the Case, the Information had been for
printing and publishing a certain *true* Libel, would
that be the same thing? Or could Mr. Attorney support such an Information by any Precedent in the English Law? No, the Falsehood makes the Scandal, and
both make the Libel. And to shew the Court that I am
in good Earnest, and to save the Court's Time, and Mr.
Attorney's Trouble, I will agree, that if he can prove
the Facts charged upon us, to be false, I'll own them
to be scandalous, seditious, and a Libel. So the Work
seems now to be pretty much shortened, and Mr.
Attorney has now only to prove the Words false, in
order to make us Guilty.

Mr. Attorney. We have nothing to prove; you have
confessed the Printing and Publishing . . .

Mr. Chief Justice. You cannot be admitted, Mr.
Hamilton, to give the Truth of a Libel in Evidence. A
Libel is not to be justified; for it is nevertheless a Libel
that it is true.

Mr. Hamilton. I am sorry the Court has so soon resolved upon that Piece of Law; I expected first to have
been heard to that Point. I have not in all my Reading
met with an Authority that says, we cannot be admitted to give the Truth in Evidence, upon an information
for a Libel . . .

Mr. Chief Justice. Mr. Hamilton, the Court have delivered their Opinion, and we expect you will use us
with good Manners; you are not to be permitted to argue against the Opinion of the Court.

Mr. Hamilton.   With Submission, I have seen the Practice in very great Courts, and never heard it deemed unmannerly to - - - - - -

Mr. Chief Justice.   After the Court have declared their Opinion, it is not good Manners to insist upon a Point, in which you are over-ruled.

Mr. Hamilton.   I will say no more at this Time; the Court I see is against us in this Point; and that I hope I may be allowed to say.

Mr. Chief Justice.   Use the Court with good Manners, and you shall be allowed all the Liberty you can reasonably desire.

Mr. Hamilton.   I thank your Honour. Then, Gentlemen of the Jury, it is to you we must now appeal, for Witness, to the Truth of the Facts we have offered, and are denied the Liberty to prove; and let it not seem strange, that I apply my self to you in this Manner, I am warranted so to do, both by Law and Reason. The Last supposes you to be summoned, out of the Neighbourhood where the Fact is alleged to be committed; and the Reason of your being taken out of the Neighbourhood is, because you are supposed to have the best Knowledge of the fact that is to be tried. And were you to find a Verdict against my client, you must take upon you to say, the Papers referred to in the Information, and which we acknowledge we printed and published, are false, scandalous and seditious: but of this I can have no Apprehension. You are Citizens of New-York; you are really what the Law supposes you to be, honest and lawful Men; and, according to my Brief, the Facts which we offer to prove were not committed in a Corner; they are notoriously known to be true; and therefore in your Justice lies our Safety. And as we are denied the Liberty of giving Evidence, to prove the Truth of what we have published, I will beg Leave to lay it down as a standing Rule in such Casess, That the suppressing of Evidence ought always to be taken for the strongest Evidence; and I hope it will have that Weight with you. But since we are not admitted to examine our Witnesses, I will endeavor to shorten the Dispute with Mr. Attorney, and to that End, I desire he would favor us with some Standard Definition of a Libel, by which it may be certainly known, whether a Writing be a Libel, yea or not.

Mr. Attorney.   The Books, I think, have given a very full definition of a Libel; they say it is ". . . in a strict Sense taken for a malicious Defamation, expressed either in Printing or Writing, and tending either to blacken the Memory of one who is dead, or the Reputation of one who is alive, and to expose him to publick Hatred, Contempt or Ridicule. But it is said, That in a larger Sense the Notion of a Libel may be applied to any Defamation whatsoever, expressed either by Signs or Pictures, as by fixing up a Gallows against a Man's Door, or by painting him in a shameful and ignominious Manner. And since the chief Cause for which the Law so severely punishes all Offences of this Nature, is the direct Tendency of them to a Breach of Publick Peace, by provoking the Parties injured, their Friends and Families to Acts of Revenge, which it would be impossible to restrain by the severest Laws, were there no Redress from Publick Justice for Injuries of this kind . . . "

Mr. Hamilton.   Ay, Mr. Attorney; but what certain Standard Rule have the Books laid down, by which we can certainly know, whether the Words or the Signs are malicious? Whether they are defamatory? Whether they tend to the Breach of the Peace, and are a sufficient Ground to provoke a Man, his Family, or Friends to Acts of Revenge, especially those of the ironical sort of Words? And what Rule have you to know when I write ironically? I think it would be hard, when I say, such a Man is a very worthy honest Gentleman, and of fine Understanding, that therefore I meant he was a Knave or a fool.

Mr. Attorney.   I think the Books are very full; it is said in 1 Hawk, p. 193. just now read, "That such Scandal as is expressed in a scoffing and ironical Manner, makes a Writing as properly a Libel, as that which is expressed in direct Terms . . . " I think nothing can be plainer or more full than these Words.

Mr. Hamilton.   I agree the Words are very plain and I shall not scruple to allow (when we are agreed that the Words are false and scandalous, and were spoken in an ironical and scoffing Manner, &c.) that they are really libellous; but here still occurs the Uncertainty, which makes the Difficulty to know, what Words are scandalous and what not; for you say, they may be scandalous, true or false; besides, how shall we know whether the Words were spoke in a scoffing and ironical Manner, or seriously? Or how can you know whether the Man did not think as he wrote? For by your Rule, if he did, it is no Irony, and consequently no Libel. But under Favour, Mr. Attorney, I think the same Book, and the same Section will shew us the only Rule by which all these Things are to be known. The Words are these; " . . . which Kind of Writing is as well Understood to mean only to upbraid the Parties with the Want of these Qualities, as if they had directly and expressly done so." Here it is plain, the Words are scandalous, scoffing and ironical, only as they are Understood. I know no Rule laid down in the Books but this, I mean, as the Words are *understood*.

Mr. Chief Justice.   Mr. Hamilton, do you think it so hard to know, when Words are ironical, or spoke in a scoffing Manner?

Mr. Hamilton.   I own it may be known; but I insist, the only Rule to know is, as I do or can *understand* them; I have no other Rule to go by, but as I understand them.

Mr. Chief Justice.   That is certain. All Words are libellous, or not, as they are understood. Those who are to judge of the Words, must judge whether they are scandalous or ironical, tend to the Breach of the Peace, or are seditious: There can be no Doubt of it.

Mr. Hamilton.   I thank your Honour; I am glad to find the Court of this Opinion. Then it follows that those twelve Men must understand the Words in the Information to be scandalous, that is to say, *false*; for I think it is not pretended they are of the ironical Sort; and when they understand the Words to be so, they will say we are guilty of Publishing a false Libel, and not otherwise.

Mr. Chief Justice.   No, Mr. Hamilton the Jury may find that Zenger printed and published those Papers, and leave it to the Court to judge whether they are libellous; you know this is very common; it is in the Nature of a special Verdict, where the Jury leave the Matter of Law to the Court.

Mr. Hamilton.   I know, may it please Your Honour, the Jury may do so; but I do likewise know, they may do otherwise. I know they have the Right beyond all

Dispute, to determine both the Law and the Fact, and where they do not doubt of the Law, they ought to do so. This of leaving it to the Judgment of the Court, whether the Words are libellous or not, in Effect renders Juries useless (to say no worse) in many Cases; but this I shall have Occasion to speak to by and by . . . May it please Your Honour, I was saying, That notwithstanding all the Duty and Reverence claimed by Mr. Attorney to Men in Authority, they are not exempt from observing the Rules of Common Justice, even in their private or public Capacities; the Laws of our Mother Country know no Exemption. It is true, Men in Power are harder to be come at for Wrongs they do, either to a private Person, or to the Publick; especially a Governor in the Plantations, where they insist upon an Exemption from answering Complaints of any Kind in their own Government. We are indeed told, and it is true they are obliged to answer a Suit in the King's Courts at Westminster, for a Wrong done to any Person here: But do we not know how impracticable this is to most Men among us, to leave their Families (who depend upon their Labour and Care for their Livelihood) and carry Evidences to Britain, and at a great, nay, a far greater Expense than almost any of us are able to bear, only to prosecute a Governour for an Injury done here. But when the Oppression is general, there is no Remedy even that Way, no, our Constitution has (blessed be God) given us an Opportunity, if not to have such Wrongs redressed, yet by our Prudence and Resolution we may in a great Measure prevent the committing of such Wrongs, by making a Governour sensible that it is to his interest to be just to those under his Care; for such is the Sense that Men in General (I mean Freemen) have of common Justice, that when they come to know, that a chief Magistrate abuses the Power with which he is trusted, for the good of the People, and is attempting to turn that very Power against the Innocent, whether of high or low degree, I say, Mankind in general seldom fail to interpose, and as far as they can, prevent the Destruction of their fellow Subjects. And has it not often been seen (and I hope it will always be seen) that when the Representatives of a free People are by just Representations or Remonstrances, made sensible of the Sufferings of their Fellow-Subjects, by the Abuse of Power in the Hands of a Governour, they have declared (and loudly too) that they were not obliged by any Law to support a Governour who goes about to destroy a Province or Colony, or their Priviledges, which by His Majesty he was appointed, and by the Law he is bound to protect and encourage. But I pray it may be considered of what Use is this mighty Priviledge, if every Man that suffers must be silent? And if a Man must be taken up as a Libeller, for telling his Sufferings to his Neighbour? I know it may be answer'd, "Have you not a Legislature? Have you not a House of Representatives, to whom you may complain?" And to this I answer, we have. But what then? Is an Assembly to be troubled with every Injury done by a Governour? Or are they to hear of nothing but what those in the Administration will please to tell them? Or what Sort of a Tryal must a Man have? And how is he to be remedied; especially if the Case were, as I have known it to happen in America in my Time; That a Governour who has Places (I will not [say] Pensions, for I believe they seldom give that to another which they can take to themselves) to bestow, and can or will keep the same Assembly (after he has modeled them so as to get a Majority of the House in his Interest) for near twice Seven Years together? I pray, what Redress is to be expected for an honest Man, who makes his Complaint against a Governour to an Assembly who may properly enough be said, to be made by the same Governour against whom the Complaint is made? The Thing answers it self. No, it is natural, it is a Priviledge, I will go farther, it is a Right which all Freemen claim, and are entitled to complain when they are hurt; they have a Right publickly to remonstrate the Abuses of Power, in the strongest Terms, to put their Neighbours upon their Guard, against the Craft or open Violence of Men in Authority, and to assert with Courage the Sense they have of the Blessings of Liberty, the Value they put upon it, and their Resolution at all Hazards to preserve it, as one of the greatest Blessings Heaven can bestow . . . I beg leave to insist, That the Right of complaining or remonstrating is natural; And the Restraint upon this natural Right is the Law only, and that those Restraints can only extend to what is false; For as it is Truth alone which can excuse or justify any Man for complaining of a bad Administration, I as frankly agree, that nothing ought to excuse a Man who raises a false Charge or Accusation, even against a private Per-

son, and that no manner of Allowance ought to be made to him who does so against a publick Magistrate. Truth ought to govern the whole Affair of Libels, and yet the Party accused runs Risque enough even then; for if he fails of proving every Tittle of what he has wrote, and to the Satisfaction of the Court and Jury too, he may find to his Cost, that when the Prosecution is set on Foot by Men in Power, it seldom wants Friends to Favour it. And from thence (it is said) has arisen the great Diversity of Opinions among Judges, about what words were or were not scandalous or libellous. I believe it will be granted, that there is not greater Uncertainty in any Part of the Law, than about Words of Scandal; it would be mispending of the Court's Time to mention the Cases; they may be said to be numberless; and therefore the uttermost Care ought to be taken in following Precedents . . .

  If then upon the whole there is so great an Uncertainty among Judges (learned and great Men) in Matters of this Kind; If Power has had so great an Influence on Judges; how cautious ought we to be in determining by their Judgments, especially in the Plantations, and in the Case of Libels? There is Heresy in Law, as well as in Religion, and both have changed very much; and we well know that it is not two Centuries ago that a Man would have been burnt as an Heretick, for owning such Opinions in Matters of Religion as are publickly wrote and printed at this Day. They were fallible Men, it seems, and we take the Liberty not only to differ from them in religious Opinion, but to condemn them and their Opinions too; and I must presume, that in taking these Freedoms in thinking and speaking about Matters of Faith and Religion, we are in the right: For, tho' it is said there are very great Liberties of this Kind taken in New-York, yet I have heard of no Information prefered by Mr. Attorney for any Offences of this Sort. From which I think it is pretty clear, That in New-York a Man may make very free with his God, but he must take special Care what he says of his Governour. It is agreed upon by all Men that this is a Reign of Liberty, and while Men keep within the Bounds of Truth, I hope they may with Safety both speak and write their Sentiments of the Conduct of Men in Power, I mean of that Part of their Conduct only, which affects the Liberty or Property of the People under their Administration; were this to be denied, then the next Step may make them Slaves. For what Notions can be entertained of Slavery, beyond that of suffering the greatest Injuries and Oppressions, without the Liberty of complaining; or if they do, to be destroyed, Body and Estate, for so doing?

It is said and insisted upon by Mr. Attorney: That Government is a sacred Thing; That it is to be supported and reverenced; It is Government that protects our Persons and Estates; That prevents Treasons, Murders, Robberies, Riots, and all the Train of Evils that overturns Kingdoms and States, and ruins particular Persons; and if those in the Administration, especially the Supream Magistrate, must have all their Conduct censured by private Men, Government cannot subsist. This is called a Licentiousness not to be tollerated. It is said That it brings the Rulers of the People into Contempt, and their Authority not to be regarded, and so in the End the Laws cannot be put in Execution. These I say, and such as these, are the general Topicks insisted upon by Men in Power, and their Advocates. But I wish it might be considered at the same Time, How often it has happened, that the Abuse of Power has been the primary Cause of these Evils, and that it was the Injustice and Oppression of these great Men, which has commonly brought them into Contempt with the People. The Craft and Art of such Men is great, and who, that is the least acquainted with History or Law, can be ignorant of the specious Pretences, which have often been made use of by Men in Power, to introduce arbitrary Rule, and destroy the Liberties of a free People . . .

I hope to be pardon'd Sir for my Zeal upon this Occasion; it is an old and wise Caution, That when our Neighbours House is on Fire, we ought to take Care of our own. For tho' Blessed be God, I live in a Government where Liberty is well understood, and freely enjoy'd; yet Experience has shewn us all (I'm sure it has to me) that a bad Precedent in one Government, is soon set up for an Authority in another; and therefore I cannot but think it mine, and every Honest Man's Duty, that (while we pay all due Obedience to Men in Authority) we ought at the same Time to be upon our Guard against Power, wherever we apprehend that it may affect ourselves or our Fellow-Subjects . . .

But to conclude; the Question before the Court

and you, Gentlemen of the Jury, is not of small nor private Concern, it is not the Cause of a poor Printer, nor of New-York alone, which you are now trying: No! It may in its Consequence, affect every Freeman that lives under a British Government on the main of America. It is the best Cause. It is the Cause of Liberty; and I make no Doubt but your upright Conduct, this Day, will not only entitle you to the Love and Esteem of your Fellow-Citizens; but every Man who prefers Freedom to a Life of Slavery will bless and honour You, as Men who have baffled the Attempt of Tyranny; and by an impartial and uncorrupt Verdict, have laid a noble Foundation for securing to ourselves, our Posterity, and our Neighbours, That, to which Nature and the Laws of our Country have given us a Right, — The Liberty — both of exposing and opposing arbitrary Power (in these Parts of the World, at least) by speaking and writing Truth.

Jonathan Blenman: Remarks on the trial of John Peter Zenger (1737)

As the doctrines contained in that trial, or rather in the speech of Mr. Hamilton, are of so new a cast and so absolutely contradictory to all the resolutions and judgments that have been settled and established for so many ages and by judges of the highest reputation and most unquestionable characters for their integrity, virtues, and abilities, it could not be imagined so wild and idle an harangue could have had any weight or have met with any reception here, where the laws relating to libels have been so often canvassed and are generally so well understood. Therefore, the person to whom these *Remarks* were sent never thought of making any other use of them than to satisfy his own curiosity and that of his friends. But seeing, to his great surprise, that this extraordinary declamation has been mentioned with an air of applause and triumph in the paper called *Common-Sense* as striking out some new lights with regard to the doctrine of libels and, upon the credit of that recommendation the whole trial, not only twice printed here, but retailed out in scraps in the public newspapers, whereby many well-meaning people may be deceived and led into wrong notions concerning the laws of their country in this point, he has thought fit to communicate these *Remarks* to the public in order to remove any mistakes or errors that persons may fall into for want of an adequate judgment in these matters. If such false opinions should happen to influence the conduct or practice of any, the consequences may be very dangerous, it being an established maxim in our law that neither ignorance nor mistake is an escuse to anyone who has broke it, from the penalty of it.

. . . My intention is to consider things, not persons, having no other knowledge of the gentleman principally concerned than what is derived from the paper now before me, and being wholly a stranger to the merit of those disputes that give rise to the prosecution of this printer.

Much less shall I turn advocate for any lawless power in Governors. God forbid I should be guilty of such a prostitution who know by experience of what stuff they are commonly made, the wrong impressions they are apt to receive of themselves and others, their passions, prejudices and pursuit. Although when all reasonable allowances are made for certain circumstances that attend their mission from home and their situation abroad, a considerate person may be tempted to think it is well they are no worse than they are . . .

But to come to my Remarks on Zenger's Trial. In considering the defense made for the defendant by his counsel, Mr. Hamilton, upon "not guilty" pleaded to an "information for printing and publishing a libel," it is not to the purpose to enquire how far the matters charged in the information are in their nature libellous, nor whether the innuendoes are properly used to apply the matter to persons, things and places. It is only necessary to examine the truth of this single proposition, upon which the whole defense is grounded and to which the several parts of it refer: namely, that the several matters charged in the information are not and cannot be libellous because they are true in fact.

This is the cardinal point upon which the learned gentleman's whole argument turns and which he lays down over and over as the first principle that governs the doctrine of libels. Accordingly he confesses the printing and publishing of the papers laid in the information and puts it upon the King's Counsel to prove the facts contained in them to be false, alleging at the same time that unless that were done, the defendant could not be guilty. But if the same were proved to be false, he would own the papers containing them to be libels . . .

I would be glad to know, by the way, how this undertaking gentleman could have proved the truth of divers facts contained in the paper which the defendant published, supposing the court had been so much overseen as to let him into a proof of this sort. Could he prove, for example, that judges were arbitrarily displaced and new courts erected in the province of New York without consent of the Legislature? For I am credibly informed there never was a pretence or surmise of more than one judge being displaced or more than one court erected under Mr. Cosby's Administration, both which happened upon one and the same occasion. Now I would not have this esteemed a captious exception when I have to deal with a man of law who must or ought to know that if such a justification as he offered were at all allowable it ought to be full and express so as to leave no room for a libeller to multiply and exaggerate facts at his please when he is disposed to traduce persons in authority, there being a manifest difference between a single act of power without or against law (from which perhaps few governments have been free) and an habitual abuse of power in repeated instances of the same species. I would further ask how he could prove that the law itself was at an end and that trials by juries were taken away when a governor pleased, for if I mistake not, he was, at that time speaking to a jury in a regular court of law and in a prosecution which the Governor had much at heart. As the Gentleman himself insinuates, he would have been highly pleased to convict his client, yet would not attempt it but in the ordinary course of a trial by a jury and then too could not find a jury that would convict him. I think I am warranted in putting these questions, even by the authority of the barrister himself who says, "Truth ought to govern the whole affair of libels, and yet the party accused runs risk enough even then, for if he fails of proving every tittle he has wrote and to the satisfaction of the court and jury too, he may find to his cost etc."

But for the present I will suppose Mr. Hamilton was able to prove all these things, nay, that the jury knew them all to be true. I will go farther and allow that juries in criminal cases may determine both law and fact when they are complicated, if they will take such a decision upon their consciences (which is almost the only point in which I can have the honor of agreeing with him), yet after all these concessions, the main question rests still between us: whether a writing can be a libel in legal acceptance if the matter contained in it be true. He is pleased indeed to express his dislike of infamous papers even when they are true if levelled against private vices and fault. In this case, he calls them base, unworthy, scandalous, unmanly and unmannerly. But surely it might be expected when a point of law was in question that he would have told us whether they were lawful or unlawful . . . But it is plain he was aware of the consequence of being explicit upon this head, for had he owned such writings to be lawful, because true, he would have alarmed the common sense of mankind by opening a door for exposing at mercy the frailties, vices, defects and misfortunes of every person high and low which must inevitably destroy the peace of families and beget ill blood and disorders.

If, on the other hand, he had acknowledged such writings to be unlawful inasmuch as they concerned private miscarriages and transactions, but that every man might write as much truth as he pleased about the administration of the government — not only by pointing out faults and mistakes — but by publishing his own comment and inferences in order to fill the minds of the people with all the jealousies and apprehensions his imagination can form, it must have shocked men of understanding to be thus told that the law had provided against private quarrels and breaches of the peace occasioned by virulent writing, but had taken no care to prevent sedition and public disturbance arising from the same cause . . .

The authorities cited by Mr. Hamilton to support the proposition formerly stated (whether falsity in fact be essential to a libel so that the truth of the fact may be given in evidence to prove a writing to be no libel) consists principally of four cases which I shall consider in the order as they were produced.

The first is the Case of John de Northampton, 18 Edward III . . . John de Northampton, an attorney of the King's Bench, wrote a letter to one Ferrers, one of the King's Council, that neither Sir William Scot, Chief Justice, nor his fellows, the King's justices, nor their clerks, any great thing would do by the commandment

of our Lord, the King etc which said John, being called confessed the letter . . . Here, says the barrister, by this judgment it appears the libellous words were utterly false, and there the falsehood was the crime and is the ground for the judgment. For my own part, I can neither see truth nor falsehood in the words at the time they were wrote, for they refer to a future contingency that might or might not be as he said. And, in this respect, they were the same as if the man had said the roof of Westminster Hall would fall upon Sir William Scott and his fellows. Besides, the words taken by themselves have no ill meaning, for I imagine it will be allowed that most of the great things which judges do as judges are such as ought neither to be done, nor left undone by the King's Commandment . . .

I would not have this construction of the case, plain and natural as it is, pass merely upon my own credit, for I shall show that this case was so understood by one of the greatest lawyers of his time . . .

21 James I . . . The plaintiff brought an action upon the case against the defendant for delivering of a scandalous writing to the Prince. Noy, for the plaintiff cited 18 Edward III (when) a letter was sent to Ferrers, one of the King's Council, the effect of which was that Scot, Chief Justice, and his companions of the same Bench would not do a vain thing at the command of the king. Yet, because he sent such a letter to the King's Council, although he spake no ill, yet because it might incense the King against the judges, he was punished. If no ill was said, will it be pretended that the falsehool of what was said could be a reason for punishing a man? Is it not ridiculous to say that the falsehood of innocent or insignificant words can be criminal? . . .

And is it not high time to ask whether such gross misrepresentations of the books can proceed from ignorance or disingenuity? Be that as it will, it might certainly be expected that a proposition advanced with so much assurance by a man of years and reading, should have been supported by some one authority in point rather than by a series of low prevarication and quibble. Could he not find in all the book cases and trials at large concerning libels (which are sufficient of themselves to make a large volume) one example of proof being received to the truth or falsity contained in a libellous writing? Indeed there is nothing like it to be found, though the occasions have been many where such proof might be had, if it were proper – nay where the truth of the thing was notorious to all men and yet no question ever moved concerning it . . .

If anything can be necessary further to expose Mr. Hamilton's doctrine of libels after answering his own cases, it is only to subjoin some others that will show how much he is mistaken in almost everything he has offered on the subject. I shall, therefore, mention a very few that will bear a particular application to his crude notions without entering into a multitude of others to tire the reader.

15 Charles II The King v. Pym.

Pym was indicted at Exeter for a libel which he delivered to a parson to be published in church there, and was to this effect: "You are desired to bewail the sodomitry, wickedness, whoredom, lewdness that is of late broken out in this formerly well-governed city, that God would turn their hearts from committing those wickednesses which go unpunished by the magistrates." Pym confessed the indictment and was fined £100. He afterwards brought a writ of error and assigned for error that this was no offence because, though he says "go unpunished by the magistrate," yet he does not say that the magistrate knew of it, and wickedness unknown can't be punished. It was answered by the Court that this contains matter of great scandal to the government of the city, for it makes the late government better than the present . . .

This case was adjudged about four years after the Restoration when the memory of the preceding usurpation was fresh in everybody's mind. It is strange, therefore, Mr. Pym did not put himself on his trial at Exeter, for it was evident beyond contradiction to the people of that age from their own knowledge, as it is now to us from history, that the wickedness specified in the libel was restrained by a stricter hand before than after the Restoration. But this notorious truth, it seems did not avail Mr. Pym . . .

The case of Tutchin is strong against him, a case adjudged since the Revolution before that learned and upright judge, Sir John Holt. It plainly shows the fallacy that runs throughout his whole argument.

The points insisted on by this Chief Justice in his Charge to the Jury were these: to say that corrupt officers are appointed to administer affairs is certainly a reflection on the government. "If people should not be called to an account for possessing the people with an ill opinion of the government, no government can subsist. Now you are to consider whether these words I have read to you do not tend to beget an ill opinion of the administration of the government — to tell us that those that are employed know nothing of the matter and those that do know are not employed. Men are not adapted to offices, but offices to men, out of a particular regard to their interest and not to their fitness for the place! This is the purport of these papers." If this was the purport of the papers and so criminal as has been just said, it is amazing surely that Mr. Tutchin did not offer to prove the truth of these allegations and thereby take out their sting! Could not he possibly think of as many corrupt or incompetent officers — ecclesiastical, civil or military — in England preferred by interest rather than merit, as there were judges displaced and courts erected in New York? Or, if he was restrained by the hard-hearted judge from desporting himself in this pleasant and spacious field, could he not apply to the private knowledge which the jurors (as well as the rest of mankind) had of these matters, . . . "Lay your hands upon your hearts, gentlemen, and recollect. Do none of you know; nay, do not all of you know certain persons who shall be nameless, that have been lately promoted by a favor and interest to places of trust and profit, both in church and state, army and navy, whom you must know and believe in your consciences to be ill men and no way qualified for such preferment, as my sagacious client has most seasonably remonstrated to the neighbors by virtue of that right which every free born subject has of publishing his complaints when the matters so published can be supported with the truth?" But is Lord Holt asleep all this time? Can any reasonable man who has but common notions of judicature imagine that this great judge would suffer such trash as this to be thrown out in any court where he sat in judgment? But what must he have said if the libellers before him had offered to prove " . . . that the law itself was at an end, that trials by juries were taken away when a minister pleased, that no man could call anything his own or enjoy any liberty longer than those in the administration would condescend to let him do it?" Would he have said that the things did not tend to possess the people with an ill opinion of the government and that governments might well subsist, though men should not be called to an account for publishing the like? Or would he have said it was no matter what opinion the people had of the government, nor whether it subsisted or not, provided the assertions were true and so have discharged the man as a publisher of precious and useful truths to put the neighbors on their guard . . .

But this lawyer seems to be above having his points of law decided by the authorities of the law and has something in reserve which may serve to overthrow not only what has been offered in this paper, but even all the books of the law. This is what he calls the "reason of the thing," but is truly and properly a sketch of his own politics . . . Now is it not a sad case that he should want to be told that human laws don't strictly regard the moral pravity of actions, but their tendency to hurt the community whose peace and safety are their principal objects, so that by this standard only are punishments measured. If this profound sophister is of another opinion, let him give a reason why it should be a greater crime in our law for a man to counterfeit a silver shilling than to cut his father's throat.

The right of remonstrating or publishing just complaints, the barrister thinks, the right of all freemen, and so think I, provided such remonstrances and complaints are made in a lawful way. But when he comes to explain, it is not a court of justice, it is not an house of representatives, it is not a legislature that is to be troubled (as he phrases it) with these things. Who then, I pray, is to be troubled with them, for the King, it seems, is out of the question? Let the barrister speak for himself: "They have a right publicly to remonstrate against the abuses of power, in the strongest terms, to put their neighbors upon their guard," etc and, in another place, he speaks of it as a hardship " . . . if a man must be taken up as a libeller for telling his sufferings to his neighbor."

Now though I wish and hope as earnestly as he can do that a free people may never want the means of uttering their just complaints and of redressing their wrongs too, when their complaints are not heard. Yet, I always thought these things were better understood than expressed in a court of law, and I shall probably remain in that opinion 'til the learned Gentleman can produce something from the Common or Statute Law to show that a British subject has a right of appealing publicly to his neighbors (that is, to the collective body of the people) when he is injured in his person, rights or possessions . . .

I know the Law Books assert the right of complaining to the magistrates and courts of justice, to the Parliament, to the King himself, but a right of complaining to the neighbors is what has not occurred to me. After all, I would not be thought to derogate by anything I have said or shall say from that noble privileges of a free people, the liberty of the press. I think it the bulwark of all other liberty and the surest defense against tyranny and oppression. But still it is a two-edged weapon, capable of cutting both ways and is not therefore to be trusted in the hands of every discontented fool or designing knave. Men of sense and address (who alone deserve public attention) will ever be able to convey proper ideas to the people in time of danger without running counter to all order and decency or crying "fire" and "murder" through the streets if they chance to awake from a frightful dream. But I must again urge that these points are not fit to be discussed in a court of justice whose jurisdiction is circumscribed by positive and known laws . . .

I have hitherto been taught to believe that when a brave and free people have resorted to measures unauthorized by the ordinary course of the laws, such measures have been justified by the extraordinary necessity of the case which excluded all other means of redress. And as far as I understand the Constitution and have heard accounts of the British colonies, such a case can not well happen and has never yet happened among them . . . And I imagine it may be affirmed (without catching an occasion of offering incense to majesty) that if one half of the facts contained in Zenger's papers, and vouched for true by his Council, had been fairly represented and proved at home, Mr. Cosby would not have continued much longer in his government . . . I am the more emboldened to say this much because, though it is my lot to dwell in a colony where liberty has not always been well understood — at least not freely enjoyed — yet I have known a governor brought to justice within these last twenty years who was not only supported by a council and assembly, besides a numerous party here, but also by powerful friend at home, all which advantages were not able to screen him from censure, disgrace and a removal from the trust he had abused . . .

In a word, I shall agree with the Barrister (and so take my leave of him) that "the liberty of exposing and opposing arbitrary power" is the right of a free people, and he ought at the same time to admit that the order of things and the peace of society require that extraordinary means should not be used for this purpose 'till the ordinary have failed in the experiment. The supreme magistrate of an independent kingdom or state can not always be controlled by the one, and then the other is justified by that consideration. But in colonies that are from their creation subordinate to their Mother Country, there is no person who is not controllable by regular and well-known methods of proceeding. Consequently, there can be no absolute necessity of flying to extremities, at least in the first instance. From all which, I conceive, it follows that local considerations upon which the gentleman lays so great stress, conclude directly against him. I hope the security which the British Constitution affords to every man's person, property and reputation, as well as to the public tranquility is not lessened by any distance from the fountain of power and justice, but that a libel is a libel and punishable as such in America as well as in Europe . . .

Remonstrance of the upper inhabitants of South Carolina (1767)

The Remonstrance and petition of the inhabitants of the upper and interior parts of this province on behalf of themselves, and all the other settlers of the back-country humbly showeth that for many years past, the back parts of this province hath been infested with an infernal gang of villains, who have committed such horrid depredations on our properties and estates, such insults on the persons of many settlers, and perpetrated such shocking outrages throughout the back settlements, as is past description.

Charles Woodmason, *The Carolina Backcountry on the Eve of the Revolution,* Richard J. Hooker (ed.), Chapel Hill, 1953, pp. 213–59. Reprinted here by permission of the publishers: the Institute of Early American History and Culture at Williamsburg, Virginia, and the University of North Carolina Press.

Our large stocks of cattle are either stolen and destroyed — our cow pens are broken up — and all our valuable horses are carried off. Houses have been burned by these rogues, and families stripped and turned naked into the woods. Stores have been broken open and rifled by them (wherefrom several traders are absolutely ruined). Private houses have been plundered, and the inhabitants wantonly tortured in the indian manner for to be made confess where they secreted their effects from plunder. Married women have been ravished, virgins deflowered, and other unheard of cruelties committed by these barbarous ruffians who, by being let loose among us (and connived at) by the Acting Magistrates, have hereby reduced numbers of individuals to poverty — and for these three years last past have laid (in a manner) this part of the province under contribution.

No trading persons (or others) or with money or goods, no responsible persons and traders dare keep cash, or any valuable articles by them. Nor can women stir abroad, but with a guard, or in terror. The chastity of many beauteous maidens have been threatened by these rogues. Merchants stores are obliged for to be kept constantly guarded (which enhances the price of goods), and thus we live not as under a British government (every man sitting in peace and security under his own vine and his own fig tree), but as if we were in Hungary or Germany, and in a state of war — continually exposed to the incursions of Hussars and Pandours. Obliged to be constantly on the watch and on our guard against these intruders, and having it not in our power to call what we possess our own, not even for an hour; as being liable daily and hourly to be stripped of our property.

Representations of these grievances and vexations have often been made by us to those in power — but without redress. Our cries must have pierced their ears, though not entered into their hearts, for instead of public justice being executed on many of these notorious robbers (who have been taken by us at much labor and expense and committed) and on others (who with great difficulty and charge have been arraigned and convicted), we have to lament that such have from time to time been pardoned; and afresh set loose among us to repeat their villanies, and strip us of the few remaining cattle, horses, and moveables which after their former visits they had left us.

Thus distressed, thus situated and unrelieved by government, many among us have been obliged to punish some of these Banditti and their accomplices in a proper manner — necessity (that first principle) compelling them to do what was expected that the executive branch of the legislature would *long ago* have done.

We are Free-Men — British Subjects — Not Born Slaves. We contribute our proportion in all public taxations, and discharge our duty to the public equally with our fellow provincials. Yet we do not participate with them in the rights and benefits which they enjoy, though equally entitled to them.

Property is of no value, except it be secure. How ours is secured appears from the forementioned circumstances, and from our now being obliged to defend our families by our own strength: as legal methods are beyond our reach — or not as yet extended to us.

We may be deemed too bold in saying "That the present constitution of this province is very defective, and become a burden rather than being beneficial to the back-inhabitants." For instance, to have but one place of judicature in this large and growing colony, and that seated not central but in a nook by the seaside. The back-inhabitants to travel two, three hundred miles to carry down criminals, prosecute offenders, appear as witnesses (though secluded to serve as jurors), attend the courts and suits of law — the Governor and Court of Ordinary — all land matters, and on every public occasion are great grievances, and call loudly for redress. For 'tis not only loss of time which the poor settlers sustain therefrom, but the toil of traveling and heavy expenses therefrom arising. Poor suitors are often driven to great distress, even to the spending their last shilling or to sell their only horse for to defray their traveling and town costs; after which they are obliged to trudge home on foot and beg for subsistence by the way. And after being subpoenaed, and then attending court as witnesses or as constables, they oft are never called for on trials but are put off to next court, and then the same services must be repeated. These are circumstances experienced by no individuals under British government save those in South Carolina.

It is partly owing to these burdens on our should-

ers that the gangs of robbers who infest us have so long reigned without repression. For if a party hath twenty cattle or the best of his stallions stolen from him, the time and charge consequent on a prosecution of the offenders is equal to or greater than his loss — as, to prosecute would make him doubly a sufferer. And poor persons have not money to answer the cravings of rapacious lawyers. As proceedings at law are now managed, it may cost a private person fifty pounds to bring a villain to justice, and in civil cases the recovery of twenty pounds will frequently be attended with seventy pounds costs — if not treble that sum . . .

If we are thus insecure, if our lives and properties are thus at stake, if we cannot be protected, if these villains are suffered to range the country uncontrolled and no redress to be obtained for our losses, all of us and our families must quit the province and retire where there are laws, religion and government . . .

By poor persons being obliged to travel to Charlestown to obtain patents for small tracts of land, or to renew their warrants, His Majesty's kindness to his subjects is defeated — as it causes land to come as dear, or prove as expensive in running out, as if for to be purchased. The same fees being paid on a grant of ten, as on one of ten thousand acres. The like grievance exists in respect to the proving of wills, or taking out letters of administration the fees on which are treble to what is charged at home, even though clogged with stamps. When effects of a deceased party doth not exceed forty or fifty pounds, half this sum must be expended in court fees — no distinction being made, it being alike the same, if the effects are fifty or fifty thousand pounds. These are great hardships on the poor — especially as the fees now claimed at the public offices are double to what were formerly demanded, which merits the serious attention of the legislature.

As the laws are now modeled, any malicious, malevolent party may arrest any stranger, any innocent person, for any sum whatever, without showing cause of action, or making oath of his debt, or giving security for joining issue; which often prevents persons from getting bail, for though the debt or balance may not be sixpence, yet the sum alleged may be six thousand pounds. This intimidates persons from becoming securities, and subjects many to wrongful and injurious imprisonment; whereby their credit and families are entirely ruined — health impaired, lives sacrificed — by lying in a close and stinking jail crowded with thieves and vagabonds! No distinction made of parties, not hardly even of the sexes — who can boast of British liberty, that is not safe one hour from so dreadful an oppression! A stranger, or vagrant in this province who can pay a lawyer ten pounds, may at his pleasure or for his frolic send to prison (at 200 miles distance) the best person here among us, without his knowing on what account or for what reason, and this in as arbitrary a manner as in France, by a *lettre de Cachet*, or in Spain, by warrant from the Inquisition. Most sore are these evils! Especially too when a poor wretch who has inadvertantly broke the peace (for which in Britain he would be ordered a few lashes or a small fine and be dismissed) must lie five or six months in this loathsome jail amidst thieves and robbers, in the heat of summer, and then afterward be discharged by proclamation. Punishments ought to bear some proportion to trespass — nor should small and great offences be treated with equal severity. To be confined six months in Charlestown jail at two- or three-hundred miles distance from friends or family, and to live in this hot clime on bread and water is a far heavier punishment than for to be in the French King's Gallies, or a slave in Barbary. And for persons to lie there session after session for small sums, or petty offences, is contrary to all humanity. And more so (as we observed) when persons of every class and each sex are promiscuously confined together in a space where they have not room to lie, and no distinction made between offenders — but thieves and murderers, debtors to the King, offenders in penal laws, vagrants and idle persons are closely huddled in one mixed crowd . . .

By our birth-right, as Britons, we ought for to be tried by a jury of our peers. This is the glorious liberty of free born subjects — the darling privilege that distinguishes Britain from all other nations. But we poor distressed settlers enjoy only the shadow, not the substance of this happiness. For can we truly be said to be tried by our peers when few or no persons on this north side of Santee River (containing half the province) are on the jury list? The juries of every court are generally composed of the inhabitants of Charlestown or its environs, persons who never perhaps traveled beyond Charlestown Neck, who know not even the geog-

raphy, much less the persons and concerns of the back country. These determine boundaries of our lands, without a view, and decide on matters of which they have no proper conception. We think these proceedings as absurd as if affairs of shipping and trade were to be settled by twelve residents in our woods, who never saw a town, the sea, or a ship in their lives . . .

Nor can we be said to possess our legal rights as freeholders when we are so unequally represented in Assembly — the south side of Santee River electing forty-four members, and the north side, with these upper parts of the province (containing two thirds of the white inhabitants), returning but six. It is to this great disproportion of representatives on our part, that our interests have been so long neglected, and the back country disregarded. But it is the number of free men, not black slaves, that constitute the strength and riches of a state.

The not laying out the back country into parishes is another most sensible grievance. This evil we apprehend to arise from the selfish views of those whose fortune and estates are in or near Charlestown — which makes them endeavor that all matters and things shall center there, however detrimental to the body politic. Hence it arises that assemblies are kept sitting for six months, when the business brought before them might be dispatched in six weeks, to oblige us (against inclination) to choose such persons for representatives who live in or contiguous to Charlestown; and to render a seat in the Assembly too heavy a burden for any country planter of small estate for to bear. From this our non-representation in the House, we conceive it is: that sixty thousand pounds public money (of which we must pay the greater part, as being levied on the consumer) hath lately been voted for to build an exchange for the merchants, and a ball-room for the ladies of Charlestown, while near sixty thousand of us back settlers have not a minister or a place of worship to repair to! As if we were not worth even the thought of, or deemed as savages, and not Christians!

To leave our native countries, friends, and relations — the service of God — the enjoyment of our civil and religious rights for to breathe here (as we hoped) a purer air of freedom, and possess the utmost enjoyment of liberty and independency — and instead hereof to be set adrift in the wild woods among

indians, and out casts — to live in a state of heathenism — without law, or government or even the appearance of religion — exposed to the insults of lawless and
impudent persons — to the depredations of thieves and
robbers — and to be treated by our fellow provincials
who hold the reins of things, as persons hardly worthy
the public attention, not so much as their Negroes.
These sufferings have broken the hearts of hundreds of
our new settlers, made others quit the province, some
return to Europe (and therefrom prevent others coming this way) and deterred numbers of persons of fortune and character (both at home and in America)
from taking up of lands here, and settling this our back
country, as otherwise they would have done . . .

Oppression will make wise men mad. And many
sober persons among us are become almost desperate
in seeing the non-attention given to these and other
matters of serious concern, and which so nearly affects
the foundation of things. They seem weary of living
(as they have done for years past) without exercise of
their civil and religious rights which they ought to
share in common with the lower settlements, and being
deemed and treated as if not members of the same
body politic. For can we vote for members of assembly, or choose vestrymen, or elect parish officers when
we have no churches to repair to, or they are situated
one, two hundred miles from us? Can our poor be taken charge of when there hath been neither minister,
church wardens, or vestry in St. Marks or St. Matthews
parish for these three years past? Nor either a church
built or parish laid out in any of the upper parts of the
province? Does not hereby a great and heavy incum-
brance fall on the generous and humane? On all who
have feelings for the sufferings of others? For the
poor, the sick, the aged and infirm must be relieved
and supported in some manner and not left to perish.
What care is, or can be, taken of poor orphans and
their effects (no proper laws or provisions being yet
made on this head)? Are they not liable to become the
prey of every invader? Nor is here any security to the
merchant or trader who may credit out their goods, as
knaves and villains may remove with their substance
unmolested into the neighboring provinces and there
bid defiance to their creditors.

Herefrom, no credit can be given among us, for
no writ can be obtained without going to Charlestown,

no attachment can be sworn out, but in Charlestown —
and while these are preparing your debtor has taken
flight and is quite out of reach. And no marriage license can be obtained but in Charlestown, and there
every person must repair to get married, that would
marry judicially and according to law, for we have not
churches wherein to publish Banns, or ministers to
marry persons. Wherefrom, the generality marry each
other, which causes the vilest abominations, and that
whoredom and adultery overspreads our land. Thus
we live and have lived for years past as if without God
in the world, destitute of the means of knowledge,
without law or gospel, esteem, or credit. For we know
not even the laws of this country we inhabit, for where
are they to be found but in the Secretary's office in
Charlestown? The printing a code of the laws hath
been long petitioned for, often recommended by the
Crown, and delineated in the presentments of Grand
Juries, as a matter long wanting and of the utmost consequence. But like all other their presentments, it lies
totally unregarded.

It is notorious that through the want of churches
and ministers, new sects have arisen, now greatly prevail, especially those called New Lights. Prophaneness
and infidelity abound, ignorance, vice, and idleness
prevail. And to the great indifference shown by all
ranks to promote the interests of religion and virtue, it
is in great measure owing that such few checks have
been given to the villains and outlaws who have de-
voured us. For the common people hardly know the
first principles of religion, and so corrupt are their
morals that a reformation of manners among them in
our time is more to be wished for than expected.

Through want of churches and ministers many
persons go into the north province, there to be married
by Magistrates; which hath encouraged many of our
Magistrates (so venal are they) for to take on them also
to solemnize marriages, and this without any previous
publication of Banns or any set form, but each after
his own fancy, which occasions much confusion as
they ask no questions but couple persons of all ages
and every complexion to the ruin and grief of many
families. Their example have been followed by the
low Lay Teachers of every petty sect, and also copied
by itinerant and straggling preachers of various denominations who traverse the back country (sent this way

from Pennsylvania and New England to poison the minds of the people). From these irregular practices the sacred bond of marriage is so greatly slighted as to be productive of many great and innumerable evils. For many loose wretches are fond of such marriages on supposition that they are only temporary, or *Durante Placit*, dissoluble whenever their interests or passions incite them to separate. Thus they live *Ad Libitum*: quitting each other at pleasure, intermarrying year after year with others, changing from hand to hand as they remove from place to place, and swapping away their wives and children as they would horses or cattle. Great scandal arises herefrom to the back country, and loss to the community, for the issue of such are too often exposed deserted and disowned. Beggars are hereby multiplied. Concubinage established (as it were) by law. The most sacred obligations are hereby trampled on, and bastardy, adultery, and other heinous vices become so common, so openly practiced and avowed as to lose the stigma annexed to their commission. These are some of the main roots from whence the reigning gangs of horse thieves have sprung up from.

Through the non-establishment of public schools a great multitude of children are now grown up in the greatest ignorance of every thing, save vice — in which they are adepts. Consequently they lead idle and immoral lives, for they have no sort of education, naturally follow hunting, shooting, racing, drinking, gaming, and every species of wickedness. Their lives are only one continual scene of depravity of manners and reproach to the country, being more abandoned to sensuality and more rude in manners than the poor savages around us. They will learn no trade or mechanic arts whereby to obtain an honest livelihood, or practice any means of industry; or if they know, they will not practice them, but range the country with their horse and gun, without home or habitation: all persons, all places, all women being alike to them. These are other deep roots from which the hordes of mulattos and villains we are pestered with have shot up. Whereas, had we churches and ministers, schools and catechists, children would be early taught the principles of religion and goodness, and their heads and hands be employed in exercises of the manual and useful arts. Tradesmen would increase, manufac-

tures be followed up, agriculture be improved, the country wear a new face, and peace and plenty smile around us.

But in our present unsettled situation, when the bands of society and government hang loose and ungirt about us, when no regular police is established but every one left to do as seemeth him meet, there is not the least encouragement for any individual to be industrious, emulous in well doing, or enterprising in any attempt that is laudable or public spirited. Cunning, rapine, fraud and violence are now the studies and pursuits of the vulgar. If we save a little money for to bring down to town wherewith to purchase slaves — should it be known — our houses are beset and robbers plunder us, even of our clothes. If we buy liquor for to retail, or for hospitality, they will break into our dwellings and consume it. If we purchase bedding, linen, or decent furniture they have early notice, and we are certain for to be stripped of it. Should we raise fat cattle or prime horses for the market, they are constantly carried off though well guarded (as a small force is insufficient for their security). Or if we collect gangs of hogs for to kill and to barrel up for sale, or plant orchards or gardens, the rogues and other idle, worthless, vagrant people with whom we are overrun are continually destroying of them, and subsisting on the stocks and labors of the industrious planter.

If we are in any wise injured in our persons, fame, or fortune, what remedy have we? What redress can be obtained without traveling two hundred miles to Charlestown? Where through the chicanery of lawyers, slowness of law proceedings, and expenses thence arising we are greater sufferers than before, and only thereby add evil to evil. Nay, we have had, and daily do see, those very horses and creatures which have been stolen from us (and for which we have endeavored to bring villains to justice). We have seen these our creatures sold before our faces for to raise money to fee lawyers to plead against us and to save rogues from the halter. And what defense are the laws (as they are now dispensed) to us, against such as are below the law? . . .

As the back country is now daily increasing by imports of people from Ireland and elsewhere (most of whom are very poor), the number of the idle and worthless must also increase if our settlements long remain in their present neglected state. Many of these new settlers greatly repent their coming out here to languish away life in a country that falls so very short of their expectations. And the sober part of them would more willingly return than remain here. They have indeed land given them, and may with industry raise a bare subsistence. But they are discouraged from any bold pursuits, or exerting their laudable endeavors to make improvements through the uncertainty that attends us all, ie. whether in the end they may reap the fruits of their labor, for such number of idle and vagrant persons from the northern colonies traverse and infest this province that if a spot of ground be planted (especially with fruit trees for cider, etc.) the proprietor cannot be certain of gathering the produce, but may see it carried off before his face without control. So great is the weakness of government in these parts that our magistrates are weary of committing persons to Charlestown for petty offences, and they have no authority to inflict punishments . . .

Property being thus insecure, no improvements are attempted. No new plans can take place, nothing out of the common road can be executed, till legislation is extended to us. A damp is now put on all spirited endeavors to make matters run in their proper channel. And (shameful to say) our lands (some of the finest in America) lie useless and uncleared, being rendered of small value from the many licentious persons intermixed among us, whom we cannot drive off without force or violence.

But these our lands would be of infinite value, and (in time) the most desirable in the province, were proper regulations to take place, and good manners and order be introduced among us. Our soil is not only fruitful, but capable of producing any grain whatever. Our vales and woods are delightful. Our hills healthful and pleasant. This single consideration merits the public attention: for, was the country to be once cleared of lawless and idle people (or were they only for to be put under proper restraint), were courts of justice once established, the roads repaired and improved, bridges built in proper places and traveling rendered safe and commodious, we should no longer be pestered with insolvent and licentious persons from the neighboring governments. Nor would this province

be the sink (as now it is) of the refuse of other colonies. Such abandoned wretches would no longer seek shelter or find protection here, nor set bad examples to our rising progeny: we should chase them away as beasts of prey. And was the country once cleared of such vermin, it would induce genteel persons to make the tour of their native country, and not embark annually for Rhode Island or New York for the benefit of cool air. They may breathe equal as salubrious on our hills, and the specie which is now carried out of the province by our traveling gentry (never to return!) would circulate among the poor back inhabitants and quickly find its way down to Charlestown . . .

By our urging of these particulars, and thus bringing them home to the attention of the legislature, we do not presume to reflect on or to censure the conduct, much less to prescribe or dictate, to those in authority. But we humbly submit ourselves and our cause to the wisdom of our superiors, professing ourselves dutiful and loyal subjects to His Majesty King George, true lovers of our country, zealous for its true interests, the rights and liberties of the subject, and the stability of our present happy constitution in church and state . . .

SUGGESTIONS FOR FURTHER READING

Carl Bridenbaugh, *Myths and Realities*, Atheneum, New York, 1963.

Richard M. Brown, *The South Carolina Regulators*, Harvard University Press, Cambridge, 1963.

Philip D. Curtin, *The Atlantic Slave Trade*, University of Wisconsin Press, Madison, 1969.

Carl N. Degler, *Neither Black nor White*, Macmillan, New York, 1971.

Edwin S. Gaustad, "Society and the Great Awakening in New England," *William and Mary Quarterly*, 11 (1954).

L. C. Gray, "Economic Efficiency and Competitive Advantages of Slavery Under the Plantation System," *Agricultural History*, 4 (1930).

Jack P. Greene, *The Quest for Power*, University of North Carolina Press, Chapel Hill, 1963.

Winthrop Jordan, *White Over Black*, Pelican, New York, 1968.

Stanley Nider Katz, *Newcastle's New York: Anglo-American Politics, 1732–1753*, Belknap Press, Cambridge, 1968.

William Howland Kenney, 3rd, "George Whitefield, 1 Dissenter Priest of the Great Awakening, 1739–41," *William and Mary Quarterly,* **26** (1969).

Leonard W. Labaree, "The Conservative Attitude Toward the Great Awakening," *William and Mary Quarterly,* **1** (1944).

Lawrence H. Leder, *Liberty and Authority: Early American Political Ideology, 1689–1763,* Quadrangle, Chicago, 1968.

Leonard Levy, "Did the Zenger Case Really Matter? Freedom of the Press in Colonial New York," *William and Mary Quarterly,* **17** (1960).

Sidney Mead, *The Lively Experiment,* Harper & Row, New York, 1963.

Perry Miller, *Jonathan Edwards,* William Sloane Associates, New York, 1959.

Gary B. Nash, "The Transformation of Urban Politics 1700–1765," *Journal of American History,* **60** (1973).

Abbot E. Smith, *Colonists in Bondage, 1607–1776,* Peter Smith, New York, 1947.

Lawrence Towner, "The Sewall-Saffin Dialogue on Slavery," *William and Mary Quarterly,* **25** (1968).

Carl Ubbelohde, *The American Colonies and the British Empire,* T. Y. Crowell, New York, 1968.

THE ORIGINS OF POLITICAL LIBERALISM

Chapter 3   1641-1721

The conflicts in England over parliamentary power and religious reform led to the outbreak of civil war in 1642 with the King and his supporters fighting a coalition of Puritans and Parliament men. During the next five decades the actual form of English government changed four times as Englishmen struggled to achieve a balance between the requirements of stability and their demands for a new political structure. The victory of the King's enemies brought an end to the Civil War, and Charles I was executed. England then became a republic ruled through the Long Parliament until Oliver Cromwell assumed control as Lord Protector under a new frame of government. Cromwell's death in 1659 left Englishmen without a satisfactory alternative to the monarchy which had been destroyed ten years earlier so Parliament invited Charles's son, Charles II, to the throne. While the failure to establish a new order in England led to the restoration of the monarch, the fundamental issues which had been troubling Englishmen since the beginning of the century had not been resolved. When James II succeeded his brother in 1685 the smoldering conflicts between England's upper-class leaders and its monarch flared up. James' threat to re-establish the Catholic Church led Parliament to force his abdication. The vacant throne was then offered on well-defined terms to James' son-in-law and daughter, William and Mary, and the English people were given a Bill of Rights detailing their "laws and liberties." English government was stabilized at last in 1688 with a constitutional monarchy.

In a sense, modern English political thought began with the execution of Charles I. Kings had been murdered before. Kings had been assassinated, and kings had fallen in battle, but Charles I was the first European king who was brought to trial, convicted, and executed as a traitor to his people. Even though the monarchy was restored eleven years later, the chain of hereditary rulers whose title to the crown was a birthright, not a summons from Parliament, would never be restored. Englishmen had to find a new basis for their government.

Fundamental political questions were debated freely during these years wherever people gathered to consider the implications of their new situation. Soldiers in Oliver Cromwell's New Model army argued over who should vote in the famous debates at Putney. Thomas Hobbes wrote his masterpiece, *The Leviathan,* in response to the turmoil of the Commonwealth period when Parliament seemed more inclined to dispute within than rule without. The derangement of social order which horrified Hobbes stimulated others to pursue their important truths. Groups like James Harrington's Rota Club met regularly to consider the nature of republican government while the great Puritan movement broke into a dozen factions when it at last got the chance to determine the form of the English Church. A generation later, during the crises of James II's brief reign, John Locke synthesized some of the major conclusions from this forty-year political forum in his *Second Treatise of Government*. Diverse as these discussions were, they sprang from a common impulse: the need to articulate a rational basis for government. No longer could English rulers expect the mindless consent of their people. The mystic bonds of custom and reverence had been weakened by years of strife and were severed completely with Charles I's execution. The English had to work out new explanations for their laws and their government which were compatible with the changes in their society. They had to make explicit and reasonable what had before been unexamined and natural.

Seventeenth century Englishmen raised three fundamental questions: What was the theoretical basis for all government, who should govern, and what rights did the people have regardless of who governed them? This last question of rights had been a source of constant friction before the Civil War. The Stuart kings had angered their subjects by asserting the royal prerogative in areas where Englishmen felt that ancient laws protected their liberties. These confrontations came at a time when Englishmen were trying to reconstruct their church, enlarge the scope of economic activity, and influence England's foreign policies. Wherever they reached, a royal "no" interfered. The new circumstances of modern life aggravated this conflict, for the kings and their subjects were moving into areas of concern which called for a clarification of Englishmen's rights. Instead the disputes led to a power struggle within the kingdom. What was needed was a new definition of the role of government, for only by determining the purpose of government can rights be defined and limits assigned to government power.

Christian political theory had long held that government existed for the good of the people, as defined by the church. However, in England, some men were moving away from the traditional religious view that society was fatally marred by human corruption and hence rulers existed to control men's passions. The kind of government appropriate to the fallen sons and daughters of Adam did not appeal to the people who were responding to the new possibilities for enhancing the quality of their lives. They sought a new rationale for the power that some people are allowed to exercise over others. Many writers showed just how far they had moved from their religious moorings by discussing all questions of civil power in purely secular terms. To determine the basis of government they explored the nature of man and the human needs out of which, they theorized, government developed. They joined the purpose of government and the rights of the governed in a single analysis of man's nature. The important implications of this approach were that they were asserting that government rested on the nature of things rather than Biblical authority. They also implied that men consented to be governed because they recognized their own needs. These political theorists of the 17th century had taken a long step away from the old Christian theory of social control or the Puritan ideal of a corporate body covenanted to do God's will. In place of God's demands upon society as a whole, they put the individual's demands upon his government. Man wrenched from the context of society became the focal point of this new liberal political theory.

With a new rationale, Englishmen could turn to the question of who should govern. The first two Stuart kings had believed that they ruled through their kingly prerogative and the powers attached to the office of kingship. English common law judges and Parliamentary leaders had insisted, in opposition to James and Charles, that England was governed by law and that both the king and his people were subject to the ancient laws of the kingdom. Although this dispute involved conflicting versions of English history, it also showed that important groups within the country were determined to challenge the king's power. The success of the Parliamentary forces in the Civil War guaranteed that Parliament would play a larger part in governing England, but Parliament itself was far from representative of the whole people. One of its houses conferred power upon the eldest sons of noble families, and the other — although called the House of Commons — was filled with wealthy gentry, merchants, and the younger sons of noble families. The initiators of the Civil War wished to transfer the balance of ruling power to Parliament, but few of them thought of including the poor and unrepresented. As Harrington had predicted, political power was conferred upon those with economic power. England at the end of its revolutionary period resolved the questions of who should govern with a balanced sovereignty of king, lords, and the representatives of the most important economic groups to have survived two generations of civil discord.

For Englishmen these issues of the 17th century were settled by the accession of William and Mary, but the importance of the questions raised and the forceful reasoning used in their argumentation gave the political writing of this period an enduring significance. The theories of the Commonwealth men nourished a cen-

tury of English republican thought. Hobbes and Locke laid the basis for modern political theory when they made man's nature — rather than high moral purposes — the determining factor in civil society. The political literature from England's remarkable 17th century became an essential part of English and American education. For Englishmen, however, it represented the justification for the political arrangement of the status quo, whereas Americans, prompted to examine the basis of their own position within the British Empire, extracted the radical elements in these writings. Under new pressures, living with different social realities, 18th century Americans educated in the English political tradition picked up the threads of this earlier discourse and carried many of the liberal political theories to their logical conclusions.

The readings in this chapter are extracts from political philosophies, two of them among the greatest in western literature. Thomas Hobbes (1588-1679) published his masterpiece, *The Leviathan*, in 1659, and John Locke's *Second Treatise of Government* appeared in 1689. Although they were separated by thirty years, they are part of the same search for fundamental political principles which absorbed English thinkers throughout the 17th century. Hobbes and Locke (1632-1704), unlike their Puritan contemporaries, conducted their inquiries as modern men deliberately charting new courses. Both asked the same questions of why men form governments and how the legitimate powers of government can be determined from these original purposes. Despite a parade of Biblical references, neither man relied upon any particularly religious concept. They started with man, not God, and asked what was, not what *ought* to be. They returned to the presumed origins of government for their answers, but not origins in the historical sense of how primitive man actually formed civil units, but rather the theoretical origins discovered when one asks why, given the nature of man as we know him, would he enter organized society. Writing at a time when people accepted the traditional arrangements of power, both Hobbes and Locke sought to shift the ground of political speculation from custom to reason. In other words, they abstracted political values from any given society with its existing arrangements and tied them to philosophical definitions, although their particular definitions turned out to be quite different.

Despite some allusions to Hobbes, Locke was actually writing to answer Richard Filmer, whose *Patriachia* held up the family with its patriarchal authority as the proper model for society. Like his admirers, the supporters of Parliament, Locke rejected the paternalism and authoritarian cast of Filmer's concepts. Men in Locke's state of nature were not arranged in subordinate family roles around a towering father figure. They were equals who came together on terms of parity and created government by consent. Locke was writing to justify and explain these Whig or Parliamentary claims to share the rule of England with the King. His contemporaries understood this, but Locke proved too much. By couching his argument in universal terms and speaking about man as man, his arguments had an irrepressible, radical element in them which could be turned on any ruler group.

In fact this radical strain in Locke was developed early in the 18th century by men who came to recognize that all governments could be abusive. For the great majority of Englishmen — the unpropertied, the inarticulate, and those disenfranchised because they were not members of the Church of England — the sovereignty of Parliament proved almost as absolute as the King's had been a century earlier. For them there was still great meaning in Locke's concepts of government by consent and man's natural, inalienable rights. Where Locke had laid great stress on the origins of government, these radical Whigs, as they were called, were more concerned with the role of the people once government had been established. They examined the problem of power itself and the relationship between the governed and the governing, whether the government be monarchical or republican.

Two writers in particular, John Trenchard (1662-1723) and Thomas Gordon (d. 1750), were popular in America. In their collaborations, they developed themes that were congenial to Americans who found themselves in very much the same relationship to Parliament as that of England's own disenfranchised. The last reading in this chapter is taken from Trenchard and Gordon's *Cato's Letters*, a series of magazine articles which was widely published in the colonies. Several of the offending issued of Zenger's *New-York Journal*, in fact, had been devoted to publishing *Cato's Letters*.

Thomas Hobbes: *The Leviathan* (1651)

Nature has made men so equal in the faculties of body and mind as that though there be found one man sometimes manifestly stronger in body, or of quicker mind than another, yet when all is reckoned together, the

Cambridge University Press, New York, 1904. Chapters 13, 14, 17, and 18.

difference between man and man is not so considerable as that one man can thereupon claim to himself
any benefit to which another may not pretend as well
as he. For as to the strength of body, the weakest has
strength enough to kill the strongest, either by secret
machination or by confederacy with others that are in
the same danger with himself . . .

As to the faculties of the mind (setting aside the
arts grounded upon words, and especially that skill of
proceeding upon general and infallible rules called Science which very few have, and but in few things as being not a native faculty born with us, nor attained (as
Prudence) while we look after somewhat else), I find
yet a greater equality amongst men than that of
strength. For prudence is but experience which equal
time equally bestows on all men in those things they
equally apply themselves unto. That which may perhaps make such equality incredible is but a vain concept of one's own wisdom which almost all men think
they have in a greater degree than the vulgar; that is,
than all men but themselves and a few others whom by
fame, or for concurring with themselves, they approve.
For such is the nature of men that howsoever they may
acknowledge many others to be more witty or more
eloquent or more learned, yet they will hardly believe
there be many so wise as themselves, for they see their
own wit at hand, and other men's at a distance. But
this proves rather that men are in that point equal than
unequal. For there is not ordinarily a greater sign of
the equal distribution of anything than that every man
is contented with his share.

From this equality of ability arises equality of
hope in the attaining of our ends. And, therefore, if
any two men desire the same thing which, nevertheless, they cannot both enjoy, they become enemies,
and in the way to their end (which is principally their
own conservation and sometimes their delectation
only) endeavor to destroy or subdue one another. And
from hence it comes to pass that where an invader has
no more to fear than another man's single power, if
one plant, sow, build, or possess a convenient seat,
others may probably be expected to come prepared
with forces united to dispossess and deprive him, not
only of the fruit of his labor, but also of his life or liberty. And the invader again is in the like danger of
another.

And from this diffidence of one another, there is
no way for any man to secure himself so reasonable as
anticipation; that is, by force or wiles to master the
persons of all men he can so long 'til he sees no other
power great enough to endanger him. And this is no
more than his own conservation requires and is generally allowed. Also because there be some that taking
pleasure in contemplating their own power in the acts
of conquest, which they pursue farther than their security requires, if others that would otherwise be glad to
be at ease within modest bounds should not by invasion increase their power, they would not be able long
time, by standing only on their defence, to subsist.
And by consequence such augmentation of dominion
over men, being necessary to a man's conservation, it
ought to be allowed him.

Again, men have no pleasure (but on the contrary
a great deal of grief) in keeping company where there
is no power able to overawe them all. For every man
looks that his companion should value him at the same
rate he sets upon himself. And upon all signs of contempt, or undervaluing, naturally endeavors as far as he
dares (which amongst them that have no common
power to keep them in quiet is far enough to make
them destroy each other) to extort a greater value
from his contemners by damage, and from others by
the example.

So that in the nature of man we find three principal causes of quarrel: first, competition; secondly,
diffidence; thirdly, glory.

The first makes men invade for gain; the second,
for safety; and the third, for reputation. The first use
violence to make themselves masters of other men's
persons, wives, children and cattle; the second, to defend them; the third, for trifles as a word, a smile, a
different opinion, and any other sign of undervalue,
either direct in their persons or by reflection in their
kindred, their friends, their nation, their profession or
their name.

Hereby it is manifest that during the time men
live without a common power to keep them all in awe,
they are in that condition which is called war, and such
a war as is of every man against every man . . . In such
condition, there is no place for industry, because the
fruit thereof is uncertain, and, consequently, no culture of the earth, no navigation, nor use of the

commodities that may be imported by sea, no commodious building, no instruments of moving and removing such things as require much force, no knowledge of the face of the earth, no account of time, no arts, no letters, no society; and which is worst of all, continual fear and danger of violent death. And the life of man, solitary, poor, nasty, brutish, and short.

It may seem strange to some man that has not well weighed these things that nature should thus dissociate and render men apt to invade and destroy one another, and he may, therefore, not trusting to this inference made from the passions, desire perhaps to have the same confirmed by experience. Let him therefore consider with himself, when taking a journey, he arms himself and seeks to go well accompanied. When going to sleep, he locks his doors; when even in his house, he locks his chests, and this when he knows there be laws and public officers armed to revenge all injuries [which] shall be done him. What opinion he has of his fellow subjects when he rides armed; of his fellow citisens, when he locks his doors; and of his children and servants, when he locks his chests. Does he not there as much accuse mankind by his actions, as I do by my words? But neither of us accuse man's nature in it. The desires and other passions of man are in themselves no sin. No more are the actions that proceed from those passions 'til they know a law that forbids them which 'til laws be made they cannot know, nor can any law be made 'til they have agreed upon the person that shall make it.

It may peradventure be thought there was never such a time, nor condition of war as this, and I believe it was never generally so, over all the world, but there are many places where they live so now. For the savage people in many places of America, except the government of small families, the concord whereof depends on natural lust, have no government at all and live at this day in that brutish manner as I said before. Howsoever, it may be perceived what manner of life there would be, where there were no common power to fear, by the manner of life which men that have formerly lived under a peaceful government used to degenerate into in a civil war.

But though there had never been any time wherein particular men were in a condition of war one against another, yet in all times, kings and persons of sovereign authority, because of their independency, are in continual jealousies and in the state and posture of Gladiators having their weapons pointing and their eyes fixed on one another, that is, their forts, garrisons, and guns upon the frontiers of their kingdoms and continual spies upon their neighbors, which is a posture of war. But because they uphold thereby the industry of their subjects, there does not follow from it that misery which accompanies the liberty of particular men.

To this war of everyman against everyman this also is consequent: that nothing can be unjust. The notions of right and wrong, justice and injustice have there no place. Where there is no common power, there is no law. Where no law, no injustice. Force and fraud are in war the two cardinal virtues. Justice and injustice are none of the faculties, neither of the body nor mind. If they were, they might be in a man that were alone in the world as well as his senses and passions. They are qualities that relate to men in society, not in solitude. It is consequent also to the same condition that there be no propriety, no dominion, no *mine* and *thine* distinct, but only that to be every man's that he can get, and for so long as he can keep it. And thus much for the ill condition which man by mere nature is actually placed in, though with a possibility to come out of it, consisting partly in the passions, partly in his reason.

The passions that incline men to peace are fear of death, desire of such things as are necessary to commodious living, and a hope by their industry to obtain them. And reason suggests convenient articles of peace upon which men may be drawn to agreement. These articles are they which otherwise are called the laws of nature, whereof I shall speak more particularly, in the two following chapters.

Of the first and second natural laws and of contracts.

The right of nature which writers commonly call *jus naturale* is the liberty each man has to use his own power as he will himself for the preservation of his own nature, that is to say, of his own life, and, consequently, of doing anything which in his own judgment and reason he shall conceive to be the aptest means thereunto.

By liberty is understood, according to the proper signification of the word, the absence of external impediments, which impediments may often take away part of a man's power to do what he would, but cannot hinder him from using the power left him, according as his judgment and reason shall dictate to him.

A law of nature, *lex naturalis*, is a precept or general rule, found out by reason, by which a man is forbidden to do that which is destructive of his life or takes away the means of preserving the same, and to omit that by which he thinks it may be best preserved.

For though they that speak of this subject used to confound *jus* and *lex*, right and law, yet they ought to be distinguished, because right consists in liberty to do or to forbear, whereas law determines and binds to one of them, so that law and right differ as much as obligation and liberty which in one and the same matter are inconsistent.

And because the condition of man (as has been declared in the precedent chapter) is a condition of war of everyone against everyone, in which case everyone is governed by his own reason and there is nothing he can make use of that may not be a help unto him in preserving his life against his enemies, it follows that in such a condition, everyman has a right to everything, even to one another's body. And, therefore, as long as this natural right of everyman to everything endures, there can be no security to any man (how strong or wise soever he be) of living out the time which nature ordinarily allows men to live. And, consequently, it is a precept or general rule of reason *that every man ought to endeavor peace as far as he has hope of obtaining it and when he cannot obtain it that he may seek and use all helps and advantages of war.* The first branch of which rule contains the first and fundamental law of nature which is to seek peace and follow it; The second, the sum of the right of nature which is by all means we can to defend ourselves.

From this fundamental law of nature by which men are commanded to endeavor peace is derived this second law: *that a man be willing when others are so too, as far forth, as for peace and defense of himself he shall think it necessary, to lay down this right to all things and be contented with so much liberty against other men as he would allow other men against himself.* For as long as everyman holds this right of doing anything he likes, so long are all men in the condition of war. But if other men will not lay down their right as well as he, then there is no reason for anyone to divest himself of his, for that were to expose himself to prey (which no man is bound to), rather than to dispose himself to peace. This is that law of the Gospel: whatsoever you require that others should do to you, that do you to them . . .

To lay down a man's right to anything is to divest himself of the liberty of hindering another of the benefit of his own right to the same, for he that renounces or passes away his right gives not to any other man a right which he had not before. Because there is nothing to which everyman had not right by nature, but only stands out of his way that he may enjoy his own original right without hindrance from him, not without hindrance from another. So that the effect which redounds to one man by another man's defect of right is but so much diminution of impediments to the use of his own right original.

Right is laid aside either by simply renouncing it or by transferring it to another. By simply renouncing when he cares not to whom the benefit thereof redoundeth; by transferring when he intends the benefit thereof to some certain person or persons. And when a man has in either manner abandoned or granted away his right, then is he said to be obliged or bound not to hinder those to whom such right is granted or abandoned from the benefit of it, and, that he ought and it is his duty, not to make void that voluntary act of his own and that such hindrance is injustice and injury as being *sine jure*, the right being before renounced or transferred. So that injury or injustice, in the controversies of the world, is somewhat like to that which in the disputation of scholars is called absurdity. For, as it is there called an absurdity to contradict what one maintained in the beginning, so in the world it is called injustice and injury voluntarily to undo that which from the beginning he had voluntarily done. The way by which a man either simply renounces or transfers his right is a declaration or signification by some voluntary and sufficient sign or signs that he does so renounce or transfer, or has so renounced or transferred, the same to him that accepts it. And these signs are either words only or actions only, or (as it happens most often) both words and actions. And the same are the bonds by which men are bound and obliged: bonds that have their strength not from their own nature (for nothing is more easily broken than a man's word), but from fear of some evil consequence upon the rupture.

Whensoever a man transfers his right or renounces it, it is either in consideration of some right reciprocally transferred to himself or for some other good he hopes for thereby. For it is a voluntary act and of the voluntary acts of everyman the object is some good to himself. And therefore there be some rights which no man can be understood by any words or other signs to have abandoned or transferred. As first a man cannot lay down the right of resisting them that assault him by force to take away his life, because he cannot be understood to aim thereby at any good to himself. The same may be said of wounds and chains and imprisonment, both because there is no benefit consequent to such patience, as there is to the patience of suffering another to be wounded or imprisoned, as also because a man cannot tell when he sees men proceed against him by violence whether they intend his death or not. And lastly, the motive and end for which this renouncing and transferring of rights is introduced is nothing else but the security of a man's person in his life and in the means of so preserving life as not to be weary of it. Therefore, if a man by words or other signs, seems to despoil himself of the end for which those signs were intended, he is not to be understood as if he meant it, or that it was his will, but that he was ignorant of how such words and actions were to be intended.

The mutual transferring of right is that which men call contract . . . One of the contractors may deliver the thing contracted for on his part and leave the other to perform his part at some determinate time after and in the meantime be trusted, and then the contract on his part is called pact or convenant. Or both parts may contract now to perform hereafter, in which cases he that is to perform in time to come, being trusted, his performance is called keeping of promise or faith, and the failing of performance (if it be voluntary), violation of faith . . .

If a covenant be made wherein neither of the parties perform presently, but trust one another in the condition of mere nature (which is a condition of war of everyman against everyman) upon any reasonable

suspicion, it is void. But if there be a common power set over them both with right and force sufficient to compel performance, it is not void, for he that performs first has not assurance the other will perform after, because the bonds of words are too weak to bridle men's ambition, avarice, anger, and other passions without the fear of some coercive power, which in the condition of mere nature, where all men are equal and judge of the justness of their own fears, cannot possibly be supposed. And, therefore, he which performs first does but betray himself to his enemy, contrary to the right (he can never abandon) of defending his life and means of living.

But in a civil estate where there is a power set up to constrain those that would otherwise violate their faith that fear is no more reasonable, and for that cause he which by the convenant is to perform first is obliged so to do . . .

The matter or subject of a covenant is always something that falls under deliberation, for the covenant is an act of the will, that is to say, an act and the last act of deliberation and is, therefore, always understood to be something to come and which is judged possible for him that covenants to perform. And, therefore, to promise that which is known to be impossible is no covenant, but if that proves impossible afterwards which before was thought possible, the covenant is valid and binds (though not to the thing itself, yet to the value) or if that also be impossible to the unfeigned endeavor of performing as much as is possible, for to more no man can be obliged.

Men are freed of their covenants two ways: by performing or by being forgiven. For performance is the natural end of obligation, and forgiveness, the restitution of liberty as being a retransferring of that right in which the obligation consisted.

Covenants entered into by fear in the condition of mere nature are obligatory. For example if I covenant to pay a ransom or service for my life to an enemy, I am bound by it. For it is a contract wherein one receives the benefit of life, the other to receive money or service for it, and, consequently, where no other law (as in the condition of mere nature) forbids the performance, the covenant is valid. Therefore, prisoners of war, if trusted with the payment of their ransom, are obliged to pay it, and if a weaker prince makes a disadvantageous peace with a stronger for fear, he is bound to keep it, unless (as has been said before) there arises some new and just cause of fear to renew the war. And, even in commonwealths, if I be forced to redeem myself from a thief by promising him money, I am bound to pay it 'til the civil law discharges me. For whatsoever I may lawfully do without obligation, the same I may lawfully covenant to do through fear, and what I lawfully covenant, I cannot lawfully break.

A former covenant makes void a later, for a man that has passed away his right to one man today has it not to pass tomorrow to another, and, therefore, the later promise passes not right, but is null. A covenant not to defend myself from force by force is always void, for (as I have showed before) no man can transfer or lay down his right to save himself from death, wounds, and imprisonment, the avoiding whereof is the only end of laying down any right. Therefore, the promise of not resisting force in no covenant transfers any right, nor is obliging. For, though a man may covenant thus, "unless I do so, or so, kill me," he cannot covenant thus, "unless I do so, or so, I will not resist you when you come to kill me." For man by nature chooses the lesser evil which is danger of death in resisting rather than the greater which is certain and present death in not resisting. And this is granted to be true by all men in that they lead criminals to execution and prison with armed men, notwithstanding that such criminals have consented to the law by which they are condemned . . .

From that law of nature by which we are obliged to transfer to another such rights, as being retained hinder the peace of mankind, there follows a third which is this: that men perform their covenants made, without which covenants are in vain and but empty words, and the right of all men to all things remaining, we are still in the condition of war.

And in this law of nature consists the fountain and original of justice. For where no covenant has preceded, there has no right been transferred and everyman has right to everything, and, consequently, no action can be unjust. But when a covenant is made, then to break it is unjust, and the definition of injustice is no other than the not performance of covenant. And whatsoever is not unjust is just . . .

Of the causes, generation, and definition of a commonwealth.

The final cause, end, or design of men (who naturally love liberty and dominion over others) in the introduction of that restraint upon themselves in which we see them live in commonwealths is the foresight of their own preservation and of a more contented life thereby; that is to say, of getting themselves out from that miserable condition of war which is necessarily consequent (as has been shown) to the natural passions of men when there is no visible power to keep them in awe and tie them by fear of punishment to the performance of their covenants and observation of those laws of nature set down in the fourteenth and fifteenth chapters.

For the laws of nature as justice, equity, modesty, mercy, and in sum doing to others as we would be done to, of themselves, without the terror of some power to cause them to be observed, are contrary to our natural passions that carry us to partiality, pride, revenge, and the like. And covenants without the sword are but words and of no strength to secure a man at all. Therefore, notwithstanding the laws of nature which everyone has then kept when he has the will to keep them, when he can do it safely, if there be no power erected, or not great enough for our security, everyman will and may lawfully rely on his own strength and art for caution against all other men. And in all places where men have lived by small families to rob and spoil one another has been a trade and so far from being reputed against the law of nature that the greater spoils they gained, the greater was their honor, and men observed no other laws therein, but the laws of honor, that is, to abstain from cruelty, leaving to men their lives and instruments of husbandry. And as small families did then, so now do cities and kingdoms which are but greater families, (for their own security) enlarge their dominions upon all pretences of danger and fear of invasion or assistance that may be given to invaders endeavor as much as they can to subdue, or weaken their neighbors by open force and secret arts for want of other caution, justly; and are remembered for it in after ages with honor.

Nor is it the joining together of a small number of men that gives them this security, because in small numbers small additions on the one side or the other make the advantage of strength so great as is sufficient to carry the victory, and, therefore, gives encouragement to an invasion. The multitude sufficient to confide in for our security is not determined by any certain number, but by comparison with the enemy we fear and is then sufficient when the odds of the enemy is not of so visible and conspicuous moment to determine the event of war as to move him to attempt.

And be there never so great a multitude yet if their actions be directed according to their particular judgments and particular appetites, they can expect thereby no defence, nor protection, neither against a common enemy, nor against the injuries of one another. For being distracted in opinions concerning the best use and application of their strength, they do not help, but hinder one another, and reduce their strength by mutual opposition to nothing whereby they are easily, not only subdued by a very few that agree together, but also when there is no common enemy, they make war upon each other for their particular interests. For if we could suppose a great multitude of men to consent in the observation of justice and other laws of nature without a common power to keep them all in awe, we might as well suppose all mankind to do the same, and then there neither would be, nor need to be any civil government, or commonwealth at all, because there would be peace without subjection.

Nor is it enough for the security which men desire should last all the time of their life that they be governed and directed by one judgment for a limited time, as in one battle or one war. For, though they obtain a victory by their unanimous endeavor against a foreign enemy, yet afterwards, when either they have no common enemy, or he that by one part is held for an enemy is by another part held for a friend, they must needs by the difference of their interests dissolve and fall again into a war amongst themselves.

It is true that certain living creatures, as bees and ants, live sociably one with another (which are, therefore, by Aristotle numbered amongst political creatures) and yet have no other direction than their particular judgments and appetites nor speech whereby one of them can signify to another what he thinks expedient for the common benefit and, therefore, some man may perhaps desire to know why mankind cannot do the same. To which I answer:

First, that men are continually in competition for honor and dignity which these creatures are not, and, consequently, amongst men there arises on that ground envy and hatred and finally, war, but amongst these not so.

Secondly, that amongst these creatures the common good differs not from the private and being by nature inclined to their private, they procure thereby the common benefit. But man, whose joy consists in comparing himself with other men, can relish nothing but what is eminent.

Thirdly, that these creatures having not (as man) the use of reason do not see, nor think they see, any fault in the administration of their common business, whereas amongst men there are very many that think themselves wiser and abler to govern the public good, better than the rest, and these strive to reform and innovate, one this way, another that way, and thereby bring it into distraction and civil war.

Fourthly, that these creatures, though they have some use of voice in making known to one another their desires and other affections, yet they want that art of words by which some men can represent to others that which is good in the likeness of evil and evil in the likeness of good and augment or diminish the apparent greatness of good and evil, discontenting men and troubling their peace at their pleasure.

Fifthly, irrational creatures cannot distinguish between injury and damage, and, therefore, as long as they be at ease, they are not offended with their fellows, whereas man is then most troublesome when he is most at ease, for then it is that he loves to show his wisdom and control the actions of them that govern the commonwealth.

Lastly, the agreement of these creatures is natural; that of men is by covenent only which is artificial. And, therefore, it is no wonder if there be somewhat else required (besides covenant) to make their agreement constant and lasting which is a common power to keep them in awe and to direct their actions to the common benefit.

The only way to erect such a common power as may be able to defend them from the invasion of foreigners and the injuries of one another, and thereby to secure them in such sort as that by their own industry and by the fruits of the earth, they may nourish themselves and live contentedly is to confer all their power and strength upon one man, or upon one assembly of men that may reduce all their wills by plurality of voices unto one will which is as much as to say, to appoint one man or assembly of men to bear their person, and everyone to own and acknowledge himself to be author of whatsoever he that so beareth their person shall act or cause to be acted in those things which concern the common peace and safety, and therein to submit their wills, everyone to his will and their judgments to his judgment. This is more than concent or concord; it is a real unity of them all in one and the same person made by covenant of every man with every man in such manner as if every man should say to every man, "I authorize and give up my right of governing myself to this man or to this assembly of men on this condition that thou give up thy right to him and authorize all his actions in like manner." This done, the multitude so united in one person is called a commonwealth, in Latin, *civitas*. This is the generation of that great Leviathan or rather (to speak more reverently) of that mortal god to which we owe under the immortal God our peace and defense. For by this authority given him by every particular man in the Commonwealth, he has the use of so much power and strength conferred on him, that by terror thereof, he is enabled to form the wills of them all to peace at home and mutual aid against their enemies abroad. And in him consists the essence of the commonwealth which (to define it) is one person of whose acts a great multitude by mutual covenants, one with another, have made themselves everyone the author, to the end he may use the strength and means of them all, as he shall think expedience for their peace and common defense.

And he that carries this person is called sovereign and said to have sovereign power, and everyone besides, his subject . . .

Of the rights of sovereigns by institution.

A commonwealth is said to be instituted when a multitude of men do agree and covenant, everyone with everyone, that to whatsoever man or assembly of men shall be given by the major part the right to present the person of them all (that is to say, to be their representative) everyone, as well he that voted for it as he that voted against it, shall authorize all the actions and judgments of that man or assembly of men in the same manner as if they were his own, to the end, to live peaceably amongst themselves and be protected against other men.

From this institution of a commonwealth are derived all the rights and faculties of him, or them, on whom the sovereign power is conferred by the consent of the people assembled.

First, because they covenant, it is to be understood they are not obliged by former covenant to anything repugnant hereunto. And, consequently, they that have already instituted a commonwealth, being thereby bound by covenant to own the actions and judgments of one, cannot lawfully make a new covenant amongst themselves to be obedient to any other in anything whatsoever without his permission. And, therefore, they that are subjects to a monarch cannot without his leave cast off monarchy and return to the confusion of a disunited multitude, nor transfer their person from him that beareth it to another man or other assembly of men, for they are bound, every man to every man to own and be reputed author of all that he that already is their sovereign shall do and judge fit to be done, so that any one man dissenting, all the rest should break their covenant made to that man which is injustice. And they have also every man given the sovereignty to him that bears their person, and, therefore, if they depose him, they take from him that which is his own and so again it is injustice. Besides, if he that attempts to depose his sovereign be killed or punished by him for such attempt, he is author of his own punishment, as being by the institution, author of all his sovereign shall do. And because it is injustice for a man to do anything for which he may be punished by his own authority, he is also upon that title unjust. And whereas some men have pretended for their disobedience to their sovereign a new covenant, made not with men, but with God, this also is unjust, for there is no covenant with God but by mediation of somebody that represents God's person which none doth by God's lieutenant who has the sovereignty under God. But this pretence of covenant with God is so evident a lie, even in the pretenders' own consciences, that it is not only an act of an unjust, but also of a vile and unmanly, disposition.

Secondly, because of the right of bearing the person of them all is given to him they make sovereign by covenant only of one to another and not of him to any of them, there can happen no breach of covenant on the part of the sovereign. And, consequently, none of his subjects, by any pretence of forfeiture, can be freed from his subjection . . . The opinion that any monarch receives his power by covenant, that is to say, on condition, proceeds from want of understanding this easy truth that covenants being but words and breath have no force to oblige, contain, constrain, or protect any man but what it has from the public sword, that is, from the untied hands of that man, or assembly of men, that has the sovereignty and whose actions are avouched by them all and performed by the strength of them all in him united . . .

Thirdly, because the major part has by consenting voices declared a sovereign, he that dissented must now consent with the rest, that is, be contented to avow all the actions he shall do or else justly be destroyed by the rest. For if he voluntarily entered into the congregation of them that were assembled, he sufficiently declared thereby his will (and therefore tacitly covenanted) to stand to what the major part should ordain, and, therefore, if he refuses to stand thereto, or make protestation against any of their decrees, he does contrary to his covenant and, therefore, unjustly. And whether he be of the congregation or not, and whether his consent be asked or not, he must either submit to their decrees or be left in the condition of war he was in before, wherein he might without injustice be destroyed by any man whatsoever.

Fourthly, because every subject is by this institution author of all the actions and judgments of the sovereign instituted, it follows that whatsoever he does, it can be no injury to any of his subjects, nor ought he to be by any of them accused of injustice. For he that does anything by authority from another, does therein no injury to him by whose authority he acts. But by this institution of a commonwealth every particular man is author of all the sovereign does, and, consequently, he that complains of injury from his sovereign, complains of that whereof he himself is author, and, therefore, ought not to accuse any man but himself, no, nor himself of injury, because to do

injury to oneself is impossible. It is true that they that have sovereign power may commit iniquity, but not injustice or injury in the proper signification.

Fifthly, and, consequently, to that which was said last no man that has sovereign power can justly be put to death or otherwise in any manner by his subjects punished. For seeing every subject is author of the actions of his sovereign, he punishes another for the actions committed by himself.

And because the end of this institution is the peace and defense of them all, and whosoever has right to the end has right to the means, it belongs of right to whatsoever man, or assembly, that has the sovereignty, to be judge both of the means of peace and defense and also of the hindrances and disturbances of the same and to do whatsoever he shall think necessary to be done, both beforehand, for the preserving of peace and security by prevention of discord at home, and hostility from abroad, and, when peace and security are lost, for the recovery of the same. And, therefore,

Sixthly, it is annexed to the sovereignty to be judge of what opinions and doctrines are averse and what conducing to peace, and, consequently, on what occasions, how far, and what, men are to be trusted withall, in speaking to multitudes of people and who shall examine the doctrines of all books before they be published. For the actions of men proceed from their opinions, and in the well governing of opinions consists the well governing of men's actions in order to their peace and concord. And though in matter of doctrine, nothing ought to be regarded but the truth, yet this is not repugnant to regulating of the same by peace. For doctrine repugnant to peace can no more be true than peace and concord can be against the law of nature. It is true that in a commonwealth whereby the negligence or unskillfulness of governors and teachers, false doctrines are by time generally received. The contrary truths may be generally offensive, yet the most sudden and rough bustling in of a new truth that can be, does never break the peace, but only sometimes awake the war. For those men that are so remissly governed that they dare take up arms to defend or introduce an opinion are still in war, and their condition not peace, but only a cessation of arms for fear of one another, and they live, as it were, in the precincts of battle continually. It belongs therefore to him that has the sovereign power to be judge or constitute all judges of opinions and doctrines as a thing necessary to peace, thereby to prevent discord and civil war.

Seventhly is annexed to the sovereignty the whole power of prescribing the rules whereby every man may know what goods he may enjoy and what actions he may do without being molested by any of his fellow subjects. And this is it men call propriety. For before constitution of sovereign power (as has already been shown) all men had right to all things which necessarily caused war. Therefore, this propriety being necessary to peace, and depending on sovereign power, is the act of that power in order to the public peace. These rules of propriety (or me and you) and of good, evil, lawful and unlawful in the actions of subjects are the civil laws; that is to say, the laws of each commonwealth in particular . . .

Eighthly is annexed to the sovereignty the right of judicature, that is to say, of hearing and deciding all controversies which may arise concerning law, either civil or natural, or concerning fact. For without the decision of controversies, there is no protection of one subject against the injuries of another; the laws concerning mine and yours are in vain, and to every man remains, from the natural and necessary appetite of his own conservation, the right of protecting himself by his private strength which is the condition of war and contrary to the end for which every commonwealth is instituted.

Ninthly is annexed to the sovereignty, the right of making war and peace with other nations and commonwealths, that is to say, of judging when it is for the public good and how great forces are to be assembled, armed, and paid for that end, and to levy money upon the subjects to defray the expences thereof. For the power by which the people are to be defended consists in their armies and the strength of an army in the union of their strength under one command which command the sovereign instituted, therefore has, because the command of the militia, without other institution, makes him that has it sovereign. And, therefore, whosoever is made general of an army, he that has the sovereign power is always generallissimo.

Tenthly is annexed to the sovereignty the choosing of all councillors, ministers, magistrates, and officers, both in peace and war. For seeing the sovereign

is charged with the end which is the common peace and defense, he is understood to have power to use such means as he shall think most fit for his discharge.

Eleventhly to the sovereign is committed the power of rewarding with riches or honor, and of punishing with corporal or pecuniary punishment or with ignominy every subject according to the law he has formerly made, or if there be no law made, according as he shall judge most to conduce to the encouraging of men to serve the commonwealth or deterring of them from doing diservice to the same.

Lastly, considering what values men are naturally apt to set upon themselves, what respect they look for from others and how little they value other men from whence continually arise amongst them emulation, quarrels, factions, and at last war, to the destroying of one another, and diminution of their strength against a common enemy, it is necessary that there be laws of honor and a public rate of worth of such men as have deserved, or are able to deserve well of the commonwealth, and that there be force in the hands of some or other to put those laws in execution. But it has already been shown that not only the whole militia, or forces of the commonwealth, but also the judicature of all controversies is annexed to the sovereignty. To the sovereign, therefore, it belongs also to give titles of honor and to appoint what order of place and dignity each man shall hold and what signs of respect in public or private meetings they shall give to one another.

These are the rights which make the essence of sovereignty and which are the marks whereby a man may discern in what man or assembly of men, the sovereign power is placed and resides, for these are incommunicable and inseparable. The power to coin money, to dispose of the estate and persons of infant heirs, to have preemption in markets, add all other statute prerogatives may be transferred by the sovereign and yet the power to protect his subjects be retained. But if he transfer the militia, he retains the judicature in vain for want of execution of the laws. Or if he grant away the power of raising money, the militia is in vain. Or if he give away the government of doctrines, men will be frighted into rebellion with fear of spirits. And so if we consider any one of the said rights, we shall presently see that the holding of all the rest will produce no effect in the conservation of peace and justice, the end for which all commonwealths are instituted . . .

This great authority being indivisible and inseparably annexed to the sovereignty, there is little ground for the opinion of them that say of sovereign kings, though they be *singulis majores*, of greater power than every one of their subjects, yet they be *universis minores*, of less power than them all together. For if by "all together" they mean not the collective body as one person, then "all together and "every one" signify the same, and the speech is absurd. But if by "all together" they understand them as one person (which person the sovereign bears), then the power of all together is the same with the sovereign's power, and so again the speech is absurd, which absurdity they see well enough when the sovereignty is in an assembly of the people, but in a monarch they see it not, and yet the power of sovereignty is the same in whomsoever it be placed.

And as the power, so also the honor of the sovereign, ought to be greater than that of any or all the subjects, for in the sovereignty is the fountain of honor. The dignities of Lord, Earl, Duke, and Prince are his creatures. As in the presence of the master, the servants are equal and without any honor at all, so are the subjects in the presence of the sovereign. And though they shine some more, some less, when they are out of his sight, yet in his presence, they shine no more than the stars in presence of the sun.

But a man may here object that the condition of subjects is very miserable, as being obnoxious to the lusts and other irregular passions of him or them that have so unlimited a power in their hands. And commonly they that live under a monarch think it the fault of monarchy, and they that live under the government of democracy or other sovereign assembly attribute all the inconvenience to that form of commonwealth, whereas the power in all forms, if they be perfect enough to protect them, is the same, not considering that the estate of man can never be without some incommodity or other and that the greatest that in any form of government can possibly happen to the people in general is scarce sensible, in respect of the miseries, and horrible calamities that accompany a civil war or that dissolute condition of masterless men without subjection to laws and a coercive power to tie their hands from rapine and revenge, nor considering that the greatest pressure of sovereign governors proceeds not from any delight or profit they can expect in the damage or weakening of their subjects in whose vigor consists their own strength and glory, but in the restiveness of themselves that unwillingly contributing to their own defense make it necessary for their governors to draw from them what they can in time of peace that they may have means on any emergent occasion or sudden need to resist or take advantage of their enemies. For all men are by nature provided of notable multiplying glasses (that is, their passions and self-love) through which every little payment appears a great grievance, but are destitute of those prospective glasses (namely moral and civil science) to see a far off the miseries that hang over them and cannot without such payments be avoided.

To come now to the particulars of the true liberty of the subject, that is to say, what are the things which though commanded by the sovereign he may, nevertheless, without injustice refuse to do. We are to consider what rights we pass away when we make a commonwealth, or (which is all one) what liberty we deny ourselves by owning all the actions (without exception) of the man, or assembly we make our sovereign. For in the act of our submission consists both our obligation and our liberty which must, therefore, be inferred by arguments taken from thence, there being no obligation on any man which arises not from some act of his own, for all men equally are by nature free. And because such arguments must either be drawn from the express words, "I authorize all his actions" or from the intention of him that submits himself to his power (which intention is to be understood by the end for which he so submits), the obligation and liberty of the subject is to be derived either from those words, (or others equivalent) or else from the end of the institution of sovereignty, namely, the peace of the subjects within themselves and their defense against a common enemy . . .

The obligation of subjects to the sovereign is understood to last as long, and no longer, than the power lasts by which he is able to protect them. For the right men have by nature to protect themselves when none else can protect them can by no covenant be relinquished. The sovereignty is the soul of the commonwealth which once departed from the body, the members do no more receive their motion from it. The end of obedience is protection which, wheresoever a man sees it, either in his own or in another's sword, nature applies his obedience to it and his endeavor to maintain it. And though sovereignty in the intention of them that make it be immortal, yet is in its own nature, not only subject to violent death by foreign war, but also through the ignorance and passions of man, it has in it, from the very institution, many seeds of a natural mortality by intestine discord.

John Locke: Second treatise of government (1689)

Of the State of Nature.

4. To understand political power aright, and derive it from its original, we must consider what estate all men are naturally in, and that is, a state of perfect freedom to order their actions, and dispose of their possessions and persons as they think fit, within the bounds of the law of Nature, without asking leave or depending upon the will of any other man.

    A state also of equality, wherein all the power and jurisdiction is reciprocal, no one having more than another, there being nothing more evident than that creatures of the same species and rank, promiscuously born to all the same advantages of Nature, and the use of the same faculties, should also be equal one amongst another, without subordination or subjection, unless the lord and master of them all should, by any manifest declaration of his will, set one above another, and confer on him, by an evident and clear appointment, an undoubted right to dominion and sovereignty . . .

6. But though this be a state of liberty, yet it is not a state of license; though man in that state have an uncontrollable liberty to dispose of his person or possessions, yet he has not liberty to destroy himself, or so much as any creature in his possession, but where some nobler use than its bare preservation calls for it. The state of Nature has a law of Nature to govern it, which obliges every one and reason, which is that law, teaches all mankind who will but consult it, that being all equal and independent, no one ought to harm another in his life, health, liberty or possessions; for men being all the workmanship of one omnipotent and in-

George Routledge and Sons, London, 1884.

finitely wise Maker; all the servants of one sovereign Master, sent into the world by His order and about His business; they are His property, whose workmanship they are made to last during His, not one another's pleasure. And, being furnished with like faculties, sharing all in one community of Nature, there cannot be supposed any such subordination among us that may authorize us to destroy one another, as if we were made for one another's uses, as the inferior ranks of creatures are for ours. Every one as he is bound to preserve himself, and not to quit his station wilfully, so by the like reason, when his own preservation comes not in competition, ought he as much as he can to preserve the rest of mankind, and not unless it be to do justice on an offender, take away, or impair the life, or what tends to the preservation of the life, the liberty, health, limb, or goods of another.

7. And that all men may be restrained from invading other's rights, and from doing hurt to one another, and the law of Nature be observed, which willeth the peace and preservation of all mankind, the execution of the law of Nature is in that state put into every man's hands, whereby every one has a right to punish the transgressors of that law to such a degree as may hinder its violation. For the law of Nature would, as all other laws that concern men in this world, be in vain if there were nobody that in the state of Nature had a power to execute that law, and thereby preserve the innocent and restrain offenders; and if any one in the state of Nature may punish another for any evil he has done, every one may do so. For in that state of perfect equality, where naturally there is no superiority or jurisdiction of one over another, what any may do in prosecution of that law, every one must needs have a right to do.

8. And thus, in the state of Nature, one man comes by a power over another, but yet no absolute or arbitrary power to use a criminal when he has got him in his hands, according to the passionate heats, or boundless extravagancy of his own will, but only to retribute to him so far as calm reason and conscience dictate, what is proportionate to his transgression, which is so much as may serve for reparation and restraint. For these two are the only reasons why one man may lawfully do harm to another, which is that we call punishment. In transgressing the law of

Nature, the offender declares himself to live by another rule than that of reason and common equity, which is that measure God has set to the actions of men for their mutual security, and so he becomes dangerous to mankind; the tie which is to secure them from injury and violence being slighted and broken by him, which being a trespass against the whole species, and the peace and safety of it, provided for by the law of Nature, every man upon this score, by the right he hath to preserve mankind in general, may restrain, or where it is necessary, destroy things noxious to them, and so may bring such evil on any one who hath transgressed that law, as may make him repent the doing of it, and thereby deter him, and, by his example, others from doing the like mischief. And in this case, and upon this ground, every man hath a right to punish the offender, and be executioner of the law of Nature . . .

10.   Besides the crime which consists in violating the laws, and varying from the right rule of reason, whereby a man so far becomes degenerate, and declares himself to quit the principles of human nature and to be a noxious creature, there is commonly injury done, and some person or other, some other man, receives damage by his transgression; in which case, he who hath received any damage has (besides the right of punishment common to him, with other men) a particular right to seek reparation from him that hath done it. And any other person who finds it just may also join with him that is injured, and assist him in recovering from the offender so much as may make satisfaction for the harm he hath suffered.

11.   From these two distinct rights (the one of punishing the crime, for restraint and preventing the like offence, which right of punishing is in everybody, the other of taking reparation, which belongs only to the injured party) comes it to pass that the magistrate, who by being magistrate hath the common right of punishing put into his hands, can often, where the public good demands not the execution of the law, remit the punishment of criminal offences by his own authority, but yet cannot remit the satisfaction due to any private man for the damage he has received. That he who hath suffered the damage has a right to demand in his own name, and he alone can remit. The damnified person has this power of appropriating to

himself the goods or service of the offender by right of self-preservation, as every man has a power to punish the crime to prevent its being committed again, by the right he has of preserving all mankind, and doing all reasonable things he can in order to that end. And thus it is that every man in the state of Nature has a power to kill a murderer, both to deter others from doing the like injury (which no reparation can compensate) by the example of the punishment that attends it from everybody, and also to secure men from the attempts of a criminal who, having renounced reason, the common rule and measure God hath given to mankind, hath, by the unjust violence and slaughter he hath committed upon one, declared war against all mankind, and therefore may be destroyed as a lion or a tiger, one of those wild savage beasts with whom men can have no society nor security. And upon this is grounded that great law of Nature, "Whoso sheddeth man's blood by man shall his blood be shed." And Cain was so fully convinced that every one had a right to destroy such a criminal, that, after the murder of his brother, he cries out, "Every one that findeth me shall slay me," so plain was it writ in the hearts of all mankind.

12.   By the same reason may a man in the state of Nature punish the lesser breaches of that law, it will, perhaps, be demanded, with death? I answer: Each transgression may be punished to that degree, and with so much severity, as will suffice to make it an ill bargain to the offender, give him cause to repent, and terrify others from doing the like. Every offence that can be committed in the state of Nature may, in the state of Nature, be also punished equally, and as far forth, as it may, in a commonwealth. For though it would be beside my present purpose to enter here into the particulars of the law of Nature, or its measures of punishment; yet it is certain there is such a law, and that too as intelligible and plain to a rational creature and a studier of that law as the positive laws of commonwealths, nay, possibly plainer; as much as reason is easier to be understood than the fancies and intricate contrivances of men, following contrary and hidden interests put into words; for truly so are a great part of the municipal laws of countries, which are only so far right as they are founded on the law of Nature, by which they are to be regulated and interpreted.

13. To this strange doctrine — viz., That in the state of Nature every one has the executive power of the law of Nature, I doubt not but it will be objected that it is unreasonable for men to be judges in their own cases, that self-love will make men partial to themselves and their friends; and, on the other side, ill-nature, passion, and revenge will carry them too far in punishing others, and hence nothing but confusion and disorder will follow, and that therefore God hath certainly appointed government to restrain the partiality and violence of men. I easily grant that civil government is the proper remedy for the inconveniences of the state of Nature, which must certainly be great where men may be judges in their own case, since it is easy to be imagined that he who was so unjust as to do his brother an injury will scarce be so just as to condemn himself for it. But I shall desire those who make this objection to remember that absolute monarchs are but men; and if government is to be the remedy of those evils which necessarily follow from men being judges in their own cases, and the state of Nature is therefore not to be endured, I desire to know what kind of government that is, and how much better it is than the state of Nature, where one man commanding a multitude has the liberty to be judge in his own case, and may do to all his subjects whatever he pleases without the least question or control of those who execute his pleasure? and in whatsoever he doth, whether led by reason, mistake, or passion, must be submitted to? which men in the state of Nature are not bound to do one to another. And if he that judges, judges amiss in his own or any other case, he is answerable for it to the rest of mankind.

14. It is often asked as a mighty objection, where are, or ever were, there any men in such a state of Nature? To which it may suffice as an answer at present, that since all princes and rulers of "independent" governments all through the world are in a state of Nature, it is plain the world never was, nor never will be, without numbers of men in that state. I have named all governors of "independent" communities, whether they are, or are not, in league with others; for it is not every compact that puts an end to the state of Nature between men, but only this one of agreeing together mutually to enter into one community, and make one body politic; other promises and compacts men may make one with another, and yet still be in the state of Nature. The promises and bargains for truck, &c., between the two men in Soldania, in or between a Swiss and an Indian, in the woods of America, are binding to them, though they are perfectly in a state of Nature in reference to one another for truth, and keeping of faith belongs to men as men, and not as members of society . . .

Of the State of War.

16. The state of war is a state of enmity and destruction; and therefore declaring by word or action, not a passionate and hasty, but sedate, settled design upon another man's life puts him in a state of war with him against whom he has declared such an intention, and so has exposed his life to the other's power to be taken away by him, or any one that joins with him in his defence, and espouses his quarrel; it being reasonable and just I should have a right to destroy that which threatens me with destruction; for by the fundamental law of Nature, man being to be preserved as much as possible, when all cannot be preserved, the safety of the innocent is to be preferred, and one may destroy a man who makes war upon him, or has discovered an enmity to his being, for the same reason that he may kill a wolf or a lion, because they are not under the ties of the common law of reason, have no other rule but that of force and violence, and so may be treated as a beast of prey, those dangerous and noxious creatures that will be sure to destroy him whenever he falls into their power.

17. And hence it is that he who attempts to get another man into his absolute power does thereby put himself into a state of war with him; it being to be understood as a declaration of a design upon his life. For I have reason to conclude that he who would get me into his power without my consent would use me as he pleased when he had got me there, and destroy me too when he had a fancy to it; for nobody can desire to have me in his absolute power unless it be to compel me by force to that which is against the right of my freedom — i.e., make me a slave. To be free from such force is the only security of my preservation, and reason bids me look on him as an enemy to my preservation who would take away that freedom which is the fence to it; so that he who makes an attempt to enslave

me thereby puts himself into a state of war with me. He that in the state of Nature would take away the freedom that belongs to any one in that state must necessarily be supposed to have a design to take away everything else, that freedom being the foundation of all the rest; as he that in the state of society would take away the freedom belonging to those of that society or commonwealth must be supposed to design to take away from them everything else, and so be looked on as in a state of war.

18. This makes it lawful for a man to kill a thief who has not in the least hurt him, nor declared any design upon his life, any farther than by the use of force, so to get him in his power as to take away his money, or what he pleases, from him; because using force, where he has no right to get me into his power, let his pretence be what it will, I have no reason to suppose that he who would take away my liberty would not, when he had me in his power, take away everything else. And, therefore, it is lawful for me to treat him as one who has put himself into a state of war with me — i.e., kill him if I can; for to that hazard does he justly expose himself whoever introduces a state of war, and is aggressor in it.

19. And here we have the plain difference between the state of Nature and the state of war, which however some men have confounded, are as far distant as a state of peace, goodwill, mutual assistance, and preservation; and a state of enmity, malice, violence, and mutual destruction are one from another. Men living together according to reason without a common superior on earth, with authority to judge between them, is properly the state of Nature. But force, or a declared design of force upon the person of another, where there is no common superior on earth to appeal to for relief, is the state of war; and it is the want of such an appeal gives a man the right of war even against an aggressor, though he be in society and a fellow-subject. Thus, a thief whom I cannot harm, but by appeal to the law, for having stolen all that I am worth, I may kill when he sets on me to rob me but of my horse or coat, because the law, which was made for my preservation, where it cannot interpose to secure my life from present force, which if lost is capable of no reparation, permits me my own defence and the right of war, a liberty to kill the

aggressor, because the aggressor allows not time to appeal to our common judge, nor the decision of the law, for remedy in a case where the mischief may be irreparable. Want of a common judge with authority puts all men in a state of Nature; force without right upon a man's person makes a state of war both where there is, and is not, a common judge . . .

Of Slavery.

22. The natural liberty of man is to be free from any superior power on earth, and not to be under the will or legislative authority of man, but to have only the law of Nature for his rule. The liberty of man in society is to be under no other legislative power but that established by consent in the commonwealth, nor under the dominion of any will, or restraint of any law, but what that legislative shall enact according to the trust put in it. Freedom, then, is not what Sir Robert Filmer tells us (O. A., 55): "A liberty for every one to do what he lists, to live as he pleases, and not to be tied by any laws;" but freedom of men under government is to have a standing rule to live by, common to every one of that society, and made by the legislative power erected in it. A liberty to follow my own will in all things where that rule prescribes not, not to be subject to the inconstant, uncertain, unknown, arbitrary will of another man, as freedom of nature is to be under no other restraint but the law of Nature.

23. This freedom from absolute, arbitrary power is so necessary to, and closely joined with, a man's preservation, that he cannot part with it but by what forfeits his preservation and life together. For a man, not having the power of his own life, cannot by compact or his own consent enslave himself to any one, nor put himself under the absolute, arbitrary power of another to take away his life when he pleases. Nobody can give more power than he has himself, and he that cannot take away his own life cannot give another power over it. Indeed, having by his fault forfeited his own life by some act that deserves death, he to whom he has forfeited it may, when he has him in his power, delay to take it, and make use of him to his own service; and he does him no injury by it. For, whenever he finds the hardship of his slavery outweigh the value of his life, it is in his power, by resisting the will of his

master, to draw on himself the death he desires.

24. This is the perfect condition of slavery, which is nothing else but the state of war continued between a lawful conqueror and a captive, for if once compact enter between them, and make an agreement for a limited power on the one side, and obedience on the other, the state of war and slavery ceases as long as the compact endures; for, as has been said, no man can by agreement pass over to another that which he hath not in himself — a power over his own life.

I confess, we find among the Jews, as well as other nations, that men did sell themselves; but is plain this was only to drudgery, not to slavery; for it is evident the person sold was not under an absolute, arbitrary, despotical power, for the master could not have power to kill him at any time, whom at a certain time he was obliged to let go free out of his service; and the master of such a servant was so far from having an arbitrary power over his life that he could not at pleasure so much as maim him, but the loss of an eye or tooth set him free (Exod. xxi.).

Of Property.

25. Whether we consider natural reason, which tells us that men, being once born, have a right to their preservation, and consequently to meat and drink and such other things as Nature affords for their subsistence, or "revelation," which gives us an account of those grants God made of the world to Adam, and to Noah and his sons, it is very clear that God, as King David says (Psalm cxv. 16), "has given the earth to the children of men," given it to mankind in common. But, this being supposed, it seems to some a very great difficulty how any one should ever come to have a property in anything, I will not content myself to answer, that, if it be difficult to make out "property" upon a supposition that God gave the world to Adam and his posterity in common, it is impossible that any man but one universal monarch should have any "property" upon a supposition that God gave the world to Adam and his heirs in succession, exclusive of all the rest of his posterity; but I shall endeavour to show how men might come to have a property in several parts of that which God gave to mankind in common, and that without any express compact of all the commoners.

26. God, who hath given the world to men in common, hath also given them reason to make use of it to the best advantage of life and convenience. The earth and all that is therein is given to men for the support and comfort of their being. And though all the fruits it naturally produces, and beasts it feeds, belong to mankind in common, as they are produced by the spontaneous hand of Nature, and nobody has originally a private dominion exclusive of the rest of mankind in any of them, as they are thus in their natural state, yet being given for the use of men, there must of necessity be a means to appropriate them some way or other before they can be of any use, or at all beneficial, to any particular men. The fruit or venison which nourishes the wild Indian, who knows no enclosure and is still a tenant in common, must be his, and so his — i.e., a part of him, that another can no longer have any right to it before it can do him any good for the support of his life.

27. Though the earth and all inferior creatures be common to all men, yet every man has a "property" in his own "person." This nobody has any right to but himself. The "labour" of his body and the "work" of his hands, we may say, are properly his. Whatsoever, then, he removes out of the state that Nature hath provided and left it in, he hath mixed his labour with it, and joined to it something that is his own, and thereby makes it his property. It being by him removed from the common state Nature placed it in, it hath by this labour something annexed to it that excludes the common right of other men. For this "labour" being the unquestionable property of the labourer, no man but he can have a right to what that is once joined to, at least where there is enough, and as good left in common for others.

28. He that is nourished by the acorns he picked up under an oak, or the apples he gathered from the trees in the wood, has certainly appropriated them to himself. Nobody can deny but the nourishment is his. I ask, then, when did they begin to be his? when he digested? or when he ate? or when he boiled? or when he brought them home? or when he picked them up? And it is plain, if the first gathering made them not his, nothing else could. That labour put a distinction between them and common. That added something to

them more than Nature, the common mother of all, had done, and so they became his private right. And will any one say he had no right to those acorns or apples he thus appropriated because he had not the consent of all mankind to make them his? Was it a robbery thus to assume to himself what belonged to all in common? If such a consent as that was necessary, man had starved, notwithstanding the plenty God had given him . . .

30. Thus this law of reason makes the deer that Indian's who hath killed it; it is allowed to be his goods who hath bestowed his labour upon it, though, before, it was the common right of every one. And amongst those who are counted the civilized part of mankind, who have made and multiplied positive laws to determine property, this original law of Nature for the beginning of property, in what was before common, still takes place, and by virtue thereof, what fish any one catches in the ocean, that great and still remaining common of mankind; or what ambergris any one takes up here is by the labour that removes it out of that common state Nature left it in, made his property who takes that pains about it. And even amongst us, the hare that any one is hunting is thought his who pursues her during the chase. For being a beast that is still looked upon as common, and no man's private possession, whoever has employed so much labour about any of that kind as to find and pursue her has thereby removed her from the state of Nature wherein she was common, and hath began a property.

31. It will, perhaps, be objected to this, that if gathering the acorns or other fruits of the earth, &c., makes a right to them, then any one may engross as much as he will. To which I answer, Not so. The same law of Nature that does by this means give us property, does also bound that property too. "God has given us all things richly" (1 Tim. vi. 12). Is the voice of reason confirmed by inspiration? But how far has He given it us — "to enjoy?" As much as any one can make use of to any advantage of life before it spoils, so much he may by his labour fix a property in. Whatever is beyond this is more than his share, and belongs to others. Nothing was made by God for man to spoil or destroy. And thus considering the plenty of natural provisions there was a long time in the world, and the few spend-

ers, and to how small a part of that provision the industry of one man could extend itself and engross it to the prejudice of others, especially keeping within the bounds set by reason of what might serve for his use, there could be then little room for quarrels or contentions about property so established.

32. But the chief matter of property being now not the fruits of the earth and the beasts that subsist on it, but the earth itself, as that which takes in and carries with it all the rest; I think it is plain that property in that too is acquired as the former. As much land as a man tills, plants, improves, cultivates, and can use the product of, so much is his property. He by his labour does, as it were, enclose it from the common. Nor will it invalidate his right to say everybody else has an equal title to it, and therefore he cannot appropriate, he cannot enclose, without the consent of all his fellow-commoners, all mankind. God, when He gave the world in common to all mankind, commanded man also to labour, and the penury of his condition required it of him. God and his reason commanded him to subdue the earth — i.e., improve it for the benefit of life and therein lay out something upon it that was his own, his labour. He that, in obedience to this command of God, subdued, tilled, and sowed any part of it, thereby annexed to it something that was his property, which another had no title to, nor could without injury take from him . . .

36. The measure of property Nature, well set, by the extent of men's labour and the conveniency of life. No man's labour could subdue or appropriate all, nor could his enjoyment consume more than a small part; so that it was impossible for any man, this way, to entrench upon the right of another or acquire to himself a property, to the prejudice of his neighbour, who would still have room for as good and as large a possession (after the other had taken out his) as before it was appropriated. Which measure did confine every man's possession to a very moderate proportion, and such as he might appropriate to himself without injury to anybody in the first ages of the world, when men were more in danger to be lost, by wandering from their company, in the then vast wilderness of the earth than to be straitened for want of room to plant in. And the same measure may be allowed still, without prejudice

to anybody, as full as the world seems. For, supposing a man or family, in the state they were at first, peopling of the world by the children of Adam or Noah, let him plant in some inland vacant places of America. We shall find that the possessions he could make himself, upon the measures we have given, would not be very large, nor, even to this day, prejudice the rest of mankind or give them reason to complain or think themselves injured by this man's encroachment, though the race of men have now spread themselves to all the corners of the world, and do infinitely exceed the small number was at the beginning. Nay, the extent of ground is of so little value without labour that I have heard it affirmed that in Spain itself a man may be permitted to plough, sow, and reap, without being disturbed, upon land he has no other title to, but only his making use of it. But, on the contrary, the inhabitants think themselves beholden to him who, by his industry on neglected, and consequently waste land, has increased the stock of corn, which they wanted. But be this as it will, which I lay no stress on, this I dare boldly affirm, that the same rule of propriety — viz., that every man should have as much as he could make use of, would hold still in the world, without straitening anybody, since there is land enough in the world to suffice double the inhabitants, had not the invention of money, and the tacit agreement of men to put a value on it, introduced (by consent) larger possessions and a right to them; which, how it has done, I shall by-and-by show more at large.

37. This is certain, that in the beginning, before the desire of having more than men needed had altered the intrinsic value of things, which depends only on their usefulness to the life of man, or had agreed that a little piece of yellow metal, which would keep without wasting or decay, should be worth a great piece of flesh or a whole heap of corn, though men had a right to appropriate by their labour, each one to himself, as much of the things of Nature as he could use, yet this could not be much, nor to the prejudice of others, where the same plenty was still left, to those who would use the same industry.

Before the appropriation of land, he who gathered as much of the wild fruit, killed, caught, or tamed as many of the beasts as he could — he that so employed his pains about any of the spontaneous

products of Nature as any way to alter them from the state Nature put them in, by placing any of his labour on them, did thereby acquire a propriety in them; but if they perished in his possession without their due use — if the fruits rotted or the venison putrefied before he could spend it, he offended against the common law of Nature, and was liable to be punished: he invaded his neighbour's share, for he had no right farther than his use called for any of them, and they might serve to afford him conveniences of life.

38. The same measures governed the possession of land, too. Whatsoever he tilled and reaped, laid up and made use of before it spoiled, that was his peculiar right; whatsoever he enclosed, and could feed and make use of, the cattle and product was also his. But if either the grass of his enclosure rotted on the ground, or the fruit of his planting perished without gathering and laying up, this part of the earth, notwithstanding his enclosure, was still to be looked on as waste, and might be the possession of any other. Thus, at the beginning, Cain might take as much ground as he could till and make it his own land, and yet leave enough to Abel's sheep to feed on: a few acres would serve for both their possessions. But as families increased and industry enlarged their stocks, their possessions enlarged with the need of them; but yet it was commonly without any fixed property in the ground they made use of till they incorporated, settled themselves together, and built cities, and then, by consent, they came in time to set out the bounds of their distinct territories and agree on limits between them and their neighbours, and by laws within themselves settled the properties of those of the same society . . .

39. And thus, without supposing any private dominion and property in Adam over all the world, exclusive of all other men, which can no way be proved, nor any one's property be made out from it, but supposing the world, given as it was to the children of men in common, we see how labour could make men distinct titles to several parcels of it for their private uses, wherein there could be no doubt of right, no room for quarrel.

40. Nor is it so strange as, perhaps, before consideration, it may appear, that the property of labour should

be able to overbalance the community of land, for it is labour indeed that puts the difference of value on everything; and let any one consider what the difference is between an acre of land planted with tobacco or sugar, sown with wheat or barley, and an acre of the same land lying in common without any husbandry upon it, and he will find that the improvement of labour makes the far greater part of the value. I think it will be but a very modest computation to say, that of the products of the earth useful to the life of man, nine-tenths are the effects of labour . . .

44. From all which it is evident, that though the things of Nature are given in common, man (by being master of himself, and proprietor of his own person, and the actions or labour of it) had still in himself the great foundation of property; and that which made up the great part of what he applied to the support or comfort of his being, when invention and arts had improved the conveniencies of life, was perfectly his own, and did not belong in common to others.

45. Thus labour, in the beginning, gave a right of property, wherever any one was pleased to employ it, upon what was common, which remained a long while, the far greater part, and is yet more than mankind makes use of. Men at first, for the most part, contented themselves with what unassisted Nature offered to their necessities; and though afterwards, in some parts of the world, where the increase of people and stock, with the use of money, had made land scarce, and so of some value, the several communities settled the bounds of their distinct territories, and, by laws, within themselves, regulated the properties of the private men of their society, and so, by compact and agreement, settled the property which labour and industry began. And the leagues that have been made between several states and kingdoms, either expressly or tacitly disowning all claim and right to the land in the other's possession, have, by common consent, given up their pretences to their natural common right, which originally they had to those countries; and so have, by positive agreement, settled a property amongst themselves, in distinct parts of the world; yet there are still great tracts of ground to be found, which the inhabitants thereof, not having joined with the rest of mankind in the consent of the use of their common money, lie

waste, and are more than the people who dwell on it, do, or can make use of, and so still lie in common; though this can scarce happen amongst that part of mankind that have consented to the use of money.

46. The greatest part of things really useful to the life of man, and such as the necessity of subsisting made the first commoners of the world look after — as it doth the Americans now — are generally things of short duration, such as — if they are not consumed by use — will decay and perish of themselves. Gold, silver, and diamonds are things that fancy or agreement hath put the value on, more than real use and the necessary support of life. Now of those good things which Nature hath provided in common, every one hath a right (as hath been said) to as much as he could use, and had a property in all he could effect with his labour; all that his industry could extend to, to alter from the state Nature had put it in, was his. He that gathered a hundred bushels of acorns or apples had thereby a property in them; they were his goods as soon as gathered. He was only to look that he used them before they spoiled, else he took more than his share, and robbed others. And, indeed, it was a foolish thing, as well as dishonest, to hoard up more than he could make use of. If he gave away a part to anybody else, so that it perished not uselessly in his possession, these he also made use of. And if he also bartered away plums that would have rotted in a week, for nuts that would last good for his eating a whole year, he did no injury; he wasted not the common stock; destroyed no part of the portion of goods that belonged to others, so long as nothing perished uselessly in his hands. Again, if he would give his nuts for a piece of metal, pleased with its colour, or exchange his sheep for shells, or wool for a sparkling pebble or a diamond, and keep those by him all his life, he invaded not the right of others; he might heap up as much of these durable things as he pleased; the exceeding of the bounds of his just property not lying in the largeness of his possession, but the perishing of anything uselessly in it.

47. And thus came in the use of money; some lasting thing that men might keep without spoiling, and that, by mutual consent, men would take in exchange for the truly useful but perishable supports of life . . .

Of Paternal Power.

54. Though I have said above "That all men by nature are equal," I cannot be supposed to understand all sorts of "equality." Age or virtue may give men a just precedency. Excellency of parts and merit may place others above the common level. Birth may subject some, and alliance or benefits others, to pay an observance to those to whom Nature, gratitude, or other respects, may have made it due; and yet all this consists with the equality which all men are in in respect of jurisdiction or dominion one over another, which was the equality I there spoke of as proper to the business in hand, being that equal right that every man hath to his natural freedom, without being subjected to the will or authority of any other man.

57. For law, in its true notion, is not so much the limitation as the direction of a free and intelligent agent to his proper interest, and prescribes no farther than is for the general good of those under that law. Could they be happier without it, the law, as a useless thing, would of itself vanish; and that ill deserves the name of confinement, which hedges us in only from bogs and precipices. So that however it may be mistaken, the end of law is not to abolish or restrain, but to preserve and enlarge freedom. For in all the states of created beings, capable of laws, where there is no law there is no freedom. For liberty is to be free from restraint and violence from others, which cannot be where there is no law; and is not, as we are told, "a liberty for every other man's humour might domineer over him? But a liberty to dispose and order freely as he lists his person, actions, possessions, and his whole property within the allowance of those laws under which he is, and therein not to be subject to the arbitrary will of another, but freely follow his own.

58. The power, then, that parents have over their children arises from that duty which is incumbent on them, to take care of their offspring during the imperfect state of childhood. To inform the mind, and govern the actions of their yet ignorant nonage, till reason shall take its place and ease them of that trouble, is what the children want, and the parents are bound to. For God having given man an understanding to direct his actions, has allowed him a freedom of will and liberty of acting, as properly belonging thereunto, within

the bounds of that law he is under. But whilst he is in an estate wherein he has no understanding of his own to direct his will, he is not to have any will of his own to follow. He that understands for him must will for him too; he must prescribe to his will, and regulate his actions, but when he comes to the estate that made his father a free man, the son is a free man too.

59. This holds in all the laws a man is under, whether natural or civil. Is a man under the law of Nature? What made him free of that law? what gave him a free disposing of his property, according to his own will, within the compass of that law? I answer, an estate wherein he might be supposed capable to know that law, that so he might keep his actions within the bounds of it. When he has acquired that state, he is presumed to know how far that law is to be his guide, and how far he may make use of his freedom, and so comes to have it; till then, somebody else must guide him, who is presumed to know how far the law allows a liberty. If such a state of reason, such an age of discretion made him free, the same shall make his son free too. Is a man under the law of England? what made him free of that law — that is, to have the liberty to dispose of his actions and possessions, according to his own will, within the permission of that law? a capacity of knowing that law. Which is supposed, by that law, at the age of twenty-one, and in some cases sooner. If this made the father free, it shall make the son free too . . .

60. But if through defects that may happen out of the ordinary course of Nature, any one comes not to such a degree of reason wherein he might be supposed capable of knowing the law, and so living within the rules of it, he is never capable of being a free man, he is never let loose to the disposure of his own will; because he knows no bounds to it, has not understanding, its proper guide, but is continued under the tuition and government of others all the time his own understanding is incapable of that charge. And so lunatics and idiots are never set free from the government of their parents . . .

61. Thus we are born free as we are born rational; not that we have actually the exercise of either: age that brings one, brings with it the other too. And thus we see how natural freedom and subjection to parents may

consist together, and are both founded on the same principle. A child is free by his father's title, by his father's understanding, which is to govern him till he hath it of his own . . .

63. The freedom then of man, and liberty of acting according to his own will, is grounded on his having reason, which is able to instruct him in that law he is to govern himself by, and make him know how far he is left to the freedom of his own will. To turn him loose to an unrestrained liberty, before he has reason to guide him, is not the allowing him the privilege of his nature to be free, but to thrust him out amongst brutes, and abandon him to a state as wretched and as much beneath that of a man as theirs. This is that which puts the authority into the parents' hands to govern the minority of their children. God hath made it their business to employ this care on their offspring, and hath placed in them suitable inclinations of tenderness and concern to temper this power, to apply it as His wisdom designed it, to the children's good as long as they should need to be under it . . .

Of Political or Civil Society.

77. God, having made man such a creature that, in His own judgment, it was not good for him to be alone, put him under strong obligations of necessity, convenience, and inclination, to drive him into society, as well as fitted him with understanding and language to continue and enjoy it. The first society was between man and wife, which gave beginning to that between parents and children, to which, in time, that between master and servant came to be added. And though all these might, and commonly did, meet together and make up but one family, wherein the master or mistress of it had some sort of rule proper to a family, each of these, or all together, came short of "political society," as we shall see if we consider the different ends, ties, and bounds of each of these.

78. Conjugal society is made by a voluntary compact between man and woman, and though it consist chiefly in such a communion and right in one another's bodies as is necessary to its chief end, procreation, yet it draws with it mutual support and assistance, and a communion of interests too, as necessary not only to unite their care and affection, but also necessary to

their common offspring, who have a right to be nourished and maintained by them till they are able to provide for themselves.

79. For the end of conjunction between male and female being not barely procreation, but the continuation of the species, this conjunction betwixt male and female ought to last, even after procreation, so long as is necessary to the nourishment and support of the young ones, who are to be sustained by those that got them till they are able to shift and provide for themselves . . .

86. Let us therefore consider a master of a family with all these subordinate relations of wife, children, servants and slaves, united under the domestic rule of a family, which what resemblance soever it may have in its order, offices, and number too, with a little commonwealth, yet is very far from it both in its constitution, power, and end; or if it must be thought a monarchy, and the paterfamilias the absolute monarch in it, absolute monarchy will have but a very shattered and short power, when it is plain by what has been said before, that the master of the family has a very distinct and differently limited power both as to time and extent over those several persons that are in it; for excepting the slave (and the family is as much a family, and his power as paterfamilias as great, whether there be any slaves in his family or no) he has no legislative power of life and death over any of them, and none too but what a mistress of a family may have as well as he. And he certainly can have no absolute power over the whole family who has but a very limited one over every individual in it. But how a family, or any other society of men differ from that which is properly political society, we shall best see by considering wherein political society itself consists.

87. Man being born, as has been proved, with a title to perfect freedom and an uncontrolled enjoyment of all the rights and privileges of the law of Nature, equally with any other man, or number of men in the world, hath by nature a power not only to preserve his property — that is, his life, liberty, and estate against the injuries and attempts of other men, but to judge of and punish the breaches of that law in others, as he is persuaded the offence deserves, even with death itself, in crimes where the heinousness of the fact, in his

opinion, requires it. But because no political society can be, nor subsist, without having in itself the power to preserve the property, and in order thereunto punish the offences of all those of that society, there, and there only, is political society where every one of the members hath quitted this natural power, resigned it up into the hands of the community in all cases that exclude him not from appealing for protection to the law established by it. And thus all private judgment of every particular member being excluded, the community comes to be umpire, and by understanding indifferent rules and men authorized by the community for their execution, decides all the differences that may happen between any members of that society concerning any matter of right, and punishes those offences which any member hath committed against the society with such penalties as the law has established; whereby it is easy to discern who are, and are not, in political society together. Those who are united into one body, and have a common established law and judicature to appeal to, with authority to decide controversies between them and punish offenders, are in civil society one with another; but those who have no such common appeal, I mean on earth, are still in the state of Nature, each being where there is no other, judge for himself and executioner; which is, as I have before showed it, the perfect state of Nature . . .

89. Wherever, therefore, any number of men so unite into one society as to quit every one his executive power of the law of Nature, and to resign it to the public, there and there only is a political or civil society. And this is done wherever any number of men, in the state of Nature, enter into society to make one people one body politic under one supreme government; or else when any one joins himself to, and incorporates with any government already made. For hereby he authorizes the society, or which is all one, the legislative thereof, to make laws for him as the public good of the society shall require, to the execution whereof his own assistance (as to his own decrees) is due. And this puts men out of a state of Nature into that of a commonwealth, by setting up a judge on earth with authority to determine all the controversies and redress the injuries that may happen to any member of the commonwealth, which judge is the legislative or magistrates appointed by it. And wherever there are any

number of men, however associated, that have no such decisive power to appeal to, there they are still in the state of Nature.

90. And hence it is evident that absolute monarchy, which by some men is counted for the only government in the world, is indeed inconsistent with civil society, and so can be no form of civil government at all. For the end of civil society being to avoid and remedy those inconveniencies of the state of Nature which necessarily follow from every man's being judge in his own case by setting up a known authority to which every one of that society may appeal upon any injury received, or controversy that may arise, and which every one of the society ought to obey. Wherever any persons are who have not such an authority to appeal to, and decide any difference between them there, those persons are still in the state of Nature. And so is every absolute prince in respect of those who are under his dominion.

91. For he being supposed to have all, both legislative and executive, power in himself alone, there is no judge to be found, no appeal lies open to any one, who may fairly and indifferently, and with authority decide, and from whence relief and redress may be expected of any injury or inconveniency that may be suffered from him, or by his order. So that such a man, however entitled, Czar, or Grand Signior, or how you please, is as much in the state of Nature, with all under his dominion, as he is with the rest of mankind. For wherever any two men are, who have no standing rule and common judge to appeal to on earth, for the determination of controversies of right betwixt them, there they are still in the state of Nature, and under all the inconveniencies of it . . .

Of the Beginning of Political Societies.

95. Men being, as has been said, by nature all free, equal, and independent, no one can be put out of this estate and subjected to the political power of another without his own consent, which is done by agreeing with other men, to join and unite into a community for their comfortable, safe, and peaceable living, one amongst another, in a secure enjoyment of their properties, and a greater security against any that are not of it. This any number of men may do, because it injures

not the freedom of the rest; they are left, as they were, in the liberty of the state of Nature. When any number of men have so consented to make one community or government, they are thereby presently incorporated, and make one body politic, wherein the majority have a right to act and conclude the rest.

96. For, when any number of men have, by the consent of every individual, made a community, they have thereby made that community one body, with a power to act as one body, which is only by the will and determination of the majority. For that which acts any community, being only the consent of the individuals of it, and it being one body, must move one way, it is necessary the body should move that way whither the greater force carries it, which is the consent of the majority, or else it is impossible it should act or continue one body, one community, which the consent of every individual that united into it agreed that it should; and so every one is bound by that consent to be concluded by the majority. And therefore we see that in assemblies empowered to act by positive laws where no number is set by that positive law which empowers them, the act of the majority passes for the act of the whole, and of course determines as having, by the law of Nature and reason, the power of the whole.

97. And thus every man, by consenting with others to make one body politic under one government, puts himself under an obligation to every one of that society to submit to the determination of the majority, and to be concluded by it; or else this original compact, whereby he with others incorporates into one society, would signify nothing, and be no compact if he be left free and under no other ties than he was in before in the state of Nature. For what appearance would there be of any compact? What new engagement if he were no farther tied by any decrees of the society than he himself thought fit and did actually consent to? This would be still as great a liberty as he himself had before his compact, or any one else in the state of Nature, who may submit himself and consent to any acts of it if he thinks fit.

98. For if the consent of the majority shall not in reason be received as the act of the whole, and conclude

every individual; nothing but the consent of every individual can make anything to be the act of the whole, which, considering the infirmities of health and avocations of business, which in a number though much less than that of a commonwealth, will necessarily keep many away from the public assembly; and the variety of opinions and contrariety of interests which unavoidably happen in all collections of men, it is next impossible ever to be had. And, therefore, if coming into society be upon such terms, it will be only like Cato's coming into the theatre, *tantum ut exiret*. Such a constitution as this would make the mighty leviathan of a shorter duration than the feeblest creatures, and not let it outlast the day it was born in, which cannot be supposed till we can think that rational creatures should desire and constitute societies only to be dissolved. For where the majority cannot conclude the rest, there they cannot act as one body, and consequently will be immediately dissolved again.

99. Whosoever, therefore, out of a state of Nature unite into a community, must be understood to give up all the power necessary to the ends for which they unite into society to the majority of the community, unless they expressly agreed in any number greater than the majority. And this is done by barely agreeing to unite into one political society, which is all the compact that is, or needs be, between the individuals that enter into or make up a commonwealth. And thus, that which begins and actually constitutes any political society is nothing but the consent of any number of freemen capable of majority, to unite and incorporate into such a society. And this is that, and that only, which did or could give beginning to any lawful government in the world . . .

Of the Ends of Political Society and Government.

123. If man in the state of Nature be so free as has been said, if he be absolute lord of his own person and possessions, equal to the greatest and subject to nobody, why will he part with his freedom, this empire, and subject himself to the dominion and control of any other power? To which it is obvious to answer, that though in the state of Nature he hath such a right, yet the enjoyment of it is very uncertain and constant-

ly exposed to the invasion of others; for all being kings as much as he, every man his equal, and the greater part no strict observers of equity and justice, the enjoyment of the property he has in this state is very unsafe, very insecure. This makes him willing to quit this condition which, however free, is full of fears and continual dangers; and it is not without reason that he seeks out and is willing to join in society with others who are already united, or have a mind to unite for the mutual preservation of their lives, liberties and estates, which I call by the general name — property.

124. The great and chief end, therefore, of men uniting into commonwealths, and putting themselves under government, is the preservation of their property; to which in the state of Nature there are many things wanting.

Firstly, There wants an established, settled, known law, received and allowed by common consent to be the standard of right and wrong, and the common measure to decide all controversies between them. For though the law of Nature be plain and intelligible to all rational creatures, yet men, being biased by their interest, as well as ignorant for want of study of it, are not apt to allow of it as a law binding to them in the application of it to their particular cases.

125. Secondly: in the state of Nature there wants a known and indifferent judge, with authority to determine all differences according to the established law. For every one in that state being both judge and executioner of the law of Nature, men being partial to themselves, passion and revenge is very apt to carry them too far, and with too much heat in their own cases, as well as negligence and unconcernedness, make them too remiss in other men's.

126. Thirdly: in the state of Nature there often wants power to back and support the sentence when right, and to give it due execution. They who by any injustice offended will seldom fail where they are able by force to make good their injustice. Such resistance many times makes the punishment dangerous, and frequently destructive to those who attempt it.

127. Thus mankind, notwithstanding all the privileges of the state of Nature, being but in an ill condition while they remain in it are quickly driven into society. Hence it comes to pass, that we seldom find any number of men live any time together in this state. The inconveniencies that they are therein exposed to by the irregular and uncertain exercise of the power every man has of punishing the transgressions of others, make them take sanctuary under the established laws of government, and therein seek the preservation of their property. It is this makes them so willingly give up every one his single power of punishing to be exercised by such alone as shall be appointed to it amongst them, and by such rules as the community, or those authorized by them to that purpose, shall agree on. And in this we have the original right and rise of both the legislative and executive power as well as of the governments and societies themselves . . .

131. But though men when they enter into society give up the equality, liberty, and executive power they had in the state of Nature into the hands of the society, to be so far disposed of by the legislative as the good of the society shall require, yet it being only with an intention in every one the better to preserve himself, his liberty and property (for no rational creature can be supposed to change his condition with an intention to be worse), the power of the society or legislative constituted by them can never be supposed to extend farther than the common good, but is obliged to secure every one's property by providing against those three defects above mentioned that made the state of Nature so unsafe and uneasy. And so, whoever has the legislative or supreme power of any commonwealth, is bound to govern by established standing laws, promulgated and known to the people, and not by extemporary decrees, by indifferent and upright judges, who are to decide controversies by those laws; and to employ the force of the community at home only in the execution of such laws, or abroad to prevent or redress foreign injuries and secure the community from inroads and invasion. And all this to be directed to no other end but the peace, safety, and public good of the people.

Of the Forms of a Commonwealth.

132.   The majority having, as has been showed, upon men's first uniting into society, the whole power of the community naturally in them, may employ all that power in making laws for the community from time to time, and executing those laws by officers of their own appointing, and then the form of the government is a perfect democracy; or else may put the power of making laws into the hands of a few select men, and their heirs or successors, and then it is an oligarchy; or else into the hands of one man, and then it is a monarchy; if to him and his heirs, it is a hereditary monarchy; if to him only for life, but upon his death the power only of nominating a successor, to return to them, an elective monarchy.   And so accordingly of these make compounded and mixed forms of government, as they think good.   And if the legislative power be at first given by the majority to one or more persons only for their lives, or any limited time, and then the supreme power to revert to them again, when it is so reverted the community may dispose of it again anew into what hands they please, and so constitute a new form of government . . .

Of the Extent of the Legislative Power.

135.   Though the legislative, whether placed in one or more, whether it be always in being or only by intervals, though it be the supreme power in every commonwealth; yet, first, it is not, nor can possibly be, absolutely arbitrary over the lives and fortunes of the people.   For it being but the joint power of every member of the society given up to that person or assembly which is legislator, it can be no more than those persons had in a state of Nature before they entered into society, and gave it up to the community.   For nobody can transfer to another more power than he has in himself, and nobody has an absolute arbitrary power over himself, or over any other, to destroy his own life, or take away the life or property of another.   A man, as has been proved, cannot subject himself to the arbitrary power of another; and having, in the state of Nature, no arbitrary power over the life, liberty, or possession of another, but only so much as the law of Nature gave him for the preservation of himself and the rest of mankind, this is all he doth, or can give up to

the commonwealth, and by it to the legislative power, so that the legislative can have no more than this.   Their power in the utmost bounds of it is limited to the public good of the society.   It is a power that hath no other end but preservation, and therefore can never have a right to destroy, enslave, or designedly to impoverish the subjects; the obligations of the law of Nature cease not in society, but only in many cases are drawn closer, and have, by human laws, known penalties annexed to them to enforce their observation.   Thus the law of Nature stands as an eternal rule to all men, legislators as well as others.   The rules that they make for other men's actions must, as well as their own and other men's actions, be conformable to the law of Nature — i.e., to the will of God, of which that is a declaration, and the fundamental law of Nature being the preservation of mankind, no human sanction can be good or valid against it . . .

137.   Absolute arbitrary power, or governing without settled standing laws, can neither of them consist with the ends of society and government, which men would not quit the freedom of the state of Nature for, and tie themselves up under were it not to preserve their lives, liberties, and fortunes; and by stated rules of right and property to secure their peace and quiet.   It cannot be supposed that they should intend, had they a power so to do, to give any one or more an absolute arbitrary power over their persons and estates, and put a force into the magistrate's hand to execute his unlimited will arbitrarily upon them; this were to put themselves into a worse condition than the state of Nature, wherein they had a liberty to defend their right against the injuries of others, and were upon equal terms of force to maintain it, whether invaded by a single man or many in combination . . . yet he can command anything, and hang for the least disobedience.   Because such a blind obedience is necessary to that end for which the commander has his power — viz., the preservation of the rest, but the disposing of his goods has nothing to do with it.

140.   It is true governments cannot be supported without great charge, and it is fit every one who enjoys his share of the protection should pay out of his estate his proportion for the maintenance of it.   But still it must be with his own consent — i.e., the consent of the

majority, giving it either by themselves or their representatives chosen by them; for if any one shall claim a power to lay and levy taxes on the people by his own authority, and without such consent of the people, he thereby invades the fundamental law of property, and subverts the end of government. For what property have I in that which another may by right take when he pleases to himself?

141. Fourthly. The legislative cannot transfer the power of making laws to any other hands, for it being but a delegated power from the people, they who have it cannot pass it over to others. The people alone can appoint the form of the commonwealth, which is by constituting the legislative, and appointing in whose hands that shall be. And when the people have said, "We will submit, and be governed by laws made by such men, and in such forms," nobody else can say other men shall make laws for them; nor can they be bound by any laws but such as are enacted by those whom they have chosen and authorized to make laws for them.

142. These are the bounds which the trust that is put in them by the society and the law of God and Nature have set to the legislative power of every commonwealth, in all forms of government. First: They are to govern by promulgated established laws, not to be varied in particular cases, but to have one rule for rich and poor, for the favourite at Court, and the countryman at plough. Secondly: These laws also ought to be designed for no other end ultimately but the good of the people. Thirdly: They must not raise taxes on the property of the people without the consent of the people given by themselves or their deputies . . .

202. Wherever law ends tyranny begins, if the law be transgressed to another's harm. And whosoever in authority exceeds the power given him by the law, and makes use of the force he has under his command to compass that upon the subject which the law allows not, ceases in that to be a magistrate and, acting without authority, may be opposed as any other man who by force invades the right of another . . .

203. May the commands, then, of a prince be opposed? May he be resisted as often as any one shall find himself aggrieved, and but imagine he has not right done him? . . .

204. To this I answer that force is to be opposed to nothing but to unjust and unlawful force; whoever makes any opposition in any other case draws on himself a just condemnation both from God and man.

John Trenchard and Thomas Gordon: Cato's Letters (1721)

Of the natural Honesty of the People, and their reasonable Demands. How important it is to every Government to consult their Affections and Interest.

Sir,
I have observed, in a former Letter, that the People, when they are not misled or corrupted, generally make a sound Judgment of Things. They have natural Qualifications equal to those of their Superiors; and there is oftner found a great Genius carrying a Pitch-Fork, than carrying a White Staff. The poor Cook preferred by the Grand Seignior to be his first Vizier, in order to cure the publick Disorder and Confusion, occasioned by the Ignorance, Corruption and Neglect of the former Ministry, made good effectually his own Promise, and did Credit to his Master's Choice: He remedied the publick Disorders, and proved, says Sir Paul Ricaut, an able and excellent Minister of State.

Besides, there are not such mighty Talents requisite for Government, as some, who pretend to them without possessing them, would make us believe: Honest Affections, and common Qualifications, are sufficient; and the Administration has been always best executed, and the publick Liberty best preserved, near the Origin and Rise of States, when plain Honesty and common Sense alone governed the public Affairs, and the Morals of Men were not corrupted with Riches and Luxury, nor their Understandings perverted by Subtleties and Distinctions. Great Abilities have, for the most part, if not always, been employed to mislead the honest but unwary Multitude, and to draw them out of the open and plain Paths of publick Virtue and publick Good.

The People have no Biafs to be Knaves; the Security of their Persons and Property is their highest Aim. No Ambition prompts them; they cannot come to be great Lords, and to possess great Titles, and therefore

T. Woodward, J. Walthoe, and J. Peele, London, 1755, I, pp. 177–79, 184–85, 190–91, 147–61; II, pp. 130–33, 244–51.

desire none. No aspiring or unsociable Passions incite them; they have no Rivals for Place, no Competitor to pull down; they have no darling Child, Pimp, or Relation to raise: They have no Occasion for Dissimulation or Intrigue; they can serve no End by Faction; they have no Interest, but the general Interest.

The same can rarely be said of Great Men, who, to gratify private Passion, often bring down publick Ruin; who, to fill their private Purses with many Thousands, frequently load the People with many Millions; who oppress for a Mistress, and to save a Favourite, destroy a Nation; who too often make the Publick sink and give way to their private Fortune; and for a private Pleasure, create a general Calamity . . .

The first Principles of Power are in the People; and all the Projects of Men in Power ought to refer to the People, to aim solely at their Good, and end in it: And whoever will pretend to govern them without regarding them, will soon repent it. Such Feats of Errantry may do perhaps in Asia; but in Countries where the People are free, it is Madness to hope to rule them against their Wills. They will know, that Government is appointed for their Sakes, and will be saucy enough to expect some Regard and some Good from their own Delegates . . .

Dominion that is not maintained by the Sword, must be maintained by Consent; and in this latter Case, what Security can any Man at the Head of Affairs expect, but from pursuing the People's Welfare, and seeking their good Will? The Government of One for the Sake of One, is Tyranny; and so is the Government of a Few for the Sake of Themselves: But Government executed for the Good of All, and with the Consent of All, is Liberty; and the Word Government is prophaned, and its Meaning Abused, when it signifies any Thing else.

In free Countries, the People know all this. They have their Five Senses in as great Perfection, as have those who would treat them as if they had none. They are not wont to hate their Governors, till their Governors deserve to be hated; and when this happens to be the Case, not absolute Power itself, nor the Affections of a Prince invested with it, can protect or employ Ministers detested by the People. Even the Grand Seignior, with all his boundless Authority, is frequently forced to give up his first Minister (who is sometimes his Son-in-Law, or Brother-in-Law) a Sacrifice to appease the People's Rage.

The People, rightly managed, are the best Friends to Princes; and, when injured and oppressed, the most formidable Enemies. Princes, who have trusted to their Armies or their Nobility, have been often deceived and ruined; but Princes, who have trusted wholly to the People, have seldom been deceived or deserted: The Reason is, that in all Governments, which are not Violent and Military, the People have more Power than either the Grandees or the Soldiery; and their Friendship is more sincere, as having nothing to desire but Freedom from Oppression. And whilst a Prince is thus beloved by his People, it will rarely happen that any can be so rash and precipitate as to conspire against him . . .

Considerations on the destructive Spirit of arbitrary Power. With the Blessings of Liberty, and our own Constitution.

Sir,
The Good of the Governed being the sole End of Government, they must be the greatest and best Governors, who make their People great and happy; and they the worst who make their People little, wicked, and miserable. Power in a free State, is a Trust committed by All to One or a Few, to watch for the Security, and pursue the Interest of All: And, when that Security is not sought, nor that Interest obtained, we know what Opinion the People will have of their Governors.

It is the hard Fate of the World, that there should be any Difference in the Views and Interests of the Governors and Governed; and yet it is so in most Countries. Men who have a Trust frankly bestowed upon them by the People, too frequently betray that Trust, become Conspirators against their Benefactors, and turn the Sword upon those who gave it; insomuch that in the greatest Part of the Earth, People are happy if they can defend themselves against their Defenders.

Let us look round this Great World, and behold what an immense Majority of the whole Race of Men crouch under the Yoke of a few Tyrants, naturally as low as the meanest of themselves, and, by being Tyrants, worse than the worst; who, as Mr. Sidney observes, use their Subjects like Asses and Mastiff Dogs, to work and to fight, to be oppressed and killed for them . . .

Yet this cruel Spirit in Tyrants is not always owing naturally to the Men, since they are naturally like other Men; but it is owing to the Nature of the Dominion which they exercise. Good Laws make a good Prince, if he has a good Understanding; but the best Men grow mischievous when they are set above Laws. Claudius was a very harmless Man, while he was a private Man; but when he came to be a Tyrant, he proved a bloody one, almost as bloody as his Nephew and Predecessor Caligula; who had also been a very good Subject, but when he came to be the Roman Emperor, grew the professed Executioner of Mankind.

There is something so wanton and monstrous in lawless Power, that there scarce ever was a human Spirit that could bear it; and the Mind of Man, which is weak and limited, ought never to be trusted with a Power that is boundless. The State of Tyranny is a State of War; and where it prevails, instead of an Intercourse of Confidence and affection, as between a lawful Prince and his Subjects, nothing is to be seen but Jealousy, Mistrust, Fear, and Hatred: An arbitrary Prince and his Slaves often destroy one another, to be safe: They are continually plotting against his Life; he is continually shedding their Blood, and plundering them of their Property . . .

But neither Bashaws, nor Armies, could keep that People in such abject Slavery, if their Priests and Doctors had not made Passive Obedience a Principle of their Religion. The holy Name of God is prophaned, and his Authority belied, to bind down Wretchedness upon his Creatures, and to secure the Tyrant that does it. The most consummate of all Wickedness, and the highest of all Evils, are sanctified by the Teachers of Religion, and made by them a Part of it. Yes, Turkish Slavery is confirmed, and Turkish Tyranny defended, by Religion! . . .

As arbitrary Power in a single Person has made greater Havock in human Nature, and thinned Mankind more, than all the Beasts of Prey and all the Plagues and Earthquakes that ever were; let those Men consider what they have to answer for, who would countenance such a monstrous Evil in the World, or would oppose those that would oppose it. A Bear, a Lion, or a Tyger, may now and then pick up single Men in a Wood, or a Desert; an Earthquake sometimes may bury a Thousand or Two Inhabitants in the Ruins of a Town; and the Pestilence may once in many Years carry off a much greater Number: But a Tyrant shall, out of a wanton personal Passion, carry Fire and Sword

through a whole Continent, and deliver up a Hundred Thousand of his Fellow Creatures to the Slaughter in one Day, without any Remorse or further Notice, than that they died for his Glory. I say nothing of the moral Effect of Tyranny; though 'tis certain that Ignorance, Vice, Poverty, and Vileness, always attend it . . .

Power is like Fire; it warms, scorches, or destroys, according as it is watched, provoked, or increased. It is as dangerous as useful. Its only Rule is the Good of the People; but because it is apt to break its Bounds, in all good Governments nothing, or as little as may be, ought to be left to Chance, or the Humours of Men in Authority: All should proceed by fixed and stated Rules, and upon any Emergency, new Rules should be made . . .

Cautions against the natural Encroachments of Power.

Sir,
Considering what sort of a Creature Man is, it is scarce possible to put him under too many Restraints, when he is possessed of great Power: He may possibly use it well; but they act most prudently, who, supposing that he would use it ill, inclose him within certain Bounds, and make it terrible to him to exceed them.

Men that are above all Fear, soon grow above all Shame . . .

It is nothing strange, that Men, who think themselves unaccountable, should act unaccountably, and that all Men would be unaccountable if they could: Even those who have done nothing to displease, do not know but some Time or other they may; and no Man cares to be at the entire Mercy of another. Hence it is that if every Man had his Will, all Men would exercise Dominion, and no Man would suffer it. It is therefore owing more to the Necessities of Men, than to their Inclinations, that they have put themselves under the Restraint of Laws, and appointed certain Persons, called Magistrates, to execute them; otherwise they would never be executed, scarce any Man having such a Degree of Virtue as willingly to execute the Laws upon himself; but on the contrary, most Men thinking them a Grievance, when they come to meddle with themselves and their Property. *Suarum legum auctor et everfor,* was the Character of Pompey: He made Laws when they suited his Occasions, and broke them when they thwarted his Will. And it is the Character of almost every Man possessed of Pompey's Power: They intend them for a Security to themselves, and for a Terror to others. This shews the Distrust that Men have of Men; and this made a great Philosopher call the State of Nature, a State of War; which Definition is true in a restrained Sense, since human Societies and human Laws are the Effect of Necessity and Experience: Whereas were all Men left to the boundless Liberty which they claim from Nature, every Man would be interfering and quarrelling with another; every Man would be plundering the Acquisitions of another; the Labour of one Man would be the Property of another; Weakness would be the Prey of Force; and one Man's Industry would be the Cause of another Man's Idleness.

Hence grew the Necessity of Government, which was the mutual Contract of a Number of Men, agreeing upon certain Terms of Union and Society, and putting themselves under Penalties, if they violated these Terms, which were called Laws, and put into the Hands of one or more Men to execute. And thus Men quitted Part of their Natural Liberty to acquire Civil Security. But frequently the Remedy proved worse than the Disease; and human Society had often no Enemies so great as their own Magistrates; who, wherever they were trusted with too much Power, always abused it . . .

The World is governed by Men, and Men by their Passions; which, being boundless and insatiable, are always terrible when they are not controuled. Who was ever satiated with Riches, or surfeited with Power, or tired with Honours? There is a Tradition concerning Alexander, that having penetrated to the Eastern Ocean, and ravaged as much of this World as he knew, he wept that there was never another World for him to conquer. This, whether true or no, shews the Spirit of the Man, and indeed of human Nature, whose Appetites are infinite . . .

Political Jealousy, therefore, in the People, is a necessary and laudable Passion. But in a Chief Magistrate, a Jealousy of his People is not so justifiable, their Ambition being only to preserve themselves; whereas it is natural for Power to be striveing to enlarge itself, and to be encroaching upon those that have none. The most laudable Jealousy of a Magistrate is to be jealous *for* his People; which will shew that he loves them, and has used them well: But to be jealous *of* them, would denote that he has evil Designs against them, and has used them ill. The People's Jealousy

tends to preserve Liberty; and the Prince's to destroy it . . . Now, because Liberty chastises and shortens Power, therefore Power would extinguish Liberty; and consequently Liberty has too much Cause to be exceeding jealous, and always upon her Defence. Power has many Advantages over her; it has generally numerous Guards, many Creatures, and much Treasure; besides, it has more Craft and Experience, less Honesty and Innocence: And whereas Power can, and for the most part does, subsist where Liberty is not, Liberty cannot subsist without Power; so that she has, as it were, the Enemy always at her Gates.

Some have said, that Magistrates being accountable to none but God, ought to know no other Restraint. But this Reasoning is as frivolous as it is wicked; for no good Man cares how many Punishments and Penalties lie in his Way to an Offence which he does not intend to commit: A Man who does not mean to commit Murder, is not sorry that Murder is punished with Death. And as to wicked Men, their being accountable to God, whom they do not fear, is no Security to us against their Folly and Malice; and to say that we ought to have no Security against them, is to insult common Sense, and give the Lie to the first Law of Nature, that of Self-Preservation. Human Reason says, that there is no Obedience, no Regard due to those Rulers, who govern by no Rule but their Lust. Such Men are no Rulers; they are Outlaws; who, being at Defiance with God and Man, are protected by no Law of God . . .

To conclude: Power, without Controul, appertains to God alone; and no Man ought to be trusted with what no Man is equal to. In Truth there are so many Passions, and Inconsistencies, and so much Selfishness, belonging to human Nature, that we can scarce be too much upon our Guard against each other. The only Security which we can have that Men will be honest, is to make it their Interest to be honest; and the best Defence which we can have against their being Knaves, is to make it terrible to them to be Knaves. As there are many Men wicked on some Stations, who would be innocent in others; the best Way is to make Wickedness unsafe in any Station.

Of the Equality and Inequality of Men.

Sir,
Men are naturally equal, and none ever rose above the rest but by Force or Consent: No Man was ever born

above all the rest, nor below them all; and therefore there never was any Man in the World so good or so bad, so high or so low, but he had his Fellow. Nature is a kind and benevolent Parent; she constitutes no particular Favourites with Endowments and Privileges above the rest; but for the most part sends all her Offspring into the World furnished with the Elements of Understanding and Strength to provide for themselves: She gives them Heads to consult their own Security, and Hands to execute their own Counsels; and according to the Use that they make of their Faculties, and of the Opportunities that they find, Degrees of Power and Names of Distinction grow amongst them, and their natural Equality is lost.

Thus Nature, who is their Parent, deals with Men: But Fortune, who is their Nurse, is not so benevolent and impartial; she acts wantonly and capriciously, often cruelly; and counterplotting Justice as well as Nature, frequently sets the Fool above the wise Man, and the best below the worst.

And from hence it is, that the most Part of the World, attending much more to the noisy Conduct and glaring Effects of Fortune, than to the quiet and regular Proceedings of Nature, are misled in their Judgment upon this Subject: They confound Fortune with Nature, and too often ascribe to Natural Merit and Excellency the Works of Contrivance or Chance. This, however, shews that Reason and Equity run in our Heads, while we endeavour to find a just Cause for Things that are not just; and this is the Source of the Reverence which we pay to Men whom Fortune sometimes lifts on high, though Nature had placed them below. The Populace rarely see any Creature rise, but they find a Reason for it in his Parts; when probably the true one will be found in his own Baseness, or another Man's Folly.

From the same Reasoning may be seen why it is, that, let who will be at the Head of a Party, he is always extolled by his Party as superior to the rest of Mankind; and let who will be the first Man of his Country, he will never fail being complimented by Many as the first of his Species. But the Issue and their own Behaviour constantly shew that the highest are upon a level with the rest, and often with the lowest. Men that are high are almost ever seen in a false Light; the most Part see them at a great Distance, and through a magnifying Medium; some are dazled with their Splen-

dor, many are awed by their Power. Whatever appears shining or terrible appears great, and is magnified by the Eye and the Imagination.

That Nature has made Men equal, we know and feel; and when People come to think otherwise, there is no Excess of Folly and Superstition which they may not be brought to practice. Thus they have made Gods of dead Men, and paid divine Honours to many while they were yet living: They saw them to be but Men, yet they worshipped them as Gods. And even they who have not gone so far, have yet, by their wild Notions of Inequality, done as much Mischief; they have made Men, and often wicked Men, to be Vice-Gods; and then made God's Power (falsly so called) as irresistible in the Hands of Men as in his own, and much more frightful.

It is evident to common Sense, that there ought to be no Inequality in Society, but for the sake of Society; but these Men have made one Man's Power and Will the Cause of all Men's Misery. They gave him as far as they could the Power of God, without obliging him to practice the Mercy and Goodness of God . . . Men naturally as great and brave as himself, and many more wise.

Whoever pretends to be naturally superior to other Men, claims from Nature what she never gave to any Man. He sets up for being more than a Man; a Character with which Nature has nothing to do. She has thrown her Gifts in common amongst us; and as the highest Offices of Nature fall to the Share of the Mean as well as of the Great, her vilest Offices are performed by the Great as well as by the Mean: Death and Diseases are the Portion of Kings as well as of Clowns; and the Corpse of a Monarch is no more exempted from Stench and Putrefaction, than the Corpse of a Slave.

Mors aequo pulsat pede.

All the Arts and Endowments of Men to acquire Preheminence and Advantages over one another, are so many Proofs and Confessions that they have not such Preheminence and Advantages from Nature; and all their Pomp, Titles, and Wealth, are Means and Devices to make the World think that they who possess them are superior in Merit to those that want them. But it is not much to the Glory of the upper Part of Mankind, that their boasted and superior Merit is often the Work of Heralds, Artificers, and Money; and that many derive their whole Stock of Fame from Ancestors, who lived an Age or many Ages ago . . .

All Government proved to be instituted by Men, and only to intend the general Good of Men

Sir,

. . . The Experience of every Age convinces us, that we must not judge of Men by what they ought to do, but by what they will do; and all History affords but few Instances of Men trusted with great Power without abusing it, when with Security they could. The Servants of Society, that is to say, its Magistrates, did almost universally serve it by seizing it, selling it, or plundering it; especially when they were left by the Society unlimited as to their Duty and Wages. In that Case, these faithful Stewards generally took all; and being Servants, made Slaves of their Masters.

For these Reasons, and convinced by woful and eternal Experience, Societies found it necessary to lay Restraints upon their Magistrates or publick Servants, and to put Checks upon those who would otherwise put Chains upon them; and therefore these Societies set themselves to model and form national Constitutions with such Wisdom and Art, that the publick Interest should be consulted and carried on at the same Time, when those entrusted with the Administration of it were consulting and pursuing their own.

Hence grew the Distinction between Arbitrary and Free Governments: Not that more or less Power was vested in the one than in the other; nor that either of them lay under less or more Obligations, in Justice, to protect their Subjects, and study their Ease, Prosperity and Security, and to watch for the same. But the Power and Sovereignty of Magistrates in free Countries was so qualified, and so divided into different Channels, and committed to the Direction of so many different Men, with different Interests and Views, that the Majority of them could seldom or never find their Account in betraying their Trust in fundamental Instances. Their Emulation, Envy, Fear, or Interest, always made them Spies and Checks upon one another. By all which Means, the People have often come at the Heads of those who forfeited their Heads, by betraying the People.

In despotick Governments, Things went far otherwise, those Governments having been framed otherwise; if the same could be called Governments, where the Rules of publick Power were dictated by private and lawless Lust; where Folly and Madness often swayed the Scepter, and blind Rage weilded the Sword.

The whole Wealth of the State, with its Civil or Military Power, being in the Prince, the People could have no Remedy but Death and Patience, while he oppressed them by the Lump, and butchered them by Thousands: Unless perhaps the Ambition or personal Resentments of some of the Instruments of his Tyranny procured a Revolt, which rarely mended their Condition.

The only Secret therefore in forming a Free Government, is to make the Interests of the Governors and of the Governed the same, as far as human Policy can contrive. Liberty cannot be preserved any other Way. Men have long found, from the Weakness and Depravity of themselves and one another, that most Men will act for Interest against Duty, as often as they dare. So that to engage them to their Duty, Interest must be linked to the Observance of it, and Danger to the Breach of it. Personal Advantages and Security, must be the Rewards of Duty and Obedience; and Disgrace, Torture, and Death, the Punishment of Treachery and Corruption.

Human Wisdom has yet found out but one certain Expedient to effect this; and that is, to have the Concerns of all directed by all, as far as possibly can be: And where the Persons interested are too numerous, or live too distant to meet together on all Emergencies, they must moderate Necessity by Prudence, and act by Deputies whose Interest is the same with their own, and whose Property is so intermingled with theirs, and so engaged upon the same Bottom, that Principals and Deputies must stand and fall together. When the Deputies thus act for their own Interest, by acting for the Interest of their Principals; when they can make no Law but what they themselves, and their Posterity, must be subject to; when they can give no Money, but what they must pay their Share of; when they can do no Mischief, but what must fall upon their own Heads in common with their Countrymen; their Principals may then expect good Laws, little Mischief, and much Frugality.

Here therefore lies the great Point of Nicety and Care, in forming the Constitution, that the Persons entrusted and representing, shall either never have an Interest detached from the Persons entrusting and represented, or never the Means to pursue it. Now to compass this great Point effectually, no other Way is left, but one of these two, or rather both; namely, to make the Deputies so numerous, that there may be no Possibility of corrupting the Majority; or, by changing them so often, that there is no sufficient Time to corrupt them, and to carry the Ends of that Corruption. The People may be very sure, that the major Part of their Deputies being honest, will keep the rest so; and that they will all be honest, when they have no Temptations to be Knaves . . .

An Enquiry into the Nature and Extent of Liberty; with its Loveliness and Advantages, and the vile Effects of Slavery.

Sir,

I Have shewn in a late Paper, wherein consists the Difference between Free and Arbitrary Governments, as to their Frame and Constitution; and in this and the following, I shall shew their different Spirit and Effects. But first I will shew wherein Liberty itself consists.

By Liberty, I understand the Power which every Man has over his own Actions, and his Right to enjoy the Fruits of his Labour, Art, and Industry, as far as by it he hurts not the Society, or any Members of it, by taking from any Member, or by hindering him from enjoying what he himself enjoys. The Fruits of a Man's honest Industry are the just Rewards of it, ascertained to him by natural and eternal Equity, as is his Title to use them in the Manner which he thinks fit: And thus, with the above Limitations, every Man is sole Lord and Arbiter of his own private Actions and Property — A Character of which no Man living can divest him but by Usurpation, or his own Consent.

The entering into political Society, is so far from a Departure from this natural Right, that to preserve it, was the sole Reason why Men did so; and mutual Protection and Assistance is the only reasonable Purpose of all reasonable Societies. To make such Protection practicable, Magistracy was formed, with Power to defend the Innocent from Violence, and to punish those that offered it; nor can there be any other Pretence for Magistracy in the World. In order to this good End, the Magistrate is intrusted with conducting and applying the united Force of the Community; and with exacting such a Share of every Man's Property, as is necessary to preserve the Whole, and to defend every Man and his Property from foreign and domestick Injuries. These are Boundaries of the Power of the Magistrate, who deserts his Function whenever he breaks them. By the Laws of Society, he is more limited and restrained than any Man amongst them; since, while they

are absolutely free in all their Actions, which purely concern themselves; all his Actions, as a publick Person, being for the sake of the Society, must refer to it, and answer the Ends of it.

It is a mistaken Notion in Government, that the Interest of the Majority is only to be consulted, since in Society every Man has a Right to every Man's Assistance in the Enjoyment and Defence of his private Property; otherwise the greater Number may fell the lesser, and divide their Estates amongst themselves; and so, instead of a Society, where all peaceable Men are protected, become a Conspiracy of the Many against the Minority. With as much Equity may one Man wantonly dispose of all, and Violence may be sanctified by mere Power.

And it is as foolish to say, that Government is concerned to meddle with the private Thoughts and Actions of Men, while they injure neither the Society, or any of its Members. Every Man is, in Nature and Reason, the Judge and Disposer of his own domestick Affairs; and, according to the Rules of Religion and Equity, every Man must carry his own Conscience. So that neither has the Magistrate a Right to direct the private Behaviour of Men; nor has the Magistrate, or any Body else, any manner of Power to model People's Speculations, no more than their Dreams. Government being intended to protect Men from the Injuries of one another, and not to direct them in their own Affairs, in which no one is interested but themselves; it is plain, that their Thoughts and domestick Concerns are exempted intirely from its Jurisdiction: In Truth, Men's Thoughts are not subject to their own Jurisdiction.

Idiots and Lunaticks indeed, who cannot take Care of themselves, must be taken Care of by others: But whilst Men have their five Senses, I cannot see what the Magistrate has to do with Actions by which the Society cannot be affected; and where he meddles with such, he meddles impertinently or tyrannically . . .

True and impartial Liberty is therefore the Right of every Man to pursue the natural, reasonable, and religious Dictates of his own Mind; to think what he will, and act as he thinks, provided he acts not to the Prejudice of another; to spend his own Money himself, and lay out the Produce of his Labour his own Way; and to labour for his own Pleasure and Profit, and not for others who are idle, and would live and riot by pillaging and oppressing him, and those that are like him.

So that Civil Government is only a partial Restraint put by the Laws of Agreement and Society upon natural and absolute Liberty, which might otherwise grow licentious: And Tyranny is an unlimited Restraint put upon natural Liberty, by the Will of one or a few. Magistracy, amongst a free People, is the Exercise of Power for the sake of the People; and Tyrants abuse the People, for the sake of Power. Free Government is the protecting the People in their Liberties by stated Rules; Tyranny is a brutish Struggle for unlimited Liberty to one or a few, who would rob all others of their Liberty, and act by no Rule but lawless Lust.

So much for an Idea of Civil Liberty. I will now add a Word or two, to shew how much it is the Delight and Passion of Mankind; and then shew its Advantages.

The Love of Liberty is an Appetite so strongly implanted in the Nature of all living Creatures, that even the Appetite of Self-preservation, which is allowed to be the strongest, seems to be contained in it; since by the Means of Liberty, they enjoy the Means of preserving themselves, and of satisfying their Desires in the Manner which they themselves chuse and like best. Many Animals can never be tamed, but feel the Bitterness of Restraint in the midst of the kindest Usage; and rather than bear it, grieve or starve themselves to Death; and some beat out their Brains against their Prisons.

Where Liberty is lost, Life grows precarious, always miserable, often intolerable. Liberty is, to live upon one's own Terms; Slavery is, to live at the mere Mercy of another; and a Life of Slavery is to those who can bear it, a continual State of Uncertainty and Wretchedness, often an Apprehension of Violence, often the lingring Dread of a violent Death; But by others, when no other Remedy is to be had, Death is reckoned a good one. And thus to many Men, and to many other Creatures as well as Men, the Love of Liberty is beyond the Love of Life.

This Passion for Liberty in Men, and their Possession of it, is of that Efficacy and Importance, that it seems the Parent of all the Virtues: And therefore, in free Countries there seems to be another Species of Mankind, than is to be found under Tyrants. . .

SUGGESTIONS FOR FURTHER READING

Zera Fink, *The Classical Republicans*, Northwestern University Press, Evanston, 1945.

Crawford B. MacPherson, *The Political Theory of Possessive Individualism*, Oxford University Press, New York, 1962. *The Real World of Democracy*, Oxford University Press, New York, 1970.

Lee McDonald, *Western Political Theory: the Modern Age*, Harcourt, Brace & World, New York, 1962.

Caroline Robbins, *The Eighteenth-Century Commonwealthman*, Atheneum, New York, 1959.

Quentin Skinner, "History and Ideology in the English Revolution," *Historical Journal*, 8 (1965).

Leo Strauss, *The Political Philosophy of Hobbes*, University of Chicago Press, Chicago, 1939: *Natural Right and History*, University of Chicago Press, Chicago, 1939.

A.S.P. Woodhouse (ed.), *Puritanism and Liberty*, University of Chicago Press, Chicago, 1938.

AMERICAN CULTURE AND THE REVOLUTION

Chapter 4   1763-1777

American culture originated in an interaction between the traditions that the colonists brought with them and their experiences in creating new communities in the wilderness during a period when Europe itself was undergoing the stress of adapting to great changes. All three elements — the values and models brought from Europe, the constant necessity of adapting these to a new environment, and the intellectual and material developments throughout the western world — made their impress upon American society. As we have seen, the common man's access to land in the New World worked to undermine his sense of community as well as the values of a traditional hierarchical social structure. This process was in turn fortified by the radicalism of Enlightenment thought which attacked the philosophical underpinnings of status, hereditary privileges, authoritarian institutions, and prescriptive rights. Because the American colonies were physically separated from England, the significant differences which had developed between the two societies were not brought out into the open until an issue arose demanding a response from both. Such an issue developed at the conclusion of the French and Indian War in 1763, when English statesmen, burdened with a monumental national debt, attempted to raise money in the colonies by use of the sovereign authority of Parliament. Englishmen had always assumed that Parliament possessed an absolute sovereignty over the colonies, but they had rarely asserted it. The colonial spokesmen, working under different assumptions, were outraged and expressed their opposition in terms of their American experiences.

In England, personal liberties were but a part of a complex system of rights and privileges which included a respect for hereditary power, a reverence for the historic origins of English law, and an acceptance of a hierarchy of ranks. Although English theorists talked about all government resting on the consent of the governed, few Englishmen had the right to vote, much less hold office. Consent of the governed was translated into "tacit consent," and the right of representation into "virtual representation" — vague, ill-defined phrases which permitted Englishmen to talk about rights which they did not actually possess, at least not in the active, functioning sense that Americans had given to them. English usages had been the origin of American liberties, but, in America, theories of political rights had been consistently used to expand political participation. In a flood of pamphlets and legislative resolutions in the 1760's, Americans made explicit these differences. Raising fundamental questions about their status in the empire, American writers moved on to consider the nature of all civil power. As the English rebuttals were quick to point out, the colonists based their contentions upon abstract principles, not charter provisions and constitutional precedents. Try as they might, however, the English government could not contain the dispute within the limits of legal and historical arguments, for their American antagonists insisted upon talking about inalienable rights and laws of nature.

Abstract as American principles appeared in English eyes, they were in fact based upon actual colonial practices. Since all of the colonies had to build new institutions, the political aspirations of common men were much more easily fulfilled than they could be in England where an old system stood in the way. A colonial elite exercised an inordinate share of power, but, in contrast to England, the upper class in America had to accommodate the interests and ambitions of their large constituency. In their campaign against parliamentary taxation, the upper class leaders cultivated the support of laboring men, small farmers, mechanics and tradesmen with the inevitable consequence of reducing the social distance between these groups. The pamphlet warfare of the 1760's and 1770's also played a part in blurring class distinctions with its appeal to what Americans had in common. Initially, American writers attacked the new colonial policies for being contrary to the rights of Englishmen, but when it became apparent that the colonists' opinions were not shared by the English jurists and parliamentary leaders who alone were capable of defining Englishmen's rights, American pamphleteers claimed that Parliament's policies violated those universal and inalienable rights which were rooted in the nature of man rather than the history of a particular nation. It took a decade of agitation before the colonists had a clear sense of their position, but once they grasped it, the colonial leaders were able to count on widespread support for their revolutionary rationale because it rested upon a set of political and social convictions that had grown slowly throughout the colonial period. Wealthy colonial leaders and ordinary people alike stood to gain from an assertion of their rights.

By 1763 the thirteen continental colonies had acquired a maturity which made a determined stand against British authority possible. The colonies were self-sufficient and prosperous. Each had one or more ports through which they could trade in a thriving commerce that laced Tenerife, Kingston, St. Pierre, Glasgow, Charleston, Philadelphia, London, and Liverpool together into one mercantile system. There were several cosmopolitan centers in the colonies where legislatures sat, business was transacted, and the learned professions pursued. Each colony had assiduously acquired all but perfect autonomy in local matters. Each had produced an impressive leadership group — men who were gifted parliamentarians, accomplished polemicists, and effective political in-fighters.

The colonies were socially mature too. Their taxes and tithes supported an educated clergy, judicial systems, schools, and charitable institutions. Colonial educational aspirations nourished by a prosperous economy led to the founding of new colleges. By 1766, seven of the thirteen colonies had places for educating laymen and training clergymen. Even more indicative of their social maturity, the colonists were learning to live with religious pluralism. Jewish and Catholic congregations were tolerated, and the number of different Protestant churches and sects within most colonies was making total religious disestablishment a reasonable possibility. Pennsylvania had gone beyond official tolerance to the guarantee of full religious liberty for her diverse citizenry, and her remarkable success offered the kind of utilitarian argument that Americans found most persuasive. Although the Great Awakening had stirred up conflict in the 1740's, when the boiling emotions from this series of revivals had simmered down the colonists were able to accept dissent even within their own denominations.

This maturity drew the American colonies into the larger intellectual community of Western Europe. European learned societies formed in response to the growing interest in science had a fair representation of members from America. In Benjamin Franklin the colonists had a major contributor to the scientific achievements of the century. A common interest in collecting and classifying specimens of plant and animal life had led to dozens of correspondences among gifted amateurs on both sides of the Atlantic. The diverse ethnic strains in the colonial population were reflected in international connections which opened Americans to friendships, scholarly efforts, and trade relations difficult to confine to England's concept of her colonies' proper role in the world.

What all this added up to was a society with the moral, material, and intellectual resources to wage a successful war for independence if pushed that far. Without this inner assurance of competence, it is extremely doubtful that the colonial leaders would have openly challenged the world's greatest power. Unfortunately, the English statesmen who initiated the policies that began the decade of colonial agitation were completely out of touch with the societies that had come to maturity in Britain's North American empire. They made little effort to understand when challenged to do so. What they had learned from the recent fighting of the French and Indian War was that the American colonists flouted the Navigation Laws, frustrated military operations, traded with the enemy in the West Indies, and enjoyed a prosperity that was virtually tax-free. Thus enlightened, a succession of English ministers tried to tap the potential of the colonies in order to increase royal revenues. The effort, as we know, boomeranged because the colonists retaliated with their own campaign to hold fast to the freedom they had so long enjoyed.

After the Revolution had been won, these shared values that crystallized under the pressure of conflict with Great Britain formed the ideological basis of the new American nation. The individualism, egalitarianism, and self-determination which had already developed in the colonies were now brought together into an integrated theory. Fundamental to this new ideology was the conviction that man — despite his many imperfections — was capable of running his own affairs, choosing his own form of government, determining his own religious faith, and making his own personal decisions. From this it followed that men could live peacefully with minimal social restraint. Government existed not to restrain, educate, and direct the members of society, but rather to preserve their natural rights. All having an equal stake in seeing that government fulfills these tasks should, therefore, have equal access to political rights and privileges. This liberal consensus, as historians call it, unified the colonists and provided enough cohesion to sustain the loose confederation of states through the war. The American's distrust of government power, so evident in their revolutionary pamphlets, underlay their preference for written constitutions. By carefully defining the rights of citizens and the limits of government the drafters of the state constitutions sought to protect the people from the arbitrary abuse of power which they singled out as the cause of their break with England. The absence of external control

which had characterized colonial history predisposed
Americans, once independent, to favor local autonomy,
and this attitude in turn determined the looseness of
the states' union under the Articles of Confederation.

From the first decade when the colonies formed
an independent confederation of states down to the
present, the Declaration of Independence has acted
as the single most important statement of American
political faith. As a nation of immigrants with diverse
religious and ethnic backgrounds, the United States
has needed a tie to bind its parts together and has
found one in its revolutionary rhetoric. In this fact we
have one of the most distinguishing characteristics of
America. Unfortunately it has also been a persistent
source of tension. Where other people are united by
a common birthplace, a common language, the same
ruler, or one religion, Americans had to create their
national unity. The creed of the Declaration of Independence was universal in its application and well-
suited to a country growing through immigration.
The difficulties arose in hitching America's identity to
the twin stars of freedom and equality. Making a
common commitment to the political ideals of the
Revolution their unifier meant that Americans had to
work hard for social cohesion by living up to a most
exacting set of principles. The implications of this were
obvious at once. When Northerners abolished slavery in
the 1780's and Southerners joined anti-slavery societies,
they were acknowledging the incongruity of American
ideals and the widespread use of slave labor in America.
John Adams' wife suggested that the Continental Congress
give some thought to sharing men's freedoms with
women, and religious dissenters harassed by laws favoring
established churches were quick to see the application
of political principles to religious issues. Every denial
of equality, every impediment in the pursuit of happiness
became an indictment of American good faith. Thus
the Declaration of Independence, initially the eloquent
expression of American political aspirations, became a
factor in the nation's development, a rallying point for
a country in search of national unity and a demanding
standard to live up to.

As the pamphlets of the period show, the colonists did not have a full-blown theory of the rights of man when they began protesting British policies. They formed their rationale for liberty and government as the conflict with England developed. First they tried to protect certain practices on utilitarian grounds, enlisting the aid of English merchants to convince Parliament of the foolishness of taxing a trade beneficial to both sides. The famous Stamp Act was repealed because of colonial and domestic pressure, but Parliament's determination to enforce its new statutes led to a succession of additional grievances — customs inspections without due regard for individual property rights, high-handed legal proceedings, legislation which smacked of discriminatory restrictions on colonial freedoms, and threats to subordinate the powerful colonial legislatures to the executive authority of the governors. These measures prompted appeals to the rights which the colonists were supposed to enjoy as English citizens, then to the principles which they believed underlay traditional English concepts of liberty under the law, and only as a last resort to an alternative theory of government.

In the first two readings the struggle over conflicting views of parliamentary sovereignty is explored through an exchange between Rhode Island's Governor Stephen Hopkins (1707–1785) and Martin Howard, Jr. (d. 1781), a prominent lawyer of Newport. Rhode Island and Connecticut were the only two colonies with charters permitting elected governors, and hence Hopkins represented the popular colonial position in his *The Rights of Colonies Examined*. His spirited defense of liberty raised the familiar cry that historical rights and privileges were being flouted by the new Parliamentary acts. At the time Hopkins wrote, the Stamp Act had not yet been passed, and he was reacting to the Revenue Act of 1764 which provided for more efficient enforcement of the navigation system and laid a heavy duty on the importation of foreign molasses. Hopkins' suggestion that the colonists possessed rights independent of those conferred upon them by charter or Parliamentary law prompted Martin

Howard to examine the implications of this position. Like many other colonial conservatives, Howard believed that a vigorous assertion of Parliament's sovereignty would not only strengthen Great Britain's control over the colonies, but could also check the lamentable levelling tendencies in the colonies. In his *Letter from a Gentleman at Halifax*, Howard laid bare the dilemma for all who protested the new measures: if the colonists enjoyed rights stemming from the English constitution and their English charters, upon what ground could they protest laws coming from that same authority?

Stephen Hopkins: *The rights of colonies examined (1764)*

> "Mid the low murmurs of submissive fear
> And mingled rage, my Hampden rais'd his voice,
> And to the laws appeal'd; —— "

Liberty is the greatest blessing that men enjoy, and slavery the heaviest curse that human nature is capable of. — This being so, makes it a matter of the utmost importance to men, which of the two shall be their portion. Absolute liberty is, perhaps, incompatible with any kind of government. — The safety resulting from society, and the advantage of just and equal laws, hath caused men to forego some part of their natural liberty, and submit to government. This appears to be the most rational account of its beginning; although, it must be confessed, mankind have by no means been agreed about it. Some have found its origin in the divine appointment; others have thought it took its rise from power; enthusiasts have dreamed that dominion was founded in grace.

Leaving these points to be settled by the descendants of Filmer, Cromwell and Venner, we will consider the British constitution, as it at present stands, on revolution principles; and from thence endeavor to find

John Russell Bartlett (ed.), *Records of the Colony of Rhode Island and Providence Plantations*, A. C. Greene and Brothers, Providence, 1861, *VI*, 416–26.

the measure of the magistrate's power and the people's obedience.

This glorious constitution, the best that ever existed among men, will be confessed by all, to be founded by compact, and established by consent of the people. By this most beneficent compact, British subjects are to be governed only agreeably to laws to which themselves have some way consented; and are not to be compelled to part with their property, but as it is called for by the authority of such laws. The former, is truly liberty; the latter, is really to be possessed of property, and to have something that may be called one's own.

On the contrary, those who are governed at the will of another, or of others, and whose property may be taken from them by taxes, or otherwise, without their own consent, and against their will, are in the miserable condition of slaves. "For liberty solely consists in an independency upon the will of another; and by the name of slave, we understand a man who can neither dispose of his person or goods, but enjoys all at the will of his master," says Sidney, on government. These things premised, whether the British American colonies, on the continent, are justly entitled to like privileges and freedom as their fellow subjects in Great Britain are, shall be the chief point examined.

In discussing this question, we shall make the colonies in New England, with whose rights we are best acquainted, the rule of our reasoning; not in the least doubting but all the others are justly entitled to like rights with them.

New England was first planted by adventurers, who left England, their native country, by permission of King Charles the First; and, at their own expense, transported themselves to America, with great risk and difficulty settled among savages, and in a very surprising manner formed new colonies in the wilderness. Before their departure, the terms of their freedom, and the relation they should stand in to the mother country, in their emigrant state, were fully settled; they were to remain subject to the King, and dependent on the kingdom of Great Britain. In return, they were to receive protection, and enjoy all the rights and privileges of free-born Englishmen.

This is abundantly proved by the charter given to the Massachusetts colony, while they were still in England, and which they received and brought over with them, as the authentic evidence of the conditions they removed upon. The colonies of Connecticut and Rhode Island, also, afterwards obtained charters from the crown, granting them the like ample privileges.

By all these charters, it is in the most express and solemn manner granted, that these adventurers, and their children after them for ever, should have and enjoy all the freedom and liberty that the subjects in England enjoy; that they might make laws for their own government, suitable to their circumstances; not repugnant to, but as near as might be, agreeably to the laws of England; that they might purchase lands, acquire goods, and use trade for their advantage, and have an absolute property in whatever they justly acquired. These, with many other gracious privileges, were granted them by several kings . . .

There is not any thing new or extraordinary in these rights granted to the British colonies; the colonies from all countries, at all times, have enjoyed equal freedom with the mother state. Indeed, there would be found very few people in the world, willing to leave their native country, and go through the fatigue and hardship of planting in a new uncultivated one, for the sake of losing their freedom. They who settle new countries, must be poor; and, in course, ought to be free. Advantages, pecuniary or agreeable, are not on the side of emigrants; and surely they must have something in their stead . . .

If it were possible a doubt could yet remain, in the most unbelieving mind, that these British colonies are not every way justly and fully entitled to equal liberty and freedom with their fellow subjects in Europe, we might show, that the Parliament of Great Britain, have always understood their rights in the same light.

By an act passed in the thirteenth year of the reign of His late Majesty King George the Second, entitled An act for naturalizing foreign Protestants, &c. and by another act passed in the twentieth year of the same reign, for nearly the same purposes, by both which it is enacted and ordained, "that all foreign Protestants, who had inhabited, and resided for the space of seven years, or more, in any of His Majesty's colonies, in America," might, on the conditions therein mentioned, be naturalized, and thereupon should "be deemed, adjudged and taken to be His Majesty's natural born subjects of the kingdom of Great Britain, to all intents, constructions and purposes, as if they, and every one of them, had been, or were born within the same."

No reasonable man will here suppose the Parliament intended by these acts to put foreigners, who had been in the colonies only seven years, in a better condition than those who had been born in them, or had removed from Britain thither, but only to put these foreigners on an equality with them; and to do this, they are obliged to give them all the rights of natural born subjects of Great Britain.

From what hath been shown, it will appear beyond a doubt, that the British subjects in America, have equal rights with those in Britain; that they do not hold those rights as a privilege granted them, nor enjoy them as a grace and favor bestowed; but possess them as an inherent indefeasible right; as they, and their ancestors, were free-born subjects, justly and naturally entitled to all the rights and advantages of the British constitution.

And the British legislative and executive powers have considered the colonies as possessed of these rights, and have always heretofore, in the most tender and parental manner, treated them as their dependent, though free, condition required. The protection promised on the part of the crown, with cheerfulness and great gratitude we acknowledge, hath at all times been given to the colonies. The dependence of the colonies to Great Britain, hath been fully testified by a constant and ready obedience to all the commands of His present Majesty, and his royal predecessors; both men and money having been raised in them at all times when called for, with as much alacrity and in as large proportions as hath been done in Great Britain, the ability of each considered.

It must also be confessed with thankfulness, that the first adventurers and their successors, for one hundred and thirty years, have fully enjoyed all the freedoms and immunities promised on their first removal from England. But here the scene seems to be unhappily changing.

The British ministry, whether induced by a jealousy of the colonies, by false informations, or by some alteration in the system of political government, we have no information; whatever hath been the motive, this we are sure of, the Parliament in their last session, passed an act, limiting, restricting and burdening the trade of these colonies, much more than had ever been done before; as also for greatly enlarging the power and jurisdiction of the courts of admiralty in the colonies; and also came to a resolution, that it might be necessary to establish stamp duties, and other internal taxes, to be collected within them. This act and this resolution, have caused great uneasiness and consternation among the British subjects on the continent of America; how much reason there is for it, we will endeavor, in the most modest and plain manner we can, to lay before our readers.

In the first place, let it be considered, that although each of the colonies hath a legislature within itself, to take care of its interests, and provide for its peace and internal government; yet there are many things of a more general nature, quite out of the reach of these particular legislatures, which it is necessary should be regulated, ordered and governed. One of this kind is, the commerce of the whole British empire, taken collectively, and that of each kingdom and colony in it, as it makes a part of that whole. Indeed, every thing that concerns the proper interest and fit government of the whole commonwealth, of keeping the peace, and subordination of all the parts towards the whole, and one among another, must be considered in this light. Amongst these general concerns, perhaps, money and paper credit, those grand instruments of all commerce, will be found also to have a place. These, with all other matters of a general nature, it is absolutely necessary should have a general power to direct them; some supreme and over ruling authority, with power to make laws, and form regulations for the good of all, and to compel their execution and observation. It being necessary some such general power should exist somewhere, every man of the least knowledge of the British constitution, will be naturally led to look for, and find it in the Parliament of Great Britain; that grand and august legislative body, must, from the nature of their authority, and the necessity of the thing, be justly vested with this power. Hence, it becomes the indispensable duty of every good and loyal subject, cheerfully to obey and patiently submit to all the acts, laws, orders and regulations that may be made and passed by Parliament, for directing and governing all these general matters.

Here it may be urged by many, and indeed, with great appearance of reason, that the equity, justice, and beneficence of the British constitution, will require, that the separate kingdoms and distant colonies, who are to obey and be governed by these general laws and regulations, ought to be represented, some way or other, in Parliament; at least whilst these general matters are under consideration. Whether the colonies will ever be admitted to have representatives in Parliament, — whether it be consistent with their distant and dependent state, — and whether if it were admitted, it would be to their advantage, — are questions we will pass by; and observe, that these colonies ought in justice, and for the very evident good of the whole commonwealth, to have notice of every new measure about to be pursued, and new act that is about to be passed, by which their rights, liberties, or interests will be affected; they ought to have such notice, that they may appear and be heard by their agents, by council, or written representation, or by some other equitable and effectual way . . .

Had the colonies been fully heard, before the late act had been passed, no reasonable man can suppose it ever would have passed at all, in the manner it now stands; for what good reason can possibly be given for making a law to cramp the trade and ruin the interests of many of the colonies, and at the same time, lessen in a prodigious manner the consumption of the British manufactures in them? These are certainly the effects this act must produce; a duty of three pence per gallon on foreign molasses, is well known to every man in the least acquainted with it, to be much higher than that article can possibly bear; and therefore must operate as an absolute prohibition. This will put a total stop to our exportation of lumber, horses, flour and fish, to the French and Dutch sugar colonies; and if any one supposes we may find a sufficient vent for these articles in the English islands in the West Indies, he only verifies what was just now observed, that he wants truer information. Putting an end to the importation of foreign molasses, at the same time puts an end to all the costly distilleries in these colonies, and to the rum trade to the coast of Africa, and throws it into the hands of the French. With the loss of the foreign molasses trade, the codfishery of the English, in America, must also be lost, and thrown also into the

hands of the French. That this is the real state of the whole business, is not fancy; this, nor any part of it, is not exaggeration, but a sober and melancholy truth. . .

By the same act of Parliament, the exportation of all kinds of timber, or lumber, the most natural produce of these new colonies, is greatly encumbered and uselessly embarrassed, and the shipping it to any part of Europe, except Great Britain, prohibited. This must greatly affect the linen manufactory in Ireland, as that kingdom used to receive great quantities of flax seed from America, many cargoes, being made of that and of barrel staves, were sent thither every year; but, as the staves can no longer be exported thither, the ships carrying only flax seed casks, without the staves, which used to be intermixed among them, must lose one half of their freight, which will prevent their continuing this trade, to the great injury of Ireland, and of the plantations. And what advantage is to accrue to Great Britain, by it, must be told by those who can perceive the utility of this measure.

Enlarging the power and jurisdiction of the courts of vice admiralty in the colonies, is another part of the same act, greatly and justly complained of. Courts of admiralty have long been established in most of the colonies, whose authority were circumscribed within moderate territorial jurisdictions; and these courts have always done the business necessary to be brought before such courts for trial, in the manner it ought to be done, and in a way only moderately expensive to the subjects; and if seizures were made, or informations exhibited, within reason, or contrary to law, the informer, or seizor, was left to the justice of the common law, there to pay for his folly, or suffer for his temerity.

But now, this course is quite altered; and a custom house may make a seizure in Georgia, of goods ever so legally imported, and carry the trial to Halifax, at fifteen hundred miles distance; and thither the owner must follow him to defend his property; and when he comes there, quite beyond the circle of his friends, acquaintance and correspondents, among total strangers, he must there give bond, and must find sureties to be bound with him in a large sum, before he shall be admitted to claim his own goods; when this is complied with, he hath a trial, and his goods aquitted. If the judge can be prevailed on, (which it is very well known may too easily be done,) to certify there was *only* probable cause for making the seizure, the unhappy owner shall not maintain any action against the illegal seizor, for damages, or obtain any other satisfaction; but he may return to Georgia quite ruined, and undone, in conformity to an act of Parliament. . .

The resolution of the House of Commons, come into during the same session of Parliament, asserting their rights to establish stamp duties, and internal taxes, to be collected in the colonies without their own consent, hath much more, and for much more reason, alarmed the British subjects in America, than any thing that had ever been done before. These resolutions, carried into execution, the colonies cannot help but consider as a manifest violation of their just and long enjoyed rights. For it must be confessed by all men, that they who are taxed at pleasure by others, cannot possibly have any property, can have nothing to be called their own; they who have no property, can have no freedom, but are indeed reduced to the most abject slavery; are in a condition far worse than countries conquered and made tributary; for these have only a fixed sum to pay, which they are left to raise among themselves, in the way that they may think most equal and easy; and having paid the stipulated sum, the debt is discharged, and what is left is their own. This is much more tolerable than to be taxed at the mere will of others, without any bounds, without any stipulation and agreement, contrary to their consent, and against their will.

If we are told that those who lay these taxes upon the colonies, are men of the highest character for their wisdom, justice and integrity, and therefore cannot be supposed to deal hardly, unjustly, or unequally by any; admitting, and really believing that all this is true, it will make no alteration in the nature of the case; for one who is bound to obey the will of another, is as really a slave, though he may have a good master, as if he had a bad one. . .

Whatever burdens are laid upon the Americans, will be so much taken off the Britons; and the doing this, will soon be extremely popular; and those who put up to be members of the House of Commons, must obtain the votes of the people, by promising to take more and more of the taxes off them, by putting it on the Americans. This must assuredly be the case, and it will not be in the power even of the Parliament

to prevent it; the people's private interest will be concerned, and will govern them; they will have such, and only such representatives as will act agreeably to this their interest; and these taxes laid on Americans, will be always a part of the supply bill, in which the other branches of the legislature can make no alteration; and in truth, the subjects in the colonies will be taxed at the will and pleasure of their fellow subjects in Britain. — How equitable, and how just this may be, must be left to every impartial man to determine.

But it will be said, that the monies drawn from the colonies by duties, and by taxes, will be laid up and set apart to be used for their future defence.

This will not at all alleviate the hardship, but serves only more strongly to mark the servile state of the people. Free people have ever thought, and always will think, that the money necessary for their defence, lies safest in their own hands, until it be wanted immediately for that purpose. . .

We are not insensible, that when liberty is in danger, the liberty of complaining is dangerous; yet, a man on a wreck was never denied the liberty of roaring as loud as he could, says Dean Swift. And we believe no good reason can be given, why the colonies should not modestly and soberly inquire, what right the Parliament of Great Britain have to tax them. We know such inquiries, by a late letter writer, have been branded with the little epithet of *mushroom policy;* and he insinuates, that for the colonies to pretend to claim any privileges, will draw down the resentment of the Parliament on them. — Is the defence of liberty become so contemptible, and pleading for just rights so dangerous? Can the guardians of liberty be thus ludicrous? Can the patrons of freedom be so jealous and so severe? If the British House of Commons are rightfully possessed of a power to tax the colonies in America, this power must be vested in them in the British constitution, as they are one branch of the great legislative body of the nation; as they are the representatives of all the people in Britain, they have, beyond doubt, all the power such a representation can possibly give; yet, great as this power is, surely it cannot exceed that of their constituents. And can it possibly be shown that the people in Britain have a sovereign authority over their fellow subjects in America? Yet such is the authority that must be exercised in taking peoples' estates from them by taxes, or etherwise, without their consent. In all aids granted to the crown, by the Parliament, it is said with the greatest propriety, "We freely give unto Your Majesty;" for they give their own money, and the money of those who have entrusted them with a proper power for that purpose. But can they, with the same propriety, give away the money of the Americans, who have never given any such power? Before a thing can be justly given away, the giver must certainly have acquired a property in it; and have the people in Britain justly acquired such a property in the goods and estates of the people in these colonies, that they may give them away at pleasure?

. . . Indeed, it must be absurd to suppose, that the common people of Great Britain have a sovereign and absolute authority over their fellow subjects in America, or even any sort of power whatsoever, over them; but it will be still more absurd to suppose they can give a power to their representatives, which they have not themselves. If the House of Commons do not receive this authority from their constituents, it will be difficult to tell by what means they obtained it, except it be vested in them by mere superiority and power.

Should it be urged, that the money expended by the mother country, for the defence and protection of America, and especially during the late war, must justly entitle her to some retaliation from the colonies; and that the stamp duties and taxes, intended to be raised in them, are only designed for that equitable purpose; if we are permitted to examine how far this may rightfully vest the Parliament with the power of taxing the colonies, we shall find this claim to have no sort of equitable foundation. In many of the colonies, especially those in New England, who were planted, as is before observed, not at the charge of the crown or kingdom of England, but at the expense of the planters themselves; and were not only planted, but also defended against the savages, and other enemies, in long and cruel wars, which continued for an hundred years, almost without intermission, solely at their own charge; and in the year 1746, when the Duke D'Anville came out from France, with the most formidable French fleet that ever was in the American seas, enraged at these colonies for the loss of Louisbourg, the year before, and with orders to make an attack on them; even

in this greatest exigence, these colonies were left to the protection of Heaven and their own efforts.

These colonies having thus planted and defended themselves, and removed all enemies from their borders, were in hopes to enjoy peace, and recruit their state, much exhausted by these long struggles; but they were soon called upon to raise men, and send out to the defence of other colonies, and to make conquests for the crown; they dutifully obeyed the requisition, and with ardor entered into those services, and continued in them, until all encroachments were removed, and all Canada, and even the Havana, conquered. They most cheerfully complied with every call of the crown; they rejoiced, yea, even exulted, in the prosperity and exaltation of the British empire.

But these colonies, whose bounds were fixed, and whose borders were before cleared from enemies, by their own fortitude, and at their own expense, reaped no sort of advantage by these conquests; they are not enlarged, have not gained a single acre of land, have no part in the Indian or interior trade; the immense tracts of land subdued, and no less immense and profitable commerce acquired, all belong to Great Britain; and not the least share or portion to these colonies, though thousands of their men have lost their lives, and millions of their money have been expended in the purchase of them for great part of which we are yet in debt, and from which we shall not in many years be able to extricate ourselves. Hard will be the fate, yea, cruel the destiny, of these unhappy colonies, if the reward they are to receive for all this, is the loss of their freedom; better for them Canada still remained French; yea, far more eligible that it should remain so, than that the price of its reduction should be their slavery.

If the colonies are not taxed by Parliament, are they therefore exempted from bearing their proper share in the necessary burdens of government? This by no means follows. Do they not support a regular internal government in each colony, as expensive to the people here, as the internal government of Britain is to the people there? Have not the colonies here, at all times when called upon by the crown, raised money for the public service, done it as cheerfully as the Parliament have done on like occasions? Is not this the most easy, the most natural, and most constitutional way of raising money in the colonies? What occasion then to distrust the colonies? what necessity to fall on an individious and unconstitutional method, to compel them to do what they have ever done freely? Are not the people in the colonies as loyal and dutiful subjects as any age or nation ever produced? and are they not as useful to the kingdom, in this remote quarter of the world, as their fellow subjects are who dwell in Britain? The Parliament, it is confessed, have power to regulate the trade of the whole empire; and hath it not full power, by this means, to draw all the money and all the wealth of the colonies into the mother country, at pleasure? What motive, after all this, can remain, to induce the Parliament to abridge the privileges, and lessen the rights of the most loyal and dutiful subjects; subjects justly entitled to ample freedom, who have long enjoyed, and not abused or forfeited their liberties, who have used them to their own advantage, in dutiful subserviency to the orders and interests of Great Britain? Why should the gentle current of tranquility, that has so long run with peace through all the British states, and flowed with joy and with happiness in all her countries, be at last obstructed, be turned out of its true course, into unusual and winding channels, by which many of those states must be ruined; but none of them can possibly be made more rich or more happy.

Martin Howard, Jr.: A letter from a gentleman at Halifax (1765)

My Dear Sir,
I thank you very kindly for the pamphlets and newspapers, you was so obliging as to send me. I will, according to your request, give you a few miscellaneous strictures on that pamplet wrote by Mr. H--p---s, your governor, entitled, "The rights of colonies examined."

However disguised, polished, or softened the expression of this pamphlet may seem, yet every one must see, that its professed design is sufficiently prominent throughout, namely, to prove, that the colonies have rights independant of, and not controulable by, the authority of parliament. It is upon this dangerous and indiscreet position I shall communicate to you my real sentiments.

To suppose a design of enslaving the colonies by parliament, is too presumptuous; to propagate it in print, is perhaps dangerous. Perplexed between a de-

sire of speaking all he thinks, and the fear of saying too much, the honourable author is obliged to entrench himself in obscurity and inconsistency in several parts of his performance: I shall bring one instance.

In page eleven, he says, "It is the indispensible duty of every good and loyal subject chearfully to obey, and patiently submit to, all the laws, orders, &c. that may be passed by parliament."

I do not much admire either the spirit or composition of this sentence. Is it the duty only of good and loyal subjects to obey? Are the wicked and disloyal subjects absolved from this obligation? else why is this passage so marvellously penned: *Philolevtherus Lipsiensis* would directly pronounce this a figure in rhetorick, called nonsense.---Believe me, my friend, I did not quote this passage to shew my skill in criticism, but to point out a contradiction between it, and another passage in page twenty, which runs thus: "It must be absurd to suppose, that the common people of Great-Britain have a sovereign and absolute authority over their fellow subjects of America, or even any sort of power whatsoever over them; but it will be still more absurd to suppose, they can give a power to their representatives, which they have not themselves," &c. Here it is observable, that the first cited passage expresses a full submission to the authority of parliament; the last is as explicit a denial of that authority. The sum of his honour's argument is this: The people of Great-Britain have not any sort of power over the Americans; the house of commons have no greater authority than the people of Great-Britain, who are their constituents; *ergo*, the house of commons have not any sort of power over the Americans. This is indeed a curious invented syllogism, the sole merit of which is due to the first magistrate of an English colony.

I have endeavoured to investigate the true natural relation, if I may so speak, between colonies and their mother state, abstracted from compact or positive institution, but here I can find nothing satisfactory; till this relation is clearly defined upon a rational and natural principle, our reasoning upon the measure of the colonies obedience will be desultory and inconclusive. Every connection in life has its reciprocal duties; we know the relation between a parent and child, husband and wife, master and servant, and from thence are able to deduce their respective obligations; but we have no notices of any such precise natural relation between a mother state and its colonies, and therefore cannot reason with so much certainty upon the power of the one, or the duty of the others . . . The honourable author has not freed this subject from any of its embarrassments: Vague and diffuse talk of rights and privileges, and ringing the changes upon the words liberty and slavery, only serve to convince us, that words may affect without raising images, or affording any repose to a mind philosophically inquisitive. For my own part, I will shun the walk of metaphyticks in my enquiry, and be content to consider the colonies rights upon the footing of their charters, which are the only plain avenues, that lead to the truth of this matter.

The several New-England charters ascertain, define and limit the respective rights and privileges of each colony, and I cannot conceive how it has come to pass that the colonies now claim any other or greater rights than are therein expresly granted to them. I fancy when we speak, or think of the rights of free-born Englishmen, we confound those rights which are personal, with those which are political: There is a distinction between these, which ought always to be kept in view.

Our personal rights, comprehending those of life, liberty and estate, are secured to us by the common law, which is every subject's birthright, whether born in Great-Britain, on the ocean, or in the colonies; and it is in this sense we are said to enjoy all the rights and privileges of Englishmen. The political rights of the colonies, or the powers of government communicated to them, are more limited, and their nature, quality and extent depend altogether upon the patent or charter which first created and instituted them. As individuals, the colonists participate of every blessing the English constitution can give them: As corporations created by the crown, they are confined within the primitive views of their institution. Whether therefore their indulgence is scanty or liberal, can be no cause of complaint; for when they accepted of their charters, they tacitly submitted to the terms and conditions of them.

The colonies have no rights independant of their charters, they can claim no greater than those give them, by those the parliamentary jurisdiction over them is not taken away, neither could any grant of the king abridge that jurisdiction, because it is founded upon common law, as I shall presently shew, and was prior to any charter or grant to the colonies: Every Englishman, therefore, is subject to this jurisdiction, and it follows him wherever he goes. It is of the essence of government, that there should be a supreme head, and it would be a solecism in politicks to talk of members independant of it.

With regard to the jurisdiction of parliament, I shall endeavour to shew, that it is attached to every English subject, wherever he be: And I am led to do this from a clause in page nine of his honour's pamphlet, where he says, "That the colonies do not hold their rights, as a privilege granted them, nor enjoy them as a grace and favour bestowed; but possess them, as an inherent, indefeasible right." This postulatum cannot be true with regard to political rights, for I have already shewn, that these are derived from your charters, and are held by force of the king's grant; therefore these inherent, indefeasible rights, as his honour calls them, must be personal ones, according to the distinction already made. Permit me to say, that inherent and indefeasible as these rights may be, the jurisdiction of parliament, over every English subject, is equally as inherent and indefeasible: That both have grown out of the same stock, and that if we avail ourselves of the one, we must submit to, and acknowlege the other.

It might here be properly enough asked, Are these personal rights self-existent? Have they no original source? I answer, They are derived from the constitution of England, which is the common law; and from the same fountain is also derived the jurisdiction of parliament over us.

But to bring this argument down to the most vulgar apprehension: The common law has established it as a rule or maxim, that the plantations are bound by British acts of parliament, if particularly named: And surely no Englishman, in his senses, will deny the force of a common law maxim. One cannot but smile at the inconsistency of these inherent, indefeasible men: If one of them has a suit at law, in any part of New-England, upon a question of land property, or merchandize, he appeals to the common law, to support his claim, or defeat his adversary; and yet is so profoundly stupid as to say, that an act of parliament does not bind him; when, perhaps, the same page in a law book, which points him out a remedy for a libel, or a slap in the face, would inform him that it does.——In a word, the force of an act of parliament, over the colonies, is predicated upon the common law, the origin and basis of all those inherent rights and privileges which constitute the boast and felicity of a Briton.

Can we claim the common law as an inheritance, and at the same time be at liberty to adopt one part of it, and reject the other? Indeed we cannot: The common law, pure and indivisible in its nature and essence, cleaves to us during our lives, and follows us from Nova Zembla to Cape Horn: And therefore, as the jurisdiction of parliament arises out of, and is supported by it, we may as well renounce our allegiance, or change our nature, as to be exempt from the jurisdiction of parliament: Hence, it is plain to me, that in denying this jurisdiction, we at the same time, take leave of the common law, and thereby, with equal temerity and folly, strip ourselves of every blessing we enjoy as Englishmen: A flagrant proof this, that shallow draughts in politicks and legislation confound and distract us, and that an extravagant zeal often defeats its own purposes.

I am aware that the foregoing reasoning will be opposed by the maxim, "That no Englishman can be taxed but by his own consent, or by representatives."

It is this dry maxim, taken in a literal sense, and ill understood, that, like the song of Lillibullero, has made all the mischief in the colonies: And upon this, the partizans of the colonies rights chiefly rest their cause. I don't despair, however, of convincing you, that this maxim affords but little support to their argument, when rightly examined and explained.

It is the opinion of the house of commons, and may be considered as a law of parliament, that they are the representatives of every British subject, wheresoever he be. In this view of the matter then, the aforegoing maxim is fully vindicated in practice, and the whole benefit of it, in substance and effect, extended and applied to the colonies. Indeed the maxim must be considered in this latitude, for in a literal sense or construction it ever was, and ever will be, impracticable. Let me ask, is the isle of Man, Jersey, or Guernsey, represented? What is the value or amount of each man's representation in the kingdom of Scotland, which contains near two millions of people, and yet not more than three thousand have votes in the elec-

tion of members of parliament? But to shew still further, that, in fact and reality, this right of representation is not of that consequence it is generally thought to be, let us take into the argument the moneyed interest of Britain, which, though immensely great, has no share in this representation; a worthless freeholder of forty shillings *per annum* can vote for a member of parliament, whereas a merchant, tho' worth one hundred thousand pounds sterling, if it consist only in personal effects, has no vote at all: But yet let no one suppose that the interest of the latter is not equally the object of parliamentary attention with the former.——Let me add one example more: Copyholders in England of one thousand pounds sterling *per annum*, whose estates in land are nominally, but not intrinsically, inferior to a freehold, cannot, by law, vote for members of parliament; yet we never hear that these people "murmur with submissive fear, and mingled rage:" They don't set up their private humour against the constitution of their country, but submit with chearfulness to those forms of government which providence, in its goodness, has placed them under.

Suppose that this Utopian privilege of representation should take place, I question if it would answer any other purpose but to bring an expence upon the colonies, unless you can suppose that a few American members could bias the deliberations of the whole British legislature. In short, this right of representation is but a phantom, and, if possessed in its full extent, would be of no real advantage to the colonies; they would, like Ixion, embrace a cloud in the shape of Juno.

In addition to this head, I could further urge the danger of innovations; every change in a constitution, in some degree, weakens its original frame; and hence it is that legislators and statesmen are cautious in admitting them: The goodly building of the British constitution will be best secured and perpetuated by adhering to its original principles. Parliaments are not of yesterday, they are as antient as our Saxon ancestors. Attendance in parliament was originally a duty arising from a tenure of lands, and grew out of the feudal system; so that the privilege of fitting in it, is territorial, and confined to Britain only. Why should the beauty and symmetry of this body be destroyed, and its purity defiled, by the unnatural mixture of representatives from every part of the British dominions . . . The freedom and happiness of every British subject depends, not upon his share in elections, but upon the sense and virtue of the British parliament, and these depend reciprocally upon the sense and virtue of the whole nation. When virtue and honour are no more, the lovely frame of our constitution will be dissolved. Britain may one day be what Athens and Rome now are; but may heaven long protract the hour!

The jurisdiction of parliament being established, it will follow, that this jurisdiction cannot be apportioned; it is transcendant and entire, and may levy internal taxes as well as regulate trade; there is no essential difference in the rights: A stamp duty is confessedly the most reasonable and equitable that can be devised, yet very far am I from desiring to see it established among us, but I fear the shaft is sped, and it is now too late to prevent the blow . . .

Enlarging the power of the court of admiralty, is much complain'd of by the honourable author. I shall open my mind to you freely on this head.

It is notorious, that smuggling, which an eminent writer calls a crime against the law of nature, had well nigh become established in some of the colonies. Acts of parliament had been uniformly dispensed with by those whose duty it was to execute them; corruption, raised upon the ruins of duty and virtue, had almost grown into a system; courts of admiralty, confined within small territorial jurisdictions, became subject to mercantile influence; and the king's revenue shamefully sacrificed to the venality and perfidiousness of courts and officers. — If, my friend, customs are due to the crown; if illicit commerce is to be put an end to, as ruinous to the welfare of the nation: — If, by reason of the interested views of traders, and the connivance of courts and custom-house officers, these ends could not be compassed or obtained in the common and ordinary way; tell me, what could the government do, but to apply a remedy desperate as the disease: There is, I own, a severity in the method of prosecution, in the new established court of admiralty, under Doctor Spry, here; but it is a severity we have brought upon ourselves. When every mild expedient, to stop the atrocious and infamous practice of smuggling, has been try'd in vain, the government is justifiable in making laws against it, even like those of Draco, which were

written in blood. The new instituted court of admiralty, and the power given to the seizer, are doubtlese intended to make us more circumspect in our trade, and to confine the merchant, from motives of fear and dread, within the limits of a fair commerce. "The English constrain the merchant, but it is in favour of commerce," says the admired Secondat. This is the spirit of the new regulations, both with regard to the employing of cutters, and the enlarged power of the admiralty; and both measures are justifiable upon the same principles, as is the late act for preventing murder, which executes and dissects the murderer at surgeons-hall in twenty-four hours after conviction.

But notwithstanding the severity of this act, let me add, that no harm can accrue to the honest and fair trader, so long as the crown fills the admiralty department with an upright judge. . .

I am not enough skilled in trade to know whether the act, so much complained of, will do most good or most harm; and I with others were as diffident of their knowledge in this particular. To comprehend the general trade of the British nation, much exceeds the capacity of any one man in America, how great soever he be. Trade is a vast, complicated system, and requires such a depth of genius, and extent of knowledge, to understand it, that little minds, attached to their own sordid interest, and long used to the greatest licentiousnes in trade, are, and must be, very incompetent judges of it. Sir Andrew Freeport is no inhabitant of Rhode-Island colony. For my own part, I am still willing to leave management of trade with that people, who, according to the same admired author just quoted, "know better than any people upon earth, how to value at the same time these three great advantages, religion, commerce, and liberty."

Here I would just observe, that, from the intelligence I have gained, the beloved article of melasses is now plentier and cheaper, in all the New-England colonies, than when it was avowedly smuggled; and so far is the linen manufacture of Ireland from being ruined, as his honour intimates, that never was a greater demand for flax-feed than during the last fall, notwithstanding the clause in the act relating to lumber. How senseless is it to imagine that the prohibiting a few dunnage staves to be carried to Ireland, will ruin the manufactures of that kingdom.

Believe me, my Friend, it gives me great pain to see so much ingratitude in the colonies to the mother country, whose arms and money so lately rescued them from a French government. I have been told, that some have gone so far as to say, that they would, as things are, prefer such a government to an English one. — Heaven knows I have but little malice in my heart, yet, for a moment, I ardently wish that these spurious, unworthy sons of Britain could feel the iron rod of a Spanish inquisitor, or a French farmer of the revenue; it would indeed be a punishment suited to their ingratitude. Here I cannot but call to mind the adder in one of the fables of Pilpay, which was preparing to sting the generous traveller who had just rescued him from the flames.

You'l easily perceive, that what I have said is upon the general design of his honour's pamphlet; if he had divided his argument with any precision, I would have followed him with somewhat more of method; The dispute between Great-Britain and the colonies consists of two parts; first, the jurisdiction of parliament, — and, secondly, the exercise of that jurisdiction. His honour hath blended these together, and no where marked the division between them: The first I have principally remarked upon: As to the second, it can only turn upon the expediency or utility of those schemes which may, from time to time, be adopted by parliament, relative to the colonies. Under this head, I readily grant, they are at full liberty to remonstrate, petition, write pamphlets and newspapers, without number, to prevent any improper or unreasonable imposition: Nay, I would have them do all this with that spirit of freedom which Englishmen always have, and I hope ever will, exert; but let us not use our liberty for a cloak of maliciousness. Indeed I am very sure the loyalty of the colonies has ever been irreproachable; but from the pride of some, and the ignorance of others, the cry against mother country has spread from colony to colony; and it is to be feared, that prejudices and resentments are kindled among them which it will be difficult ever, thoroughly, to sooth or extinguish. It may become necessary for the supreme legislature of the nation to frame some code, and therein adjust the rights of the colonies, with precision and certainty, otherwise Great-Britain will always be teazed with new claims about liberty and privileges.

I have no ambition in appearing in print, yet if you think what is here thrown together is fit for the publick eye, you are at liberty to publish it: I the more chearfully acquiesce in this, because it is with real concern I have observed, that, notwithstanding the abuse poured forth in pamphlets and news-papers against the mother country, not one filial pen in America hath, as yet, been drawn, to my knowledge, in her vindication.

The second pair of readings deals with a religious issue which got sucked into the vortex of colonial discontent. For almost a century there had been talk of sending a bishop of the Church of England to the colonies. Since the episcopal structure of the Anglican church requires a bishop to officiate at the confirmation of new members and the ordination of new clergymen, the colonial church suffered from a lack of a bishop. However, outside the church, non-Anglicans viewed an American bishop as a threat to their own religious freedom. The Congregational descendents of the Puritans were particularly hostile to the prospect, but Presbyterians and Baptists were equally alarmed at the thought of introducing the ecclesiastical hierarchy of the Church of England into the colonies. The reason for this was both religious and political. Church and state were joined in all European countries because their mutually supportive roles were considered essential to maintaining religious faith and social cohesion. Religious uniformity undergirt political stability while government support for the church ensured the inculcation of morality so important in keeping order. They shared social functions. In the colonies no corresponding social unity had ever been created, and the controlling functions of church and state were viewed with suspicion. Strong government came to be associated with incursions upon individual freedom, and strong churches conjured up ecclesiastical courts which interfered with people's private lives and conferred political preference on loyal sons of the established church.

When a new effort was made in 1767 to secure a bishop for the colonial church, colonists already stirred up about the Stamp Act, the Declaratory Act, and the Townshend Acts were quick to resent it. The first reading of this section is from Thomas Bradbury Chandler (1726-1790) whose *Appeal to the Public in behalf of the Church of England in America* triggered off a vigorous newspaper campaign attack on the pretensions of the Church of England. Regular columns were started in Boston, Philadelphia, and New York. The next reading presents extracts from *The American Whig,* which appeared in the *New York Gazette.* William

Livingston (1723-1790), the author, was a well-known colonial writer and an active New York political figure. He had long made the cause of religious liberty his own, and drew upon the writings of Trenchard and Gordon and the English Dissenters who suffered under civil disabilities because they were not members of the Church of England. This exchange between Chandler and Livingston shows how a variety of different events and interests were gradually interwoven into a larger attack upon the political and social ideals which Great Britain represented. Taxes on molasses and tea affected a relatively small portion of the population, but the creation of a strong imperial government in the colonies threatened a diverse range of colonial concerns.

Thomas Bradbury Chandler: An appeal to the public in behalf of the Church of England in America (1767)

In Order to judge properly of the Subject before us, it is necessary to premise, and it should be well considered, that the Church of England is *Episcopal,* and consequently holds the Necessity of Bishops to govern the Church, and to confer Ecclesiastical Powers upon others. Of this there can be no Dispute, since many of her public Offices, and indeed the whole System of her Conduct with Regard to the Clergy is founded on this Principle. . .

And her Practice of admitting none to officiate as Clergymen, who have not been ordained by Bishops, is a Proof, that she esteems every other Ordination to be, at least, irregular and defective. . .

It is an essential Doctrine of the Church of England, that none can have any Authority in the Christian Church, but those who derive it from Christ, either *mediately* or *immediately* . . . As Christ is the great Founder of the Church, so he is the only Fountain of Ecclesiastical Authority. Whatever general Laws he was pleased to injoin, must be of indispensible Obligation to all his Followers. . .

Our present Inquiry therefore, leads us to the Consideration of those Powers only, which, being inseparable from the Office, and peculiar to it, all Bishops, as such, are equally possessed of, and without which they would cease to be Bishops: and these will be found to be the Powers of *Government, Ordination,* and *Confirmation.*

The Power or Right of Government is necessarily included in the Superiority of their Office. For in every Society, where there is a Subordination of Offices, that which constitutes the highest Office is the legal Possession of the highest Power; and the superintending and governing Power, being superior to all others, must of Consequence belong to the highest Office. In the Christian Church, the Apostles were invested with this Power by Christ — as it was intended for perpetual Use, they conveyed it to their Successors. . . And, through all the Ages of the Church, it has been transmitted down and maintained by the Episcopal Order; who, in the exercise of it, have occasionally and frequently taken the Advice of their Presbyters. The Bishop may communicate this Power, in some Degree, to the Presbyters or others as he shall think proper; but in such Cases, it must be exercised in Subordination to him, for he can never divest himself of his controlling and superintending Authority. . .

In the preceding Sections I have endeavoured to give a *Summary* of the Arguments in Favour of Episcopacy, and to prove, with all possible Brevity, that the Powers of ordaining, confirming and governing the Church, belong rightfully to Bishops, and are not to be exercised by any of an inferior Order. . . If, according to the Doctrine and Belief of the Church of England, none have a Right to govern the Church but Bishops, nor to ordain, nor to confirm; then the American Church, while without Bishops, must be without Government, without Ordination and Confirmation.

Was there no other Disadvantage attending our Want of Bishops, than that it necessarily prevents our having Confirmation administered, we should esteem it a great Grievance. For in Proportion to our Opinion of the Usefulness of this sacred Institution, must be the Hardship of being excluded from the Enjoyment of it — especially, when it is considered that our Enjoyment of it would not interfere with either the civil or religious Rights or Privileges of any. I will not, however, enlarge on this Subject, but proceed immediately to Matters of greater Consequence; and such are the Church's Want of Government and or-

daining Powers.

When it is said, that the Church of England in America, without Bishops, must be without Government, this is to be understood in a Qualified Sense. For where there is absolutely no Government at all, there can be nothing but Disorder and Confusion, without any Appearance of Regularity; which, I trust, is not yet the Case of the Church in America. . .

The State of the Church in America is, at present, really this: The Clergy are independent of each other, and have no Ecclesiastical Superiors to unite or control them; and the People are sensible of their Want of Power, and find themselves free from all Restraints of Ecclesiastical Authority. They both consider themselves as accountable to God for their religious Behaviour, and, in some Sense, to the World for the Consistency of their Characters. They have the Rubrics of the Church of England, whereby they profess to govern themselves, and to which, for the most Part, they strictly adhere, in the public Offices of Religion; and they endeavour to conform to the *Canons,* so far as the Circumstances of the Church in this country will admit of. But after all, Men's governing themselves by certain Rules and Laws, (if the Expression may be allowed of) and their being governed by others, who have a proper Authority, although according to the same Laws, are Things that will ever be found to be different. In the former Case, some Appearance of Order may be maintained, but the Body is without Strength, and liable to be destroyed by innumerable Accidents; whereas it is only in the latter Case, that Health and Vigour and Permanency can be reasonably expected.

The Government of the Church may be naturally divided into Two Branches, and considered as relating to the Clergy, or the Laity; and it may be proper to take a short View of it, with Reference to both. Religion being a Matter of free Choice, for which we are ordinarily accountable only to him, who will hereafter judge us for our moral Behaviour — and the Church, considered with Relation to civil Power, being in the very Nature of it a voluntary Society; it is left to Men's Consciences, whether they will become Members of it

New York, 1767, pp. 3–5, 14–19, 26–35, 44–48, 54–59, 78–79, 93–97.

or not. But after they are become Members, the Laws of the Church are in Force against them, and they are subject, in Ecclesiastical Matters, to the Authority of those who govern it.

What the just Penalties of Disobedience are, we must learn from the Nature of the Church itself. In Civil Society, the Magistrate is armed with the Sword of Justice, and "he is the Minister of God, a Revenger to execute Wrath upon him that doeth Evil," according to the Degree and Nature of his Offences. But the Power of the Church is of a spiritual Nature, and the utmost Effect of it in this World, is the cutting off and rejecting those Members which are incurably and dangerously corrupted. This Punishment which has commonly been known by the Name of Excommunication, however it was dreaded in the purest Ages of Christianity, has lost much of its Force in this; wherein Altars are set up against Altars, and Churches against Churches, and those who are rejected by one, may be received by another. A Disposition to slight the highest Punishment which the Church can inflict has become general, and there appears to be no Remedy for it, unless in the Use of Reason and Persuasion. But we live in an Age, in which the Voice of Reason will not be heard, nor the Strength of Arguments regarded, although supported by the Declarations of Heaven, on the Subject of Church Discipline. Nay, a Man would be generally esteemed to be either wrong-headed, or mean-spirited, or both, who should profess much Reverence for Ecclesiastical Authority; and the Charge of Priest-Craft, so long hackneyed by Infidels and Libertines, would be sure to fall upon the Clergy, should they have Courage to speak up in Defence of it.

In this State of Things, the Restoration of the primitive Discipline seems to be a Matter rather to be wished for and desired, than to be rationally attempted by those in Authority. Accordingly no Attempts of this Nature will be made under an American Episcopate; the Discipline of the Church, so far as it relates to the private Members, will be left as it is, and nothing farther will be done than refusing the Communion to disorderly and scandalous Persons, which every Clergyman may now refuse, and ought to refuse, agreeably to the Rubrics.

But with Regard to the Clergy, it is proposed that a strict Discipline be established, and that the Bishop's Power over them shall be as full and complete, as the Laws and Canons of the Church direct. Of the Necessity of this, none can be more sensible than the Clergy themselves, who, in all their Addresses in Favour of an Episcopate, have proposed and requested that this may be the Case. The general Character of the American Clergy, the Author believes, if he may judge from a large and extensive Acquaintance with them, and he hopes it may be thought excusable in him, on this Occasion, although one of the Number, to declare his Belief of it, to be truly respectable. They are found and steady in their Principles, and regular in their Behaviour. In so large a Body, some Exceptions from the general Character must be expected; but it is rather to be wondered that their Number is so small, considering all Things.

Indeed we have heard much of the profligate Behaviour of the Clergy to the Southward, and in the Islands; but this, perhaps, may have been owing to the Conduct of a few Individuals, reported and aggravated with a malicious Intention. . .

But after all, whatever may be the Proportion between the virtuous and vicious Clergymen in America, as there are undoubtedly some of both Characters; the Want of Bishops to superintend and govern them, is obvious at first View. If one Sort have no Need of a Bishop to keep them to their Duty, yet some Cases will arise in the Discharge of it in which his Direction will be useful — and many Cases, wherein his Support and Encouragement will be needful — and in all Cases, his Friendship and Patronage will give Life and Spirit to them in undergoing the Difficulties, and in performing the Duties, of their Station. . .

If a Clergyman shall disgrace his Profession in an open and scandalous Manner, a Bishop residing in the Country can suspend him immediately; and if upon Trial the Case shall be found to deserve it, he can proceed to deprive him of his Benefice, and not only silence and depose him, but excommunicate him from the Society of Christians. The Consideration of this, and that they are under the Eye of their Bishop, one main Branch of whose Business is to inspect and enquire into their Conduct, will naturally tend to make the Clergy in general, more regular and diligent in the Discharge of the Duties of their Office, and more careful and circumspect in their whole Behaviour. In a Word, of those whose Characters are justly exceptionable, some may probably be reformed by a Bishop; and as to others, they may be easily displaced, unless it be the Fault of the People themselves.

But a greater Disadvantage, if possible, than the Want of a regular Government, attends the Church of England in America in its present State, I mean the Want of Ordination: for none can be admitted to Holy Orders without crossing the Atlantic, with great Hazard and Expence. The Danger of such a Voyage may, to some, appear to be trifling; but the Apprehension of it, together with a natural Aversion to the Sea, has been known to deter many worthy Persons, who have been desirous of obtaining Ordination in the Church, from attempting it — the Fear and Apprehension of Danger, in such Cases, whether rightly founded or not, having always the same Effect. But what real Foundation there is for such an Apprehension, will be best discovered from Experience and Facts. Now the exact Number of those that have gone Home for Ordination, from these Northern Colonies (excepting some who have failed lately, who cannot properly be included in this Account) is Fifty-two. Of these Forty-two have returned safely, and Ten have miscarried; the Voyage, or Sickness occasioned by it, having proved fatal to near a fifth Part of them.

The Expence of this Voyage cannot be reckoned at less, upon an Average, than One Hundred Pounds Sterling to each Person. To Men of Fortune this is an inconsiderable Sum; but Men of Fortune must not be expected to devote themselves to the Service of the Church in America, where the Prospect is so discouraging, and so many disagreeable Circumstances are known to attend it. The Expence must therefore generally fall upon such, as having already expended the greatest Part of their Pittance in their Education, will find it extremely hard to raise a Sum sufficient for the Purpose.

Under these Discouragements, there has always been great Difficulty in supplying the Church with Clergymen, and there always must be. In what Manner the Church is supplied at present, the following Instances will sufficiently testify. In the Province of New-Jersey there are Twenty-one Churches and Congregations; Eleven of these are intirely destitute of a Minister, and there are but Five Clergymen to do the Duties of the other Ten. In Pennsylvania, including the Lower Counties, the Case is similar. In the City of Philadel-

phia there are Three Churches and Congregations, and but Two Clergymen; in the Rest of the Province the Number of Churches is Twenty-six, and that of the Clergy is but Seven.

If some of the Colonies are better supplied, perhaps others may be found which are provided for not so well. In North-Carolina, the late Governor Dobbs informed the Society, in his Letter dated March 29th, 1764, "that there were then but Six Clergymen in that Province, although there were Twenty-nine Parishes, and each Parish contained a whole County."

If we pursue the History of the Church from this Period, we shall meet with no Instance, in which any large Number of People proselyted to the Christian Religion, or any considerable Colonies, settled by a Christian Country, have been without a Bishop, the Dutch Colonies excepted, which do not desire them. It has been the Practice of all Christian Nations, to provide for and maintain the national Religion, and to render it as respectable as possible, in the most distant Colonies; wherein, either a Regard for their Religion, or Reasons of Policy, and probably both, have led them to take equal Care for the Establishment of Ecclesiastical, as of Civil Government. As to America, in particular, wherever we meet with French or Spanish Settlements, we find Bishops. In Canada, a Country less populous than many of the British Colonies, when we took Possession of it, there was a compleat Ecclesiastical Establishment under an Episcopate. . .

This universal Practice of all Nations and Ages, has proceeded from Two general Principles that are deeply founded in human Nature, and human Policy. The first is inseparable from our Nature, and necessarily leads Men to exert themselves, for the Preservation and Security of whatever they esteem and hold to be valuable, in Proportion as they judge of its Usefulness and Importance. The other seems to be a fundamental Principle of sound and consistent Policy, which necessarily requires the Protection and Security of the national Religion. For as some Religion has been ever thought, by the wisest Legislators, to be necessary for the Security of Civil Government, and accordingly has always been interwoven into the Constitution of it; so, in every Nation, that Religion which is thus distinguished, must be looked upon as, in the Opinion of the Legislature, the best fitted for this great Purpose.

Wherever therefore the national Religion is not made, in some Degree, a national Concern, it will commonly be considered as an Evidence, that those who have the Direction of the national Affairs do not esteem their Religion — or, that they are negligent of the Duty they owe to God and the Public, as the Guardians of its Happiness.

Are we then, from the present State of the Church of England in America, immediately to form so harsh a Conclusion, concerning those who have the Direction of our national Affairs? Must we necessarily suppose, that they have no Esteem and Affection for that Religion, which is so closely allied and connected with the Constitution of the State? Has the Conduct of the Church of England been such, with Regard to the Government — or, are its Principles such, that it is not intitled to the same Care and Protection, which other Kingdoms and States have ever afforded to the national Religion, whether Christian, Mahometan, or Pagan? Neither of these, it is hoped, can be said properly.

Although the Church of England in America appears not hitherto to have been made a national Concern; yet many Reasons may be assigned for this Neglect, owing to the peculiar Circumstances of the English Nation and Colonies, which will account for, although, perhaps, not altogether excuse it. The Colonies were generally settled by private Adventurers; and some of them, by those who had an Aversion to Episcopal Government. The Propriety of not sending a Bishop to Colonies of the latter Sort, will be disputed by none: and as to the others, their Beginnings were small, and for some Time an Episcopate was not greatly wanted.

Besides, it ought to be considered, that the Changes of Government — the Revolutions of Power — the Opposition of contending Parties at Home — the Intrigues of foreign Courts — and the Attacks of neighbouring Kingdoms and States, have generally been more than sufficient to employ the public Attention, almost ever since the Rise of our Colonies. Accordingly we have found, that even the commercial and political Importance of these Colonies, has been but little known or regarded, until of very late Years. In these Circumstances, it is not to be wondered, that the Case of the Church in America, has not been attended to; especially as the Members of it, not excepting the

Clergy, have been careless themselves, and not made those Representations in Favour of it, which they ought to have made.

To this may be added, that so long as no regular Plan for an American Episcopate was settled and proposed, a Fear of infringing the religious Rights of Protestant Dissenters in this Country, for which both our Civil and Ecclesiastical Rulers have to tender a Regard, must have created an almost insuperable Difficulty in carrying into Execution a Work of this Nature.

Our own Negligence in this Country has been confessed; and I wish as much could be fairly said in Excuse for it. How can the Necessities of the Church here be known, at a Distance, unless those who reside here will be at the Trouble of representing them? And from whom can such Representations be properly expected, but from the Clergy, and other Friends and Members of the Church? . . .

This Argument taken from the Number of those who belong to the Church of England in America, will receive great additional Force, from a Consideration of the State of the Blacks in our Islands and Colonies; who were found, in the above-mentioned Survey, to be about Eight Hundred and Forty-four Thousand. Although many of these, it is to be feared, through the Neglect of their Masters, are not Christians at all; yet, as they are connected with, and under the immediate Government of, Persons who profess Christianity, they may be said, in an imperfect Sense, to belong to the respective religious Classes of their Owners. However, their Situation is undoubtedly such, that in Proportion as a Sense of Religion prevails in their Masters, they will receive Benefit. Now as these are known chiefly to belong to the Professors of the Church, if an Episcopate will naturally tend to improve the State of Religion in the Church of England, it must consequently, (to say nothing of a particular Care which will probably be extended to them, when Bishops shall be settled) have a general good Effect upon more than half a Million of poor Creatures, Sharers with us of the same common Nature — sent into the World as Probationers and Candidates for the same glorious Immortality — whom Christ equally purchased by his precious blood-shedding — who notwithstanding, as they are bred up in Ignorance and Darkness, are suffered, to the eternal Disgrace of their Owners, to walk on "in the Shadow of Death," without a Ray of rational religious Hope to chear them.

This Consideration must make a deep Impression upon the Minds of all serious Christians, and lead them to encourage and help forward every Work, which has any probable Appearance of promoting the Spiritual Interests, of so many of these wretched Outcasts of Humanity. If it is the Duty of Christians to communicate "the glad Tidings of Salvation" to Heathens in general; it is a Duty more peculiarly incumbent upon us, to extend the Gospel to such of them as are under our immediate Government and Inspection, and who wear out, under the hard Yoke of Bondage, their Strength and very Lives in our Service.

Another Argument for granting an American Episcopate, arises from the Obligations of Gratitude; a national Sense of which, it is humbly conceived, ought, at this Time, to have a peculiar Efficacy in Favour of Religion in the American Plantations. By a signal Interposition of Divine Providence, the British Arms in America have triumphed over all that opposed them, our Colonies have been prodigiously extended, and our new Acquisitions, together with our old Settlements, have been secured, not only by Treaty, but by a total Annihilation of that Power on this Continent, whereby our former Safety was chiefly endangered.

Every wise Nation sees and acknowledges the Hand of God in the Production of such Events; and every religious Nation will endeavour to make some suitable Returns to him for such extraordinary Favours. And what Returns are proper to be made in such Cases, one Moment's serious Reflection will clearly discover. The Circumstances of Things evidently point out two Duties to our Governors, on this Occasion, both of them important in themselves, and of indispensible Obligation: One is, the farther Security and Support of the true Religion in America, in those Places where it already is; and the other, the Propagation of it in those Places, to which it has not hitherto been extended.

As America is the Region, wherein the Divine Goodness has been more remarkably displayed, in Favour of the British Nation; so, America is evidently the very Ground, on which some suitable Monument of religious Gratitude ought to be erected. It necessarily follows, that the State of the national Religion

here has a Right, on this Occasion, to the peculiar Attention and Consideration of those, who are intrusted with the Direction of our public Affairs. . .

We are very sensible that a Work of this Nature will have many to oppose it. Some will oppose it from an Enmity to all Religion. Others will oppose it from an Enmity, either open or secret, to the Protestant Religion; of which the Church of England is confessedly the strongest Barrier against Popery. There are others again who heretofore have opposed it, from an Apprehension, that either the Property or religious Liberty of their Friends might be affected by it; as it was not so well known, with what Powers and with what Views it had been requested that Bishops might be sent to us. But this has been so often and explicitly mentioned of late, that it can hardly be supposed, that any Persons of Power and Influence can remain ignorant of our true Plan.

However, for the Sake of others, and of such as mistake it, it may be proper, in a Work of this Nature, to make the following Declaration to the Public, (and I appeal to every Reader, who is acquainted with the Matter, for the Truth of it) that it has been long settled by our Friends and Superiors at Home, and the Clergy of this Country have often signified their entire Approbation and Acquiescence therein — That the Bishops to be sent to America, shall have no Authority, but purely of a Spiritual and Ecclesiastical Nature, such as is derived altogether from the Church and not from the State — That this Authority shall operate only upon the Clergy of the Church, and not upon the Laiety nor Dissenters of any Denomination — That the Bishops shall not interfere with the Property or Privileges, whether civil or religious, of Churchmen or Dissenters — That, in particular, they shall have no Concern with the Probate of Wills, Letters of Guardianship and Administration, or Marriage-Licences, nor be Judges of any Cases relating thereto — But, that they shall only exercise the original Powers of their Office as before stated, i. e. ordain and govern the Clergy, and administer Confirmation to those who shall desire it.

This, without any Reservation or Equivocation, is the exact Plan of an American Episcopate which has been settled at Home; and it is the only one, on which Bishops have been requested here, either in our general or more particular Addresses. And so far is it from

being our Desire to molest the Dissenters, or any Denominations of Christians, in the Enjoyment of their
present religious Privileges, that we have carefully consulted their Safety and Security, and studied not to
injure, but oblige them. . .

Surely the Dissenters in America now, when the
English Episcopal Government is so much milder than
heretofore, will not oppose the every Existence of
Bishops in the same Country with themselves—especially
as no Obedience or Submission at all from them is
required or expected. . .   Some of them indeed
formerly have had an aversion to the Idea of Bishops
in America, on the Supposition that they must become
subject to their Authority. But the Plan which is now
fixed, must effectually obviate all their Objections
and dissipate their Fears. As the Bishops proposed
will have no Power over them, or Concern with them,
there can be nothing to alarm them. Our Ordinations
cannot hurt them; any more than their Ordinations
can injure us. They can have no more Reason to
complain of Confirmation, or of any other Episcopal
Office performed in our Churches by Bishops, than
they now have to complain, that Preaching and the
common Administration of the Sacraments are practiced in them by Presbyters. And as to such Discipline
and Government as is intended to be exercised under
an Episcopate, they will have no Reasons to be dissatisfied therewith; any more than we now have to be
dissatisfied with the Discipline exercised by them —
but on the other Hand, they will have many Reasons
to be pleased with it. . .

If our American Bishops are to have no Authority over Dissenters, nor indeed to exercise Discipline
over our own People, the Clergy excepted; then the
frightful Objection of Spiritual Courts intirely vanishes.
For if no Authority of this Kind will be claimed or
exercised by them, we may be sure that no Courts will
be erected for the Exercise of it.

What Foundation there is for Complaint of the
Spiritual Courts in England, I know not. Perhaps
they may have used too great Severity in some particular Instances. But this Complaint is not unfrequently made, of our common Courts of Justice. Cruelty
and Severity is by no Means the Character of the
English Bishops, nor is it connected with the Exercise
of their Authority, more than with that of the civil

Magistrate: and in all Courts, whether Ecclesiastical or
others, where an Injury is suffered, the Laws of England
have provided a Remedy.

If some of the Laws which relate to these Courts,
are imagined to bear hard upon British Liberty, this, by
the Way, is not necessarily to be considered as the
Fault of the Bishops — it ought to be charged to the
Account of the Legislature in general, and not of a
particular Branch of it. But be this as it may, it is probable that these, and all other Ecclesiastical Laws, as well
as our Liturgy and public Offices, and our Translation
of the Bible, will be reviewed, as soon as it shall be
thought that there is good Sense and Candour enough
in the Body of the Nation to admit of it . . .

But as Ignorance is ever suspicious, it may farther
be asked, Shall we not be taxed in this Country for the
Support of Bishops, if any shall be appointed? I answer,
Not at all. But should a general Tax be laid upon the
Country, and thereby a Sum be raised sufficient for the
Purpose: and even supposing we should have three
Bishops on the Continent, which are the most that have
been mentioned; yet I believe such a Tax would not
amount to more than Four Pence in One Hundred
Pounds. And this would be no mighty Hardship upon
the Country. He that could think much of giving the
Six Thousandth Part of his Income to any Use, which
the Legislature of his Country should assign, deserves
not to be considered in the Light of a good Subject, or
Member of Society . . .

That an American Episcopate is reasonable and
proper in itself, and that such an Episcopate as is now
proposed has a natural Tendency to produce no ill
Consequences, has, I trust, been sufficiently proved.
There is not the least Prospect at present, that Bishops
in this Country will acquire any Influence or Power,
but what shall arise from a general Opinion of their
Abilities and Integrity, and a Conviction of their Usefulness; and of this, no Persons need dread the Consequences. But should the Government see fit hereafter to invest them with some Degree of civil Power
worthy of their Acceptance, which it is impossible
to say they will not, although there is no Appearance
that they ever will; yet as no new Powers will be
created in Favour of Bishops, it is inconceivable
that any would thereby be injured. All that the
Happiness and Safety of the Public require, is, that

the legislative and executive Power be placed in the Hands of such Persons, as are possessed of the greatest Abilities, Integrity and Prudence: and it is hoped that our Bishops will always be thought to deserve this Character . . .

William Livingston: *The American Whig (1768)*

By this time I suppose Dr. Chandler's *Appeal* has safely crossed the Atlantic, and if properly introduced to his superiors with those usual private advices of his brethren on this side of the water (which for a particular reason it is their interest should ever remain private), of what success it promises to the cause of episcopacy in America and how by the aid of a bishop it is like to expand the gentle bosom of the church so as to receive thousands and ten thousands of Fanatics, Enthusiasts, Methodists, Deists, Iroquois Indians and West-India Blacks. If this, I say, has been properly managed, it will doubtless answer what without breach of charity we may suppose at least a secondary motive of the reverend author in composing it: namely to demonstrate to his benefactors that his doctrine had not been bestowed in vain. It certainly breaths a noble zeal for the church . . . It sagaciously distinguishes between a primitive Christian and a modern English bishop. It assumes an unusual moderation; and so naturally counterfeits the voice of a sheep that it is not every reader who will discriminate it from that of a wolf. In fine, it bemoans with deeper moans than any of the most moanful shepherds in pastoral, the numberless souls already perished through the neglect of his all important plan and congratulates posterity, if not on the hopes of rescuing them out of purgatory, at least on the prospect of speedily introducing a kind of millenium by the episcopal triple discharge of ordination, confirmation and government, by virtue of which are to be converted Jews and Infidels, together with all and singular the Whites, Blacks and Browns, farther than from Dan to Beersheba, even from Lake Superior to Pensacola . . .

For my own part with respect to any execution this remarkable performance is like to do among ourselves where almost every intelligent reader is able,

A Collection of Tracts from the Late Newspapers, John Holt, New York, 1768. 1, 3–7, 19–20, 59–62, 74–75, 196–202.

from his own personal knowledge, to contradict the facts upon which great part of it, and by far the most plausible part is founded, I should have been very willing to leave the author to triumph in his imaginary victory. But when I consider that it will chiefly be read in a country where, with a moderate share of address, people may be made to believe that a man can jump into a quarter bottle — that thousands of Negroes who never so much as heard of Gospel are, notwithstanding, "virtual Churchmen" — that what must inevitably ruin a country is absolutely necessary to its welfare . . . I cannot but think it my duty to administer an antidote to the poison and to show as well the falsity of the facts as the futility of the reasoning by which the *Appeal* may impose on the weak and credulous. I shall, therefore, without any apology of this man's "having a tremor in his hand," or that one a torpor in his head, think myself sufficiently authorized as a friend of truth and of society to prevent to the utmost of my power the fatal, the tremendous mischiefs which the *Appeal* is so artfully calculated to introduce . . .

Considering the encroachments that have lately been made on our civil liberties and that we can scarcely obtain redress against one injurious project, but another is forming against us, considering the poverty and distress of the colonies by the restriction on our trade and how peculiarly necessary it is in these times of common calamity to be united amongst ourselves, one could scarcely have imagined that the most ambitious ecclesiastic should be so indifferent about the true interest of his native country as to sow, at this critical juncture, the seeds of universal discord, and, besides the deprivation of our civil liberties, lend his helping hand to involve us in ecclesiastical bondage into the bargain. Is this a time to think of episcopal places, of pontifical revenues, of spiritual courts and all the pomp, grandeur, luxury and regalia of an American Lambeth? 'Tis true, the pamphlet is specious and appears to ask nothing but what is highly reasonable. Could any man, above the capacity of an Idiot, really persuade himself the Doctor and the Convention would content themselves with a bishop so limited and curtailed as he is pleased to represent his future lordship, it were manifest injustice to deny them what in their opinion their eternal salvation so greatly depends upon. But it is not the "primitive Christian" bishop they want. It is the modern, splendid, opulent, court-favored, law-dignified, superb, magnificent, powerful prelate on which their hearts are so intent. And that such a bishop would be one of the worst commodities that can possibly be imported into a new country and must inevitably prove absolute desolation and ruin to this, I shall abundantly evince in the course of these speculations.

As civil and religious liberty is the foundation of public happiness and the common birthright of mankind, it is the duty and interest of every individual to keep a watchful eye over and to cherish it with the utmost care and tenderness. Would we preserve the invaluable jewel and act the part of true friends to our country, we ought to maintain a scared jealousy that it be not ravished from us by open violence, nor undermined by secret artifice and fraud . . . So jealous and tenacious are mankind of their liberty that every attempt to deprive them of it by open violence is generally fruitless. A direct attack will be resented and repelled with heroic bravery, and next to life and property, men will most zealously contend for its preservation. Conscious of this, those in all ages who have commenced tyrants and undertaken to enslave mankind have ever had recourse to artifice and under pretext of the public good have, by insensible degrees, introduced alterations into the civil and religious constitutions of their country, til the deluded people are gradually wormed out of their liberty and at last find the shackles of slavery effectually rivetted.

This being the case, every new project proposed to the public, every attempted innovation, ought to be critically canvassed and examined even in their remotest tendency and consequences and adopted, if at all, with the utmost caution and reserve. Barely the novelty of any proposal is in this light sufficient to alarm our jealousy and excite our vigilance. However plausible it may appear at first view, or disguised with the colorable pretence of being friendly to liberty and promotive of public happiness, if we hastily acquiesce in, or without examination rashly receive it, we shall probably lament our folly and when too late feel the fatal effects of our temerity.

What led me into these reflections was the reading Dr. Chandler's pleas for an American Episcopate lately published in New York. The scheme for sending bishops into the colonies has, it seems, been long under consideration. 'Tis about fifty years since it was first started and some provision made for carrying it into execution. It has been lately revived and, we hear, the advocates of it, both here and in England, have sanguine expectations of its speedy accomplishment. This revival of the project, the Doctor tells us, is in consequence of some late applications from these parts. No less than seven petitions, we are told, have been transmitted by a certain convention of the episcopal clergy here to some of the most respectable personages in England earnestly soliciting bishops for America, representing the deplorable condition of an unmitered church, boasting of their incredible numbers in the colonies, their distinguished and unshaken loyalty and not sparing very injurious reflections upon the other denominations as seditious incendiaries and disaffected to the king and government. With what truth these aspersions are cast upon you, my dear countrymen, and what at this juncture so vehemently urged, you must judge for yourselves. If they are just and you are indeed such factious incendiaries, such disloyal subjects to the best of kings as these addresses are said to insinuate, it highly concerns you to repent and reform. If not you will resent them in a manner becoming an injured people conscious of their own innocence, when basely and falsely traduced . . .

The first settlers of the Northern colonies fled from the cruel persecution of the Church of England to this country which then was an uncultivated wilderness. The Indians soon became jealous of the new settlers and gave them all the disturbance in their power. But those brave sons of religion and liberty chose rather to run the risque of the rage and malice of the Indian savages, than of the perfidious and persecuting bishops. They continued to settle the country, and God, in whom they trusted, appeared for their defense and drove out the heathens from before them.

As America is a new country and the settlers generally poor, they are obliged to be very laborious in order to procure a tolerable subsistence for themselves and families. They have ever been, and still are, too much engaged in business to get acquainted with the parties and controversies that continued in the Mother Country and particularly in the Church of

England, especially as they hoped that their great enemies the diocesan bishops would be contented since they had, in effect, procured them to be banished from the land of their nativity. Indeed, we could not but hope they would have suffered us to live in peace in these remote parts of the earth and that the vast Atlantic Ocean would have served for a partition between us to all generations . . .

It is storied in their own history that when the Emperor Constantine endowed the church with lands and possessions, the voice of an Angel was heard in the air crying "Hodie venenum infunditur in ecclesiam (This day poison is poured into the church)" and bitter experience has confirmed the truth of these words, whatever we believe concerning the being by whom they were uttered. Of this execrable potion, the bishop of Rome took the first draught, and all Christendom furnishes instances of priests who long to tipple this "wine of fornication." Our wise and pious reformers began, therefore, with absolutely renouncing the cup, and tis too, too evident, that in spite of the admonitions of prophecy, the principles of sound policy, and the experience of every age since, this destructive bowl was stirred up in which spiritual gifts and worldly benefits are absurdly compounded together, that some of the Protestant clergy are as desirous to take the intoxicating sip as those who with the "scarlet whore" have often got drunk and defiled the nations.

To this, I impute all the prayers, entreaties, conjurations, sighs and lamentations of a certain class of priests for the introduction of a "spiritual Generalissimo" into this country. I am sensible that they disavow all noxious designs and that like other sots they palliate their inordinate thirst after the insalutary dose by pretences that seem friendly to health and consistent with sobriety and innocence. But as all attempts from an order who abjur the roughness of violence will be dictated by the "wisdom of the serpent" and cunningly affect the "harmlessness of the dove," we ought, for preventing the success of their machinations, to set a double guard upon our privileges. Of all thraldom, spiritual thraldom is the worst, and, if ever any sect acquires a dominion in this country, the fires of persecution must burn with hotter vengeance here than in any other part of the world, because our numerous persuasions afford the most plentiful fuel. Cowards

are malicious, and the fears of the assuming denomination will never be quieted 'til the throne they erect is free from all danger. Which of our numerous persuasions bids fairest to lord it over the rest, I have shown in some former papers, and for that very reason, they of all others ought to be content with their lot. Guaranteed on every side against oppression, what have Episcopalians to fear? In the distribution of power they have so immoderate a share that the very desire to have more is not only inconsistent with all Christian moderation, but gives just grounds for suspicion that they are meditating an offensive war.

But conscience is pleaded. For what? That the church, says Dr. Chandler, may be better governed. Over whom is this government to be exercised? Not, says he, over the laity (a sure proof this that the government is not deduced from the scriptures), but only over the clergy. Let them behave better. This is in their own power and if any remain incorrigible, my Lord of Landaff and the rest of the society at home, upon proper complaint (which complaint every man is invited to make) will soon bring the delinquents to reason. As to the matter of ordination, the candidate's conscience is relievable by a trip to London. Nor need the laity be afflicted if he makes any difficulty, for those must be small motions of the spirit indeed towards the work of the ministry which the sight of salt water will subdue. And with respect to confirmation, since we have so long been without it and no man is so shamelessly uncharitable as to suppose it necessary to salvation and that our ancestors have all perished for want of it, the conscience bound on account of this defect can be on no very pitiable rack of pain. Besides, what is most fatal to this plea is that the majority of the continent have consciences too, and by those very consciences think themselves bound to oppose the unseasonable introduction of proud prelates into this country. That it is a fact that thousands have horrors at the bare prospect, the Doctor can want no proof at this day. And if the minority have such unconscionable consciences as not to possess their souls in patience 'til God, in his wise providence and for the punishment of our sins, opens a wider door for these right reverend fathers and their lay and clerical officers and attendants, they can have no Christian consciences at all . . .

We should esteem it the palladium of our liberties if the King's judges held their commissions by the tenure of good behavior. And to the preservation of the morals of our clergy, it is essential that their subsistence depend upon the same honorable condition. A bishop and his officers, independent of the people! I tremble at the thought of such a powerful spy in a country just forming a state of soundness and stability. Rouse then Americans! You have as much to fear from such a minister of the Church as you had lately from a minister of state. And whether this project is not a device of the latter, by dividing us to favor his designs, though he is now in disgrace, is submitted to your wisdom to discern and prevent . . .

If any man doubts my prediction and fondly presumes upon the charitable indulgence of ecclesiastical clemency after it is exalted to the power of applying punishments at will and pleasure which must inevitably be the case upon the introduction of spiritual lords into a country where they will find no laymen for their match, let him learn wisdom from history. Without the knowledge of mankind, it is impossible to govern them well. This necessary accomplishment seldom falls to the lot of speculative mortals immured in a study. Hence their conceit, contraction and obstinacy. Give the reins to one of these bookworms, and he will attempt to drive the chariot of the sun. Let him be an ecclesiastic besides, and impelled by the two irresistible momentums of "the glory of God and the salvation of souls," and how can he refrain from adopting the popish comment upon the text, "compelt them to come in!" He will compel them with a witness. The dignity of the end justifies all sorts of means. Mines and galleys, fire and faggot, pains and penalties, the rack and the cross, have all been applied instead of reason and argument. Thus mankind will ever be pillaged and butchered as often as they are subjected to the unbridled power of zealots who, as we said of Archbishop Laud, by the pride of a good conscience will be more obstinately in the wrong.

There can be no dependence for the continuation of our liberties, if ever a lordly clergyman is clothed with sufficient power to put down all opposers. Give him that, and his conscience will set it to work. Nay,

judging from experience, he will think himself conscience-bound, by the sword of the spirit, to brandish for our conviction, a sort of weapons of a very different nature . . .

It being impossible, as the laws now stand, to introduce a bishop into America who will not have authority the instant he arrives to set up an ecclesiastical court to which all denominations will be equally subject, the Doctor's plea can have no validity at all, since no man can plead conscience for a measure mischievous or dangerous to his neighbor. As the law now stands, we cannot have an Episcopate in this country but upon terms more mischievous than beneficial. I have already shown that bishops will necessarily bring with them the ecclesiastical courts and subjugate the colonies to the pride and tyranny of the clergy. Evils of all others to be most dreaded and which to prevent and abhor, I hope, is as consistent with the character of a churchman as of any other denomination. All who expect to better their circumstance by his lordship's favor will fret at the opposition and be apt to deny the moderate Episcopalians who disapprove their ambition and indiscretion to be true sons of the church . . .

As to Americans, what is the language of their charters, the commissions and instructions to their governors, the statute of naturalization and the colony laws unrepealed, with the constant usage of government, in appointing persons to places both of trust and profit without any religious discrimination but that if they are Protestants and good subjects, nothing more will be expected? Depending upon this, people of different nations came out and settled this wilderness and thereby acquired dominion for Great Britain which, if she had been left to herself, she never could have peopled. The Americas have, therefore, a compact to plead for their immunities and all the benefits which flow from this country, whether they respect extent of commerce, wealth, or the augmentation of the number of British subjects.

. . . Away then with every ill-policied intolerant, contemptible priestly project, contrived in a conclave, convocation, convention or any other nest of narrow-minded, proud, ignorant, inflammatory parsons. No bishop without a spiritual court. 'Tis by this rod, the Church of England, according to the present state of the law, corrects her disorderly professors. And if a

number of these judicatories are once set up in America,
farewell to those emigrations from Europe which have
proved such fruitful nurseries to this country. The
bare apprehension, if it spreads accross the Atlantic,
will do us more harm than many are aware of. Assure
yourself, Sir, that it is not the church, nor even the
majority of our clergy, that wish success to this silly
scheme. To those only who are in the pay of the
Society, and of these, to such as are discontented with
their allowance, it is to be imputed. All the rest of the
Episcopal clergy are quiet and the body of the laity
with the missionaries had been so too. For the satisfaction of the weaker sort who think otherwise I shall
in some future letters abundantly show that, whether
the non-Episcopalians are right or wrong in this controversy, we shall be wrong if we persist in teasing
the government to patronize a scheme that may, if it
proceeds, involve us either in the calamities of a civil
war or by driving the present inhabitants out, or stop-
ping further importations into the country, prevent
the settlement of our lands and by sinking their value,
plunge us into ruin and perhaps drag the nation after
us into the same pit of destruction.

No word figured more prominently in the revolutionary polemics than liberty. Liberty, indeed, had come to represent all that the colonists sought in their unhappy conflict with the mother country — liberty from trade restrictions, liberty from unjust taxation, liberty from symbols of church authority, liberty from distant rule. The American discontent with imperial interference was widespread, but it took skilled writers to weave these many grievances into a theory of opresion. Such a writer was John Dickinson (1732-1808), whose *Letters from a Farmer in Pennsylvania* appeared in 1768 after the Townshend Acts had placed an indirect duty on tea, paints, and glass items. The English government had been led to believe that the colonists would accept an indirect tax when they would not accept a direct tax such as the Stamp Act imposed. In fact, the colonial statements of the period indicate that all taxation was offensive and that only regulation of the overall imperial trade system was acceptable. Enormously popular, Dickinson's *Letters* were important because he took the different measures recently passed by Parliament and related them to an overall plan to check colonial rights. It was the knitting together of the disparate threads of British rule that brought diverse groups together to make a concerted effort to oppose the threat of tyranny. Dickinson's eventual refusal to sign the Declaration of Independence — despite the effectiveness of his *Letters* in persuading others to back independence — is a reminder of how reluctant many of the principal leaders of colonial opposition were to break with the mother country.

In vain did colonial conservatives argue that liberty was at best a qualified virtue and that it could not exist at all without a recognized sovereign power whose right to rule was unquestioned. When Church of England clergymen tried to teach loyalty and submission as prime religious values, they lost their congregations. During the turbulent months of 1775, after the skirmishes at Lexington and Concord, Jonathan Boucher (1730–1804), one of the most outspoken critics of the protesters, preached to his congregation at Annapolis, Maryland, with a brace of loaded pistols at his side. Although Boucher too was

to join the Loyalists who left their homes rather than be unfaithful to the British government, as long as he had a pulpit he preached the uncomfortable truths of a Christian's duty to his sovereign. The last reading comes from his sermon, *On Civil Liberty, Passive Obedience and Non-Resistance.* Anglican clergymen were in a minority, however; the majority of colonial churchmen preached a doctrine which placed individual consciences above the authority of particular governments. More often than not, their message complemented the concept of natural rights which the colonial leaders were developing.

John Dickinson: Letters from a farmer in Pennsylvania to the inhabitants of the British Colonies (1769)

LETTER 1

My Dear Countrymen,

I am a farmer, settled after a variety of fortunes, near the banks, of the river Delaware, in the province of Pennsylvania. I received a liberal education, and have been engaged in the busy scenes of life: But am now convinced, that a man may be as happy without bustle, as with it. My farm is small, my servants are few, and good; I have a little money at interest; I wish for no more: my employment in my own affairs is easy; and with a contented grateful mind, I am compleating the number of days allotted to me by divine goodness . . .

From infancy I was taught to love humanity and liberty. Inquiry and experience have since confirmed my reverence for the lessons then given me, by convincing me more fully of their truth and excellence. Benevolence towards mankind excites wishes for their welfare, and such wishes endear the means of fulfilling them. Those can be found in liberty alone, and therefore her sacred cause ought to be espoused by every man, on every occasion, to the utmost of his power: as a charitable but poor person does not withhold his mite; because he cannot relieve all the distresses of the miserable, so let not any honest man suppress his sentiments concerning freedom, however small their influence is likely to be. Perhaps he may "touch some wheel" that will have an effect greater than he expects . . .

With a good deal of surprise I have observed, that little notice has been taken of an act of parliament, as injurious in its principle to the liberties of these colonies, as the Stamp-act was: I mean the act for suspending the legislation of New-York.

The assembly of that government compiled with a former act of parliament, requiring certain provisions to be made for the troops in America, in every particular, I think, except the articles of salt, pepper, and vinegar. In my opinion they acted imprudently, considering all circumstances, in not complying so far, as would have given satisfaction, as several colonies did: but my dislike of their conduct in that instance, has not blinded me so much, that I cannot plainly perceive, that they have been punished in a manner pernicious to American freedom, and justly alarming to all the colonies.

If the British Parliament has a legal authority to order, that we shall furnish a single article for the troops here, and to compel obedience to that order; they have the same right to order us to supply those troops with arms, cloaths, and every necessary, and to compel obedience to that order also; in short, to lay any burdens they please upon us. What is this but taxing us at a certain sum, and leaving to us only the manner of raising it? How is this mode more tolerable than the Stamp Act? Would that act have appeared more pleasing to Americans, if being ordered thereby to raise the sum total of the taxes, the mighty privilege had been left to them, of saying how much should be paid for an instrument of writing on paper, and how much for another on parchment?

An act of parliament commanding us to do a certain thing if it has any validity, is a tax upon us for the expence that accrues in complying with it, and for this reason, I believe, every colony on the continent, that chose to give a mark of their respect for Great-Britain, in complying with the act relating to the troops, cautiously avoided the mention of that act, lest their conduct should be attributed to its supposed obligation.

The matter being thus stated, the assembly of New-York either had, or had not a right to refuse submission to that act. If they had, and I imagine no American will say, they had not, then the parliament had no right to compel them to execute it.—If they had not that right, they had no right to punish them for not

executing it; and therefore had no right to suspend their legislation, which is a punishment. In fact, if the people of New-York cannot be legally taxed but by their own representatives, they cannot be legally deprived of the privileges of making laws, only for insisting on that exclusive privilege of taxation. If they may be legally deprived of such a case of the privilege of making laws, why may they not, with equal reason, be deprived of every other privilege? Or why may not every colony be treated in the same manner, when any of them shall dare to deny their assent to any impositions that shall be directed? Or what signifies the repeal of the Stamp-act, if these colonies are to lose their other privileges, by not tamely surrendering that of taxation?

There is one consideration arising from this suspicion, which is not generally attended to, but shews its importance very clearly. It was not necessary that this suspension should be caused by an act of parliament. The crown might have restrained the governor of New-York, even from calling the assembly together, by its prerogative in the royal governments. This step, I suppose, would have been taken, if the conduct of the assembly of New-York, had been regarded as an act of disobedience to the crown alone but it is regarded as an act of "disobedience to the authority of the British Legislature." This gives the suspension a consequence vastly more affecting. It is a parliamentary assertion of the supreme authority of the British legislature over these colonies in the part of taxation; and is intended to compel New-York unto a submission to that authority. It seems therefore to me as much a violation of the liberty of the people of that province, and consequently of all these colonies, as if the parliament had sent a number of regiments to be quartered upon them til they should comply. For it is evident, that the suspension is meant as a compulsion; and the method of compelling is totally indifferent. It is indeed probable, that the sight of red coats, and the beating of drums would have been most alarming, because people are generally more influenced by their eyes and ears than by their reason: But whoever seriously considers the matter, must perceive, that a dreadful stroke is aimed at the liberty of these colonies: For the cause of one is the cause of all. If the parliament may lawfully deprive New-York of any of its rights, it may deprive any, or all the other colonies of their rights; and nothing can possibly so much encourage such attempts, as a mutual inattention to the interest of each other. To divide, and thus to destroy, is the first political maxim in attacking those who are powerful by their union. He certainly is not a wise man, who folds his arms and reposeth himself at home, seeing with unconcern the flames that have invaded his neighbour's house, without any endeavours to extinguish them . . .

A Farmer

LETTER II.

Beloved countrymen,

There is another late act of parliament, which seems to me to be as destructive to the liberty of these colonies, as that inserted in my last letter; that is, the act for granting the duties on paper, glass, &c. It appears to me to be unconstitutional.

The parliament unquestionably possesses a legal authority to regulate the trade of Great-Britain, and all its colonies. Such an authority is essential to the relation between a mother country and its colonies; and necessary for the common good of all. He, who considers these provinces as states distinct from the British Empire, has very slender notions of justice or of their interests. We are but parts of a whole; and therefore there must exist a power somewhere, to preside, and preserve the connection in due order. This power is lodged in the parliament; and we are as much dependant on Great-Britain, as a perfectly free people can be on another . . . . Never did the British parliament, till the period abovementioned, think of imposing duties in America for the purpose of raising a revenue. Mr. Greenville's sagacity first introduced this language, in the preamble to the 4th of Geo. III. Ch. 15, which has these words — "And whereas it is just and necessary that a revenue be raised in your Majesty's said dominions in America, for defraying the expences of defending, protecting and securing the same: We your Majesty's most dutiful and loyal subjects, the commons of Great Britain, in parliament assembled, being desirous to make some provision in the present session of parliament, towards raising the said revenue in America, have resolved to give and grant unto your Majesty the several rates and duties herein after mentioned," &c. . . .

Here we may observe an authority expressly claimed to impose duties on these colonies; not for the regulation of trade; not for the preservation or promotion of a mutually beneficial intercourse between the several constituent parts of the empire, heretofore the sole objects of parliamentary institutions; but for the single purpose of levying money upon us.

This I call an innovation; and a most dangerous innovation. It may perhaps be objected, that Great-Britain has a right to lay what duties she pleases upon her exports, and it makes no difference to us, whether they are paid here or there.

To this I answer. These colonies require many things for their use, which the laws of Great-Britain prohibit them from getting any where but from her. Such are paper and glass.

That we may be legally bound to pay any general duties on these commodities, relative to the regulation of trade, is granted; but we being obliged by her laws to take them from Great Britain, any special duties imposed on their exportation to us only, with intention to raise a revenue from us only, are as much taxes upon us, as those imposed by the Stamp-act.

What is the difference in substance and right, whether the same sum is raised upon us by the rates mentioned in the Stamp-act, on the use of the paper, or by these duties, on the importation of it. It is nothing but the edition of a former book, with a new title page.

Suppose the duties were made payable in Great-Britain?

It signifies nothing to us, whether they are to be paid here or there. Had the Stamp-act directed, that all the paper should be landed in Florida, and the duties paid there, before it was brought to the British Colonies, would the act have raised less money upon us, or have been less destructive of our rights? By no means: For as we were under a necessity of using the paper, we should have been under the necessity of paying the duties. Thus, in the present case, a like necessity will subject us, if this act continues in force, to the payment of the duties now imposed.

Why was the Stamp-act then so pernicious to freedom? It did not enact, that every man in the colonies should buy a certain quantity of paper-- No: It only directed, that no instrument of writing should be valid in law, if not made on stamp paper, &c.

The makers of that act knew full well, that the confusions that would arise upon the disuse of writings would compel the colonies to use the stamp paper, and therefore pay the taxes imposed. For this reason the Stamp-act was said to be a law that would execute itself. For the very same reason, the last act of parliament, if it is granted to have any force here, will execute itself, and will be attended with the very same consequences to American Liberty.

Our great advocate, Mr. Pitt, in his speeches on the debate concerning the repeal of the Stamp-act, acknowledged, that Great Britain could restrain our manufactures. His words are these — "This kingdom, as the supreme governing and legislative power, has always bound the colonies by her regulations and restrictions in trade, in navigation, in manufactures — in every thing, except that of taking their money out of their pockets, without their consent." Again he says, "We may bind their trade, confine their manufactures, and exercise every power whatever, except that of taking money out of their pockets, without their consent."

Here then, let my countrymen, rouse yourselves, and behold the ruin hanging over their heads. If they once admit, that Great-Britain may lay duties upon her exportations to us, for the purpose of levying money on us only, she then will have nothing to do, but to lay those duties on the articles which she prohibits us to manufacture — and the tragedy of American liberty is finished. We have been prohibited from procuring manufactures, in all cases, any where but from Great-Britain, (excepting linens, which we are permitted to import directly from Ireland). We have been prohibited, in some cases, from manufacturing for ourselves; We are therefore exactly in the situation of a city besieged, which is surrounded by the works of the besiegers in every part but one. If that is closed up, no step can be taken, but to surrender at discretion. If Great-Britain can order us to come to her for necessaries we want, and can order us to pay what taxes she pleases before we take them away, or when we have them here, we are as abject slaves, as France and Poland can shew . . .   A Farmer

LETTER III.

My dear countrymen,

. . . Sorry I am to learn, that there are some few persons, shake their heads with solemn motion, and pretend to wonder what can be the meaning of these letters. "Great-Britain, they say, is too powerful to contend with; she is determined to oppress us; it is in vain to speak of right on one side, when there is power on the other; when we are strong enough to resist, we shall attempt it; but now we are not strong enough, and therefore we had better be quiet; it signifies nothing to convince us that our rights are invaded, when we cannot defend them, and if we should get into riots and tumults about the late act, it will only draw down heavier displeasure upon us."

What can such men design? What do their grave observations amount to, but this — "that these colonies, totally regardless of their liberties, should commit them, with humble resignation, to chance, time, and the tender mercies of ministers."

Are these men ignorant, that usurpations, which might have been successfully opposed at first, acquire strength by continuance, and thus become irresistible? Do they condemn the conduct of these colonies, concerning the Stamp-act? Or have they forgot its successful issue? Ought the colonies at that time, instead of acting as they did, to have trusted for relief, to the fortuitous events of futurity? If it is needless "to speak of rights" now, it was as needless then. If the behaviour of the colonies was prudent and glorious then, and successful too; it will be equally prudent and glorious to act in the same manner now, if our rights are equally invaded, and may be as successful. Therefore it becomes necessary to enquire, whether "our rights are invaded." To talk of "defending" them, as if they could be no otherwise "defended" than by arms, is as much out of the way, as if a man having a choice of several roads to reach his journey's end, should prefer the worst, for no other reason, than because it is the worst.

As to "riots and tumults," the gentlemen who are so apprehensive of them, are much mistaken, if they think, that grievances cannot be redressed without such assistance.

I will now tell the gentlemen, what is "the meaning of these letters." The meaning of them is, to convince the people of these colonies, that they are at this moment exposed to the most imminent dangers; and to persuade them immediately, vigourously, and unanimously, to exert themselves, in the most firm, but most peaceable manner for obtaining relief.

The cause of liberty is a cause of too much dignity, to be sullied by turbulence and tumult. It ought to be maintained in a manner suitable to her nature. Those who engage in it, should breathe a sedate, yet fervent spirit, animating them to actions of prudence, justice, modesty, bravery, humanity, and magnanimity . . .

I hope, my dear countrymen, that you will in every colony be upon your guard against those who may at any time endeavour to stir you up, under pretences of patriotism, to any measures disrespectful to our sovereign and our mother country. Hot, rash, disorderly proceedings, injure the reputation of a people as to wisdom, valour and virtue, without procuring them the least benefit. I pray God, that he may be pleased to inspire you and your posterity to the latest ages with that spirit, of which I have an idea, but find a difficulty to express: to express in the best manner I can, I mean a spirit that shall so guide you, that it will be impossible to determine, whether an American's character is most distinguishable for his loyalty to his sovereign, his duty to his mother country, his love of freedom, or his affection for his native soil.

Every government, at some time or other, falls into wrong measures; these may proceed from mistake or passion. — But every such measure does not dissolve the obligation between the governors and the governed; the mistake may be corrected; the passion may pass over.

It is the duty of the governed, to endeavour to rectify the mistake, and appease the passion. They have not at first any other right, than to represent their grievances, and to pray for redress, unless an emergency is so pressing, as not to allow time for receiving an answer to their applications which rarely happens. If their applications are disregarded, then that kind of opposition becomes justifiable, which can be made without breaking the laws, or disturbing the public peace. This consists in the prevention of the oppressors reaping advantage from their oppressions, and not in their punishment. For experience may teach them what reason did not; and harsh methods, cannot be proper, till milder ones have failed.

If at length it becomes undoubted, that an invet-

erate resolution is formed to annihilate the liberties of the governed, the English history affords frequent examples of resistance by force. What particular circumstances will in any future case justify such resistance, can never be ascertained till they happen. Perhaps it may be allowable to say, generally, that it never can be justifiable, until the people are fully convinced, that any further submission will be destructive to their happiness.

When the appeal is made to the sword, highly probable it is, that the punishment will exceed the offence; and the calamities attending on war out weigh those preceding it. These considerations of justice and prudence, will always have great influence with good and wise men.

To these reflections on this subject, it remains to be added, and ought for ever to be remembered; that resistance in the case of colonies against their mother country, is extremely different from the resistance of a people against their prince. A nation may change their King or race of Kings, and retain their antient form of government, be gainers by changing. Thus Great-Britain, under the illustrious house of Brunswick, a house that seems to flourish for the happiness of mankind, has found a felicity, unknown in the reigns of the Stuarts. But if once we are separated from our mother country, what new form of government shall we accept, or when shall we find another Britain to supply our loss? Torn from the body to which we are united by religion, liberty, laws, affections, relations, language, and commerce, we must bleed at every vein.

In truth, the prosperity of these provinces is founded in their dependance on Great-Britain; and when she returns to "her old good humour, and old good nature," as Lord Clerendon expresses it, I hope they will always esteem it their duty and interest, as it most certainly will be, to promote her welfare by all the means in their power . . .

The constitutional modes of obtaining relief, are those which I would wish to see pursued on the present occasion, that is, by petitioning of our assemblies, or, where they are not permitted to meet, of the people to the powers that can afford us relief.

We have an excellent prince, in whose good dispositions towards us we may confide. We have a generous, sensible, and humane nation, to whom we may apply. They may be deceived: they may, by artful men, be provoked to anger against us; but I cannot yet believe they will be cruel or unjust; or that their anger will be implacable. Let us behave like dutiful children, who have received unmerited blows from a beloved parent. Let us complain to our parents; but let our complaints speak at the same time, the language of affliction and veneration.

If, however, it shall happen by an unfortunate course of affairs, that our applications to his Majesty and the parliament for the redress, prove ineffectual, let us then take another step, by withholding from Great-Britain, all the advantages she has been used to receive from us. Then let us try, if our ingenuity, industry, and frugality, will not give weight to our remonstrances. Let us all be united with one spirit in one cause. Let us invent; let us work; let us save; let us at the same time, keep up our claims, and unceasingly repeat our complaints; but above all, let us implore the protection of that infinite good and gracious Being, "by whom kings reign and princes decree justice."

A Farmer

LETTER IV.

My dear countrymen,

An objection, I hear, has been made against my second letter, which I would willingly clear up before I proceed. "There is," say these objectors, "a material difference between the Stamp-act and the late act for laying a duty on paper, &c. that justifies the conduct of those who opposed the former, and yet are willing to submit to the latter. The duties imposed by the Stamp-act were internal taxes; but the present are external, and therefore the parliament may have a right to impose them."

To this I answer, with a total denial of the power of parliament to lay upon these colonies any "tax" whatever.

This point, being so important to this, and to succeeding generations, I wish to be clearly understood.

To the word "tax," I annex that meaning which the constitution and history of England require to be annexed to it; that is — that it is an imposition on the subject, for the sole purpose of levying money.

Whenever we speak of "taxes" among Englishmen, let us therefore speak of them with reference to the principles on which, and the intentions with which they have been established. This will give certainty to

our expression, and safety to our conduct . . . A "tax" means an imposition to raise money. Such persons therefore as speak of internal and external "taxes," I pray may pardon me, if I object to that expression, as applied to the privileges and interests of these colonies. There may be internal and external impositions, founded on different principles, and having different tendencies, every "tax" being an imposition, tho' every imposition is not a "tax." But all taxes are founded on the same principles; and have the same tendency.

External impositions, for the regulation of our trade, do not "grant to his Majesty the property of the colonies." They only prevent the colonies acquiring property, in things not necessary, in a manner judged to be injurious to the welfare of the whole empire. But the last statute respecting us, "grants to his Majesty the property of the colonies," by laying duties on the manufactures of Great-Britain which they must take, and which she settled on them on purpose that they should take . . .

A Farmer

LETTER IX.

My dear countrymen,

I have made some observations on the purposes for which money is to be levied upon us by the late act of parliament. I shall now offer to your consideration some further reflections on that subject: And, unless I am greatly mistaken, if these purposes are accomplished according to the expressed intention of the act, they will be found effectually to supersede that authority in our respective assemblies, which is essential to liberty. The question is not, whether some branches shall be lopt off — The ax is laid to the root of the tree; and the whole body must infallibly perish, if we remain idle spectators of the work.

No free people ever existed, or can ever exist, without keeping, to use a common, but strong expression, " the purse strings," in their own hands. Where this is the case, they have a constitutional check upon the administration, which may thereby be brought into order without violence: But where such a power is not lodged in the people, oppression proceeds uncontrolled in its career, till the governed, transported into rage, seek redress in the midst of blood and confusion . . .

It has been for a long time, and now is, a constant instruction to all governors, to obtain a permanent support for the offices of government. But as the author of "the administration of the colonies" says, "this order of the crown is generally, if not universally, rejected by the legislatures of the colonies."

They perfectly know how much their grievances would be regarded, if they had no other method of engaging attention, than by complaining. Those who rule are extremely apt to think well of the constructions made by themselves in support of their own power. These are frequently erroneous, and pernicious to those they govern . . .

There are two other considerations relating to this head, that deserve the most serious attention.

By the late act, the officers of the customs are "impowered to enter into any house, warehouse, shop, cellar, or other place, in the British colonies or plantations in America, to search for or seize prohibited or unaccustomed goods," &c., on "writs granted by the superior or supreme court of justice, having jurisdiction within such colony or plantation respectively."

If we only reflect that the judges of these courts are to be during pleasure — that they are to have "adequate provision" made for them, which is to continue during their complaisant behavior — that they may be strangers to these colonies — what an engine of oppression may this authority be in such hands?

I am well aware, that writs of this kind may be granted at home, under the seal of the court of exchequer: But I know also, that the greatest asserters of the rights of Englishmen have always strenuously contended, that such a power was dangerous to freedom, and expressly contrary to the common law, which ever regarded a man's house as his castle, or a place of perfect security.

If such power was in the least degree dangerous there, it must be utterly destructive to liberty here. For the people there have two securities against the undue exercise of this power by the crown, which are wanting with us, if the late act takes place. In the first place, if any injustice is done there, the person injured may bring his action against the offender, and have it tried before independent judges, who are no parties in committing the injury. Here he must have it tried before dependent judges, being the men who granted the writ.

To say, that the cause is to be tried by a jury, can never reconcile men who have any idea of freedom, to

such a power. For we know that sheriffs in almost every colony on this continent, are totally dependent on the crown; and packing of the juries has been frequently practised even in the capital of the British empire. Even if juries are well inclined, we have too many instances of the influence of over-bearing unjust judges upon them. The brave and wise men who accomplished the revolution, thought the independency of judges essential to freedom.

The other security which the people have at home, but which we shall want here, is this.

If this power is abused there, the parliament, the grand resource of the oppressed people, is ready to afford relief. Redress of grievances must precede grants of money. But what regard can we expect to have paid to our assemblies, when they will not hold even the puny privilege of French parliaments — that of registering, before they are put in execution, edicts that take away our money.

The second consideration above hinted at, is this. There is a confusion in our laws, that is quite unknown in Great-Britain. As this cannot be described in a more clear or exact manner, than has been done by the ingenious author of the history of New-York, I beg leave to use his words. "The state of our laws opens a door to much controversy. The uncertainty, with respect to them, renders property precarious, and greatly exposes us to the arbitrary decision of bad judges. The common law of England is generally received, together with such statutes as were enacted before we had a legislature of our own, but our courts exercise a sovereign authority, in determining what parts of the common and statute law ought to be extended: For it must be admitted that the difference of circumstances necessarily requires us, in some cases to reject the determination of both. In many instances, they have also extended even acts of parliament, passed since we had a distinct legislature, which is greatly adding to our confusion. The practice of our courts is no less uncertain than the law. Some of the English rules are adopted, others rejected. Two things therefore seem to be absolutely necessary for the public security. First, the passing an act for settling the extent of the English laws. Secondly, that the courts ordain a general sett of rules for the regulation of the practice."

How easy it will be, under this "state of our laws," for an artful judge, to act in the most arbitrary manner, and yet cover his conduct under specious pretences; and how difficult it will be for the injured people to obtain relief, may be readily perceived. We may take a voyage of 3000 miles to complain; and after the trouble and hazard we have undergone, we may be told, that the collection of the revenue, and maintenance of the prerogative, must not be discouraged — and if the misbehavior is so gross and to admit of no justification, it may be said, that it was an error in judgment only, arising from the confusion of our laws, and the zeal of the King's servants to do their duty . . .

A Farmer

LETTER XII

My dear countrymen,

Our vigilance and our union are success and safety. Our negligence and our division are distress and death. They are worse — they are shame and slavery. Let us equally shun the benumbing stillness and the feverish activity of that ill informed zeal, which busies itself in maintaining little, mean, and narrow opinions. Let us, with a truly wise generosity and charity, banish and discourage all illiberal distinctions, which may arise from differences in situation, forms of government, or modes of religion. Let us consider ourselves as men — freemen — Christian freemen — separate from the rest of the world and firmly bound together by the same rights, interests and dangers. Let these keep our attention inflexibly fixed on the great objects, which we must continually regard, in order to preserve those rights, to promote those interests, and to avert those dangers.

Let these truths be indelibly impressed on our minds — that we cannot be happy, without being free — that we cannot be free, without being secure in our property — that we cannot be secure in our property, if without our consent, others may, as by right, take it away — that taxes imposed on us by parliament, do thus take it away — that duties laid for the sole purpose of raising money, are taxes — that attempts to lay such duties should be instantly and firmly opposed — that this opposition can never be effectual, unless it is the united effort of these provinces . . .

A Farmer

A View of the Causes and Consequences of the American Revolution, G. G. & J. Robinson, London, 1797, pp. 506-555.

Jonathan Boucher: On civil liberty, passive obedience and nonresistance (1775)

. . . It has just been observed, that the liberty inculcated in the Scriptures, is wholly of the spiritual or religious kind. This liberty was the natural result of the new religion in which mankind were then instructed; which certainly gave them no new civil privileges. They remained subject to the governments under which they lived, just as they had been before they became Christians, and just as others were who never became Christians; with this difference only, that the duty of submission and obedience to Government was enjoined on the converts to Christianity with new and stronger sanctions. The doctrines of the Gospel make no manner of alteration in the nature or form of Civil Government; but enforce afresh, upon all Christians, that obedience which is due to the respective Constitutions of every nation is which they may happen to live. Be the supreme power lodged in one or in many, be the kind of government established in any country absolute or limited, this is not the concern of the Gospel. It's single object, with respect to these public duties, is to enjoin obedience to the laws of every country, in every kind or form of government.

The only liberty or freedom which converts to Christianity could hope to gain by becoming Christians, was the being exempted from sundry burthensome and servile Jewish ordinances, on the one hand; and on the other, from Gentile blindness and superstition. They were also in some measure perhaps made more free in the inner man; by being endowed with greater firmness of mind in the cause of truth, against the terrors and the allurements of the world; and with such additional strength and vigour as enabled them more effectually to resist the natural violence of their lusts and passions. On all these accounts it was that our Savior so emphatically told the Jews, that the truth (of which himself was now the preacher) would make them free.   And on the same principle St. James terms the Gospel the perfect law of liberty . . .

Obedience to Government is every man's duty, because it is every man's interest: but it is particularly incumbent on Christians, because (in addition to it's moral fitness) it is enjoined by the positive commands of God: and therefore, when Christians are disobedient to human ordinances, they are also disobedient to God. If the form of government under which the good providence of God has been pleased to place us be mild and free, it is our duty to enjoy it with gratitude and with thankfulness; and, in particular, to be careful not to abuse it by licentiousness. If it be less indulgent and less liberal than in reason it ought to be, still it is our duty not to disturb and destroy the peace of the community, by becoming refractory and rebellious subjects, and resisting the ordinances of God. However humiliating such acquiescence may seem to men of warm and eager minds, the wisdom of God in having made it our duty is manifest. For, as it is the natural temper and bias of the human mind to be impatient under restraint, it was wise and merciful in the blessed Author of our religion not to add any new impulse to the natural force of this prevailing propensity, but, with the whole weight of his authority, altogether to discountenance every tendency to disobedience.

If it were necessary to vindicate the Scriptures for this their total unconcern about the principle which so many other writings seem to regard as the first of all human considerations, it might be observed, that, avoiding the vague and declamatory manner of such writings, and avoiding also the useless and impracticable subtleties of metaphysical definitions, these Scriptures have better consulted the great general interests of mankind, by summarily recommending and enjoining a conscientious reverence for law whether human or divine. To respect the laws, is to respect liberty in the only rational sense in which the term can be used; for liberty consists in a subserviency to law. "Where there is no law," says Mr. Locke, "there is no freedom." The mere man of nature (if such an one there ever was) has no freedom: all his lifetime he is subject to bondage. It is by being included within the pale of civil polity and government that he takes his rank in society as a free man.

Hence it follows, that we are free, or otherwise, as we are governed by law, or by the mere arbitrary will, or wills, or any individual, or any number of individuals. And liberty is not the setting at nought and despising established laws — much less the making our own wills the rule of our own actions, or the actions of others — and not bearing (whilst yet we dictate to others) the being dictated to, even by the laws of the land; but it is the being governed by laws, and by law only . . . .

The more carefully well-devised restraints of law

are enacted, and the more rigorously they are executed in any country, the greater degree of civil liberty does that country enjoy. To pursue liberty, then, in a manner not warranted by law, whatever the pretence may be, is clearly to be hostile to liberty: and those persons who thus promise you liberty, are themselves the servants of corruption.

"Civil liberty (says an excellent writer) is a "severe and a restrained thing; implies, in the notion of it, authority, settled subordinations, subjection, and obedience; and is altogether as much hurt by too little of this kind, as by too much of it. And the love of liberty, when it is indeed the love of liberty, which carries us to withstand tyranny, will as much carry us to reverence authority, and to support it; for this most obvious reason, that one is as necessary to the being of liberty, as the other is destructive of it. And, therefore, the love of liberty which does not produce this effect, the love of liberty which is not a real principle of dutiful behaviour towards authority, is as hypocritical as the religion which is not productive of a good life. Licentiousness is, in truth, such an excess of liberty as is of the same nature with tyranny. For, what is the difference betwixt them, but that one is lawless power exercised under pretence of authority, or by persons vested with it; the other, lawless power exercised under pretence of liberty, or without any pretence at all? A people, then, must always be less free in proportion as they are more licentious; licentiousness being not only different from liberty, but directly contrary to it — a direct breach upon it."

True liberty, then, is a liberty to do every thing that is right, and the being restrained from doing any thing that is wrong. So far from our having a right to do every thing that we please, under a notion of liberty, liberty itself is limited and confined — but limited and confined only by laws which are at the same time both it's foundation and it's support. It can, however, hardly be necessary to inform you, that ideas and notions respecting liberty, very different from these, are daily suggested in the speeches and the writings of the times; and also that some opinions on the subject of government at large, which appear to me to be particularly loose and dangerous, are advanced in the sermon now under consideration; and that, therefore, you will acknowledge the propriety of my bestowing some farther notice on them both.

It is laid down in this sermon, as a settled maxim; that the end of government is "the common good of mankind." I am not sure that the position itself is indisputable; but, if it were, it would by no means follow that, "this common good being matter of common feeling, government must therefore have been instituted by common consent." There is an appearance of logical accuracy and precision in this statement; but it is only an appearance. The position is vague and loose; and the assertion is made without an attempt to prove it. If by men's "common feelings" we are to understand that principle in the human mind called common sense, the assertion is either un-meaning and insignificant, or it is false. In no instance have mankind ever yet agreed as to what is, or is not, "the common good." A form or mode of government cannot be named, which these "common feelings" and "common consent," the sole arbiters, as it seems, of "common good," have not, at one time or another, set up and established, and again pulled down and reprobated. What one people in one age have con-curred in establishing as the "common good," another in another age have voted to be mischievous and big with ruin. The premises, therefore, that "the common good is matter of common feeling," being false, the consequence drawn from it, viz. that government was instituted by "common consent," is of course equally false.

This popular notion, that government was origi-nally formed by the consent or by a compact of the people, rests on, and is supported by, another similar notion, not less popular, nor better sounded. This other notion is, that the whole human race is born equal; and that no man is naturally inferior, or, in any respect, subjected to another; and that he can be made subject to another only by his own consent. The position is equally ill-founded and false both in its premises and conclusions. In hardly any sense that can be imagined is the position strictly true; but, as applied to the case under consideration, it is dem-onstrably not true . . .

It was the purpose of the Creator, that man should be social: but, without government, there can be no society; nor, without some relative inferiority and superiority, can there be any government. A musical instrument composed of chords, keys, or pipes, all perfectly equal in size and power, might as well be expected to produce harmony, as a society composed of members all perfectly equal to be productive of order and peace. If (according to the idea of the advocates of this chimerical scheme of equality) no man could rightfully be compelled to come in and be a member even of a government to be formed by a regular compact, but by his own individual consent; it clearly follows, from the same principles, that neither could he rightfully be made or compelled to submit to the ordinances of any government already formed, to which he has not individually or actually consented. On the principle of equality, neither his parents, nor even the vote of a majority of the society, (however virtuously and honourably that vote might be obtained,) can have any such authority over any man. Neither can it be maintained that acquiescence implies consent; because acquiescence may have been extorted from impotence or incapacity. Even an explicit consent can bind a man no longer than he chooses to be bound. The same principle of equality that exempts him from being governed without his own consent, clearly entitles him to recall and resume that consent whenever he sees fit, and he alone has a right to judge when and for what reasons it may be resumed.

Any attempt, therefore, to introduce this fantastic system into practice, would reduce the whole business of social life to the wearisome, confused, and useless talk of mankind's first expressing, and then with-drawing, their consent to an endless succession of schemes of government. Governments, though al-ways forming, would never be completely formed: for, the majority to-day, might be the minority to-morrow; and, of course, that which is now fixed might and would be soon unfixed. Mr. Locke indeed says, that, "by consenting with others to make one body-politic under government, a man puts himself under an obligation to every one of that society to submit to the determination of the majority, and to be concluded by it." For the sake of the peace of society, it is undoubtedly reasonable and necessary that this should be the case: but, on the principles of the system now under consideration, before Mr. Locke or any of his followers can have authority to say that it actually is the case, it must be stated and proved that every individual man, on entering into the social compact, did first consent, and declare his consent, to be concluded and bound in all cases by the vote of the majority. In making such a declaration, he would certainly consult both his interest and his duty; but at the same time he would also completely relinquish the principle of equality, and eventually subject himself to the possibility of being governed by ignorant and corrupt tyrants. . .

. . . This long enquiry concerning the divine origin and authority of government might perhaps have been deemed rather curious than useful, were it not of acknowledged moment, that some dangerous inferences which are usually drawn from the contrary opinion should be obviated. One of these dangerous inferences it seems to have been the aim of the sermon now before me to inculcate. Government being assumed to be a mere human ordinance, it is thence inferred, that "rulers are the servants of the public:" and, if they be, no doubt it necessarily follows, that they may (in the coarse phrase of the times) be cashiered or continued in pay, be reverenced or resisted, according to the mere whim or caprice of those over whom they are appointed to rule. Hence the author of this sermon also takes occasion to enter his protest against "passive obedience and non-resistance." . . . Whilst the right of resistance has thus incessantly been delivered from the pulpit, insisted on by orators, and inculcated by statesmen, the contrary position is still (I believe) the dictate of religion, and certainly the doctrine of the established Church, and still also the law of the land.

You are not now to learn my mind on this point. As, however, the subject has again been forced on me, let me be permitted again to obviate, if I can, some fresh misrepresentations, and again to correct some new mistakes.

All government, whether lodged in one or in many, is, in it's nature, absolute and irresistible. It is not within the competency even of the supreme power to limit itself; because such limitation can emanate only from a superior. For any government to make itself irresistible, and to cease to be absolute, it must cease to be supreme; which is but saying, in other words, that it must dissolve itself, or be destroyed. If, then, to resist government be to destroy it, every man who is a subject must necessarily owe to the government under which he lives an obedience either active or passive: active, where the duty enjoined may be

performed without offending God; and passive, (that is to say, patiently to submit to the penalties annexed to disobedience,) where that which is commanded by man is forbidden by God. No government upon earth can rightfully compel any one of it's subjects to an active compliance with any thing that is, or that appears to his conscience to be, inconsistent with, or contradictory to, the known laws of God: because every man is under a prior and superior obligation to obey God in all things. When such cases of incompatible demands of duty occur, every well-informed person knows what he is to do; and every well-principled person will do what he ought, viz. he will submit to the ordinances of God, rather than comply with the commandments of men. In thus acting he cannot err and this alone is "passive obedience;" which I entreat you to observe is so far from being "unlimited obedience," (as it's enemies wilfully persist to miscall it,) that it is the direct contrary. Resolute not to disobey God, a man of good principles determines, in case of competition, as the lesser evil, to disobey man: but he knows that he should also disobey God, were he not, at the same time, patiently to submit to any penalties incurred by his disobedience to man.

. . . In the present state of things, when a resistance is recommended, it must be, not against the king alone, but against the laws of the land. To encourage undistinguishing multitudes, by the vague term of resistance, to oppose all such laws as happen not to be agreeable to certain individuals, is neither more nor less than, by a regular plan, to attempt the subversion of the government: and I am not sure but that such attacks are more dangerous to free than to absolute governments.

Even the warmest advocates for resistance acknowledge, that, like civil liberty, the term is incapable of any accurate definition. Particular cases of injury and oppression are imagined: on which arguments are founded, to shew that mankind must be determined and governed, not by any known and fixed laws, but "by a law antecedent and paramount to all positive laws of men;" "by their natural sense and feelings." These unwritten, invisible, and undefinable "antecedent laws;" this indescribable "natural sense and feelings;" these "hidden powers and mysteries" in our Constitution, are points too refined and too subtle for argument. Indeed it can be to little purpose to argue, either on resistance or on any other subject, with men who are so weak as to declaim, when it is incumbent on them to reason.

Without any encouragement, mankind, alas! are, of themselves, far too prone to be presumptuous and self-willed; always disposed and ready to despise dominion, and to speak evil of dignities. There is, says a learned writer, such a "witchcraft in rebellion, as to tempt men to be rebels, even though they are sure to be damned for it." What dreadful confusions and calamities must have been occasioned in the world, had such strong and dangerous natural propensities been directly encouraged by any positive law!

. . . Mr. Locke, like many inferior writers, when defending resistance, falls into inconsistencies, and is at variance with himself. "Rebellion being," as he says, "an opposition not to persons, but to authority, which is founded only in the constitution and laws of the government, those, whoever they be, who by force break through, and by force justify their violation of them, are truly and properly rebels." To this argument no one can object: but it should be attended to, that, in political consideration, it is hardly possible to dissociate the ideas of authority in the abstract from persons vested with authority. To resist a person legally vested with authority, is, I conceive, to all intents and purposes, the same thing as to resist authority. Nothing, but it's success, could have rescued the revolution from this foul imputation, had it not been for the abdication. Accordingly this great event has always hung like a mill-stone on the necks of those who must protest against rebellions; whilst yet their system of politics requires that they should approve of resistance, and the revolution.

The resistance which your political counsellors urge you to practise, (and which no doubt was intended to be justified by the sermon which I have now been compelled to notice,) is not a resistance exerted only against the persons invested with the supreme power either legislative or executive, but clearly and literally against authority. Nay, if I at all understand the following declaration made by those who profess that they are the disciples of Mr. Locke, you are encouraged to resist not only all authority over us as it now exists, but any and all that it is possible to constitute. "Can men who exercise their reason believe, that the Divine Author of our existence intended a

part of the human race to hold an absolute property in, and an unbounded power over, others marked out by his infinite wisdom and goodness as the objects of a legal domination never rightfully resistible, however severe and oppressive?" It might be hazardous, perhaps, for me, even under shelter of a Scripture phrase, to call these words great swelling words; because they are congressional words. That they have excited a very general panic, and many apprehensions of a real impending slavery, is no more than might have been expected in a country where there is literally "absolute property in, and unbounded power over, human beings." How far this was intended, I presume not to judge. But, involved and obscure as the language (in which these extraordinary sentiments are couched) must be confessed to be, the declaration certainly points at all government: and it's full meaning amounts to a denial of that just supremacy which "the Divine Author of our existence" has beyond all question given to "one part of the human race" to hold over another. Without some paramount and irresistible power, there can be no government. In our Constitution, this supremacy is vested in the King and the Parliament; and, subordinate to them, in our Provincial Legislatures. If you were now released from this constitutional power, you must differ from all others "of the human race," if you did not soon find yourselves under a necessity of submitting to a power no less absolute, though vested in other persons, and a government differently constituted. And much does it import you to consider, whether those who are now so ready to promise to make the grievous yoke of your fathers lighter, may not themselves verify Rehoboam's assertion, and make you feel that their little fingers are thicker than your father's loins . . .

O my brethren, consult your own hearts, and follow your own judgments! and learn not your "measures of obedience" from men who weakly or wickedly imagine there can be liberty unconnected with law—and whose aim it is to drive you on, step by step, to a resistance which will terminate, if it does not begin, in rebellion! On all such trying occasions, learn the line of conduct which it is your duty and interest to observe, from our Constitution itself: which, in this particular, is a fair transcript or exemplification of the ordinance of God . . .

Principle never lay far beneath the surface of the conflict between Great Britain and her continental American colonies. For the English government, the principle was one of due submission to established authorities and historic political arrangements. Charters flowing from the sovereignty of the English King had conferred whatever rights and privileges the colonists had, and the English Parliament and judicial courts alone had the recognized authority to amplify and interpret these earlier documents. For the colonists, the principle was that of their rights as individuals. If they did not possess them as English citizens, they possessed them as natural men, and it was upon their Lockean faith in the natural, inalienable rights of man that the Americans put forth a theoretical argument for republican government. It was at this point that American moves toward independence took on revolutionary overtones, for the Americans then were not just defending a break with a particular king, they were endorsing a philosophy of self-government.

Arrived at over almost a decade of continuous political agitation, the American concept of government was very simply set forth by Thomas Jefferson in the opening words of the second paragraph of the Declaration of Independence:

> We hold these truths to be self evident: That all men are created equal; that they are endowed by their Creator with certain unalienable rights; that among these are life, liberty, and the pursuit of happiness; that, to secure these rights, governments are instituted among men, deriving their just powers from the consent of the governed; that whenever any form of government becomes destructive of these ends, it is the right of the people to alter or to abolish it.

In these straightforward statements the Americans asserted their determination to put into practice what had formerly been confined to theory. Power, they were saying, can only be rightfully used when it is limited to specific "natural" goals. The mere possession of power, however dignified by time and tradition, can not make it legitimate.

The first pamphlet to extol the positive benefits of independence came from the pen of Thomas Paine (1737–1809), an English radical who had come to America expressly to participate in the political agitation. *Common Sense* appeared in the early months of 1776 when the colonists were caught between their loyalty and fear of Great Britain and their unwillingness to back down from a full assertion of their rights under the British rule. Paine's clear, forceful writing helped make *Common Sense* so popular that it went through twenty-five editions in six months. His arguments were persuasive to thoughtful men, however, because he found a place for American yearnings for self-government within the philosophical teachings of the Enlightenment. Paine urged Americans to act upon the ideas philosophers merely talk about, in particular the belief in natural social laws that had universal applicability and rose above the pretension of any particular government. Not since the Puritans arrived to found a Bible Commonwealth had the colonists been given a mission of such high moral purpose. *Common Sense,* from which the reading in this section is taken, has been credited with mobilizing public opinion behind independence, a task Paine accomplished by joining a solution to the imperial impasse to a concept of national destiny which could bind the colonies together in a cause of great significance.

Thomas Paine: *Common Sense (1776)*

Some writers have so confounded society with government, as to leave little or no distinction between them; whereas they are not only different, but have different origins. Society is produced by our wants and government by our wickedness; the former promotes our happiness positively by uniting our affections, the latter negatively by restraining our vices. The one

Moncure Daniel Conway (ed.), *The Writings of Thomas Paine*, G. P. Putnam & Sons, New York, 1894, I, 69–76, 84–95, 99–102, 107–120.

encourages intercourse, the other creates distinctions. The first is a patron, the last a punisher.

Society in every state is a blessing, but government, even in its best state, is but a necessary evil; in its worst state an intolerable one: for when we suffer, or are exposed to the same miseries by a government, which we might expect in a country without government, our calamity is heightened by reflecting that we furnish the means by which we suffer. Government, like dress, is the badge of lost innocence; the palaces of kings are built upon the ruins of the bowers of paradise. For were the impulses of conscience clear, uniform and irresistibly obeyed, man would need no other law-giver; but that not being the case, he finds it necessary to surrender up a part of his property to furnish means for the protection of the rest; and this he is induced to do by the same prudence which in every other case advises him, out of two evils to choose the least. Wherefore, security being the true design and end of government, it unanswerably follows that whatever form thereof appears most likely to ensure it to us, with the least expence and greatest benefit, is preferable to all others.

In order to gain a clear and just idea of the design and end of government, let us suppose a small number of persons settled in some sequestered part of the earth, unconnected with the rest; they will then represent the first peopling of any country, or of the world. In this state of natural liberty, society will be their first thought. A thousand motives will excite them thereto; the strength of one man is so unequal to his wants, and his mind so unfitted for perpetual solitude, that he is soon obliged to seek assistance and relief of another, who in his turn requires the same. Four or five united would be able to raise a tolerable dwelling in the midst of a wilderness, but one man might labor out the common period of life without accomplishing any thing; when he had felled his timber he could not remove it, nor erect it after it was removed; hunger in the mean time would urge him to quit his work, and every different want would call him a different way. Disease, nay even misfortune, would be death; for though neither might be mortal, yet either would disable him from living, and reduce him to a state in which he might rather be said to perish than to die.

Thus necessity, like a gravitating power, would soon form our newly arrived emigrants into society, the reciprocal blessings of which would supercede, and render the obligations of law and government unnecessary while they remained perfectly just to each other; but as nothing but Heaven is impregnable to vice, it will unavoidably happen that in proportion as they surmount the first difficulties of emigration, which bound them together in a common cause, they will begin to relax in their duty and attachment to each other: and this remissness will point out the necessity of establishing some form of government to supply the defect of moral virtue.

Some convenient tree will afford them a State House, under the branches of which the whole colony may assemble to deliberate on public matters. It is more than probable that their first laws will have the title only of regulations and be enforced by no other penalty than public disesteem. In this first parliament every man by natural right will have a seat.

But as the colony increases, the public concerns will increase likewise, and the distance at which the members may be separated, will render it too inconvenient for all of them to meet on every occasion as at first, when their number was small, their habitations near, and the public concerns few and trifling. This will point out the convenience of their consenting to leave the legislative part to be managed by a select number chosen from the whole body, who are supposed to have the same concerns at stake which those have who appointed them, and who will act in the same manner as the whole body would act were they present. If the colony continue increasing, it will become necessary to augment the number of representatives, and that the interest of every part of the colony may be attended to, it will be found best to divide the whole into convenient parts, each part sending its proper number: and that the elected might never form to themselves an interest separate from the electors, prudence will point out the propriety of having elections often: because as the elected might by that means return and mix again with the general body of the electors in a few months, their fidelity to the public will be secured by the prudent reflection of not making a rod for themselves. And as this frequent interchange will establish a common interest with every part of the community, they will mutually and naturally support each other, and on this, (not on the unmeaning name of king,) depends the strength of government, and the happiness of the governed.

Here then is the origin and rise of government; namely, a mode rendered necessary by the inability of moral virtue to govern the world; here too is the design and end of government, viz. freedom and security. And however our eyes may be dazzled with show, or our ears deceived by sound; however prejudice may warp our wills, or interest darken our understanding, the simple voice of nature and reason will say, 'tis right.

I draw my idea of the form of government from a principle in nature which no art can overturn, viz. that the more simple any thing is, the less liable it is to be disordered, and the easier repaired when disordered; and with this maxim in view I offer a few remarks on the so much boasted Constitution of England. That it was noble for the dark and slavish times in which it was erected, is granted. When the world was overrun with tyranny the least remove therefrom was a glorious rescue. But that it is imperfect, subject to convulsions, and incapable of producing what it seems to promise, is easily demonstrated.

Absolute governments, (though the disgrace of human nature) have this advantage with them, they are simple; if the people suffer, they know the head from which their suffering springs; know likewise the remedy; and are not bewildered by a variety of causes and cures. But the Constitution of England is so exceedingly complex, that the nation may suffer for years together without being able to discover in which part the fault lies; some will say in one and some in another, and every political physician will advise a different medicine.

I know it is difficult to get over local or long standing prejudices, yet if we will suffer ourselves to examine the component parts of the English Constitution, we shall find them to be the base remains of two ancient tyrannies, compounded with some new Republican materials.

First.   The remains of monarchical tyranny in the person of the king.

Secondly.   The remains of aristocratical tyranny in the persons of the peers.

Thirdly.   The new Republican materials, in the persons of the Commons, on whose virtue depends the freedom of England.

The two first, by being hereditary, are independent of the people; wherefore in a constitutional sense they contribute nothing towards the freedom of the State.

To say that the Constitution of England is an union of three powers, reciprocally checking each other, is farcical; either the words have no meaning, or they are flat contradictions . . .

That the crown is this overbearing part in the English Constitution needs not be mentioned, and that it derives its whole consequence merely from being the giver of places and pensions is self-evident; wherefore, though we have been wise enough to shut and lock a door against absolute Monarchy, we at the same time have been foolish enough to put the crown in possession of the key.

The prejudice of Englishmen, in favor of their own government, by king, lords and Commons, arises as much or more from national pride than reason. Individuals are undoubtedly safer in England than in some other countries: but the will of the king is as much the law of the land in Britain as in France, with this difference, that instead of proceeding directly from his mouth, it is handed to the people under the formidable shape of an act of Parliament. For the fate of Charles the First hath only made kings more subtle — not more just . . .

Mankind being originally equals in the order of creation, the equality could only be destroyed by some subsequent circumstance: the distinctions of rich and poor may in a great measure be accounted for, and that without having recourse to the harsh illsounding names of oppression and avarice. Oppression is often the consequence, but seldom or never the means of riches; and though avarice will preserve a man from being necessitously poor, it generally makes him too timorous to be wealthy.

But there is another and greater distinction for which no truly natural or religious reason can be assigned, and that is the distinction of men into kings and subjects. Male and female are the distinctions of nature, good and bad the distinctions of heaven; but how a race of men came into the world so exalted above the rest, and distinguished like some new species, is worth inquiring into, and whether they are the means of happiness or of misery to mankind.

In the early ages of the world, according to the scripture chronology there were no kings; the consequence of which was, there were no wars; it is the pride of kings which throws mankind into confusion. Holland, without a king hath enjoyed more peace for this last century than any of the monarchical governments in Europe. Antiquity favors the same remark; for the quiet and rural lives of the first Patriarchs have a happy something in them, which vanishes when we come to the history of Jewish royalty.

Government by kings was first introduced into the world by the heathens, from whom the children of Israel copied the custom. It was the most prosperous invention the devil ever set on foot for the promotion of idolatry. The heathens paid divine honors to their deceased kings, and the Christian world has improved on the plan by doing the same to their living ones. How impious is the title of sacred majesty applied to a worm, who in the midst of his splendor is crumbling into dust!

As the exalting one man so greatly above the rest cannot be justified on the equal rights of nature, so neither can it be defended on the authority of scripture; for the will of the Almighty as declared by Gideon, and the prophet Samuel, expressly disapproves of government by kings. All anti-monarchical parts of scripture, have been very smoothly glossed over in monarchical governments, but they undoubtedly merit the attention of countries which have their governments yet to form. "Render unto Cesar the things which are Cesar's," is the scripture doctrine of courts, yet is is no support of monarchical government, for the Jews at that time were without a king, and in a state of vassalage to the Romans . . .

If we inquire into the business of a king, we shall find that in some countries they may have none; and after sauntering away their lives without pleasure to themselves or advantage to the nation, withdraw from the scene, and leave their successors to tread the same idle round. In absolute monarchies the whole weight of business civil and military lies on the king; the children of Israel in their request for a king urged this plea, "that he may judge us, and go out before us and fight our battles." But in countries where he is neither a judge nor a general, as in England, a man would be puzzled to know what is his business . . .

Men fall out with names without understanding them. For 'tis the republican and not the monarchical part of the Constitution of England which Englishmen glory in, viz. the liberty of choosing an House of Commons from out of their own body — and it is easy to see that when republican virtues fail, slavery ensues. Why is the Constitution of England sickly, but because monarchy hath poisoned the Republic; the crown has engrossed the Commons.

In England a king hath little more to do than to make war and give away places; which, in plain terms, is to empoverish the nation and set it together by the ears. A pretty business indeed for a man to be allowed eight hundred thousand sterling a year for, and worshipped into the bargain! Of more worth is one honest man to society, and in the sight of God, than all the crowned ruffians that ever lived.

In the following pages I offer nothing more than simple facts, plain arguments, and common sense: and have no other preliminaries to settle with the reader, than that he will divest himself of prejudice and prepossession, and suffer his reason and his feelings to determine for themselves: that he will put on, or rather that he will not put off, the true character of a man, and generously enlarge his views beyond the present day.

Volumes have been written on the subject of the struggle between England and America. Men of all ranks have embarked in the controversy, from different motives, and with various designs; but all have been ineffectual, and the period of debate is closed. Arms as the last resource decide the contest; the appeal was the choice of the king, and the continent has accepted the challenge . . .

The sun never shone on a cause of greater worth. 'Tis not the affair of a city, a county, a province, or a kingdom; but of a continent — of at least one eighth part of the habitable globe. 'Tis not the concern of a day, a year, or an age; posterity are virtually involved in the contest, and will be more or less affected even to the end of time, by the proceedings now. Now is the seed-time of continental union, faith and honor. The least fracture now will be like a name engraved with the point of a pin on the tender rind of a young oak; the wound would enlarge with the tree, and posterity read it in full grown characters.

By referring the matter from argument to arms, a new era for politics is struck — a new method of thinkings has arisen. All plans, proposals, &c. prior to the nineteenth of April, i.e. to the commencement of hostilities, are like the almanacks of the last year; which though proper then, are superceded and useless now. Whatever was advanced by the advocates on either side of the question then, terminated in one and the same point, viz. a union with Great Britain; the only difference between the parties was the method of effecting it; the one proposing force, the other friendship; but it has so far happened that the first has failed, and the second has withdrawn her influence.

As much has been said of the advantages of reconciliation, which, like an agreeable dream, has passed away and left us as we were, it is but right that we should examine the contrary side of the argument, and inquire into some of the many material injuries which these colonies sustain, and always will sustain, by being connected with and dependant on Great Britain. To examine that connection and dependance, on the principles of nature and common sense, to see what we have to trust to, if separated, and what we are to expect, if dependant.

I have heard it asserted by some, that as America has flourished under her former connection with Great Britain, the same connection is necessary towards her future happiness, and will always have the same effect. Nothing can be more fallacious than this kind of argument. We may as well assert that because a child has thrived upon milk, that it is never to have meat, or that the first twenty years of our lives is to become a precedent for the next twenty. But even this is admitting more than is true; for I answer roundly, that America would have flourished as much, and probably much more, had no European power taken any notice of her. The commerce by which she hath enriched herself are the necessaries of life, and will always have a market while eating is the custom of Europe.

But she has protected us, say some. That she hath engrossed us is true, and defended the continent at our expense as well as her own, is admitted; and she would have defended Turkey from the same motive, viz. for the sake of trade and dominion.

Alas! we have been long led away by ancient prejudices and made large sacrifices to superstition. We have boasted the protection of Great Britain, without considering, that her motive was interest not attachment; and that she did not protect us from our enemies on our account; but from her enemies on her own account, from those who had no quarrel with us on any other account, and who will always be our enemies on the same account. Let Britain waive her pretensions to the continent, or the continent throw off the dependance, and we should be at peace with France and Spain, were they at war with Britain. The miseries of Hanover's last war ought to warn us against connections.

It hath lately been asserted in Parliament, that the colonies have no relation to each other but through the parent country, i.e. that Pennsylvania and the Jerseys, and so on for the rest, are sister colonies by the way of England; this is certainly a very roundabout way of proving relationship, but it is the nearest and only true way of proving enmity (or enemyship, if I may so call it.) France and Spain never were, nor perhaps ever will be, our enemies as Americans, but as our being the subjects of Great Britain.

But Britain is the parent country, say some. Then the more shame upon her conduct. Even brutes do not devour their young, nor savages make war upon their families; wherefore, the assertion, if true, turns to her reproach; but it happens not to be true, or only partly so, and the phrase parent or mother country hath been jesuitically adopted by the king and his parasites, with a low papistical design of gaining an unfair bias on the credulous weakness of our minds. Europe, and not England, is the parent country of America. This new world hath been the asylum for the persecuted lovers of civil and religious liberty from every part of Europe. Hither have they fled, not from the tender embraces of the mother, but from the cruelty of the monster; and it is so far true of England, that the same tyranny which drove the first emigrants from home, pursues their descendants still.

In this extensive quarter of the globe, we forget the narrow limits of three hundred and sixty miles (the extent of England) and carry our friendship on a larger scale; we claim brotherhood with every European Christian, and triumph in the generosity of the sentiment.

It is pleasant to observe by what regular gradations we surmount the force of local prejudices, as we enlarge our acquaintance with the world. A man born in any town in England divided into parishes, will naturally associate most with his fellow parishioners (because their interests in many cases will be common) and distinguish him by the name of neighbor; if he meet him but a few miles from home, he drops the narrow idea of a street, and salutes him by the name of townsman; if he travel out of the county and meet him in any other, he forgets the minor divisions of street and town, and calls him countryman, i.e. countyman; but if in their foreign excursions they should associate in France, or any other part of Europe, their local remembrance would be enlarged into that of Englishman. And by a just parity of reasoning, all Europeans meeting in America, or any other quarter of the globe, are countrymen; for England, Holland, Germany, or Sweden, when compared with the whole, stand in the same places on the larger scale, which the divisions of street, town, and county do on the smaller ones; distinctions too limited for continental minds. Not one third of the inhabitants, even of this province, Pennsylvania, are of English descent. Wherefore, I reprobate the phrase of parent or mother country applied to England only, as being false, selfish, narrow and ungenerous ...

Much hath been said of the united strength of Britain and the colonies, that in conjunction they might bid defiance to the world. But this is mere presumption; the fate of war is uncertain, neither do the expressions mean any thing; for this continent would never suffer itself to be drained of inhabitants, to support the British arms in either Asia, Africa or Europe.

Besides, what have we to do with setting the world at defiance? Our plan is commerce, and that, well attended to, will secure us the peace and friendship of all Europe; because it is the interest of all Europe to have America a free port. Her trade will always be a protection, and her barrenness of gold and silver secure her from invaders.

I challenge the warmest advocate for reconciliation to show a single advantage that this continent can reap by being connected with Great Britain. I repeat the challenge; not a single advantage is derived. Our corn will fetch its price in any market in Europe, and our imported goods must be paid for buy them where we will.

But the injuries and disadvantages which we sustain by that connection, are without number; and our duty to mankind at large, as well as to ourselves, instruct us to renounce the alliance: because, any submission to, or dependence on, Great Britain, tends directly to involve this continent in European wars and quarrels, and set us at variance with nations who would otherwise seek our friendship, and against whom we have neither anger nor complaint. As Europe is our market for trade, we ought to form no partial connection with any part of it. It is the true interest of America to steer clear of European contentions, which she never can do, while, by her dependence on Britain, she is made the make-weight in the scale of British politics.

Europe is too thickly planted with kingdoms to be long at peace, and whenever a war breaks out between England and any foreign power, the trade of America goes to ruin, because of her connection with Britain. The next war may not turn out like the last, and should it not, the advocates for reconciliation now will be wishing for separation then, because neutrality in that case would be a safer convoy than a man of war. Every thing that is right or reasonable pleads for separation. The blood of the slain, the weeping voice of nature cries, 'Tis time to part. Even the distance at which the Almighty hath placed England and America is a strong and natural proof that the authority of the one over the other, was never the design of heaven. The time likewise at which the continent was discovered, adds weight to the argument, and the manner in which it was peopled, encreases the force of it. The Reformation was preceded by the discovery of America: As if the Almighty graciously meant to open a sanctuary to the persecuted in future years, when home should afford neither friendship nor safety.

The authority of Great Britain over this continent, is a form of government, which sooner or later must have an end. And a serious mind can draw no true pleasure by looking forward, under the painful and positive conviction that what he calls "the present constitution" is merely temporary. As parents, we can have no joy, knowing that this government is not sufficiently lasting to insure any thing which we may bequeath to posterity. And by a plain method of argument, as we are running the next generation into debt, we ought to do the work of it, otherwise we use them meanly and pitifully. In order to discover the line of our duty rightly, we should take our children in our hand, and fix our station a few years farther into life; that eminence will present a prospect which a few present fears and prejudices conceal from our sight.

Though I would carefully avoid giving unnecessary offence, yet I am inclined to believe, that all those who espouse the doctrine of reconciliation, may be included within the following descriptions.

Interested men, who are not to be trusted, weak men who cannot see, prejudiced men who will not see, and a certain set of moderate men who think better of the European world than it deserves; and this last class, by an ill-judged deliberation, will be the cause of more calamities to this continent than all the other three . . .

Men of passive tempers look somewhat lightly over the offences of Great Britain, and, still hoping for the best, are apt to call out, Come, come, we shall be friends again for all this. But examine the passions and feelings of mankind: bring the doctrine of reconciliation to the touchstone of nature, and then tell me whether you can hereafter love, honor, and faithfully serve the power that hath carried fire and sword into your land? If you cannot do all these, then are you only deceiving yourselves, and by your delay bringing ruin upon posterity. Your future connection with Britain, whom you can neither love nor honor, will be forced and unnatural, and being formed only on the plan of present convenience, will in a little time fall into a relapse more wretched than the first . . .

Dearly, dearly do we pay for the repeal of the acts, if that is all we fight for; for, in a just estimation 'tis as great a folly to pay a Bunker Hill price for law as for land. As I have always considered the independancy of this continent, as an event which sooner or later must arrive, so from the late rapid progress of the continent to maturity, the event cannot be far off. Wherefore, on the breaking out of hostilities, it was not worth the while to have disputed a matter which time would have finally redressed, unless we meant to be in earnest: otherwise it is like wasting an estate on a suit at law, to regulate the trespasses of a tenant whose lease is just expiring. No man was a warmer wisher for a reconciliation than myself, before the

fatal nineteenth of April, 1775, but the moment the event of that day was made known, I rejected the hardened, sullen-tempered Pharaoh of England for ever; and disdain the wretch, that with the pretended title of Father of his people can unfeelingly hear of their slaughter, and composedly sleep with their blood upon his soul.

But admitting that matters were now made up, what would be the event? I answer, the ruin of the continent. And that for several reasons.

First. The powers of governing still remaining in the hands of the king, he will have a negative over the whole legislation of this continent. And as he hath shown himself such an inveterate enemy to liberty, and discovered such a thirst for arbitrary power, is he, or is he not, a proper person to say to these colonies, *You shall make no laws but what I please!?* And is there any inhabitant of America so ignorant as not to know, that according to what is called the *present Constitution,* this continent can make no laws but what the king gives leave to; and is there any man so unwise as not to see, that (considering what has happened) he will suffer no law to be made here but such as suits *his* purpose? We may be as effectually enslaved by the want of laws in America, as by submitting to laws made for us in England. After matters are made up (as it is called) can there be any doubt, but the whole power of the crown will be exerted to keep this continent as low and humble as possible? Instead of going forward we shall go backward, or be perpetually quarrelling, or ridiculously petitioning. We are already greater than the king wishes us to be, and will he not hereafter endeavor to make us less? To bring the matter to one point, Is the power who is jealous of our prosperity, a proper power to govern us? Whoever says No, to this question is an independent for independency means no more than this, whether we shall make our own laws, or whether the king, the greatest enemy this continent hath, or can have, shall tell us *there shall be no laws but such as I like.*

But the king, you will say, has a negative in England; the people there can make no laws without his consent. In point of right and good order, it is something very ridiculous that a youth of twenty-one (which hath often happened) shall say to several millions of people older and wiser than himself, "I forbid this or that act of yours to be law." But in this place I decline this sort of reply, though I will never cease to expose the absurdity of it, and only answer that England being the king's residence, and America not so, makes quite another case. The king's negative here is ten times more dangerous and fatal than it can be in England; for there he will scarcely refuse his consent to a bill for putting England into as strong a state of defense as possible, and in America he would never suffer such a bill to be passed.

America is only a secondary object in the system of British politics. England consults the good of this country no further than it answers her own purpose. Wherefore, her own interest leads her to suppress the growth of ours in every case which doth not promote her advantage, or in the least interferes with it. A pretty state we should soon be in under such a second hand government, considering what has happened! Men do not change from enemies to friends by the alteration of a name: And in order to show that reconciliation now is a dangerous doctrine, I affirm, that it would be policy in the king at this time to repeal the acts, for the sake of reinstating himself in the government of the provinces; In order that he may accomplish by craft and subtlety, in the long run, what he cannot do by force and violence in the short one. Reconciliation and ruin are nearly related.

Secondly. That as even the best terms which we can expect to obtain can amount to no more than a temporary expedient, or a kind of government by guardianship, which can last no longer than till the colonies come of age, so the general face and state of things in the interim will be unsettled and unpromising. Emigrants of property will not choose to come to a country whose form of government hangs but by a thread, and who is every day tottering on the brink of commotion and disturbance; and numbers of the present inhabitants would lay hold of the interval to dispose of their effects, and quit the continent.

But the most powerful of all arguments is, that nothing but independance, i. e. a continental form of government, can keep the peace of the continent and preserve it inviolate from civil wars . . .

But where, say some, is the king of America? I'll tell you, friend, he reigns above, and doth not make havoc of mankind like the royal brute of Great Britain. Yet that we may not appear to be defective even in earthly honors, let a day be solemnly set apart for proclaiming the charter; let it be brought forth placed on the divine law, the Word of God; let a crown be placed thereon, by which the world may know, that so far as we approve the monarchy, that in America the law is king. For as in absolute governments the king is law, so in free countries the law ought to be king; and there ought to be no other . . .

A government of our own is our natural right: and when a man seriously reflects on the precariousness of human affairs, he will become convinced, that it is infinitely wiser and safer, to form a Constitution of our own in a cool deliberate manner, while we have it in our power, than to trust such an interesting event to time and chance. If we omit it now, some Massanello may hereafter arise, who, laying hold of popular disquietudes, may collect together the desperate and the discontented, and by assuming to themselves the powers of government, finally sweep away the liberties of the continent like a deluge. Should the government of America return again into the hands of Britain, the tottering situation of things will be a temptation for some desperate adventurer to try his fortune; and in such a case, what relief can Britain give? Ere she should hear the news, the fatal business might be done; and ourselves suffering like the wretched Britons under the oppression of the conqueror. Ye that oppose independance now, ye know not what ye do: ye are opening a door to eternal tyranny, by keeping vacant the seat of government. There are thousands and tens of thousands, who would think it glorious to expel from the continent, that barbarous and hellish power, which hath stirred up the indians and the negroes to destroy us; the cruelty hath a double guilt, it is dealing brutally by us, and treacherously by them.

To talk of friendship with those in whom our reason forbids us to have faith, and our affections wounded through a thousand pores instruct us to detest, is madness and folly. Every day wears out the little remains of kindred between us and them; and can there be any reason to hope, that as the relationship expires, the affection will increase, or that we shall agree better when we have ten times more and greater concerns to quarrel over than ever?

Ye that tell us of harmony and reconciliation,

can ye restore to us the time that is past? Can ye give
to prostitution its former innocence? neither can ye
reconcile Britain and America. The last cord now is
broken, the people of England are presenting addresses against us. There are injuries which nature
cannot forgive; she would cease to be nature if she
did. As well can the lover forgive the ravisher of his
mistress, as the continent forgive the murders of
Britain. The Almighty hath implanted in us these
unextinguishable feelings for good and wise purposes.
They are the guardians of his image in our hearts. They
distinguish us from the herd of common animals. The
social compact would dissolve, and justice be extirpated
from the earth, or have only a casual existence were we
callous to the touches of affection. The robber and
the murderer would often escape unpunished, did not
the injuries which our tempers sustain, provoke us
into justice.

O! ye that love mankind! Ye that dare oppose
not only the tyranny but the tyrant, stand forth! Every
spot of the old world is overrun with oppression.
Freedom hath been hunted round the globe. Asia and
Africa have long expelled her. Europe regards her like
a stranger, and England hath given her warning to depart. O! receive the fugitive, and prepare in time an
asylum for mankind.

In the months that followed the adoption of the Declaration of Independence by the Second Continental Congress, the individual colonies formed their own governments, producing constitutions which detailed the political arrangements of the new republics. In addition to drafting a constitution, the Virginia convention drew up a Declaration of Rights which was widely distributed throughout the other states and became a model for similar bills of rights for Massachusetts, Pennsylvania, Delaware, Maryland, North Carolina, and New Hampshire. These bills of rights made explicit the philosophical underpinnings of the new American political institutions. The Declaration of Independence had set forth the revolutionary proposition that government existed only to protect the rights of the governed; the bills of rights detailed those specific rights which the new state governments would protect.

The drafting of these bills of rights to protect people from the unjust exercise of power pushed to the foreground the question of religious liberty. The presence of many different religious groups prevented the establishment of a single state religion, but many Americans, believing that the maintenance of religion was absolutely essential to law and public morality, favored a multiple-establishment in which tax funds would be distributed to all churches proportional to their membership. Representatives of the major Protestant denominations favored this solution, but religious groups like the Quakers and Baptists had always favored a complete separation of church and state. Additional support for this position came from the rationalists who wanted to free the individual conscience and untie the traditional knot between government and religion.

The first battleground for total disestablishment developed in Virginia. In spite of the guarantee of religious liberty in the Virginia Declaration of Rights, it took a protracted campaign to divest the Virginia Episcopal Church, the former Anglican church, of its colonial privileges. The campaign itself was of great interest because it brought together two very dissimilar groups — the simple, usually poor pietists who had suffered harassment from the official church, and sophisticated men like James Madison and Thomas Jefferson who viewed the cause of religious liberty as a step toward man's liberation from superstition and bigotry. The pietists — many of whom had been converted during the Great Awakening — were heirs of the traditional Baptist view that the purity of true churches could only be preserved if they remained independent of all government interference. The rationalists, on the other hand, were more concerned with saving man, the citizen, from the stultifying influence of authoritarian churches.

The climax of their long struggle for religious liberty came with the defeat of the Virginia Bill Establishing a Provision for Teachers of the Christian Religion. Church conservatives, aided by the vigorous oratory of Patrick Henry, had proposed an annual tax for the support of the Christian religion. Hotly debated throughout the state, the issue turned on whether or not churches could survive without some sort of civil establishment. By extending tax revenues to all Christian religions in the state, the bill's proponents hoped that they had found a compromise between the unpopular single establishment and the conversion of all churches into voluntary associations bereft of public support. The Pietists and the Rationalists were determined to settle for nothing less than the complete separation of church and state. Their victory, repeated in most of the other states, carried one step further the breach in America between individual and social purposes. With the ratification of the federal Bill of Rights in 1791, the possibility of federal support for religion was extinguished, but church establishments in the old Puritan colonies of Massachusetts and Connecticut continued on into the 19th century. A memorial opposing the Virginia assessment bill is presented in the following reading.

The difficulty of giving concrete expression to the lofty ideals of the Declaration of Independence touched the issue of slavery as well. The colonists' rationale for self-government rested on assertions of inalienable, natural rights which were flatly contradicted by the existence of slavery. The Declaration had asserted unambiguously that in everything that pertained to government, men were equal, yet a third of the delegates were slave-holders. Contemporaries were well aware of the irony of their assertions, and many of the revolutionary radicals wanted to make the commitment to equality explicit as a means to ending slavery rather than wait for the extinction of the institution before affirming natural rights. In the Virginia state constitutional convention, delegates argued for a week before they adopted an opening statement on human equality. In Delaware, the declaration of equality was dropped altogether, but in Massachusetts the constitutional assertion of human equality was used by several different slaves as the basis for successful litigation against their masters. Abolitionist societies waged vigorous and successful campaigns against slavery in the Northern colonies, and antislavery sentiment even spread to the South where schemes for gradual abolition were debated and the terms for personal manumission were liberalized. Although the optimism about the speedy eradication of slavery was ill-founded, contemporaries were well aware of the incongruity between slavery and their natural-rights convictions.

The tension between the ideals used to justify the American Revolution and the actual social practices of the new nation was keenly felt in the closing years of the 18th century. Americans had been unified and their cause ennobled by their commitment to idealistic political principles, but they were reluctant to make substantial sacrifices to implement these principles once independence had been won. Slavery and religious intolerance were only the most important in a whole range of colonial practices which were incompatible with the nation's new status as the world's champion of freedom, equality, and justice. At a more profound level, however, the Americans were becoming trapped in their own ideological cage, for the more they removed the traditional restraints upon human behavior the more difficult they were making the imposition of the high moral standards implied in their national creed.

Presbytery of Hanover County, Virginia, memorial to the General Assembly of Virginia (1777)

Gentlemen— The united clergy of the Presbyterian church of Virginia assembled in Presbytery beg leave to address your honorable house upon a few important subjects in which we find ourselves interested as citizens of this State . . .

We have understood that a comprehensive incorporating act had been and is at present in aggitation, whereby ministers of gospel as such, of certain descriptions, shall have legal advantages which are not proposed to be extended to the people at large of any denomination. A proposition has been made by some gentlemen in the house of delegates, we are told, to extend the grace to us amongst others in our professional capacity. If this be so we are bound to acknowledge with gratitude our obligations to such gentlemen for their inclination to favor us with the sanction of public authority in the discharge of our duty. But as the scheme of incorporating clergymen, independent of the religious communities to which they belong, is inconsistent with our ideas of propriety, we request the liberty of declining any such solitary honor should it be again proposed. To form clergymen into a distinct order in the community, and especially where it would be possible for them to have the principal direction of a considerable public estate by such incorporation, has a tendency to render them independent, at length, of the churches whose ministers they are; and this has been too often found by experience to produce ignorance, immorality and neglect of the duties of their station.

Besides, if clergymen were to be erected by the State into a distinct political body, detached from the rest of the citizens, with the express design of "enabling them to direct spiritual matters," which we all possess without such formality, it would naturally tend to introduce the antiquated and absurd system in which government is owned in effect to be the fountain head of spiritual influences to the church. It would establish an immediate, a peculiar, and for that very reason, in our opinion, illicit connection

Charles F. James, *Documentary History of the Struggle for Religious Liberty in Virginia*, J. P. Bell, Lynchburg, Virginia, 1900, Appendices.

between government and such as were thus distinguished. The Legislature in that case would be the head of the religious party, and its dependent members would be entitled to all decent reciprocity to a becoming paternal and fostering care. This we suppose would be given a preference, and creating a distinction between citizens equally good, on account of something entirely foreign from civil merit, which would be a source of endless jealousies, and inadmissible in a Republic of any other well directed government. The principle, too, which this system aims to establish is both false and dangerous to religion, and we take this opportunity to remonstrate and protest against it. The real ministers of true religion derive their authority to act in the duties of their profession from a higher source than any Legislature on earth, however respectable. Their office relates to the care of the soul, and preparing it for a future state of existence, and their administrations are, or ought to be, of a spiritual nature suited to this momentous concern. And it is plain from the very nature of the case that they should neither expect nor receive from government any commission or direction in this respect. We hope, therefore, that the house of delegates share so large a portion of that philosophic and liberal discernment which prevails in America at present, as to see this matter in its proper light — and that they will understand too well the nature of their duty, as the equal and common guardians of the chartered rights of all the citizens, to permit a connection of this kind we have just now mentioned to subsist between them and the spiritual instructors of any religious denomination in the State. The interference of government in religion cannot be indifferent to us, and as it will probably come under consideration at the present session of the Assembly, we request the attention of the honorable House to our sentiments upon this head.

We conceive that human legislation ought to have affairs alone for its concern. Legislators in free States possess delegated authority for the good of the community at large in its political and civil capacity.

The existence, preservation and happiness of society should be their only object, and to this their public cares should be confined. Whatever is not materially connected with this lies not within their province as statesmen. The thoughts, the intentions,

the faith and the consciences of men, with their modes of worship, lie beyond their reach, and are ever to be referred to a higher and more penetrating tribunal. These internal and spiritual matters cannot be measured by human rule, nor be amenable to human laws. It is the duty of every man for himself to take care of his immortal interests in a future state, where we are to account for our conduct as individuals; and it is by no means the business of the Legislature to attend to this, for there governments and states, as collective bodies, shall no more be known.

Religion, therefore, as a spiritual system, and its ministers in a professional capacity, ought not to be under the direction of the State.

Neither is it necessary for their existence that they should be publicly supported by legal provision for the purpose, as tried experience hath often shown; although it is absolutely necessary to the existence and welfare of every political combination of men in society to have the support of religion and its solemn institutions, as it affects the conduct of rational beings more than human laws can possibly do. On this account it is wise policy in legislators to seek its alliance and solicit its aid in a civil view, because of its happy influence upon the morality of its citizens, and its tendency to preserve the veneration of an oath, or an appeal to heaven, which is the cement of the social union. It is upon this principle alone, in our opinion, that a legislative body has right to interfere in religion at all, and of consequence we suppose that this interference ought only to extend to the preserving of the public worship of the Deity, and the supporting of institutions for inculcating the great fundamental principles of all religion, without which society could not easily exist. Should it be thought necessary at present for the Assembly to exert the right of supporting religion in general by an assessment on all the people, we would wish it to be done on the most liberal plan. A general assessment of the kind we have heard proposed is an object of such consequence that it excites much anxious speculation amongst your constituents.

We therefore earnestly pray that nothing may be done in the case inconsistent with the proper objects of human legislation, or the Declaration of Rights, as published at the Revolution. We hope that the assessment will not be proposed under the idea of supporting religion as a spiritual system, relating to the care of the soul, and preparing it for its future destiny. We hope that no attempt will be made to point out articles of faith that are not essential to the preservation of society; or to settle modes of worship; or to interfere in the internal government of religious communities; or to render the ministers of religion independent of the will of the people whom they serve. We expect from our representatives that careful attention to the political equality of all the citizens which a republic ought ever to cherish, and no scheme of an assessment will be encouraged which will violate the happy privilege we now enjoy of thinking for ourselves in all cases where conscience is concerned . . .

SUGGESTIONS FOR FURTHER READING

Charles M. Andrews, *The Colonial Background of the American Revolution*, Yale University Press, New Haven, 1924.

Bernard Bailyn, *The Ideological Origins of the American Revolution*, Harvard University Press, Cambridge, 1967.

Thomas C. Barrow, "The American Revolution as a Colonial War for Independence," *William and Mary Quarterly*, 25 (1968), 452–64.

Carl Becker, *The Declaration of Independence*, Vintage, New York, 1942.

Carl Bridenbaugh, *Mitre and Sceptre*, Oxford University Press, New York, 1962.

John G. Buchanan, "Drumfire from the Pulpit: Natural Law in Colonial Election Sermons in Massachusetts," *American Journal of Legal History*, 12 (1968).

Richard Buel, Jr. "Democracy and the American Revolution: A Frame of Reference," *William and Mary Quarterly*, 21 (1964).

R. Freeman Butts, *The American Tradition in Religion and Education*, Beacon Press, Boston, 1950.

Oliver M. Dickerson, *The Navigation Acts and the American Revolution*, A. S. Barnes, Cranbury, New Jersey, 1951.

Cecelia Kenyon, "Republicanism and Radicalism in the American Revolution: An Old-Fashioned Interpretation," *William and Mary Quarterly*, 19 (1962).

Staughton Lynd, *Intellectual Origins of American Radicalism*, Vintage, New York, 1968.

Edmund Morgan, *The Stamp Act Crisis*, Collier, New York, 1953.

William H. Nelson, "The Revolutionary Character of the American Revolution," *American Historical Review*, 70 (1965).

Robert Allen Rutland, *The Birth of the Bill of Rights*, 1776–1791, Collier, New York, 1955.

Gordon S. Wood, "Rhetoric and Reality in the American Revolution," *William and Mary Quarterly*, 23 (1966).

Arthur Zilversmit, *The First Emancipation: The Abolition of Slavery in the North*, University of Chicago Press, Chicago, 1967.

THE CONSTITUTION,
ITS CRITICS,
AND ITS INTERPRETERS

Chapter 5 1787-1819

The American revolutionary movement was a strong
unifier of public sentiment. Despite their separate histories, the colonists demonstrated a keen sense of kin-
ship which created a solidarity that lasted throughout
the War. Once independence had been won, however,
the diversity of opinion and personal assertiveness more
characteristic of Americans reappeared. The general
principles of republican self-government were widely
affirmed, but they in themselves were no blueprint for
the political structure to be raised. The questions of
exactly how the Americans should govern themselves
or which means were most suitable for achieving common goals remained to be answered.

The most immediate problem facing American
leaders when peace came was how to correct the shortcomings of their confederation. The Articles of Confederation, which were not ratified until 1781, had
only formalized the very loose working relationship of
the war. The states participated in the Confederation
on an equal footing. Regardless of its population, each
state had one vote in all decisions. Laws made by the
Congress of the United States were only binding on the
states as political units. Congress could take no direct
action against individual Americans. In fact, there were
no citizens of the United States, but rather citizens of
particular states that were confederated. There was no
executive or judiciary for the Confederation, only the
single deliberative body of Congress, and if any state
flouted a Congressional measure, compliance could be

enforced only by a major aggressive act such as a boycott or invasion. The Articles further protected state sovereignty by specifying that important decisions required nine of the states to agree and amendments to the Articles needed unanimous approval.

There were practical objections to government under the Articles which almost all public figures agreed must be corrected. The inability of Congress to raise taxes — they could only requisition the individual states — had prevented the repayment of the national war debt and left some influential Americans embittered about their government. Foreign creditors had also lost faith in the word of Congress and were unlikely to lend money in the future to private or public borrowers. Individual state legislatures were passing regulations and taxes obstructing interstate commerce which Congress was helpless to control. Abroad, American diplomats were getting nowhere in their efforts to secure commercial treaties with European countries. Why should English or Spanish statesmen negotiate treaties when they knew full well that Congress could not force the individual states to honor national commitments? Several attempts to change specific articles had foundered on the requirement for unanimous approval, but finally agreement was reached to hold a special convention to amend the Articles in 1787.

While most Americans agreed that the Articles needed amending, those who spearheaded the drive for a convention felt that the entire concept behind the Articles was inadequate. They found no expression in the loose confederation of states for the nationalistic spirit which fighting the war against England had engendered. Their wartime experience had made them sensitive to the weaknesses of a confederation which maximized local autonomy and frustrated general action. In the post-war period many other Americans, accustomed to economic legislation from Great Britain, were disappointed when the new American government failed to respond to the dislocations in the economy. Similarly, the weakness of the central government caused others to fear outbreaks of lawlessness. When hard-pressed farmers in western Massachusetts closed down the county courts by force of arms, people in

many states became thoroughly alarmed about the apparent weaknesses of the Confederation.

Each of these fundamental criticisms of the Articles pointed to the limitations inherent in the radical liberalism set forth in the Declaration of Independence. The concept of governments existing solely to protect the inalienable rights of men overlooked too many of the other functions of government, such as giving expression to national goals, promoting the power, glory, or prosperity of a nation, and maintaining a particular social order. The conflict over amending the Articles of Confederation, therefore, went deeper than dispute over correcting some obvious flaws in tax and regulatory powers. It reflected two opposing republican positions — the one favoring republican government as a means of limiting all government to the minimal power needed to protect personal liberties, and the other replacing the sovereignty of king or Parliament with the sovereignty of the electorate. In the latter view, republican government is not necessarily weaker than monarchical government; it is just more responsive to the governed.

At Philadelphia the convention leaders began with the assumption that the American situation called for a central government which could act with strength and vigor. Although instructed to amend the Articles, the fifty-five delegates side-stepped these instructions and spent four months drafting an entirely new frame of government. The preamble to their draft constitution described the result as a move to "create a more perfect union." This was certainly the most significant difference between the old Confederation and their proposals. Where the Articles had left state sovereignty intact, the Constitution created a national government which was supreme in certain specified areas and empowered to act directly upon individual citizens of the United States. As astute politicians, the delegates knew full well the vitality of the existing state governments, but their hope was to create a new kind of federalism where local autonomy could be preserved without sacrificing the goal of an effective national government.

During the ensuing two years, the states held special ratification conventions to consider the proposed

Constitution. Those who opposed the Constitution did so in terms of the dominant attitudes of the revolutionary period: distrust of power, support of local government, and the endorsement of equal rights. The Constitution's defenders emphasized the need for energetic government if America were to prosper. In general, those who favored the strict limitation of civil power favored preserving state sovereignty, apparently assuming that localized centers of power could be more easily watched by the electorate. Those who wanted strong government favored centering a great deal more power at the national level. The ratification of the Constitution was a victory for a well-organized group of national-minded political leaders. The majority of American voters no doubt agreed that they needed a stronger national government, but disagreement lay dormant on a number of unsettled questions about American life and politics.

Although the Constitution created a lasting frame of government for the United States, it left unresolved the question of what the role of the people should be. All other societies in the Western World exercised strict control over the people and restricted the exercise of power to the upper class. Riots, rebellions, and even civil wars had marked the histories of European countries, but few had thought of preventing these disruptions by decreasing social control. Popular disturbances had seemed to prove the need for continued restraint. The idea of limiting government's coercive power rested on the new social theory that average men and women possessed enough good sense and self-control to lead their lives without authoritarian institutions to guide them. Those who had faith in the common man felt that he was also capable of playing a larger part in his own government. The Revolution had brought many new people into contact with political processes, and common men were acquiring an awareness of the part which they could play in them. Yet the most influential Americans at the time of the ratification of the new Constitution were not democrats. They recognized the right of the people to select public officials and to enjoy equal protection under the law, but once the elections were over, they believed

that the people should leave the actual governing to those elected to office.

When the Constitution was criticized for its failure to protect individual liberties, the pro-Constitution Federalists were willing to make an agreement with the anti-Federalists to add a Bill of Rights, but the Founding Fathers shied away from the democratic principle of equal power as well as equal rights. While despising inherited privileges, they accepted as natural the deference which a poor, uneducated man paid to his superiors. Even those who granted that the average person might possess political wisdom feared that unalloyed majority rule was inherently dangerous, giving to mere numbers the power to run roughshod over the rights of individuals. They also feared what unpropertied men would do to property rights. The primary goals of the founding fathers were the securing of order, justice, and freedom under the law; only secondarily were they concerned with extending the limits of political power. In this they reflected the unspoken assumptions of their social position which were essentially liberal rather than democratic. If government kept open the avenues to property and protected it once acquired, those with ability, ambition, and energy would rightfully prosper. It was this type of person who was the principle beneficiary of American institutions.

Although slavery did not become an issue during the ratification process, the Founding Fathers failed to embed the principles of the Declaration of Independence in the permanent frame of government for the United States. The expiring Congress of the old Confederation, meeting while the Constitutional Convention was being held, banned the extension of slavery into the public domain of the Northwest Territory, but left the spread of slavery into the Southwest Territory unchecked. The Founding Fathers tacitly accepted the perpetuation of slavery in the Constitution with an arrangement for proportional representation for the South's slave population, and the slave trade itself was protected for another twenty years. The reality of slavery apparently overpowered the delegates' moral scruples about its continuance in America. The revolutionary zeal for abolishing slavery was already dying out and stayed alive only among the reforming fringe of American society.

After the Constitution had been ratified, the new national government generated a fresh set of public concerns. The debates over the Constitution had brought to the surface political differences which formed a groundwork for partisan politics, and the need for organizing support for national policies gave parties a function. Local interests which formerly had been large enough to dominate state politics were now part of the many factors playing upon federal decisions. Political groups eager to control the new office of President put together coalitions that cut across state lines to form national constituencies. The Constitution itself contributed to political divisions when groups started arguing about the implementation of its provisions.

The Constitution embodied both the pessimism and the optimism in American culture. The pessimism was reflected in the acceptance of the ugly reality of slavery and in the distrust of human nature evident in the provisions for fractured and limited powers, intra-governmental checking devices, and the various curbs on majority rule. The optimism can be found in the high degree of individual freedom provided for and in the creation of a stronger union which transferred power from state units to national majorities of self-governing citizens. Both the optimism and the pessimism have persisted in the American outlook; both were to be put under new pressures. At the inauguration of George Washington, America had passed from the days when an elite minority could self-confidently control the political process and take for granted the support of its deferential followers, but the people were not yet ready for the free-wheeling, every-man's-opinion-is-as-good-as-the-next's style that would come with the presidency of Andrew Jackson. The direction, however, was set. The ambitions of the free white man in America increased steadily while social problems like slavery, whose solution demanded restraint of the individual, went unattended. The Constitution also solved the immediate problem of whether America was to develop as a nation or as a group of states, even though the exercise of national power would be challenged for another seventy years.

Although the delegates gathering in Philadelphia in May of 1787 had been instructed to consider ways to amend the Articles of Confederation, those who wanted to draft an entirely new frame of government dominated the proceedings from the very beginning, carrying the other delegates with them in their insistence that America needed a central government empowered to act directly upon its citizens and not through sovereign states. Meeting daily in secret sessions, the delegates hammered out a new constitution through the long, hot Philadelphia summer. Only one issue threatened to disrupt the working relationship among those thirty who regularly attended the sessions, and this was the distribution of power between population and states. Virginia's delegation, which had seized the initiative the opening day, maintained that representation in the national legislature must be based upon population. Alarmed, the delegates from Connecticut and New Jersey threatened to leave the convention rather than see the separate identity of the states wiped out. The result of this impasse was the famous compromise dividing the legislative power into two houses representative of population and states. After this compromise, other arrangements were easier to make, and by September the new document was ready for submission to the old Congress of the United States.

One of the most radical proposals of the convention hardly attracted notice at all. This was the convention's final suggestion that each state hold a special convention to consider ratification of the proposed constitution and that the new government go into operation upon acceptance by the ninth state. With this the Philadelphia delegates had brilliantly maneuvered themselves free of the unanimity provision of the Articles. State politicians who had expected to attack the new constitution from their fortified positions in the state legislatures were faced with accepting the suggestion or repudiating an appeal to the people's decision through special conventions. Rather than take so unpopular a position, they worked instead to get their men elected to the state ratifying conventions.

Particularly important in their campaign to defeat the Constitution were the *Letters from the Federal Farmer* written by one of Virginia's Revolutionary leaders, Richard Henry Lee (1732-1794). The general themes of Lee's attack were picked up by a variety of anti-Federalist writers. For a time it looked as though the anti-Federalists might succeed in getting a second convention summoned, ostensibly to draft a national bill of rights. As the constitution's promoters well knew, there was no way to limit discussion to a bill of rights, for any new convention would be as capable of throwing out the whole constitutional plan as they had been to ignore their instructions to amend the Articles. Hence the Federalists were adamantly opposed to a new convention and risked everything on a favorable decision from the state ratifying conventions.

The nationalists who had dominated the Philadelphia convention knew that they faced formidable obstacles in the ratification process, but they had the advantage of organization and speed. The small states of Connecticut, New Jersey, and Delaware had no place to go but into the new union, and by January of 1788, each had ratified the Constitution along with Pennsylvania and Georgia. With five states safely in, the anti-Federalists intensified their efforts and the remaining state conventions witnessed stiff opposition. By summer of 1788, eight states had ratified the Constitution, but New York and Virginia, both essential to the union, were led by men implacably opposed to a strong national government. Alexander Hamilton (1757-1804), looking forward to a close battle at the Albany convention, enlisted the help of both his fellow New Yorker John Jay and Virginia's James Madison (1751-1836) to prepare a series of articles in support of the Constitution. Beginning in October of 1787, *The Federalist Papers* appeared twice a week in New York newspapers and were rushed into book form for distribution in Virginia. Although it is difficult to assess their influence in securing the two states' approval for the Constitution, *The Federalist Papers* offered a brilliant explanation of the principles behind the Constitution. They also rank as one of America's few contributions to political philosophy. In the extracts from *The Federalist Papers* presented in this section, Madison and Hamilton explain why a new form of government is necessary and how the Constitution compliments America's political disposition. They never answer the anti-Federalists directly, but rather present a coherent statement of the theory behind the new federal arrangement. Madison's Federalist No. 10 is a small masterpiece in itself, addressed to the principal fear of his generation — that a popular form of government could not maintain freedom and order in a country as large as the United States.

Richard Henry Lee: Letters of a Federal farmer (1788)

LETTER I

Dear Sir,

. . . The present moment discovers a new face in our affairs. Our object has been all along, to reform our federal system, and to strengthen our governments — to establish peace, order and justice in the community — but a new object now presents. The plan of government now proposed is evidently calculated totally to change, in time, our condition as a people. Instead of being thirteen republics, under a federal head, it is clearly designed to make us one consolidated government. Of this, I think, I shall fully convince you, in my following letters on this subject. This consolidation of the states has been the object of several men in this country for some time past. Whether such a change can ever be effected, in any manner; whether it can be effected without convulsions and civil wars; whether such a change will not totally destroy the liberties of this country — time only can determine .

To have a just idea of the government before us, and to shew that a consolidated one is the object in view, it is necessary not only to examine the plan, but also its history, and the politics of its particular friends.

The confederation was formed when great confidence was placed in the voluntary exertions of individuals, and of the respective states; and the framers of it, to guard against usurpation, so limited, and checked the powers, that, in many respects, they are inadequate

Paul Leicester Ford (ed.), *Pamphlets on the Constitution of the United States*, Brooklyn, 1888, pp. 282–319.

to the exigencies of the union. We find, therefore, members of congress urging alterations in the federal system almost as soon as it was adopted. It was early proposed to vest congress with powers to levy an impost, to regulate trade, &c. but such was known to be the caution of the states in parting with power, that the vestment even of these, was proposed to be under several checks and limitations. During the war, the general confusion, and the introduction of paper money, infused in the minds of people vague ideas respecting government and credit. We expected too much from the return of peace, and of course we have been disappointed. Our governments have been new and unsettled; and several legislatures, by making tender, suspension, and paper money laws, have given just cause of uneasiness to creditors. By these and other causes, several orders of men in the community have been prepared, by degrees, for a change of government; and this very abuse of power in the legislatures, which in some cases has been charged upon the democratic part of the community, has furnished aristocratical men with those very weapons, and those very means, with which, in great measure, they are rapidly effecting their favourite object. And should an oppressive government be the consequence of the proposed change, prosperity may reproach not only a few overbearing, unprincipled men, but those parties in the states which have misused their powers . . .

The plan proposed appears to be partly federal, but principally however, calculated ultimately to make the states one consolidated government.

The first interesting question, therefore suggested, is, how far the states can be consolidated into one entire government on free principles. In considering this question extensive objects are to be taken into view, and important changes in the forms of government to be carefully attended to in all their consequences. The happiness of the people at large must be the great object with every honest statesman, and he will direct every movement to this point. If we are so situated as a people, as not to be able to enjoy equal happiness and advantages under one government, the consolidation of the states cannot be admitted.

There are three different forms of free government under which the United States may exist as one nation; and now is, perhaps, the time to determine to which we will direct our views. 1. Distinct republics connected under a federal head. In this case the respective state governments must be the principal guardians of the peoples rights, and exclusively regulate their internal police; in them must rest the balance of government . . . Under this federal modification of government, the powers of congress would be rather advisory or recommendatory than coercive. 2. We may do away the federal state governments, and form or consolidate all the states into one entire government, with one executive, one judiciary, and one legislature, consisting of senators and representatives collected from all parts of the union: In this case there would be a compleat consolidation of the states. 3. We may consolidate the states as to certain national objects, and leave them severally distinct independent republics, as to internal police generally . . .

Touching the first, or federal plan, I do not think much can be said in its favor: The sovereignity of the nation, without coercive and efficient powers to collect the strength of it, cannot always be depended on to answer the purposes of government; and in a congress of representatives of foreign states, there must necessarily be an unreasonable mixture of powers in the same hands.

As to the second, or compleat consolidating plan, it deserves to be carefully considered at this time by every American: If it be impracticable, it is a fatal error to model our governments, directing our views ultimately to it.

The third plan, or partial consolidation, is, in my opinion, the only one that can secure the freedom and happiness of this people. I once had some general ideas that the second plan was practicable, but from long attention, and the proceedings of the convention, I am fully satisfied, that this third plan is the only one we can with safety and propriety proceed upon. Making this the standard to point out, with candor and fairness, the parts of the new constitution which appear to be improper, is my object. The convention appears to have proposed the partial consolidation evidently with a view to collect all powers ultimately, in the United States into one entire government; and from its views in this respect, and from the tenacity of the small states to have an equal vote in the senate,

probably originated the greatest defects in the proposed plan.

Independent of the opinions of many great authors, that a free elective government cannot be extended over large territories, a few reflections must evince, that one government and general legislation alone never can extend equal benefits to all parts of the United States: Different laws, customs, and opinions exist in the different states, which by a uniform system of laws would be unreasonably invaded. The United States contain about a million of square miles, and in half a century will, probably, contain ten millions of people; and from the center to the extremes is about 800 miles.

Before we do away the state governments or adopt measures that will tend to abolish them, and to consolidate the states into one entire government several principles should be considered and facts ascertained . . .

The Federal Farmer.

LETTER II

Dear Sir,
The essential parts of a free and good government are a full and equal representation of the people in the legislature, and the jury trial of the vicinage in the administration of justice — a full and equal representation, is that which possesses the same interests, feelings, opinions, and views the people themselves would were they all assembled — a fair representation, therefore, should be so regulated, that every order of men in the community, according to the common course of elections, can have a share in it — in order to allow professional men, merchants, traders, farmers, mechanics, &c. to bring a just proportion of their best informed men respectively into the legislature, the representation must be considerably numerous . . .

There are other considerations which tend to prove that the idea of one consolidated whole, on free principles, is ill-founded — the laws of a free government rest on the confidence of the people, and operate gently — and never can extend the influence very far — if they are executed on free principles, about the centre, where the benefits of the government induce the people to support it voluntarily;

yet they must be executed on the principles of fear and force in the extremes — This has been the case with every extensive republic of which we have any accurate account.

There are certain unalienable and fundamental rights, which in forming the social compact, ought to be explicitly ascertained and fixed — a free and enlightened people, in forming this compact, will not resign all their rights to those who govern, and they will fix limits to their legislators and rulers, which will soon be plainly seen by those who are governed, as well as by those who govern: and the latter will know they cannot be passed unperceived by the former, and without giving a general alarm. These rights should be made the basis of every constitution; and if a people be so situated, or have such different opinions that they cannot agree in ascertaining and fixing them, it is a very strong argument against their attempting to form one entire society, to live under one system of laws only . . .

It is in connection with these, and other solid principles, we are to examine the constitution. It is not a few democratic phrases, or a few well formed features, that will prove its merits; or a few small omissions that will produce its rejection among men of sense; they will enquire what are the essential powers in a community, and what are nominal ones; where and how the essential powers shall be lodged to secure government, and to secure true liberty.

The Federal Farmer.

LETTER III

Dear Sir,

. . . I will examine, first, the organization of the proposed government, in order to judge; 2d, with propriety, what powers are improperly, at least prematurely lodged in it. I shall examine, 3d, the undefined powers; and 4th, those powers, the exercise of which is not secured on safe and proper ground.

First. As to the organization — the house of representatives, the democrative branch, as it is called, is to consist of 65 members: that is, about one representative for fifty thousand inhabitants, to be chosen biennially — the federal legislature may increase this number to one for each thirty thousand inhabitants, abating fractional numbers in each state. — Thirty-three representatives will make a quorum for doing business, and a majority of those present determine the sense of the house. — I

have no idea that the interests, feelings, and opinions of three or four millions of people, especially touching internal taxation, can be collected in such a house. — In the nature of things, nine times in ten, men of the elevated classes in the community only can be chosen — Connecticut, for instance, will have five representatives — not one man in a hundred of those who form the democrative branch in the state legislature, will, on a fair computation, be one of the five. — The people of this country, in one sense, may all be democratic; but if we make the proper distinction between the few men of wealth and abilities, and consider them, as we ought, as the natural aristocracy of the country, and the great body of the people, the middle and lower classes, as the democracy, this federal representative branch will have but very little democracy in it, even this small representation is not secured on proper principles . . .

In considering the practicability of having a full and equal representation of the people from all parts of the union, not only distances and different opinions, customs and views, common in extensive tracts of country, are to be taken into view, but many differences peculiar to Eastern, Middle, and Southern States. These differences are not so perceivable among the members of congress, and men of general information in the states, as among the men who would properly form the democratic branch. The Eastern states are very democratic, and composed chiefly of moderate freeholders, they have but few rich men and no slaves; the Southern states are composed chiefly of rich planters and slaves; they have but few moderate freeholders, and the prevailing influence, in them is generally a dissipated aristocracy: The Middle states partake partly of the Eastern and partly of the Southern character.

Perhaps, nothing could be more disjointed, unweildly and incompetent to doing business with harmony and dispatch, than a federal house of representatives properly numerous for the great objects of taxation, &c. collected from the federal states . . .

The house of representatives is on the plan of consolidation, but the senate is entirely on the federal plan; and Delaware will have as much constitutional influence in the senate, as the largest state in the union: and in this senate are lodged legislative, executive and judicial powers: Ten states in this union urge that they are small states, nine of which were present in the convention. — They were interested in collecting large powers into the hands of the senate, in which each state still will have its equal share of power. I suppose it was impracticable for the three large states, as they were called, to get the senate formed on any other principles: But this only proves, that we cannot form one general government on equal and just principles — and proves, that we ought not to lodge in it such extensive powers before we are convinced of the practicability of organizing it on just and equal principles . . .

There were various interests in the convention, to be reconciled, especially of large and small states; of carrying and non-carrying states; and of states more and states less democratic — vast labour and attention were by the convention bestowed on the organization of the parts of the constitution offered; still it is acknowledged there are many things radically wrong in the essential parts of this constitution — but it is said that these are the result of our situation: On a full examination of the subject, I believe it; but what do the laborious inquiries and determination of the convention prove? If they prove anything, they prove that we cannot consolidate the states on proper principles: The organization of the government presented proves, that we cannot form a general government in which all power can be safely lodged; and a little attention to the parts of the one proposed will make it appear very evident, that all the powers proposed to be lodged in it, will not be then well deposited, either for the purposes of government, or the preservation of liberty . . . The plan does not present a well balanced government: The senatorial branch of the legislative and the executive are substantially united, and the president, or the state executive magistrate, may aid the senatorial interest when weakest, but never can effectually support the democratic, however it may be opposed; — the excellency, in my mind, of a well-balanced government is that it consists of distinct branches, each sufficiently strong and independant to keep its own station, and to aid either of the other branches which may occasionally want aid . . .

In addition to the insecurity and inconveniences attending this organization beforementioned, it may be observed, that it is extremely difficult to secure the people against the fatal effects of corruption and influence. The power of making any law will be in the president, eight senators, and seventeen representatives, relative to the important objects enumerated in the constitution. Where there is a small representation a sufficient number to carry any measure, may, with ease, be influenced by bribes, offices and civilities; they easily form private juntoes, and out-door meetings, agree on measures, and carry them by silent votes.

Impressed, as I am, with a sense of the difficulties there are in the way of forming the parts of a federal government on proper principles, and seeing a government so unsubstantially organized, after so arduous an attempt has been made, I am led to believe, that powers ought to be given to it with great care and caution.

In the second place it is necessary, therefore, to examine the extent, and the probable operations of some of those extensive powers proposed to be vested in this government. These powers legislative, executive, and judicial, respect internal as well as external objects. Those respecting external objects, as all foreign concerns, commerce, imposts, all causes arising on the seas, peace and war, and Indian affairs, can be lodged no where else, with any propriety, but in this government. Many powers that respect internal objects ought clearly to be lodged in it; as those to regulate trade between the states, weights and measures, the coin or current monies, post-offices, naturalization, &c. These powers may be exercised without essentially effecting the internal police of the respective states: But powers to lay and collect internal taxes, to form the militia, to make bankrupt laws, and to decide on appeals, questions arising on the internal laws of the respective states, are of a very serious nature, and carry with them almost all other powers. These taken in connection with the others, and powers to raise armies and build navies, proposed to be lodged in this government, appear to me to comprehend all the essential powers in this community, and those which will be left to the states will be of no great importance.

A power to lay and collect taxes at discretion, is, in itself, of very great importance. By means of taxes, the government may command the whole or any part of the subject's property. Taxes may be of various kinds; but there is a strong distinction between external and internal taxes. External taxes are import duties, which are laid on imported goods; they may usually be collected in a few seaport towns, and of a few individuals, though ultimately paid by the consumer; a few officers can collect them, and they can be carried no higher than trade will bear, or smuggling permit — that in the very nature of commerce, bounds are set to them. But internal taxes, as poll and land taxes, excises, duties on all written instruments, &c. may fix themselves on every person and species of property in the community; they may be carried to any lengths, and in proportion as they are extended, numerous officers must be employed to assess them, and to enforce the collection of them . . .

Should the general government think it politic, as some administration (if not all) probably will, to look for a support in a system of influence, the government will take every occasion to multiply laws, and officers to execute them, considering these as so many necessary props for its own support. Should this system of policy be adopted, taxes more productive than the impost duties will, probably, be wanted to support the government, and to discharge foreign demands, without leaving any thing for the domestic creditors. The internal sources of taxation then must be called into operation, and internal tax laws and federal assessors and collectors spread over this immense country. All these circumstances considered, is it wise, prudent, or safe, to vest the powers of laying and collecting internal taxes in the general government, while imperfectly organized and inadequate; and to trust to amending it hereafter, and making it adequate to this purpose? It is not only unsafe but absurd to lodge power in a government before it is fitted to receive it? It is confessed that this power and representation ought to go together. Why give the power first? Why give the power to the few, who, when possessed of it, may have address enough to prevent the increase of representation? Why not keep the power, and, when necessary, amend the constitution, and add to its other parts this power, and a proper increase of representation at the same time? Then men who may want the power will be under strong inducements to let in the people, by their representatives, into the government, to hold their due proportion of this power. If a proper representation be impracticable, then we shall see this power resting in the states, where

it at present ought to be, and not inconsiderately given up.

When I recollect how lately congress, conventions, legislatures, and people contended in the cause of liberty, and carefully weighed the importance of taxation, I can scarcely believe we are serious in proposing to vest the powers of laying and collecting internal taxes in a government so imperfectly organized for such purposes. Should the United States be taxed by a house of representatives of two hundred members, which would be about fifteen members for Connecticut, twenty-five for Massachusetts, &c. still the middle and lower classes of people could have no great share, in fact, in taxation. I am aware it is said, that the representation proposed by the new constitution is sufficiently numerous; it may be for many purposes; but to suppose that this branch is sufficiently numerous to guard the rights of the people in the administration of the government, in which the purse and sword is placed, seems to argue that we have forgot what the true meaning of representation is. I am sensible also, that it is said that congress will not attempt to lay and collect internal taxes; that it is necessary for them to have the power, though it cannot probably be exercised. I admit that it is not probable that any prudent congress will attempt to lay and collect internal taxes, especially direct taxes: but this only proves, that the power would be improperly lodged in congress, and that it might be abused by imprudent and designing men . . .

The power in the general government to lay and collect internal taxes, will render its powers respecting armies, navies and the militia, the more exceptionable. By the constitution it is proposed that congress shall have power "to raise and support armies, but no appropriation of money to that use shall be for a longer term than two years; to provide and maintain a navy; to provide for calling forth the militia to execute the laws of the union; suppress insurrections, and repel invasions: to provide for organizing, arming, and disciplining the militia;" reserving to the states the right to appoint the officers, and to train the militia according to the discipline prescribed by congress; congress will have unlimited power to raise armies, and to engage officers and men for any number of years; but a legislative act applying money for their support can have operation for no longer term than two years, and if a subsequent congress do not within the two years renew the appropriation, or further appropriate monies for the use of the army, the army will be left to take care of itself. When an army shall once be raised for a number of years, it is not probable that it will find much difficulty in getting congress to pass laws for applying monies to its support. I see so many men in America fond of a standing army, and especially among those who probably will have a large share in administering the federal system; it is very evident to me, that we shall have a large standing army as soon as the monies to support them can be possibly found. An army is not a very agreeable place of employment for the young gentlemen of many families. A power to raise armies must be lodged some where; still this will not justify the lodging this power in a bare majority of so few men without any checks; or in the government in which the great body of the people, in the nature of things, will be only nominally represented. In the state governments the great body of the people, the yeomanry, &c. of the country, are represented: It is true they will chuse the members of congress, and may now and then chuse a man of their own way of thinking; but it is not impossible for forty, or thirty thousand people in this country, one time in ten to find a man who can possess similar feelings, views, and interests with themselves: Powers to lay and collect taxes and to raise armies are of the greatest moment; for carrying them into effect, laws need not be frequently made, and the yeomanry, &c. of the country ought substantially to have a check upon the passing of these laws; this check ought to be placed in the legislatures, or at least, in the few men the common people of the country, will, probably, have in congress, in the true sense of the word, "from among themselves." It is true, the yeomanry of the country possess the lands, the weight of property, possess arms, and are too strong a body of men to be openly offended — and, therefore, it is urged, they will take care of themselves, that men who shall govern will not dare pay any disrespect to their opinions. It is easily perceived, that if they have not their proper negative upon passing laws in congress, or on the passage of laws relative to taxes and armies, they may in twenty or thirty years be by means imperceptible to them, totally deprived of that boasted weight and strength . . .

The Federal Farmer.

LETTER IV

Dear Sir,

. . . There are certain rights which we have always held sacred in the United States, and recognized in all our constitutions, and which, by the adoption of the new constitution in its present form, will be left unsecured. By article 6, the proposed constitution, and the laws of the United States, which shall be made in pursuance thereof; and all treaties made, or which shall be made under the authority of the United States, shall be the supreme law of the land; and the judges in every state shall be bound thereby; anything in the constitution or laws of any state to the contrary notwithstanding.

It is to be observed that when the people shall adopt the proposed constitution it will be their last and supreme act; it will be adopted not by the people of New Hampshire, Massachusetts, &c., but by the people of the United States; and wherever this constitution, or any part of it, shall be incompatible with the ancient customs, rights, the laws or the constitutions heretofore established in the United States, it will entirely abolish them and do them away: And not only this, but the laws of the United States which shall be; made in pursuance of the federal constitution will be also supreme laws, and wherever they shall be incompatible with those customs, rights, laws or constitutions heretofore established, they will also entirely abolish them and do them away.

By the article before recited, treaties also made under the authority of the United States, shall be the supreme law: It is not said that these treaties shall be made in pursuance of the constitution — nor are there any constitutional bounds set to those who shall make them: The president and two-thirds of the senate will be empowered to make treaties indefinitely, and when these treaties shall be made, they will also abolish all laws and state constitutions incompatible with them. This power in the president and senate is absolute, and the judges will be bound to allow full force to whatever rule, article or thing the president and senate shall establish by treaty, whether it be practicable to set any bounds to those who make treaties, I am not able to say; if not, it proves that this power ought to be more safely lodged.

The federal constitution, the laws of congress made in pursuance of the constitution, and all treaties must have full force and effect in all parts of the United States; and all other laws, rights and constitutions which stand in their way must yield: It is proper the national laws should be supreme, and superior to state or district laws; but then the national laws ought to yield to unalienable or fundamental rights — and national laws, made by a few men, should extend only to a few national objects. This will not be the case with the laws of congress: To have any proper idea of their extent, we must carefully examine the legislative, executive and judicial powers proposed to be lodged in the general government, and consider them in connection with a general clause in art. I, sect. 8, in these words (after enumerating a number of powers) "To make all laws which shall be necessary and proper for carrying into execution the foregoing powers, and all other powers vested by this constitution in the government of the United States, or in any department or officer thereof." — The powers of this government as has been observed, extend to internal as well as external objects, and to those objects to which all others are subordinate; it is almost impossible to have a just conception of their powers, or of the extent and number of the laws which may be deemed necessary and proper to carry them into effect, till we shall come to exercise those powers and make the laws . . .

It is said that when people make a constitution, and delegate powers, that all powers are not delegated by them to those who govern, is reserved in the people; and that the people, in the present case, have reserved in themselves, and in their state governments, every right and power not expressly given by the federal constitution to those who shall administer the national government. It is said, on the other hand, that the people, when they make a constitution, yield all power not expressly reserved to themselves. The truth is, in either case, it is mere matter of opinion, and men usually take either side of the argument, as will best answer their purposes: But the general presumption being, that men who govern, will in doubtful cases, construe laws and constitutions most favourably for increasing their own powers; all wise and prudent people, in forming constitutions, have drawn the line, and carefully described the powers parted with and the powers reserved. By the state constitutions, certain rights have been reserved in the people; or rather, they have been

recognized and established in such a manner, that state legislatures are bound to respect them, and to make no laws infringing upon them. The state legislatures are obliged to take notice of the bills of rights of their respective states. The bills of rights, and the state constitutions, are fundamental compacts only between those who govern, and the people of the same state.

In the year 1788 the people of the United States made a federal constitution, which is a fundamental compact between them and their federal rulers; these rulers, in the nature of things, cannot be bound to take notice of any other compact. It would be absurd for them, in making laws, to look over thirteen, fifteen, or twenty state constitutions, to see what rights are established as fundamental, and must not be infringed upon, in making laws in the society. It is true, they would be bound to do it if the people, in their federal compact, should refer to the state constitutions, recognize all parts not inconsistent with the federal constitution, and direct their federal rulers to take notice of them accordingly; but this is not the case, as the plan stands proposed at present; and it is absurd, to suppose so unnatural an idea is intended or implied. I think my opinion is not only founded in reason, but I think it is supported by the report of the convention itself. If there are a number of rights established by the state constitutions, and which will remain sacred, and the general government is bound to take notice of them — it must take notice of one as well as another; and if unnecessary to recognize or establish one by the federal constitution, it would be unnecessary to recognize or establish another by it. If the federal constitution is to be construed so far in connection with the state constitution, as to leave the trial by jury in civil causes, for instance, secured; on the same principles it would have left the trial by jury in criminal causes, the benefits of the writ of habeas corpus, &c. secured; they all stand on the same footing; they are the common rights of Americans, and have been recognized by the state constitutions . . .

It is true, we are not disposed to differ much, at present, about religion; but when we are making a constitution, it is to be hoped, for ages and millions yet unborn, why not establish the free exercise of religion, as a part of the national compact. There are other essential rights, which we have justly understood to be the rights of freemen; as freedom from hasty and unreasonable search warrants, warrants not founded on oath, and not issued with due caution, for searching and seizing men's papers, property, and persons. The trials by jury in civil causes, it is said, varies so much in the several states, that no words could be found for the uniform establishment of it. If so, the federal legislation will not be able to establish it by any general laws. I confess I am of opinion it may be established, but not in that beneficial manner in which we may enjoy it, for the reasons beforementioned. When I speak of the jury trial of the vicinage, or the trial of the fact in the neighborhood, I do not lay so much stress upon the circumstance of our being tried by our neighbours: in this enlightened country men may be probably impartially tried by those who do not live very near them: but the trial of facts in the neighbourhood is of great importance in other respects. Nothing can be more essential than the cross examining witnesses, and generally before the triers of the facts in question . . .

The trial by jury is very important in another point of view. It is essential in every free country, that common people should have a part and share of influence, in the judicial as well as in the legislative department. To hold open to them the offices of senators, judges, and offices to fill which an expensive education is required, cannot answer any valuable purposes for them; they are not in a situation to be brought forward and to fill those offices; these, and most other offices of any considerable importance, will be occupied by the few. The few, the well born, &c. as Mr. Adams calls them, in judicial decisions as well as in legislation, are generally disposed, and very naturally too, to favour those of their own description.

The trial by jury in the judicial department, and the collection of the people by their representatives in the legislature, are those fortunate inventions which have procured for them, in this country, their true proportion of influence, and the wisest and most fit means of protecting themselves in the community. Their situation, as jurors and representatives, enables them to acquire information and knowledge in the affairs and government of the society; and to come forward, in turn, as the centinels and guardians of each other. I am very sorry that even a few of our countrymen should consider jurors and representatives in a different point of view, as ignorant, troublesome bodies, which ought not to have any share in the concerns of government . . .

It may also be worthy our examination, how far the provision for amending this plan, when it shall be adopted, is of any importance. No measures can be taken towards amendments, unless two-thirds of the congress, or two-thirds of the legislature of the several states shall agree. — While power is in the hands of the people, or democratic part of the community, more especially as at present, it is easy, according to the general course of human affairs, for the few influential men in the community, to obtain conventions, alterations in government, and to persuade the common people that they may change for the better, and to get from them a part of the power: But when power is once transferred from the many to the few, all changes become extremely difficult; the government, is this case, being beneficial to the few, they will be exceedingly artful and adroit in preventing any measures which may lead to a change; and nothing will produce it, but great exertions and severe struggles on the part of the common people. Every man of reflection must see, that the change now proposed, is a transfer of power from the many to the few, and the probability is, the artful and ever active aristocracy, will prevent all peaceful measures for changes, unless when they shall discover some favorable moment to increase their own influence. I am sensible, thousands of men in the United States, are disposed to adopt the proposed constitution, though they perceive it to be essentially defective, under an idea that amendments of it, may be obtained when necessary. This is a pernicious idea, it argues a servility of character totally unfit for the support of free government; it is very repugnant to that perpetual jealousy respecting liberty, so absolutely necessary in all free states, spoken of by Mr. Dickinson. — However, if our countrymen are so soon changed, and the language of 1774, is become odious to them, it will be in vain to use the language of freedom, or to attempt to rouse them to free enquiries: But I shall never believe this is the case with them, whatever present appearances may be, till I shall have very strong evidence indeed of it.

The Federal Farmer.

Alexander Hamilton: The Federalist. No. 1 (1787)

After an unequivocal experience of the inefficiency of the subsisting federal government, you are called upon to deliberate on a new Constitution for the United States of America. The subject speaks its own importance; comprehending in its consequences nothing less than the existence of the Union, the safety and welfare of the parts of which it is composed, the fate of an empire in many respects the most interesting in the world. It has been frequently remarked that it seems to have been reserved to the people of this country, by their conduct and example, to decide the important question, whether societies of men are really capable or not of establishing good government from reflection and choice, or whether they are forever destined to depend for their political constitutions on accident and force. If there be any truth in the remark, the crisis at which we are arrived may with propriety be regarded as the era in which that decision is to be made; and a wrong election of the part we shall act may, in this view, deserve to be considered as the general misfortune of mankind.

This idea will add the inducements of philanthropy to those of patriotism, to heighten the solicitude which all considerate and good men must feel for the event. Happy will it be if our choice should be directed by a judicious estimate of our true interests, unperplexed and unbiassed by considerations not connected with the public good. But this is a thing more ardently to be wished than seriously to be expected. The plan offered to our deliberations affects too many particular interests, innovates upon too many local institutions, not to involve in its discussion a variety of objects foreign to its merits, and of views, passions and prejudices little favorable to the discovery of truth.

Among the most formidable of the obstacles which the new Constitution will have to encounter may readily be distinguished the obvious interest of a certain class of men in every State to resist all changes which may hazard a diminution of the power, emolument, and consequence of the offices they hold under the State establishments; and the perverted ambition of another class of men, who will either hope to ag-

grandize themselves by the confusions of their country, or will flatter themselves with fairer prospects of elevation from the subdivision of the empire into several partial confederacies than from its union under one government.

It is not, however, my design to dwell upon observations of this nature. I am well aware that it would be disingenuous to resolve indiscriminately the opposition of any set of men (merely because their situations might subject them to suspicion) into interested or ambitious views. Candor will oblige us to admit that even such men may be actuated by upright intentions; and it cannot be doubted that much of the opposition which has made its appearance, or may hereafter make its appearance, will spring from sources, blameless at least, if not respectable — the honest errors of minds led astray by preconceived jealousies and fears . . .

. . . An enlightened zeal for the energy and efficiency of government will be stigmatized as the offspring of a temper fond of despotic power and hostile to the principles of liberty. An over-scrupulous jealousy of danger to the rights of the people, which is more commonly the fault of the head than of the heart, will be represented as mere pretence and artifice, the stale bait for popularity at the expense of the public good. It will be forgotten, on the one hand, that jealousy is the usual concomitant of love, and that the noble enthusiasm of liberty is apt to be infected with a spirit of narrow and illiberal distrust. On the other hand, it will be equally forgotten that the vigor of government is essential to the security of liberty; that, in the contemplation of a sound and well-informed judgment, their interest can never be separated; and that a dangerous ambition more often lurks behind the specious mask of zeal for the rights of the people than under the forbidding appearance of zeal for the firmness and efficiency of government. History will teach us that the former has been found a much more certain road to the introduction of despotism than the latter, and that of those men who have overturned the liberties of republics, the greatest number have begun their career by paying an obsequious court to the people; commencing demagogues, and ending tyrants . . .

I propose, in a series of papers, to discuss the following interesting particulars: The utility of the Union to your political prosperity — The insufficiency

---

Henry Cabot Lodge (ed.), *The Federalist*, G. P. Putnam's Sons, New York, 1888, pp. 3–7, 51–59, 86–91, 232–39, 322–27.

of the present Confederation to preserve that Union — The necessity of a government at least equally energetic with the one proposed, to the attainment of this object — The conformity of the proposed Constitution to the true principles of republican government — Its analogy to your own State constitution — and lastly, The additional security which its adoption will afford to the preservation of that species of government, to liberty, and to property.

In the progress of this discussion I shall endeavor to give a satisfactory answer to all the objections which shall have made their appearance, that may seem to have any claim to your attention.

It may perhaps be thought superfluous to offer arguments to prove the utility of the Union, a point, no doubt, deeply engraved on the hearts of the great body of the people in every State, and one, which it may be imagined, has no adversaries. But the fact is, that we already hear it whispered in the private circles of those who oppose the new Constitution, that the thirteen States are of too great extent for any general system, and that we must of necessity resort to separate confederacies of distinct portions of the whole. The doctrine will, in all probability, be gradually propagated, till it has votaries enough to countenance an open avowal of it. For nothing can be more evident, to those who are able to take an enlarged view of the subject, than the alternative of an adoption of the new Constitution or a dismemberment of the Union . . .

James Madison: The Federalist. No. 10 (1787)

Among the numerous advantages promised by a well-constructed Union, none deserves to be more accurately developed than its tendency to break and control the violence of faction. The friend of popular governments never finds himself so much alarmed for their character and fate, as when he contemplates their propensity to this dangerous vice. He will not fail, therefore, to set a due value on any plan which, without violating the principles to which he is attached, provides a proper cure for it. The instability, injustice, and confusion introduced into the public councils, have, in truth, been the mortal diseases under which popular governments have everywhere perished; as they continue to be the favorite and fruitful topics

from which the adversaries to liberty derive their most specious declamations. The valuable improvements made by the American constitutions on the popular models, both ancient and modern, cannot certainly be too much admired; but it would be an unwarrantable partiality, to contend that they have as effectually obviated the danger on this side, as was wished and expected. Complaints are everywhere heard from our most considerate and virtuous citizens, equally the friends of public and private faith, and of public and personal liberty, that our governments are too unstable, that the public good is disregarded in the conflicts of rival parties, and that measures are too often decided, not according to the rules of justice and the rights of the minor party, but by the superior force of an interested and overbearing majority. However anxiously we may wish that these complaints had no foundation, the evidence of known facts will not permit us to deny that they are in some degree true. It will be found, indeed, on a candid review of our situation, that some of the distresses under which we labor have been erroneously charged on the operation of our governments; but it will be found, at the same time, that other causes will not alone account for many of our heaviest misfortunes; and, particularly, for that prevailing and increasing distrust of public engagements, and alarm for private rights, which are echoed from one end of the continent to the other. These must be chiefly, if not wholly, effects of the unsteadiness and injustice with which a factious spirit has tainted our public administrations.

By a faction, I understand a number of citizens, whether amounting to a majority or minority of the whole, who are united and actuated by some common impulse of passion, or of interest, adverse to the rights of other citizens, or to the permanent and aggregate interests of the community.

There are two methods of curing the mischiefs of faction: the one, by removing its causes; the other, by controlling its effects.

There are again two methods of removing the causes of faction: the one, by destroying the liberty which is essential to its existence; the other, by giving to every citizen the same opinions, the same passions, and the same interests.

It could never be more truly said than of the first

remedy, that it was worse than the disease. Liberty is to faction what air is to fire, an aliment without which it instantly expires. But it could not be less folly to abolish liberty, which is essential to political life, because it nourishes faction, than it would be to wish the annihilation of air, which is essential to animal life, because it imparts to fire its destructive agency.

The second expedient is as impracticable as the first would be unwise. As long as the reason of man continues fallible, and he is at liberty to exercise it, different opinions will be formed. As long as the connection subsists between his reason and his self-love, his opinions and his passions will have a reciprocal influence on each other; and the former will be objects to which the latter will attach themselves. The diversity in the faculties of men, from which the rights of property originate, is not less an insuperable obstacle to a uniformity of interests. The protection of these faculties is the first object of government. From the protection of different and unequal faculties of acquiring property, the possession of different degrees and kinds of property immediately results; and from the influence of these on the sentiments and views of the respective proprietors, ensues a division of the society into different interests and parties.

The latent causes of faction are thus sown in the nature of man; and we see them everywhere brought into different degrees of activity, according to the different circumstances of civil society. A zeal for different opinions concerning religion, concerning government, and many other points, as well of speculation as of practice; an attachment to different leaders ambitiously contending for pre-eminence and power; or to persons of other descriptions whose fortunes have been interesting to the human passions, have, in turn, divided mankind into parties, inflamed them with natural animosity, and rendered them much more disposed to vex and oppress each other than to co-operate for their common good. So strong is this propensity of mankind to fall into mutual animosities, that where no substantial occasion presents itself, the most frivolous and fanciful distinctions have been sufficient to kindle their unfriendly passions and excite their most violent conflicts. But the most common and durable source of factions have been the various and unequal distribution of property. Those who hold

and those who are without property have ever formed distinct interests in society. Those who are creditors, and those who are debtors, fall under a like discrimination. A landed interest, a manufacturing interest, a mercantile interest, a moneyed interest, with many lesser interests, grow up of necessity in civilized nations, and divide them into different classes, actuated by different sentiments and views. The regulation of these various and interfering interests forms the principal task of modern legislation, and involves the spirit of party and faction in the necessary and ordinary operations of the government.

No man is allowed to be a judge in his own cause, because his interest would certainly bias his judgment, and, not improbably, corrupt his integrity. With equal, nay with greater reason, a body of men are unfit to be both judges and parties at the same time; yet what are many of the most important acts of legislation, but so many judicial determinations, not indeed concerning the rights of single persons, but concerning the rights of large bodies of citizens? And what are the different classes of legislators but advocates and parties to the causes which they determine? Is a law proposed concerning private debts? It is a question to which the creditors are parties on one side and the debtors on the other. Justice ought to hold the balance between them. Yet the parties are, and must be, themselves the judges; and the most numerous party, or, in other words, the most powerful faction must be expected to prevail. Shall domestic manufactures be encouraged, and in what degree, by restrictions on foreign manufactures? are questions which would be differently decided by the landed and the manufacturing classes, and probably by neither with a sole regard to justice and the public good. The apportionment of taxes on the various descriptions of property is an act which seems to require the most exact impartiality; yet there is, perhaps, no legislative act in which greater opportunity and temptation are given to a predominant party to trample on the rules of justice. Every shilling with which they overburden the inferior number, is a shilling saved to their own pockets.

It is in vain to say that enlightened statesmen will be able to adjust these clashing interests, and render them all subservient to the public good. Enlightened statesmen will not always be at the helm. Nor, in many cases, can such an adjustment be made at all without taking into view indirect and remote considerations, which will rarely prevail over the immediate interest which one party may find in disregarding the rights of another or the good of the whole.

The inference to which we are brought is, that the causes of faction cannot be removed, and that relief is only to be sought in the means of controlling its effects.

If a faction consists of less than a majority, relief is supplied by the republican principle, which enables the majority to defeat its sinister views by regular vote. It may clog the administration, it may convulse the society; but it will be unable to execute and mask its violence under the forms of the Constitution. When a majority is included in a faction, the form of popular government, on the other hand, enables it to sacrifice to its ruling passion or interest both the public good and the rights of other citizens. To secure the public good and private rights against the danger of such a faction, and at the same time to preserve the spirit and the form of popular government, is then the great object to which our inquiries are directed. Let me add that it is the great desideratum by which this form of government can be rescued from the opprobrium under which it has so long labored, and be recommended to the esteem and adoption of mankind.

By what means is this object attainable? Evidently by one of two only. Either the existence of the same passion or interest in a majority at the same time must be prevented, or the majority, having such coexistent passion or interest, must be rendered, by their number and local situation, unable to concert and carry into effect schemes of oppression. If the impulse and the opportunity be suffered to coincide, we well know that neither moral nor religious motives can be relied on as an adequate control. They are not found to be such on the injustice and violence of individuals, and lose their efficacy in proportion to the number combined together, that is, in proportion as their efficacy becomes needful.

From this view of the subject it may be concluded that a pure democracy, by which I mean a society consisting of a small number of citizens, who assemble and administer the government in person, can admit of no cure for the mischiefs of faction. A common passion or interest will, in almost every case, be felt by a majority of the whole; a communication and concert result from the form of government itself; and there is nothing to check the inducements to sacrifice the weaker party or an obnoxious individual. Hence it is that such democracies have ever been spectacles of turbulence and contention; have ever been found incompatible with personal security or the rights of property; and have in general been as short in their lives as they have been violent in their deaths. Theoretic politicians, who have patronized this species of government, have erroneously supposed that by reducing mankind to a perfect equality in their political rights, they would, at the same time, be perfectly equalized and assimilated in their possessions, their opinions, and their passions.

A republic, by which I mean a government in which the scheme of representation takes place, opens a different prospect, and promises the cure for which we are seeking. Let us examine the points in which it varies from pure democracy, and we shall comprehend both the nature of the cure and the efficacy which it must derive from the Union.

The two great points of difference between a democracy and a republic are: first, the delegation of the government, in the latter, to a small number of citizens elected by the rest; secondly, the greater number of citizens, and greater sphere of country, over which the latter may be extended.

The effect of the first difference is, on the one hand, to refine and enlarge the public views, by passing them through the medium of a chosen body of citizens, whose wisdom may best discern the true interest of their country, and whose patriotism and love of justice will be least likely to sacrifice it to temporary or partial considerations. Under such a regulation, it may well happen that the public voice, pronounced by the representatives of the people, will be more consonant to the public good than if pronounced by the people themselves, convened for the purpose. On the other hand, the effect may be inverted. Men of factious tempers, of local prejudices, or of sinister designs, may, by intrigue, by corruption, or by other means, first obtain the suffrages, and then betray the interests, of the people. The question resulting is, whether small or extensive republics are more favorable to the election of proper guardians of the public weal; and it is clearly decided in favor of the latter by two obvious considerations:

In the first place, it is to be remarked that, however small the republic may be, the representatives must be raised to a certain number, in order to guard against the cabals of a few; and that, however large it may be, they must be limited to a certain number, in order to guard against the confusion of a multitude. Hence, the number of representatives in the two cases not being in proportion to that of the two constituents, and being proportionally greater in the small republic, it follows that, if the proportion of fit characters be not less in the large than in the small republic, the former will present a greater option, and consequently a greater probability of a fit choice.

In the next place, as each representative will be chosen by a greater number of citizens in the large than in the small republic, it will be more difficult for unworthy candidates to practise with success the vicious arts by which elections are too often carried; and the suffrages of the people being more free, will be more likely to centre in men who possess the most attractive merit and the most diffusive and established characters.

It must be confessed that in this, as in most other cases, there is a mean, on both sides of which inconveniences will be found to lie. By enlarging too much the number of electors, you render the representative too little acquainted with all their local circumstances and lesser interests; as by reducing it too much, you render him unduly attached to these, and too little fit to comprehend and pursue great and national objects. The federal Constitution forms a happy combination in this respect; the great and aggregate interests being referred to the national, the local and particular to the State legislatures.

The other point of difference is, the greater number of citizens and extent of territory which may be brought within the compass of republican than of democratic government; and it is this circumstance principally which renders factious combinations less to be dreaded in the former than the latter. The smaller the society, the fewer probably will be the distinct parties and interests composing it; the fewer the distinct parties and interests, the more frequently will a majority be found of the same party; and the smaller the number of individuals composing a majority, and the smaller the compass within which they are placed, the more easily will they concert and execute their plans of oppression. Extend the sphere, and you take in a greater variety of parties and interests; you make it less probable that a majority of the whole will have a common motive to invade the rights of other citizens; or if such a common motive exists, it will be more difficult for all who feel it to discover their own strength, and to act in unison with each other. Besides other impediments, it may be remarked that, where there is a consciousness of unjust or dishonorable purposes, communication is always checked by distrust in proportion to the number whose concurrence is necessary.

Hence, it clearly appears, that the same advantage which a republic has over a democracy, in controlling the effects of faction, is enjoyed by a large over a small republic, — is enjoyed by the Union over the States composing it. Does the advantage consist in the substitution of representatives whose enlightened views and virtuous sentiments render them superior to local prejudices and to schemes of injustice? It will not be denied that the representation of the Union will be most likely to possess these requisite endowments. Does it consist in the greater security afforded by a greater variety of parties, against the event of any one party being able to outnumber and oppress the rest? In an equal degree does the increased variety of parties comprised within the Union, increase the security. Does it, in fine, consist in the greater obstacles opposed to the concert and accomplishment of the secret wishes of an unjust and interested majority? Here, again, the extent of the Union gives it the most palpable advantage.

The influence of factious leaders may kindle a flame within their particular States, but will be unable to spread a general conflagration through the other States. A religious sect may degenerate into a political faction in a part of the Confederacy; but the variety of sects dispersed over the entire face of it must secure the national councils against any danger from that source. A rage for paper money, for an abolition of debts, for an equal division of property, or for any other improper or wicked project, will be less apt to pervade the whole body of the Union than a particular member of it; in the same proportion as such a malady is more likely to taint a particular county or district, than an entire State.

In the extent and proper structure of the Union, therefore, we behold a republican remedy for the diseases most incident to republican government. And according to the degree of pleasure and pride we feel in being republicans, ought to be our zeal in cherishing the spirit and supporting the character of Federalists.

Alexander Hamilton: The Federalist. No. 15, (1787)

. . . The great and radical vice in the construction of the existing Confederation is in the principle of legislation for States or Governments, in their corporate or collective capacities, and as contradistinguished from the individuals of which they consist. Though this principle does not run through all the powers delegated to the Union, yet it pervades and governs those on which the efficacy of the rest depends. Except as to the rule of appointment, the United States has an indefinite discretion to make requisitions for men and money; but they have no authority to raise either, by regulations extending to the individual citizens of America. The consequence of this is, that though in theory their resolutions concerning those objects are laws, constitutionally binding on the members of the Union, yet in practice they are mere recommendations which the States observe or disregard at their option.

It is a singular instance of the capriciousness of the human mind, that after all the admonitions we have had from experience on this head, there should still be found men who object to the new Constitution, for deviating from a principle which has been found the bane of the old, and which is in itself evidently incompatible with the idea of Government; a principle, in short, which, if it is to be executed at all, must substitute the violent and sanguinary agency of the sword to the mild influence of the magistracy.

There is nothing absurd or impracticable in the idea of a league or alliance between independent nations for certain defined purposes precisely stated in a treaty regulating all the details of time, place, circumstance, and quantity; leaving nothing to future discretion; and depending for its execution on the good faith of the parties. Compacts of this kind exist among all civilized nations, subject to the usual vicissitudes of peace and war, of observance and non-observance, as the interests or passions of the contracting powers dictate. In the early part of the present century there was an epidemical rage in Europe for this species of compacts, from which the politicians of the times fondly hoped for benefits which were never realized. With a view to establishing the equilibrium of power and the peace of that part of the world, all the resources of negotiation were exhausted, and triple and quadruple alliances were formed; but they were scarcely formed before they were broken, giving an instructive but afflicting lesson to mankind, how little dependence is to be placed on treaties which have no other sanction than the obligations of good faith, and which oppose general considerations of peace and justice to the impulse of any immediate interest or passion.

If the particular States in this country are disposed to stand in a similar relation to each other, and to drop the project of a general discretionary superintendence, the scheme would indeed be pernicious, and would entail upon us all the mischiefs which have been enumerated under the first head; but it would have the merit of being, at least, consistent and practicable. Abandoning all views towards a confederate government, this would bring us to a simple alliance offensive and defensive; and would place us in a situation to be alternate friends and enemies of each other, as our mutual jealousies and rivalships, nourished by the intrigues of foreign nations, should prescribe to us.

But if we are unwilling to be placed in this perilous situation; if we still will adhere to the design of a national government, or, which is the same thing, of a superintending power, under the direction of a common council, we must resolve to incorporate into our plan those ingredients which may be considered as forming the characteristic difference between a league and a government; we must extend the authority of the Union to the persons of the citizens, the only proper objects of government.

Government implies the power of making laws. It is essential to the idea of a law, that it be attended with a sanction; or, in other words, a penalty or punishment for disobedience. If there be no penalty annexed to disobedience, the resolutions or commands which pretend to be laws will, in fact, amount to nothing more than advice or recommendation. This penalty, whatever it may be, can only be inflicted in two ways: by the agency of the courts and ministers of justice, or by military force; by the coercion of the magistracy, or by the coercion of arms. The first kind can evidently apply only to men; the last kind must of necessity, be employed against bodies politic, or communities, or States. It is evident that there is no process of a court by which the observance of the laws can, in the last resort, be enforced. Sentences may be denounced against them for violations of their duty; but these sentences can only be carried into execution by the sword. In an association where the general authority is confined to the collective bodies of the communities that compose it, every breach of the laws must involve a state of war; and military execution must become the only instrument of civil obedience. Such a state of things can certainly not deserve the name of government, nor would any prudent man choose to commit his happiness to it.

There was a time when we were told that breaches, by the States, of the regulations of the federal authority were not to be expected; that a sense of common interest would preside over the conduct of the respective members, and would beget a full compliance with all the constitutional requisitions of the Union. This language, at the present day, would appear as wild as a great part of what we now hear from the same quarter will be thought, when we shall have received further lessons from that best oracle of wisdom, experience. It at all times betrayed an ignorance of the true springs by which human conduct is actuated, and belied the original inducements to the establishment of civil power. Why has government been instituted at all? Because the passions of men will not conform to the dictates of reason and justice, without constraint. Has it been found that bodies of men act with more rectitude or greater disinterestedness than individuals? The contrary of this has been inferred by all accurate observers of the conduct of mankind; and the inference is founded upon obvious reasons. Regard to reputation has a less active influence, when the infamy of a bad action is to be divided among a number, than when it is to fall singly upon one. A spirit of faction, which

is apt to mingle its poison in the deliberations of all bodies of men, will often hurry the persons of whom they are composed into improprieties and excesses, for which they would blush in a private capacity.

In addition to all this, there is, in the nature of sovereign power, an impatience of control, that disposes those who are invested with the exercise of it, to look with an evil eye upon all external attempts to restrain or direct its operations. From this spirit it happens, that in every political association which is formed upon the principle of uniting in a common interest a number of lesser sovereignties, there will be found a kind of eccentric tendency in the subordinate or inferior orbs, by the operation of which there will be a perpetual effort in each to fly off from the common centre. This tendency is not difficult to be accounted for. It has its origin in the love of power. Power controlled or abridged is almost always the rival and enemy of that power by which it is controlled or abridged. This simple proposition will teach us, how little reason there is to expect, that the persons intrusted with the administration of the affairs of the particular members of a confederacy will at all times be ready, with perfect good-humor, and an unbiased regard to the public weal, to execute the resolutions or decrees of the general authority. The reverse of this results from the constitution of human nature.

If, therefore, the measures of theConfederacy cannot be executed without the intervention of the particular administrations, there will be little prospect of their being executed at all. The rulers of the respective members, whether they have a constitutional right to do it or not, will undertake the judge of the propriety of the measures themselves. They will consider the conformity of the thing proposed or required to their immediate interests or aims; the momentary conveniences or inconveniences that would attend its adoption. All this will be done; and in a spirit of interested and suspicious scrutiny, without that knowledge of national circumstances and reasons of state, which is essential to a right judgment, and with that strong predilection in favor of local objects, which can hardly fail to mislead the decision. The same process must be repeated in every member of which the body is constituted; and the execution of the plans, framed by the councils of the whole, will always fluctuate on the discretion of the ill-informed and prejucided opinion of every part. Those who have been conversant in the proceedings of popular assemblies; who have seen how difficult it often is, where there is no exterior pressure of circumstances, to bring them to harmonious resolutions on important points, will readily conceive how impossible it must be to induce a number of such assemblies, deliberating at a distance from each other, at different times, and under different impressions, long to cooperate in the same views and pursuits.

In our case, the concurrence of thirteen distinct sovereign wills is requisite, under the Confederation, to the complete execution of every important measure that proceeds from the Union. It has happened as was to have been foreseen. The measures of the Union have not been executed; the delinquencies of the States have, step by step, matured themselves to an extreme, which has, at length, arrested all the wheels of the national government, and brought them to an awful stand. Congress at this time scarcely possess the means of keeping up the forms of administration, till the States can have time to agree upon a more substantial substitute for the present shadow of a federal government. Things did not come to this desperate extremity at once. The causes which have been specified produced at first only unequal and disproportionate degrees of compliance with the requisitions of the Union. The greater deficiencies of some States furnished the pretext of example and the temptation of interest to the complying, or to the least delinquent States. Why should we do more in proportion than those who are embarked with us in the same political voyage? Why should we consent to bear more than our proper share of the common burden? These were suggestions which human selfishness could not withstand, and which even speculative men, who looked forward to remote consequences, could not, without hesitation, combat. Each State, yielding to the persuasive voice of immediate interest or convenience, has successively withdrawn its support, till the frail and tottering edifice seems ready to fall upon our heads, and to crush us beneath its ruins.

James Madison: The Federalist. No. 39 (1787).

The last paper having concluded the observations which were meant to introduce a candid survey of the plan of government reported by the convention, we now proceed to the execution of that part of our undertaking.

The first question that offers itself is, whether the general form and aspect of the government be strictly republican. It is evident that no other form would be reconcilable with the genius of the people of America; with the fundamental principles of the Revolution; or with that honorable determination which animates every votary of freedom, to rest all our political experiments on the capacity of mankind for self-government. If the plan of the convention, therefore, be found to depart from the republican character, its advocates must abandon it as no longer defensible.

What, then, are the distinctive characters of the republican form? . . . If we resort for a criterion to the different principles on which different forms of government are established, we may define a republic to be, or at least may bestow that name on, a government which derives all its powers directly or indirectly from the great body of the people, and is administered by persons holding their offices during pleasure, for a limited period, or during good behavior. It is essential to such a government that it be derived from the great body of the society, not from an inconsiderable porportion, or a favored class of it; otherwise a handful of tyrannical nobles, exercising their oppressions by a delegation of their powers, might aspire to the rank of republicans, and claim for their government the honorable title of republic. It is sufficient for such a government that the persons administering it be appointed, either directly or indirectly, by the people; and that they hold their appointments by either of the tenures just specified; otherwise every government in the United States, as well as every other popular government that has been or can be well organized or well executed, would be degraded from the republican character. According to the constitution of every State in the Union, some or other of the officers of government are appointed indirectly only by the people. According to most of them, the chief magistrate himself is so appointed. And according to one, this mode of appointment is extended to one of the coordinate branches of the legislature. According to all the constitutions, also, the tenure of the highest offices is extended to a definite period, and in many instances, both within the legislative and executive departments, to a period of years. According to the provisions of most of the constitutions, again, as well as according to the most respectable and received opinions on the subject, the members of the judiciary department are to retain their offices by the firm tenure of good behavior.

On comparing the Constitution planned by the convention with the standard here fixed, we perceive at once that it is, in the most rigid sense, conformable to it. The House of Representatives, like that of one branch at least of all the State legislatures, is elected immediately by the great body of the people. The Senate, like the present Congress, and the Senate of Maryland, derives its appointment indirectly from the people. The President is indirectly derived from the choice of the people, according to the example in most of the States. Even the judges, with all other officers of the Union, will, as in the several States, be the choice, though a remote choice, of the people themselves. The duration of the appointments is equally conformable to the republican standard, and to the model of State constitutions. The House of Representatives is periodically elective, as in all the States; and for the period of two years, as in the State of South Carolina. The Senate is elective, for the period of six years; which is but one year more than the period of the Senate of Maryland, and but two more than that of the Senates of New York and Virginia. The President is to continue in office for the period of four years; as in New York and Delaware the chief magistrate is elected for three years, and in South Carolina for two years. In the other States the election is annual. In several of the States, however, no constitutional provision is made for the impeachment of the chief magistrate. And in Delaware and Virginia he is not impeachable till out of office. The President of the United States is impeachable at any time during his continuance in office. The tenure by which the judges are to hold their places, is, as it unquestionably ought to be, that of good behavior. The tenure of the ministerial offices generally, will be a subject of legal regulation, conformably to the reason of the case and the example of the State constitutions.

Could any further proof be required of the republican complexion of this system, the most decisive one might be found in its absolute prohibition of titles of nobility, both under the federal and the State governments; and in its express guaranty of the republican form to each of the latter.

"But it was not sufficient," say the adversaries of the proposed Constitution, "for the convention to adhere to the republican form. They ought, with equal care, to have preserved the federal form, which regards the Union as a Confederacy of sovereign states; instead of which, they have framed a national government, which regards the Union as a consolidation of the States." And it is asked by what authority this bold and radical innovation was undertaken? The handle which has been made of this objection requires that it should be examined with some precision . . .

First. — In order to ascertain the real character of the government, it may be considered in relation to the foundation on which it is to be established; to the sources from which its ordinary powers are to be drawn; to the operation of those powers; to the extent of them; and to the authority by which future changes in the government are to be introduced.

On examining the first relation, it appears, on one hand, that the Constitution is to be founded on the assent and ratification of the people of America, given by deputies elected for the special purpose; but, on the other, that this assent and ratification is to be given by the people, not as individuals composing one entire nation, but as composing the distinct and independent States to which they respectively belong. It is to be the assent and ratification of the several States, derived from the supreme authority in each State, — the authority of the people themselves. The act, therefore, establishing the Constitution, will not be a national, but a federal act.

That it will be a federal and not a national act, as these terms are understood by the objectors; the act of the people, as forming so many independent States, not as forming one aggregate nation, is obvious from this single consideration, that it is to result neither from the decision of a majority of the people of the Union, nor from that of a majority of the States. It must result from the unanimous assent of the several States that are parties to it, differing no otherwise from their ordinary assent than in its being expressed, not by the legislative authority, but by that of the people themselves. Were the people regarded in this transaction as forming one nation, the will of the majority of the whole people of the United States would bind the minority, in the same manner as the majority in each State must bind the minority; and the will of the majority must be determined either by a comparison of the individual votes, or by considering the will of the majority of the States as evidence of the will of a majority of the people of the United States. Neither of these rules has been adopted. Each State, in ratifying the Constitution, is considered as a sovereign body, independent of all others, and only to be bound by its own voluntary act. In this relation, then, the new Constitution will, if established, be a federal, and not a national constitution.

The next relation is, to the sources from which the ordinary powers of government are to be derived. The House of Representatives will derive its powers from the people of America; and the people will be represented in the same proportion, and on the same principle, as they are in the legislature of a particular State. So far the government is national, not federal. The Senate, on the other hand, will derive its powers from the States, as political and coequal societies; and these will be represented on the principle of equality in the Senate, as they now are in the existing Congress. So far the government is federal, not national. The executive power will be derived from a very compound source. The immediate election of the President is to be made by the States in their political characters. The votes allotted to them are in a compound ratio, which considers them partly as distinct and coequal societies, partly as unequal members of the same society. The eventual election, again, is to be made by that branch of the legislature which consists of the national representatives; but in this particular act they are to be thrown into the form of individual delegations, from so many distinct and coequal bodies politic. From this aspect of the government, it appears to be of a mixed character, presenting at least as many federal as national features.

The difference between a federal and national government, as it relates to the operation of the government, is supposed to consist in this, that in the former the powers operate on the political bodies composing the Confederacy, in their political capacities; in the latter, on the individual citizens composing the nation, in their individual capacities. On trying the Constitution by this criterion, it falls under the national, not the federal character; though perhaps not so completely as has been understood. In several cases, and particularly in the trial of controversies to which States may be parties, they must be viewed and proceeded against in their collective and political capacities only. So far the national countenance of the government on this side seems to be disfigured by a few federal features. But this blemish is perhaps unavoidable in any plan; and the operation of the government on the people, in their individual capacities, in its ordinary and most essential proceedings, may, on the whole, designate it, in this relation, a national government.

But if the government be national with regard to the operation of its powers, it changes its aspect again when we contemplate it in relation to the extent of its powers. The idea of a national government involves in it, not only an authority over the individual citizens, but an indefinite supremacy over all persons and things, so far as they are objects of lawful government. Among a people consolidated into one nation, this supremacy is completely vested in the national legislature. Among communities united for particular purposes, it is vested partly in the general and partly in the municipal legislatures. In the former case, all local authorities are subordinate to the supreme; and may be controlled, directed, or abolished by it at pleasure. In the latter, the local or municipal authorities form distinct and independent portions of the supremacy, no more subject, within their respective spheres, to the general authority, than the general authority is subject to them, within its own sphere. In this relation, then, the proposed government cannot be deemed a national one; since its jurisdiction extends to certain enumerated objects only, and leaves to the several States a residuary and inviolable sovereignty over all other objects. It is true that in controversies relating to the boundary between the two jurisdictions, the tribunal which is ultimately to decide, is to be established under the general government. But this does not change the principle of the case. The decision is to be impartially made, according to the rules of the Constitution; and all the usual and most effectual precautions are taken to secure this impartiality. Some such tribunal is clearly essential to prevent an appeal to the sword and a dissolution of the compact; and that it ought to be established under the general rather than under the local governments, or, to speak more properly, that it could be safely established under the first alone, is a position not likely to be combated.

If we try the Constitution by its last relation to the authority by which amendments are to be made, we find it neither wholly national nor wholly federal. Were it wholly national, the supreme and ultimate authority would reside in the majority of the people of the Union; and this authority would be competent at all times, like that of a majority of every national society, to alter or abolish its established government. Were it wholly federal, on the other hand, the concurrence of each State in the Union would be essential to every alteration that would be binding on all. The mode provided by the plan of the convention is not founded on either of these principles. In requiring more than a majority, and particularly in computing the proportion by States, not by citizens, it departs from the national and advances towards the federal character; in rendering the concurrence of less than the whole number of States sufficient, it loses again the federal and partakes of the national character.

The proposed Constitution, therefore, is, in strictness, neither a national nor a federal Constitution, but a composition of both. In its foundation it is federal, not national; in the sources from which the ordinary powers of the government are drawn, it is partly federal and partly national; in the operation of these powers, it is national, not federal; in the extent of them, again, it is federal, not national; and, finally, in the authoritative mode of introducing amendments, it is neither wholly federal nor wholly national.

James Madison: The Federalist. No. 51 (1787)

To what expedient, then, shall we finally resort, for maintaining in practice the necessary partition of power among the several departments, as laid down in the Constitution? The only answer that can be given is, that as all these exterior provisions are found to be inadequate, the defect must be supplied, by so contriving the interior structure of the government as that its several constituent parts may, by their mutual relations, be the means of keeping each other in their proper places. Without presuming to undertake a full development of this important idea, I will hazard a few general observations, which may perhaps place it in a clearer light, and enable us to form a more correct judgment of the principles and structure of the government planned by the convention.

In order to lay a due foundation for that separate and distinct exercise of the different powers of government, which to a certain extent is admitted on all hands to be essential to the preservation of liberty, it is evident that each department should have a will of its own; and consequently should be so constituted that the members of each should have as little agency as possible in the appointment of the members of the others. Were this principle rigorously adhered to, it would require that all the appointments for the supreme executive, legislative, and judiciary magistracies should be drawn from the same fountain of authority, the people, through channels having no communication whatever with one another. Perhaps such a plan of constructing the several departments would be less difficult in practice than it may in contemplation appear. Some difficulties, however, and some additional expense would attend the execution of it. Some deviations, therefore, from the principle must be admitted. In the constitution of the judiciary department in particular, it might be inexpedient to insist rigorously on the principle: first, because peculiar qualifications being essential in the members, the primary consideration ought to be to select that mode of choice which best secures these qualifications; secondly, because the permanent tenure by which the appointments are held in that department, must soon destroy all sense of dependence on the authority conferring them.

It is equally evident, that the members of each department should be as little dependent as possible on those of the others, for the emoluments annexed to their offices. Were the executive magistrate, or the judges, not independent of the legislature in this particular, their independence in every other would be merely nominal.

But the great security against a gradual concentration of the several powers in the same department, consists in giving to those who administer each department the necessary constitutional means and personal motives to resist encroachments of the others. The provision for defence must in this, as in all other cases, be made commensurate to the danger of attack. Ambition must be made to counteract ambition. The interest of the man must be connected with the constitutional rights of the place. It may be a reflection of human nature, that such devices should be necessary to control the abuses of government. But what is government itself, but the greatest of all reflections on human nature? If men were angels, no government would be necessary. If angels were to govern men, neither external nor internal controls on government would be necessary. In framing a government which is to be administered by men over men, the great difficulty lies in this: you must first enable the government to control the governed; and in the next place oblige it to control itself. A dependence on the people is, no doubt, the primary control on the government; but experience has taught mankind the necessity of auxiliary precautions.

This policy of supplying, by opposite and rival interests, the defect of better motives, might be traced through the whole system of human affairs, private as well as public. We see it particularly displayed in all the subordinate distributions of power, where the constant aim is to divide and arrange the several offices in such a manner as that each may be a check on the other — that the private interest of every individual may be a sentinel over the public rights. These inventions of prudence cannot be less requisite in the distribution of the supreme powers of the State.

But it is not possible to give to each department an equal power of self-defence. In republican government, the legislative authority necessarily predominates. The remedy for this inconveniency is to divide the legislature into different branches; and to render them, by different modes of election and different principles of action, as little connected with each other as the nature of their common functions and their common dependence on the society will admit. It may even be necessary to guard against dangerous encroachments by still further precautions. As the weight of the legislative authority requires that it should be thus divided, the weakness of the executive may require, on the

other hand, that it should be fortified. An absolute negative on the legislature appears, at first view, to be the natural defence with which the executive magistrate should be armed. But perhaps it would be neither altogether safe nor alone sufficient. On ordinary occasions it might not be exerted with the requisite firmness, and on extraordinary occasions it might be perfidiously abused. May not this defect of an absolute negative be supplied by some qualified connection between this weaker department and the weaker branch of the stronger department, by which the latter may be led to support the constitutional rights of the former, without being too much detached from the rights of its own department?

If the principles of which these observations are founded be just, as I persuade myself they are, and they be applied as a criterion to the several State constitutions, and to the federal Constitution, it will be found that if the latter does not perfectly correspond with them, the former are infinitely less able to bear such a test.

There are, moreover, two considerations particularly applicable to the federal system of America, which place that system in a very interesting point of view.

First. In a single republic, all the power surrendered by the people is submitted to the administration of a single government; and the usurpations are guarded against by a division of the government into distinct and separate departments. In the compound republic of America, the power surrendered by the people is first divided between two distinct governments, and then the portion allotted to each subdivided among distinct and separate departments. Hence a double security arises to the rights of the people. The different governments will control each other, at the same time that each will be controlled by itself.

Second. It is of great importance in a republic not only to guard the society against the oppression of its rulers, but to guard one part of the society against the injustice of the other part. Different interests necessarily exist in different classes of citizens. If a majority be united by a common interest, the rights of the minority will be insecure. There are but two methods of providing against this evil: the one by creating a will in the community independent of the majority — that is, of the society itself; the other, by comprehending in the society so many separate descriptions of citizens as will render an unjust combination of a majority of the whole very improbable, if not impracticable. The first method prevails in all governments possessing an hereditary or self-appointed authority. This, at best, is but a precarious security; because a power independent of the society may as well espouse the unjust views of the major, as the rightful interests of the minor party, and may possibly be turned against both parties. The second method will be exemplified in the federal republic of the United States. Whilst all authority in it will be derived from and dependent on the society, the society itself will be broken into so many parts, interests, and classes of citizens, that the rights of individuals, or of the minority, will be in little danger from interested combinations of the majority. In a free government the security for civil rights must be the same as that for religious rights. It consists in the one case in the multiplicity of interests, and in the other in the multiplicity of sects. The degree of security in both cases will depend on the number of interests and sects; and this may be presumed to depend on the extent of country and number of people comprehended under the same government. This view of the subject must particularly recommend a proper federal system to all the sincere and considerate friends of republican government, since it shows that in exact proportion as the territory of the Union may be formed into more circumscribed Confederacies, or States, oppressive combinations of a majority will be facilitated; the best security, under the republican forms, for the rights of every class of citizens, will be diminished; and consequently the stability and independence of some member of the government, the only other security, must be proportionally increased. Justice is the end of government. It is the end of civil society. It ever has been and ever will be pursued until it be obtained, or until liberty be lost in the pursuit. In a society under the forms of which the stronger faction can readily unite and oppress the weaker, anarchy may as truly be said to reign as in a state of nature, where the weaker individual is not secured against the violence of the stronger; and as, in the latter state, even the stronger individuals are prompted, by the uncertainty of their condition, to submit to a government which may protect the weak

as well as themselves; so, in the former state, will the more powerful factions or parties be gradually induced, by a like motive, to wish for a government which will protect all parties, the weaker as well as the more powerful. It can be little doubted that if the State of Rhode Island was separated from the Confederacy and left to itself, the insecurity of rights under the popular form of government within such narrow limits would be displayed by such reiterated oppressions of factious majorities that some power altogether independent of the people would soon be called for by the voice of the very factions whose misrule had proved the necessity of it. In the extended republic of the United States, and among the great variety of interests, parties, and sects which it embraces, a coalition of a majority of the whole society could seldom take place on any other principles than those of justice and the general good; whilst there being thus less danger to a minor from the will of a major party, there must be less pretext, also, to provide for the security of the former, by introducing into the government a will not dependent on the latter, or, in other words, a will independent of the society itself. It is no less certain than it is important, notwithstanding the contrary opinions which have been entertained, that the larger the society, provided it lie within a practical sphere, the more duly capable it will be of self-government. And happily for the republican cause, the practicable sphere may be carried to a very great extent, by a judicious modification and mixture of the federal principle.

Quite unexpectedly, the Constitution became a source of conflict even after ratification. Implicit in the idea of having a constitution is the fact that its arrangement of rights and powers takes precedence over state laws, presidential programs or congressional measures. The Constitution thus stands as a limitation on the powers of the states, of the national government and of the people themselves. But unfortunately the language of its provisions could be variously interpreted so that there was no clear-cut knowledge of what the Constitution did or did not permit.

The issue of constitutional interpretation developed during the first administration under the new government. George Washington had brought into his cabinet two men of unusual capabilities, Thomas Jefferson (1743–1826) and Alexander Hamilton. Hamilton, as Secretary of the Treasury, took the initiative in Washington's administration and introduced a bold and innovative fiscal program to fund the entire wartime debt of the states and the confederation. Once funded, the debt was to be used as a means of strengthening the national economy. Although Congress passed the necessary laws to implement Hamilton's program, there were bitter fights over parts of his program, and when he proposed that Congress incorporate a quasi-public Bank, his opponents raised the cry that it was unconstitutional. Congress passed the bank bill, but Washington was disturbed at the thought of signing into law a measure that exceeded the bounds so carefully laid in Philadelphia. He therefore asked members of his cabinet to give him their views on the question of the bank's constitutionality.

In the first two readings, Jefferson and Hamilton present their opposing views on the constitutional grant of powers to Congress. Behind their legalistic and philological quibbles lie two basically different attitudes toward the role of government and the future of the American republic. As a firm believer in defining the limits of government power, Jefferson recognized that the Constitution could only bind men to its limitations if its words were strictly interpreted. Hence he was loath to extend to Congress any power

beyond that absolutely necessary to fulfill its designated functions. Hamilton, on the other hand, favored vigorous, effective government and saw the Constitution as an obstacle to efficient government unless men were willing to broadly interpret its grants of power. Although Washington finally signed the bank bill, the opposing interpretations of the Constitution presented by Jefferson and Hamilton continued to play a part in the political divisions of the United States through the first half of the 19th century.

As the bank issue made clear, there was no agreement upon what grounds legislation could be declared unconstitutional or, even more interestingly, which agency of government was expected to determine constitutionality. Many contemporaries assumed that this would be the responsibility of the Supreme Court, but the Constitution did not state so explicitly, and men who had served as delegates to the Philadelphia convention, such as some of the disputants in the bank controversy, did not agree.

In 1803 a case came before the Supreme Court which gave the new Chief Justice of the United States, John Marshall (1755–1835), an opportunity to assert the Court's authority to determine the constitutionality of federal laws. The case itself was highly partisan. Departing President John Adams made a number of last minute appointments to the federal judiciary. These so-called Midnight Judges offended the new president, Thomas Jefferson, and he requested his secretary of state, James Madison, not to deliver those appointments still remaining at the state department. One of the appointees, William Marbury, applied to the Supreme Court for a writ of mandamus to force Madison to deliver his commission. Marshall, though a Federalist and Adams appointee like Marbury, decided to turn the case into a vehicle for asserting the Court's right of judicial review. In a closely reasoned argument he declared the Judiciary Act of 1789 null and void on grounds that it flouted the specific provisions of the Constitution. The decision in *Marbury v. Madison* is best remembered for Marshall's examination of the concept of a written constitution. His argument, which follows in the third reading, demonstrates the distinction between republics and democracies as contemporaries understood it. Republics filtered power through a set of fundamental laws, or a constitution, whereas in democracies power flowed unrestrained from the will of the majority.

The last reading in this section is an extract from another famous Marshall decision, *McCulloch v. Maryland*. In this case Marshall struck down a state law as unconstitutional and, incidentally, vindicated Hamilton's broad interpretation of Congress's powers. During the presidency of James Madison, a second Bank of the United States was incorporated with the blessings of the Jeffersonian Republicans who had become reconciled to parts of Hamilton's fiscal program. The state legislatures, however, opposed the B.U.S. because its branches competed with banks incorporated under state law. The Maryland legislature actually passed a stamp tax act directed against any bank operating in Maryland and not chartered by the State of Maryland. Only the Bank of the United States fell into this category. The cashier of the Baltimore branch of the B.U.S., James William McCulloch, refused to pay the tax — for which he was arrested, tried, and convicted of violating the Maryland bank act. The Maryland Court of Appeals upheld McCulloch's conviction, but, on appeal to the United States Supreme Court, Marshall reversed the lower court's decision on the grounds that the Maryland law was unconstitutional. Marshall's decision set strict limits upon state sovereignty under the Constitution, but conflicts over state and federal powers continued to plague American politics in those areas where the Constitution was silent. Throughout the remainder of his career as Chief Justice, Marshall continued to interpret the Constitution so as to strengthen the Supreme Court, bind men and institutions to written contracts, and protect the federal government from the encroachments of the states.

Thomas Jefferson: Opinion on the constitutionality of a national bank (1791)

. . . I consider the foundation of the Constitution as laid on this ground: That "all powers not delegated to

Paul L. Ford, *The Writings of Thomas Jefferson*, G. P. Putnam's Sons, New York, 1892–99, V, 284–89.

the United States, by the Constitution, nor prohibited by it to the States, are reserved to the States or to the people." To take a single step beyond the boundaries thus specially drawn around the powers of Congress, is to take possession of a boundless field of power, no longer susceptible of any definition.

The incorporation of a bank, and the powers assumed by this bill, have not, in my opinion, been delegated to the United States, by the Constitution.

I. They are not among the powers specially enumerated: for these are:

1. A power to lay taxes for the purpose of paying the debts of the United States; but no debt is paid by this bill, nor any tax laid. Were it a bill to raise money, its origination in the Senate would condemn it by the Constitution.

2. "To borrow money." But this bill neither borrows money nor ensures the borrowing it. The proprietors of the bank will be just as free as any other money holders, to lend or not to lend their money to the public. The operation proposed in the bill, first, to lend them two millions, and then to borrow them back again, cannot change the nature of the latter act, which will still be a payment, and not a loan, call it by what name you please.

3. To "regulate commerce with foreign nations, and among the States, and with the Indian tribes." To erect a bank, and to regulate commerce, are very different acts. He who erects a bank, creates a subject of commerce in its bills; so does he who makes a bushel of wheat, or digs a dollar out of the mines; yet neither of these persons regulates commerce thereby. To make a thing which may be bought and sold, is not to prescribe regulations for buying and selling. Besides, if this was an exercise of the power regulating commerce, it would be void, as extending as much to the internal commerce of every State, as to its external. For the power given to Congress by the Constitution does not extend to the internal regulation of the commerce of a State, (that is to say of the commerce between citizen and citizen,) which remain exclusively with its own legislature; but to its external commerce only, that is to say, its commerce with another State, or with foreign nations, or with the Indian tribes. Accordingly the bill does not propose the measure as a regulation of trade, but as "productive of considerable advantages to

trade." Still less are these powers covered by any other of the special enumerations.

II. Nor are they within either of the general phrases, which are the two following:

1. To lay taxes to provide for the general welfare of the United States, that is to say, "to lay taxes for the purpose of providing for the general welfare." For the laying of taxes is the *power*, and the general welfare the *purpose* for which the power is to be exercised. They are not to lay taxes ad libitum for any purpose they please; but only to pay the debts or provide for the welfare of the Union. In like manner, they are not to do anything they please to provide for the general welfare, but only to lay taxes for that purpose. To consider the latter phrase, not as describing the purpose of the first, but as giving a distinct and independent power to do any act they please, which might be for the good of the Union, would render all the preceding and subsequent enumerations of power completely useless.

It would reduce the whole instrument to a single phrase, that of instituting a Congress with power to do whatever would be for the good of the United States; and, as they would be the sole judges of the good or evil, it would be also a power to do whatever evil they please.

It is an established rule of construction where a phrase will bear either of two meanings, to give it that which will allow some meaning to the other parts of the instrument, and not that which would render all the others useless. Certainly no such universal power was meant to be given them. It was intended to lace them up straitly within the enumerated powers, and those without which, as means, these powers could not be carried into effect. It is known that the very power now proposed as a means was rejected as an end by the Convention which formed the Constitution. A proposition was made to them to authorize Congress to open canals, and an amendatory one to empower them to incorporate. But the whole was rejected, and one of the reasons for rejection urged in debate was, that then they would have a power to erect a bank, which would render the great cities, where there were prejudices and jealousies on the subject, adverse to the reception of the Constitution.

2. The second general phrase, is, "to make all laws necessary and proper for carrying into execution the enumerated powers." But they can all be carried into execution without a bank. A bank therefore is not necessary, and consequently not authorized by this phrase.

It has been urged that a bank will give great facility or convenience in the collection of taxes. Suppose this were true: yet the Constitution allows only the means which are "necessary," not those which are merely "convenient" for effecting the enumerated powers. If such a latitude of construction be allowed to this phrase as to give any non-enumerated power, it will go to every one, for there is not one which ingenuity may not torture into a convenience in some instance or other, to some one of so long a list of enumerated powers. It would swallow up all the delegated powers, and reduce the whole to one power, as before observed. Therefore it was that the Constitution restrained them to the necessary means, that is to say, to those means without which the grant of power would be nugatory.

But let us examine this convenience and see what it is. The report on this subject, page 3, states the only general convenience to be, the preventing the transportation and re-transportation of money between the States and the treasury, (for I pass over the increase of circulating medium, ascribed to it as a want, and which, according to my ideas of paper money, is clearly a demerit.) Every State will have to pay a sum of tax money into the treasury; and the treasury will have to pay, in every State, a part of the interest on the public debt, and salaries to the officers of government resident in that State. In most of the States there will still be a surplus of tax money to come up to the seat of government for the officers residing there. The payments of interest and salary in each State may be made by treasury orders on the State collector. This will take up the greater part of the money he has collected in his State, and consequently prevent the great mass of it from being drawn out of the State. If there be a balance of commerce in favor of that State against the one in which the government resides, the surplus of taxes will be remitted by the bills of exchange drawn for that commercial balance. And so it must be if there was a bank. But if there be no balance of commerce, either direct or circuitous, all the banks in the world could not bring up the surplus of taxes but in the form of money. Treasury orders then, and bills of exchange may prevent the displacement of the main mass of the money collected, without the aid of any bank; and where these fail, it cannot be prevented even with that aid.

Perhaps, indeed, bank bills may be a more convenient vehicle than treasury orders. But a little difference in the degree of convenience, cannot constitute the necessity which the constitution makes the ground for assuming any non-enumerated power.

Besides; the existing banks will, without a doubt, enter into arrangements for lending their agency, and the more favorable, as there will be a competition among them for it; whereas the bill delivers us up bound to the national bank, who are free to refuse all arrangement, but on their own terms, and the public not free, on such refusal, to employ any other bank. That of Philadelphia, I believe, now does this business, by their post-notes, which, by an arrangement with the treasury, are paid by any State collector to whom they are presented. This expedient alone suffices to prevent the existence of that necessity which may justify the assumption of a non-enumerated power as a means for carrying into effect an enumerated one. The thing may be done, and has been done, and well done, without this assumption; therefore, it does not stand on that degree of necessity which can honestly justify it.

It may be said that a bank whose bills would have a currency all over the States, would be more convenient than one whose currency is limited to a single State. So it would be still more convenient that there should be a bank, whose bills should have a currency all over the world. But it does not follow from this superior conveniency, that there exists anywhere a power to establish such a bank; or that the world may not go on very well without it.

Can it be thought that the Constitution intended that for a shade or two of convenience, more or less, Congress should be authorised to break down the most ancient and fundamental laws of the several States; such as those against Mortmain, the laws of Alienage, the rules of descent, the acts of distribution, the laws of escheat and forfeiture, the laws of monopoly? Nothing but a necessity invincible by any other means, can justify such a prostitution of laws, which con-

stitute the pillars of our whole system of jurisprudence. Will Congress be too straight-laced to carry the constitution into honest effect, unless they may pass over the foundation-laws of the State government for the slightest convenience of theirs?

The negative of the President is the shield provided by the constitution to protect against the invasions of the legislature: 1. The right of the Executive. 2. Of the Judiciary. 3. Of the States and State legislatures. The present is the case of a right remaining exclusively with the States, and consequently one of those intended by the Constitution to be placed under its protection.

It must be added, however, that unless the President's mind on a view of everything which is urged for and against this bill, is tolerably clear that it is unauthorised by the Constitution; if the pro and the con hang so even as to balance his judgment, a just respect for the wisdom of the legislature would naturally decide the balance in favor of their opinion. It is chiefly for cases where they are clearly misled by error, ambition, or interest, that the Constitution has placed a check in the negative of the President.

Alexander Hamilton: *Opinion as to the constitutionality of the Bank of the United States (1791)*

The Secretary of the Treasury having perused with attention the papers containing the opinions of the Secretary of State and the Attorney-General, concerning the constitutionality of the bill for establishing a national bank, proceeds, according to the order of the President, to submit the reasons which have induced him to entertain a different opinion.

It will naturally have been anticipated, that in performing this task he would feel uncommon solicitude. Personal considerations alone, arising from the reflection that the measure originated with him, would be sufficient to produce it. The sense which he has manifested of the great importance of such an institution to the successful administration of the department of serious ill consequences to result from a failure of the measure, do not permit him to be without anxiety on public accounts. But the chief solicitude arises from

Henry Cabot Lodge (ed.), *The Works of Alexander Hamilton*, G. P. Putnam's Son, III, 445–58.

a firm persuasion, that principles of construction like those espoused by the Secretary of State and the Attorney-General would be fatal to the just and indispensable authority of the United States.

In entering upon the argument, it ought to be premised that the objections of the Secretary of State and the Attorney-General are founded on a general denial of the authority of the United States to erect corporations. The latter, indeed, expressly admits, that if there be anything in the bill which is not warranted by the Constitution, it is the clause of incorporation.

Now it appears to the Secretary of the Treasury that this general principle is inherent in the very definition of government, and essential to every step of the progress to be made by that of the United States, namely: That every power vested in a government is in its nature sovereign, and includes, by force of the term, a right to employ all the means requisite and fairly applicable to the attainment of the ends of such power, and which are not precluded by restrictions and exceptions specified in the Constitution, or not immoral, or not contrary to the essential ends of political society.

This principle, in its application to government in general, would be admitted as an axiom; and it will be incumbent upon those who may incline to deny it, to prove a distinction, and to show that a rule which, in the general system of things, is essential to the preservation of the social order, is inapplicable to the United States.

The circumstance that the powers of sovereignty are in this country divided between the National and State governments, does not afford the distinction required. It does not follow from this, that each of the portion of powers delegated to the one or to the other, is not sovereign with regard to its proper objects. It will only follow from it, that each has sovereign power as to certain things, and not as to other things. To deny that the Government of the United States has sovereign power, as to its declared purposes and trusts, because its power does not extend to all cases, would be equally to deny that the State governments have sovereign power in any case, because their power does not extend to every case. The tenth section of the first article of the Constitution exhibits a long list of very important things which they may not do. And

thus the United States would furnish the singular spectacle of a political society without sovereignty, or of a people governed, without government.

If it would be necessary to bring proof to a proposition so clear, as that which affirms that the powers of the Federal Government, as to its objects, were sovereign, there is a clause of its Constitution which would be decisive. It is that which declares that the Constitution, and the laws of the United States made in pursuance of it, and all treaties made, or which shall be made, under their authority, shall be the supreme law of the land. The power which can create the supreme law of the land in any case, is doubtless sovereign as to such case.

This general and indisputable principle puts at once an end to the abstract question, whether the United States have power to erect a corporation; that is to say, to give a legal or artificial capacity to one or more persons, distinct from the natural. For it is unquestionably incident to sovereign power to erect corporations, and consequently to that of the United States, in relation to the objects intrusted to the management of the government. The difference is this: where the authority of the government is general, it can create corporations in all cases; where it is confined to certain branches of legislation, it can create corporations only in those cases.

Here, then, as far as concerns the reasonings of the Secretary of State and the Attorney-General, the affirmative of the constitutionality of the bill might be permitted to rest. It will occur to the President, that the principle here advanced has been untouched by either of them.

For a more complete elucidation of the point, nevertheless, the arguments which they had used against the power of the government to erect corporations, however foreign they are to the great and fundamental rule which has been stated, shall be particularly examined. And after showing that they do not tend to impair its force, it shall also be shown that the power of incorporation, incident to the governmant in certain cases, does fairly extend to the particular case which is the object of the bill.

The first of these arguments is, that the foundation of the Constitution is laid on this ground: "That all powers not delegated to the United States by the

Constitution, nor prohibited by it to the States, are reserved to the States, or to the people." Whence it is meant to be inferred, that Congress can in no case exercise any power not included in those enumerated in the Constitution. And it is affirmed, that the power of erecting a corporation is not included in any of the enumerated powers.

The main proposition here laid down, in its true signification, is not to be questioned. It is nothing more than a consequence of this republican maxim, that all government is a delegation of power. But how much is delegated in each case is a question of fact, to be made out by fair reasoning and construction, upon the particular provisions of the Constitution, taking as guides the general principles and general ends of governments.

It is not denied that there are implied, as well as express powers, and that the former are as effectually delegated as the latter. And for the sake of accuracy it shall be mentioned that there is another class of powers, which may be properly denominated resulting powers. It will not be doubted that if the United States should make a conquest of any of the territories of its neighbors, they would possess sovereign jurisdiction over the conquered territory. This would be rather a result from the whole mass of the powers of the government, and from the nature of political society, than a consequence of either of the powers specially enumerated.

But be this as it may, it furnishes a striking illustration of the general doctrine contended for; it shows an extensive case, in which a power of erecting corporations is either implied in, or would result from, some or all of the powers vested in the National Government. The jurisdiction acquired over such conquered country would certainly be competent to any species of legislation.

To return: — It is conceded that implied powers are to be considered as delegated equally with express ones. Then it follows, that as a power of erecting a corporation may as well be implied as any other thing, it may as well be employed as an instrument or means of carrying into execution any of the specified powers, as any other instrument or means whatever. The only question must be in this, as in every other case, whether the means to be employed, or, in this instance, the corporation to be erected, has a natural relation to any of the acknowledged objects or lawful ends of the government. Thus a corporation may not be erected by Congress for superintending the police of the city of Philadelphia, because they are not authorized to regulate the police of that city. But one may be erected in relation to the collection of taxes, or to the trade with foreign countries, or to the trade between the States, or with the Indian tribes; because it is the province of the Federal Government to regulate those objects, and because it is incident to a general sovereign or legislative power to regulate a thing, to employ all the means which relate to its regulation to the best and greatest advantage.

A strange fallacy seems to have crept into the manner of thinking and reasoning upon this subject. Imagination appears to have been unusually busy concerning it. An incorporation seems to have been regarded as some great independent substantive thing; as a political end of peculiar magnitude and moment; whereas it is truly to be considered as a quality, capacity, or means to an end. Thus a mercantile company is formed, with a certain capital, for the purpose of carrying on a particular branch of business. Here the business to be prosecuted is the end. The association in order to form the requisite capital, is the primary mean. Suppose that an incorporation were added to this, it would only be to add a new quality to that association, to give it an artificial capacity, by which it would be enabled to prosecute the business with more safety and convenience . . .

Through this mode of reasoning respecting the right of employing all the means requisite to the execution of the specified powers of the government, it is to be objected, that none but necessary and proper means are to be employed; and the Secretary of State maintains, that no means are to be considered necessary but those without which the grant of the power would be nugatory. Nay, so far does he go in his restrictive interpretation of the word, as even to make the case of necessity which shall warrant the constitutional exercise of the power to depend on casual and temporary circumstances; an idea which alone refutes the construction. The expediency of exercising a particular power, at a particular time, must indeed, depend on circumstances; but the constitutional right of exercising it must be uniform and invariable, the same to-day as to-morrow.

All the arguments, therefore, against the constitutionality of the bill derived from the accidental existence of certain State banks — instutions which happen to exist to-day, and, for aught that concerns the government of the United States, may disappear to-morrow — must not only be rejected as fallacious, but must be viewed as demonstrative that there is a radical source of error in the reasoning.

It is essential to the being of the national government, that so erroneous a conception of the meaning of the word necessary should be exploded.

It is certain, that neither the grammatical nor popular sense of the term requires that construction. According to both, necessary often means no more than needful, requisite, incidental, useful, or conductive to. It is a common mode of expression to say, that it is necessary for a government or a person to do this or that thing, when nothing more is intended or understood, than that the interests of the government or person require, or will be promoted by, the doing of this or that thing. The imagination can be at no loss for exemplifications of the use of the word in this sense. And it is the true one in which it is to be understood as used in the Constitution. The whole turn of the clause containing it indicates, that it was the intent of the Convention, by that clause, to give a liberal latitude to the exercise of the specified powers. The expressions have peculiar comprehensiveness. They are, "to make all laws necessary and proper for carrying into execution the foregoing powers, and all other powers vested by the Constitution in the Government of the United States, or in any department or officer thereof."

To understand the word as the Secretary of State does, would be to depart from its obvious and popular sense, and to give it a restrictive operation, an idea never before entertained. It would be to give it the same force as if the word absolutely or indispensably had been prefixed to it.

Such a construction would beget endless uncertainty and embarrassment. The cases must be palpable and extreme, in which it would be pronounced, with certainty, that a measure was absolutely necessary, or one, without which the exercise of a given power would be nugatory. There are few measures of any government which would stand so severe a test. To insist upon it, would be to make the criterion of the exercise of any implied power, a case of extreme necessity; which is rather a rule to justify the overleaping of the bounds of constitutional authority, than to govern the ordinary exercise of it.

It may be truly said of every government, as well as of that of the United States, that it has only a right to pass such laws as are necessary and proper to accomplish the objects intrusted to it. For no government has a right to do merely what it pleases. Hence, by a process of reasoning similar to that of the Secretary of State, it might be proved that neither of the State governments has the right to incorporate a bank. It might be shown that all the public business of the State could be performed without a bank, and inferring thence that it was unnecessary, it might be argued that it could not be done, because it is against the rule which has been just mentioned. A like mode of reasoning would prove that there was no power to incorporate the inhabitants of a town, with a view to a more perfect police. For it is certain that an incorporation may be dispensed with, though it is better to have one. It is to be remembered that there is no express power in any State constitution to erect corporations.

The degree in which a measure is necessary can never be a test of the legal right to adopt it; that must be a matter of opinion, and can only be a test of expediency. The relation between the measure and the end; between the nature of the means employed towards the execution of a power, and the object of that power, must be the criterion of constitutionality, not the more or less of necessity or utility.

The practice of the government is against the rule of construction advocated by the Secretary of State. Of this, the act concerning light-houses, beacons, buoys, and public piers is a decisive example. This, doubtless, must be referred to the powers of regulating trade, and is fairly relative to it. But it cannot be affirmed that the exercise of that power in this instance was strictly necessary, or that the power itself would be nugatory, without that of regulating establishments of this nature.

This restrictive interpretation of the word necessary is also contrary to this sound maxim of construction; namely, that the powers contained in a constitution of government, especially those which concern the general administration of the affairs of a country, its finances, trade, defence, etc., ought to be construed liberally in advancement of the public good. This rule does not depend on the particular form of a government, or on the particular demarcation of the boundaries of its powers, but on the nature and objects of government itself. The means by which national exigencies are to be provided for, national inconveniences obviated, national prosperity promoted, are of such infinite variety, extent, and complexity, that there must of necessity be great latitude of discretion in the selection and application of those means. Hence, consequently, the necessity and propriety of exercising the authorities intrusted to a government on principles of liberal construction.

But while on the one hand the construction of the Secretary of State is deemed inadmissible, it will not be contended, on the other, that the clause in question gives any new or independent power. But it gives an explicit sanction to the doctrine of implied powers, and is equivalent to an admission of the proposition that the government, as to its specified powers and objects, has plenary and sovereign authority, in some cases paramount to the States; in others, co-ordinate with it. For such is the plain import of the declaration, that it may pass all laws necessary and proper to carry into execution those powers.

It is no valid objection to the doctrine to say, that it is calculated to extend the power of the General Government throughout the entire sphere of State legislation. The Same thing has been said, and may be said, with regard to every exercise of power by implication or construction.

The moment the literal meaning is departed from, there is a chance of error and abuse. And yet an adherence to the letter of its powers would at once arrest the motions of government. It is not only agreed, on all hands, that the exercise of constructive powers is indispensable, but every act which has been passed is more or less an exemplification of it. One has been already mentioned — that relating to light-houses, etc.; that which declares the power of the President to remove officers at pleasure, acknowledges the same truth in another and a signal instance.

The truth is, that difficulties on this point are inherent in the nature of the Federal Constitution; they result inevitably from a division of the legislative power. The consequence of this division is, that there will be cases clearly within the power of the National Government; others, clearly without its powers; and a third class, which will leave room for controversy and difference of opinion, and concerning which a reasonable latitude of judgment must be allowed.

But the doctrine which is contended for is not chargeable with the consequences imputed to it. It does not affirm that the National Government is sovereign in all respects, but that it is sovereign to a certain extent — that is, to the extent of the objects of its specified powers.

It leaves, therefore, a criterion of what is constitutional, and of what is not so. This criterion is the end, to which the measure relates as a means. If the end be clearly comprehended within any of the specified powers, and if the measure have an obvious relation to that end, and is not forbidden by any particular provision of the Constitution, it may safely be deemed to come within the compass of the national authority. There is also this further criterion, which may materially assist the decision: Does the proposed measure abridge a pre-existing right of any State or of any individual? If it does not there is a strong presumption in favor of its constitutionality, and slighter relations to any declared object of the Constitution may be permitted to turn the scale . . .

Marbury v. Madison

The question, whether an act repugnant to the constitution can become the law of the land, is a question deeply interesting to the United States; but, happily, not of an intricacy proportioned to its interest. It seems only necessary to recognize certain principles, supposed to have been long and well established, to decide it.

That the people have an original right to establish, for their future government, such principles as, in their opinion, shall most conduce to their own happiness, is the basis on which the whole American fabric has been erected. The exercise of this original right is a very great exertion; nor can it nor ought it to be frequently repeated. The principles, therefore, so established, are deemed fundamental. And as the authority from which they proceed is supreme, and can seldom act, they are designed to be permanent.

This original and supreme will organizes the government, and assigns to different departments their respective powers. It may either stop here, or establish certain limits not to be transcended by those departments.

The government of the United States is of the latter description. The powers of the legislature are defined and limited; and that those limits may not be mistaken, or forgotten, the constitution is written. To what purpose are powers limited, and to what purpose is that limitation committed to writing, if these limits may, at any time, be passed by those intended to be restrained? The distinction between a government with limited and unlimited powers is abolished, if those limits do not confine the persons on whom they are imposed, and if acts prohibited and acts allowed, are of equal obligation. It is a proposition too plain to be contested, that the constitution controls any legislative act repugnant to it; or, that the legislature may alter the constitution by an ordinary act.

Between these alternatives there is no middle ground. The constitution is either a superior paramount law, unchangeable by ordinary means, or it is on a level with ordinary legislative acts, and, like other acts, is alterable when the legislature shall please to alter it.

If the former part of the alternative be true, then a legislative act contrary to the constitution, is not law; if the latter part be true, then written constitutions are absurd attempts, on the part of the people, to limit a power in its own nature illimitable.

Certainly all those who have framed written constitutions contemplate them as forming the fundamental and paramount law of the nation, and, consequently, the theory of every such government must be, that an act of the legislature, repugnant to the constitution, is void.

This theory is essentially attached to a written constitution, and is consequently to be considered, by this court, as one of the fundamental principles of our society. It is not, therefore, to be lost sight of in the further consideration of this subject.

If an act of the legislature, repugnant to the con-stitution, is void, does it, notwithstanding its invalidity, bind the courts, and oblige them to give it effect? Or, in other words, though it be not law, does it constitute a rule as operative as if it was a law? This would be to overthrow in fact what was established in theory; and would seem, at first view, an absurdity too gross to be insisted on. It shall, however, receive a more attentive consideration.

It is emphatically the province and duty of the judicial department to say what the law is. Those who apply the rule to particular cases, must of necessity expound and interpret that rule. If two laws conflict with each other, the courts must decide on the operation of each.

So if a law be in opposition to the constitution; if both the law and the constitution apply to a particular case, so that the court must either decide that case conformably to the law, disregarding the constitution, or conformably to the constitution, disregarding the law, the court must determine which of these conflicting rules governs the case. This is of the very essence of judicial duty.

If, then, the courts are to regard the constitution, and the constitution is superior to any ordinary act of the legislature, the constitution, and not such ordinary act, must govern the case to which they both apply.

Those, then, who controvert the principle that the constitution is to be considered, in court, as a paramount law, are reduced to the necessity of maintaining that courts must close their eyes on the constitution, and see only the law.

This doctrine would subvert the very foundation of all written constitutions. It would declare that an act which, according to the principles and theory of our government, is entirely void, is yet, in practice, completely obligatory. It would declare that if the legislature shall do what is expressly forbidden, such act, notwithstanding the express prohibition, is in reality effectual. It would be giving to the legislature a practical and real omnipotence, with the same breath which professes to restrict their powers within narrow limits. It is prescribing limits, and declaring that those limits may be passed at pleasure.

That it thus reduces to nothing what we have deemed the greatest improvement on political institutions, a written constitution, would of itself be sufficient, in America, where written constitutions have been viewed with so much reverence, for rejecting the construction. But the peculiar expressions of the constitution of the United States furnish additional arguments in favor of its rejection.

The judicial power of the United States is extended to all cases arising under the constitution.

Could it be the intention of those who gave this power, to say that in using it the constitution should not be looked into? That a case arising under the constitution should be decided without examining the instrument under which it arises?

This is too extravagant to be maintained.

In some cases, then, the constitution must be looked into by the judges. And if they can open it at all, what part of it are they forbidden to read or to obey?

There are many other parts of the constitution which serve to illustrate this subject.

It is declared that "no tax or duty shall be laid on articles exported from any State." Suppose a duty on the export of cotton, of tobacco, or of flour; and a suit instituted to recover it. Ought judgment to be rendered in such a case? ought the judges to close their eyes on the constitution, and only see the law.

The constitution declares "that no bill of attainder or ex post facto law shall be passed."

If, however, such a bill should be passed, and a person should be prosecuted under it, must the court condemn to death those victims whom the constitution endeavors to preserve?

"No person," says the constitution, "shall be convicted of treason unless on the testimony of two witnesses to the same overt act, or on confession in open court."

Here the language of the constitution is addressed especially to the courts. It prescribes, directly for them, a rule of evidence not to be departed from. If the legislature should change that rule, and declare one witness, or a confession out of court, sufficient for conviction, must the constitutional principle yield to the legislative act?

From these, and many other selections which might be made, it is apparent that the framers of the constitution contemplated that instrument as a rule for the government of courts, as well as of the legislature.

Why otherwise does it direct the judges to take an oath to support it? This oath certainly applies in an especial manner to their conduct in their official character. How immoral to impose it on them, if they were to be used as the instruments, and the knowing instruments, for violating what they swear to support!

The oath of office, too, imposed by the legislature, is completely demonstrative of the legislative opinion on this subject. It is in these words: "I do solemnly swear that I will administer justice without respect to persons, and do equal right to the poor and to the rich; and that I will faithfully and impartially discharge all the duties incumbent on me as _____ , according to the best of my abilities and understanding, agreeably to the constitution and laws of the United States."

Why does a judge swear to discharge his duties agreeably to the constitution of the United States, if that constitution forms no rule for his government — if it is closed upon him, and cannot be inspected by him?

If such be the real state of things, this is worse than solemn mockery. To prescribe, or to take this oath, becomes equally a crime.

It is also not entirely unworthy of observation, that in declaring what shall be the supreme law of the land, the constitution itself is first mentioned; and not the laws of the United States generally, but those only which shall be made in pursuance of the constitution, have that rank.

Thus, the particular phraseology of the constitution of the United States confirms and strengthens the principle, supposed to be essential to all written constitutions, that a law repugnant to the constitution is void; and that courts, as well as other departments, are bound by that instrument.

McCulloch v. Maryland (1819)

Marshall, C. J., delivered the opinion of the court.

In the case now to be determined, the defendant, a sovereign state, denies the obligation of a law enacted by the legislature of the Union; and the plaintiff, on his part, contests the validity of an act which has been passed by the legislature of that State. The constitution

4 Wheaton 316

of our country, in its most interesting and vital parts, is to be considered; the conflicting powers of the government of the Union and of its members, as marked in that constitution, are to be discussed; and an opinion given, which may essentially influence the great operations of the government. No tribunal can approach such a question without a deep sense of its importance, and of the awful responsibility involved in its decision. But it must be decided peacefully, or remain a source of hostile legislation, perhaps of hostility of a still more serious nature; and if it is to be so decided, by this tribunal alone can the decision be made. On the supreme court of the United States has the constitution of our country devolved this important duty.

The first question made in the cause is, has congress power to incorporate a bank?

It has been truly said, that this can scarcely be considered as an open question, entirely unprejuiced by the former proceedings of the nation respecting it. The principle now contested was introduced at a very early period of our history, has been recognized by many successive legislatures, and has been acted upon by the judicial department, in cases of peculiar delicacy, as a law of undoubted obligation . . .

In discussing this question, the counsel for the State of Maryland have deemed it of some importance, in the construction of the constitution, to consider that instrument not as emanating from the people, but as the act of sovereign and independent States. The powers of the general government, it has been said, are delegated by the States, who alone are truly sovereign; and must be exercised in subordination to the States, who alone possess supreme dominion.

It would be difficult to sustain this proposition. The convention which framed the constitution was, indeed, elected by the state legislatures. But the instrument, when it came from their hands, was a mere proposal, without obligation, or pretensions to it. It was reported to the then existing congress of the United States, with a request that it might "be submitted to a convention of delegates, chosen in each State, by the people thereof, under the recommendation of its legislature, for their assent and ratification." This mode of proceeding was adopted; and by the convention, by congress, and by the State legislatures, the instrument was submitted to the people. They acted upon it, in

the only manner in which they can act safely, effectively, and wisely, on such a subject, by assembling in convention. It is true, they assembled in their several States; and where else should they have assembled? No political dreamer was ever wild enough to think of breaking down the lines which separate the States, and of compounding the American people into one common mass. Of consequence, when they act, they act in their States. But the measures they adopt do not, on that account, cease to be the measures of the people themselves, or become the measures of the State governments.

From these conventions the constitution derives its whole authority. The government proceeds directly from the people; is "ordained and established" in the name of the people; and is declared to be ordained, "in order to form a more perfect union, establish justice, insure domestic tranquillity, and secure the blessings of liberty to themselves and to their posterity." The assent of the States, in their sovereign capacity, is implied in calling a convention, and thus submitting that instrument to the people. But the people were at perfect liberty to accept or reject it; and their act was final. It required not the affirmance, and could not be negatived, by the State governments. The constitution, when thus adopted, was of complete obligation, and bound the State sovereignties.

It has been said, that the people had already surrendered all their powers to the State sovereignties, and had nothing more to give. But, surely, the question whether they may resume and modify the powers granted to government, does not remain to be settled in this country. Much more might the legitimacy of the general government be doubted, had it been created by the States. The powers delegated to the State sovereignties were to be exercised by themselves, not by a distinct and independent sovereignty, created by themselves. To the formation of a league, such as was the confederation, the State sovereignties were certainly competent. But when, "in order to form a more perfect union," it was deemed necessary to change this alliance into an effective government, possessing great and sovereign powers, and acting directly on the people, the necessity of referring it to the people, and of deriving its powers directly from them, was felt and acknowledged by all.

The government of the Union, then, (whatever may be the influence of this fact on the case,) is, emphatically and truly, a government of the people. In form and in substance it emanates from them. Its powers are granted by them, and are to be exercised directly on them, and for their benefit.

This government is acknowledged by all to be one of enumerated powers. The principle, that it can exercise only the powers granted to it, would seem too apparent to have required to be enforced by all those arguments which its enlightened friends, while it was depending before the people, found it necessary to urge. That principle is now universally admitted. But the question respecting the extent of the powers actually granted, is perpetually arising, and will probably continue to arise, as long as our system shall exist.

In discussing these questions, the conflicting powers of the general and State governments must be brought into view, and the supremacy of their respective laws, when they are in opposition, must be settled.

If any one proposition could command the universal assent of mankind, we might expect it would be this: that the government of the Union, though limited in its powers, is supreme within its sphere of action. This would seem to result necessarily from its nature. It is the government of all; its powers are delegated by all; it represents all, and acts for all. Though any one State may be willing to control its operations, no State is willing to allow others to control them. The nation, on those subjects on which it can act, must necessarily bind its component parts. But this question is not left to mere reason: the people have, in express terms, decided it, by saying, "this constitution, and the laws of the United States, which shall be made in pursuance thereof," "shall be the supreme law of the land," and by requiring that the members of the State legislatures, and the officers of the executive and judicial departments of the States, shall take the oath of fidelity to it.

The government of the United States, then, though limited in its powers, is supreme; and its laws, when made in pursuance of the constitution, form the supreme law of the land, "any thing in the constitution or laws of any State, to the contrary notwithstanding."

Among the enumerated powers, we do not find that of establishing a bank or creating a corporation.

But there is no phrase in the instrument which, like the articles of confederation, excludes incidental or implied powers; and which requires that every thing granted shall be expressly and minutely described. Even the 10th amendment, which was framed for the purpose of quieting the excessive jealousies which had been excited, omits the word "expressly," and declares only that the powers "not delegated to the United States, nor prohibited to the States, are reserved to the States or to the people;" thus leaving the question, whether the particular power which may become the subject of contest, has been delegated to the one government, or prohibited to the other, to depend on a fair construction of the whole instrument. The men who drew and adopted this amendment, had experienced the embarrassments resulting from the insertion of this word in the articles of confederation, and probably omitted it to avoid those embarrassments. A constitution, to contain an accurate detail of all the subdivisions of which its great powers will admit, and of all the means by which they may be carried into execution, would partake of the prolixity of a legal code, and could scarcely be embraced by the human mind. It would probably never be understood by the public. Its nature, therefore, requires, that only its great outlines should be marked, its important objects designated, and the minor ingredients which compose those objects be deduced from the nature of the objects themselves. That this idea was entertained by the framers of the American constitution, is not only to be inferred from the nature of the instrument, but from the language. Why else were some of the limitations, found in the 9th section of the 1st article, introduced? It is also, in some degree, warranted by their having omitted to use any restrictive term which might prevent its receiving a fair and just interpretation. In considering this question, then, we must never forget, that it is a constitution we are expounding.

Although, among the enumerated powers of government, we do not find the word "bank," or "incorporation," we find the great powers to lay and collect taxes; to borrow money; to regulate commerce; to declare and conduct a war; and to raise and support armies and navies. The sword and the purse, all the external relations, and no inconsiderable portion of the industry of the nation, are intrusted to its government. It can never be pretended that these vast powers draw after them others of inferior importance, merely because they are inferior. Such an idea can never be advanced. But it may, with great reason, be contended, that a government, intrusted with such ample powers, on the due execution of which the happiness and prosperity of the nation so vitally depends, must also be intrusted with ample means for their execution . . .

But the constitution of the United States has not left the right of congress to employ the necessary means, for the execution of the powers conferred on the government, to general reasoning. To its enumeration of powers is added that of making "all laws which shall be necessary and proper, for carrying into execution the foregoing powers, and all other powers vested by this constitution, in the government of the United States, or in any department thereof."

The counsel for the State of Maryland have urged various arguments, to prove that this clause, though in terms a grant of power, is not so in effect; but is really restrictive of the general right, which might otherwise be implied, of selecting means for executing the enumerated powers.

In support of this proposition, they have found it necessary to contend, that this clause was inserted for the purpose of conferring on congress the power of making laws. That, without it, doubts might be entertained, whether congress could exercise its powers in the form of legislation.

But could this be the object for which it was inserted? A government is created by the people, having legislative, executive, and judicial powers . . . After allowing each house to prescribe its own course of proceeding, after describing the manner in which a bill should become a law, would it have entered into the mind of a single member of the convention, that an express power to make laws was necessary to enable the legislature to make them? That a legislature, endowed with legislative powers, can legislate, is a proposition too self-evident to have been questioned.

But the argument on which most reliance is placed, is drawn from the peculiar language of this clause. Congress is not empowered by it to make all laws, which may have relation to the powers conferred on the government, but such only as may be "necessary and proper" for carrying them into execution. The word "necessary" is considered as controlling the whole sentence, and as limiting the right to pass laws for the execution of the granted powers, to such as are indispensable, and without which the power would be nugatory. That it excludes the choice of means, and leaves to congress, in each case, that only which is most direct and simple . . .

Let this be done in the case under consideration. The subject is the execution of those great powers on which the welfare of a nation essentially depends. It must have been the intention of those who gave those powers, to insure, as far as human prudence could insure, their beneficial execution. This could not be done by confining the choice of means to such narrow limits as not to leave it in the power of congress to adopt any which might be appropriate, and which were conducive to the end. This provision is made in a constitution intended to endure for ages to come, and, consequently, to be adapted to the various crises of human affairs. To have prescribed the means by which government should, in all future time, execute its powers, would have been to change, entirely, the character of the instrument, and give it the properties of a legal code. It would have been an unwise attempt to provide, by immutable rules, for exigencies which, if foreseen at all, must have been seen dimly, and which can be best provided for as they occur. To have declared that the best means shall not be used, but those alone without which the power given would be nugatory, would have been to deprive the legislature of the capacity to avail itself of experience, to exercise its reason, and to accommodate its legislation to circumstances . . .

In ascertaining the sense in which the word "necessary" is used in this clause of the constitution, we may derive some aid from that with which it is associated. Congress shall have power "to make all laws which shall be necessary and proper to carry into execution" the powers of the government. If the word "necessary" was used in that strict and rigorous sense for which the counsel for the State of Maryland contend, it would be an extraordinary departure from the usual course of the human mind, as exhibited in composition, to add a word, the only possible effect of which is to qualify that strict and rigorous meaning; to present to the mind the idea of some choice of means of legislation not straitened and compressed within the narrow limits for which gentlemen contend . . .

After the most deliberate consideration, it is the unanimous and decided opinion of this court, that the act to incorporate the Bank of the United States is a law made in pursuance of the constitution, and is a part of the supreme law of the land . . .

It being the opinion of the court, that the act incorporating the bank is constitutional; and that the power of establishing a branch in the State of Maryland might be properly exercised by the bank itself we proceed to inquire: —

Whether the State of Maryland may, without violating the constitution, tax that branch?

That the power of taxation is one of vital importance; that it is retained by the States; that it is not abridged by the grant of a similar power to the government of the Union; that it is to be concurrently exercised by the two governments; are truths which have never been denied. But, such is the paramount character of the constitution, that its capacity to withdraw any subject from the action of even this power, is admitted. The States are expressly forbidden to lay any duties on imports or exports, except what may be absolutely necessary for executing their inspection laws. If the obligation of this prohibition must be conceded — if it may restrain a State from the exercise of its taxing power on imports and exports, the same paramount character would seem to restrain, as it certainly may restrain, a State from such other exercise of this power, as is in its nature incompatible with, and repugnant to, the constitutional laws of the Union. A law absolutely repugnant to another, as entirely repeals that other as if express terms of repeal were used.

On this ground, the counsel for the bank place its claim to be exempted from the power of a State to tax its operations. There is no express provision for the case; but the claim has been sustained on a principle which so entirely pervades the constitution, is so intermixed with the materials which compose it, so interwoven with its web, so blended with its texture, as to be incapable of being separated from it without rending it into shreds.

This great principle is, that the constitution and the laws made in pursuance thereof are supreme; that they control the constitution and laws of the respective States, and cannot be controlled by them. From this, which may be almost termed an axiom, other propositions are deduced as corollaries, on the truth or error of which, and on their application to this case, the cause has been supposed to depend. These are,

1 That a power to create implies a power to preserve. 2 That a power to destroy, if wielded by a different hand, is hostile to, and incompatible with, these powers to create and to preserve. 3 That where this repugnancy exists, that authority which is supreme must control, not yield, to that over which it is supreme.

These propositions, as abstract truths, would, perhaps, never be controverted. Their application to this case, however, has been denied; and, both in maintaining the affirmative and the negative, a splendor of eloquence and strength of argument, seldom, if ever, surpassed, have been displayed.

The power of congress to create, and of course to continue, the bank, was the subject of the preceding part of this opinion; and is no longer to be considered as questionable.

That the power of taxing it by the States may be exercised so as to destroy it, is too obvious to be denied. But taxation is said to be an absolute power, which acknowledges no other limits than those expressly prescribed in the constitution, and like sovereign power of every other description, is trusted to the discretion of those who use it. But the very terms of this argument admit that the sovereignty of the State, in the article of taxation itself, is subordinate to, and may be controlled by, the constitution of the United States. How far it has been controlled by that instrument, must be a question of construction. In making this construction, no principle not declared, can be admissible, which would defeat the legitimate operations of a supreme government. It is of the very essence of supremacy to remove all obstacles to its action within its own sphere, and so to modify every power vested in subordinate governments, as to exempt its own operations from their own influence. This effect need not be stated in terms. It is so involved in the declaration of supremacy, so necessarily implied in it, that the expression of it could not make it more certain. We must, therefore, keep it in view while construing the constitution.

The argument on the part of the State of Maryland is, not that the States may directly resist a law of congress, but that they may exercise their acknowledged powers upon it, and that the constitution leaves them this right in the confidence that they will not abuse it . . .

The sovereignty of a State extends to every thing which exists by its own authority, or is introduced by its permission; but does it extend to those means which are employed by congress to carry into execution powers conferred on that body by the people of the United States? We think it demonstrable that it does not. Those powers are not given by the people of a single State. They are given by the people of the United States, to a government whose laws, made in pursuance of the constitution, are declared to be supreme. Consequently, the people of a single State cannot confer a sovereignty which will extend over them.

If we measure the power of taxation residing in a State, by the extent of sovereignty which the people of a single State possess, and can confer on its government, we have an intelligible standard applicable to every case to which the power may be applied. We have a principle which leaves the power of taxing the people and property of a State unimpaired; which leaves to a State the command of all its resources, and which places beyond its reach all those powers which are conferred by the people of the United States on the government of the Union, and all those means which are given for the purpose of carrying those powers into execution. We have a principle which is safe for the States, and safe for the Union. We are relieved, as we ought to be, from clashing sovereignty; from interfering powers; from a repugnancy between a right in one government to pull down what there is an acknowledged right in another to build up; from the incompatibility of a right in one government to destroy what there is a right in another to preserve. We are not driven to the perplexing inquiry, so unfit for the judicial department, what degree of taxation is the legitimate use, and what degree may amount to the abuse of the power. The attempt to use it on the means employed by the government of the Union, in pursuance of the constitution, is itself an abuse, because it is the usurpation of a power which the people of a single State cannot give . . .

That the power to tax involves the power to destroy; that the power to destroy may defeat and render useless the power to create; that there is a plain repugnance, in conferring on one government a power to control the constitutional measures of another, which other, with respect to those very measures, is declared to be supreme over that which exerts the control, are propositions not to be denied. But all inconsistencies are to be reconciled by the magic of the word confidence. Taxation, it is said, does not necessarily and unavoidably destroy. To carry it to the excess of destruction would be an abuse, to presume which, would banish that confidence which is essential to all government.

But is this a case of confidence? Would the people of any one State trust those of another, with a power to control the most insignificant operations of their state government? We know they would not. Why, then, should we suppose that the people of any one State should be willing to trust those of another with a power to control the operations of a government to which they have confided their most important and most valuable interests? In the legislature of the Union alone, are all represented. The legislature of the Union alone, therefore, can be trusted by the people with the power of controlling measures which concern all, in the confidence that it will not be abused. This, then, is not a case of confidence, and we must consider it as it really is.

If we apply the principle for which the State of Maryland contends, to the constitution generally, we shall find it capable of changing totally the character of that instrument. We shall find it capable of arresting all the measures of the government, and of prostrating it at the foot of of the States. The American people have declared their constitution, and the laws made in pursuance thereof, to be supreme; but this principle would transfer the supremacy, in fact, to the States.

If the States may tax one instrument, employed by the government in the execution of its powers, they may tax any and every other instrument. They may tax the mail; they may tax the mint; they may tax patent rights; they may tax the papers of the customhouse; they may tax judicial process; they may tax all the means employed by the government, to an excess which would defeat all the ends of government. This was not intended by the American people. They did not design to make their government dependent on the State . . .

It has also been insisted, that, as the power of

taxation in the general and state governments is acknowledged to be concurrent, every argument which would sustain the right of the general government to tax banks chartered by the States, will equally sustain the right of the States to tax banks chartered by the general government.

But the two cases are not on the same reason. The people of all the States have created the general government, and have conferred upon it the general power of taxation. The people of all the States, and the States themselves, are represented in congress, and, by their representatives, exercise this power. When they tax the chartered institutions of the States, they tax their constituents; and these taxes must be uniform. But, when a State taxes the operations of the government of the United States, it acts upon institutions created, not by their own constituents, but by people over whom they claim no control. It acts upon the measures of a government created by others as well as themselves, for the benefit of others in common with themselves. The difference is that which always exists, and always must exist, between the action of the whole on a part, and the action of a part on the whole; between the laws of a government declared to be supreme, and those of a government which, when in opposition to those laws, is not supreme.

SUGGESTIONS FOR FURTHER READING

Douglass Adair, "The Tenth Federalist Revisited," *William and Mary Quarterly*, **8** (1951).

Edwin S. Corwin, "Marbury v. Madison and the Doctrine of Judicial Review," *Michigan Law Review*, **12** (1914); "The Progress of Constitutional Theory between the Declaration of Independence and the Philadelphia Convention," *American Historical Review*, **30** (1925).

Martin Diamond, "Democracy and the Federalists: A Reconsideration of the Framers' Intent," *American Political Science Review*, **53** (1959).

Richard T. Ellis, *The Jeffersonian Crisis*, Oxford University Press, New York, 1971.

Max Farrand, *The Framing of the Constitution*, Yale University Press, New Haven, 1913.

Merrill Jensen, *The New Nation,* Vintage, New York, 1950.

Staughton Lynd, *Class Conflict, Slavery and the United States Constitution*, Bobbs-Merrill, Indianapolis, 1968.

Alpheus T. Mason, *The States Rights Debate*, Prentice Hall, Englewood Cliffs, N. J., 1964.

Andrew C. McLaughlin, *The Foundations of American Constitutionalism*, Fawcett, New York, 1961.

John P. Roche, "The Founding Fathers: A Reform Caucus in Action," *American Political Science Review*, **55** (1961).

James Morton Smith, "The Transformation of Republican Thought, 1763–1787," *Indiana Historical Society Lectures*, Indiana Historical Society, Indianapolis, 1970.

Benjamin F. Wright, *Consensus and Continuity, 1776–1787*, W. W. Norton, New York, 1958.

THE FRENCH REVOLUTION AND AMERICAN NATIONALISM

Chapter 6   1789-1824

During the first quarter century under the Constitution,
the American people enjoyed the blessings of liberty
at the high price of public turmoil and strident partisan
politics. There was far from a consensus on the most
important issues facing the people, and the newness of
the nation magnified the importance of every decision.
The Constitution had redressed the balance between
individual freedom and social control somewhat, but
it had left a host of other questions unresolved. As
the debates over ratification had shown, there was
still a difference of opinion about the true nature of
republican government. The individual citizens enjoyed
a wider range of guaranteed personal freedoms under
their state and national constitutions than before.
Colonial religious toleration had been transformed
into religious liberty, and the permissible range of
economic activities was very broad. These freedoms,
however, had been extended on the assumption that
law and order could be maintained without authoritarian institutions of church and state. This was still
viewed as something of a debatable proposition, and
any civil disorder could stir up instant support for
more social control. The centralized power lodged
in the new federal government created new sources
of conflict. Sectional tensions, particularly those
generated by the fundamental differences between
the southern plantation economy and northeastern
commercial interests, were becoming greater. But
above all, determining what course the new American

nation should take in relation to other countries caused the most dissension. Between 1789 and 1815 foreign policy decisions touched the most vital areas of national concern, including the defining of America's future role in the world.

The American Revolution coincided with a period of unrest throughout western Europe. The kings and oligarchies which had so long monopolized power were plagued with serious problems — exhausted treasuries, crop failures, population pressures, and insistent attacks from subjects who were excluded from political power. These predominantly middle class critics who were working to liberalize European society saw the American Revolution as a reflection of their own political aspirations. They eagerly hailed America's victory as the opening event in a new enlightened period when the people would exert their true sovereignty. Their prophecies appeared to be fulfilled by events. There was trouble in Geneva, a serious effort to reform the Dutch Republic, and finally, in 1789, the outbreak of the French Revolution, which spread war and revolution over half of Europe. Americans, for their part, were flattered to be considered civilization's torchbearers. French radical reformers justified their revolution with a new philosophy which some Americans enthusiastically endorsed and others just as emphatically rejected. These opposing American reactions to the rationale to the French Revolution exercised an inflammatory influence upon domestic politics and turned every question of foreign policy into a heated partisan issue.

The underlying premise of the radical reformers of Europe was that human institutions no less than the physical universe could be understood through the scientific method. These enlightened revolutionary thinkers taught that there were natural laws of cause and effect in society which operated as surely as the laws of gravity. Inquiry and reason, in their hands, became weapons to destroy what they considered to be man's chains of superstition, bigotry, and oppression. The truth revealed by enlightened inquiry was that the environment was the primary influence upon men. Rejecting religious explanations of evil as coming from man's corrupt nature, they believed that evil was the result of ignorance and could be eradicated. By changing man's environment — his education, his government, and the socializing institutions in his world — man himself could be transformed. Here were grounds for boundless optimism, and by combining the emphasis upon the determining role of the environment with the belief in natural social laws, these radical reformers created the idea of progress. Where classical writers had described human history in terms of cycles of repeating stages and Christians had written history as a chronicle of human corruption redeemable only through divine intervention, Enlightenment philosophers saw man's history as developmental and progressive. Man could now perfect himself through study and social engineering.

Most educated Americans were impressed by man's new found mastery over his ancient enemies of hunger, disease, ignorance, and oppression, and many believed too that their age represented the dawn of a new era in which the capacity for human achievement was unlimited. These new theories were congenial to all who welcomed further reforms, but placing the American Revolution in the context of a world-wide revolutionary movement had distrubing, radical implications. It suggested that what was truly authentic about the American Revolution were the social and political changes it wrought and implied that America's destiny was linked with that of other people engaged in throwing off their present rulers. When the French Revolution began, during George Washington's first administration, these implications were made explicit. Just as European reformers had earlier seized upon the American Revolution as their cause, so in the 1790's those Americans in favor of a more progressive society quickly espoused the French Revolution, seeing it as a kind of second chapter in the historic epic begun by America. Since many leaders of the French Revolution, like Lafayette, had fought in America, it was easy to conceive of

Americans and Frenchmen tied together by a common commitment to "liberty, equality, and fraternity." The French Revolution became important to American domestic issues because it brought out into the open a number of important differences among Americans. It also acted as a catalyst in the formation of political parties.

The American Revolution had effected political change, but it had not explicitly dealt with social values. For all their bold revolutionary writings, the Americans had left unanswered some important questions. Would American politics continue to be dominated by a wealthy and well-educated elite making decisions for a voting, but otherwise passive, electorate? Did the high-sounding phrases of the Declaration of Independence mean that American society would purge itself of class distinctions? Could the absolute claims for inalienable personal freedoms be guaranteed without disrupting the social order? The reason that the French Revolution inspired such ardent support from many Americans is because it represented the triumph of the common man over aristocrats, kings and prelates, but not all Americans thrilled to the advance of ordinary men and women.

Even in American society, the people of low and middling means were made to feel inferior to the important few. Churches, schools, civil courts, and government, while more open to popular participation than anywhere else in the Western World, were based upon the assumption that those with the advantages of wealth, education, and distinguished family connections should be entrusted with power. Deference was still considered the proper response of the common man to his superiors. It was in this context that many ordinary Americans responded to the ideas spread by the French Revolution. They had been drawn into a consideration of social values through their own experiences in the American Revolution and welcomed the support of a well-constructed philosophical system for their own drive toward social equality. If the environment truly determined what a man became, then upper class pretensions to innate superiority were false, even old-fashioned. The past which had always been carried so lightly in America now appeared to many to be totally expendable.

Other Americans — those with strong ties to an upper class position or to traditional concepts of loyalty and respect for authority — saw the danger of French radicalism. They disliked the suggestion that what was truly significant about the American Revolution was its importance in a world revolutionary movement. In their memory the Revolution was not a landmark on the road towards equality, but rather a testimony to Americans' determination to govern themselves. This conservative position was the one held by the Federalists, the party of Washington and his successor in the presidency, John Adams. The Federalist were appalled at the violence which accompanied the French Revolution. To them it proved what happened when men tampered with age-old institutions, and they vowed to fight any effort to use the French Revolution as an excuse to radicalize American society. They obviously did not believe in man's perfectibility or the inevitable progress of human history, retaining instead the religious perspective of man's unchanging nature. The Federalists tended to accept society as it was, which meant that there would always be the rich and poor, always the social problems of poverty, disease, and ignorance. Although they were aware of the differences between America and Europe, they expected their country to become more like traditional European societies with time. Indeed, now that the United States was independent, these conservatives renewed their identification with England.

Economic influences also played a part in these differing responses to the Enlightenment philosophy. Washington's secretary of the treasury, Alexander Hamilton, had initiated a fiscal program which relied heavily upon English credit and revenue from Anglo-American commerce. The bankers and merchants of the eastern seaboard, already inclined towards conservative social values, supported Hamilton's pro-English program.

These opposing reactions to the French Revolution

provided the ideological basis for the political parties that emerged during Washington's presidency, but the parties drew members because of the succession of domestic issues which could easily be engrafted on to the philosophical ones. Thomas Jefferson, who had been in France as United States minister when the French Revolution broke out, immediately characterized it as an echo of American aspirations. Coming back home to become Washington's secretary of state, Jefferson gathered around him those who believed that America was destined to be a new kind of society where men might live freely and peacefully without the oppression of government or the antagonisms of class. In their view, Hamilton's policies were leading to the dangerous entrenchment of the moneyed interests in the national government. With the help of his fellow Virginian, Congressman James Madison, Jefferson created a party in opposition to the Federalists, one that was committed to the old American revolutionary ideals of limiting government, promoting popular political participation, and guaranteeing the personal freedoms of ordinary men. Most of Jefferson's followers were small scale farmers. They distrusted banks, government fiscal policies, and Alexander Hamilton. Personal interests do not, however, explain the line-up between Jeffersonians and Federalists. Jefferson, the champion of revolutionary ideals, was a cultivated and wealthy slave-owning Virginian, and many an ardent Federalist eked out a meager living from the rocky soil of New England.

Party disputes were aggravated by the fact that the French Revolution plunged Europe into protracted warfare which threatened to involve the United States. In 1778, when the French publicly recognized the rebellious American colonies, the two countries had entered into a mutual aid treaty. Must the United States now come to the aid of France's revolutionary government? Such a course could be disastrous for the United States, particularly during the first years under a new Constitution. Naturally the pro-French Jeffersonians wanted to fulfill the most generous reading of the treaty, for they feared the extinction of France's

reforms should she succumb to her reactionary enemies. The pro-English Federalists, however, wanted to avoid war and alignment with revolutionary France and sought to settle old disputes with Great Britain even at the risk of a break with France. Washington and Adams tried to pursue policies of neutrality, but their partiality to England made them perceive neutrality differently from the French partisans and rendered their policies suspect.

The Federalists wanted to keep the public discussion of these controversial subjects to a minimum, but the Jeffersonians insisted upon taking their opposition politics to the people. They encouraged popular participation and feared that without check the already-powerful men of wealth would manipulate government policies to their own advantage. Public meetings, parades, and bonfire rallies accompanied the critical events of the 1790's. Opposition newspapers were started, publishing bold, often scurrilous attacks on national heroes, even the revered Washington. This development pushed to the fore the question of what, if any, limitations should be placed on public demonstrations and popular political activity. The Federalists were alarmed by the violent language used by their critics and insisted that no society could maintain law and order with such invective inflaming the masses. Fortunately for them, the French government, frustrated by American neutrality, began attacking American ships and insulting American diplomats. When public opinion in 1799 swung towards a repudiation of the French Revolution, the Federalists in Congress secured the passage of the Alien and Sedition Acts, which set prison penalties for the crime of criticizing government officials and threatened aliens with deportation.

Since the principal critics of the government were Jeffersonian Republicans, the Sedition Act looked like a politically-inspired measure to silence opposition. At least Jefferson and his friends interpreted the law this way and fought against it vigorously. Jeffersonians in Congress argued for free speech on the premise that since the people were sovereign there could be no legislative interference with their right to discuss the politics of the men they chose to represent them. Seditious libel, they said, in effect, was no crime in a popular form of government. The issues of political participation and free speech came to a head in the presidential election of 1800, when Jefferson defeated Adams and brought to an end the Federalist domination of national politics. Despite the frenzy generated by the campaign issues, power passed peacefully from one party to another. The new Constitution had stood its first major test of stability, and the common men in America had elected their champion to the presidency.

American statesmen had not anticipated the appearance of political parties, but retrospectively it seems inevitable. Americans in the 1790's did not have the same social expectations or political values. There existed no consensus about the implications of the American Revolution, and consequently about the proper direction for the new national government. The many economic interests, religious practices, and political goals which people use political power to protect were quite suddenly made vulnerable to a new majority that could express itself through a national legislature. The selection of presidential electors and congressmen through frequent elections created a forum for political issues which had not existed before. All these factors promoted the speedy organization of political parties. Hamilton developed a following among legislators and commercial leaders in campaigning for support for his financial program. Jefferson, thoroughly alarmed at the aristocratic bias of Hamilton's policies, carried his concerns to the people. The turbulence of the 1790's was a direct reflection of the intensity of the fears both Federalists and Republicans entertained about each other, but the election of Jefferson and the spirit of reconciliation he promoted brought to an end much of the discord that had characterized the administrations of Washington and Adams.

By 1800 most Americans had been weaned from their loyalties to France and England. The French Revolutionary governments had been displaced by the imperial rule of Napoleon, and England's ruthless use of sea power to check Napoleon's ambitions had destroyed almost all popular sympathy for Great Britain. An American economic nationalism had also developed to take the place of the earlier economic alliances with England and France. Despite shipping losses, Americans had profited from the European warfare, and during the brief respite from war in the first decade of the 19th century, the steady demand for American foodstuffs to feed Europe's growing population and for cotton to supply England's new steam-powered textile industry caused a steady expansion of American agriculture.

When war broke out again in Europe in 1806, Americans became aware that France and England were engaged in a struggle in which the United States was often a pawn and never more than a minor concern. They were quicker to resent French and English harassment on the high seas, particularly the unabated English impressment of American sailors. America, however, was also a small, relatively defenseless country, and her ability to chart an independent course between the oppressions of two powerful nations was limited. Both England and France announced their determination to seize any ship which traded with its enemy. When they both ignored American claims for the rights of neutral shippers, Jefferson initiated an embargo policy, using the closure of American ports as a means of getting the belligerents to cease their depredations. France and England were obdurate, and the closing of American ports was disastrous for much of the American economy. Northern merchant capital could be diverted into manufacturing, but the cotton producers of the South and the grain and hemp producers in the West had no such alternative. Jefferson's successor, James Madison, tried another tack, proposing a ban on American trade with the enemy of either France or England, whichever promised to cease preying on American ships. Napoleon announced his compliance with American demands, and Madison preferred to believe him. England continued to search and seize American ships and seamen, and a new Congress meeting in December of 1811 was spoiling for a fight with her. Led by young war hawks, John Calhoun and Henry Clay, Congress accepted a presidential recommendation of war, and the United States was at last dragged into the European war which had convulsed Europe since 1792.

Although a wealth of petty interests bubbled beneath the surface rhetoric vindicating American rights and national pride, the war itself was far from glorious. Americans were actually lucky to have escaped a severe beating from the English, and the peace treaty of 1814 settled few outstanding issues. Yet the nationalistic spirit in the south and west which had helped lead to war was itself heightened by the war. Andrew Jackson's stunning victory at New Orleans, fought after the peace had been signed, thrilled Americans, even in New England where the war had been unpopular. By the time a general European peace had been secured, Americans felt more keenly the bonds of their federal union. Economic self-sufficiency had become a popular goal, and Washington's farewell advice to avoid entangling alliances seemed more pertinent than ever.

During the next decade the United States acquired the social and economic cohesion to match the political union which had been created by the Constitution. Public attention turned westward as pioneers pushed into the rich valleys of the Ohio and Mississippi rivers, assured now of an outlet for their produce because of the acquisition of New Orleans in the Louisiana Purchase of 1803. Territorial expansion and the beginning of domestic manufacturing strengthened hopes for economic independence. Even the issue of slavery which touched vital areas of commitment and concern was temporarily resolved in favor of a limited expansion of the Southern slave-based economy. When Congress was asked to pass on the admission of several new states in 1820, a compromise was worked out to admit Missouri as a slave state, but to close all the rest of the Louisiana Territory north of the latitude of 36°30′ to slavery. After 1820 Congress added to the union by pairing free and slave states.

There still remained the ticklish question of the United States' official position in regard to other revolutionary efforts to establish popular governments. In the case of France, revolution had led to reaction, and Napoleon Bonaparte's career of conquest had dis-

enchanted the most ardent Gallophiles; but, after 1810, Spain's American empire was hit by a succession of revolutions which posed the problems all over again. Naturally sympathetic to colonial movements toward independence, the American government nonetheless did not act decisively until a coalition of European powers was formed to aid Spain in the recovery of her colonies. This threat of European interference in the Western Hemisphere led President Monroe to enunciate a new American foreign policy based upon a distinction between the interests of the Old World and the New.

Americans' growing sense of self-interest more and more overcame sentimental attachment to revolutionary movements. The outbreak of rebellion in Greece in 1812 aroused people's sympathies, but only prompted rhetoric from Congress. Despite the fact that Americans conceived of their political faith in terms of universal, inalienable rights, in practice they began considering their situation unique. A part of America's uniqueness was obviously its abundance, as exemplified by the vast hinterland of free land in the west. As the rich possibilities of occupying this domain were explored in the early decades of the 19th century, people in the United States began thinking more of a continental future and less of the parallels between the American Revolution and the internal struggles in other countries. Throughout the remainder of the 19th century, images of America's manifest destiny guided foreign policy.

Men and women in the 1820's had acquired that confidence in their material well-being that would become a marked feature of the American character. Political stability and economic expansion nourished national pride, and the enhanced opportunities for ordinary white families continued to erode social distinctions. Like other national groups, Americans began to take pride in what they considered to be their peculiar strengths — social equality, economic opportunity, individual resourcefulness, and free institutions. A characteristic American way, distinguishable from both America's colonial past and contemporary European societies, had formed. Although Americans con-

tinued to believe in progress and still had faith in the
capacities of the common man, they came to reject
any association of the American Revolution with a
worldwide revolutionary movement. America's mission in the future seemed best limited to American soil
which alone had proved capable to supporting free institutions. The French Revolution had acted as a catalyst in this process of Americanization, at first stimulating Americans to reflect upon the meaning of their
revolution, but finally shocking most Americans into
an awareness of the distinctiveness of their situation.
The War of 1812 only accelerated the process through
which Americans shed the internationalism of their
colonial past. The Missouri Compromise prepared
Americans domestically as the Monroe Doctrine did
internationally for a turning away from Europe. They
now saw their country as unique and were ready to
build a national identity on that perception.

In the first pair of readings, two Americans explore the meaning of the French Revolution. The first is Joel Barlow (1754–1812), who came of age in the year of American independence and committed his talents as poet and diplomat to his vision of the meaning of the American Revolution. Barlow was in Europe when the French Revolution broke out, and he hailed it as a joyous echo of American principles and an unparalleled opportunity to ring the death knell on the repressive institutions of Europe. A true son of the Enlightenment, Barlow was sure that nothing could stop social progress toward free and democratic institutions. His *Advice to the Privileged Orders* was addressed to those European aristocrats who were standing in the way of this progress. English leaders were sufficiently outraged by Barlow's book to expel him from the country.

John Adams (1735–1826), the author of the *Discourses on Davila*, from which the second selection was taken, unlike Barlow, recoiled in horror from the French Revolution and had the distinction of being one of the first to predict the violence which would accompany its course. He became thoroughly alarmed when he discovered his fellow countrymen hailing the French cause as a sister to America's Revolution. In Adams' view, Americans had fought to secure their liberties whereas the French were chasing the will o' the wisp of human equality, a mere chimera in Adams's opinion. He believed that history proved the folly of seeking a pure democracy because man's nature, as revealed in the lessons of history, rejected the equality which would alone make democracy possible. Adams wrote the *Discourses*, which were based on his reading of Henrico Caterino Davila's history of the French religious wars, while he was presiding over the Senate as vice-president. They appeared in a series of articles in the *Gazette of the United States*. His political enemies were only too happy to ballyhoo the undemocratic drift of Adams' writings, but Adams considered himself unfairly maligned since he wrote only what he believed to be true, not what he hoped was so.

Joel Barlow: *Advice to the privileged orders (1792–1793)*

The French Revolution is at last not only accomplished, but its accomplishment universally acknowledged, beyond contradiction abroad, or the power of retraction at home. It has finished its work, by organizing a government, on principles approved by reason; an object long contemplated by different writers, but never before exhibited, in this quarter of the globe. The experiment now in operation will solve a question of the first magnitude in human affairs: Whether Theory and Practice, which always agree together in things of slighter moment, are really to remain eternal enemies in the highest concerns of men?

The change of government in France is, properly speaking, a renovation of society; an object peculiarly fitted to hurry the mind into a field of thought, which can scarcely be limited by the concerns of a nation, or the improvements of an age. As there is a tendency in human nature to imitation; and, as all the apparent causes exist in most of the governments of the world, to induce the people to wish for a similar change, it becomes interesting to the cause of humanity, to take a deliberate view of the real nature and extent of this change, and find what are the advantages and disadvantages to be expected from it . . .

The Revolution in France certainly comes recommended to us under one aspect which renders it at first view extremely inviting: it is the work of argument and rational conviction, and not of the sword. The *ultima ratio regum* had nothing to do with it. It was an operation designed for the benefit of the people; it originated in the people, and was conducted by the people. It had therefore a legitimate origin; and this circumstance entitles it to our serious contemplation, on two accounts: because there is something venerable in the idea, and because other nations, in similar circumstances, will certainly be disposed to imitate it . . .

Among those whose anxieties arise only from in-

London, 1792, part 1, pp. 3–16, 26–37, 111–16; Paris, 1793, part 2, pp. 34–37.

terest, the enquiry is, how their privileges or their professions are to be affected by the new order of things. These form a class of men respectable both for their numbers and their sensibility; it is our duty to attend to their case. I sincerely hope to administer some consolation to them in the course of this essay. And though I have a better opinion of their philanthropy, than political opponents generally entertain of each other, yet I do not altogether rely upon their presumed sympathy with their fellow-citizens, and their supposed willingness to sacrifice to the public good; but I hope to convince them, that the establishment of general liberty will be less injurious to those who now live by abuses, than is commonly imagined; that protected industry will produce effects far more astonishing than have ever been calculated; that the increase of enjoyments will be such, as to ameliorate the condition of every human creature . . .

To induce the men who now govern the world to adapt these ideas, is the duty of those who now possess them.

Two very powerful weapons, the force of reason and the force of numbers, are in the hands of the political reformers. While the use of the first brings into action the second, and ensures its co-operation, it remains a sacred duty, imposed on them by the God of reason, to wield with dexterity this mild and beneficent weapon, before recurring to the use of the other; which, though legitimate, may be less harmless; though infallible in operation, may be less glorious in victory.

The tyrannies of the world, whatever be the appellation of the government under which they are exercised, are all aristocratical tyrannies. An ordinance to plunder and murder, whether it fulminate from the Vatican, or steal silently forth from the Harem; whether it come clothed in the certain science of a Bed of Justice, or in a legal solemnities of a bench of lawyers; whether it be purchased by the caresses of a woman, or the treasures of a nation, — never confines its effects to the benefit of a single individual; it goes to enrich the whole combination of conspirators, whose business it is to dupe and to govern the nation . . .

The state of human nature requires that this should be the case. Among beings so nearly equal in power and capacity as men of the same community are, it is impossible that a solitary tyrant should exist. Laws that are designed to operate

unequally on society, must offer an exclusive interest to a considerable portion of its members, to ensure their execution upon the rest. Hence has arisen the necessity of that strange complication in the governing power, which has made of politics an inexplicable science; hence the reason for arming one class of our fellow creatures with the weapons of bodily destruction, and another with the mysterious artillery of the vengeance of heaven; hence the cause of what in England is called the independence of the judges, and what on the continent has created a judiciary nobility, a set of men who purchase the privilege of being the professional enemies of the people, of selling their decisions to the rich, and of distributing individual oppression; hence the source of those Draconian codes of criminal jurisprudence which enshrine the idol Property in a bloody sanctuary, and teach the modern European, that his life is of less value than the shoes on his feet; hence the positive discouragements laid upon agriculture, manufactures, commerce, and every method of improving the condition of men; for it is to be observed, that in every country the shackles imposed upon industry are in proportion to the degree of general despotism that reigns in the government. This arises not only from the greater debility and want of enterprise in the people, but from the superior necessity that such governments are under, to prevent their subjects from acquiring that ease and information, by which they could discern the evil and apply the remedy.

To the same fruitful source of calamities we are to trace that perversity of reason, which, in governments where men are permitted to discuss political subjects, has given rise to those perpetual shifts of sophistry by which they vindicate the prerogative of kings. In one age it is the right of conquest, in another the divine right, then it comes to be a compact between king and people, and last of all, it is said to be founded on general convenience, the good of the whole community . . .

It is said to be dangerous to pull down systems that are already formed, or even to attempt to improve them; and it is likewise said, that, were they peaceable destroyed, and we had society to build up anew, it would be best to create hereditary kings, hereditary orders, and exclusive privileges.

These are sober opinions, uniting a class of reasoners too numerous and too respectable to be treated with contempt. I believe however that their number is every day diminishing, and I believe the example which France will soon be obliged to exhibit to the world on this subject, will induce every man to reject them, who is not personally and exclusively interested in their support . . .

Whether men are born to govern, or to obey, or to enjoy equal liberty, depends not on the original capacity of the mind, but on the instinct of analogy, or the habit of thinking. When children of the same family are taught to believe in the unconquerable distinctions of birth among themselves, they are completely fitted for a feudal government; because their minds are familiarised with all the gradations and degradations that such a government requires. The birthright of domineering is not more readily claimed on the one hand, than it is acknowledged on the other; and the Jamaica planter is not more habitually convinced that an European is superior to an African, than he is that a lord is better than himself.

. . . When we assert that nature has established inequalities among men, and has thus given to some the right of governing others, or when we maintain the contrary of this position, we should be careful to define what sort of nature we mean, whether the first or second nature; or whether we mean that there is but one. A mere savage, Colocolo for instance, would decide the question of equality by a trial of bodily strength, designating the man that could lift the heaviest beam to be the legislator; and unless all men could lift the same beam, they could not be equal in their rights. Aristotle would give the preference to him that excelled in mental capacity. Ulysses would make the decision upon a compound ratio of both. But there appears to me another step in this ladder, and that the habit of thinking is the only safe and universal criterion to which, in practice, the question can be referred. Indeed, when interest is laid aside, it is the only one to which, in civilized ages, it ever is referred. We never submit to a king, because he is stronger than we in bodily force, nor because he is superior in understanding or in information; but because we believe him born to govern, or at least, because a majority of the society believes it.

This habit of thinking has so much of nature in it, it is so undistinguishable from the indelible marks of the man, that it is a perfectly safe foundation for any system that we may choose to build upon it; indeed it is the only foundation, for it is the only point of contact by which men communicate as moral associates . . .

First, it is evident that all the arbitrary systems in the world are founded and supported on this second nature of man, in counteraction of the first. Systems which distort and crush and subjugate every thing that we can suppose original and characteristic in man, as an undistorted being. It sustains the most absurd and abominable theories of religion, and honors them with as many martyrs as it does those that are the most peaceful and beneficent.

But secondly, we find for our consolation, that it will likewise support systems of equal liberty and national happiness. In the United States of America, the science of liberty is universally understood, felt and practiced, as much by the simple as the wise, the weak as the strong. Their deep-rooted and inveterate habit of thinking is, that all men are equal in their rights, that it is impossible to make them otherwise; and this being their undisturbed belief, they have no conception how any man in his senses can entertain any other. This point once settled, every thing is settled. Many operations, which in Europe have been considered as incredible tales or dangerous experiments, are but the infallible consequences of this great principle. The first of these operations is the business of election, which with that people is carried on with as much gravity as their daily labor. There is no jealousy on the occasion, nothing lucrative in office; any man in society may attain to any place in the government, and may exercise its functions. They believe that there is nothing more difficult in the management of the affairs of a nation, than the affairs of a family; that it only requires more hands. They believe that it is the juggle of keeping up impositions to blind the eyes of the vulgar, that constitutes the intricacy of state. Banish the mysticism of inequality, and you banish almost all the evils attendant on human nature.

The people, being habituated to the election of all kinds of officers, the magnitude of the office makes no difficulty in the case. The president of the United States, who has more power while in office than some of the kings of Europe, is chosen with as little commotion as a churchwarden. There is a public service to be performed, and the people say who shall do it. The servant feels honored with the confidence reposed in him, and generally expresses his gratitude by a faithful performance.

Another of these operations is making every citizen a soldier, and every soldier a citizen; not only permitting every man to arm, but obliging him to arm. This fact, told in Europe previous to the French revolution, would have gained little credit; or at least it would have been regarded as a mark of an uncivilized people, extremely dangerous to a well ordered society Men who build systems on an inversion of nature, are obliged to invert every thing that is to make part of that system. It is because the people are civilized, that they are with safety armed. It is an effect of their conscious dignity, as citizens enjoying equal rights, that they wish not to invade the rights of others. The danger (where there is any) from armed citizens, is only to the government, not to the society; and as long as they have nothing to revenge in the government (which they cannot have while it is in their own hands) there are many advantages in their being accustomed to the use of arms, and no possible disadvantage.

Power, habitually in the hands of a whole community, loses all the ordinary associated ideas of power. The exercise of power is a relative term; it supposes an opposition, — something to operate upon . . .

Another consequence of the habitual idea of equality, is the facility of changing the structure of their government whenever and as often as the society shall think there is any thing in it to amend. As Mr. Burke has written no "reflections on the revolution" in America, the people there have never yet been told that they had no right "to frame a government for themselves;" they have therefore done much of this business, without ever affixing to it the idea of "sacrilege" or "usurpation," or any other term of rant to be found in that gentleman's vocabulary.

Within a few years the fifteen states have not only framed each its own state-constitution, and two successive federal constitutions; but since the settlement of the present general government in the year 1789, three of the states, Pennsylvania, South-Carolina and Georgia, have totally new modeled their own. And all this is done without the least confusion; the operation being scarcely known beyond the limits of the state where it is performed . . .

But it is said, these things will do very well for America, where the people are less numerous, less indigent, and better instructed; but they will not apply to Europe. This objection deserves a reply, not because it is solid, but because it is fashionable. It may be answered, that some parts of Spain, much of Poland, and almost the whole of Russia, are less peopled than the settled country in the United States; that poverty and ignorance are effects of slavery rather than its causes; but the best answer to be given, is the example of France. To the event of that revolution I will trust the argument. Let the people have time to become thoroughly and soberly grounded in the doctrine of equality, and there is no danger of oppression either from government or from anarchy. Very little instruction is necessary to teach a man his rights; and there is no person of common intellects in the most ignorant corner of Europe, but receives lessons enough, if they were of the proper kind. For writing and reading are not indispensible to the object; it is thinking right which makes them act right. Every child is taught to repeat about fifty Latin prayers, which set up the Pope, the Bishop, and the King, as the trinity of his adoration; he is taught that the powers that be are ordained of God, and therefore the soldier quartered in the parish has a right to cut his throat. Half this instruction, upon opposite principles, would go a great way; in that case Nature would be assisted, while here she is counteracted. Engrave it on the heart of man, that all men are equal in rights, and that the government is their own, and then persuade him to sell his crucifix and buy a musquet, — and you have made him a good citizen . . .

It is a truth, I believe, not to be called in question, that every man is born with an imprescriptible claim to a portion of the elements; which portion is termed his birth-right. Society may vary this right, as to its form, but never can destroy it in substance. She has no control over the man, till he is born; and the right being born with him, and being necessary to his existence, she can no more annihilate the one than the other, though she has the power of new-modelling both. But on coming into the world, he finds that the ground which nature had promised him is taken up, and in the occupancy of others; society has changed the form of his birth-right; the general flock of elements, from which the lives of men are to be supported, has undergone a new modification; and his portion among the rest. He is told that he cannot claim it in its present form, as an independent inheritance; that he must draw on the stock of society, instead of the stock of nature; that he is banished from the mother and must cleave to the nurse. In this unexpected occurrence he is unprepared to act but knowledge is a part of the stock of society; and an indispensable part to be allotted in the portion of the claimant is instruction relative to the new arrangement of natural right. To withhold this instruction therefore would be, not merely the omission of a duty, but the commission of a crime; and society in this case would sin against the man, before the man could sin against society.

I should hope to meet the assent of all unprejudiced readers, in carrying this idea still farther. In cases where a person is born of poor parents, or finds himself brought into the community of men without the means of subsistence, society is bound in duty to furnish him the means. She ought not only to instruct him in the artificial laws by which property is secured, but in the artificial industry by which it is obtained. She is bound, in justice as well as policy, to give him some art or trade. For the reason of his incapacity is, that she has usurped his birth-right; and this is restoring it to him in another form, more convenient for both parties. The failure of society in this branch of her duty is the occasion of much the greater part of the evils that call for criminal jurisprudence. The individual feels that he is robbed of his natural right; he cannot bring his process to reclaim it from the great community, by which he is overpowered; he therefore feels authorized in reprisal; in taking another's goods to replace his own. And it must be confessed, that in numberless instances the conduct of society justifies him in this proceeding; she has seized upon his property, and commenced the war against him.

Some, who perceive these truths, say that it is unsafe for society to publish them; but I say it is unsafe not to publish them. For the party from which the mischief is expected to arise has the knowledge of them already, and has acted upon them in all ages. It is the wife who are ignorant of these things, and not the foolish. They are truths of nature; and in them the

teachers of mankind are the only party that remains to be taught . . .

It has been the folly of all old governments, to begin every thing at the wrong end, and to erect their institutions on an inversion of principle. This is more sadly the case in their systems of jurisprudence, than is commonly imagined. Compelling justice is always mistaken for rendering justice. But this important branch of administration consists not merely in compelling men to be just to each other, and individuals to society, — this is not the whole, nor is it the principal part, nor even the beginning, of the operation. The source of power is said to be the source of justice; but it does not answer this description, as long as it contents itself with compulsion. Justice must begin by flowing from its source; and the first as well as the most important object is, to open its channels from society to all the individual members. This part of the administration being well devised and diligently executed, the other parts would lessen away by degrees to matters of inferior consideration.

It is an undoubted truth, that our duty is inseparably connected with our happiness. And why should we despair of convincing every member of society of a truth so important for him to know? Should any person object, by saying, that nothing like this, has ever yet been done; I answer that nothing like this has ever yet been tried. Society has hitherto been curst with governments, whose existence depended on the extinction of truth. Every moral light has been smothered under the bushel of perpetual imposition; from whence it emits but faint and glimmering rays, always insufficient to form any luminous system on any of the civil concerns of men. But these covers are crumbling to the dust, with the governments which they support; and the probability becomes more apparent, the more it is considered, that society is capable of curing all the evils to which it has given birth . . .

John Adams: Discourses on Davila (1790)

Men, in their primitive conditions, however savage, were undoubtedly gregarious; and they continue to be

Charles Frances Adams (ed.), *The Works of John Adams*, Little, Brown, Boston, 1851, VI, 232–51, 270–83.

social, not only in every stage of civilization, but in every possible situation in which they can be placed. As nature intended them for society, she has furnished them with passions, appetites, and propensities, as well as a variety of faculties, calculated both for their individual enjoyment, and to render them useful to each other in their social connections. There is none among them more essential or remarkable, than the passion for distinction. A desire to be observed, considered, esteemed, praised, beloved, and admired by his fellows, is one of the earliest, as well as keenest dispositions discovered in the heart of man. If any one should doubt the existence of this propensity, let him go and attentively observe the journeymen and apprentices in the first workshop, or the oarsmen in a cockboat, a family or a neighborhood, the inhabitants of a house or the crew of a ship, a school or a college, a city or a village, a savage or civilized people, a hospital or a church, the bar or the exchange, a camp or a court. Wherever men, women, or children, are to be found, whether they be old or young, rich or poor, high or low, wise or foolish, ignorant or learned, every individual is seen to be strongly actuated by a desire to be seen, heard, talked of, approved and respected, by the people about him, and within his knowledge . . .

A regard to the sentiments of mankind concerning him, and to their dispositions towards him, every man feels within himself; and if he has reflected, and tried experiments, he has found, that no exertion of his reason, no effort of his will, can wholly divest him of it. In proportion to our affection for the notice of others is our aversion to their neglect; the stronger the desire of the esteem of the public, the more powerful the aversion to their disapprobation; the more exalted the wish for admiration, the more invincible the abhorrence of contempt. Every man not only desires the consideration of others, but he frequently compares himself with others, his friends or his enemies; and in proportion as he exults when he perceives that he has more of it than they, he feels a keener affliction when he sees that one or more of them, are more respected than himself.

This passion, while it is simply a desire to excel another, by fair industry in the search of truth, and the practice of virtue, is properly called Emulation.

When it aims at power, as a means of distinction, it is Ambition. When it is in a situation to suggest the sentiments of fear and apprehension, that another, who is now inferior, will become superior, it is denominated Jealousy. When it is in a state of mortification, at the superiority of another, and desires to bring him down to our level, or to depress him below us, it is properly called Envy. When it deceives a man into a belief of false professions of esteem or admiration, or into a false opinion of his importance in the judgment of the world, it is Vanity. These observations alone would be sufficient to show, that this propensity, in all its branches, is a principal source of the virtues and vices, the happiness and misery of human life; and that the history of mankind is little more than a simple narration of its operation and effects.

There is in human nature, it is true, simple Benevolence, or an affection for the good of others; but alone it is not a balance for the selfish affections. Nature then has kindly added to benevolence, the desire of reputation, in order to make us good members of society. *Spectemur agendo* expresses the great principle of activity for the good of others. Nature has sanctioned the law of self-preservation by rewards and punishments. The rewards of selfish activity are life and health; the punishments of negligence and indolence are want, disease, and death. Each individual, it is true, should consider, that nature has enjoined the same law on his neighbor, and therefore a respect for the authority of nature would oblige him to respect the rights of others as much as his own. But reasoning as abstruse, though as simple as this, would not occur to all men. The same nature therefore has imposed another law, that of promoting the good, as well as respecting the rights of mankind, and has sanctioned it by other rewards and punishments. The rewards in this case, in this life, are esteem and admiration of others; the punishments are neglect and contempt; nor may any one imagine that these are not as real as the others. The desire of the esteem of others is as real a want of nature as hunger; and the neglect and contempt of the world as severe a pain as the gout or stone. It sooner and oftener produces despair, and a detestation of existence; of equal importance to individuals, to families, and to nations. It is a principal end of government to regulate this passion, which in its turn becomes a principal means of government. It is the only adequate instrument of order and subordination in society, and alone commands effectual obedience to laws, since without it neither human reason, nor standing armies, would ever produce that great effect. Every personal quality, and every blessing of fortune, is cherished in proportion to its capacity of gratifying this universal affection for the esteem, the sympathy, admiration and congratulations of the public. Beauty in the face, elegance of figure, grace of attitude and motion, riches, honors, every thing is weighed in the scale, and desired, not so much for the pleasure they afford, as the attention they command. As this is a point of great importance, it may be pardonable to expatiate a little upon these particulars.

Why are the personal accomplishments of beauty, elegance, and grace, held in such high estimation by mankind? Is it merely for the pleasure which is received from the sight of these attributes? By no means. The taste for such delicacies is not universal; in those who feel the most lively sense of them, it is but a slight sensation, and of shortest continuance; but those attractions command the notice and attention of the public; they draw the eyes of spectators. This is the charm that makes them irresistible. Is it for such fading perfections that a husband or a wife is chosen? Alas, it is well known, that a very short familiarity totally destroys all sense and attention to such properties; and on the contrary, a very little time and habit destroy all the aversion to ugliness and deformity, when unattended with disease or ill temper. Yet beauty and address are courted and admired, very often, more than discretion, wit, sense, and many other accomplishments and virtues, of infinitely more importance to the happiness of private life, as well as to the utility and ornament of society. Is it for the momentous purpose of dancing and drawing, painting and music, riding or fencing, that men or women are destined in this life or any other? Yet those who have the best means of education, bestow more attention and expense on those, than on more solid acquisitions. Why? Because they attract more forcibly the attention of the world, and procure a better advancement in life. Notwithstanding all this, as soon as an establishment in life is made, they are found to have answered their

end, are neglected and laid aside.

Is there any thing in birth, however illustrious or splendid, which should make a difference between one man and another? If, from a common ancestor, the whole human race is descended, they are all of the same family. How then can they distinguish families into the more or the less ancient?   The mighty secret lies in this: — An illustrious descent attracts the notice of mankind. A single drop of royal blood, however illegitimately scattered, will make any man or woman proud or vain. Why? Because, although it excites the indignation of many, and the envy of more, it still attracts the attention of the world. Noble blood, whether the nobility be hereditary or elective, and, indeed, more in republican governments than in monarchies, least of all in despotisms, is held in estimation for the same reason. It is a name and a race that a nation has been interested in, and is in the habit of respecting. Benevolence, sympathy, congratulation, have been so long associated to those names in the minds of the people, that they are become national habits. National gratitude descends from the father to the son, and is often stronger to the latter than the former. It is often excited by remorse, upon reflection on the ingratitude and injustice with which the former has been treated. When the names of a certain family are read in all the gazettes, chronicles, records, and histories of a country for five hundred years, they become known, respected, and delighted in by every body. A youth, a child of this extraction, and bearing this name, attracts the eyes and ears of all companies long before it is known or inquired whether he be a wise man or a fool . . .

This desire of the consideration of our fellow-men, and their congratulations in our joys, is not less invincible than the desire of their sympathy in our sorrows. It is a determination of our nature, that lies at the foundation of our whole moral system in this world, and may be connected essentially with our destination in a future state.

Why do men pursue riches? What is the end of avarice?

The labor and anxiety, the enterprises and adventures, that are voluntarily undertaken in pursuit of gain, are out of all proportion to the utility, convenience, or pleasure of riches. A competence to satisfy the wants of nature, food and clothes, a shelter from the seasons, and the comforts of a family, may be had for very little. The daily toil of the million, and of millions of millions, is adequate to a complete supply of these necessities and conveniences, With such accommodations, thus obtained, the appetite is keener, the digestion more easy and perfect, and repose is more refreshing, than among the most abundant superfluities and the rarest luxuries. For what reason, then, are any mortals averse to the situation of the farmer, mechanic, or laborer? Why do we tempt the seas and encompass the globe? Why do any men affront heaven and earth to accumulate wealth, which will forever be useless to them? Why do we make an ostentatious display of riches? Why should any man be proud of his purse, houses, lands, or gardens? or, in better words, why should the rich man glory in his riches? What connection can there be between wealth and pride?

The answer to all these questions is, because riches attract the attention, consideration, and congratulations of mankind; it is not because the rich have really more of ease or pleasure than the poor. Riches force the opinion on a man that he is the object of the congratulations of others, and he feels that they attract the complaisance of the public. His senses all inform him, that his neighbors have a natural disposition to harmonize with all those pleasing emotions and agreeable sensations, which the elegant accommodations around him are supposed to excite.

His imagination expands, and his heart dilates at these charming illusions. His attachment to his possessions increases as fast as his desire to accumulate more; not for the purposes of beneficence or utility, but from the desire of illustration.

Why, on the other hand, should any man be ashamed to make known his poverty? Why should those who have been rich, or educated in the houses of the rich, entertain such an aversion, or be agitated with such terror, at the prospect of losing their property? or of being reduced to live at a humbler table? in a meaner house? to walk, instead of riding? or to ride without their accustomed equipage or retinue? Why do we hear of madness, melancholy, and suicides, upon bankruptcy, loss of ships, or any other sudden fall from opulence to indigence, or mediocrity? Ask your reason, what disgrace there can be in poverty? What moral sentiment of approbation, praise, or honor can

there be in a palace? What dishonor in a cottage? What glory in a coach? What shame in a wagon? Is not the sense of propriety and sense of merit as much connected with an empty purse as a full one? May not a man be as estimable, amiable, and respectable, attended by his faithful dog, as if preceded and followed by a train of horses and servants? All these questions may be very wise, and the stoical philosophy has her answers ready. But if you ask the same questions of nature, experience, and mankind, the answers will be directly opposite to those of Epictetus, namely, — that there is more respectability, in the eyes of the greater part of mankind, in the gaudy trappings of wealth, than there is in genius or learning, wisdom or virtue.

The poor man's conscience is clear; yet he is ashamed. His character is irreproachable; yet he is neglected and despised. He feels himself out of the sight of others, groping in the dark. Mankind take no notice of him. He rambles and wanders unheeded. In the midst of a crowd, at church, in the market, at a play, at an execution, or coronation, he is in as much obscurity as he would be in a garret or a cellar. He is not disapproved, censured, or reproached; he is only not seen. This total inattention is to him mortifying, painful, and cruel.

Is there in science and letters a reward for the labor they require? Scholars learn the dead languages of antiquity, as well as the living tongues of modern nations; those of the east, as well as the west. They puzzle themselves and others with metaphysics and mathematics. They renounce their pleasures, neglect their exercises, and destroy their health, for what? Is curiosity so strong? Is the pleasure that accompanies the pursuit and acquisition of knowledge so exquisite? If Crusoe, on his island, had the library of Alexandria, and a certainty that he should never again see the face of man, would he ever open a volume? Perhaps he might; but it is very probable he would read but little. A sense of duty; a love of truth; a desire to alleviate the anxieties of ignorance, may, no doubt, have an influence on some minds. But the universal object and idol of men of letters is reputation. It is the notoriety, the celebration, which constitutes the charm that is to compensate the loss of appetite and sleep, and sometimes of riches and honors . . .

There is a voice within us, which seems to intimate, that real merit should govern the world; and that men ought to be respected only in proportion to their talents, virtues, and services. But the question always has been, how can this arrangement be accomplished? How shall the men of merit be discovered? How shall the proportions of merit be ascertained and graduated? Who shall be the judge? When the government of a great nation is in question, shall the whole nation choose? Will such a choice be better than chance? Shall the whole nation vote for senators? Will you divide the nation into districts, and let each district choose a senator? This is giving up the idea of national merit, and annexing the honor and the trust to an accident, that of living on a particular spot. A hundred or a thousand men of the first merit in a nation, may live in one city, and none at all of this description in several whole provinces. Real merit is so remote from the knowledge of whole nations, that were magistrates to be chosen by that criterion alone, and by a universal suffrage, dissensions and venality would be endless. The difficulties, arising from this source, are so obvious and universal, that nations have tried all sorts of experiments to avoid them.

As no appetite in human nature is more universal than that for honor, and real merit is confined to a very few, the numbers who thirst for respect, are out of all proportion to those who seek it only by merit. The great majority trouble themselves little about merit, but apply themselves to seek for honor, by means which they see will more easily and certainly obtain it, by displaying their taste and address, their wealth and magnificence, their ancient parchments, pictures, and statues, and the virtues of their ancestors; and if these fail, as they seldom have done, they have recourse to artifice, dissimulation, hypocrisy, flattery, imposture, empiricism, quackery, and bribery. What chance has humble, modest, obscure, and poor merit in such a scramble? Nations, perceiving that the still small voice of merit was drowned in the insolent roar of such dupes of impudence and knavery in national elections, without a possibility of a remedy, have sought for something more permanent than the popular voice to designate honor. Many nations have attempted to annex it to land, presuming that a good estate would at least furnish means of a good

education; and have resolved that those who should possess certain territories, should have certain legislative, executive, and judicial powers over the people. Other nations have endeavored to connect honor with offices; and the names and ideas at least of certain moral virtues and intellectual qualities have been by law annexed to certain offices, as veneration, grace, excellence, honor, serenity, majesty. Other nations have attempted to annex honor to families, without regard to lands or offices. The Romans allowed none, but those who had possessed curule offices, to have statues or portraits. He who had images or pictures of his ancestors, was called noble. He who had no statue or pictures but his own, was called a new man. Those who had none at all, were ignoble. Other nations have united all those institutions; connected lands, offices, and families; made them all descend together, and honor, public attention, consideration, and congratulation, along with them . . .

We are told that our friends, the National Assembly of France, have abolished all distinctions. But be not deceived, my dear countrymen. Impossibilities cannot be performed. Have they levelled all fortunes and equally divided all property? Have they made all men and women equally wise, elegant, and beautiful? Have they annihilated the names of Bourbon and Montmorenci, Rochefoucauld and Noailles, Lafayette and LaMoignon, Necker and De Calonne, Mirabeau and Bailly? Have they committed to the flames all the records, annals, and histories of the nation? All the copies of Mererai, Daniel, DeThou, Velly, and a thousand others? Have they burned all their pictures, and broken all their statues? Have they blotted out of all memories, the names, places of abode, and illustrious actions of all their ancestors? Have they not still princes of the first and second order, nobles and knights? Have they no record nor memory who are the men who compose the present national assembly? Do they wish to have that distinction forgotten? Have the French officers who served in America melted their eagles and torn their ribbons?

All the miracles enumerated in our last number, must be performed in France, before all distinctions can be annihilated, and distinctions in abundance would be found, after all, for French gentlemen, in the history of England, Holland, Spain, Germany,

Italy, America, and all other countries on the globe.

The wisdom of nations has remarked the universal consideration paid to wealth; and that the passion of avarice excited by it, produced treachery, cowardice, and a selfish, unsocial meanness, but had no tendency to produce those virtues of patience, courage, fortitude, honor, or patriotism, which the service of the public required in their citizens in peace and war.

The wisdom of nations has observed that the general attention paid to birth produced a different kind of sentiments, — those of pride in the maxims and principles of religion, morals, and government as well as in the talents and virtues, which first produced illustration to ancestors.

As the pride of wealth produced nothing but meanness of sentiment and a sordid scramble for money; and the pride of birth produced some degree of emulation in knowledge and virtue; the wisdom of nations has endeavored to employ one prejudice to counteract another; the prejudice in favor of birth, to moderate, correct, and restrain the prejudice in favor of wealth.

The national assembly of France is too enlightened a body to overlook the inquiry: What effect on the moral character of the nation would be produced, by destroying, if that were possible, all attention to families, and setting all the passions of the pursuit of gain? Whether universal venality and an incorrigible corruption in elections would not be the necessary consequence? It may be relied on, however, that the intentions of that august and magnanimous assembly are misunderstood and misrepresented. Time will develop their designs, will show them to be more judicious than to attempt impossibilities so obvious as that of the abolition of all distinctions . . .

God, in the constitution of nature, has ordained that every man shall have a disposition to emulation, as well as imitation, and consequently a passion for distinction; and that all men shall not have equal means and opportunities of gratifying it. Shall we believe the national assembly capable of resolving that no man shall have any desire of distinction; or that all men shall have equal means of gratifying it? Or that no man shall have any means of gratifying it? What would this be better than saying, "if we had been called to the councils of the celestials, we could have given better advice in the constitution of human nature?" If nature and that assembly could be thus at variance, which however is not credible, the world would soon see which is the most powerful . . .

Frenchmen! Act and think like yourselves! confessing human nature, be magnanimous and wise. Acknowledging and boasting yourselves to be men, avow the feelings of men. The affectation of being exempted from passions is inhuman. The grave pretension to such singularity is solemn hypocrisy. Both are unworthy of your frank and generous natures. Consider that government is intended to set bounds to passions which nature has not limited; and to assist reason, conscience, justice, and truth, in controlling interests, which, without it, would be as unjust as uncontrollable.

Americans! Rejoice, that from experience you have learned wisdom; and instead of whimsical and fantastical projects, you have adopted a promising essay towards a well-ordered government. Instead of following any foreign example, to return to the legislation of confusion, contemplate the means of restoring decency, honesty, and order in society, by preserving and completing, if any thing should be found necessary to complete the balance of your government. In a well-balanced government, reason, conscience, truth, and virtue, must be respected by all parties, and exerted for the public good. Advert to the principles on which you commenced that glorious self-defence, which, if you behave with steadiness and consistency, may ultimately loosen the chains of all mankind . . .

The spirit of inquiry, like a severe and searching wind, penetrates every part of the great body politic; and whatever is unsound, whatever is infirm, shrinks at the visitation. Liberty, led by philosophy, diffuses her blessings to every class of men; and even extends a smile of hope and promise to the poor African, the victim of hard, impenetrable avarice. Man, as man, becomes an object of respect. Tenets are transferred from theory to practice. The glowing sentiment, the lofty speculation, no longer serve 'but to adorn the pages of a book.' They are brought home to men's business and bosoms; and what, some centuries ago, it was daring but to think and dangerous to express, is now realized and carried into effect. Systems are analyzed into their first principles, and

principles are fairly pursued to their legitimate consequences."

This is all enchanting. But amidst our enthusiasm,
there is great reason to pause and preserve our sobriety.
It is true that the first empire of the world is breaking
the fetters of human reason and exerting the energies
of redeemed liberty. In the glowing ardor of her zeal,
she condescends, Americans, to pay the most scrupulous attention to your maxims, principles, and example. There is reason to fear she has copied from you
errors which have cost you very dear. Assist her, by
your example, to rectify them before they involve
her in calamities as much greater than yours, as her
population is more unwieldly, and her situation
more exposed to the baleful influence of rival neighbors.
Amidst all their exultations, Americans and Frenchmen should remember that the perfectibility of man
is only human and terrestrial perfectibility. Cold
will still freeze, and fire will never cease to burn;
disease and vice will continue to disorder, and death
to terrify mankind. Emulation next to self-preservation
will forever be the great spring of human actions, and
the balance of a well-ordered government will alone be
able to prevent that emulation from degenerating into
dangerous ambition, irregular rivalries, destructive
factions, wasting seditions, and bloody, civil wars.

The great question will forever remain, who shall
work? Our species cannot all be idle. Leisure for
study must ever be the portion of a few. The number
employed in government must forever be very small.
Food, raiment, and habitations, the indispensable
wants of all, are not to be obtained without the continual toil of ninety-nine in a hundred of mankind. As
rest is rapture to the weary man, those who labor little
will always be envied by those who labor much, though
the latter in reality be probably the most enviable.
With all the encouragements, public and private, which
can ever be given to general education, and it is
scarcely possible they should be too many or too
great, the laboring part of the people can never be
learned. The controversy between the rich and the
poor, the laborious and the idle, the learned and the
ignorant, distinctions as old as the creation, and as
extensive as the glove, distinctions which no art or
policy, no degree of virtue or philosophy can ever
wholly destroy, will continue, and rivalries will spring

out of them. These parties will be represented in the
legislature, and must be balanced, or one will oppress
the other. There will never probably be found any
other mode of establishing such an equilibrium, than
by constituting the representation of each an independent branch of the legislature, and an independent
executive authority, such as that in our government,
to be a third branch and a mediator or an arbitrator
between them. Property must be secured, or liberty
cannot exist. But if unlimited or unbalanced power
of disposing property, be put into the hands of those
who have no property, France will find, as we have
found, the lamb committed to the custody of the
wolf. In such a case, all the pathetic exhortations and
addresses of the national assembly to the people, to
respect property, will be regarded no more than the
warbles of the songsters of the forest. The great art
of lawgiving consists in balancing the poor against the
rich in the legislature, and in consistuting the legislative a perfect balance against the executive power,
at the same time that no individual or party can become its rival. The essence of a free government
consists in an effectual control of rivalries. The executive and the legislative powers are natural rivals;
and if each has not an effectual control over the other,
the weaker will ever be the lamb in the paws of the
wolf. The nation which will not adopt an equilibrium
of power must adopt a despotism. There is no other
alternative. Rivalries must be controlled, or they will
throw all things into confusion; and there is nothing
but despotism or a balance of power which can control them. Even in the simple monarchies, the nobility
and the judicatures constitute a balance, though a
very imperfect one, against the royalties . . .

Instead of throwing false imputations on republican
governments; instead of exciting or fomenting a vulgar
malignity against the most respectable men and
families, let us draw the proper inferences from history
and experience; let us lay it down for a certain fact,
that emulation between individuals, and rivalries among
families never can be prevented. Second, let us adopt
it as a certain principle, that they ought not to be prevented, but directed to virtue, and then stimulated and
encouraged by generous applause and honorable rewards.
And from these premises let the conclusion be, as it
ought to be, that an effectual control be provided in the

constitution, to check their excesses and balance their weights. If this conclusion is not drawn, another will follow of itself; the people will be the dupes, and the leaders will worry each other and the people too, till both are weary and ashamed, and from feeling, not from reasoning, set up a master and a despot for a protector . . .

The French Revolution proved to be a catalyst in the formation of political parties in the new nation. Divided American opinion on a whole range of questions polarized around conflicting responses to the French people's efforts to remake their society. The pair of readings that follows presents the diverging viewpoints of Federalists and Jeffersonians on the issue of partisan politics itself. In the Federalist view, set forth by Noah Webster (1758-1843), party factions had developed because average Americans had become actively involved in public issues through their emotional attachment to the revolutionaries of France. This undesirable political turmoil could have been avoided if the people had left governing to those whom they had elected. Webster, who had fought in the American Revolution, used all of his considerable prestige as author, lecturer, and dictionary editor to dissuade Americans from identifying their revolution with that of France. Webster's *The Revolution in France* shows how many American patriots still retained an essentially conservative view of society.

William Manning (1747-1814), the author of *The Key of Libberty,* from which the second reading is taken, found a different reason for the formation of parties in America. In his eyes, they were the result of the organized efforts of the well-born and well-educated to dominate the lower classes. When John Adams defeated Manning's beloved Thomas Jefferson for the presidency in 1796, Manning sat down at his family's century old Massachusetts farm and composed a treatise on how the poor should organize to oppose the rich. He sent his manuscript to the only Jeffersonian newspaper in Boston, but the editor had been indicted for seditious libel under the new Sedition Act, and Manning's wisdom was never published during his lifetime.

Noah Webster: The revolution in France considered in respect to its progress and its effects

The Revolution of France, like that of Rome, is fruitful in lessons of instruction, of which all enlightened nations should avail themselves, and which may be of great use to the United States of America.

The most important truth suggested by the foregoing remarks is, that party spirit is the source of faction and faction is death to the existing government. The history of the Jacobins is the most remarkable illustration of this truth . . . When government is radically bad, it is meritorious to reform it; when there is no other expedient to rid a people of oppression, it is necessary to change the government; but when a people have freely and voluntarily chosen and instituted a constitution of government, which guarantees all their rights, and no corruption appears in the administration, there can be no necessity for a change; and if in any particular, it is thought to require amendment, a constitutional mode is provided, and there is no necessity for recurring to extraordinary expedients. In America therefore there can exist no necessity for private societies to watch over the government. Indeed to pretend that a government that has been in operation but five or six years, and which has hitherto produced nothing but public prosperity and private happiness, has need of associations in all parts of the country to guard its purity, is like a jealous husband who should deem it necessary, the day after his nuptials, to set a centinel over his wife to secure her fidelity.

If the government of America wants a reform, the best mode of effecting this, is the constitutional mode. If it is become absolutely necessary to overthrow it, the most direct mode of doing it, is to organize a party for the purpose, by condensing its scattered forces into union and system. But if the point is admitted, that the government does not require any essential alteration, which cannot be effected in a legal way, it follows of course that the establishment of private societies is not necessary. For the same reason that such societies were found useful in France, they ought to be avoided like a pestilence in America; because a total renovation was judged necessary in that country; and such a total renovation is judged not necessary in America — because a republican government was to be established in that country; and in this, it is already established on principles of liberty and equal rights.

As the tendency of such associations is probably not fully understood by most of the persons composing them in this country, and many of whom are doubtless well-meaning citizens; it may be useful to trace the progress of party-spirit to faction first, and then of course to tyranny.

My first remark is, that contentions usually spring out of points which are trifling, speculative, or of doubtful tendency. Among trifling causes I rank personal injuries. It has frequently happened that an affront offered by one leading man in a state to another, has disquieted the whole state, and even caused a revolution. The real interest of the people has nothing to do with private resentments, and ought never to be affected by them, yet nothing is more common. And republics are more able to suffer changes and convulsions, on account of personal quarrels, than any other species of government; because the individuals, who have acquired the confidence of the people, can always fabricate some reasons for rousing their passions — some pretext of public good may be vented, when the man has his own passions to gratify — the minds of the populace are easily enflamed — and strong parties may be raised on the most frivolous occasions. I have known an instance in America of a man's intriguing for and obtaining an election to an important trust; which he immediately resigned, and confessed he had done it solely to gratify his own will and mortify his enemies. Yet had the man been disposed, he might have used his influence to strengthen a party, and given trouble to the state.

Another cause of violent parties is frequently a difference of opinion on speculative questions, or those whose real tendency to secure public happiness is equivocal. — When measures are obviously good, and clearly tend to advance public weal, there will seldom be much division of opinion on the propriety of adopting them. All parties unite in pursuing the public interest, when it is clearly visible. But when it is doubtful what will be the ultimate effect of a measure, men will differ in opinion, and probably the parties will be nearly equal. It is on points of private local utility, or on those of doubtful tendency, that men split into parties . . .

Nothing is more dangerous to the cause of truth and liberty than a party-spirit. When men are once united, in whatever form, or upon whatever occasion, the union creates a partiality or friendship for each member of the party or society. A coalition for any purpose creates an attachment, and inspires a confidence in the individuals of the party, which does not die with the cause which united them; but continues, and extends to every other object of social intercourse.

Thus we see men first united in some system of religious faith, generally agree in their political opinions. Natives of the same country, even in a foreign country, unite and form a separate private society. The Masons feel attached to each other, tho in distant parts of the world.

The same may be said of Episcopalians, Quakers, Presbyterians, Roman Catholics, Federalists, and Antifederalists, Mechanic societies, Chambers of Commerce, Jacobin and Democratic societies. It is altogether immaterial what circumstance first unites a number of men into a society; whether they first rally round the church, a square and compass, a cross, or a cap; the general effect is always the same; while the union continues, the members of the association feel a particular confidence in each other, which leads them to believe each others opinions, to catch each others passions, and to act in concert on every question in which they are interested.

Hence arises what is called bigotry or illiberality. Persons who are united on any occasion, are more apt to believe the prevailing opinions of their society, than the prevailing opinions of another society. They examine their own creeds more fully, (and perhaps with a mind predisposed to believe them,) than they do the creeds of other societies. Hence the full persuasion in every society that theirs is right; and if right, others of course are wrong. Perhaps therefore I am warranted in saying, there is a species of bigotry in every society on earth — and indeed in every man's own particular faith. While each man and each society is freely indulged in his own opinion, and that opinion is mere speculation, there is peace, harmony, and good understanding. But the moment a man or a society attempts to oppose the prevailing opinions of another man or society, even his arguments rouse passion; it being difficult for two men of opposite creeds to dispute for any time, without getting angry. And when one party attempts in practice to interfere with the opinions of another party, violence most generally succeeds.

These remarks are so consonant to experience and common observation, that I presume no man can deny them; and if true, they deserve the serious attention of every good citizen of America . . .

The principal danger to which our government is exposed will probably arise from another quarter; the spirit of party, which is now taking the form of system. While a jealousy and opposition to the national constitution exist only in the legislatures of the several states, they will be restrained and moderated by the public dignity of those bodies, and by legal or constitutional forms of proceeding. Opposition thus tempered loses its terrors.

But opposition that is raised in private societies of men, who are self-created, unknown to the laws of the country, private in their proceedings, and perhaps violent in their passions, the moment it ceases to be insignificant, becomes formidable to government and freedom. The very people who compose these societies, are not aware of the possible consequences that may flow from their associations. They are few of them persons of extensive historical knowlege; and they do not percieve, that under pretence of securing their rights and liberties, they are laying the foundation of factions which will probably end in the destruction of liberty and a free government. They do not consider, that when men become members of a political club, they lose their individual independence of mind; that they lose their impartiality of thinking and acting; and become the dupes of other men. The moment a man is attached to a club, his mind is not free: He receives a bias from the opinions of the party: A question indifferent to him, is no longer indifferent, when it materially effects a brother of the society. He is not left to act for himself; he is bound in honor to take part with the society — his pride and his prejudices, if at war with his opinions, will commonly obtain the victory; and rather than incur the ridicule or censure of his associates, he will countenance their measures, at all hazards; and thus an independant freeman is converted into a mere walking machine, a convenient engine of party leaders.

It is thus that private associations may always

influence public measures; and if they are formed for the express purpose of discussing political measures, they may prove pernicious to the existing government . . .

Private associations of men for the purposes of promoting arts, sciences, benevolence or charity are very laudable, and have been found beneficial in all countries. But whenever such societies attempt to convert the private attachment of their members into an instrument of political warfare, they are, in all cases, hostile to government. They are useful in pulling down bad governments; but they are dangerous to good government, and necessarily destroy liberty and equality of rights in a free country. I say necessarily; for it must occur to any man of common reflection, that in a free country, each citizen, in his private capacity, has an equal right to a share of influence in directing public measures; but a society, combined for the purpose of augmenting and extending its influence, acquires an undue proportion of that general influence which is to direct the will of the state. Each individual member of the state should have an equal voice in elections; but the individuals of a club have more than an equal voice, because they have the benefit of another influence; that of extensive private attachments which come in aid of each man's political opinion. And just in proportion as the members of a club have an undue share of influence, in that proportion they abridge the rights of their fellow citizens. Every club therefore formed for political purposes, is an aristocracy established over their brethren. It has all the properties of an aristocracy, and all the effects of tyranny. It is only substituting the influence of private attachments, in lieu of the influence of birth and property among the nobility of Europe; and the certain effect of private intrigue in lieu of the usurped power and rights of feudal lords; the effects are the same. It is a literal truth, which cannot be denied, evaded, or modified, that the Democratic clubs in the United States, while running mad with the abhorrence of aristocratic influence, are attempting to establish precisely the same influence under a different name. And if any thing will rescue this country from the jaws of faction, and prevent our free government from falling a prey, first to civil dissensions, and finally to some future Sylla and Marius, it must be either the good sense of a great majority of Americans, which will discourage private political associations, and render them contemptible; or the controling power of the laws of the country, which in an early stage, shall demolish all such institutions, and secure to each individual in the great political family, equal rights and an equal share of influence in his individual capacity.

And it appears very clear from history and observation, that in a popular government, it is not difficult to inflame the passions of a people with imaginary as well as real evils. In Europe, the people have real evils to extirpate. The passions of Americans are inlisting on one side or the other of the present contest in France. We feel no loss of personal liberty as yet, in consequence of the combination against France; but artful men address the passions of our citizens; they teach them to fear, that if France should be reduced, the combined powers will attack liberty in America. Cool men who reflect upon the difficulties of such an attempt, consider all such apprehensions as groundless and idle. But two or three hundred men collected, might have their passions so wrought upon by an artful or noisy declaimer, as to believe the danger real. They then grow violent, and denounce as enemies, all who are cool or moderate enough to entertain no such fears. Thus two parties are formed on a mere imaginary evil, and when the parties are formed, some badge of distinction, a button or a cockade is assumed, to widen the breach, and create disaffection, suspicion and hostile passions. All this is very visible in America; and because some men are too rational to be alarmed at chimeras, too temperate to commit themselves hastily, or too respectable not to despise little badges of distinction, the livery of faction, they are insulted as enemies to the rights of the people: And whenever opportunities offer, they fall a prey to the fury of popular passion. This is the triumph of passion over reason; of violence, over moderation. Should the present controversy in Europe continue two or three years longer, I should not be surprised to see party spirit in America, which grew originally out of a mere speculative question, proceed to open hostility and blood shed. People are easily made to believe their government is bad, or not so good as they might

expect from change; they may be made to fear corruption, which they do not see, and which does not exist; and to risk real evils at the present moment, to guard against possible evils, a century hence. All this may be done, if restless daring men will take pains to manage popular passions . . .

Those who suppose France now in possession of a free government are most egregiously mistaken. At no period has France experienced a despotism so severe and bloody, as the present authority of the convention, backed by a full treasury and more than a million of disciplined troops. This severe tyranny has imprisoned and executed more French citizens in 18 months past, than had been thrown into the Bastile for three centuries, preceding its demolition . . .

Americans! be not deluded. In seeking liberty, France has gone beyond her. You, my countrymen, if you love liberty, adhere to your constitution of government. The moment you quit that sheet-anchor, you are afloat among the surges of passion and the rocks of error; threatened every moment with ship-wreck. Heaven grant that while Europe is agitated with a violent tempest, in which palaces are shaken, and thrones tottering to their base, the republican government of America, in which liberty and the rights of man are embarked, fortunately anchored at an immense distance, on the margin of the gale, may be enabled to ride out from the storm, and land us safely on the shores of peace and political tranquillity.

William Manning: The Key of Libberty (1798)

To all the Republicans, Farmers, Mecanicks, and Labourers In America your Canded attention is Requested to the Sentiments of a Labourer.

I am not a Man of Larning my selfe for I neaver had the advantage of six months schooling in my life. I am no travelor for I neaver was 50 Miles from whare I was born in no direction, & I am no grate reader of antiant history for I always followed hard labour for a living. But I always thought it My duty to search into & see for my selfe in all maters that consansed

Samuel Eliot Morison, "William Manning's The Key of Libberty'," *William and Mary Quarterly*, 13(1956), 202–54. Reprinted by permission of Samuel Eliot Morison and the Institute of Early American History and Culture of Williamsburg, Virginia.

me as a member of society, & when the war began between Brittan & Amarica I was in the prime of Life & highly taken up with Libberty & a free Government. I See almost the first blood that was shed in Concord fite & scores of men dead, dying & wounded in the Cause of Libberty, which caused serious sencations in my mind.

But I beleived then & still believ it is a good cause which we aught to defend to the very last, & I have bin a Constant Reader of publick Newspapers & closely attended to men & measures ever sence, through the war, through the operation of paper money, framing Constitutions, makeing & constructing Laws, & seeing what selfish & contracted ideayes of interests would influence the best picked men & bodyes of men.

I have often thought it was imposable ever to seport a free Government, but firmly believing it to be the best sort & the ondly one approved off by heaven it was my unweryed study & prayers to the almighty for many years to find out the real cause & a remidy and I have for many years bin satisfyed in my own mind what the causes are & what would in a grate measure prove a reamidy provided it was carried into efect . . .

A General Description of the Causes that Ruen Republicks

The Causes that I shall Indeavor to Make appear are a Conceived Difference of Interests Between those that Labour for a Living & those that git a Living without Bodily Labour.

This is no new docterin if I may judge from the many scraps of history I have Seen of antiant Republicks. The best information I ever had on this Subject & the greatest colection of historical accounts was by a writer who wrote ten long numbers in the Chronicle in December [17]85 & January 86 stileing himselfe a Free Republican.

In his 4 first numbers he recites a long & blody history about the fudes & animosityes, contentions & blood sheds that hapned in the antiant Republicks of Athens, Greesh & Roome & many other nations, between the few & Many, the Perthiens,* & Plebians,

*This is probably as near as the author could get to "patricians."

Rich & poor, Dettor & Creditor, &cc, In his 5th No. he draws the dividing line between the few & the many as they apply to us in Amarica—amongue the few he reacons the marchent, phesition the lawyer & divine and all in the literary walkes of Life, the Juditial & Executive oficers & all the rich who could live with out bodily labour, so that the hole controvercy was between those that labour for a living & those who do not. Then tryes to prove that unless these few can have wait or influence in the Government according to their property & high stations in life it can not be free. Then goes on to shew how a government aught to be ballenced and proposes grate alterations in the Constitution of Masachusets — better to acomidate the Interests of the few — wishes to have the Senet represent the hole property of the State & the Representitives the persons ondly, & the Govenour to have as compleet a nagative on both as the King of Ingland has on the Parlement, which he thinks cant be so long as the people vote annully for Governour & Senetors.

These Sentiments being urged in such a masterly manner just before the adoption of the federal Constitution, & have bin so closely followed by the administration eversence, (although they are directly contrary to the prinsaples of a free government & no dout written to destroy it) yet if they ware republished they would be of servis to the people in many things & convince the author (if he is yet alive) that his unweried resarches for his ten numbers ware not intirely lost . . .

I have often Looked over those ten Nos. & Searched other historyes to satisfy my selfe as to the truth of his asertions, but am very far from thinking as he doth — that the destruction of free governments arises from the Licentiousness of the Many or their Representatives, but on the conterary shall indever to prove that their destruction always arises from the ungoverned dispositions & Combinations of the few, & the ignorance of the Many . . .

1. A Description of Mankind & Nesecaty of government

To search into & know our selves is of the greatest importance, & the want of it is the cause of the gratest evils suffered in Society. If we knew what alterations might be made in our Minds & Conduct

by alterations in our Edication, age, Circumstances, &
Conditions in this Life, we should be vastly less sen-
sorious on others for their conduct, & more cautious
of of trusting them when their was no need of it.

Men are born & grow up in this world with a vast
veriaty of capacityes, strength & abilityes both of
Body & Mind, & have strongly implanted within them
numerous pashons & lusts continually urging them to
fraud violence & acts of injustis toards one another.
He has implanted in him a sence of Right & Rong,
so that if he would always follow the dictates of
Contiance & Consider the advantages of Society &
mutual assistance he would need no other Law or
Government. Yet as he is sentanced by the just decrees
of heaven to hard Labour for a Living in this world,
& has so strongly implanted in him a desire to Selfe
Seporte, Selfe Defence, Selfe Love, Selfe Conceit,
Selfe Importance, & Selfe agrandisement, that it
Ingroses all his care and attention so that he can see
nothing beyond Selfe — for Selfe (as once described
by a Divine) is like an object plased before the eye
that hinders the sight of every thing beyond . . .

The most comprehensive description of Man I
ever saw was by a writer as followeth: —Viz—Man is
a being made up of Selfe Love seeking his own hapiness to the misery of all around him, who would
Damne a world to save him selfe from temporal or
other punishment, & he who denyes this to be his
real carrictor is ignorant of him selfe, or else is more
than a man . . .

From this disposition of Man or the depravity of
the human hart, arises not ondly the advantage but
the absolute nesecaty of Sivil government—without
it Mankind would be continually at war on their
own spetia, stealing roving fighting with & killing one
another. This all Nations on Earth have bin convinced
off, and have established it in some form or other, &
their soul aime in doing it is their safty & hapyness.
But for want of wisdom or some plan to curb the
ambition & govern those to hoom they gave power,
they have often bin brought to suffer as Much under
their governments as they would without any—and it
still remains uncartain wheather any such plan can be
found out or not.

2dly. A Description of a free Government & its administration
Their are many sorts of governments, or rather names
by which they are distinguished. Such as Dispotick,
Monorcal, & Aristrocraticle. In these the power to
govern is in the hands of one or a few to govern as they
pleas, consiquently they are masters & not servents so,
that the government is not free.

Their are also sundry names by which free governments are described, such as Democratical, Republican,
Elective, all which I take to be senominus tarmes, or
that all those nations who ever adopted them aimed
at nearly the same thing, viz. to be governed by known
Laws in which the hole nation had a Voice in making,
by a full and fair Representation, & in which all the
officers in every department of Government are (or
aught to be) servents & not masters. Grate panes has
bin taken & the wisdom of many Nations & States
have bin put to the racke, to delineate the rights of
the peopel & powers of government & forme Constitutions so that the blessings of government might be
injoyed without being oppresed by them, and it is
thought that it has bin much improved upon sence
the Amarican Revolution . . .

The soul end of Government is the protection of
Life, Liberty & property. The poor mans shilling aught
to be as much the care of government as the rich mans
pound. Every person in the Nation aught to be com-
peled to do justis & have it dun to him promptly &
without delay. All taxes for the seport of government
aught to be layed equilly according to the property
each person purseses & the advantages he receives
from it, and the peopel aught to seport just so many
persons in office as is absolutely nesecary and no
more, & pay them just so much saleryes as will command sefitiant abilityes, & no more.

Also in free Government the most sacred regard
must be paid to the Constitutions established by the
peopel to gard their rights. No law aught or can be
made or constructed conterary to the true meening
thereof without becomeing a nullity & those becomeing gilty who does it, let them be either
Lejeslative Juditial or Executive officers or bodyes
of men. And no parte of the Constitution can be

constructed conterary to the declared Rights of the people.

In short a free Government is one In which all the laws are made judged & executed according to the will & interest of a majority of the hole peopel and not by the craft cunning & arts of the few. To seport such a government it is absolutely nesecary to have a larger degree or better meens of knowledge amongue the peopel than we now have, which I shall indevor to make appear before I close.

3dly. Shews how the Few & Many Differ in their Interests in its operation

In the swet of thy face shall thou git thy bread until thou return to the ground, is the erivarsable sentance of Heaven on Man for his rebellion. To be sentanced to hard Labour dureing life is very unplesent to humane Nature. Their is a grate avartion to it purceivable in all men — yet it is absolutely nesecary that a large majority of the world should labour, or we could not subsist. For Labour is the soul parrant of all property — the land yealdeth nothing without it, & their is no food, clothing, shelter, vessel, or any nesecary of life but what costs Labour & is generally esteemed valuable according to the Labour it costs. Therefore no person can posess property without labouring, unless he git it by force or craft, fraud or fortun out of the earnings of others.

But from the grate veriety of capacietyes strength & abilityes of men, their always was, & always will be, a very unequel distribution of property in the world. Many are so rich that they can live without Labour. Also the marchent, phisition, lawyer & divine, the philosipher and school master, the Juditial & Executive Officers, & many others who could honestly git a living without bodily labours. As all these professions require a considerable expence of time & property to qualify themselves therefor, & as no person after this qualifying himselfe & making a pick on a profession by which he meens to live, can desire to have it dishonourable or unproductive, so all these professions naturally unite in their skems to make their callings as honourable & lucrative as possable. Also as ease & rest from Labour are reaconed amongue the gratest pleasurs of Life, pursued by all with the greatest avidity & when

attained at once creates a sense of superiority & as pride & ostentation are natural to the humain harte, these ordirs of men generally asotiate together and look down with two much contempt on those that labour.

On the other hand the Labourer being contious that it is Labour that seports the hole, & that the more there is that live without Labour & the higher they live or the grater their salleryes & fees are, so much the harder he must work, or the shorter he must live, this makes the Labourer watch the other with a jelous eye & often has reason to complain of real impositions . . .

The Reasons why a free government has always failed is from the unreasonable demands & desires of the few. They cant bare to be on a leavel with their fellow cretures, or submit to the determinations of a Lejeslature whare (as they call it) the Swinish Multitude are fairly represented, but sicken at the eydea, & are ever hankering & striving after Monerca or Aristocracy whare the people have nothing to do in maters of government but to seport the few in luxury & idleness.

For these & many other reasons a large majority of those that live without Labour are ever opposed to the prinsaples & operation of a free Government, & though the hole of them do not amount to one eighth part of the people, yet by their combinations, arts & skeems have always made out to destroy it soner or later, which I shall indeavour to prove by considering —

4thly The Meens by which the few Destroy it

This I will indever to do by making a few remarks on the doings of the few on the eight following things, Viz. 1t on the Ignorance of the Many — 2d on the Combinations of the few. 3 on Larning — 4 on knowledge — 5t on Constitutions 6tly on Money or the Medium — 7th on Elections 8thly on wars.

1. On the Ignorance of the Many

Solomon said, Train up a Child in the way he should go, & when he is old he will not depart from it. And it is as true that if a child is trained up in the way he should not go, when he is old he will keep to it. It is the universal custom & practis of monorcal & dispotick government to train up their subjects as much in ignorance as they can in matters of government, & to teach them to reverance & worship grate men in office, & to take for truth what ever they say without examining for themselves.

Consiquently when ever Revolutions are brought about & free governments established it is by the influence of a few leeding men, who after they have obtained their object (like other men) can neaver receiv compensation & honours anough from the people for their services, & the people being brought up from their uths to reverance & respect such men they go on old ways & neglect to search & see for themselves & take care of their own interists. Also being naturally very fond of being flattered, they redily hear to measures proposed by grate men who they are convinced have done them good services. This is the prinsaple ground on which the few work to Destroy a free government.

2. *On the Combinations of the Few*

In a free government the few, finding their scheems & vues of interest borne down by the many, to gain the power they cant constitutionally obtain, Always indevour to git it by cunning & corruption, contious at the same time that userpation when once began the safety of the userper consists ondly in grasping the hole. To efect this no cost nor pains is spared, but they first unite their plans & scheems by asotiations, conventions, & coraspondances with each other. The Marchents asotiate by themselves, the Phitisians by themselves, The Ministers by themselves, the Juditial & Executive Officers are by their professions often called together & know each others minds, & all letirary men & the over grown rich, that can live without labouring, can spare time for consultation. All being bound together by common interest, which is the stronges bond of union, join in their secret coraspondance to counter act the interests of the many & pick their pockets, which is efected ondly for want of the meens of knowledge amongue them.

3. *On Larning*

Larning is of the gratest importance to the seport of a free government, & to prevent this the few are always crying up the advantages of costly collages, national acadimyes & grammer schooles, in ordir to make places for men to live without work, & so strengthen their

party. But are always opposed to cheep schools & woman schools, the ondly or prinsaple means by which larning is spred amongue the Many.

4. *On Knowledge*

The gratest & best meens of obtaining the knowledge nesecary for a free man to have, is by the Liberty of the Press, or publick Newspapers. To counter act and destroy this priviledge the few spare no pains to make them as costly as posable & to contradict everything in them that favours the interests of the Many, puting Darkness for Light, & Light for Darkness, falsehood for truth & truth for falsehood, &cc.

5. *On Constitutions & Laws*

The few have a grate advantage over the Many in forming & constructing Constitutions & Laws, & are highly interested in haveing them numerous, intricate & as inexplicit as possable. By this they take to themselves the right of giving them such explanations as suits their interests, & make places for numerous lawyers & Juditial & Executive officers, which ads grately to their strength by numbers . . .

These ordirs of men ar made up prinsaply of Cincinaty, & by the funding sistim have risen like a black cloud over the Continant, & have gained welth like the Nabobs of the East. They have got the prinsaple command of our funds, & not ondly swindle honest individuals out of their property, but by their bribery & corruption have grate influence in our elections, & agitate our public Counsels. By their land speculations & bribery they shook the government of Jorgia almost to its foundation & agitated the federal Government so that one of the Senetors chellenged one of the Representitives for a Duel, right in the midst of one of the most important debates they Ever was or ever will be ingaged in.

On Doctors

The Doctors have established their Meditial Societyes & have both their State & County Meetings, by which they have so nearly enielated Quacary of all kinds, that a poor man cant git so grate cures of them now for a ginna, as he could 50 years ago of an old Squaw for halfe a pint of Rhum. The bisness of a Midwife could be purformed 50 years ago for halfe a doller & now it costs a poor man 5 hole ones.

On Marchents

The Marchents have organised themselves & have their Chambers of Commerce & corraspondance from one end of the Continent to the other. Although they are in many respects a grate advantage to the Many, by making vent for our produce & furnishing us with nesecaryes & conveniences from other cuntryes, yet if we should be drawn into a war by their adventures we should pay very dear for all the advantages we receive from them. Besides, forron trade not well regulated is the most dangerous to the interest of the Many of any thing we have to fear. Our money may be all carried off from amongue us for that which will do us no good . . .

On Literary Men & Coledges

The true prinsaples of Republicanisam & a free govern- may be taught to the Uths in some of our Coleges & Acadimies for aught I know, but it is evident that other political prinsaples are admited in many of them, or we should not be stunded with Exhibitions in fa- vour of Monocyes & runing down Republican prin- saples as we often be. One thing is prity cartain, that the Schollers are taught to keep up the dignity of their professions, for if we apply for a preacher or a School Master, we are told the price So Much, & they cant go under, for it is agreed upon & they shall be disgrased if they take less, let their abilityes for the servis be what they will.

On Ministers of the Gospel

The Ministers of the Congeragational ordir & others for aught I know have formed them selves in to Societyes & many of them are incorporated & have their State & County Meetings which may be of grate service or absolutely nesecary in their Sacred functions. But it is no brech of Charity to sepose that they have some political purposes in them, nor do I deny their right to meddle in politicks. But as they receive their seport for teaching piety, religion, morality & things relitive to another world, & their hearers being not all

of them capable of desarning betwen divinity & poli- ticks, they aught when ever they teach obediance to the sivil Laws or reprove for disobediance &cc., to teach & explain to them the true prinsaples of our free government as Established in our Constitutions. Insted of preaching about & praying for Officers of govern- ment as infalible beings, or so perfect that we aught to submit to & prais them for all they do, (when in fact they are all our servents & at all times accountable to the peopel) they aught to teach their hearers to be watchfull of men in power, & to gard their own Rights & priviledges, with a jelous eye, & teach them how to do it in a Constitutional way . . .

On Lawyers

The Lawyers have established their Bar Meetings & become the most formidable & influential ordir of any in the Government, & though they are nither Juditial nor Executive officers, but a kind of Mule ordir, in- gendered by, & many times overawing both. This ordir of men git their living intirely from the quarrils follyes disputes & destreses of the Many & the intri- cacy of our Laws, & it is from the arts & doings of these men, that the Juditial & Executive officers are furnished with the chief of their bisness & imploy. Consiquently they are bound together by the strongest bonds of union.

Many have bin the complantes against the Lawyers in years bak & of the intricacy of our lawsm & much time spent & pains taken by the Lejeslature to remidy the evil. But all to little or nor purpose, & the soul reason is because we send these fee officers as Repre- sentitives to make our laws. Unless the peopel can be brought to calculate more upon the opporation of these little selfish prinsaples on mankind, & purge the Lejeslatures from fee officers, they cannot be governed by laws very long.

Thus we see all the ordirs of the few compleetly organised, & they have of late got so monstrusly crouded with numbers that it is imposable for them all to git a living by their profissions, & being in want of imploy they are aiding in all the plans & scheems of Cincinaty to influence the Many.

I would not be understood to be against the asotiations of any ordirs of men, for to hinder it would hinder their improvements in their professions, & hinder them from being servisable to the Many. Their need ondly one Society more being established, or proper meens of information amongue the Many to hinder their being daingerous in politicks. In ordir to promote those meens of information among the peopel their has bin many sociatyes established, by Constitutial, Democracticle & other names, made up of men of Republican prinsaples & grate abilityes who did all in their power to inliten the peopel into their true Interests. But for want of the Society I have mentioned, or a proper chanel of conveying their sentiments to the peopel, & by the joint exertions of a majority of the other ordirs I have mentioned to hinder their usefulness & pregidis the minds of the peopel against them, have brought them almost into disuse. But I have no dout but that they will revive again when they think they can do any good. But before I proseed to describe the Society or meens of Knowlidge I have mentioned I must make sundry Remarks on what has bin & provibly may be done by the joint exertion of the few to inslave the Many, unless they meet with a check.

On Larning

No person who is a frind to Libberty will be against a large expence in Larning, but it aught to be promoted in the cheepest & best manner possable, which in my oppinnion would be: — For every State to maintain as many Coledges in conveniant parts thereof as would be attended upon to give the highest Degrees of Larning, & for every County to keep as many Grammer Schools or Acadimies in conveniant parts thereof as would be attended too by both sects summer & winter, & no student or scholer to pay anything for tuition, and for the County Schooles to pay a particuler attention to teaching the Inglish langueg & qualifying its scholers to teach & govern Common Schools for little children . . .

If this method of Larning was established we should soone have a plenty of school masters & mistrises as cheep as we could hire other labour, & Labour & Larning would be conected together & lesen the number of those that live without work. Also we should have a plenty of men to fill the highest offices of State for less than halfe we now give. But insted of this mode of Larning the few are always striving to

oblige us to maintain grait men with grate salleryes & to maintain Grammer Schools in every town to teach our Children a b c all which is ondly to give imploy to gentlemens sons & make places for men to live without worke. For their is no more need of a mans haveing a knowledge of all the languages to teach a Child to read write & cifer than their is for a farmer to have the marinors art to hold plow . . .

On Elections

The hole interest of the Many lays in giting and keeping fully & fairly represented in the several branches of government, & this depends intirely in the Electors haveing a knoledge of the carictor, abilityes & politicle sentiments of those they vote for, & it is imposible for all to have a personal knoledge of them. In large towns their are some instances wheir the electors do not all know those they vote for in them. The State Senetors are more unknown, the govenour & federal Representitives are furder off still, & the Electors of president, being chosen ondly for a single Act & not accountable for his Conduct in that all Important Act. I have often wondered that under the present meens of knowledge, and in opposition to the numerous arts of flatery, deception thretnings & falsehoods practised by the few in elections, that the Many git so fully represented as they do . . .

On the Name of Washington

Grate use has bin made of this name to deceive the peopel & make them content with the Administration of Government, & much time has bin spent in our Legislative bodyes, & sacred pulpets, in the most fulsome & sickish praises & adulations of Warshington for what he aught to have bin bannished for, which has deceived thousands & thousands of honest peopel into their measures, which was prinsaply done, by pretending (in adition to his real services in the war) that he was the cause of all the prosperity we ware under, for all are sonsable that the times have bin veri prosporous to the interests of the Many . . .

On partyes

Much has bin said of late about partyes & Many are the names by which they are described, such as Monorcal &

Republican, Aristocratical, & Demacratical, Royallests, & Jacobines, Toryes & Whigs, the few & the Many, all which names appear to me to describe but two sets of men differing about one & the same thing, or that the causes of their disputes arise from the conceived differance of interests I have bin discribing & the unreasonable desires of the few to tironise over & inslave the many, & the glorious Revolution that has lately taken place in France has alarmed the few to a very high degree. When it first brock out almost all the kings of Urope openly combined to destroy them or restore Monorca & tirony over them again, & so grate was their confidence of suckses that they agreed amongue themselves how to divide the taritory & Spoils. But as the Lord is always on the side of a people contending for their Rights & Libbertyes, he so inspired france with wisdom & corage that they have already cut & tore them to peaces, so that they have all but one bin obliged to make peace with them on their own tarmes.

But all this has not discoraged that party. They are yet in hopes of efecting by bribery & corruption what they cant do by force of armes, for their combinations are extended far & wide & are not confined to Urope & Emarica, but are extending to every part of the world. Gog & magog are gathered together, to destroy the Rights of Man & banish Libberty

Thus haveing indevoured to shew the causes that ruen all free governments and the circumstances we are brought into by them I request your canded atention to what I shall propose as a

Reamidy Against It

The ondly Remidy against these evils is by improveing our Rights as freemen in elections, nor do we need any other if we ware posesed of knowledge anough to act rationally in them. For as I have before shewed, the duty of a Representitive or any person chosen into office is to act as all his Constitutiants would if they ware all present & all knew what was for their own interests. And as men being elected into neavour so high offices, remain men still and are moved by the same prinsaples & passions as other men are, so that the temtation & emolument of 25 thousand dollors a year or any other some & to be worshiped into the bargain hath ten thousand charme with it, so that the love of office will compel tham to aim at pleasing their Constituants. Consiquently if elections are closely attended to by all the peopel & they look well ever after their Representitives, their is no dainger but that they will do their duty. Therefore the ondly Remidi is knowledge . . .

The Knowledge nesecary for every freeman to have is A Knowledge of Manking — A Knowledge of the differend interest that influence all ordirs of men — A Knowledge of the prinsaples of the government & Constitution he lives under — A Knowledge of all the laws that immediately consarnes his conduct & interests — A knowledge that when laws are once constitutially made, they must be obayed, let them be neaver so rong in his mind, and that their is no remidy for greevences but by petitioning the authority that made them & useing his Right in Elections — A knowledge of the true prinsaples, caricter & abilityes of all those he votes for into any kind of office — A knowledge of the existing sentiments wishes & circumstances, of all those of his interest in the town, county, State or Nation to which he belongs, so that he may unite in the choice of the ablest & best men to take care of & defend their interests. Also Unite in petitioning for redress of grevances. Also a knowledge of the moste interesting debates in the Legeslature & the side his own Representitive takes in the desition. He aught to have all this knowledge independant of any ordirs of men, or individuals who may be interested to deceive or misleed him.

As all new things make a grate stir at first, so it may be expected this will, & many objicttions raised against it. The ordirs of the few may denounce it as dangerous to Government. But if all the powers of Hell should rise up & assume the wisdom & grateness of Angels & try to overthrow it they aught not to be heard to nor minded, for it is perfectly Constitutianal, & what all the ordirs of the few have practised upon (as I have before shewen) & their opposition to it arises holly from selfeish vues . . .

Such a Society would convince the world that Emarica can & will be free, & would do more to prevent a war with france than all we have in our power to do other ways.

And I have often had it impressed on my mind that in some such way as this Society might be orga-

nised throughout the world as well as government, &
by sotial corraspondance & mutual consestions all
differences might be settled, so that wars might be
bannished from the Earth. For it is from the pride &
ambition of rulers & the ignorance of the peopel that
wars arise, & no nation as a nation ever got anithing
by making war on others, for what evr their conquests
may have bin the plunder goes to a few individuals, &
always increases the misiryes of more than it helpes.

For the prinsapel hapiness of a Man in this world
is to eat & drink & injoy the good of his Labour, & to
feal that his Life Libberty & property is secure, & not
in the abundance he poseses nor in being the instrument of other mens miseryes. All the advantage of
national dealings is commerce & the exchange of the
produce of one cuntry for another, which if it might
be carried on without wars would increase the hapiness
of all Nations. But as it is in general conducted it ads
to the miseryes of mankind.

Thus my frinds I have tryed to describe to you
(not in the language & stile of the Larned for I am not
able) But in as plane a manner as I am capable, the
Causes that have always destroyed free governments,
& the daingerous circumstances we are brought into by
said Causes. Also described what I think would prove
a Remidy, which is not a costly one, for if it should
once become general, confident I am that each penny
laid out in it would soone save pounds. I have also
placed a Constitution at the close of this adress with a
Covenant ready for signing, which though an imperfect
one may answer for the beginning of said Society. And
unless you see more dificulty in applying the Reamidy
or less need of it than I do, you will immediately put
it on foot & neaver give over untill such a Society is
established on such a strong & lasting foundation that
the gates of hell can never prevail against it — which
may the Almighty grant is the sincear desire of

A Labourer.

The French Revolutionary events made a great impression upon people in the United States in large part because they became vehicles for furious debates over unresolved issues in American public life. This was particularly true of the conflicting viewpoints on popular political participation. Men who had been relatively passive during the colonial period became actively involved in political life during the Revolution. Much to the dismay of their social superiors, they continued to be so. As early as 1794 members of the House of Representatives had sought a Congressional resolution censuring "self-created societies" which they believed responsible for the uprising among farmers in Western Pennsylvania. After this so-called Whiskey Rebellion, popular demonstrations increased. Bonfires and parades were organized to mark the victories of the armies of the French Revolution and when Washington's emissary, John Jay, negotiated a very unpopular treaty with Great Britain, Jay was hung in effigy from Maine to Virginia. Democratic societies had spread to all of the states, and every act of government was being exposed to public scrutiny in a dozen or more opposition newspapers. Added to this lively display of popular political participation was the congregation in cities of foreign immigrants, many of them political refugees from France and Ireland.

Flouting the sensibilities of conservative Americans, the members of Democratic Clubs openly identified themselves with the Jacobins of France who by this time were aggressively campaigning against the Christian religion. At Harvard and Yale, undergraduates were said to be hailing one another as "Volney," "Voltaire," and "Rousseau," all considered to be free-thinking philosophers. In the frontier community of Lexington, Kentucky, the Democratic Club was threatening to cooperate with Frenchmen to liberate New Orleans from the Spanish. Only the negotiation of a treaty with Spain opening up New Orleans to Mississippi traffic seems to have stopped this wild scheme.

There was no consensus in the United States upon the role of the people or of political parties in public life. Conservatives condemned both, maintaining that society benefitted from leaving government to duly elected officials whose record in office should be discussed only when new officials were to be elected. Radicals claimed that participation in public life was an inalienable right along with free and open discussion of all foreign and domestic issues facing the country. Probably most Americans were not sure how they felt. Certainly factions implied political skullduggery, and organized parties — as distinguished from opposing sides on a given issue — were too new to have been accepted or rejected. The very uncertainty of public attitudes towards popular politics increased the tension, which was at an all-time high when the Federalist leaders in Congress finally succeeded in getting through four acts restricting the activity of aliens and specifying punishments for printed criticism of government.

Jefferson, who had been presiding over the Senate during the passage of the Alien and Sedition Acts, returned home to Virginia thoroughly alarmed at the new federal statutes. Convinced that they were unconstitutional and clearly designed to silence him and his supporters, he turned to the only alternative source of legitimate power he knew — that of the states. During the summer months, working hastily and in secret, he prepared a series of resolutions denouncing the Alien and Sedition Acts which were subsequently adopted by the Kentucky and Virginia legislatures. The actual prosecutions under the new federal statute confirmed Jefferson 's worst fears. During 1799 and 1800 the five major Republican newspaper publishers were indicted along with four other Jeffersonian publishers, a United States Congressman, and several pro-Jefferson writers, including a distinguished English-born publicist, Thomas Cooper (1759–1839). Cooper's case was notable because of the role which the presiding judge, Samuel Chase, played in obtaining a conviction. The Sedition Law had included a provision that if the defendant could prove the truth of his offensive statements the jury could find him innocent of seditious libel. This was the principle which John Peter Zenger's lawyer had argued for, but according to Judge Chase's interpretation, the truth as a defense provision meant that the defendant had to prove the truth of everything charged against him.

In this way, Chase reversed the common law principle that the burden of proof rests with the prosecution.

Despite the vigor with which Federalist grand juries went after newspaper publishers who had criticized John Adams' administration, the Jeffersonians were not intimidated. Aware that the Federalists had the better of common law precedents, the Jeffersonians attacked the central assumption behind all seditious libel laws — which is that government needs to be protected from criticism. Moving to a new position, Jeffersonian congressmen and writers argued that the intention to bring the government into disrespect — far from being a crime — was a substantial part of the political process of republican self-government. The citizen, in this view, was the custodian of government rather than the other way around. This new definition of freedom of speech was hammered out in congressional debates, before juries in seditious libel trials, and finally in separate political treaties. In the following readings, defendant Thomas Cooper and Judge Samuel Chase argue their respective positions.

The lines on this issue were sharply drawn in the presidential campaign of 1800. The incumbent John Adams, though at odds with other Federalist leaders, defended the party's twelve year record of strengthening the central government, pursuing a pro-English foreign policy, and supressing dissent. For conservatives, those Americans with pro-French sympathies had come to represent anarchy and atheism, and Federalist propagandists accused Jefferson of favoring both. Jeffersonian Republicans were equally alarmed by the dangerous aristocratic and militaristic tendencies of the Federalists. After a mud-slinging campaign conducted through the press, pulpit, and public rallies, Jefferson won the presidency. The American people had endorsed a new style of politics — the culmination of a process started almost two centuries earlier.

United States Circuit Court: Trial of Thomas Cooper (1800)

An indictment had been found against Thomas Cooper under the Sedition Act which made it a crime to be

John Davison Lawson, *American State Trials*, Thomas Law, St. Louis, 1914–1936, X, 785–809.

punished by fine and imprisonment for any one to print or publish any false, scandalous and malicious writings against the Government, Congress or the President, with intent to defame them, to bring them into contempt or to excite the hatred of the people against them, for the following seditious libel against John Adams, President of the United States.

The libelous matter set out in the indictment was as follows:

"Nor do I see any impropriety in making this request of Mr. Adams. At that time he had just entered into office; he was hardly in the infancy of political mistakes; even those who doubted his capacity thought well of his intentions. Nor were we yet saddled with the expense of a permanent navy, or threatened, under his auspies, with the existence of a standing army. Our credit was not yet reduced so low as to borrow money at eight per cent in time of peace, while the unnecessary violence of official expressions might justly have provoked a war. Mr. Adams had not yet projected his embassies to Prussia, Russia and the Sublime Porte, nor had he yet interfered, as President of the United States, to influence the decisions of a court of justice—a stretch of authority which the monarch of Great Britain would have shrunk from—an interference without precedent, against law and against mercy. This melancholy case of Jonathan Robbins, a native citizen of America, forcibly impressed by the British, and delivered up, with the advice of Mr. Adams, to the mock trial of a British court-martial, had not yet astonished the republican citizens of this free country; a case too little known, but of which the people ought to be fully apprised, before the election, and they shall be" . . .

Mr. Rawle read that part of the publication which is included in the indictment.

Mr. Cooper. Gentlemen of the jury: If it were true, as it is not true, that, in the language of the Attorney General of the district, I have been guilty of publishing with the basest motives a foul and infamous libel on the character of the President; of exciting against him the hatred and contempt of the people of this country, by gross and malicious falsehoods — then, indeed, would it be his duty to bring before me this tribunal, it would be yours to convict, and the duty of the court to punish me.

But I hope, in the course of this trial, I shall be enabled to prove to your satisfaction, that I have published nothing which truth will not justify. That the assertions for which I am indicted are free from malicious imputation, and that my motives have been honest and fair.

You will observe, gentlemen of the jury, that the law requires it to be proved as a necessary part of the charge, that the passages for which I am indicted should be false and scandalous, and published from malicious motives. And before you will be able, consistently with your oaths, to convict upon this indictment, you must be thoroughly satisfied that both these parts of the charge are well founded. Nor does it appear to be that the expression of the act, to bring the President into contempt, can be fulfilled, if the accusation, as in the present instance, related to an examination of his public conduct, and no improper motives are imputed to him. And that I have carefully avoided imputing any impropriety of intention to the Presidnet, even in the very paper complained of; that the uniform tenor of my conduct and language has been to attribute honesty of motive even where I have strongly disapproved of the tendency of his measures, I can abundantly show.

You, and all who hear me, well know that this country is divided, and almost equally divided, into two grand parties; usually termed, whether properly or improperly, Federalists and Anti-Federalists; and that the governing powers of the country are ranked in public opinion under the former denomination — of these divisions, the one wishes to increase, the other to diminish, the powers of the executive; the one thinks that the people (the democracy of the country) has too much, the other too little, influence on the measures of government. The one is friendly, the other hostile, to a standing army and a permanent navy. The one thinks them necessary to repel invasions and aggressions from without, and commotion within; the other, that a well-organized militia is a sufficient safeguard for all that an army could protect, and that a navy is more dangerous and expensive than any benefit derived from it can compensate; the one thinks the liberties of our country endangered by the licentiousness, the other, by the restrictions of the press. Such are some among the leading features of these notorious divisions of political party. It is evident, gentlemen of the jury, that each will view with a jealous eye the positions of the other, and

that there cannot but be a bias among the partisans of the one side, against the principles and doctrines inculcated by the other. In the present instance, I fear it cannot but have its effects; for, without impeaching the integrity of any person directly concerned in the progress of the present trial, I may fairly state that, under the Sedition Law, a defendant, such as I stand before you, is placed in a situation unknown in any other case.

Directly or indirectly, the public, if not the private, character of the Presidnet of the United States is involved in the present trial. Who nominates the judges who are to preside? the juries who are to judge of the evidence? the marshal who has the summoning of the jury? the President. Suppose a case of arbitration concerning the property of any one of you, where the adverse party should claim the right of nominating the persons whose legal opinions are to decide the law of the question, and of the very man who shall have the appointment of the arbitrators — what would you say to such a trial? and yet in fact such is mine, and such is the trial of every man who has the misfortune to be indicted under this law. But although I have a right to presume something of political bias against my opinions, from the court who try me, to you who sit there as jurymen, I am still satisfied you will feel that you have some character to support and some character to lose; and whatever your opinions may be on the subjects alluded to in the indictment, you will reverence as you ought the sacred obligation of the oath you have taken.

Gentlemen of the jury, I acknowledge, as freely as any of you can, the necessity of a certain degree of confidence in the executive government of the country. But this confidence ought not to be unlimited, and need not be paid up in advance; let it be earned before it be reposed; let it be claimed by the evidence of benefits conferred, of measures that compel approbation, of conduct irreproachable. It cannot be exacted by the guarded provisions of sedition laws, by attacks on the freedom of the press, by prosecutions, pains and penalties on those which boldly express the truth, or who may honestly and innocently err in their political sentiments. Let this required confidence be the meed of desert, and the public will not be backward to pay it.

But in the present state of affairs, the press is open to those who will praise, while the threats of the law hang over those who blame the conduct of the men in power. Indiscriminate approbation of the measures of the executive is not only unattacked, but fostered, and received with the utmost avidity; while those who venture to express a sentiment of opposition must do it in fear and trembling, and run the hazard of being dragged like myself before the frowning tribunal, erected by the Sedition Law. Be it so; but surely this anxiety to protect public character must arise from fear of attack. That conduct which will not bear investigation will naturally shun it; and whether my opinions are right or wrong, as they are stated in the charge, I cannot help thinging they would have been better confuted by evidence and argument than by indictment. Fines and imprisonment will produce conviction neither in the mind of the sufferer nor of the public.

Nor do I see how the people can exercise on rational grounds their elective franchise, if perfect freedom of discussion of public characters be not allowed. Electors are bound in conscience to reflect and decide who best deserves their suffrages; but how can they do it, if these prosecutions *in terrorem* close all the avenues of information, and throw a veil over the grossest misconduct of our periodical rulers? . . .

The first article selected for accusation is, that, at the time I allude to, he was but in the infancy of political mistake. Why this expression should have been fixed on as seditious, I know not, unless it be that *quem deus vult perdere prius dementat*; for have we advanced so far on the road to despotism in this republican country, that we dare not say our President may be mistaken? Is a plain citizen encircled at once by the mysterious attribute of political infallibility the instant he mounts the presidential chair? If so, then indeed may it be seditious to say he is mistaken; but before you can condemn me for this kind of sedition, you must become catholic believers in this new-fangled doctrine of infallibility. I know that in England the king can do no wrong, but I did not know til now that the President of the United States had the same attribute.

I have said (and I am accused for saying it) "that even those who doubted his capacity thought well of his intentions." Is it a crime to doubt the capacity of the President? Suppose I had said that there were some who did not give him credit for capacity sufficient for the office he holds, is that a crime? Or if in them, is it a crime in me, who have not said it? Nor can the word capacity here be fairly construed into any other than a comparative meaning; for surely no one who has read his Defense, as it is called, of the American Constitution, or who reflects that he has had abilities enough to raise himself to his present situation, can say that he is devoid either of industry or talents. But those who voted for his opponent must have believed Mr. Adams of inferior capacity to that gentleman. Of that number was I; of that number was at least one-half of the people of the United States. If it be a crime thus to have thought and thus to have spoken, I fear I shall continue in this respect incorrigible. But if of two constructions the one is absurd, improbable and unfavorable, surely it should be rejected in favor of that meaning which was most likely to have occurred, and which in its effects will do least injury to a defendant like myself. This is common, this is legal charity.

Nor had we yet, under his auspices, been saddled with the expense of a permanent navy.

Gentlemen, is it true or not that we are saddled with the expense of a permanent navy? Is it necessary that I should enter into a detail of authorities to prove that the sun shines at noon-day? But farther, is it true that we incur this expense under his auspices and sanction?

I have before me two publications. The one the Gazette of the United States, published by Mr. Fenno in this city; and another, in a form more portable and convenient, purporting to be a selection of addresses and answers to and from the President during the summer of 1798. Not having been able to procure office copies of the documents I wished to refer to, I must offer in evidence such publications as I can find; that class of publications, upon which in fact the mind of the public is usually made up; and upon whose authority the electors of this country determine the characters whom they honor with their suffrage. Indeed, if the opinion that fell from the court this morning be accurate, that no man should hazard an assertion but upon sufficient and legal evidence, and if documents from the public offices in proof of notorious facts are required as such evidence, than are the mouths of the people completely shut up on every question of public conduct or public character . . .

Judge Chase. What is it that you say, sir, fell from the court? They have not yet decided what was or what not proper evidence for you to adduce. The court said, if you thought the public documents at your service, you were mistaken. If you undertake to publish, without having proper evidence before you to justify your assertions, you do it at your own risk. Most assuredly, in common traverses, you could not offer the evidence you mention. But we acknowledge that, in such a case as this, great latitude may be given. If you say the President did write a letter, you must prove it. We should incline to admit gazettes and acts of public authority and notoriety. You might read the speech of the President to both Houses of Congress in evidence. If you want to prove that the President advocated a navy, you may read the journals of Congress or any authentic public document.

Mr. Cooper. If I am defeated in my endeavors to procure these documents, I must offer such evidence as I can procure; . . .

Judge Chase. You may read anything and everything you please.

Mr. Cooper. (went on to argue at length, from a copious collection from the public documents of the day, that the policy of the President had been to saddle upon the country a permanent navy and army, and to keep down the liberties of the citizens by his arbitrary interference in the case of Jonathan Robbins.)

Gentlemen, I have gone through all the charges, and I am satisfied that I have brought in support of my assertions the best evidence the nature of my case would admit of. It is true, by resorting to Danbury for depositions and to Charlestown for records, I might have made the evidence in the last charge more

complete; but I did not and do not think them necessary to produce further conviction on your minds than you feel on the subject already. This is an important point under the law in question. If such strictness of testimony is required, there is an end at once of all political conversation in promiscuous society. The time, the labor, the difficulty, the expense, the harassment and fatigue of minds as well as of body, which such doctrine would occasion to every citizen whom a corrupt administration might determine to ruin, would be an engine of oppression of itself sufficiently powerful to establish a perfect despotism over the press; and would be a punishment for innocence before trial, too severe to be inflicted on sedition itself. I think you must feel the truth of these remarks. The proceedings on this trial irresistibly suggest them . . .

Gentlemen, if the assertions I have made are true, whatever the motives of them may be, you cannot find me guilty. But I think it impossible, if you consider the paper altogether, that you can ascribe the publication of it to malice. It is on the force of it not voluntary, but compelled. I have, in the very outset of the paper, spoken well of the President. I have been in the habit of thinking his intentions right, and his public conduct wrong: and that this has been the general tenor of my language and behavior, I believe I can even now bring proof enough from among my friends and my neighbors.

Judge Chase. This is not necessary. It is your conduct, not your character, that is in question. If this prosecution were for a crime against the United States, you might give evidence to your character, and show that you have always been a good citizen; but this is an indictment for a libel against the President, where your general character is not in question.

Mr. Cooper. I am satisfied. I shall fatigue the jury no longer; but rest my defense here.

Mr. Rawle. Gentlemen of the jury: The defense you have just heard is one of the most extraordinary and unexampled I ever remember to have witnessed in a court of justice. It is no less than to call into decision whether Thomas Cooper, the defendant, or the President of the United States, to whom this country has thought proper to confide its most important interests, is best qualified to judge whether the measures adopted by our government are calculated to preserve the peace and promote the happiness of America. This, however, does not seem to me the real point which you are to try; . . .

The defendant is allowed, under the third section of that act, to give in evidence the truth of the matters charged as a libel in the publication, and the jury have a right to determine the law and the fact under the direction of the court. The true spirit of the law is that the defendant shall not be found guilty of publishing defamatory writings, unless they be false, nor, although they may be false, shall he be considered as guilty under the law, unless the intent of the publication appear to be malicious . . .

The defendant has undertaken to satisfy the mind of the jury that, in this publication, he had no malicious intention against the President of the United States; I join issue with him on the point, and request your particular attention to it. He alleges that he did not impute improper motives to the President, and attempts to substantiate his allegation by referring you to his declaration in the outset, where he says that "I cannot believe him (the President) capable of such gross misrepresentations, for I still think well of his intentions, however I may disapprove of his conduct;" but to this I shall add that he goes on and concludes with a paragraph, evincing in the clearest manner a settled design to persuade the public that the President of the United States is not fit for the high office he bears, and of this you must be fully convinced from the whole tenor of the expressions which have been read to you in the indictment . . .

It is very far from my views to press hard upon any part of his long address to you, or to make use against him of any unguarded expression, which, on more deliberate consideration, he might have omitted or corrected; yet, when I cannot but observe, from the whole tenor of his present argument, as well as from his publication, that his object is not so much to convince you, gentlemen of the jury, that his assertions are true, as to cast an unmerited reflection on the general character and conduct of the President, I cannot help suspecting him of the motives he disclaims, and I must do my duty by exposing the design as well as the fallacy of the justification he has set up . . .

Whether the reflections he has thrown upon the conduct of government, in so many instances throughout his defense as well as in his publication, evince the regard he professes to entertain for the intentions of the President, is to me, as it will be to you, extremely dubious; nor have those professions been confirmed by the singular manner in which he has cited and selected the passages on which his defense has been grounded . . .

The nature of his defense, though he has stated his opinion of the good intentions of the President, evidently shows that he meant to justify his own conduct and language throughout. You, gentlemen of the jury, under the direction of the court, will decide whether he has presented to you such a justification as will entitle him to your verdict in his favor.

Judge Chase. Gentlemen of the jury: When men are found rash enough to commit an offense such as the traverser is charged with, it becomes the duty of the government to take care that they should not pass with impunity. It is my duty to state to you the law on which this indictment is preferred, and the substance of the accusation and defense.

Thomas Cooper, the traverser, stands charged with having published a false, scandalous and malicious libel against the President of the United States, in his official character as President. There is no civilized country that I know of, that does not punish such offenses; and it is necessary to the peace and welfare of this country, that these offenses should meet with their proper punishment, since ours is a government founded on the opinions and confidence of the people. The Representatives and the President are chosen by the people. It is a government made by themselves; and their officers are chosen by themselves; and, therefore, if any improper law is enacted, the people have it in their power to obtain the repeal of such law, or even of the Constitution itself, if found defective, since provision is made for its amendment. Our government, therefore, is really republican; the people are truly represented, since all power is derived from them. It is a government of representation and responsibility. All officers of the government are liable to be displaced or removed, or their duration in office limited by elections at fixed periods. There is one department only, the judiciary, which is not subject to such removal; their offices being held "during good behavior," and therefore they can only be removed for misbehavior.

All governments which I have ever read or heard of punish libels against themselves. If a man attempts to destroy the confidence of the people in their officers, their supreme magistrate, and their legislature, he effectually saps the foundation of the government. A republican government can only be destroyed in two ways; the introduction of luxury, or the licentiousness of the press. This latter is the more slow, but most sure and certain, means of bringing about the destruction of the government. The legislature of this country, knowing this maxim, has thought proper to pass a law to check this licentiousness of the press . . .

Thomas Cooper, then, stands indicted for having published a false, scandalous and malicious libel upon the President of the United States, with intent to defame the President, to bring him into contempt and disrepute, and to excite against him the hatred of the good people of the United States. This is the charge. The traverser has pleaded not guilty, and that he has not published, etc., with these views: he has also pleaded in justification (which the law provides for), that the matters asserted by him are true, and that he will give the same in evidence.

It is incumbent on the part of the prosecution to prove two facts: 1st. That the traverser did publish the matters contained in the indictment. 2d. That he did publish with intent to defame, etc.

For the intent is as much a fact as the other, and must be proved in the same manner as other facts; and must be proved as stated in the law of Congress — the mere publication is no offense; and in making up your verdict, though you consider them separately, you must take the whole tenor and import of the publication, since the offense is committed by the two coupled together.

First, then, as to the publication.

The fact of writing and publishing is clearly proved; nay, in fact, it is not denied . . .

For he justifies the publication in all its parts, and declares it to be founded in truth. It is proved most clearly to be his publication. It is your business to consider the intent as coupled with that, and view the whole together. You must take that publica-

tion, and compare it with the indictment; if there are doubts as to the motives of the traverser, he has removed them; for, though he states in his defense that he does not arraign the motives of the President, yet he has boldly avowed that his own motives in this publication were to censure the conduct of the President, which his conduct, as he thought, deserved. Now, gentlemen, the motives of the President, in his official capacity, are not a subject of inquiry with you. Shall we say to the President, you are not fit for the government of this country? It is no apology for a man to say, that he believes the President to be honest, but that he has done acts which prove him unworthy the confidence of the people, incapable of executing the duties of his high station, and unfit for the important office to which the people have elected him. The motives and intent of the traverser, not of the President, are the subject to be inquired into by you.

Now we will consider this libel as published by the defendant, and observe what were his motives. You will find the traverser speaking of the President in the following words: "Even those who doubted his capacity, thought well of his intentions." This the traverser might suppose would be considered as a compliment as to the intentions of the President; but I have no doubt that it was meant to carry a sting with it which should be felt; for it was in substance saying of the President, "you may have good intentions, but I doubt your capacity."

He then goes on to say, "Nor were we yet saddled with the expense of a permanent navy, nor threatened, under his (the President's) auspices, with the existence of a standing army. Our credit was not yet reduced so low as to borrow money at eight per cent in time of peace." Now, gentlemen, if these things were true, can any one doubt what effect they would have on the public mind? If the people believed those things, what would be the consequence? What! the President of the United States saddle us with a permanent navy, encourage a standing army, and borrow money at a large premium? And are we told, too, that this is in time of peace? If you believe this to be true, what opinion can you, gentlemen, form of the President? One observation must strike you, viz.: That these charges are made not only against the President, but against yourselves who elect the

House of Representatives, for these acts cannot be done without first having been approved of by Congress. Can a navy be built, can an army be raised, or money borrowed, without the consent of Congress?

The President is further charged for that "the unnecessary violence of his official expressions might justly have provoked a war." This is a very serious charge indeed. What, the President, by unnecessary violence, plunge this country into a war! and that a just war? It cannot be — I say, gentlemen, again, if you believe this, what opinion can you form of the President? Certainly the worst you can form. You would certainly consider him totally unfit for the high station which he has so honorably filled, and with such benefit to his country.

Take this publication in all its parts, and it is the boldest attempt I have known to poison the minds of the people. He asserts that Mr. Adams has countenanced a navy, that he has brought forward measures for raising a standing army in the country . . .

There is no subject on which the people of America feel more alarm, than the establishment of a standing army. Once persuade them that the government is attempting to promote such a measure, and you destroy their confidence in the government. Therefore, to say, that under the auspices of the President, we were saddled with a standing army, was directly calculated to bring him into contempt with the people, and excite their hatred against him . . .

You will please to notice, gentlemen, that the traverser in his defense must prove every charge he has made to be true; he must prove it to the marrow. If he asserts three things, and proves but one, he fails; if he proves but two, he fails in his defense, for he must prove the whole of his assertions to be true. If he were to prove, that the President had done everything charged against him in the first paragraph of the publication—though he should prove to your satisfaction, that the President had interfered to influence the decisions of a court of justice, that he had delivered up Jonathan Robbins without precedent, against law and against mercy, this would not be sufficient, unless he proved at the same time, that Jonathan Robbins was a native American, and had been forcibly impressed, and compelled to serve on board of a British ship of war. If he fails, therefore, gentle-

men, in this proof, you must then consider whether his intention in making these charges against the President were malicious or not. It is not necessary for me to go more minutely into an investigation of the defense. You must judge for yourselves— you must find the publication, and judge of the intent with which that publication was made, whether it was malice or not? If you believe that he has published it without malice, or an intent to defame the President of the United States, you must acquit him; if he has proved the truth of the facts asserted by him, you must find him not guilty.

The Jury retired and returned with a verdict of Guilty . . . The Court sentenced Mr. Cooper to pay a fine of four hundred dollars; to be imprisoned for six months, and at the end of that period to find surety for his good behavior, himself in a thousand and two sureties in five hundred dollars each.

Having resolved the domestic questions of free speech, popular participation, and the role of political parties, Americans had yet to define their position toward foreign revolutions. American enthusiasm for the French Revolution had pushed to the fore a number of domestic issues, but diplomatic policies remained ambiguous. Federalists and Jeffersonians alike had concentrated on American rights as neutral shippers during the subsequent war period, leaving unresolved the question of whether or not to extend aid to future revolutionary regimes. Theoretically most Americans believed self-government to be morally superior to the existing monarchical regimes, but the high cost of involvement in European warfare had been clearly demonstrated. The issue, however, continued to arise after the general peace of Europe. With the restoration of the monarchy in France, the reactionary forces had the upper hand throughout Europe, drawing sharper the lines between popular and traditional governments.

Americans were confronted with the question anew in Latin America, where the colonists had cast off Spanish sovereignty in a series of revolutions beginning in 1810. Harassed by problems at home, the Spanish government had been unable to reassert its control, but in 1822 a group of European diplomats gathered to consider forming an alliance to regain Spain's New World possessions for her. United States leaders naturally preferred having free and independent neighbors, yet America was in no position to tackle the combined powers of the European continent. England, however, also had much to gain from the breakup of the Spanish New World empire, for she would have access to the ports of Latin America. The English foreign secretary, sensing a community of interests with the United States, proposed a joint declaration warning the so-called Holy Alliance to stay out of Latin America. Largely because of the persuasion of John Quincy Adams, President James Monroe (1758–1831) decided to take unilateral action instead. Explaining his position in a message to Congress, Monroe based American opposition to the Holy Alliance's interference on the grounds that Europe and the Western Hemisphere represented different spheres of interest. England's concurrence in the American position gave the presidential statement some bite, and the Alliance dropped its plans. Being merely an explanation to Congress, Monroe's new doctrine had no legal status, but it was indicative of the withdrawal of American sympathies from Europe.

The national revolutionary movements were not, however, over. In the 1820's, the Greeks began fighting for their independence from Turkey. At first the Greek revolt seemed doomed to failure, but the longer the Greeks held out against the Turks, the more their revolt took on the aura of man's indomitable struggle for freedom. Throughout the Western world, where classical Greek was still a part of an educated person's learning, people pressured their governments to help the Greeks. In America, funds were raised, public meetings held, and thousands memorialized Congress to do something for the brave defenders of Greek liberties. In the House of Representatives members engaged in a long debate in which they tried to assess the relationship of the United States to revolutionary movements in the light of President Monroe's new doctrine. The last two readings present Monroe's message to Congress and extracts from the House debates on the Greek cause. Participating in these debates were Daniel Webster of Massachusetts, Joel R. Poinsett of South Carolina, Henry W. Dwight of Massachusetts, George Cary of Georgia, Silas Wood of New York, Henry Clay of Kentucky, Ichabod Bartlett of New Hampshire, Alfred Cuthbert of Georgia, and John Randolph and Alexander Smyth of Virginia.

James Monroe: Seventh Annual Message to Congress (1823).

Fellow-Citizens of the Senate and House of Representatives:

James D. Richardson (ed.), *A Compilation of the Messages and Papers of the President,* 1789–1897, Government Printing Office, Washington, 1896, II, 775–79.

Many important subjects will claim your attention during the present session, of which I shall endeavor to give, in aid of your deliberations, a just idea in this communication. I undertake this duty with diffidence, from the vast extent of the interests on which I have to treat and of their great importance to every portion of our Union. I enter on it with zeal from a thorough conviction that there never was a period since the establishment of our Revolution when, regarding the condition of the civilized world and its bearing on us, there was greater necessity for devotion in the public servants to their respective duties, or for virtue, patriotism, and union in our constituents . . .

It is by such knowledge that local prejudices and jealousies are surmounted, and that a national policy, extending its fostering care and protection to all the great interests of our Union, is formed and steadily adhered to.

A precise knowledge of our relations with foreign powers as respects our negotiations and transactions with each is thought to be particularly necessary. Equally necessary is it that we should form a just estimate of our resources, revenue, and progress in every kind of improvement connected with the national prosperity and public defense. It is by rendering justice to other nations that we may expect it from them. It is by our ability to resent injuries and redress wrongs that we may avoid them . . .

At the proposal of the Russian Imperial Government, made through the minister of the Emperor residing here, a full power and instructions have been transmitted to the minister of the United States at St. Petersburg to arrange by amicable negotiation the respective rights and interests of the two nations on the northwest coast of this continent. A similar proposal had been made by His Imperial Majesty to the Government of Great Britain, which has likewise been acceded to. The Government of the United States has been desirous by this friendly proceeding of manifesting the great value which they have invariably attached to the friendship of the Emperor and their solicitude to cultivate the best understanding with his Government. In the discussions to which this interest has given rise and in the arrangements by which they may terminate the occasion has been

judged proper for asserting, as a principle in which the rights and interests of the United States are involved, that the American continents, by the free and independent condition which they have assumed and maintain, are henceforth not to be considered as subjects for future colonization by any European powers . . .

The ministers who were appointed to the Republics of Colombia and Buenos Ayres during the last session of Congress proceeded shortly afterwards to their destinations. Of their arrival there official intelligence has not yet been received. The minister appointed to the Republic of Chile will sail in a few days. An early appointment will also be made to Mexico. A minister has been received from Colombia, and the other Governments have been informed that ministers, or diplomatic agents of inferior grade, would be received from each, accordingly as they might prefer the one or the other . . .

A strong hope has been long entertained, founded on the heroic struggle of the Greeks, that they would succeed in their contest and resume their equal station among the nations of the earth. It is believed that the whole civilized world take a deep interest in their welfare. Although no power has declared in their favor, yet none, according to our information, has taken part against them. Their cause and their name have protected them from dangers which might ere this have overwhelmed any other people. The ordinary calculations of interest and of acquisition with a view to aggrandizement, which mingles so much in the transactions of nations, seem to have had no effect in regard to them. From the facts which have come to our knowledge there is good cause to believe that their enemy has lost forever all dominion over them; that Greece will become again an independent nation. That she may obtain that rank is the object of our most ardent wishes.

It was stated at the commencement of the last session that a great effort was then making in Spain and Portugal to improve the condition of the people of those countries, and that it appeared to be conducted with extraordinary moderation. It need scarcely be remarked that the result has been so far very different from what was then anticipated. Of events in that quarter of the glove, with which we have so much intercourse and from which we derive our origin, we have always been anxious and interested spectators. The citizens of the United States cherish sentiments the most friendly in favor of the liberty and happiness of their fellow-men on that side of the Atlantic. In the wars of the European powers in matters relating to themselves we have never taken any part, nor does it comport with our policy so to do. It is only when our rights are invaded or seriously menaced that we resent injuries or make preparation for our defense. With the movements in this hemishere we are of necessity more immediately connected, and by causes which must be obvious to all enlightened and impartial observers. The political system of the allied powers is essentially different in this respect from that of America. This difference proceeds from that which exists in their respective Governments; and to the defense of our own, which has been achieved by the loss of so much blood and treasure, and matured by the wisdom of their most enlightened citizens, and under which we have enjoyed unexampled felicity, this whole nation is devoted. We owe it, therefore, to candor and to the amicable relations existing between the United States and those powers to declare that we should consider any attempt on their part to extend their system to any portion of this hemisphere as dangerous to our peace and safety. With the existing colonies or dependencies of any European power we have not interfered and shall not interfere. But with the Governments who have declared their independence and maintained it, and whose independence we have, on great consideration and on just principles, acknowledged, we could not view any interposition for the purpose of oppressing them, or controlling in any other manner their destiny, by any European power in any other light than as the manifestation of an unfriendly disposition toward the United States. In the war between those new Governments and Spain we declared our neutrality at the time of their recognition, and to this we have adhered, and shall continue to adhere, provided no change shall occur which, in the judgment of the competent authorities of this Government, shall make a corresponding change on the part of the United States indispensable to their security.

The late events in Spain and Portugal shew that Europe is still unsettled. Of this important fact no stronger proof can be adduced than that the allied powers should have thought it proper, on any principle satisfactory to themselves, to have interposed by force in the internal concerns of Spain. To what extent such interposition may be carried, on the same principle, is a question in which all independent powers whose governments differ from theirs are interested, even those most remote, and surely none more so than the United States. Our policy in regard to Europe, which was adopted at an early stage of the wars which have so long agitated that quarter of the globe, nevertheless remains the same, which is, not to interfere in the internal concerns of any of its powers; to consider the government de facto as the legitimate government for us; to cultivate friendly relations with it, and to preserve those relations by a frank, firm, and manly policy, meeting in all instances the just claims of every power, submitting to injuries from none. But in regard to those continents circumstances are eminently and conspicuously different. It is impossible that the allied powers should extend their political system to any portion of either continent without endangering our peace and happiness; nor can anyone believe that our southern brethren, if left to themselves, would adopt it of their own accord. It is equally impossible, therefore, that we should behold such interposition in any form with indifference. If we look to the comparative strength and resources of Spain and those new Governments, and their distance from each other, it must be obvious that she can never subdue them. It is still the true policy of the United States to leave the parties to themselves in the hope that others powers will pursue the same course.

If we compare the present condition of our Union with its actual state at the close of our Revolution, the history of the world furnishes no example of a progress in improvement in all the important circumstances which constitute the happiness of a nation which bears any resemblance to it. At the first epoch our population did not exceed 3,000,000. By the last census it amounted to about 10,000,000, and, what is more extraordinary, it is almost altogether native, for the immigration from other countries has been inconsiderable. At the first epoch half the territory within our acknowledged limits was uninhabited and a wilderness.

Since then new territory has been acquired of vast extent, comprising within it many rivers, particularly the Mississippi, the navigation of which to the ocean was of the highest importance to the original States. Over this territory our population has expanded in every direction, and new States have been established almost equal in number to those which formed the first bond of our Union. This expansion of our population and accession of new States to our Union have had the happiest effect on all its highest interests. That it has eminently augmented our resources and added to our strength and respectability as a power is admitted by all. But it is not in these important circumstances only that this happy effect is felt. It is manifest that by enlarging the basis of our system and increasing the number of States the system itself has been greatly strengthened in both its branches. Consolidation and disunion have thereby been rendered equally impracticable. Each Government, confiding in its own strength has less to apprehend from the other, and in consequence each, enjoying a greater freedom of action, is rendered more efficient for all the purposes for which it was instituted. It is unnecessary to treat here of the vast improvement made in the system itself by the adoption of this Constitution and of its happy effect in elevating the character and in protecting the rights of the nation as well as of individuals. To what, then, do we owe these blessings? It is known to all that we derive them from the excellence of our institutions. Ought we not, then, to adopt every measure which may be necessary to perpetuate them?

The House of Representatives: Debates on the Greek cause (1824)

Mr. Webster rose and said . . . The question which is now to be discussed is the American question in relation to this affair — What is it best for us to do in the present aspect of things respecting Greece? And surely, sir, this is a question that comprehends something more than a mere pecuniary calculation. Whenever my mind turns to that question, I cannot forget the age I live in, as well as the peculiar position of our own country.

Annals of Congress, 18th Congress, lst Session, Gales and Seaton, Washington, D.C., 1824, pp. 1085–94, 1103–12, 1132–35, 1165–68, 1170–74, 1209–13.

At the commencement of the present session of Congress, Mr. W. said, the President of the United States, in the discharge of the high duties of his station, deemed it incumbent upon him to introduce the subject to the consideration of the National Legislature; and, in his communication, he had expressed an opinion that there was reason to hope that the Greeks would be successful in the present struggle with their oppressors, and that the power that has so long crushed them had lost its dominion over them forever. The same communication contained other matters of great importance, in relation to a rumored combination of foreign Sovereigns to interfere in the concerns of South America. Under these circumstances, said Mr. W., I thought it was proper and becoming that that communication should receive a response from this House. . . The policy of this Government is peace, for peace is to us the greatest source of national increase and aggrandizement. The most sanguine projector cannot furnish more brilliant or exalted prospects than those which must be realized by these States if they can preserve their pacific relations towards the rest of the world. Time, peace, industry, and the arts, are raising this Government by a certain and irresistible progress. It is our true policy, Mr. W. said, to grow, not to acquire; we are to attain to greatness by internal development, not by external accretion — and he should be the last to turn aside the wise policy of the country from its wonted and proper channel. But, said he, that policy, while it is pacific, should at the same time be liberal; he spoke now in relation to those great questions which are at this hour agitating Europe and the world — questions which are concerned wherever a nation attempts to obtain its freedom — the question, in a word, between regulated and unregulated power. Wherever it is disputed, whether a nation shall or shall not possess a constitution, our side of that question ought to be known and declared; we are bound to bring, in aid of its decision, that moral force which must ever reside in the opinion of a free and an intelligent nation. He had said that the policy of this Government was a pacific but a liberal policy; he should endeavor to show that in both of these characters it sanctioned the adoption of the resolution now on the table.

The age, said he, is a peculiar one — it has a marked and striking character, and the position and circumstances of our country are no less so. Had we enjoyed the option, in which period of the world's history, as thus far disclosed, our personal lot should be cast, none of us, surely, would wish to have been born in any other time, or in any other country. There has occurred no age that may be compared with the present, whether in the interest excited by what now is, or the prospects it holds out as to what shall be. The attitude of the United States, meanwhile, is solemn and impressive. Ours is now the great Republic of the earth; its free institutions are matured by the experiment of half a century; nay, as a free Government, it goes farther back — the benefits of a free Constitution have virtually been enjoyed here for two centuries. As a free Government, as the freest Government, its growth and strength compel it, willing or unwilling, to stand forth to the contemplation of the world, We cannot obscure ourselves, if we would; a part we must take, honorable or dishonorable, in all that is done in the civilized world. Now, it will not be denied, that within the last ten years, there has been agitated, in that world, a question of vast moment — a question pregnant with consequences favorable or unfavorable to the prevalence, nay, to the very existence, of civil liberty. It is a question which comes home to us. It calls on us for the expression of our opinion on the great question now before us. Assuredly, if there is any general tendency in the minds and affairs of men, which may be said to characterize the present age, it is the tendency to limited Governments. The enlightened part of mankind have very distinctly evinced a desire to take a share, at least, in the government of themselves. The men of this age will not be satisfied even with kind masters. They have shown, (except where force has been interposed to crush them,) that they will not be contented without a participation in the Government. This is so strongly marked a feature in the social condition of this age, that it can have escaped the observation of none to whom I address myself. It cannot be denied that while this is the prevailing spirit, there is an antagonist principle also at work. This, sir, said Mr. W., is a state of things in which we, as a nation, have, we must have, an interest. The doctrines advanced (and which are promptly supported by a great force) go to prostrate the liberties of the entire civilized world, whether existing under an absolute, a monarchical, or a republican form of government. They are doctrines which have been conceived with great sagacity, they are pursued with unbroken perseverance, and they bring to their support a million and a half of bayonets.

And, here, said Mr. W., let me not be misunderstood, I am not about to declaim against crowned heads, nor enter on a tirade against other forms of government, but I ask that the declarations of the Congress of European Sovereigns, which is promulgated as that which is to form a part of the public law of civilized Europe, may be subjected to a close examination.

The entire overthrow of the late French Emperor, left the European world in a state of very strong excitement. In September, 1815, the Sovereigns, who had, by their united exertions, succeeded in putting down the French power, entered into, and published to the world, an instrument of agreement, which has since been familiarly known by the title of the "Holy Alliance." . . . Was this an alliance of nation with nation? No, Mr. W. said, it was an alliance of crowns against the people; of sovereigns against their own subjects; it was, in a word, the union of the physical force of all Governments against the rights of the people in all countries. What was the natural tendency of such an alliance? It was to put an end to all nations, as such. Extend the principles of that alliance, and the nations are no more — there are only Kings. It divided society horizontally, (if such a figure was allowed to him,) and left all the sovereigns above, and all the people below; it set up the one above all rule or restraint, and put down the other to be trampled beneath their feet. Not satisfied with demanding from the subject allegiance to his own master, it exacted a double, a triple, a quadruple, and he believed, indeed, a quintuple allegiance. According to its principle, all people owe allegiance to all sovereigns. What must be, what has been, the practical operation of such principles? They lead, necessarily, to mutual distrust, to general discontent, and to universal war . . . What was to be the limit to such a principle, or to the practice growing out of it? If this principle is allowed, what, said Mr. W., becomes of our example? Why are we not as legitimate objects for the operation of the principle as any who attempt to set a republican example on the other side of the Atlantic? We certainly did not subscribe to this principle in the days of the Revolution. We did think that when oppressed we might lawfully resist oppression; and I trust we are not so sick of our liberty and its effects as to be unwilling, by our example, and by the most public expression of our opinion, to recommend to others the same doctrine . . . Though there should be no French, or Russian, or Prussian, or Austrian, or English policy, (though this latter I never will believe,) there will at least be an American policy . . . Is it not time to step forth, and at least declare that we condemn and deny such monstrous opinions? How can reformation of Government ever begin but with the people? The radical defect of this system is, that it divides civilization — it would allow it to go on in all other matters, but not in principles of Government and civil liberty. But human knowledge is all connected — that knowledge is fast spreading — the great mass of society which holds, and ever must hold, the physical, is fast obtaining the intellectual power of society . . .

But now, it may be asked, what is all that to us? The question is easily answered. We are one of the nations. Our system of Government is, throughout, utterly hostile to that system, and if we are safe from its effects we may thank our situation or our courage. The age we live in, and our own active character, have connected us with all the nations of the world, and we, as a nation, have precisely the same interest in international law as a private individual has in the laws of his country.

But, apart from the soundness of the policy, on general principles there is a ground of duty in this matter. What do we not, as a people, owe to the principle of lawful resistance? to the principle that society shall govern itself? These principles have raised us to a state of prosperity, in which our course is rapid and irresistible. We are borne on as by a mighty current, and if we would stop long enough to take an observation, that we may measure our national course, before we can effect it, we find we have already moved a vast distance from the point at which it was commenced. This course we cannot check; it is the course of things, and it will go on. Shall we not, thus situated, give to others who are struggling for these very principles, the cheering aid of our example and opinion?

But, whatever we do in this matter, it behooves us

to do on principle. If, on the subject of the rumored combination against South America, we take any stand, it must be on principle that that stand is taken. The near approach, or the remote distance of danger, may change policy, but cannot touch principle; and the same reasons of an abstract kind, that would lead us to protest in the case of the whole Southern Continent, bind us to protest in the case of the smallest Republic in Italy.

A second question, however, may here be asked. What can we do? This thunder is at a distance — the wide Atlantic rolls between — we are safe: would you have us go to war? Would you have us send armies into Europe? No: I would not. But this reasoning mistakes the age. Formerly, indeed, there was no making an impression on a nation but by bayonets, and subsidies, by fleets and armies: but the age has undergone a change: there is a force in public opinion which, in the long run, will outweigh all the physical force that can be brought to oppose it. Until public opinion is subdued, the greatest enemy of tyranny is not yet dead. What is the soul, the informing spirit of our institutions, of our entire system of government? Public opinion. While this acts with intensity, and moves in the right direction, the country must ever be safe — let us direct the force, the vast moral force of this engine, to the aid of others. Public opinion is the great enemy of the Holy Alliance . . .

Sir, I am not one of those who are for withholding aid when it is most urgently needed, and when the stress is past, and the aid no longer necessary, overwhelming the sufferer with caresses. I will not stand by and see my fellow man drowning without stretching out a hand to help him, till he has by his own efforts and presence of mind reached the shore in safety, and then encumber him with aid. With suffering Greece, now is the crisis of her fate — her great, it may be, her last struggle. Sir, while we sit here deliberating, her destiny may be decided. The Greeks, contending with ruthless oppressors, turn their eyes to us, and invoke us by their ancestors, by their slaughtered wives and children, by their own blood, poured out like water, by the hecatombs of dead they have heaped up as it were to heaven, they invoke, they implore of us some cheering sound, some look of sympathy, some token of compassionate regard. They look to us as the great

Republic of the earth — and they ask us by our common faith, whether we can forget that they are struggling, as we once struggled, for what we now so happily enjoy? I cannot say, sir, that they will succeed: that rests with Heaven. But for myself, sir, if I should to-morrow hear that they have failed — that their last phalanx had sunk beneath the Turkish scimetar, that the flames of their last city had sunk in its ashes, and that naught remained but the wide melancholy waste where Greece once was, I should still reflect, with the most heartfelt satisfaction, that I have asked you, in the name of seven millions of freemen, that you would give them at least the cheering of one friendly voice . . .

Mr. Poinsett, of South Carolina, then rose, and addressed the House as follows:

To view this question calmly and dispassionately as a statesman ought to do, requires us to exercise the utmost control over our feelings.

It is impossible to contemplate the contest between the Greeks and the Turks, so eloquently described by the gentleman from Massachusetts, without feeling the strongest indignation at the barbarous atrocities committed by the infidel oppressor, and the deepest interest in the cause of a brave people struggling alone, against fearful odds, to shake off the yoke of despotism.

Our sympathies are always with the oppressed — our feelings are always engaged in the cause of liberty. In favor of Greece, they are still more strongly excited by recollections, which the scholar cherishes with delight, and which are associated in our minds with every pure and exalted sentiment.

The descendants of that illustrious people, to whom we owe our arts, our sciences, and, except our religion, every thing which gives a charm to life, must command our warmest interest: but the Greeks have other claims to our sympathies. They are not only heirs of the immortal fame of their ancestors — they are the rivals of their virtues. In their heroic struggle for freedom, they have exhibited a persevering courage, a spirit of enterprise, and a contempt of danger and of suffering worthy the best days of ancient Greece. The enthusiasm and liberality manifested in their cause, by our fellow-citizens throughout the Union, are, in the highest degree, honorable to their feelings. As men, we must applaud their generosity, and may imitate their example. But the duty of a statesman is a stern duty. As Representatives of the people, we have no right to indulge our sympathies, however noble, or to give way to our feelings, however generous. We are to regard only the policy of a measure submitted to our consideration. Our first, and most important duty, is to maintain peace, whenever that can be done consistently with the honor and safety of the nation; and we ought to be slow to adopt any measure which might involve us in a war, except where those great interests are concerned. The gentleman disclaims any such intention. He does not believe that we run the slightest risk, by adopting the resolution on your table. He considers it as a pacific measure, and relies entirely upon the discretion of the President, to accept or reject our recommendation, as the interests of the country may require. The object of passing such a resolution, can only be to give an impulse to the Executive, and to induce him, by an expression of the opinion of this House, to send a commission to Greece. I have as great a reliance upon the discretion of the Executive as the gentleman from Massachusetts. I believe that he would resist the suggestion of this House in favor of any measure, if he thought the public interest required him to do so. But, unless we wish and expect him to act upon our recommendation, we ought not to throw upon him, alone, the responsibility of resisting the strong public feeling, which has been excited on this subject. The question for us to consider appears to me to be, whether, if the power rested with us, we would exercise it to this extent. I think we could not do so, without incurring some risk of involving the country in a war foreign to its interests. Let us suppose that these commissioners were to fall into the hands of the Turks; an event by no means impossible, in the present state of Greece — what would be their fate? The Porte has not been remarkable for its strict observance of the laws of nations, in its intercourse with the Powers of Europe; and it is not probable, that such a Court would be very scrupulous in its conduct towards a nation whose flag it has never acknowledged. Or, let us imagine, what is much more probable, that on the rumor of our having taken any measure in favor of Greece, the barbarous and infuriated Janissaries at Smyrna were to assassinate our Consul and fellow-citizens residing there; might not a war grow out of such acts? . . .

It appears to me, that in the consideration of this question we have been misled by comparing this revolution with that of Spanish America. And I have heard it argued that, as we sent commissioners to Buenos Ayres without rousing the jealousy of any nation, and recognised the independence of those Governments without exciting the hostility of Spain, we may do the same in relation to Greece, without offending any nation in Europe.

Independently of the different attitude it becomes us to assume towards America, there is no similarity in the two cases. When we adopted the first measures, Buenos Ayres had been independent, de facto, for more than eight years, and Spain had not, during the whole of that period, made the slightest effort to recover possession of that country. When we recognised the independence of the American Governments south of us, they were all free, from the Sabine to the La Plata. The tide could not be rolled back; but, in whatever light Spain may have regarded our conduct on those occasions, the situation of the internal concerns of that country prevented any manifestation of its resentment. No, sir; it is to Europe that we must look for a case parallel to that of Greece. Let us suppose that the Italian States had made an attempt to shake off the iron yoke of Austria, would there be any doubt as to the course of policy this country ought to pursue in that case? Or, if Poland were again to make a desperate effort to recover its liberties, and to re-establish its political existence, that gallant nation sould have a claim to our sympathies. Yet, I apprehend we should hesitate before we took any step which might offend the Emperor of Russia . . .

In this hemisphere we have already taken the station which it becomes us to hold. We have been the first to recognise the free States of North and South America, and the honor and safety of this country requires us to defend them from the attacks of the confederated monarchs of Europe. We are called upon, by every consideration, to resist them, should they attempt to extend their plans of conquest and legitimacy to America; for, if they succeed in that unhallowed enterprise, the independence of nations will be but a name.

That there are indications of such intentions, no one will deny. The King of Spain has proclaimed his determination to employ force to recover his American dominions. Even he is not weak enough to undertake an enterprise of such magnitude with the resources of Spain alone. The Envoy of the Emperor of Russia, sent to congratulate Ferdinand on his restoration to the fulness of his legitimate authority, or, in other words, to the right of tyrannizing over his subjects without control, expresses the wishes of his august master that the benefits now enjoyed by his subjects in Europe may be extended to his dominions in America. In reply to our call for information upon that subject, the President indirectly tells us, that some combined movement against America is to be apprehended. Indeed, we may see the storm gathering in all the signs of the times.

And at this portentous crisis, when we may be compelled to take up arms to defend our rights and liberties on this side of the Atlantic, shall we extend our operations to the remotest corner of Europe? When, to preserve our political existence, we ought to concentrate our strength, shall we diffuse and weaken it by engaging in a distant war? Shall we, in short, so give way to feelings of mere charity and generosity, as to lose sight of the higher obligations of prudence and self-defence?

The gentleman from Massachusetts has painted in true colors the fearful combination of Sovereigns against the liberties of mankind. But, if there is danger, and I agree with him that it is imminent and appalling, it is here that we ought to meet it. A very slight examination of our resources, of the nature and character of our Government and institutions, will convince us, that, in a distant war, foreign to our interests, this nation is weak as an infant. For purpose of defence, in a war that would unite all our resources, and rouse the energies of the people, we are strong as Hercules.

I repeat, that if there is danger to be apprehended from the avowed principles of the Holy Alliance, it is in America that we must resist them. Like the generous animal, which is the emblem of this country, let us not go forth to seek enemies. If they threaten us, let our warning be heard over the waves, in the voices of millions of freemen, resolved to maintain their liberties. If they approach our shores with hostile intent, we may arise in the collected strength of a great nation, and hurl destruction on the foes of freedom and of America . . .

Mr. Randolph then rose and said, that this was perhaps one of the finest and the prettiest themes for declamation ever presented to a deliberative assembly. But it appeared to him in a light very different from any that had as yet been thrown upon it. He looked at the measure as one fraught with deep and deadly danger to the best interests and to the liberties of the American people . . .

I was delegated to this House to guard the interests of the people of the United States, not to guard the rights of other people; and if it was doubted, even in the case of England, that land fertile above all others (not excepting Greece herself) in great men—if it was doubtful whether her interference in the politics of the Continent, though separated from it only by a narrow frith, were either for her honor or advantage; if the effect of that interference has been a monumental debt, that paralyzes the arm that certainly would have struck for Spain, can it be for us to seek in the very bottom of the Mediterranean for a quarrel with the Ottoman Porte? And this while we have an ocean rolling between? While we are in that sea without a single port in which to refit a ship? And while the Powers of Barbary lie in succession in our path? Shall we open this Pandora's box of political evils? It has been wisely and truly said, that it is possible the mere rumor of our interference may produce at Constantinople, or at Smyrna, that which will drive us at once into a war. We all know the connexion that subsists between the Barbary States and what we may denominate the Mother Power. Are we prepared for a war with these pirates? (not that we are not perfectly competent to such a war, but) does it suit our finances? Does it, sir, suit our magnificent project of roads and canals? Does it suit the temper of our people? Does it promote their interests? Will it add to their happiness? Sir, why did we remain supine, while Piedmont and Naples were crushed by Austria? Why did we stand aloof, while the Spanish peninsula was again reduced under legitimate government? If we did not interfere then, why now? . . .

Mr. Wood, of New York, rose and observed, that he had no idea that any thing that he had to say would change a single vote on the question, but that the subject had created great excitement in the community, and that what he should say, would be merely in justification of the vote which he deemed it his duty to give.

He observed, that the resolution, as explained by its advocates, implies that the United States are the guardians of liberty, and are bound to propagate it among all nations . . .

Before we admit this doctrine, it would be well to examine what was our duty as a nation. The duties of every nation are limited to the prosperity and security of its own citizens; it owes nothing to other nations but the duties of humanity. This is more particularly the case with a government like ours, which is only intrusted with certain specific powers.

The Government of the United States is bound to employ the treaty-making power, so as to secure a market to our own citizens for the encouragement of their industry, by stipulations with other nations for the mutual exchange of their productions, and to employ their power over imports, so as to foster domestic industry, and prevent its being overwhelmed by an unequal competition in our own markets.

The Government is also bound to provide a navy and army, with such national establishments as are necessary to repel or redress injury from other nations, and this is the limit of its authority in relation to other nations. We have no authority from the Constitution to embark in wars of ambition, or to propagate the principles of religion or liberty by the sword.

Because the world is full of oppression, is this Government the Hercules that is to free it from the monsters of tyranny and slavery? And are we bound to emulate the chivalrous achievements of the renowned Knight of LaMancha, by engaging in conflict with every windmill that we may, in the delirium of our frenzy, imagine to be a tyrant?

It will be asked, is our Government to be of no use to mankind? I answer yes; but not by its fleets and armies—not by embarking in a military crusade to establish the empire of our principles—not by establishing a corps of diplomatic apostles of liberty, but by the moral influence of its example.

It presents to the world a model by which the rights of men may be secured, and the benefit of good government may be obtained, with the least sacrifice of individual independence. It excites inquiry—it invites examination; the knowledge of it will be conveyed, by our flag, to every region of the earth. Foreigners will visit our shores; they will examine its structure; they will witness its practical operation; they will discover its excellence; and it will thus diffuse a spirit of reformation throughout the world.

Much has been said, during this debate, about the spirit of the age. The present age is distinguished from the last by liberality of sentiment in religion and politics. The American Revolution, Bible societies, and Christian missions, aided by the extension of commerce, have produced this change. It does not need the aid of physical means—such aid would obstruct its influence. This moral influence is all powerful, but does not irritate—does not excite alarm—does not provoke opposition. But, let it be connected with physical means, and it instantly will meet with resistance. Let it, then, operate as it has done, and we may expect it will continue to produce more and more important results, till the governments of the world are reformed . . .

Sir, it is very doubtful whether the Greeks possess the elementary principles that are necessary to form a free State. If a people possess the elements of freedom, they cannot be long held in slavery; and if they are destitute of these, no efforts they may make will terminate in the establishment of free institutions.

The love of liberty is so ingrained into the heart of every American, that we are apt to overlook the difficulties in the way of free government, and to conclude that every effort in favor of liberty will be successful.

It is a deception to compare the situation of other countries with ours, at the commencement of our Revolution.

We inherited the principles of liberty from our ancestors; we were educated in the free principles of the common law. We enjoyed the protection of person and property, the right of suffrage, and trial by jury; in which it would require a century for any people who have been born under the civil law to be instructed, and much longer to acquire by their own exertions.

Sir, are gentlemen aware of the value of the inheritance which they have derived from their ancestors? The privilege we enjoy is the result of a struggle of virtuous and enlightened men for more than six hundred years, with ignorance, superstition, and tyranny. They were extorted by piecemeal, with incredible labor and perseverance. It was more than two hundred years from the Great Charter to the Bill of Rights. From the time of the Great Charter to the American Revolution, distinguished individuals continued the conflict, breaking one fetter after another, until their persevering efforts terminated in a complete emancipation of this country from the shackles of superstition and tyranny, and in the establishment of civil and religious liberty, by political institutions conformable to the principles of natural liberty and calculated to secure it.

Sir, the peace of the country was endangered at the commencement of the French revolution, by disregarding those difficulties. A brief examination of the principles that are essential to the structure of every free government, will enable us to calculate the chances of a struggle in favor of liberty with ancient institutions, with more correctness.

Political writers agree, with one voice, that no people can be free, who have not intelligence to understand their rights, and virtue to submit to the restraints of law, as well as to aid their execution by the moral force of public sentiment; but they seem to have overlooked the influence of property in society. Experience proves, that intelligence and virtue may be overborne by the influence of property, secured to a few by the laws of the society.

Property is the basis of power in society. This is a law of our nature, and founded in the moral constitution of man. Men will be governed by their wants, and will be subservient to those who feed them, or who furnish them with the means of feeding themselves. The condition of the real property of any country will control and modify the government. The possession of the whole country by a few persons, secured by the laws of primogeniture and restraints against alienation, will necessarily lead to monarchy or aristocracy; an equality of property in a soil, or the power of acquiring it, will lead to a republic. The first was the plan of the feudal system; the second is the plan embraced by the constitutions and laws of the States that compose our Union. The hereditary descent of property and established ranks, with exclusive privileges, lie at the foundation of the European Governments—the great mass of the people are tenants, laborers, and artisans, without any interest in the soil.

Before free Governments can be established in those countries, the existing establishments must be rased to their foundations, and the whole structure of society must be reorganized; the restraints on alienation must be removed, ranks abolished, and equality of civil privileges established . . .

Do the Greeks possess the elementary principles of freedom? This is very doubtful.

Mr. Cuthbert, (who had, by the custom of the House, the right to the floor, having last evening moved that the Committee rise,) in introducing his remarks, observed . . . that it would be conceded by gentlemen on the other side, that this was a measure which had its origin, principally, in feeling. That a very strong popular excitement did exist at this moment on the subject, could not be denied; and how far the feelings of a virtuous, intelligent, and reflecting people, ought to influence their legislators, he should not undertake to determine; he did not, for a moment, suppose that a legislative body was the only assemblage of citizens who were competent to judge and determine a question of this kind. But there was a wide and important distinction between assemblages of the people, gathered together in masses without responsibility, and those who were bound by their office and their oath to deliberate with their calmest judgment, and whose decisions were to be followed with momentous consequences.

The people, gathered in large assemblies, feel a generous pride in expressing their warmest feelings. The noble glow of sympathy catches from heart to heart; the feeling rises with the numbers who partake in it, till each man feels his bosom swell with a big emotion, the result of the congregated feeling. But, sir, while such meetings are held, and such emotions experienced, do the people, sir, expect that you shall be governed, in solemn acts of legislation, by the resolutions they pass? Were you to yield yourselves to such a governance, you would

betray the confidence reposed in you. Not that you have more wisdom than they, but that you are intrusted with the administration of their Government. They tell you that they love liberty—that they deplore the calamities and sufferings of the oppressed Greeks—that they rejoice and exult in all their triumphs. Well, sir, what is the conslusion? This: that if sound wisdom shall direct you to engage in any active measures on the subject, you have an ardent and an energetic people to back you. Ought you not to pause, Mr. Chairman, before you commit such a people, noble, gallant, generous, now enjoying unprecedented happiness, and in the full possession of all the blessings of peace, to all the privations, the untried horrors of war? To judge of your duty, select any individual who has been a member of one of these popular meetings, who has been the most enthusiastic of all who were present, and who there passed resolutions, couched in the most glowing language; select him from that meeting, (where he was without responsibility,) place him in the solitude of his chamber, tell him he must now act, and act under the whole responsibility of the happiness or the distress of his country—passion departs—he begins to pause, and to reflect, and he invokes, not passion, but wisdom, for his guide. It is thus that these very people expect and demand of you to act.

What does such a reflection naturally suggest to us? That we should make a comparison between our Government, and those under which this very nation of the Greeks once lived. Shall I be told that it is but the declamation of a school boy to talk of ancient Greece? I answer, that sentiment is worthy only of those enslaved countries where it is the fashion, because it is the interest of their oppressors, to cast every species of ridicule and sneer upon republican governments. Shall we on this account, deny ourselves the solid benefit of the experience of other republics? Those who live under the monarchical governments of Europe are liable to be misled on this subject, by the cant of their writers—from the humblest journal of the day, to the largest and weightiest tome that engrosses the shelf of their libraries, all hold one language—a regular war is waged with the principles of free government; if we join in the adoption of such anti-republican sentiments, we aid this bank of conspirators in the servile design of degrading and debasing the human family. No, sir. We are warranted in appealing for facts to aid us to the history of Greece—it is our duty to look carefully at that history. And what do we find, sir? that the Grecian Republics had all the soul and fire of liberty, but that they wanted intelligence, and a regular plan in its enjoyment and its preservation. Hence, we see them split up into contending factions; and so bitter were their mutual hatred and animosity, and so fierce the rage of their contests, that, in some instances whole communities were destroyed, wars of annihilation were carried on between neighboring States, and scenes occurred on the Grecian soil, over which freedom and humanity mingle their tears. But how, sir, is the case with us? Under an administration of mild and equal laws, we are at this hour in the enjoyment of the utmost practicable measure of personal liberty. We are blessed with profound peace, and the humblest and most timid man among us is in the full possession of absolute security in person and property...

How cautious, then, should we be that we do not, by bringing disaster on our hitherto happy experiment, blast the rising cause of freedom (check it, rather, for rise it will) throughout the world. Let us take care that we do not make our case a warning against free governments, instead of the strongest of arguments in their favor. And what, sir, is the process by which you are to spread the influence of your free principles and free institutions? Not by wars, but by a friendly intercourse with Europe, by writings, by personal conversation, and by the speeches of your statesmen. By means like these, the rapid contagion of enlightened principles will spread from land to land. Men easily imbibe right principles on politics, when once they are suggested to them. The plainest and the humblest peasant can be made to understand that men are born equal, and have equal rights; all he needs is to be convinced that these principles, so true and so plain in themselves can be carried out into a practical government. The literati of Europe know this, and some of them spread the truth in their writings. Their statesmen know it, too, and some of these, too, recommend it. The honest

common people acknowledge the truth, and long for its benefits. They have the demonstration of the truth brought to their very senses: they see and know our seamen, our merchants, and their families, and they know that there does exist a country that fosters in its bosom a free, proud, and energetic people, who know how to protect their rights and their honor. Such a state of things now exists that these people inhale some notions of freedom with the very atmosphere they breathe—and as they breathe in they come to love those rights. Despotism, on the other hand, is founded on the ignorance, prejudice, timidity, and depression of the people: but that ignorance is dissipating—those prejudices are weakening—that fear is dispelling—the people are fast rising in the scale of being. How unwise would it be, nay, how wicked, to abandon all these gradual but powerful effects of our Government and condition, in order to assume another character. What will be the effect of war on this influence? It will counteract it at once, by conjuring up in opposition all the angry and resentful passions. Why should we so effectually advance the dearest interests of despotism? Think you that their monarchs will fail to direct these passions against the cause of freedom? Sir, we can give no physical, no warlike aid to liberty that will not injure her cause.

There is another consideration that calls upon us to pause and reflect, before we take any step that may commit the nation. Monarchy can go to war from policy or ambition, and if they do not find it suits their views they can, with almost equal ease, withdraw from the contest. But it is far otherwise with Republics. In these, before you enter into a war, you must convince the mass of the nation that the war is virtuous and just in its principles, and unavoidable without disgrace. When a free people have become, by reflection, convinced of this, they become reckless of consequences; you rouse a deeper spirit; you concentrate a mightier wrath than a despotic Government can ever know. There is a moral force that mingles with the physical, and propels it with redoubled energy. But, if the war is unreasonable, unjust, unnecessary, when any calamity happens in its prosecution they at once look back to its origin, re-examine its principle;

they ask, in a spirit of discontent and indignation, why was it not avoided; and they wreak their vengeance on its authors. You cannot, then, enter with too much caution on steps that have war in their probable or possible results . . .

Mr. Clay then rose, and commenced his speech by distinctly stating the original resolution, as moved by Mr. Webster, and the amendment proposed by Mr. Poinsett. The resolution proposed providing the means to defray the expense of a mission, whenever the President, who knows, or ought to know, the dispositions of all the European Powers, Turkish or Christian, shall deem it proper to send one. The amendment goes to withold any appropriation, and to make a public declaration of our sympathy with the Greeks, and our good wishes for their cause. And how, sir, (asked Mr. C.,) has this simple, modest, unpretending, this harmless proposition been treated? It has been argued, as if it proposed aid to the Greeks; as if it proposed the recognition of their Government; as an act of unjustifiable interference; as a measure of war. And those who thus argue the question, while they themselves give unbounded range to their imagination in conceiving and setting in array the monstrous consequences which are to grow out of so simple a proposal, impute to us who are its advocates, Quixotism! Quixotism! While they are taking the most extravagant and unlimited range, and arguing any thing and every thing but the question before the House, they accuse us of enthusiasm, of giving the reins to feeling, of being carried away by our imagination. No, sir, the proposition on your table is no proposition for aid, nor for recognition, nor for interference, nor for war . . .

The measure, sir, has been unwarrantably magnified. Gentlemen speak of the watchful jealousy of the Turks, and seem to think that the lightest movements in this body will be matter of speculation at Constantinople. He could assure the gentlemen that the European Powers attached no such vast importance to our acts and deliberations as some seemed to suppose. The Turk will in all probability never hear of the gentlemen's names who either advocate or oppose the resolution. The resolution is certainly not without its value, but that value is wholly a moral value; it throws our little tribute into the vast stream of public opinion, which, sooner or later, must regulate the physical action upon the great interests of the civilized world. But, sir, rely upon it the Turk is not about to declare war because this unoffending proposition has been offered by my honorable friend from Massachusetts, of whom, however eminent in our own country, the Sublime Porte has never yet heard. The Allied Powers are not going to be thrown into a state of alarm by a resolution appropriating two or three thousand dollars to send an agent to Greece.

The question has been argued as if the Greeks were likely to be exposed to increased sufferings in consequence of such a measure; as if the Turkish scimetar would be sharpened by its influence, and dyed deeper and yet deeper in Christian blood . . .

But, sir, so far from this resolution being likely if passed, to produce injury to the Greeks, it is likely to have a directly opposite effect. Sir, the Turk, with all his power, and in all the elevation of his despotic throne, is at last but man; he is made as we are, of flesh, of muscle, of bones, and sinews; he can feel; and, sir, he has felt the uncalculating valor of American freedom in some of his dominions; and when he is made to understand, that not only the Executive of this Government, but that this nation—that our entire political fabric, base, column, and entablature, rulers and people, with heart, soul, mind, and strength, are all on the side of the nation he is crushing, he will be more likely to restrain, than to increase his atrocities upon suffering and bleeding Greece . . .

It has been admitted by all that there is impending over this country a threatening storm, which is likely to call into action all our vigor, courage, and resources. Is it a wise way of preparing for this awful event, to talk to this nation of its incompetency to resist European aggression, to lower its spirit, to weaken its moral force, and do what we can to prepare it for base submission and easy conquest? If, sir, there be any reality in this menacing danger, I would rather adjure the nation to remember that it contains a million of freemen capable of bearing arms, and ready to exhaust their last drop of blood and their last cent, in defending their country, its institutions, and its liberty. Sir, are these to be conquered by all Europe united? But I am quite sure that that danger, so far at least as this resolution is concerned, is perfectly ideal and imaginary. But, if it were otherwise, any danger is best guarded against by invigorating our minds to meet it—by teaching our heads to think, our hearts to conceive, and our arms to execute the high and noble deeds which belong to the character and glory of our country. Sir, the experience of the world may instruct us that conquests are achieved when they are boldly and firmly determined on; and that men become slaves as soon as they have ceased to resolve to live freemen. If we wish to cover ourselves with the best of all armor against perils, let us not discourage our people, let us stimulate their ardor, let us sustain their resolution, let us show them that we feel as they feel, and that we are prepared to live or die like freemen. Surely, sir, we need no long or learned lectures about the influence of property or of rank; let us rather remember that we can bring into the field a million of bayonets; let us remember that we are placed over a nation capable of doing and of suffering all things for its liberty . . .

Mr. A. Smyth, of Virginia, addressed the Chair. He said, that, being deeply impressed with the importance of the question before the Committee, he would solicit respectfully the attention of members, while he delivered his observations . . .

We are sitting in judgment on the Russian and the Turk. But what right have we to judge of their acts, unless they affect us? And we are about to take measures on our own behalf. What right have we to judge between the Turk and his revolted subjects, unless our own interest or safety is concerned? We should not take it well that our proceedings should be denounced by foreign Governments. We do not take it well that the Russian Minister, at the Court of Spain, denounces the United States as the source of all the evils which have disturbed the nations and sovereigns of Europe; and we should take it worse were the like denunciations made by his master. What have we to do with the oppressions of the Government of China, India, Turkey, or France, unless we are about to relieve the oppressed? We have nothing to do with the wrongs committed by other Governments against those whom they govern, but to avoid their example.

You profess to interfere on behalf of the Greeks for liberty and religion. What have you to do with the liberty of any people, except the people you govern, unless the subjection of a neighboring foreign people endangers your safety? You have nothing to do with religion, even here, and why should you meddle with it elsewhere? . . .

Sir, the present is a time of imminent danger, and, therefore, a time for caution. Remember the words of Washington: "Why quit your own, to stand on foreign ground?" Meddle not with Greece. I tell you, that Greece cannot exist as a Republic; and if allowed to become a separate nation, under a prince of her own, it must be under the control of Russia. From the position of Greece, between Russia, Austria, and Turkey, it cannot maintain itself as an independent nation. The revolt of Greece would not have been allowed to continue until this time, but that Austria and Russia cannot agree what shall become of that country, which each of them desires to possess. Can it be supposed that the allied, who are not disposed to allow the independence of South America, who scarcely tolerate us, will permit two or three millions of half civilized people, in their vicinity, to form a Republic? It is not to be expected. The most that can be done for the advantage of the Greeks, is to assist them to obtain favorable terms from the Turks. Our interference may furnish a pretext to men of blood—to come upon us; and, whatever may be said of the strength of the United States, I am not for exposing it to trial, in a contest with the allies . . .

The cause of freedom, the hope of mankind, depends on the ultimate success of the hitherto successful experiment in the science of government, making in the United States. When we consider the importance of the interests confided to us, it must appear unpardonable wantonly to hazard the success of that experiment. If there be a mode of destroying civil liberty, it is by leading this Government into unnecessary wars. There can be no increase of the happiness of this people. Individuals may experience wants; but, as a nation, we have nothing more to ask of Heaven. All we have to ask of other nations is, friendship and "let us alone." What shall we deserve if, without necessity, we plunge this happy people into war and distress? Whatever may be said of the valor of our people, and the glory of the nation, I should be very unwilling to engage in a war with Europe. We might defend ourselves. I think we should successfully defend ourselves. I am no prophet of evil. We do not act on our own responsibility; we act for an immortal people. This people are to be immortal; but whether in freedom or abject subjection, is uncertain. This people are to be responsible for our acts, with their treasure and their blood. I am not disposed to bring upon them a trial, such as Spain passed through, in the war waged against that nation, for the purpose of placing Joseph Bonaparte on the Throne . . .

Sir, our course, I think, is plain. Let us be moderate and just. Let us offer no aggression; throw out no menaces, and give the Allies no pretext to quarrel with us . . .

SUGGESTIONS FOR FURTHER READING

Samuel F. Bemis, "Washington's Farewell Address: A Foreign Policy of Independence," *American Historical Review*, **39** (1934).

William N. Chambers, *Political Parties in a New Nation: The American Experience, 1776–1809*, Oxford U. Press, New York, 1963.

Marcus Cunliffe, *The Nation Takes Shape*, The University of Chicago Press, Chicago, 1959.

Noble Cunningham, *The Jeffersonian Republicans, 1789–1801*, University of North Carolina Press, Chapel Hill, 1957.

George Dangerfield, *The Awakening of American Nationalism, 1815–1828*, Harper, New York, 1965.

Manning J. Dauer, *The Adams Federalists*, The Johns Hopkins Press, Baltimore, 1953.

Philip F. Detweiler, "The Congressional Debate on Slavery and the Declaration of Independence, 1819–1821," *American Historical Review*, **63** (1958).

Durand Echeverria, *Mirage in the West*, Princeton University Press, Princeton, 1957.

Felix Gilbert, *The Beginnings of American Foreign Policy*, Harper, New York, 1961.

Zoltan Haraszti, *John Adams and the Prophets of Progress*, Grosset & Dunlap, New York, 1952.

Adrienne Koch and Harry Ammon, "The Virginia and Kentucky Resolutions: An Episode in Jefferson's and Madison's Defense of Civil Liberties," *William and Mary Quarterly*, 5 (1948).

Stephen G. Kurtz, *The Presidency of John Adams*, University of Pennsylvania Press, Philadelphia, 1957.

Leonard W. Levy, "Liberty and the First Amendment: 1790–1800," *American Historical Review*, **67** (1962).

John C. Miller, *Alexander Hamilton and the Growth of the New Nation*, Harper, New York, 1959.

Robert R. Palmer, *The Age of the Democratic Revolution*, I, Princeton University Press, Princeton, 1959.

Dexter Perkins, *A History of the Monroe Doctrine*, Little, Brown, Boston, 1963.

Julius W. Pratt, "The Ideology of American Expansion," *Essays in Honor of William E. Dodd*, University of Chicago Press, Chicago, 1935.

Marshall Smelzer, "George Washington and the Alien and Sedition Laws," *American Historical Review*, **59** (1954).

James Morton Smith, "The Sedition Law, Free Speech and the American Political Process," *William and Mary Quarterly*, **9** (1952).

THE FLOWERING
OF LIBERALISM
IN THE
JACKSONIAN PERIOD

Chapter 7   1820-1840

The political and social structure of America in the
Jacksonian period was more egalitarian than it had ever
been before or would ever be again during the century
that followed. There were few towering fortunes, little
poverty, and many opportunities for sharing in the
country's remarkable material prosperity. The rapid
agricultural expansion of the first three decades of the
19th century had brought eight new states into the
union, most of them characterized by the eighty-acre
farms that government land offices sold for $100.
Manufacturing, though still not a major force in the
economy, stimulated enterprise and investment and
frequently rewarded individual initiative with financial success. Factories and shops were small, making
competition brisk among many firms. The categories
of employee and employer more often marked the
stages in a man's life than the distinctions of birth.
Western states coming into the union provided for
universal manhood suffrage, prompting the older states
to reconsider their constitutions. Political participation was open to most free men, and political parties
were learning how to bring the power of organized
groups to bear on the decision-making process.

Andrew Jackson was the embodiment of this
democratization of American society. More a symbol
than a cause of social equality, Jackson nonetheless
represented the mobility and ambitions of his time.
He was the first American president who was born
poor, and he came to the presidency with none of the

establishment credentials of his six predecessors. Before Jackson, every president except Washington had previously served as vice president or secretary of state. The United States might easily have followed the example of England and continued to choose for the chief executive men who had been carefully groomed for leadership. Jackson's example checked this possibility. His personality and reputation as a military hero carried him into the White House where his popularity laid the foundation for the Democratic party. Like the typical American, Jackson was impressed by money but distrustful of the wealthy, confident of the native ability of average men, and impatient with the pretensions of the well-born. The fact that he was derided by members of the upper class did not seem to bother Jackson. He was content to be the leader of the great majority — those Americans of middling means and undistinguished origins.

More than ever before the individual became the focus of American institutions in the 1820's and 1830's. No superior wisdom, no claim of family, no transcending social purpose was deemed more important than the free development of the individual. Economists taught that no economic planning could possibly stimulate production and commerce better than the undirected competition of individuals pursuing their own self-interest. Prevailing democratic theory held that political decisions could be arrived at similarly through the mechanism of votes registering the desires of the greatest number in the society. Free economic and political institutions seeemed to offer solutions to the thorny problems of human society. There were, of course, those who rejected the proposition that because men have equal rights they are equally endowed with the judgment necessary for wise political decisions. They lamented the decline of the authority of social institutions and harkened back to an older tradition that placed its emphasis upon checking man's passions rather than liberating his energies. Some recognized that the majority too can be a tyrant, but the circumstances of American life in the first half of the 19th century worked against these conservative critics.

Even the churches followed the libertarian and individualistic cast of prevailing social values. The separation of church and state had put religion on a voluntary basis for membership and financial support. Congregations flourished or failed to the extent that they were able to attract and keep members. More and more the churches spoke to the needs of the individual rather than to problems of the society as a whole. Preachers directed their reforming efforts towards personal vices to the exclusion of social ills, and individuals were left to follow their own preferences in matters of conscience, unfettered by a demanding social ethic.

The most effective means of recruiting church members proved to be the revival techniques which had been developed during the Great Awakening in the 1730's. In the new settlements of the West, families travelled many miles to hear itinerant preachers exhort thousands at great camp meetings. These revivalists appealed to the feelings of their listeners, winning converts through their vivid sermons which reduced complex moral problems to simple choices. Inevitably they encouraged the idea that if one's heart were in the right place all would be well, a point of view that completely undercut the study of doctrine and theology. Instincts and intuitions, they implied, were better guides to moral decisions than painstaking, often painful, assessments of human situations. By the first decade of the 19th century the pietistic, revival-oriented churches like the Baptists and Methodists had far more members than the churchly religious bodies that had dominated in the colonial period. The pietists' emphasis upon the teaching of a simple Christian message unsupported by church discipline or learned doctrine soon colored all of American Christianity and sank deep into American culture.

Because American energies were absorbed in the pursuit of profit in these years, economics came into its own as the science of wealth. Some hoped that a true knowledge of economic principles would take such issues as tariffs, banking, and monetary control out of the reach of partisan politics and place them in the antiseptic and passionless realm of rational inquiry. Scholarly opinion held that there were laws governing society just as there were laws governing the physical world. Once discovered and explained, these laws could determine government economic policies. Unfortunately, the learned economists disagreed. One group, following in the footsteps of the great Scottish scholar, Adam Smith, believed that competition and self-interest were the true regulators of economic activity, and that the invisible hand of the market could best settle questions about investments, wages, prices, and supply and demand. Everything, these men said, could be safely left to the inexorable workings of economic laws if legislators were wise enough to adopt a let-alone, *laissez faire* attitude.

The opposing group of economic thinkers, while admitting much of Smith's reasoning, rejected the atomization of the national economy into thousands of unregulated egotistical operators. They insisted that an economy must be thought of as a whole unit requiring direction and regulatory legislation. While they endorsed as much freedom as they felt was consonant with their aims, these economists wished to develop comprehensive national programs rather than rely upon the automatic operation of free choice and competition. Actually two concepts of government hovered behind this dispute over economic policy. The first, drawing support from the success of individual initiative in America, insisted upon restricting government activity to the absolute minimum necessary to protect personal freedom. The opposing political philosophy was the more traditional one which Hamilton had represented in an earlier period. It called for government to give overall direction, establish priorities, supply incentives, and protect vital national interests. While competition, in this view, might be counted upon to achieve certain ends, it was never considered as anything but a means.

Jackson himself believed in limited government and pursued an economic policy of *laissez faire*. The milestones of his administration were his attacks upon national banking and federally funded internal improvements. He vetoed federal appropriations for

roads and canals and single-handedly set out to destroy the Bank of the United States. As the most powerful financial institution in the country, the bank was the government's chief means for influencing economic activity. At a more popular level, the bank was a symbol of high finance and a ready target for public hostility at a time when the country was moving away from its agrarian past into an uncertain industrial future. To the average American, the bank represented the moneyed interests, the mysteries of financial manipulation and the imagined villain of economic depressions. Since most people longed for an age which had neither banks nor business cycles, Jackson was able to mine a rich vein of public sympathy with his fight against the bank. Confident that his opinions reflected the true American principles, Jackson greatly strengthened the tendency in the United States to discuss public issues in terms of patriotism rather than policy.

Despite the egalitarianism of Jacksonian America, in the South the concentration of wealth and power in the hands of an elite ruling class continued. In large part this was a reflection of the dominant form of Southern agriculture which involved large investments of capital in slave labor. In the 1820's and 1830's the forward thrust of the entire economy came from the South, whose cotton crop was the single most important American export commodity. The success of cotton cultivation provided the impetus for a Southern expansion westward which equaled that of the North, but the price of Southern prosperity was a growing alienation from the rest of the country. Southern agriculture made the rich richer and the poor poorer. The agitation against slavery which had been noticeable in the South earlier gave way with this slave-based prosperity to a hardening in the attitude of Southern leaders. Their attention became fixed upon ways to protect the South's institutions from national interference and to preserve their sectional integrity from federal encroachments.

A look at the map of the United States in 1832 reveals the Southern problem. The Missouri Compromise forbade the introduction of slavery into most of the Louisiana territory, as the Northwest Ordinance had prohibited it in the Northwest Territory. Texas, then a possession of Mexico, blocked the expansion of the South across the Mississippi. The slave-holding states were bottled up in the Southeastern corner of the United States. Southern Congressmen clearly feared the rapid movement of free labor into the seemingly limitless western frontier and even attempted to stop it. Frustrated in this effort, Southern statesmen had two recourses for protecting their social and economic particularities from federal legislation: to build a states' right's theory into an impenetrable defense of Southern sectional autonomy or to break out of the geographic barriers to which slavery was confined. Following the first course, South Carolina attempted to define the limits of federal powers by passing an Ordinance of Nullification against the tariff of 1832. Jackson, newly elected for a second term, met this challenge with a vigorous application of executive authority, but the issue was only postponed. Simultaneously during the 1830's, pressure began building up in the South for territorial expansion. Southern planters started moving into the underpopulated Texas province of neighboring Mexico. Southern territorial ambitions fed on this new hope of carrying slavery across the Mississippi.

Jackson, despite his firm opposition to Southern nullification theories, was by no means unsympathetic to the South. A Southerner himself, he had come to the presidency as the first candidate of the Democratic party which had inherited many of the ideological commitments of the old Jeffersonian Republicans, including the strict interpretation of the Constitution and support for states' rights. Like a good many Americans outside the South, he shared Southern doubts about the constitutionality of active government involvement in the economy. These attitudes appealed to Northern farmers who wanted to keep taxes and prices down and were suspicious of national legislation backed by Eastern bankers and manufacturers. Urban workers also shared this suspicion of the capitalists. Thus, aristocratic Southern slave-holders were brought into the same political coalition of the Democratic party with mechanics and shopkeepers in

the North and small farmers north and west.

Even so, Jackson did not appeal to all segments of the American electorate, nor to all sympathies within any given group, and a new Whig party was formed during the 1830's as a political counterweight to the Democrats. Held together principally by their opposition to Jackson, the Whigs emphasized the more positive contributions of government. Inspired by Henry Clay's outline of an "American System" of mutual sectional help, the Whigs favored the idea of government providing leadership to achieve national goals. They endorsed a national bank, protective tariffs and internal improvement programs with a rhetoric of union and nationalism. The Whigs and the business interests which they represented were also the principal beneficiaries of Chief Justice John Marshall's constitutional decisions which had shored up the powers of the federal government during the vigorous assertion of sectionalism and states' rights which marked the Jacksonian period.

On the surface, Jacksonian politics seemed mired down in a succession of tedious debates about banks, tariffs, internal improvements, and western land sales, but beneath this public discourse there were unresolved questions about American government. What role should it play in American life? What rights did the states possess and what powers could the majority of the electorate wield through congressional laws? What was the nature of the United States — an association of states or a unified nation? These questions, which bore a marked similarity to those discussed during the ratification of the Constitution, arose again because of the development of the South into a closed, regional society and because in the North new economic interests were emerging which were national in scope. While the fundamental questions remained unanswered, the specific issues could still be resolved through compromise. Both political parties had national constituencies that cut across sectional lines, and widespread optimism ameliorated most national tensions. Americans in the Jacksonian period shared a common admiration for their country's free institutions. North and South, men expressed a love of personal liberty and agreed that protecting freedom and equal opportunity were the proper goals of government. Americans had faith that social problems could be solved through individual action and voluntary efforts. Until this hope was shattered, the nation was content to postpone coming to grips with the issues of slavery, states rights, and federal power.

The practice of democracy in the early 19th century encouraged Americans to believe that equality and freedom were compatible. Educated Europeans, however, continued to fear that democracy led to mob rule and eventual anarchy where the strong oppressed the weak. Those who theorized on government held that true freedom could exist only where there was some independent force in society strong enough to check the power of government. In monarchies the powerful noblemen could protect themselves and their proteges from the abuses of the king and thus make a place for freedom, but in a society of equals, who was strong enough to stand against the government? A young French aristocrat, Alexis de Tocqueville (1805–1859), came to America with the specific purposes of studying this problem. Tocqueville was convinced that all countries were moving toward such conditions of social equality, and while he believed this would improve the material well-being of the people, he was not sure of the fate of the human spirit, of human excellence, and free thought. Pursuing these questions in his book, *Democracy in America*, Tocqueville also explained a great deal about Jacksonian society. He observed customs and characteristics which familiarity obscured from Americans. Behind the political institutions he found a democratic culture which shaped American thought and behavior into a common mold. The first reading in this section is taken from *Democracy in America*.

Brilliant as Tocqueville's analysis was, it implied that American society was static when in fact America was undergoing great changes, physically and culturally. The acceptance of popular participation and the addition of new western states to the union was adding to the momentum for the democratization of American institutions. Where the colonial and early national period had witnessed the growth of political freedom and an opening up of individual opportunities, the new campaign was for equality itself, particularly the political equality represented by universal manhood suffrage. Vermont, the first of the new states to enter the union, came in with a constitution free of property qualifications and most of the new western states followed Vermont's example. Pressure built up in the older states to hold conventions to draft new constitutions. In Massachusetts and Connecticut, the tax-supported churches came under attack; in other states it was the provision of a religious test for elected officials. In all of them the question of property qualifications for voting was preeminent.

The second reading in this section comes from the debates in the New York State Constitutional Convention, in which the die-hard conservatives fought to retain a property qualification for the electorate of the upper house of the legislature. New York's distinguished chancellor, James Kent, developed in full the theory that social stability demands that those with a substantial and abiding stake in society be given some means for protecting their interests from the landless man. Kent's fears for the future — when a large urban population would have the strength of numbers — were not shared by the majority of the convention, whose spokesmen insisted that voting was a right, not a privilege. The advocates of equality, however, balked at sharing it with New York's large free black population and proposed retaining a property qualification for them. The convention's conservatives who had never associated voting privileges with equality fought this discriminatory provision, but they were defeated. The word white was introduced as a qualification at the same time possession of property was removed. Elsewhere in the Northern states black men lost the vote as the nation's democratic tide brought in an anti-Negro spirit with it. The readings begin with the convention's debate on the report from the committee on the right of suffrage. The first discussion centers on the committee's recommendation that voting privileges without property qualifications apply only to white men. The following debate deals with the elimination of the property qualification itself.

Alexis de Tocqueville: Democracy in America (1835)

Introduction

Amongst the novel objects that attracted my attention during my stay in the United States, nothing struck me more forcibly than the general equality of conditions. I readily discovered the prodigious influence which this primary fact exercises on the whole course of society, by giving a certain direction to public opinion, and a certain tenor to the laws; by imparting new maxims to the governing powers, and peculiar habits to the governed. I speedily perceived that the influence of this fact extends far beyond the political character and the laws of the country, and that it has no less empire over civil society than over the Government; it creates opinions, engenders sentiments, suggests the ordinary practices of life, and modifies whatever it does not produce. The more I advanced in the study of American society, the more I perceived that the equality of conditions is the fundamental fact from which all others seem to be derived, and the central point at which all my observations constantly terminated.

I then turned my thoughts to our own hemisphere, where I imagined that I discerned something analogous to the spectacle which the New World presented to me. I observed that the equality of conditions is daily progressing towards those extreme limits which it seems to have reached in the United States, and that the democracy which governs the American communities appears to be rapidly rising into power in Europe. I hence conceived the idea of the book which is now before the reader . . .

It appears to me beyond a doubt that sooner or later we shall arrive, like the Americans, at an almost complete equality of conditions. But I do not conclude from this that we shall ever be necessarily led to draw the same political consequences which the Americans have derived from a similar social organization. I am far from supposing that they have chosen the only form of government which a democracy may adopt; but the identity of the efficient cause of laws and manners in the two countries is sufficient to ac-

count for the immense interest we have in becoming acquainted with its effects in each of them . . .

The Striking Characteristic of the Social Condition of the Anglo-Americans in its Essential Democracy

In America there are comparatively few who are rich enough to live without a profession. Every profession requires an apprenticeship, which limits the time of instruction to the early years of life. At fifteen they enter upon their calling, and thus their education ends at the age when ours begins. Whatever is done afterwards is with a view to some special and lucrative object; a science is taken up as a matter of business, and the only branch of it which is attended to is such as admits of an immediate practical application. In America most of the rich men were formerly poor; most of those who now enjoy leisure were absorbed in business during their youth; the consequence of which is, that when they might have had a taste for study they had no time for it, and when time is at their disposal they have no longer the inclination.

There is no class, then, in America, in which the taste for intellectual pleasures is transmitted with hereditary fortune and leisure, and by which the labors of the intellect are held in honor. Accordingly there is an equal want of the desire and the power of application to these objects.

A middle standard is fixed in America for human knowledge. All approach as near to it as they can; some as they rise, others as they descend. Of course, an immense multitude of persons are to be found who entertain the same number of ideas on religion, history, science, political economy, legislation, and government. The gifts of intellect proceed directly from God, and man cannot prevent their unequal distribution. But in consequence of the state of things which we have here represented it happens that, although the capacities of men are widely different, as the Creator has doubtless intended they should be, they are submitted to the same method of treatment.

In America the aristocratic element has always been feeble from its birth; and if at the present day it is not actually destroyed, it is at any rate so completely disabled that we can scarcely assign to it any degree of influence in the course of affairs. The democratic principle, on the contrary, has gained so much strength

Colonial Press, New York, 1899, I, 3, 14, 52–53, 258–59, 263–71; II, 99–105, 307–09; I, 240–43; II, 336–47.

by time, by events, and by legislation, as to have become not only predominant by all-powerful. There is no family or corporate authority, and it is rare to find even the influence of individual character enjoy any durability.

America, then, exhibits in her social state a most extraordinary phenomenon. Men are there seen on a greater equality in point of fortune and intellect, or, in other words, more equal in their strength, than in any other country of the world, or in any age of which history has preserved the remembrance . . .

Philosophical Method Among the Americans

I think that in no country in the civilized world is less attention paid to philosophy than in the United States. The Americans have no philosophical school of their own; and they care but little for all the schools into which Europe is divided, the very names of which are scarcely known to them.

Nevertheless it is easy to perceive that almost all the inhabitants of the United States conduct their understanding in the same manner, and govern it by the same rules; that is to say, that without ever having taken the trouble to define the rules of a philosophical method, they are in possession of one, common to the whole people.

To evade the bondage of system and habit, of family-maxims, class-opinions, and, in some degree, of national prejudices; to accept tradition only as a means of information, and existing facts only as a lesson used in doing otherwise and doing better; to seek the reason of things for oneself, and in oneself alone; to tend to results without being bound to means, and to aim at the substance through the form;—such are the principal characteristics of what I shall call the philosophical method of the Americans.

But if I go further, and if I seek among these characteristics that which predominates over and includes almost all the rest, I discover, that in most of the operations of the mind, each American appeals to the individual exercise of his own understanding alone.

America is therefore one of the countries in the world where philosophy is least studied, and where the precepts of Descartes are best applied. Nor is this surprising. The Americans do not read the works of Descartes, because their social condition deters them

from speculative studies; but they follow his maxims, because this very social condition naturally disposes their understanding to adopt them.

In the midst of the continual movement which agitates a democratic community, the tie which unites one generation to another is relaxed or broken; every man readily loses the trace of the ideas of his forefathers or takes no care about them

Nor can men living in this state of society derive their belief from the opinions of the class to which they belong; for, so to speak, there are no longer any classes, or those which still exist are composed of such mobile elements, that their body can never exercise a real control over its members.

As to the influence which the intelligence of one man has on that of another, it must necessarily be very limited in a country where the citizens, placed on the footing of a general similitude, are all closely seen by each other; and where, as no signs of incontestable greatness or superiority are perceived in any one of them, they are constantly brought back to their own reason as the most obvious and proximate source of truth. It is not only confidence in this or that man which is then destroyed, but the taste for trusting the *ipse dixit* of any man whatsoever. Every one shuts himself up in his own breast, and affects from that point to judge the world.

The practice which obtains among the Americans of fixing the standard of their judgement in themselves alone, leads them to other habits of mind. As they perceive that they succeed in resolving without assistance all the little difficulties which their practical life presents, they readily conclude that every thing in the world may be explained, and that nothing in it transcends the limits of the understanding. Thus they fall to denying what they cannot comprehend; which leaves them but little faith for whatever is extraordinary, and an almost insurmountable distaste for whatever is supernatural . . .

At different periods dogmatical belief is more or less abundant. It arises in different ways, and it may change its object or its form; but under no circumstances will dogmatical belief cease to exist, or, in other words, men will never cease to entertain some implicit opinions without trying them by actual discussion. If every one undertook to form his own opinions, and to seek for truth by isolated paths struck out by himself alone, it is not to be supposed that any considerable number of men would ever unite in any common belief.

But obviously without such common belief no society can prosper—say rather no society does subsist; for without ideas held in common, there is no common action, and without common action, there may still be men, but there is no social body. In order that society should exist, and, *a fortiori*, that a society should prosper, it is required that all the minds of the citizens should be rallied and held together by certain predominant ideas; and this cannot be the case, unless each of them sometimes draws his opinions from the common source, and consents to accept certain matters of belief at the hands of the community.

If I now consider man in his isolated capacity, I find that dogmatical belief is not less indispensible to him in order to live alone, than it is to enable him to co-operate with his fellow creatures. If man were forced to demonstrate to himself all the truths of which he makes daily use, his task would never end. He would exhaust his strength in preparatory exercises, without advancing beyond them. As, from the shortness of his life, he has not the time, nor, from the limits of his intelligence, the capacity to accomplish this, he is reduced to take upon trust a number of facts and opinions which he has not had either the time or the power to verify himself, but which men of greater ability have sought out, or which the world adopts. On this groundwork he raises for himself the structure of his own thoughts; nor is he led to proceed in this manner by choice, so much as he is constrained by the inflexible law of his condition.

There is no philosopher of such great parts in the world, but that he believes a million of things on the faith of other people, and supposes a great many more truths than he demonstrates.

This is not only necessary but desirable. A man who should undertake to inquire into everything for himself, could devote to each thing but little time and attention. His task would keep his mind in perpetual unrest, which would prevent him from penetrating to the depth of any truth, or of grappling his mind indissolubly to any conviction. His intellect would be at once independent and powerless. He must therefore make his choice from among the various objects of human belief, and he must adopt many opinions without discussion, in order to search the better into that smaller number which he sets

apart for investigation. It is true, that whoever receives an opinion on the word of another, does so far enslave his mind; but it is a salutary servitude which allows him to make a good use of freedom.

A principle of authority must then always occur, under all circumstances, in some part or other of the moral and intellectual world. Its place is variable, but a place it necessarily has. The independence of individual minds may be greater or it may be less: unbounded it cannot be. Thus the question is, not to know whether any intellectual authority exists in the ages of democracy, but simply where it resides and by what standard it is to be measured . . .

When the ranks of society are unequal, and men unlike each other in condition, there are some individuals invested with all the power of superior intelligence, learning, and enlightenment, while the multitude is sunk in ignorance and prejudice. Men living at these aristocratic periods are therefore naturally induced to shape their opinions by the superior standard of a person or a class of persons, while they are averse to recognise the infallibility of the mass of the people.

The contrary takes place in ages of equality. The nearer the citizens are drawn to the common level of an equal and similar condition, the less prone does each man become to place implicit faith in a certain man or a certain class of men. But his readiness to believe the multitude increases, and opinion is more than ever mistress of the world. Not only is common opinion the only guide which private judgement retains among a democratic people, but among such a people it possesses a power infinitely beyond what it has elsewhere. At periods of equality men have no faith in one another, by reason of their common resemblance; but this very resemblance gives them almost unbounded confidence in the judgement of the public; for it would not seem probable, as they are all endowed with equal means of judging, but that the greater truth should go with the greater number.

When the inhabitant of a democratic country compares himself individually with all those about him, he feels with price that he is the equal of any one of them; but when he comes to survey the totality of his fellows, and to place himself in contrast to so huge a body, he is instantly overwhelmed by the sense of his own insignificance and weakness.

The same equality which renders him independent of each of his fellow-citizens, taken severally, exposes him alone and unprotected to the influence of the greater number.

The public has therefore among a democratic people a singular power, of which aristocratic nations could never so much as conceive an idea; for it does not persuade to certain opinions, but it enforces them, and infuses them into the faculties by a sort of enormous pressure of the minds of all upon the reason of each.

In the United States the majority undertakes to supply a multitude of ready-made opinions for the use of individuals, who are thus relieved from the necessity of forming opinions of their own. Everybody there adopts great numbers of theories on philosophy, morals, and politics, without inquiry, upon public trust; and if we look to it very narrowly, it will be perceived that religion herself holds her sway there, much less as a doctrine of revelation than as a commonly received opinion.

The fact that the political laws of the Americans are such that the majority rules the community with sovereign sway, materially increases the power which that majority naturally exercises over the mind. For nothing is more customary in man than to recognise superior wisdom in the person of his oppressor. This political omnipotence of the majority in the United States doubtless augments the influence which public opinion would obtain without it over the mind of each member of the community; but the foundations of that influence do not rest upon it. They must be sought for in the principle of equality itself, not in the more or less popular institutions which men living under that condition may give themselves. The intellectual dominion of the greater number would probably be less absolute among a democratic people governed by a king than in the sphere of a pure democracy, but it will always be extremely absolute; and by whatever political laws men are governed in the ages of equality, it may be foreseen that faith in public opinion will become a species of religion there, and the majority its ministering prophet . . .

Unlimited Power of the Majority in the United States, and its Consequences

The very essence of democratic government consists in the absolute sovereignty of the majority; for there is nothing in democratic States which is capable of resisting it. Most of the American Constitutions have sought to increase this natural strength of the majority by artificial means.

The legislature is, of all political institutions, the one which is most easily swayed by the wishes of the majority. The Americans determined that the members of the legislature should be elected by the people immediately, and for a very brief term, in order to subject them, not only to the general convictions, but even to the daily passions, of their constituents. The members of both houses are taken from the same class in society, and are nominated in the same manner; so that the modifications of the legislative bodies are almost as rapid and quite as irresistible as those of a single assembly. It is to a legislature thus constituted that almost all the authority of the government has been entrusted . . .

Custom, however, has done even more than law. A proceeding which will in the end set all the guarantees of representative government at naught is becoming more and more general in the United States; it frequently happens that the electors, who choose a delegate, point out a certain line of conduct to him, and impose upon him a certain number of positive obligations which he is pledged to fulfil. With the exception of the tumult, this comes to the same thing as if the majority of the populace held its deliberations in the market-place.

Several other circumstances concur in rendering the power of the majority in America not only preponderant, but irresistible. The moral authority of the majority is partly based upon the notion that there is more intelligence and more wisdom in a great number of men collected together than in a single individual, and that the quantity of legislators is more important than their quality. The theory of equality is in fact applied to the intellect of man: and human pride is thus assailed in its last retreat by a doctrine which the minority hesitate to admit, and in which they very slowly concur. Like all other powers, and perhaps more than all other powers, the authority of the many requires the sanction of time; at first it enforces obedience by constraint, but its laws are not respected until they have long been maintained.

The right of governing society, which the majority

supposes itself to derive from its superior intelligence, was introduced into the United States by the first settlers, and this idea, which would be sufficient of itself to create a free nation, has now been amalgamated with the manners of the people and the minor incidents of social intercourse . . .

Tyranny of the Majority

It has been asserted that a people can never entirely outstep the boundaries of justice and of reason in those affairs which are more peculiarly its own, and that consequently full power may fearlessly be given to the majority by which it is represented. But this language is that of a slave. A majority taken collectively may be regarded as a being whose opinions, and most frequently whose interests, are opposed to those of another being, which is styled a minority. If it be admitted that a man, possessing absolute power, may misuse that power by wronging his adversaries, why should a majority not be liable to the same reproach? Men are not apt to change their characters by agglomeration; nor does their patience in the presence of obstacles increase with the consciousness of their strength. And for these reasons I can never willingly invest any number of my fellow-creatures with that unlimited authority which I should refuse to any one of them . . .

Unlimited power is in itself a bad and dangerous thing; human beings are not competent to exercise it with discretion, and God alone can be omnipotent, because His wisdom and His justice are always equal to His power. But no power upon earth is so worthy of honor for itself, or of reverential obedience to the rights which it represents, that I would consent to admit its uncontrolled and all-predominant authority. When I see that the right and the means of absolute command are conferred on a people or upon a king, upon an aristocracy or a democracy, a monarchy or a republic, I recognize the germ of tyranny, and I journey onward to a land of more hopeful institutions.

In my opinion the main evil of the present democratic institutions of the United States does not arise, as is often asserted in Europe, from their weakness, but from their overpowering strength; and I am not so much alarmed at the excessive liberty which reigns in that country as at the very inadequate securities which exist against tyranny.

When an individual or a party is wronged in the United States, to whom can he apply for redress? If to public opinion, public opinion constitutes the majority; if to the legislature, it represents the majority, and implicitly obeys its injunctions; if to the executive power, it is appointed by the majority, and remains a passive tool in its hands; the public troops consist of the majority under arms; the jury is the majority invested with the right of hearing judicial cases; and in certain States even the judges are elected by the majority. However iniquitous or absurd the evil of which you complain may be, you must submit to it as well as you can.

If, on the other hand, a legislative power could be so constituted as to represent the majority without necessarily being the slave of its passions; an executive, so as to retain a certain degree of uncontrolled authority; and a judiciary, so as to remain independent of the two other powers; a government would be formed which would still be democratic without incurring any risk of tyrannical abuse.

I do not say that tyrannical abuses frequently occur in America at the present day, but I maintain that no sure barrier is established against them, and that the causes which mitigate the government are to be found in the circumstances and the manners of the country more than in its laws.

Effects of the Unlimited Power of the Majority Upon the Arbitrary Authority of the American Public

A distinction must be drawn between tyranny and arbitrary power. Tyranny may be exercised by means of the law, and in that case it is not arbitrary; arbitrary power may be exercised for the good of the community at large, in which case it is not tyrannical. Tyranny usually employs arbitrary means, but, if necessary, it can rule without them . . .

Power Exercised by the Majority in America Upon Opinion

It is in the examination of the display of public opinion in the United States that we clearly perceive how far the power of the majority surpasses all the powers with which we are acquainted in Europe. Intellectual principles exercise an influence which is so invisible, and often so inappreciable, that they baffle the toils of oppression. At the present time the most absolute monarchs in Europe are unable to prevent certain notions, which are opposed to their authority, from circulating in secret throughout their dominions, and even in their courts. Such is not the case in America; as long as the majority is still undecided, discussion is carried on; but as soon as its decision is irrevocably pronounced, a submissive silence is observed, and the friends, as well as the opponents, of the measure unite in assenting to its propriety. The reason of this is perfectly clear: no monarch is so absolute as to combine all the powers of society in his own hands, and to conquer all opposition with the energy of a majority which is invested with the right of making and of executing the laws.

The authority of a king is purely physical, and it controls the actions of the subject without subduing his private will; but the majority possess a power which is physical and moral at the same time; it acts upon the will as well as upon the actions of men, and it represses not only all contest, but all controversy.

I know no country in which there is so little true independence of mind and freedom of discussion as in America. In any constitutional state in Europe every sort of religious and political theory may be advocated and propagated abroad; for there is no country in Europe so subdued by any single authority as not to contain citizens who are ready to protect the man who raises his voice in the cause of truth from the consequences of his hardihood. If he is unfortunate enough to live under an absolute government, the people is upon his side; if he inhabits a free country, he may find a shelter behind the authority of the throne, if he require one. The aristocratic part of society supports him in some countries, and the democracy in others. But in a nation where democratic institutions exist, organized like those of the United States, there is but one sole authority, one single element of strength and of success, with nothing beyond it.

In America the majority raises very formidable barriers to the liberty of opinion: within these barriers an author may write whatever he pleases, but he will repent it if he ever step beyond them. Not that he is exposed to the terrors of an *auto-da-fé*, but he is tormented by the slights and persecutions of daily

obloquy. His political career is closed forever, since he has offended the only authority which is able to promote his success. Every sort of compensation, even that of celebrity, is refused to him. Before he published his opinions he imagined that he held them in common with many others; but no sooner has he declared them openly than he is loudly censured by his overbearing opponents, whilst those who think without having the courage to speak, like him, abandon him in silence. He yields at length, oppressed by the daily efforts he has been making, and he subsides into silence, as if he was tormented by remorse for having spoken the truth.

Fetters and headsmen were the coarse instruments which tyranny formerly employed; but the civilization of our age has refined the arts of despotism which seemed, however, to have been sufficiently perfected before. The excesses of monarchical power had devised a variety of physical means of oppression: the democratic republics of the present day have rendered it as entirely an affair of the mind as that will which it is intended to coerce. Under the absolute sway of an individual despot the body was attacked in order to subdue the soul, and the soul escaped the blows which were directed against it and rose superior to the attempt; but such is not the course adopted by tyranny in democratic republics; there the body is left free, and the soul is enslaved. The sovereign can no longer say, "You shall think as I do on pain of death;" but he says, "You are free to think differently from me, and to retain your life, your property, and all that you possess; but if such be your determination, you are henceforth an alien among your people. You may retain your civil rights, but they will be useless to you, for you will never be chosen by your fellow-citizens if you solicit their suffrages, and they will affect to scorn you if you solicit their esteem. You will remain among men, but you will be deprived of the rights of mankind. Your fellow-creatures will shun you like an impure being, and those who are most persuaded of your innocence will abandon you too, lest they should be shunned in their turn. Go in peace! I have given you your life, but it is an existence incomparably worse than death."

Effects of the Tyranny of the Majority Upon the National Character of the Americans

The tendencies which I have just alluded to are as yet very slightly perceptible in political society, but they already begin to exercise an unfavorable influence upon the national character of the Americans. I am inclined to attribute the singular paucity of distinguished political characters to the ever-increasing activity of the despotism of the majority in the United States. When the American Revolution broke out they arose in great numbers, for public opinion then served, not to tyrannize over, but to direct the exertions of individuals. Those celebrated men took a full part in the general agitation of mind common at that period, and they attained a high degree of personal fame, which was reflected back upon the nation, but which was by no means borrowed from it. . .

In absolute governments the great nobles who are nearest the throne flatter the passions of the sovereign, and voluntarily truckle to his caprices. But the mass of the nation does not degrade itself by servitude . . .

. . . In democratic republics, where public life is incessantly commingled with domestic affairs, where the sovereign authority is accessible on every side, and where its attention can almost always be attracted by vociferation, more persons are to be met with who speculate upon its foibles and live at the cost of its passions than in absolute monarchies . . .

Democratic republics extend the practice of currying favor with the many, and they introduce it into a greater number of classes at once: this is one of the most serious reproaches that can be addressed to them. In democratic States organized on the principles of the American republics, this is more especially the case, where the authority of the majority is so absolute and so irresistible that a man must give up his rights as a citizen, and almost abjure his quality as a human being, if he intends to stray from the track which it lays down . . .

Influence of Democracy on the Feelings of the Americans

The first and most intense passion which is engendered by the equality of conditions is, I need hardly say, the love of that same equality. My readers will therefore not be surprised that I speak of it before all others.

Everybody has remarked that in our time, and especially in France, this passion for equality is every day gaining ground in the human heart. It has been said a hundred times that our contemporaries are far more ardently and tenaciously attached to equality than to freedom; but as I do not find that the causes of the fact have been sufficiently analyzed, I shall endeavor to point them out.

It is possible to imagine an extreme point at which freedom and equality would meet and be confounded together. Let us suppose that all the members of the community take a part in the government, and that each one of them has an equal right to take a part in it. As none is different from his fellows, none can exercise a tyrannical power: men will be perfectly free, because they will all be entirely equal; and they will all be perfectly equal, because they will be entirely free. To this ideal state democratic nations tend. Such is the completest form that equality can assume upon earth; but there are a thousand others which, without being equally perfect, are not less cherished by those nations.

The principle of equality may be established in civil society, without prevailing in the political world. Equal rights may exist of indulging in the same pleasures, of entering the same professions, of frequenting the same places—in a word, of living in the same manner and seeking wealth by the same means, although all men do not take an equal share in the government. A kind of equality may even be established in the political world, though there should be no political freedom there. A man may be the equal of all his countrymen save one, who is the master of all without distinction, and who selects equally from among them all the agents of his power. Several other combinations might be easily imagined, by which every great quality would be united to institutions more or less free, or even to institutions wholly without freedom. Although men cannot become absolutely equal unless they be entirely free, and consequently equality, pushed to its furthest extent, may be confounded with freedom, yet there is good reason for distinguishing the one from the other. The taste which men have for liberty, and that which they feel for equality, are, in fact, two different things; and I am not afraid to add that, amongst democratic nations, they are two unequal things.

Upon close inspection, it will be seen that there is

in every age some peculiar and preponderating fact with which all others are connected; this fact almost always gives birth to some pregnant idea or some ruling passion, which attracts to itself, and bears away in its course, all the feelings and opinions of the time: it is like a great stream, towards which each of the surrounding rivulets seems to flow. Freedom has appeared in the world at different times and under various forms; it has not been exclusively bound to any social condition, and it is not confined to democracies. Freedom cannot, therefore, form the distinguishing characteristic of democratic ages. The peculiar and preponderating fact which marks those ages as its own is the equality of conditions; the ruling passion of men in those periods is the love of this equality. Ask not what singular charm the men of democratic ages find in being equal, or what special reasons they may have for clinging so tenaciously to equality rather than to the other advantages which society holds out to them: equality is the distinguishing characteristic of the age they live in; that, of itself, is enough to explain that they prefer it to all the rest . . .

That political freedom may compromise in its excesses the tranquillity, the property, the lives of individuals, is obvious to the narrowest and most un-thinking minds. But, on the contrary, none but at-tentive and clear-sighted men perceive the perils with which equality threatens us, and they commonly avoid pointing them out. They know that the calamities they apprehend are remote, and flatter themselves that they will only fall upon future genera-tions, for which the present generation takes but little thought. The evils which freedom sometimes brings with it are immediate; they are apparent to all, and all are more or less affected by them. The evils which extreme equality may produce are slowly disclosed; they creep gradually into the social frame; they are only seen at intervals, and at the moment at which they become most violent habit already causes them to be no longer felt. The advantages which freedom brings are only shown by length of time; and it is al-ways easy to mistake the cause in which they originate. The advantages of equality are instantaneous, and they may constantly be traced from their source. Political liberty bestows exalted pleasures, from time to time, upon a certain number of citizens.

Equality every day confers a number of small enjoy-ments on every man. The charms of equality are every instant felt and are within the reach of all; the noblest hearts are not insensible to them, and the most vulgar souls exult in them. The passion which equality engenders must therefore be at once strong and general. Men cannot enjoy political liberty un-purchased by some sacrifices, and they never obtain it without great exertions. But the pleasures of equality are self-proffered: each of the petty incidents of life seems to occasion them, and in order to taste them nothing is required but to live . . .

I think that democratic communities have a natural taste for freedom: left to themselves, they will seek it, cherish it, and view any privation of it with regret. But for equality, their passion is ardent, insatiable, incessant, invincible: they call for equality in freedom; and if they cannot obtain that, they still call for equality in slavery. They will endure poverty, servitude, barbarism—but they will not endure aristoc-racy. This is true at all times, and especially true in our own. All men and all powers seeking to cope with this irresistible passion, will be overthrown and destroyed by it. In our age, freedom cannot be established with-out it, and despotism itself cannot reign without its support . . .

I have shown how it is that in ages of equality every man seeks for his opinions within himself: I am now about to show how it is that, in the same ages, all his feelings are turned towards himself alone. Individualism is a novel expression, to which a novel idea has given birth. Our fathers were only acquainted with egotism. Egotism is a passionate and exaggerated love of self, which leads a man to connect everything with his own person, and to prefer himself to every-thing in the world. Individualism is a mature and calm feeling, which disposes each member of the community to sever himself from the mass of his fellow-creatures; and to draw apart with his family and his friends; so that, after he has thus formed a little circle of his own, he willingly leaves society at large to itself. Egotism originates in blind instinct: individualism proceeds from erroneous judgment more than from depraved feelings; it originates as much in the deficiencies of the mind as in the perversity of the heart. Egotism blights the germ of all virtue; individualism, at first, only saps the virtues of public life; but, in the long run, it attacks and destroys all others, and is at length absorbed in downright egotism. Egotism is a vice as old as the world, which does not belong to one form of society more that to another: individualism is of democratic origin, and it threatens to spread in the same ratio as the equality of conditions.

Amongst aristocratic nations, as families remain for centuries in the same condition, often on the same spot, all generations become as it were contemporaneous. A man almost always knows his forefathers, and respects them: he thinks he already sees his remote descendants, and he loves them. He willingly imposes duties on himself towards the former and the latter; and he will frequently sacrifice his personal gratifications to those who went before and to those who will come after him. Aristocratic institutions have, moreover, the effect of closely binding every man to several of his fellow-citizens. As the classes of an aristocratic people are strongly marked and permanent, each of them is regarded by its own members as a sort of lesser country, more tangible and more cherished than the country at large. As in aristocratic communities all the citizens occupy fixed positions, one above the other, the result is that each of them always sees a man above himself whose patronage is necessary to him, and below himself another man whose co-operation he may claim. Men living in aristocratic ages are therefore almost always closely attached to something placed out of their own sphere, and they are often disposed to forget themselves. It is true that in those ages the notion of human fellowship is faint, and that men seldom think of sacrificing themselves for mankind; but they often sacrifice themselves for other men. In democratic ages, on the contrary, when the duties of each individual to the race are much more clear, devoted service to any one man becomes more rare; the bond of human affection is extended, but it is relaxed . . .

. . . Aristocracy had made a chain of all the members of the community, from the peasant to the king: democracy breaks that chain, and severs every link of it. As social conditions become more equal, the number of persons increases who although they are neither rich enough nor powerful enough to exercise any great influence over their fellow-creatures, have nevertheless acquired or retained sufficient education and

fortune to satisfy their own wants. They owe nothing to any man, they expect nothing from any man; they acquire the habit of always considering themselves as standing alone, and they are apt to imagine that their whole destiny is in their own hands. Thus not only does democracy make every man forget his ancestors, but it hides his descendants, and separates his contemporaries from him; it throws him back forever upon himself alone, and threatens in the end to confine him entirely within the solitude of his own heart . . .

If it be true that, in ages of equality, men readily adopt the notion of a great central power, it cannot be doubted on the other hand that their habits and sentiments predispose them to recognize such a power and to give it their support . . . As the men who inhabit democratic countries have no superiors, no inferiors, and no habitual or necessary partners in their undertakings, they readily fall back upon themselves and consider themselves as being apart. I had occasion to point this out at considerable length in treating of individualism. Hence such men can never, without an effort, tear themselves from their private affairs to engage in public business; their natural bias leads them to abandon the latter to the sole visible and permanent representative of the interests of the community, that is to say, to the State. Not only are they naturally wanting in a taste for public business, but they have frequently no time to attend to it. Private life is so busy in democratic periods, so excited, so full of wishes and of work, that hardly any energy or leisure remains to each individual for public life. I am the last man to contend that these propensities are unconquerable, since my chief object in writing this book has been to combat them. I only maintain that at the present day a secret power is fostering them in the human heart, and that if they are not checked they will wholly overgrow it.

I have also had occasion to show how the increasing love of well-being, and the fluctuating character of property, cause democratic nations to dread all violent disturbance. The love of public tranquillity is frequently the only passion which these nations retain, and it becomes more active and powerful amongst them in proportion as all other passions droop and die. This naturally disposes the members of the community constantly to give or to surrender additional rights to the central power, which alone seems to be interested in defending them by the same means that it uses to defend itself. As in ages of equality no man is compelled to lend his assistance to his fellow-men, and none has any right to expect much support from them, everyone is at once independent and powerless. These two conditions, which must never be either separately considered or confounded together, inspire the citizen of a democratic country with very contrary propensities. His independence fills him with self-reliance and pride amongst his equals; his debility makes him feel from time to time the want of some outward assistance, which he cannot expect from any of them, because they are all impotent and unsympathizing. In this predicament he naturally turns his eyes to that imposing power which alone rises above the level of universal depression . . .

I believe that it is easier to establish an absolute and despotic government amongst a people in which the conditions of society are equal, than amongst any other; and I think that if such a government were once established amongst such a people, it would not only oppress men, but would eventually strip each of them of several of the highest qualities of humanity. Despotism therefore appears to me peculiarly to be dreaded in democratic ages. I should have loved freedom, I believe, at all times, but in the time in which we live I am ready to worship it. On the other hand, I am persuaded that all who shall attempt, in the ages upon which we are entering, to base freedom upon aristocratic privilege, will fail — that all who shall attempt to draw and to retain authority within a single class, will fail . . . Thus the question is not how to reconstruct aristocratic society, but how to make liberty proceed out of that democratic state of society in which God has placed us.

These two truths appear to me simple, clear, and fertile in consequences; and they naturally lead me to consider what kind of free government can be established amongst a people in which social conditions are equal.

It results from the very constitution of democratic nations and from their necessities, that the power of government amongst them must be more uniform, more centralized, more extensive, more searching, and more efficient than in other countries. Society at large is naturally stronger and more active, individuals more subordinate and weak; the former does more, the latter less; and this is inevitably the case. It is not therefore to be expected that the range of private independence will ever be as extensive in democratic as in aristocratic countries — nor is this to be desired; for, amongst aristocratic nations, the mass is often sacrificed to the individual, and the prosperity of the greater number to the greatness of the few. It is both necessary and desirable that the government of a democratic people should be active and powerful: and our object should not be to render it weak or indolent, but solely to prevent it from abusing its aptitude and its strength.

The circumstance which most contributed to secure the independence of private persons in aristocratic ages, was, that the supreme power did not affect to take upon itself alone the government and administration of the community; those functions were necessarily partially left to the members of the aristocracy: so that as the supreme power was always divided, it never weighed with its whole weight and in the same manner on each individual. Not only did the government not perform everything by its immediate agency; but as most of the agents who discharged its duties derived their power not from the State, but from the circumstance of their birth, they were not perpetually under its control. The government could not make or unmake them in an instant, at pleasure, nor bend them in strict uniformity to its slightest caprice — this was an additional guarantee of private independence. I readily admit that recourse cannot be had to the same means at the present time: but I discover certain democratic expedients which may be substituted for them. Instead of vesting in the government alone all the administrative powers of which corporations and nobles have been deprived, a portion of them may be entrusted to secondary public bodies, temporarily composed of private citizens: thus the liberty of private persons will be more secure, and their equality will not be diminished . . .

In periods of aristocracy every man is always bound so closely to many of his fellow-citizens, that he cannot be assailed without their coming to his assistance. In ages of equality every man naturally stands alone; he has no hereditary friends whose co-operation he may demand — no class upon whose sym-

pathy he may rely: he is easily got rid of, and he is
trampled on with impunity. At the present time, an
oppressed member of the community has therefore
only one method of self-defence — he may appeal to
the whole nation; and if the whole nation is deaf to
his complaint, he may appeal to mankind . . .

What the Real Advantages Are Which American Society Derives From the Government of the Democracy

. . . I am induced to remind the reader of what I have
more than once adverted to in the course of this book.
The political institutions of the United States appear
to me to be one of the forms of government which a
democracy may adopt; but I do not regard the American Constitution as the best, or as the only one, which
a democratic people may establish. In showing the
advantages which the Americans derive from the government of democracy, I am therefore very far from
meaning, or from believing, that similar advantages can
only be obtained from the same laws.

The defects and the weaknesses of a democratic
government may very readily be discovered; they are
demonstrated by the most flagrant instances, whilst
its beneficial influence is less perceptible exercised.
A single glance suffices to detect its evil consequences,
but its good qualities can only be discerned by long
observation. The laws of the American democracy
are frequently defective or incomplete; they sometimes attack vested rights, or give a sanction to others
which are dangerous to the community; but even if
they were good, the frequent changes which they
undergo would be an evil. How comes it, then, that
the American republics prosper and maintain their
position?

In the consideration of laws a distinction must
be carefully observed between the end at which they
aim and the means by which they are directed to that
end, between their absolute and their relative excellence.
If it be the intention of the legislator to favor the
interests of the minority at the expense of the majority,
and if the measures he takes are so combined as to
accomplish the object he has in view with the least
possible expense of time and exertion, the law may be
well drawn up, although its purpose be bad; and the
more efficacious it is, the greater is the mischief which
it causes.

Democratic laws generally tend to promote the
welfare of the greatest possible number; for they emanate from the majority of the citizens, who are subject to error, but who cannot have an interest opposed
to their own advantage. The laws of an aristocracy
tend, on the contrary, to concentrate wealth and
power in the hands of the minority, because an
aristocracy, by its very nature, constitutes a minority.
It may therefore be asserted, as a general proposition,
that the purpose of a democracy in the conduct of
its legislation is useful to a greater number of citizens
than that of an aristocracy. This is, however, the sum
total of its advantages.

Aristocracies are infinitely more expert in the
science of legislation than democracies ever can be.
They are possessed of a self-control which protects
them from the errors of temporary excitement, and
they form lasting designs which they mature with
the assistance of favorable opportunities. Aristocratic government proceeds with the dexterity of art;
it understands how to make the collective force of
all its laws coverge at the same time to a given point.
Such is not the case with democracies, whose laws are
almost always ineffective or inopportune. The means
of democracy are therefore more imperfect than those
of aristocracy, and the measures which it unwittingly
adopts are frequently opposed to its own cause; but
the object it has in view is more useful . . .

An analogous observation may be made respecting public officers. It is easy to perceive that the
American democracy frequently errs in the choice
of the individuals to whom it entrusts the power of
the administration; but it is more difficult to say
why the State prospers under their rule. In the first
place it is to be remarked, that if in a democratic
State the governors have less honesty and less capacity
than elsewhere, the governed, on the other hand, are
more enlightened and more attentive to their interests.
As the people in democracies is more incessantly
vigilant in its affairs and more jealous of its rights, it
prevents its representatives from abandoning that
general line of conduct which its own interest prescribes. In the second place, it must be remembered
that if the democratic magistrate is more apt to
misuse his power, he possesses it for a shorter period
of time . . .

No political form has hitherto been discovered

which is equally favorable to the prosperity and the development of all the classes into which society is divided. These classes continue to form, as it were, a certain number of distinct nations in the same nation: and experience has shown that it is no less dangerous to place the fate of these classes exclusively in the hands of any one of them than it is to make one people the arbiter of the destiny of another. When the rich alone govern, the interest of the poor is always endangered; and when the poor make the laws, that of the rich incurs very serious risks. The advantage of democracy does not consist, therefore, as has sometimes been asserted, in favoring the prosperity of all, but simply in contributing to the well-being of the greatest possible number.

The men who are entrusted with the direction of public affairs in the United States are frequently inferior, both in point of capacity and of morality, to those whom aristocratic institutions would raise to power. But their interest is identified and confounded with that of the majority of their fellow-citizens. They may frequently be faithless and frequently mistaken, but they will never systematically adopt a line of conduct opposed to the will of the majority; and it is impossible that they should give a dangerous or an exclusive tendency to the government . . .

I shall conclude by one general idea, which comprises not only all the particular ideas which have been expressed in the present chapter, but also most of those which it is the object of this book to treat of. In the ages of aristocracy which preceded our own, there were private persons of great power, and a social authority of extreme weakness. The outline of society itself was not easily discernible, and constantly confounded with the different powers by which the community was ruled. The principal efforts of the men of those times were required to strengthen, aggrandize, and secure the supreme power; and on the other hand, to circumscribe individual independence within narrower limits, and to subject private interests to the interests of the public. Other perils and other cares await the men of our age. Amongst the greater part of modern nations, the government, whatever may be its origin, its constitution, or its name, has become almost omnipotent, and private persons are falling, more and more, into the lowest stage of weakness and dependence. In olden society everything was different;

unity and uniformity were nowhere to be met with. In modern society everything threatens to become so much alike, that the peculiar characteristics of each individual will soon be entirely lost in the general aspect of the world . . . The good things and the evils of life are more equally distributed in the world: great wealth tends to disappear, the number of small fortunes to increase; desires and gratifications are multiplied, but extraordinary prosperity and irremediable penury are alike unknown. The sentiment of ambition is universal, but the scope of ambition is seldom vast. Each individual stands apart in solitary weakness; but society at large is active, provident, and powerful: the performances of private persons are insignificant, those of the State immense. There is little energy of character; but manners are mild, and laws humane. If there be few instances of exalted heroism or of virtues of the highest, brightest, and purest temper, men's habits are regular, violence is rare, and cruelty almost unknown. Human existence becomes longer, and property more secure: life is not adorned with brilliant trophies, but it is extremely easy and tranquil. Few pleasures are either very refined or very coarse; and highly polished manners are as uncommon as great brutality of tastes. Neither men of great learning, nor extremely ignorant communities, are to be met with; genius becomes more rare, information more diffused. The human mind is impelled by the small efforts of all mankind combined together, not by the strenuous activity of certain men. There is less perfection, but more abundance, in all the productions of the arts. The ties of race, of rank, and of country are relaxed; the great bond of humanity is strengthened. If I endeavor to find out the most general and the most prominent of all these different characteristics, I shall have occasion to perceive, that what is taking place in men's fortunes manifests itself under a thousand other forms. Almost all extremes are softened or blunted: all that was most prominent is superseded by some mean term, at once less lofty and less low, less brilliant and less obscure, than what before existed in the world.

. . . For myself, who now look back from this extreme limit of my task, and discover from afar, but at once, the various objects which have attracted my more attentive investigation upon my way, I am full of apprehensions and of hopes. I perceive mighty dangers which it is possible to ward off — mighty evils which may be avoided or alleviated; and I cling with a firmer hold to the belief, that for democratic nations to be virtuous and prosperous they require but to will it. I am aware that many of my contemporaries maintain that nations are never their own masters here below, and that they necessarily obey some insurmountable and unintelligent power, arising from anterior events, from their race, or from the soil and climate of their country. Such principles are false and cowardly; such principles can never produce aught but feeble men and pusillanimous nations. Providence has not created mankind entirely independent or entirely free. It is true that around every man a fatal circle is traced, beyond which he cannot pass; but within the wide verge of that circule he is powerful and free: as it is with man, so with communities. The nations of our time cannot prevent the conditions of men from becoming equal; but it depends upon themselves whether the principle of equality is to lead them to servitude or freedom, to knowledge or barbarism, to prosperity or to wretchedness.

New York: Constitutional Convention debates (1821)

Mr. N. Sanford took the floor. The question before us is the right of suffrage — who shall, or who shall not, have the right to vote. The committee have presented the scheme they thought best; to abolish all existing distinctions, and make the right of voting uniform. Is this not right? Where did these distinctions arise? They arose from British precedents. In England, they have their three estates, which must always have their separate interests represented. Here there is but one estate — the people. To me, the only qualifications seems to be, the virtue and morality of the people; and if they may be safely entrusted to vote for one class of our rulers, why not for all? In my opinion, these distinctions are fallacious. We have the experience of almost all the other states against them. The principle of the scheme now proposed, is that those who bear the burthens of the state, should choose those that rule it. There is no privilege given to property, as such; but those who contribute to the public support, we consider as entitled to a share in the election of rulers. The burthens are annual, and the elec-

tions are annual, and this appears proper. To me, and the majority of the committee, it appeared the only reasonable scheme that those who are to be affected by the acts of the government, should be annually entitled to vote for those who administer it. Our taxes are of two sorts, on real and personal property. The payment of a tax on either, we thought, equally entitled a man to a vote, and thus we intended to destroy the odious distinctions of property which now exist. But we have considered personal service, in some cases, equivalent to a tax on personal property, as in work on the high roads. This is a burthen, and should entitle those subject to it to equivalent privileges . . . But, after admitting all these persons, what restrictions, it will be said, are left on the right of suffrage? 1st. The voter must be a citizen. 2d. The service required must be performed within the year, on the principle that taxation is annual, and election annual; so that when the person ceases to contribute or serve, he ceases to vote.

A residence is also required. We proposed the term of six months, because we find it already in the constitution; but we propose this residence in the state, and not in the county or town, so that wherever a voter may be at the time of election, he may vote there, if he has been a resident of the state for six months . . . Now, sir, this scheme will embrace almost the whole male population of the state. There is perhaps no subject so purely matter of opinion, as the question how far the right of suffrage may be safely carried. We propose to carry it almost as far as the male population of the state . . .

Mr. Ross. Mr. Chairman . . . feeling a responsibility in common with the members of that committee, I may perhaps be permitted to state, as concisely as I can, in addition to the views just submitted by the honourable chairman of that committee some of the motives which led to the provisions contained in that report. The subject now submitted, may be viewed as one of deep and interesting importance; inasmuch as it discriminates who among our fellow citizens shall be allowed to exercise the high privilege of designating, by their votes, who shall represent them in their wants and their wishes, in the various and multiplied concerns of legislation and civil government. In every free state, the electors ought to form the basis, the soil from which every thing is to spring, relating to

Reports of the Proceedings and Debates of the Convention of 1821, E. and E. Horsford, Albany, N.Y., 1821, pp. 178–90, 199–201, 218–24, 239–42.

the administration of their political concerns. Otherwise it could not be denominated a government of the people. This results from the immutable principle, that civil government is instituted for the benefit of the governed. — Consequently all, at least, who contribute to the support or defence of the state, have a just claim to exercise the elective privilege, if consistent with the safety and welfare of the citizens. It is immaterial whether that support or defence of the state be by the payment of money, or by personal service, which are precisely one and the same thing: that of taxation . . . It gives a liberal extension to that privilege, which, unquestionably, a vast majority of our constituents will demand at our hands, and which we can have no wish to withhold, unless to perpetuate those odious distinctions which have hitherto so long and so justly been complained of. — This is one of the crying evils for which we were sent here to provide a remedy . . .

That all men are free and equal, according to the usual declarations, applies to them only in a state of nature, and not after the institution of civil government: for then many rights, flowing from a natural equality, are necessarily abridged, with a view to produce the greatest amount of security and happiness to the whole community. On this principle the right of suffrage is extended to white men only. But why, it will probably be asked, are blacks to be excluded? I answer, because they are seldom, if ever, required to share in the common burthens or defence of the state. There are also additional reasons; they are a peculiar people, incapable, in my judgment, of exercising that privilege with any sort of discretion, prudence, or independence. They have no just conceptions of civil liberty. They know not how to appreciate it, and are consequently indifferent to its preservation.

Under such circumstances, it would hardly be compatible with the safety of the state, to entrust such a people with this right. It is not thought advisable to permit aliens to vote, neither would it be safe to extend it to the blacks. We deny to minors this right, and why? Because they are deemed incapable of exercising it discreetly, and therefore not safely, for the good of the whole community. — Even the better part of creation, as my honourable friend from Oneida, (Mr. N. Williams,) stiles them, are not permitted to participate in this right. No sympathies seemed to be awakened in their behalf, nor in behalf of the aborigines, the original and only rightful proprietors of our soil — a people altogether more acute and discerning, and in whose judicious exercise of the right I should repose far more confidence, than in the African race. In nearly all the western and southern states, indeed many others, even in Connecticut, where steady habits and correct principles prevail, the blacks are excluded. And gentlemen have been frequently in the habit of citing the precedents of our sister states for our guide; and would it not be well to listen to the decisive weight of precedents furnished in this case also? It is true that in many of the states the black population is more numerous than in ours. Then, sir, if the exclusion be unjust or improper, that injustice would be of so much greater extent. The truth is, this exclusion invades no inherent rights, nor has it any connection at all with the question of slavery. The practice of every state in the union, is to make such exceptions, limitations, and provisions in relation to the elective privilege, under their respective constitutions, as are deemed to be necessary or consistent with public good — varied in each according to the existing circumstances under which they are made. It must therefore necessarily rest on the ground of expediency. And, sir, I fear that an extension to the blacks would serve to invite that kind of population to this state, an occurrence which I should most sincerely deplore . . .

Mr. Jay. When this Convention was first assembled, it was generally understood that provisions would be made to extend the right of suffrage, and some were apprehensive that it might be extended to a degree which they could not approve. But, sir, it was not expected that this right was in any instance to be restricted, much less was it anticipated, or desired, that a single person was to be disfranchised. Why, sir, are these men to be excluded from rights which they possess in common with their countrymen? What crime have they committed for which they are to be punished? Why are they, who were born as free as ourselves, natives of the same country, and deriving from nature and our political institutions, the same rights and privileges which we have, now to be deprived of all those rights, and doomed to remain forever as aliens among us? We are told, in reply, that other states have set us the example. It is true that other states treat this race of men with cruelty and injustice, and that we have hitherto manifested towards them a disposition to be just and liberal. Yet even in Virginia and North-Carolina, free people of colour are permitted to vote, and if I am correctly informed, exercise that privilege. In Pennsylvania, they are much more numerous than they are here, and there they are not disfranchised, nor has any inconvenience been felt from extending to all men the rights which ought to be common to all. In Connecticut, it is true, they have, for the last three years, adopted a new constitution which prevents people of colour from acquiring the right of suffrage in future, yet even there they have preserved the right to all those who previously possessed it.

Mr. Chairman, I would submit to the consideration of the committee, whether the proposition of the gentleman from Saratoga is consistent with the constitution of the United States. That instrument provides that "citizens of each state shall be entitled to all the privileges and immunities of citizens in the several states." No longer ago than last November, the legislature of this state almost unanimously resolved, that "if the provisions contained in any proposed constitution of a new state, deny to any citizens of the existing states the privileges and immunities of citizens of such new state, that such proposed constitution should not be accepted or confirmed; the same in the opinion of this legislature being void by the constitution of the United States." Now, sir, is not the right of suffrage a privilege? And can you deny it to a citizen of Pennsylvania who comes here and complies with your laws, merely because he is not six feet high, or because he is of a dark complexion?

But we are told by one of the select committee, that people of colour are incapable of exercising the right of suffrage. I may have misunderstood that gentleman; but I thought he meant to say, that they laboured under a physical disability. It is true that some philosophers have held that the intellect of a black man, is naturally inferior to that of a white one; but this idea has been so completely refuted, and is now so universally exploded, that I did not expect to have heard of it in an assembly so enlightened as this, nor do I now think it necessary to disprove it. That in general the people of colour are inferior to the whites in knowledge and in industry, I shall not deny. You made them slaves, and nothing is more true than the

ancient saying, "The day you make a man a slave takes half his worth away." Unaccustomed to provide for themselves, and habituated to regard labour as an evil, it is no wonder that when set free, they should be improvident and idle, and that their children should be brought up without education, and without prudence or forethought. But will you punish the children for your own crimes; for the injuries which you have inflicted upon their parents? Besides, sir, this state of things is fast passing away. Schools have been opened for them, and it will, I am sure, give pleasure to this committee to know, that in these schools there is discovered a thirst for instruction, and a progress in learning, seldom to be seen in the other schools of the state. They have also churches of their own, and clergymen of their own colour, who conduct their public worship with perfect decency and order, and not without ability.

This state, Mr. Chairman, has taken high ground against slavery, and all its degrading consequences and accompaniments. There are gentlemen on this floor, who, to their immortal honour, have defended the cause of this oppressed people in congress, and I trust they will not now desert them. Adopt the amendment now proposed, and you will hear a shout of triumph and a hiss of scorn from the southern part of the union, which I confess will mortify me—I shall shrink at the sound, because I fear it will be deserved. But it has been said that this measure is necessary to preserve the purity of your elections. I do not deny that necessity has no law, and that self-preservation may justify in states, as well as in individuals, an infringement of the rights of others. Were I a citizen of one of the southern states, I would not (much as I abhor slavery) advise an immediate and universal emancipation. But where is the necessity in the present instance? The whole number of coloured people in the state, whether free or in bondage, amounts to less than a fortieth part of the whole population. When your numbers are to theirs as forty to one, do you still fear them? To assert this, would be to pay them a compliment which, I am sure, you do not think they deserve. But there are a great number in the city of New-York. How many? Sir, in even that city, the whites are to the blacks as ten to one. And even of the tenth which is composed of the black population, how few are there that are entitled to vote? It has also been said that their numbers are rapidly increasing. The very reverse is the fact. During the last ten years, in which the white population had advanced with astonishing rapidity, the coloured population of the state has been stationary. This fact appears from the official returns of the last and the preceding census, and completely refutes the arguments which are founded upon this mis-statement. Will you, then, without necessity, and merely to gratify an unreasonable prejudice, stain the constitution you are about to form, with a provision equally odious and unjust, and in direct violation of the principles which you profess, and upon which you intend to form it? I trust, I am sure, you will not.

Gen. Root, after a few introductory remarks, and observations upon the order in which the amendments had been proposed . . . proceeded to explain his views of the social compact . . .

In the formation of a social compact, which generally grows out of exigency, when the people are but a little removed from their barbarous and rude state, they are not particular in enumerating the principles upon which they thus unite; but when they become more enlightened, they will undertake to say who shall belong to their family.

In my judgment, every one who is taken into the bosom of that family, and made to contribute, either in property or personal service, to the benefit of that family, should have a voice in managing its concerns. It cannot be denied, that the preservation of property is a much less consideration, than that of a security in our liberty and independence. Every member of this political family, who is worthy to be one of its members, will prize much higher the freedom of the country, than the preservation of property.

Sir, for the preservation, or protection, of property, you require a contribution in property towards the public fund—you do this in the case of an alien, who may hold property and be protected by the laws of your country, in the enjoyment of that property; but he is not allowed to vote. An alien is sometimes permitted, by a particular law to hold property; and if he is an able bodied man, he is required to fight in defence of this country, yet he is not allowed to vote. The reasons are, that notwithstanding he may live among us and enjoy the benefit

of our freedom, he may have a partiality for some foreign country; therefore, he is not to partake fully of our privileges till after a certain probationary season. The black population have a right to hold property, and are protected in the enjoyment of it by our laws: but, sir, in case of an invasion or insurrection, neither the alien nor black man is bound to defend your country. They are not called on, because it is supposed there is no reliance to be placed in them, they might desert the standard and join your enemy—they have not any anchorage in your country which the government is willing to trust.

Then under this view of the subject, it appears to me they cannot complain at being excluded from voting, inasmuch as they are not bound to assist in the defence of the country; but have their liberty secured to them. It would be improper that they should come forward and vote for the election of a commander in chief, whom they were not bound to obey. We have been told by the honourable gentleman from Westchester, (Mr. Jay) and shall be again told, that we are about to deprive these people of a franchise, with which they are now vested. Sir, it is impossible to remodel your constitution without changing the relative rights of your citizens. It is said that these people are now entitled to vote under our constitution, and that it is proposed to deprive them of this privilege—Are there not others who are in a measure disfranchised by the report of this committee, which requires nothing but a residence, and to have paid taxes, to qualify a man to vote for governor and senators? . . .

At present the number of blacks who are voters is so small, that if they were scattered all over the state, there would not be much danger to be apprehended; but if we may judge of the future by the past, I should suppose there was some cause of alarm—when a few hundred free negroes of the city of New York, following the train of those who ride in their coaches, and whose shoes and boots they had so often blacked, shall go to the polls of the election and change the political condition of the whole state. A change in the representation of that city may cause a change in your assembly, by giving a majority to a particular party, which would vary your council of appointment who make the highest officers of your government— Thus would the whole state be controlled by a few hundred of this species of population in the city of New-York.

This is not all, in time of war these people who are not called on to fight your battles, may make the majority of your legislature, which will defeat every measure for the prosecution of that war; so that instead of being an "organized corps" to fight your battles, they may be an "organized corps" to defeat the energies of the state with all its patriotic exertions . . .

Mr. R. Clarke said he rose with considerable embarrassment, knowing the weight of experience, talent, and elocution opposed to him. I am, said Mr. C. opposed to my honourable colleague (Mr. Root) on this question, to whose judgment and experience I have generally been willing to pay due deference. I am unwilling to retain the word "white," because its detention is repugnant to all the principles and notions of liberty, to which we have heretofore professed to adhere, and to our declaration of independence, which is a concise and just expose of those principles. In that sacred instrument we have recorded the following incontrovertible truths— "We hold these truths to be self-evident —that all men are created equal; that they are endowed by their Creator with certain unalienable rights; that among these are life, liberty, and the pursuit of happiness."

The people of colour are capable of giving their consent, and ever since the formation of your government they have constituted a portion of the people, from whence your legislators have derived "their just powers;" and by retaining that word, you deprive a large and respectable number of the people of this state of privileges and rights which they have enjoyed in common with us, ever since the existence of our government, and to which they are justly entitled. Sir, to this declaration we all profess to be willing to subscribe, yet by retaining this word you violate one of the most important maxims it contains.

It has been appropriately observed by the honourable gentleman from Westchester, (Mr. Jay,) that, by retaining this word, you violate the constitution of the United States. Besides the clause quoted by that honourable gentleman, I think there is another upon which it crowds very hard. Free people of colour are included in the number which regulates your represen-

tation in congress, and I wish to know how freemen can be represented when they are deprived of the privilege of voting for representatives. The constitution says, "representatives and direct taxes shall be apportioned among the different states, according to the inhabitants thereof, including all free persons," &c. All colours and complexions are here included. It is not free "white" persons. No, sir, our venerable fathers entertained too strong a sense of justice to countenance such an odious distinction.—Now, sir, taking this in connection with the declaration of independence, I think you cannot exclude them without being guilty of a palpable violation of every principle of justice. We are usurping to ourselves a power which we do not possess, and by so doing, deprive them of a privilege to which they are, and always have been, justly entitled—an invaluable right— a right in which we have prided ourselves as constituting our superiority over every other people on earth— a right which they have enjoyed ever since the formation of our government—the right of suffrage. And why do we do this? Instead of visiting the iniquities of these people upon them and their children, we are visiting their misfortunes upon them and their posterity unto the latest generation. It was not expected of us, that in forming a constitution to govern this state, we should so soon have shewn a disposition to adopt plans fraught with usurpation and injustice. Because we have done this people injustice, by enslaving them, and rendering them degraded and miserable, is it right that we should go on and continue to deprive them of their most invaluable rights, and visit upon their children to the latest posterity this deprivation? Is this just? Is it honest? Was it expected by our constituents? Will it not fix a foul stain upon the proceedings of this Convention which time will not efface.

My honourable colleague has told us "that these people are not liable to do military duty, and that as they are not required to contribute to the protection or defence of the state, they are not entitled to an equal participation in the privileges of its citizens." But, sir, whose fault is this? Have they ever refused to do military duty when called upon? It is haughtily asked, who will stand in the ranks, shoulder to shoulder, with a negro? I answer, no one in time of peace; no one when your musters and trainings are looked upon as mere pastimes; no one when your militia will shoulder their muskets and march to their trainings with as much unconcern as they would go to a sumptuous entertainment, or a splendid ball. But, sir, when the hour of danger approaches, your "white" militia are just as willing that the man of colour should be set up as a mark to be shot at by the enemy, as to be set up themselves. In the war of the revolution, these people helped to fight your battles by land and by sea. Some of your states were glad to turn out corps of coloured men, and to stand "shoulder to shoulder" with them. In your late war they contributed largely towards some of your most splendid victories. On Lake Erie and Champlain, where your fleets triumphed over a foe superior in numbers, and engines of death, they were manned in a large proportion with men of colour. And in this very house, in the fall of 1814, a bill passed receiving the approbation of all the branches of your government, authorizing the governor to accept the services of a corps of 2000 free people of colour . . .

But is said these people are incapable of exercising the right of suffrage judiciously; that they will become the tools and engines of aristocracy, and set themselves up in market, and give their votes to the highest bidder; that they have no will or judgment of their own, but will follow implicitly the dictates of the purse-proud aristocrats of the day, on whom they depend for bread. This may be true to a certain extent; but, sir, they are not the only ones who abuse this privilege; and if this be a sufficient reason for depriving any of your citizens of their just rights, go on and exclude also the many thousands of white fawning, cringing sycophants, who look up to their more wealthy and more ambitious neighbours for direction at the polls, as they look to them for bread. But although most of this unfortunate class of men may at present be in this dependent state, both in body and mind, yet we ought to remember, that we are making our constitution, not for a day, nor a year, but I hope for many generations; and there is a redeeming spirit in liberty, which I have no doubt will eventually raise these poor, abused, unfortunate people, from their present degraded state, to equal intelligence with their more fortunate and enlightened neighbors . . .

The honourable gentleman from Genesee (Mr.

Ross) has said that they were a peculiar people. We were told the other day that the people of Connecticut were a peculiar people. Indeed this is a peculiarly happy mode of evading the force of an argument. I admit that the blacks are a peculiarly unfortunate people, and I wish that such inducements may be held out, as shall induce them to become a sober and industrious class of the community, and raise them to the high standard of independent electors.

Col. Young expressed his intention to vote against the amendment proposed by the gentleman from Albany (Mr. Van Rensselaer) on the express ground that it did not contain the limitation of white. He should use no circumlocution nor disguise. He was willing to express his opinion openly and fully, and to record his name in the journals of the Convention, and thereby transmit it to posterity. He was disposed to discharge the duty which he owed to the people without fear of favour.

The gentleman who had just sat down had adverted to the declaration of independence to prove that the blacks are possessed of "certain unalienable rights." But is the right of voting a natural right? If so, our laws are oppressive and unjust. A natural right is one that is born with us. No man is born twenty-one years old, and of course all restraint upon the natural right of voting, during the period of nonage, is usurpation and tyranny. This confusion arises from mixing natural with acquired rights. The right of voting is adventitious. It is resorted to only as a means of securing our natural rights.

In forming a constitution, we should have reference to the feelings, habits, and modes of thinking of the people. The gentleman last up has alluded to the importance of regarding public sentiment. And what is the public sentiment in relation to this subject? Are the negroes permitted to a participation on social intercourse with the whites! Are they elevated to public office! No, sir— public sentiment forbids it. This they know; and hence they are prepared to sell their votes to the higher bidder. In this manner you introduce corruption into the very vitals of the government.

A few years ago a law was made requiring the clerks of the respective counties to make out a list of jurymen. Was a negro ever returned upon that list?

If he were, no jury would sit with him. Was a constable ever known to summon a negro as a jurror, even before a justice of the peace in a matter of five dollars amount? Never,— but gentlemen who would shrink from such an association, would now propose to associate with him in the important act of electing a governor of the state.

This distinction of colour is well understood. It is unnecessary to disguise it, and we ought to shape our constitution so as to meet the public sentiment. If that sentiment should alter—if the time should ever arrive when the African shall be raised to the level of the white man—when the distinctions that now prevail shall be done away—when the colours shall intermarry—when negroes shall be invited to your tables—to sit in your pew, or ride in your coach, it may then be proper to institute a new Convention, and remodel the constitution so as to conform to that state of society . . .

Mr. Jay in reply—Mr. Chairman—I am sensible that little remains to be gleaned, in a field which has been so well reaped. Still, there are some arguments which deserve a reply, and some points which have been discussed upon which a few rays of light may perhaps yet be thrown. It has been repeatedly urged, that since the whole body of the clergy, have, from reasons of political convenience, been disfranchised, we may with equal justice, and for the same reasons, disfranchise the people of colour. But is it true that the clergy are disfranchised? or that their case is similar to that of the people whose rights we are now considering? The clergy have a right to vote, and do vote; they have a right to be represented, and they are represented. The only restriction put upon them, is, that while they exercise the pastoral office, they shall exercise no other. If this be disfranchisement, the chancellor and chief justice of the state are equally disfranchised. Neither of those high officers can be a representative in the legislature unless he resigns his judical office. But if he resigns it, he immediately becomes eligible; so a clergyman, while he exercises his pastoral office, may not be elected, but if he resigns that office and ceases to be a minister of the gospel, he may, for any thing that I know to the contrary, accept any other appointment which the people shall please to bestow upon him. History proves, that the interference of the clergy in secular concerns, has usually been prejudicial

to the public: that when they mingled in the heats and asperities of political parties, they impaired their own dignity and usefulness, and occasioned dissensions and distrusts among the flocks committed to their charge. The Convention, therefore, which framed our constitution, thought it wise to set them apart, and to confine them to the high and honourable office of instructing the people in their most important duties, and to exempt them from all those offices which would expose them to the rancour of political contests. But what analogy is there between these provisions, and that by which all people of a certain complexion are to be excluded from the right of suffrage? A clergyman has that right; a black is to be excluded from it. A clergyman may not be elected, a black man may be. The disability of the clergyman is annexed to the clerical character, and ceases with it; the disability of the black man is to be annexed to his blood, is never to be removed, and is to be inseparable from him and his posterity to the latest generation. Again it has been urged, that the case of the people of colour is similar to that of the Indians. This also is a mistake. The Indian tribes are considered by us as independent nations. We send to them ambassadors, we receive ambassadors from them, and make treaties with them. They are aliens to us, and we to them.

Under these circumstances, they are no more entitled to vote at our elections, than Englishmen, Frenchmen, or other foreigner. But should an Indian forsake his tribe and settle in the county of Dutchess, his child, born there, would be as much a citizen, as either of the members from that county, and as much entitled to a vote. Another argument, sir, has been strongly pressed by the gentleman from whom I have the misfortune to differ upon this occasion. It is insisted, that this Convention, clothed with all the powers of the sovereign people of the state, have a right to construct the government in the manner they think most conducive to the general good — If, sir, right and power be equivalent terms, then I am far from disputing the rights of this assembly. We have power, sir, I acknowledge, not only to disfranchise every black family, but as many white families also as we may think expedient. We may place the whole government in the hands of a few, and thus construct an aristocracy; nay, I do not perceive why the reasons of some gentlemen would not prove, that we have power to confine the government to a single family, and then a monarchy might be the result. But, sir, right and power are not convertible terms. No man, no body of men, however powerful, have a right to do wrong. And if it be unjust to ex-clude from all participation in the government of their country, those who are the free born natives of its soil, and who possess all the qualifications required from others to whom we secure the right of suffrage, merely because their complexion displeases us, then, whatever may be our powers we have no right to commit this injustice . . .

I am told, sir, that the southern states are about to emancipate their slaves, and that we shall then be overrun by an emigration of free blacks from those parts of the union. Happy should I be, sir, if this in-telligence were confirmed. But where is the evidence of this approaching emancipation? I have heard, in-deed, that the southern planters were adopting mea-sures to rivet more firmly the fetters of slavery, but never that they were beginning to break them. I have heard of laws that forbade the ministers of the gospel to proclaim them the glad tidings of salvation. I have heard of laws to prohibit any man from imparting to them a knowledge of letters, and of the first rudiments of literature. I have heard of laws which prohibited manumission — But I have not heard of a single mea-sure which tended to prepare them for the enjoyment of freedom, or which indicated an intention of grant-ing it.

I have yet, sir, to notice the arguments of the gentleman from Saratoga, (Col. Young) — these were avowedly addressed, not to our reason, but to our prejudices, and so forcibly have they been urged, that I feel persuaded they have had more influence on the committee, than all that has been said beside on this occasion. Though repeated in various forms, they may all be summoned up in this: that we are accustomed to look upon black men with contempt — that we will not eat with them — that we will not sit with them — that we will not serve with them in the militia, or on juries, nor in any manner associate with them — and thence it is concluded, that they ought not to vote with us — how, sir, can that argument be answered by rea-son, which does not profess to be founded on reason? Why do we feel reluctant to associate with a black man? There is no such reluctance in Europe, nor in any country in which slavery is unknown. It arises

from an association of ideas. Slavery, and a black skin, always present themselves together to our minds — But with the dimunition of slavery, the prejucide has already diminished, and when slavery shall be no longer known among us, it will perhaps disappear — But, sir, what sort of argument is this? I will not eat with you, nor associate with you, because you are black; therefore I will disfranchise you. I despise you, not because you are vicious, but merely because I have an insuperable prejudice against you; — therefore I will condemn you, and your innocent posterity, to live forever as aliens in your native land. Mr. Chairman, I do trust, that this committee will not consent to violate all those principles upon which our free institu-tions are founded, or to contradict all the professions which we so profusely make, concerning the natural equality of all men, merely to gratify odious, and I hope, temporary prejudices — Nor will they endeavour to remove a slight inconvenience by so perilous a remedy as the establishment of a large, a perpetual, a degraded, and a discontented caste, in the midst of our population.

[At the conclusion of these debates, the word "white" was dropped, but later in the convention, the delegates voted to exclude all black voters except those with a freehold worth $250. After this debate, the convention turned its attention to the major recom-mendation, that of removing all property qualifications for white voters.]

Chief Justice Spencer moved to amend the amendment under consideration . . . Mr. Chairman — In presenting you the amendment . . . which I have now moved, it will be perceived that if it be adopted, there will be different qualifications for the electors of the senate, and of the governor, lieutenant-governor, and members of assembly, and all other elective officers . . . The re-port of the select committee, and the amendment of the gentleman from Delaware, propose, with the dash of the pen, to obliterate this part of our constitution, to destroy a barrier in legislation, which the wisdom of the sages and patriots of the revolution have erected for our protection. It has been insinuated, that as we have already unanimously agreed to abolish the exist-ing qualifications of electors, we in some measure stand pledged to abolish the distinction between the electors of the senate and assembly. This is not a correct deduction from the vote we have given. The vote taken implies no more than that we are willing to extend the right of suffrage, as far as may consist with the public good, but no farther. It will be perceived, that the amendment I have the honour to propose, admits all persons having an interest in real estate of the value of two hundred and fifty dollars, either in law or equity, without regard to the tenure, so that persons having a leasehold interest, or holding lands under contract for purchase, and who shall have by payments or improvements, added to the value to the amount of two hundred and fifty dollars, will be entitled to vote for senators; and the right will extend to those who hold lands in right of their wives . . .

Chancellor Kent. I am in favour of the amendment which has been submitted by my honourable colleague from Albany; and I must beg leave to trespass for a few moments upon the patience of the committee, while I state the reasons which have induced me to wish, that the senate should continue, as heretofore, the representative of the landed interest, and exempted from the control of universal suffrage . . .

We appear to be disregarding the principles of the constitution, under which we have so long and so happily lived, and to be changing some of its essential institutions. I cannot but think that the considerate men who have studied the history of republics, or are read in lessons of experience, must look with concern upon our apparent disposition to vibrate from a well balanced government, to the extremes of the democratic doctrines. Such a broad proposition as that contained in the report, at the distance of ten years past, would have struck the public mind with astonishment and terror. So rapid has been the career of our vibration.

Let us recall our attention, for a moment, to our past history.

This state has existed for forty-four years under our present constitution, which was formed by those illustrious sages and patriots who adorned the revolution. It has wonderfully fulfilled all the great ends of civil government. During that long period, we have enjoyed in an eminent degree, the blessings of civil and religious liberty. We have had our lives, our privileges, and our property, protected. We have had a succession of wise and temperate legislatures. The code of our statute law has been again and again revised and corrected, and it may proudly bear a comparison with that of any other people. We have had, during that period, (though I am, perhaps, not the fittest person to say it) a regular, stable, honest, and enlightened administration of justice. All the peaceable pursuits of industry, and all the important interests of education and science, have been fostered and encouraged. We have trebled our numbers within the last twenty-five years, have displayed mighty resources, and have made unexampled progress in the career of prosperity and greatness.

Our financial credit stands at an enviable height; and we are now successfully engaged in connecting the great lakes with the ocean by stupendous canals, which excite the admiration of our neighbours, and will make a conspicous figure even upon the map of the United States.

These are some of the fruits of our present government; and yet we seem to be dissatisfied with our condition, and we are engaged in the bold and hazardous experiment of remoddelling the constitution. Is it not fit and discreet: I speak as to wise men; is it not fit and proper that we should pause in our career, and reflect well on the immensity of the innovation in contemplation? Discontent in the midst of so much prosperity, and with such abundant means of happiness, looks like ingratitude, and as if we were disposed to arraign the goodness of Providence. Do we not expose ourselves to the danger of being deprived of the blessings we have enjoyed?—When the husbandman has gathered in his harvest, and has filled his barns and his graneries with the fruits of his industry, if he should then become discontented and unthankful, would he not have reason to apprehend, that the Lord of the harvest might come in his wrath, and with his lightning destroy them?

The senate has hitherto been elected by the farmers of the state—by the free and independent lords of the soil, worth at least $250 in freehold estate, over and above all debts charged thereon. The governor has been chosen by the same electors, and we have hitherto elected citizens of elevated rank and character. Our assembly has been chosen by freeholders, possessing a freeholder of the value of $50, or by persons renting a tenement of the yearly value of $5, and who have been rated and actually paid taxes to the state. By the report before us, we proposed to annihilate, at one stroke, all those property distinctions and to bow before the idol of universal suffrage. That extreme democratic principle, when applied to the legislative and executive departments of government, has been regarded with terror, by the wise men of every age, because in every European republic, ancient and modern, in which it has been tried, it has terminated disatrously, and been productive of corruption, injustice, violence, and tyranny. And dare we flatter ourselves that we are a peculiar people, who can run the career of history, exempted from the passions which have disturbed and corrupted the rest of mankind? If we are like other races of men, with similar follies and vices, then I greatly fear that our posterity will have reason to deplore in sackcloth and ashes, the delusion of the day.

It is not my purpose at present to interfere with the report of the committee, so far as respects the qualifications of electors for governor and members of assembly. I shall feel grateful if we may be permitted to retain the stability and security of a senate, bottomed upon the freehold property of the state. Such a body, so constituted, may prove a sheet anchor amidst the future factions and storms of the republic. The great leading and governing interest of this state, is, at present, the agricultural; and what madness would it be to commit that interest to the winds. The great body of the people, are now the owners and actual cultivators of the soil. With that wholesome population we always expect to find moderation, frugality, order, honesty, and a due sense of independence, liberty, and justice. It is impossible that any people can lose their liberties by internal fraud or violence, so long as the country is parcelled out among freeholders of moderate possessions, and those freeholders have a sure and efficient control in the affairs of the government. Their habits, sympathies, and employments, necessarily inspire them with a correct spirit of freedom and justice; they are the safest guardians of property and the laws: We certainly cannot too highly appreciate the value of the agricultural interest: It is the foundation of national wealth and power. According to the opinion of her ablest political economists, it is the surplus produce of the agriculture of England, that enables her to support her vast body of manufacturers, her formidable fleets and armies, and the crowds of persons engaged in the liberal professions, and the cultivation of the various arts.

Now, sir, I wish to preserve our senate as the representative of the landed interest. I wish those who have an interest in the soil, to retain the exclusive possession of a branch in the legislature, as a strong hold in which they may find safety through all the vicissitudes which the state may be destined, in the course of Providence, to experience. I wish them to be always enabled to say that their freeholds cannot be taxed without their consent. Then men of no property, together with the crowds of dependants connected with great manufacturing and commercial establishments, and the motley and undefinable population of crowded ports, may, perhaps, at some future day, under skilful management, predominate in the assembly, and yet we should be perfectly safe if no laws could pass without the free consent of the owners of the soil. That security we at present enjoy; and it is that security which I wish to retain.

The apprehended danger from the experiment of universal suffrage applied to the whole legislative department, is no dream of the imagination. It is too mighty an excitement for the moral constitution of men to endure. The tendency of universal suffrage, is to jeopardize the rights of property, and the principles of liberty. There is a constant tendency in human society, and the history of every age proves it; there is a tendency in the poor to covet and to share the plunder of the rich; in the debtor to relax or avoid the obligation of contracts; in the majority to tyranize over the minority, and trample down their rights; in the indolent and the profligate, to cast the whole burthens of society upon the industrious and the virtuous; and there is a tendency in ambitious and wicked men, to inflame these combustible materials. It requires a vigilant government, and a firm administration of justice, to counteract that tendency. Thou shalt not covet; thou shalt not steal; are divine injunctions induced by this miserable depravity of our nature. Who can undertake to calculate with any precision, how many millions of people, this great state will contain in the course of this and the next century, and who can estimate the future extent and magnitude of our commercial ports? The disproportion between the men of property, and the men of no property, will be in every society in a ratio to its commerce, wealth, and population. We are no longer to remain plain and simple republics of farmers, like the New-England colonists, or the Dutch settlements on the Hudson. We are fast becoming a great nation, with great commerce, manufactures, population, wealth, luxuries, and with the vices and miseries that they engender. One seventh of the population of the city of Paris at this day subsists on charity, and one third of the inhabitants of that city die in the hospitals; what would become of such a city with universal suffrage? . . .

The growth of the city of New-York is enough to startle and awaken those who are pursuing the *ignis fatuus* of universal suffrage . . .

New-York is destined to become the future London of America; and in less than a century, that city, with the operation of universal suffrage, and under skilful direction, will govern this state. The notion that every man that works a day on the road, or serves an idle hour in the militia, is entitled as of right to an equal participation in the whole power of the government, is most unreasonable, and has no foundation in justice. We had better at once discard from the report such a nominal test of merit. If such persons have an equal share in one branch of the legislature, it is surely as much as they can in justice or policy demand. Society is an association for the protection of property as well as of life, and the individual who contributes only one cent to the common stock, ought not to have the same power and influence in directing the property concerns of the partnership, as he who contributes his thousands. He will not have the same inducements to care, and diligence, and fidelity. His inducements and his temptation would be to divide the whole capital upon the principles of an agrarian law.

Liberty, rightly understood, is an inestimable blessing, but liberty without wisdom, and without justice, is no better than wild and savage licentiousness. The danger which we have hereafter to apprehend, is not the want, but the abuse, of liberty. We have to apprehend the oppression of minorities, and a disposition to encroach on private right—to disturb chartered privileges—and to weaken, degrade, and overawe the administration of justice; we have to apprehend the establishment of unequal, and con-

sequently, unjust systems of taxation, and all the mischiefs of a crude and mutable legislation. A stable senate, exempted from the influence of universal suffrage, will powerfully check these dangerous propensities, and such a check becomes the more necessary, since this Convention has already determined to withdraw the watchful eye of the judicial department from the passage of laws . . .

Gen. Root. I rejoice that this proposition has presented itself distinctly to the committee, and hope that its rejection may be had in a plain and unequivocal manner. It divides itself into two branches.—1st. Whether the senate and assembly ought to be elected by different persons, so as to possess genius and feelings hostile to each other; and 2dly. Whether it is properly provided for by the amendment that is now proposed . . .

But why must the two branches of the legislature be composed of different genius and heterogeneous materials? To constitute a sufficient check, says the gentleman:—and so, for this purpose, it must consist of discordant elements! Is this the way that government should be constituted? That the different branches, instead of harmonious movement, should be set in hostile array against each other? The honourable gentleman has adverted to the case of an individual employing two agents for the transaction of his business. Sir, I want no better example to illustrate my views of the subject, and to deduce a consequence directly the reverse of that which he has drawn. Were I that individual, I would choose men who might act in unison, and counsel each other upon the subject matter of their agency. If they possessed different tempers—opposite opinions, and hostile feelings, could I expect that the agency would be well managed? —Would not my interests be lost sight of, in their distractions and animosities? What government ever sent two ministers to negociate a treaty, and selected them for their known hostility to each other?

I agree that in a monarchical government, where little liberty is left to the people, it is necessary to have such checks as gentlemen have described. In such governments there are different orders, as lords and commons in Englend; different estates, as in the diets of Sweden, Denmark, and Germany. But the necessity in those governments bears no analogy to ours.—We have no different estates, having different interests, necessary to be guarded from encroachment by the watchful eye of jealousy.—We are all of the same estate—all commoners; nor, until we have privileged orders, and aristocratic estates to defend, can this argument apply . . .

I would admonish gentlemen of this committee, to reflect, who they are about to exclude from the right of suffrage, if the amendment under consideration should prevail.—They will exclude your honest industrious mechanics, and many farmers, for many there are, who do not own the soil which they till. And what for? Because your farmers wish it? No, sir, they wish no such thing; they wish to see the men who have defended their soil, participate equally with them in the election of their rulers . . .

And why are these men to be excluded? Not because they are not virtuous, not because they are not meritorious; but, sir, because they are poor and dependent, and can have no will of their own, and will vote as the man who feeds them and clothes them may direct, as one of the honourable gentlemen has remarked. I know of no men in this country, who are not dependant. The rich man is as much dependant upon the poor man for his labour, as the poor man is upon the rich for his wages. I know of no men, who are more dependant upon others for their bread and raiment, than the judges of your supreme court are upon the legislature, and who will pretend that this destroys their independence, or makes them subservient to the views of the legislature. Let us not, sir, disgrace ourselves in the eyes of the world, by expressing such degrading opinions of our fellow citizens. Let us grant universal suffrage, for after all, it is upon the virtue and intelligence of the people that the stability of your government must rest. Let us not brand this constitution with any odious distinctions as to property, and let it not be said of us as has been truly said of most republics, that we have been ungrateful to our best benefactors.

Mr. Buel . . . The question whether it is safe and proper to extend the right of suffrage to other classes of our citizens, besides the landholders, is decided, as I think, by the sober sense and deliberate acts of the great American people. To this authority I feel willing to bow. An examination of the constitutions of the different states, will show us that those enlightened bodies of statesmen and patriots who have from time to time been assembled for the grave and important purpose of forming and reforming the constitutions of the states—have sanctioned and established as a maxim, the opinion that there is no danger in confiding the most extensive right of suffrage to the intelligent population of these United States.

Of the twenty four states which compose this union, twelve states require only a certain time of residence as a qualification to vote for all their elective officers—eight require in addition to residence the payment of taxes or the performance of militia duty—four states only require a freehold qualification . . .

When our constitution was framed, the domain of the state was in the hands of a few. The proprietors of the great manors were almost the only men of great influence; and the landed property was deemed worthy of almost exclusive consideration. Before the revolution, freeholders only were allowed to exercise the right of suffrage. The notions of our ancestors, in regard to real property, were all derived from England. The feudal tenures were universally adopted. The law of primogeniture, by which estates decended to the eldest son, and the rule of descent by which the male branches inherited the paternal estate, to the exclusion of the female, entails, and many other provisions of feudal origin were in force. The tendency of this system, it is well understood, was to keep the lands of the state in few hands. But since that period, by the operation of wiser laws, and by the prevalence of juster principles, an entire revolution has taken place in regard to real property. Our laws for regulating descents, and for converting entailed estates into free-simple, have gradually increased the number of landholders: Our territory has been rapidly divided and subdivided: And although the landed interest is no longer controlled by the influence of a few great proprietors, its aggregate importance is vastly increased, and almost the whole community have become interested in its protection. In New-England, the inhabitants, from the earliest period, have enjoyed the system which we are progressively attaining to. There, the property of the soil has always been in the hands of the many. The great bulk of the population are farmers and freeholders, yet no provision is incorporated in their constitutions, excluding those who are not freeholders from a full participation in the right of suffrage . . .

There are in my judgment, many circumstances which will forever preserve the people of this state from the vices and the degradation of European population, beside those which I have already taken notice of. The provision already made for the establishment of common schools, will, in a very few years, extend the benefit of education to all our citizens. The universal diffusion of information will forever distinguish our population from that of Europe. Virtue and intelligence are the true basis on which every republican government must rest. When these are lost, freedom will no longer exist. The diffusion of education is the only sure means of establishing these pillars of freedom. I rejoice in this view of the subject, that our common school fund will (if the report on the legislative department be adopted,) be consecrated by a constitutional provision; and I feel no apprehension, for myself, or my posterity, in confiding the right of suffrage to the great mass of such a population as I believe ours will always be.

One ground of the argument of gentlemen who support the amendment is, that the exertion of the right of suffrage will give an undue influence to the rich over the persons who depend upon them for employment; but if the rich control the votes of the poor, the result cannot be unfavourable to the security of property. The supposition that, at some future day, when the poor shall become numerous, they may imitate the radicals of England, or the jacobins of France; that they may rise, in the majesty of their strength, and usurp the property of the landholders, is so unlikely to be realized, that we may dismiss all fear arising from that source. Before that can happen, wealth must lose all its influence; public morals must be destroyed; and the nature of our government changed, and it would be in vain to look to a senate, chosen by landholders, for security in a case of such extremity. I cannot but think, that all the dangers which it is predicted will flow from doing away the exclusive right of the landholders to elect the senators, are groundless.

I contend, that by the true principle of our government, property, as such, is not the basis of representation. Our community is an association of persons—of human beings—not a partnership founded on property. The declared object of the people of this state is associating, was, to "establish such a government as they deemed best calculated to secure the rights and liberties of the good people of the state, and most conducive to their happiness and safety." Property, it is admitted, is one of the rights to be protected and secured; and although the protection of life and liberty is the highest object of attention, it is certainly true, that the security of property is a most interesting and important object in every free government. Property is essential to our temporal happiness; and is necessarily one of the most interesting subjects of legislation. The desire of acquiring property is a universal passion. I readily give to property the important place which has been assigned to it by the honourable member from Albany (Chancellor Kent.) To property we are indebted for most of our comforts, and for much of our temporal happiness. The numerous religious, moral, and benevolent institutions which are every where established, owe their existence to wealth; and it is wealth which enables us to make those great internal improvements which we have undertaken. Property is only one of the incidental rights of the person who possess it; and, as such, it must be made secure; but it does not follow, that it must therefore be represented specifically in any branch of the government. It ought, indeed, to have an influence—and it ever will have, when properly enjoyed. So ought talents to have an influence. It is certainly as importnat to have men of good talents in your legislature, as to have men of property; but you surely would not set up men of talents as a separate order, and give them exclusive privileges.

The truth is, that both wealth and talents will ever have a great influence; and without the aid of exclusive privileges, you will always find the influence of both wealth and talents predominant in our halls of legislation . . .

Religious freedom and the separation of church and state flowed from the Lockean premises that individual rights took precedence over social goals, but it did not grow out of the specific religious tenets of the major colonial churches. Despite the freedom of worship enjoyed in Pennsylvania, New Jersey, and Rhode Island, colonial Americans did not applaud religious liberty nor practice any more tolerance than was absolutely necessary. Indeed, among people of strong religious convictions, tolerance is a maverick spirit, for if one's duty to God is of preeminent importance the way of discharging this duty cannot be left to personal whim. What colonial America offered was the space in which many different groups could enjoy their own form of orthodoxy. The Puritan Congregational churches established by law in New England had given only a grudging accommodation to Baptists and Anglicans, while the Anglicans in the South had done everything to discourage Dissenters —be they Congregationalists, Presbyterians, Baptists, or Quakers. The presence of these many diverse religious groups contributed to the separation of church and state, but only inadvertently. The major religions in America at that time—Presbyterian, Congregational, and the Episcopalian successors to the old Church of England—continued to endorse the older concept of the church serving the entire community, speaking with authority to the needs of the whole society and empowered either by government or social approval to discipline erring souls. The religious values they instilled were conservative, coming out of the accrued wisdom of the Christian heritage.

When the time for developing state and national religious policies arrived, however, no one church had commanded anywhere near a majority of church membership. Well over half of the population did not belong to any church. Except in Connecticut and Massachusetts, the proponents of religious liberty were successful in separating church and state ties. The disestablishment of religion had turned all churches into voluntary associations of like-minded people with no special claims upon society and dependent upon voluntary contributions for support. A number of important consequences flowed from this new situation. Religion, like so much else in the new nation, was put on a voluntary basis. The authority of the clergy was underminded. Christian nurture of the young was left to individual parents. Another community tie was loosened. In settled areas, changes were gradual, but the frontier areas, so long neglected when there were religious establishments, were now cut loose from all church authority. The conservative denominations—which were bound to an educated ministry, regular worship services, and the transmission of a complicated religious doctrine—could rarely afford to support their traditions beyond the limits of their own congregation's area. In the newly settled areas the people were bereft of all religious care. Into this void moved the men who had inherited the rivival techniques of the Great Awakening, itinerant Baptist ministers and Methodist circuit riders. In most cases these preachers were poor, simple, and uneducated. There were no social barriers between them and their congregations, and the persuasive powers they exercised were dramatic rather than authoritarian. Depending solely upon effective teaching, they vivified the tortures of the damned, exhorted men and women to stop sinning, and urged all to save themselves by responding to God's offer of grace. Their success was enormous. Within three decades the frontier was better know for its great camp meetings than its wild scenes of debauchery, and the revival-oriented denominations had far outstripped the older churches in membership.

At the same time a new religious subculture was created in which emotion, feeling, and the promptings of the individual Christian's heart were made the arbiters of religious truths. Left behind was the church's mission to the whole community viewed as a complex of economic, social, and political forces. Now the focus was exclusively upon the single, isolated sinner. If religion was a matter of the heart alone, then a knowledge of the historic church, of Christian dogma, of the larger world of civilized man became valueless. Increasingly too, the revivalists began preaching a different theology. Where the dominant strain of Protestantism introduced into America had stressed the submission of man to God's sovereignty, the revivalists came close to making God dependent upon people's personal choice. They tried to evoke the wrath of God, but they ended up begging people to be saved.

Charles Finney (1792–1875) was the century's most successful revivalist minister. He also developed a theory of revivals in which he explained how mankind was moving toward perfection by means of periodic revivals of religious excitement. An innovater in revival techniques, Finney used a style of preaching in which individuals in the congregation were personally exhorted. He also introduced a device known as the anxious bench, where members of the congregation believed to be in the throes of spiritual crisis were invited to sit in order to get additional ministerial help. Finney's new measures were credited with huge harvests of new converts, and there successes moved ministers in all denominations—conservative as well as revivalist—to consider their adoption. For some ministers and theologians, however, success measured by numbers was not persuasive. To them, Finney and his ilk were threatening the very foundation of Christianity in America. They themselves were trained in theology, and they believed that true Christian faith could only be transmitted through the careful instruction of each new generation. One of Finney's most articulate critics was John Nevin (1803–1886), a professor of theology of Pennsylvania's German Reformed Church. In arguments reminiscent of the Great Awakening disputes, Nevin explained why he felt that the religion of emotion-charged mass meetings or what he dubbed "the anxious-bench system" could not be considered genuine.

The readings in this section present excerpts from Finney's *Lectures on Revivals of Religion* and Nevin's scathing indictment of Finney's New Measures, *The Anxious Bench.*

Charles Finney: *Lectures on revivals of religion* (1835)*

It is supposed that the prophet Habakkuk was contemporary with Jeremiah, and that [this] prophecy

*Pp. 8–25, 30–34.

was uttered in anticipation of the Babylonish captivity. Looking at the judgments which were speedily to come upon his nation, the soul of the prophet was wrought up to an agony, and he cries out in his distress, "O Lord, revive thy work." As if he had said, "O Lord, grant that thy judgments may not make Israel desolate. In the midst of these awful years, let the judgments of God be made the means of reviving religion among us. In wrath remember mercy."

Religion is the work of man. It is something for man to do. It consists in obeying God with and from the heart. It is man's duty. It is true, God induces him to do it. He influences him by his Spirit, because of his great wickedness and reluctance to obey. If it were not necessary for God to influence men—if men were disposed to obey God, there would be no occasion to pray, "O Lord, revive thy work." The ground of necessity for such a prayer is, that men are wholly indisposed to obey; and unless God interpose the influence of his Spirit, not a man on earth will ever obey the commands of God.

A "Revival of Religion" presupposes a declension. Almost all the religion in the world has been produced by revivals. God has found it necessary to take advantage of the excitability there is in mankind, to produce powerful excitements among them, before he can lead them to obey. Men are so spiritually sluggish, there are so many things to lead their minds off from religion, and to oppose the influence of the Gospel, that it is necessary to raise an excitement among them, till the tide rises so high as to sweep away the opposing obstacles. They must be so excited that they will break over these counteracting influences, before they will obey God. Not that excited feeling is religion, for it is not; but it is excited desire, appetite and feeling that prevents religion. The will is, in a sense, enslaved by the carnal and worldly desires. Hence it is necessary to awaken men to a sense of guilt and danger, and thus produce an excitement of counter feeling and desire which will break the power of carnal and worldly desire and leave the will free to obey God . . .

There is so little principle in the church, so little firmness and stability of purpose, that unless the religious feelings are awakened and kept excited, counter worldly feeling and excitement will prevail, and men will not obey God. They have so little knowledge, and their principles are so weak, that unless they are excited, they will go back from the path of duty, and do nothing to promote the glory of God. The state of the world is still such, and probably will be till the millennium is fully come, that religion must be mainly promoted by means of revivals. How long and how often has the experiment been tried, to bring the church to act steadily for God, without these periodical excitements. Many good men have supposed, and still suppose, that the best way to promote religion, is to go along uniformly, and gather in the ungodly gradually, and without excitement. But however sound such reasoning may appear in the abstract, facts demonstrate its futility . . .

It is very desirable it should be so. It is very desirable that the church should go on steadily in a course of obedience without these excitements. Such excitements are liable to injure the health. Our nervous system is so strung that any powerful excitement, if long continued, injures our health and unfits us for duty. If religion is ever to have a pervading influence in the world, it cannot be so; this spasmodic religion must be done away. Then it will be uncalled for. Christians will not sleep the greater part of the time, and once in a while wake up, and rub their eyes, and bluster about, and vociferate a little while, and then go to sleep again. Then there will be no need that ministers should wear themselves out, and kill themselves, by their efforts to roll back the flood of worldly influence that sets in upon the church. But as yet the state of the Christian world is such, that to expect to promote religion without excitements is unphilosophical and absurd. The great political, and other worldly excitements that agitate Christendom, are all unfriendly to religion, and divert the mind from the interests of the soul. Now these excitements can only be counteracted by religious excitements. And until there is religious principle in the world to put down irreligious excitements, it is vain to try to promote religion, except by counteracting excitements. This is true in philosophy, and it is a historical fact.

It is altogether improbable that religion will ever make progress among heathen nations except through the influence of revivals. The attempt is now making to do it by education, and other cautious and gradual improvements. But so long as the laws of mind remain what they are, it cannot be done in this way. There must be excitement sufficient to wake up the dormant moral powers, and roll back the tide of degradation and sin. And precisely so far as our own land approximates to heathenism, it is impossible for God or man to promote religion in such a state of things but by powerful excitements . . .

These remarks are designed only as an introduction to the discourse. I shall now proceed with the main design, to show, what a revival of religion is not; what it is; and, the agencies employed in promoting it . . .

I said that a revival is the result of the right use of the appropriate means. The means which God has enjoined for the production of a revival, doubtless have a natural tendency to produce a revival. Otherwise God would not have enjoined them. But means will not produce a revival, we all know, without the blessing of God. No more will grain, when it is sowed, produce a crop without the blessing of God . . . It is true that religion does not properly belong to the category of cause and effect; but although it is not caused by means, yet it has its occasion, and may as naturally and certainly result from its occasion as a crop does from its cause.

I wish this idea to be impressed on all your minds, for there has long been an idea prevalent that promoting religion has something very peculiar in it, not to be judged of by the ordinary rules of cause and effect; in short, that there is no connection of the means with the result, and no tendency in the means to produce the effect. No doctrine is more dangerous than this to the prosperity of the church, and nothing more absurd.

Suppose a man were to go and preach this doctrine among farmers, about their sowing grain. Let him tell them that God is a sovereign, and will give them a crop only when it pleases him, and that for them to plow and plant and labor as if they expected to raise a crop is very wrong, and taking the work out of the hands of God, that it interferes with his sovereignty, and is going on in their own strength; and that there is no connection between the means and the result on which they can depend. And now, suppose the farmers should believe such doctrine. Why, they would starve the world to death.

Just such results will follow from the church's being persuaded that promoting religion is somehow so mysteriously a subject of Divine sovereignty, that there is no natural connection between the means and the end. What are the results? Why, generation after generation has gone down to hell. No doubt more than five thousand millions have gone down to hell, while the church has been dreaming, and waiting for God to save them without the use of means. It has been the devil's most successful means of destroying souls. The connection is as clear in religion as it is when the farmer sows his grain.

There is one fact under the government of God, worthy of universal notice, and of everlasting remembrance; which is, that the most useful and important things are most easily and certainly obtained by the use of the appropriate means. This is evidently a principle in the Divine administration . . . Hence, all the necessaries of life are obtained with great certainty by the use of the simplest means . . .

I am to show what a revival is. It is the renewal of the first love of Christians, resulting in the awakening and conversion of sinners to God. In the popular sense, a revival of religion in a community is the arousing, quickening, and reclaiming of the more or less backslidden church and the more or less general awakening of all classes, and insuring attention to the claims of God.

It presupposes that the church is sunk down in a backslidden state, and a revival consists in the return of a church from her backslidings, and in the conversion of sinners.

1. A revival always includes conviction of sin on the part of the church. Backslidden professors cannot wake up and begin right away in the service of God, without deep searchings of heart. The fountains of sin need to be broken up. In a true revival, Christians are always brought under such convictions; they see their sins in such a light, that often they find it impossible to maintain a hope of their acceptance with God. It does not always go to that extent; but there are always, in a genuine revival, deep convictions of sin, and often cases of abandoning all hope.

2. Backslidden Christians will be brought to repentance. A revival is nothing else than a new beginning of obedience to God. Just as in the case of a converted sinner, the first step is a deep repentance, a breaking down of heart, a getting down into the dust before God, with deep humility, and forsaking of sin.

3. Christians will have their faith renewed. While they are in their backslidden state they are blind to the state of sinners. Their hearts are as hard as marble. The truths of the Bible only appear like a dream. They admit it to be all true; their conscience and their judgment assent to it; but their faith does not see it standing out in bold relief, in all the burning realities of eternity. But when they enter into a revival, they no longer see men as trees walking, but they see things in that strong light which will renew the love of God in their hearts. This will lead them to labor zealously to bring others to him. They will feel grieved that others do not love God, when they love him so much. And they will set themselves feelingly to persuade their neighbors to give him their hearts. So their love to men will be renewed. They will be filled with a tender and burning love for souls. They will have a longing desire for the salvation of the whole world. They will be in an agony for individuals whom they want to have saved — their friends, relations, enemies. They will not only be urging them to give their hearts to God, but they will carry them to God in the arms of faith, and with strong crying and tears beseech God to have mercy on them, and save their souls from endless burnings.

4. A revival breaks the power of the world and of sin over Christians. It brings them to such vantage ground that they get a fresh impulse towards heaven. They have a new foretaste of heaven, and new desires after union with God; and the charm of the world is broken, and the power of sin overcome.

5. When the churches are thus awakened and reformed, the reformation and salvation of sinners will follow, going through the same stages of conviction, repentance, and reformation. Their hearts will be broken down and changed. Very often the most abandoned profligates are among the subjects. Harlots, and drunkards, and infidels, and all sorts of abandoned characters, are awakened and converted. The worst among human beings are softened, and reclaimed, and made to appear as lovely specimens of the beauty of holiness . . .

Ordinarily, there are three agents employed in the work of conversion, and one instrument. The agents are God, – some person who brings the truth to bear on the mind, – and the sinner himself. The instrument is the truth. There are always two agents, God and the sinner, employed and active in every case of genuine conversion.

1.   The agency of God is two-fold; by his Providence and by his Spirit . . . If men were disposed to obey God, the truth is given with sufficient clearness in the Bible; and from preaching they could learn all that is necessary for them to know. But because they are wholly disinclined to obey it, God clears it up before their minds, and pours in a blaze of convincing light upon their souls, which they cannot withstand, and they yield to it, and obey God, and are saved.

2.   The agency of men is commonly employed. Men are not mere instruments in the hands of God. Truth is the instrument. The preacher is a moral agent in the work; he acts; he is not a mere passive instrument; he is voluntary in promoting the conversion of sinners.

3.   The agency of the sinner himself. The conversion of a sinner consists in his obeying the truth. It is therefore impossible it should take place without his agency, for it consists in his acting right. He is influenced to this by the agency of God, and by the agency of men. Men act on their fellow-men, not only by language, but by their looks, their tears, their daily deportment. See that impenitent man there, who has a pious wife. Her very looks, her tenderness, her solemn, compassionate dignity, softened and moulded into the image of Christ are a sermon to him all the time. He has to turn his mind away, because it is such a reproach to him. He feels a sermon ringing in his ears all day long.

Mankind are accustomed to read the countenances of their neighbors. Sinners often read the state of a Christian's mind in his eyes. If his eyes are full of levity, or worldly anxiety and contrivance, sinners read it. If they are full of the Spirit of God, sinners read it; and they are often led to conviction by barely seeing the countenance of Christians.

An individual once went into a manufactory to see the machinery. His mind was solemn, as he had been where there was a revival. The people who labored there all knew him by sight, and knew who he was. A young lady who was at work saw him, and whispered some foolish remark to her companion, and laughed. The person stopped and looked at her with a feeling of grief. She stopped, her thread broke, and she was so much agitated she could not join it. She looked out at the window to compose herself, and then tried again; again and again she strove to recover her self-command. At length she sat down, overcome with her feelings. The person then approached and spoke with her; she soon manifested a deep sense of sin. The feeling spread through the establishment like fire, and in a few hours almost every person employed there was under conviction, so much so, that the owner, though a worldly man, was astounded, and requested to have the works stop and have a prayer meeting; for he said it was a great deal more important to have these people converted than to have the works go on. And in a few days, the owner and nearly every person employed in the establishment were hopefully converted. The eye of this individual, his solemn countenance, his compassionate feeling, rebuked the levity of the young woman, and brought her under conviction of sin: and this whole revival followed, probably in a great measure, from so small an incident.

If Christians have deep feeling on the subject of religion themselves, they will produce deep feeling wherever they go. And if they are cold, or light and trifling, they inevitably destroy all deep feeling, even in awakened sinners.

I knew a case, once, of an individual who was very anxious, but one day I was grieved to find that her convictions seemed to be all gone. I asked her what she had been doing. She told me she had been spending the afternoon at such a place, among some professors of religion, not thinking that it would dissipate her convictions to spend an afternoon with professors of religion. But they were trifling and vain, and thus her convictions were lost. And no doubt those professors of religion, by their folly, destroyed a soul, for her convictions did not return . . .

Mistaken notions concerning the sovereignty of God have greatly hindered revivals.

Many people have supposed God's sovereignty to be something very different from what it is. They have supposed it to be such an arbitrary disposal of events, and particularly of the gift of his Spirit, as precluded a rational employment of means for promoting a revival of religion. But there is no evidence from the Bible that God exercises any such sovereignty as that. There are no facts to prove it. But every thing goes to show that God has connected means with the end through all the departments of his government — in nature and in grace . . .

Some people are terribly alarmed at all direct efforts to promote a revival, and they cry out, "You are trying to get up a revival in your own strength. Take care, you are interfering with the sovereignty of God. Better keep along in the usual course, and let God give a revival when he thinks it is best. God is a sovereign, and it is very wrong for you to attempt to get up a revival, just because you think a revival is needed." This is just such preaching as the devil wants. And men cannot do the devil's work more effectually than by preaching up the sovereignty of God, as a reason why we should not put forth efforts to produce a revival.

You see the error of those who are beginning to think that religion can be better promoted in the world without revivals, and who are disposed to give up all efforts to produce religions awakenings. Because there are evils arising in some instances out of great excitements on the subject of religion, they are of opinion that it is best to dispense with them altogether. This cannot, and must not be. True, there is danger of abuses. In cases of great religious as well as all other excitements, more or less incidental evils may be expected of course. But this is no reason why they should be given up. The best things are always liable to abuses. Great and manifold evils have originated in the providential and moral governments of God. But these foreseen perversions and evils were not considered a sufficient reason for giving them up. For the establishment of these governments was on the whole the best that could be done for the production of the greatest amount of happiness. So in revivals of religion, it is found by experience, that in the present state of the world, religion cannot be promoted to any considerable extent without them. The evils which are sometimes complained of, when they are real, are incidental, and of small importance when compared with the amount of good produced by revivals. The sentiment should not be admitted by the church for a moment, that revivals may be given up. It is fraught with all that is dangerous to the interest of Zion, is death of the cause of missions, and brings in its train the damnation of the world . . .

A Revival of Religion is the only possible thing that can wipe away the reproach which covers the church, and restore religion to the place it ought to have in the estimation of the public. Without a revival, this reproach will cover the church more and more, until it is overwhelmed with universal contempt. You may do any thing else you please, and you can change the aspects of society in some respects, but you will do no real good; you only make it worse without a Revival of Religion. You may go and build a splendid new house of worship, and line your seats with damask, put up a costly pulpit, and get a magnificent organ, and every thing of that kind, to make a show and dash, and in that way you may procure a sort of respect for religion among the wicked, but it does no good in reality. It rather does hurt. It misleads them as to the real nature of religion; and so far from converting them, it carries them farther away from salvation. Look wherever they have surrounded the altar of Christianity with splendor, and you will find that the impression produced is contrary to the true nature of religion. There must be a waking up of energy, on the part of Christians, and an outpouring of God's Spirit, or the world will laugh at the church.

Nothing else will restore Christian love and confidence among church members. Nothing but a Revival of Religion can restore it, and nothing else ought to restore it. There is no other way to wake up that love of Christians for one another, which is sometimes felt, when they have such love as they cannot express. You cannot have such love without confidence; and you cannot restore confidence without such evidence of piety as is seen in a revival . . .

There is no other way in which a church can be sanctified, grow in grace, and be fitted for heaven. What is growing in grace? Is it hearing sermons and getting some new notions about religion? No — no such thing. The Christian who does this, and nothing more, is getting worse and worse, more and more hardened, and every week it is more difficult to rouse him up to duty . . .

There never will be a revival till somebody makes particular efforts for this end. But when the attention of a minister is directed to the state of the families in his congregation, and his heart is full of feeling of the necessity of a revival, and when he puts forth the proper efforts for this end, then you may be prepared to expect a revival. As I explained last week, the connection between the right use of means for a revival, and a revival, is as philosophically sure as between the right use of means to raise grain, and a crop of wheat . . . In raising grain, for instance, there are cases which are beyond the control of man, such as drought, hard winter, worms, and so on. So in laboring to promote a revival, there may things occur to counteract it, something or other turning up to divert the public attention from religion, which may baffle every effort. But I believe there are fewer such cases in the moral than in the natural world. I have seldom seen an individual fail, when he used the means for promoting a revival in earnest, in the manner pointed out in the word of God. I believe a man may enter on the work of promoting a revival, with as reasonable an expectation of success, as he can enter on any other work with an expectation of success . . .

Brethren, you can tell from our subject, whether you need a revival here or not, in this church, and in this city; and whether you are going to have one or not. Elders of the church, men, women, any of you, and all of you — what do you say?

Do you need a revival here?

Do you expect to have one?

Have you any reason to expect one?

You need not make any mist about it; for you know, or can know if you will, whether you have any reason to look for a revival here.

You see why you have not a revival. It is only because you do not want one. Because you are not praying for it; nor anxious for it, nor putting forth efforts for it. I appeal to your own consciences. Are you making these efforts now, to promote a revival? You know, brethren, what the truth is about it. Will you stand up and say that you have made the efforts for a revival and been disappointed — that you have cried to God, "Wilt thou not revive us?" and God would not do it?

Do you wish for a revival? Will you have one? If God should ask you this moment, by an audible voice from heaven, "Do you want a revival?" would you dare to say, Yes? "Are you willing to make the sacrifices?" would you answer, Yes? "When shall it begin?" would you answer, Let it begin tonight — let it begin here — let it begin in my heart *now*? Would you dare to say so to God, if you should hear his voice to-night? . . .

John W. Nevin: *The Anxious Bench* (1843)*

It is proposed to institute a free inquiry into the merits of the Anxious Bench, as it has been enlisted extensively of late years in the service of religion. My object will be to show, that the measure is adapted to obstruct rather than to promote the progress of true godliness, and that it deserves to be discouraged on this account . . .

It will be understood, that the Anxious Bench is made to stand, in this case, as the type and representative of the entire system of what are technically denominated in our day, "New Measures." . . .

It might answer little purpose to interpose remonstrance or inquiry, if the rage for New Measures were fairly let loose, as a sweeping wind, within our borders. It were idle to bespeak attention from the rolling whirlwind. But with the whirlwind in full view, we may be exhorted reasonably to consider and stand back from its destructive path. We are not yet committed to the cause of New Measures, in any respect. We are still free to reject or embrace them, as the interests of the Church, on calm reflection, may be found to require. In such circumstances precisely, may it be counted in all respects proper to subject the system to a serious examination.

It has been sometimes intimated, that it is not safe to oppose and condemn the use of New Measures, because of their connections and purpose. Their relation to the cause of revivals, is supposed to invest them with a sort of sacred character, which the friends of religion should at least respect, even if they may not be able in all cases, to approve. The system has taken hold of the "horns of the altar," and it seems to some like sacrilege to fall upon it there, or to force it away for the purposes of justice to any other place.

---

*Pp. 19–29, 40–43, 110–21, 128–33.

It is a serious thing, we are told, to find fault with any movement, that claims to be animated by the Spirit of God. By so doing, we render it questionable whether we have ourselves any proper sympathy with revivals, and furnish occasion to the world also to blaspheme and oppose everything of the kind. But this is tyrannical enough, to take for granted the main point in dispute, and then employ it as a considation to repress inquiry or to silence objection. If New Measures can be shown to proceed from the Holy Ghost, or to be identified in any view with the cause of revivals, they may well demand our reverence and respect. If they can be shown even to be of adiaphorous character with regard to religion, harmless at least if not positively helpful to the Spirit's work, they may then put in a reasonable plea to be tolerated in silence, if not absolutely approved. But neither the one nor the other of these positions can be successfully maintained. It is a mere trick unworthy of the gospel, for any one to confound with the sacred idea of a revival, things that do not belong to it in truth at all, for the purpose of compelling a judgment in their favor. The very design of the inquiry now proposed, is to show that the Anxious Bench, and the system to which it belongs, have no claim to be considered either salutary or safe, in the service of religion. It is believed, that instead of promoting the cause of true vital godliness, they are adapted to hinder its progress. The whole system is considered to be full of peril, for the most precious interests of the Church . . .

The case is one that calls loudly for light, and it is high time that light should be extended to it without reserve . . . If Finneyism and Winebrennerism, the Anxious Bench, revival machinery, solemn tricks for effect, decision displays at the bidding of the preacher, genuflections and prostrations in the aisle or around the altar, noise and disorder, extravagance and rant, mechanical conversions, justification by feeling rather than faith, and encouragement ministered to all fanatical impressions; if these things, and things in the same line indefinitely, have no connection in fact with true serious religion and the cause of revivals, but tend only to bring them into discredit, let the fact be openly proclaimed. Only in this way, may it be hoped that the reproach put upon revivals and other evangeli-

cal interests by some, under cover of their pretended connection with this system of New Measures in the true sense, will be in due time fairly rolled away . . .

Let us not be told then, that the Anxious Bench is a godly interest, because many seem to be convicted by its means, and some are converted in fact. All this may be, and the general operation of the system remain notwithstanding intrinsically and permanently bad.

As a general thing, the movement of coming to the Anxious Bench, gives no proper representation of the religious feeling that may be actually at work in the congregation, at the time. It is always more or less theatrical, and often has no other character whatever. A sermon usually goes before. But frequently this has no felt relation at all to the subsequent excitement, so far as its actual contents are concerned. The writer was present, not a great while ago, as a stranger, in a church, where a preacher of some little note in connection with the subject of revivals, had been introduced, under the expectation and hope, that something of the kind might be secured, at the time, by his instrumentality. The congregation had but little appearance of life at the beginning, and still less as the sermon drew towards a close. The truth is, it was a very dull discourse, at the best. The preacher was not well, and altogether he failed to make the least impression on the great body of his audience. A number were fairly asleep, and others were bordering on the same state. The preacher saw and felt, that he had preached without effect; and took occasion, after the sermon was properly ended, to express his regret in view of the fact, and to add a few valedictory remarks in the prospect of his leaving the place the next day, without any thought evidently of calling out the anxious, where not a trace of feeling had been discerned. But the new strain adopted at the close, served to rouse attention and create interest. The congregation put on a more wakeful aspect, and something like emotion could be perceived in the countenances of a few. The preacher took courage, and after a few minutes dared to try the Anxious Bench. As usual, the hymn was started, Come humble sinner, &c., and carried through, with pauses, in which sinners present were urged and pressed to seek their salvation by coming forward. Soon a female was seen going to the place, then another, and another; till at last a whole seat was filled. One old lady rose, and moved around, trying to induce others to go forward. At the close of the meeting, I retired, wondering within myself that educated men, as were both the preacher in this case and the pastor at his side, could so impose upon themselves, as to attach any importance to such a demonstration, in such circumstances. It was attempted to carry forward the work, by an appointment for the next evening. But on coming together at the time, it was found that it would not go forward, and so it was dropped altogether.

Commonly indeed, those who deal in the anxious seat, rely far less upon the presentation of truth to the understanding, than they do upon other influences, to bring persons forward. Pains are taken rather to raise the imagination and confound the judgment. Exciting appeals are made to the principle of fear. Advantage is taken in every way of the senses and nerves. Especially the mysterious force of sympathy is enlisted in support of the measure, and made to tell in many cases with immense effect.

As might be expected accordingly, the most favorable subjects for the operation of the system, are persons in whom feelings prevail over judgment, and who are swayed by impulse more than reflection. In an enlightened, well instructed congregation, the anxious bench can never be generally popular. Where it is in full favor, a large proportion of those who are brought out by it, are females and persons who are quite young. It often happens that the "bench" is filled altogether with such cases, the greater part of them perhaps mere girls and boys. So where a community is characterised by a general ignorance with regard to the nature of true religion, the measure is frequently applied with great effect; and those precisely who are the most rude and uncultivated, are the most likely in such circumstances to come under its power.

It requires then no spiritual power to use the Anxious Bench with effect. To preach the truth effectually, a man must have a certain spiritual force in himself, which others are made to feel. But nothing of this sort is needed, to secure success here. The object sought is a mere outward demonstration on the subject of religion, which may be gained by other forms of influence, just as well. It shows no inward power whatever, to be able to move a congregation in this way. It can be done without eloquence, and calls for no particular earnestness or depth of thought. It is truly wonderful indeed, with how little qualification of intellect and soul a man may be fitted to carry all before him at certain times, and to show himself off to the eyes of a bewitched multitude as "the great power of God," by having recourse to new measures. He may be vulgar, coarse and dull, and so pointless and sapless in his ordinary pulpit services, that it will be a weariness to hear him; and yet you shall find him, from time to time, throwing a whole community into excitement, gathering around him crowded houses night after night, and exercising as it might seem, for the space of three or four weeks, an irresistible sway, in favor of religion. Such cases are by no means uncommon. Some of the most successful practitioners in the art of the Anxious Bench show themselves lamentably defective in the power of serious godliness, as well as in mental cultivation generally. The general habit of their lives is worldly and vain, and their religion, apart from the occasional whirlwinds of excitement in which they are allowed to figure in their favorite way, may be said to be characteristically superficial and cold. Nay, the evidence may be palpable, that religion has nothing at all to do with the system, in cases where it is employed with the greatest apparent effect. Nothing is more common, than for those even who glory in the power of the Anxious Bench, as employed within their own communion, to look with entire distrust on its results as exhibited in the practice of other sects. What is trumpeted in the one case as a glorious revival, is allowed to pass in the other without notice as at best a questionable excitement. In this way it is practically acknowledged, that the system does not necessarily involve spiritual power. It can be made to work as well in connection with error, as in connection with truth. It is as fully at the service of quackery and imposture, as it can be available in the case of genuine religion. It is well adapted indeed to become the sport of quacks, under every name. All wild and fanatical sects employ it, with equal success . . .

Quackery consists in pretension to an inward virtue or power, which is not possessed in fact, on the ground of a mere show of the strength which such power or virtue is supposed to include. The self-styled physician, who without any knowledge of the human frame, undertakes to cure diseases by a sovereign panacea, in the shape of fluid, powder, or pill, is a quack; and there is no doubt abundance of quackery in the medical profession, under more professional forms, where practice is conducted without any true professional insight and power. Such practice may at times seem eminently successful, and yet it is quackery notwithstanding. The same false show of power may, of course, come into view in every department of life. It makes up in fact a large part of the action and business of the world. Quack lawyers, quack statesmen, quack scholars, quack teachers, quack gentlemen, quacks in a word of every name and shape, meet us plentifully in every direction. We need not be surprised then to find the evil fully at home also in the sphere of religion. Indeed it might seem to be more at home here, than any where else. Here especially the heart of man, "deceitful above all things and desperately wicked," has shown itself most ingenious in all ages, in substituting the shadow for the reality, the form for the substance, the outward for the inward . . .

Religion must have forms, as well as an inward living force. But these can have no value, no proper reality, except as they spring perpetually from the presence of that living force itself. The inward must be the bearer of the outward. Quackery however reverses the case. The outward is made to bear the inward. The shrine, consecrated with the proper ceremonies, must become a shechinah. Forms have a virtue in them, to bind and rule the force of things. Such forms may be exhibited in a ritual, or in a creed, or in a scheme of a religious experience mechanically apprehended; but in the end, the case is substantially the same. It is quackery in the garb of religion, without its inward life and power.

That old forms are liable to be thus abused, and have been extensively thus abused in fact, is easily admitted. But it is not always recollected, that new forms furnish precisely the same opportunity for the same error. It is marvellous indeed how far this seems to be overlooked, by the zealous advocates of the system of New Measures, in our own day. They propose to rouse the Church from its dead formalism. And to do this effectually, they strike off from the old ways of worship, and bring in new and strange practices, that are adapted to excite attention. These naturally produce a theatrical effect, and this is taken at once for an evidence of waking life in the congregation. One measure, losing its power in proportion as it becomes familiar, leads to the introduction of another. A few years since a sermon was preached and published by a somewhat distinguished revivalist, in which the ground was openly taken that there must be a constant succession of new measures in the Church, to keep it alive and awake; since only in this way could we hope to counteract permanently the force of that spiritual gravitation, by which the minds of men are so prone continually to sink towards the earth in the sphere of religion. The philosophy this precisely, by which the Church of Rome, from the fourth Century downward, was actuated in all her innovations. Her worship was designed to make up through the flesh, what was wanting in the spirit. The friends of new measures affect to be more free than others, from the authority of mere forms. They wish not to be fettered and cramped by ordinary methods. And yet none make more account in fact of forms. They discard old forms, only to trust the more blindly in such as are new. Their methods are held to be all sufficient, for awakening sinners and effecting their conversion! They have no faith in ordinary pastoral ministrations, comparatively speaking; no faith in the Catechism. Converts made in this way are regarded with suspicion. But they have great faith in the Anxious Bench and its accompaniments. Old measures they hold to be in their very nature unfriendly to the spirit of revivals; they are the "letter that killeth." But new measures "make alive." And yet they are *measures,* when all is done; and it is only by losing sight of the inward power of truth, that any can be led to attach to them any such importance . . .

Here is another most serious charge, demanding our special attention. I have denominated the system a heresy, not inconsiderately or for rhetorical effect simply, but with sober calculation and design. In religion, as in life universally, theory and practice are always inseparably interwined, in the ground of the soul. Every error is felt practically; and wherever obliquity in conduct comes into view, it must be referred to some corresponding obliquity in principle. It is not by accident then that the system of New Measures is found producing so largely, the evil consequences which have been thus far described. Error and heresy, I repeat it, are involved in the system itself, and cannot fail sooner or later, where it is encouraged, to evolve themselves in the most mischievous results . . .The higher force does not strictly and properly take possession of the lower, but is presumed rather to have been reduced to the possession and and service of this last, to be used by it for its own convenience. Religion does not get the sinner, but it is the sinner who "gets religion." Justification is taken to be in fact by feeling, not by faith; and in this way falls back as fully into the sphere of self-righteousness, as thought it were expected from works under any other form. In both the views which have been mentioned, as grounded either in a change of purpose or a change of feeling, religion is found to be in the end the product properly of the sinner himself. It is wholly subjective, and therefore visionary and false. The life of the soul must stand in something beyond itself. Religion involves the will; but not as self-will, affecting to be its own ground and centre. Religion involves feeling; but it is not comprehended in this as its principle. Religion is subjective also, fills and rules the individual in whom it appears; but it is not created in any sense by its subject or from its subject. The life of the branch is in the trunk. The theory we have been contemplating then, as included practically in the system of New Measures, is a great and terrible heresy; which it is to be feared is operating, in this connection, to deceive and destroy a vast multitude of souls . . .

The general system to which the Anxious Bench belongs, it may be remarked again, is unfavorable to deep, thorough and intelligent piety. This must be the case of course, if there be any truth in the observations already made with regard to its character. A system that leads to such a multitude of spurious conversations, and that makes room so largely for that low, gross, fanatical habit, which has just been described, cannot possibly be associated to any extent with the power of godliness, in its deeper and more earnest forms. The religion which it may produce, so far as it can be counted genuine, will be for the most part of a dwarfish size and sickly complexion. The "experience" of the Anxious Bench is commonly shallow. The friends of the new method often please themselves, it is true, with the idea that their awakenings include a vast amount of power in this way; and they are not backward to insinuate, that those who oppose their measures are ignorant of what pertains to the "depths" of experimental piety. Were such persons themselves experimentally acquainted with the pangs of the new birth, it is intimated, they would not be so easily offended with the noise and disorder of poor souls agonizing at the altar; and if they had ever themselves tasted the joys of pardoned sin, they might be expected to have other ears than they now have, for the shouts and hallelujahs of the redeemed, suddenly translated in these circumstances from the power of Satan into the glorious liberty of the family of God. But in fact no "experiences" are more superficial commonly, than those which belong to this whirlwind process. The foundations of the inward life are not reached and moved by it at all. All that would be wanted often to hush an "altar-full" of chaotic cries to solemn stillness, would be that the hearts of the "agonizing" mourners should be suddenly touched with some real sense of the presence of God and their own sins.

It is a different system altogether that is required, to build up the interests of Christianity in a firm and sure way. A ministry apt to teach; sermons full of unction and light; faithful, systematic instruction; zeal for the interests of holiness; pastoral visitation; catechetical training; due attention to order and discipline; patient perseverance in the details of the ministerial work; these are the agencies, by which alone the kingdom of God may be expected to go steadily forward, among any people. Where these are fully employed, there will be revivals; but they will be only as it were the natural fruit of the general culture going before, without that spasmodic, meteoric character, which too often distinguishes excitements under this name; while the life of religion will show itself abidingly at work, in the reigning temper of the Church, at all other times.

Happy the congregation, that may be placed under such spiritual auspices! . . .

We may style it, for distinction sake, the system of the Catechism. It is another system wholly from that which we have been contemplating in this tract. We find the attempt made in some cases, it is true, to incorporate the power of the Catechism with the use of new measures. But the union is unnatural, and can never be inward and complete. The two systems involve at the bottom, two different theories of religion. The spirit of the Anxious Bench is at war with the spirit of the Catechism . . .

They cannot flourish and be in vigorous force together. The Bench is against the Catechism, and the Catechism against the Bench. I mean of course not the Catechism as a mere dead form, in the way in which the original order of the Church, has been too often abused; and it is silly, if not something worse, to insist upon this view of it, when the two systems are drawn into contrast, as though there could be no other alternative to the Bench than the Catechism without life. It is the living Catechism, the Catechism awakened and active, that is intended in this opposition. As such, it stands the representative and symbol of a system, embracing its own theory of religion, and including a wide circle of agencies, peculiar to itself, for carrying this theory into effect. These agencies, in the pulpit and out of it, will be understood, and honored, and actively applied, in proportion exactly as the spirit of the system may prevail; and in the same proportion the Christianity of the Church may be expected to show itself large, deep, full, vigorous and free . . .

Such experience carrying the man beyond himself, and merging the consciousness of the particular in the consciousness of the general, may be much less ostentatious and much more quiet than the experience generated by the other view; but it will be so only because it is far less superficial, and far more full of truth. Religion in this form becomes strictly a life, the life of God in the soul. So far as this life prevails it is tranquil, profound, and free. It overcomes the world; "not by might and by power," the unequal, restless, fitful, and spasmodic efforts of the flesh, "but by the Spirit of the Lord." The believer can do all things, standing in Christ.

And as this theory of religion is the ground of all deep experience in the case of the individual Christian, so it gives rise to the most vigorous and comprehensive action, on the part of the Church, for carrying into effect the provisions of the gospel for the salvation of men. In proportion exactly as it is understood and felt, will such action display itself in all its proper forms; and under no other circumstances can any agency be employed for the same end, that will be entitled at all to take its place.

From first to last, the action now mentioned will go forward, under a due practical recognition of the truth, that both the ruin of man and his recovery rest in a ground, which is beyond himself as an individual. If saved at all, he is to be saved by the force of a spiritual constitution, established by God for the purpose, the provisions of which go far beyond the resources of his own will, and are expected to reach him, not so much through the measure of his own particular life, as by the medium of a more general life, with which he is to be filled and animated from without. This spiritual constitution is brought to bear upon him in the Church, by means of institutions and agencies which God has appointed, and clothed with power, expressly for this end. Hence where the system of the Catechism prevails, great account is made of the Church, and all reliance placed upon the means of grace comprehended in its constitution, as all sufficient under God for the accomplishment of its own purposes. The means are felt to be something more than mere devices of human ingenuity, and are honoured and diligently used accordingly as the "wisdom of God and the power of God" unto salvation. Due regard is had to the idea of the Church as something more than a bare abstraction, the conception of an aggregate of parts mechanically brought together. It is apprehended rather as an organic life, springing perpetually from the same ground, and identical with itself at every point. In this view, the Church is truly the mother of all her children. They do not impart life to her, but she imparts life to them. Here again the general is felt to go before the particular, and to condition all its manifestations. The Church is in no sense the product of individual christianity, as though a number of persons should first receive the heavenly fire in separate streams, and then come into such a spiritual connection comprising the whole; but individual christianity is the product, always and entirely, of the Church, as existing previously, and only revealing its life in this way. Christ lives in the Church, and through the Church in its particular members; just as Adam lives in the human race generically considered, and through the race in every individual man. This view of the relation of the Church to the salvation of the individual, exerts an important influence, in the case before us, on the whole system of action, by which it is sought to reach this object.

Where it prevails, a serious interest will be taken in the case of children, as proper subjects for the Christian salvation, from the earliest age. Infants born in the Church, are regarded and treated as members of it from the beginning, and this privilege is felt to be something more than an empty shadow. The idea of infant conversion is held in practical honor; and it is counted not only possible but altogether natural, that children growing up in the bosom of the Church, under the faithful application of the means of grace, should be quickened into spiritual life in a comparatively quiet way, and spring up numerously, "as willows by the water-courses," to adorn the Christian profession, without being able at all to trace the process by which the glorious change has been effected. Where the Church has lost all faith in this method of conversion, either not looking for it at all, or looking for it only in rare and extraordinary instances, it is an evidence that she is under the force of a wrong religious theory, and practically subjected, at least in some measure, to the false system whose symbol is the Bench. If conversion is not expected nor sought in this way among infants and children, it is not likely often to occur. All is made to hang methodistically on sudden and violent experiences, belonging to the individual separately taken, and holding little or no connection with his relations to the Church previously. Then as a matter of course, baptism becomes a barren sign, and the children of the Church are left to grow up like the children of the world, under general most heartless, most disastrous neglect. The exemplifications of such a connection between wrong theory and wrong practice, in this case, are within the reach of the most common observation. Only where the system of the Catechism is in honor and vigorous force, do we ever find a properly earnest and comprehensive regard exhibited for the salvation of the young; a regard, that operates, not partially and occasionally only, but follows its subjects with all-compassing interest, like the air and light of heaven, from the first breath of infancy onwards; a regard, that cannot be satisfied, in their behalf, with the spasmodic experience of the anxious bench, but travails in birth for them continually, till Christ be formed in their hearts the hope of glory.

Thus due regard is had to the family, the domestic constitution, as a vital and fundamental force, in the general organization of the Church; and all proper pains are taken to promote religion in families, as the indispensable condition of its prosperity under all other forms. Parents are engaged to pray for their children, and to watch over them with true spiritual solicitude, continually endeavoring to draw them to Christ. With such feelings, they will have of course a familiar altar, and daily sacrifices of praise and prayer, in the midst of their house. They will be careful too, to instil into the minds of their children the great truths of religion, "in the house and by the way." Catechetical instruction in particular, will be faithfully employed, from the beginning. And to crown all, the power of a pious and holy example will be sought, as necessary to impart life to all other forms of influence. All this belongs properly to the system of the Catechism . . .

In 1776, a Scottish philosopher, Adam Smith, wrote a tremendously influential treatise on economics called *An Inquiry into the Nature and Causes of the Wealth of Nations.* According to Smith, national economies grow and prosper when economic activity is left free of interference. Individuals pursuing their own self-interest, unhampered by government, will produce the goods and services needed by society, Smith said. The competition among these egocentric individuals will provide all the regulation needed, and through the workings of the free market each competitor — be he laborer, merchant, farmer of manufacturer — will serve his own and society's true interests simultaneously. Smith's theories implied that beneath the apparent chaos of thousands of daily commercial transactions there was actually an operative harmony based on the natural laws of supply and demand and the incessant competition among the members of society.

Smith's theories were congenial with American practices, particularly during the first half of the 19th century when the major economic challenge was to develop the rich national domain that stretched westward toward the Mississippi. The three major possibilities for government interference in the economy were the imposition of protective tariffs on foreign imports to prevent their underselling domestic producers, the use of national banks to stabilize currency and credit terms, and tax policies designed to raise money for internal improvement programs. The small farmer in America had little to gain from any of these. Protective tariffs invited retaliation from other countries, and he needed above all the international free trade that opened up world markets for American commodities. Usually a debtor, he favored an inflated currency and preferred the freedom of choosing from many banks. He even viewed most national internal improvement programs with suspicion, for they usually involved his paying taxes for programs aimed at a national goal in which he had little immediate interest. He might favor short-range state programs, but in general the broad rivers flowing into the Mississippi offered

him the transportation facilities he needed. Southern agricultural producers had an additional reason for favoring Adam Smith's advocacy of *laissez faire*: they wished to avoid anything which would strengthen the national government at the expense of state powers. Thus Smith's economic liberalism was particularly strong among those groups identified with Jackson's Democratic party.

Opposition to Smith came from political leaders with a national outlook and those where economic interests stood to prosper from the protection of American manufacturing and the development of a large domestic market for American goods. The intellectual heirs of Alexander Hamilton, these men, usually Whigs in politics, saw the enormous possibilites of stimulating American growth and creating economic self-sufficiency for the United States through centrally directed programs. The first reading in this secton is an extract from *The Elements of Political Economy* by Daniel Raymond (1786–1849), an American-bred economist. Raymond attacked Smith's central assumption and argued that there was a profound difference between private and national economic goals. Raymond's treatise was in turn challenged by Virginia's governor, William Branch Giles (1762–1830), in a series of articles which appeared in the *Richmond Enquirer.* Although Giles attacked Raymond on theoretical grounds rather than from the perspective of a Southern cotton-producer, the ferocity of his attack, from which the second reading is taken, shows the extent to which Smith's description of natural economic laws had become a new orthodoxy. Both men wrote while John Quincy Adams was president, but the issue became even more important during the 1830's, when Andrew Jackson repudiated the economic nationalism of his predecessors.

Daniel Raymond: The elements of political economy*
(1823)

In imposing duties on importations, governments have a two-fold object. The one is to raise a revenue; the other, to secure to its own citizens some advantage or privilege, over the citizens of foreign governments, in the domestic trade and industry of the country. All writers on political economy admit the expediency of raising a revenue by imposts. The only questions that are ever made on this branch of the subject, respect the amount of the revenue that ought to be raised by imposts, and the mode of collecting it.

But the expediency of laying import duties, for the purpose of securing the citizens some advantage, or privilege, over foreigners, in the domestic trade and industry of the country, has been vehemently controverted by many of the most celebrated and popular writers on political economy, at the head of whom stands Adam Smith . . .

Upon this question, the United States is at present divided into two parties; those who are in favour of, and those who are opposed to raising the tariff. One party contends, that the only object of imposts, should be the raising a revenue: the other, that this should be resorted to, for the purpose of creating a qualified monopoly of our own domestic trade, and for the purpose of encouraging manufacturers. The former are the partisans of a free trade—the latter, of a restricted trade . . .

Upon all subjects relating to political economy, and especially upon the subject of protecting duties, it is ever to be remembered, that the public interests are paramount to individual interests—that a private mischief, or inconvenience, must be endured for the public good; and that when a political economist has shown that public and private interests are opposed, he has made out a case, in which the interposition of the government is necessary—he cannot be required to prove that private interests ought to give way — this is to be taken for granted.

In military tactics, it is a fundamental principle, that the army is one, and the general the head; no soldier is permitted to have a right, or an interest, opposed to the general good of the army. So, in political economy, it should be a fundamental principle, that the nation is one, and the legislature the head; no citizen should be permitted to have a right, or an interest, opposed to the general good of the nation. Until this comes to be admitted, and acted upon as a fundamental principle, political economy will remain in its present crude chaotic state, and cannot be subjected to the rules of science.

It may, with as much propriety, be maintained, that the power and capacity of an army, would be augmented, by permitting every soldier to exercise and employ his military skill and prowess in what way he pleases, as that the power and capacity of a nation will be augmented, by permitting every citizen to employ his skill, industry, and capital, in what way he pleases . . .

We often hear people talk about individual rights, in a strain that would lead one to suppose, that national interests, and individual rights, were, in their opinion, often at variance. They seem to suppose, that the right of property is absolute in the indivudual, and that every one has a right to sell to whom he pleases, and to buy of whom he pleases; and that any interference by the government, in restraining the exercise of this right, is arbitrary and tyrannical. They will tell us, that government has no right to control them in the disposition of their property, merely with a view, that other citizens may derive a benefit from it.

This is a manifest error. Individual right to property is never absolute, but always relative and conditional. There is no such thing as perfect, absolute right, but in those things which are the gift of nature; such as life, liberty, strength, talents, personal beauty, &c. The right to property, is merely conventional or conditional, subject to such regulation as may be made respecting it, with a view to the general interests of the whole nation. No man has, or can have, a perfect exclusive right to property of any description. Every man in the community, has a qualified right to it, and under certain circumstances, has a right to a living out of it. The public right to every piece of property in the nation, is superior to the private right of the individual owner. Hence, the right of the public to take any man's property from him, whenever it becomes necessary for the public

*Pp. 198–208, 214–15, 222–31, 242–46, 251–53.

good. If this were not so, the social compact would not be sustained; government could not be supported.

If individual right to property was absolute, government would have no right to take an individual's property from him, for any purpose whatever. The public has no right to deprive a man of his life, his liberty, his talents, his strength, his personal beauty, or of any other gift of nature, merely for the public good, and for the plainest reason in the world, because he does not derive any of these from the public — they are the gifts of his creator, and He alone has a right to deprive him of them. No man, or body of men, has a right to take them from him, unless they have been forfeited by some crime.

Upon the same principle that God has a right to deprive a man of health and life, government has a right to deprive him of his property. The former is the bounty of God, and held subject to his will. The latter is the bounty of the government, and held subject to its will. But for the social compact no man could have an exclusive right to any spot of this earth. The right of property is therefore a conventional right, and the public grants no title to property in derogation of the public weal. An individual may have a title to property, superior to the title of any other individual, or to any number of individuals, less than the whole, but it cannot be superior to the title of the whole, because the whole includes the title of the individual himself, as well as the title of every body else. Hence the right of the public to take a man's property for the purpose of making public roads, or erecting fortifications, or for any other purpose, which the public good may require. — Hence the right of the government to levy and collect taxes in any manner the public interests may require. — Hence the right to prohibit a man from selling his property to foreigners, or to buy from them those things he may want. The government has a clear and perfect right to make any regulations respecting property, or trade, which the public interests may require.

Every question, therefore, respecting a tariff, or protecting duties, must be a question of expediency, and not a question of right.

At the head of the partisans of a free trade, as contradistinguished from a trade restricted by protecting duties, stands Adam Smith. He is supposed to have placed the subject in the strongest light, in which it is susceptible of being placed in favour of a free trade. It may, therefore, be well to examine a little into the solidity of his reasoning upon this subject. It is proper, however, to observe, that Dr. Smith's principal object in combating the restrictive system, was to show, that it had no direct tendency to increase public wealth, by increasing the quantity of gold and silver in the nation, because national wealth does not depend on the quantity of the precious metals the nation possesses . . .

In the first chapter of the fourth book of the Wealth of Nations, Dr. Smith successfully refutes the idea, that national wealth depends on the quantity of gold and silver a nation possesses, and shows, that a government has no occasion to adopt any measures with a view to increase the quantity by prohibiting its exportation, or securing a favourable balance of trade; and that all such measures are prejudicial to the nation. In the second chapter of the same book, he attempts to prove, that restraints upon the importations from foreign countries, of such goods as can be produced at home, is also prejudicial to the nation, but in this attempt he has utterly failed . . .

Thus, he says . . . "every individual is continually exerting himself to find out the most advantageous employment for whatever capital he can command. It is his own advantage, indeed, and not that of the society which he has in view. But the study of his own advantage naturally leads him to prefer that employment which is most advantageous to the society."

This is, indeed, a most extraordinary doctrine. It is, however, the necessary consequence of confounding national and individual interests and wealth. An individual may study his own advantage by smuggling goods, but it will hardly be pretended that, that is an "employment most advantageous to the society," or nation. An individual may study his own private advantage in employing his capital in the slave trade, but he would not thereby study the advantage of the nation.

It seems to be an admitted dogma with Dr. Smith, that national and individual interests are never opposed, but a more unsound doctrine in principle, or a more abominable one in its consequences, cannot well be imagined. Such a doctrine, if adopted in practice, would destroy all government, and tear up the very foundations of society.

Dr. Smith takes it for granted that it is more desirable for the individual, as well as more profitable for the nation, to employ capital in a domestic, than in a foreign trade, and thence concludes, that individuals will, if let alone by the government, of their own accord, employ their capital in the domestic occupations of the country, in preference to embarking it in foreign trade, unless there is a great disparity in the profits . . .

He says . . . "What is prudence in the conduct of every private family, can scarce be folly in that of a great kingdom. If a foreign country can supply us with a commodity cheaper than we ourselves can make it, better buy it of them, with some part of the produce of our own industry, employed in a way in which we have some advantage. The general industry of the country, being always in proportion to the capital which employs it, will not thereby be diminished, no more than that of the above mentioned artificers; but only left to find out a way in which it can be employed with the greatest advantage. It is certainly not employed to the greatest advantage, when it is thus diverted towards an object which it can buy cheaper than it can make."

It may be admitted, that if individuals, or a nation, can buy an article cheaper than they can make it, they had better buy than to make, as a general rule; but to this general rule there are many exceptions, and these exceptions will embrace the policy of protecting duties to as great an extent, as has ever been contended for by the partisans of a restricted trade . . .

It may, as an ordinary rule, be better for the tailor to buy his shoes of the shoemaker, than to make them himself, but it may be better to make than to buy them. If he has constant employment in his own trade, he had better buy his shoes than to make them. If he has not, it may be better to make than to buy them. If a tailor cannot sell his own work, he had better spend a week in making a pair of shoes, than to buy them with the price of an ordinary day's work. Whether it be better for a farmer to buy his own cloaths, and shoes, than to make them, depends entirely on circumstances. Sometimes it is better to do the one, and sometimes the other. If he can buy them with some of the produce of his own industry,

"employed in a way in which he has some advantage," better to buy than to make them; if not, he had better make than buy them. A tailor, who can find employment in his trade only one half of his time, had better employ the other half in making shoes and raising corn, than to be idle that time, and buy his shoes and corn at any price, no matter how cheap . . . But, from the general unqualified manner, in which Dr. Smith lays down the doctrine, one would be led to suppose, that in his opinion at least, it would always be better for the tailor to buy his shoes and his corn, than to make the one, and raise the other, by his own labour; and that the farmer could never be profitably employed in making clothes and shoes.

This doctrine, when rightly explained, is as applicable to nations, as to individuals. The principles which are applicable to individuals, being often applicable to nations; but in order to apply them properly, we must consider nations as individuals, distinct in all their parts, and not as part individual only. The nation must be considered as one and indivisible. Let this be done, and we shall not be embarrassed with individual interests and rights, as contradistinguished from national rights and interests. Individual interests are perpetually at variance with national interests. Hence the absurdity of supposing that, that which is beneficial to individuals, is also beneficial to the nation. An individual, or a class of the community, may be benefitted by being permitted to import goods, free of duty, but it does not necessarily follow, that the nation would be benefitted by it . . .

The question in the one case is, has the tailor full employment in his trade, and the answer to this question will determine whether he had better seize hold of the awl and the plough. So, in the case of the nation, the question is, has it full employment in raising tobacco and cotton, and in its other ordinary occupations? If it has not, it will be wiser, and more conducive to its wealth, to employ its unoccupied time in manufacturing cotton and woollen cloths, than to import them from England at any price.

As to the soundness of this principle there can be no doubt. In its application it is universal both to individuals and nations. — It is far less variable than the mariner's compass. The only difficulty consists in its application. — In knowing exactly what portion of a nation's time is unoccupied — how much surplus labour it has on hand, which might be profitably employed. The perplexity is also increased by the opposition of individual and national interests, and the difficulty of separating them. But the duty of a legislator, when these interests are once distinguished and separated, does not admit of discussion. It may with as much propriety be contended, that one class of citizens should be permitted to smuggle goods, because it is for their benefit, as that another should be permitted to import them at a low tariff, because it is for their benefit, when opposed to the general interests of the nation . . .

But the question, whether the importation of manufactures should be prohibited, or the tariff raised, does not at all depend upon the fact, that they can be procured by the consumer cheaper in foreign countries, than in his own. Buying goods where they may be had cheapest, may be the best policy for some individuals, while buying them where they come dearest, may be the best policy for the nation. Dr. Smith's doctrine cannot be admitted, till he proves, that individual interests are never at variance with national interests . . .

Suppose, this quantity of goods to be manufactured at home in consequence of prohibiting the importation of foreign goods, without withdrawing labour from other branches of industry. Now it matters not, at what price these goods come to the consumers, whether double, triple, or quadruple the price, at which they could have been procured at some other place, the saving to the nation will be, a million of dollars, just as certainly as the tailor would save the price of a pair of shoes, by making them when he had nothing else to do.

The only difficulty in comprehending this subject is in distinguishing between individual and national interests. Let it be admitted that a nation is a unity, and national interests paramount to individual interests, and the other consequences inevitably follow. The question of cheapness and dearness is altogether irrelevant, and out of the case. Dr. Smith is upon a wrong scent and his doctrine given to the winds.

It is the duty and interest of the planter to find employment for all his hands, and if this cannot be done in one branch of business, to seek out another.

So it is the duty of the legislator to find employment for all the people, and if he cannot find them employment in agriculture and commerce, he must set them to manufacturing. It is his duty to take special care that no other nation interferes with their industry. He is not to permit one half of the nation to remain idle and hungry, in order that the other half may buy goods where they may be had cheapest. A legislator may not, however, as Dr. Smith supposes the consequence of this doctrine to be, "direct private people in what manner they ought to employ their capitals." He may not direct one man to engage in this business, and another in that. Every man is to be left free to engage in what business he pleases, but he ought not to be allowed to afford patronage and support to the industry of foreigners, when his own fellow-citizens are in want of it . . .

What quantity of goods can these men manufacture in one year? What is the value of the same quantity of goods of foreign manufacture? What portion of this value did the raw material constitute? What quantity of manual labour did it require to manufacture these goods in the foreign country? In short, what is the comparative expense of manufacturing an equal quantity of goods in the two countries? The result of this inquiry will show whether these men can live by their labour, without encouragement and protection by the government, and what degree of protection is necessary to enable them to carry it on . . .

This shows the advantage of a system of political economy, which regards a nation as an individual, or unity, in opposition to a system which considers it as an indefinite number of individuals, all having distinct and separate interests, always in opposition to each other, and often in opposition to the interests of the nation . . .

Another important advantage, arising from a monopoly of the home market, is the certainty and stability of the demand for the product of industry. All fluctuations in the demand for either the necessaries or comforts of life, produce want and distress among the labourers, who supply the demand. This nation is at present groaning under the distress, caused by a fluctuation in the demand for the product of labour. The national distress in England, arises from the same cause. The consumption does not equal the production, which, as has already been shown, necessarily produces distress. This is always liable to be the case, when the consumption depends on a foreign market. This market is liable to be interrupted by foreign nations. But this is not the case with a domestic market. In this, the demand is always steady, and usually increasing. It is not liable to be interrupted by foreign nations, so long as a nation maintains its independence . . .

These are not, however, the only advantages arising from a monopoly of the home market. As such a market tends to augment the quantity of national industry, and of course national wealth, it also tends to make the people more habitually industrious; and habits of industry constitute a portion of national wealth. A man, who is industrious from habit, has a greater capacity for acquiring the necessaries and comforts of life, than one in similar circumstances, with idle habits: so of a nation . . .

From this it is not to be inferred that in all cases it would be advisable for government to secure to its own citizens the monopoly of the home trade, either by absolute prohibition of foreign importation, or by high protecting duties. All measures upon this subject should be regulated according to the existing circumstances of the nation; and the first thing to be ascertained is, whether the nation has full employment in its ordinary occupations, or whether the sum of national industry is likely to be augmented by such a measure. A great deal of mischief may be done by an imprudent restriction upon the freedom of trade — it may have the effect to diminish the consumption of the country, which will paralyze, instead of invigorating industry. But when the people of a nation have not full employment, and a measure of this description will have the effect to give employment to a portion of them, it will promote the general prosperity of the country, and augment national wealth, although it may be adverse to the interests of some individuals.

A government like ours, I know, cannot be administered upon such liberal and enlightened principles, and there is no hope that any other form of government will be better calculated to promote national prosperity and wealth. The people always look to their immediate interests, and certain classes will always have an undue influence over the government.

Individuals have always a more contracted view of public, than of their own private affairs. A man will calculate his private affairs on a scale of twenty years, with more patience, than he will calculate public affairs, upon a scale of two years. The reason is obvious. He enjoys the full and exclusive benefit of his calculations in the one case. — He shares with the whole nation, the benefit of the calculations in the other. This is the reason why private affairs are more wisely conducted than public.

Such ought not, however, to be the case with a legislator. "He who has undertaken the magnificent work of promoting national wealth and making a nation happy, should not be governed by the narrow minded views of private interest. He should not busy his thoughts with acres, but with states — not with a ship, but with navies — not with a warehouse, but with cities." Let him do this, and although he may not be able to carry a true policy to the extent that might be desired, still he will be able to carry it to a much greater extent than it has ever yet been carried . . .

William Branch Giles: Political disquisitions on Raymond's Elements of Political Economy (1825)

. . . Our fathers solemnly admonished us, to have frequent recurrence to fundamental principles; not for the purpose, as some amiable, visionary spirits seem to suppose, to alter or amend these principles; but for the purpose of correcting all aberrations from them, by the practical administrators of the government. These principles are declared to be derived from nature and from nature's God; and are, therefore, immutable and eternal. It could not be possible for our fathers under these solemn convictions, to have advised this frequent recurrence, for the purpose of changing unchangeable eternal truths; but for the opposite purpose of considering them as infallible guides! to direct the practical administrators of the several governmental institutions; and to bring them back from their wanderings, if any should occur, to the unerring truths, proclaimed in these fundamental laws. In utter disregard of this sacred injunction, as the writer conceives, our federal administration has flown far ahead of our fundamental

William Branch Giles, *Political Miscellanies*, Richmond, 1830, pp. 3–11, 16–19, 24–33, 39.

laws. The writer thinks that our liberties are in danger. That the practical administration has assailed them! That the efforts of the people in their individual capacities alone can save them! That in consequence of these lamentable fatal aberrations, a necessity has arisen for solving the great and awful political problem — Are the American people capable of self-government? Raymond's Elements of Political Economy will develop, as the writer thinks, the political elements of Mr. Adams, and Mr. Secretary Clay's practical administration. They, therefore, deserve to be read and well considered in reference to that interesting subject. Raymond is believed to be a disciple and leader of the new political school; and like most zealous sectarians, and still more the founders and leaders of sects, he is, in that respect, a fanatic . . .

One principle object of the author, corresponding precisely, as the writer conceives, with the avowals of the practical administration, appears to be, to liberate the Government of "this Union," from all limitations, and to make it one and indivisible. Another appears to be, to render its administrators irresponsible and inviolable. The first is attempted, by asserting the unity of all Governments, comprehending that of the United States; and corresponding with President Adams' notion of "a common social compact" in its application to the Government of "this Union;" forgetful of its federal ingredients; forgetful of the several common social compacts which are the basis of the several State Governments; forgetful of State sovereignties, of State rights, and even of the reserved rights of individuals . . . Upon this point, let the author be heard in his own words, and the analogy shall be sketched hereafter,

"A nation is a unity and possesses all the properties of unity. It possesses a unity of rights, a unity of interests, and a unity of possessions; and he who professes to treat of the interests of this unity, but departs from them, and treats of the interests of some constituent part of it, will just as certainly arrive at a wrong conclusion, as the arithmetician would, who, in performing an Algebraic computation, should leave out one term of the equation."

Again, "It must be remembered, that a nation is as much a unity as an individual, and must always be considered so, when treating of national interests. It possesses all the properties of unity — unity of rights, possessions, and interests." . . .

In the foregoing extracts, which are copiously made, as affording the means of correcting any possible unintentional misconstruction, the author has effected his first object. He has made a nation, an unity. One and indivisible. He lays this down, as an indispensable fundamental principle. "Upon it," he says, "every true system of political economy must be built;" of course, comprehending that of the Government of "this Union." The author effects his second object in pages 221, 222, vol. 1. "No man can be expected to forego a present advantage to himself, provided there is no immorality in the enjoyment of it, upon the ground that it may be prejudicial to posterity. He may have no posterity, or if he has, their interests at the distance of two or three generations, are too remote to influence his conduct. The influence of self-interest on human conduct, like the laws of gravitation, is in the inverse ratio of distance and quantity. Legislators, however, are not permitted to take such limited, short-sighted views of things — they are placed on a more elevated station — they move in a higher sphere — they are traitors to their high trust, if they do not look to the future as well as the present; they are in one sense, (though, in a very humble one) the vicegerents of God on earth; and, as he regulates and governs the world, by the laws of eternal justice and wisdom, in regard to the future, as well as the present; by the same laws, ought legislators to regulate and govern the nations of the earth, over whom they preside. Even according to the laws of self-interest, the remoteness of the interests of future generations, should be counterbalanced by the magnitude of those interests."

Here then, it appears, according to the new hypothesis, that legislators instead of being representatives, or servants of the people, as heretofore supposed, "are in one sense, although a very humble one, the vicegerents of God upon earth." This is the exploded doctrine of the divine rights of kings revived in the United States, and extended to all American legislators . . .

"A nation is an Unity." This is the fundamental point upon which the author has placed himself, in regard to his whole system of elementary political economy; and, like Archemides in relation to the natural world, give him this place to stand upon, and the author seems to think, he can at pleasure move the whole political world. This principle is true in one sense, but it is not true in the sense of the author. A nation may be defined to be, the land comprehended within certain geoprahical boundaries, over which one government presides; whether indivisible, or composed of different parts, and the people inhabiting the land within those boundaries. The term "nation" comprehends as well the lands, as the inhabitants thereupon, within the prescribed limits of the government. Indeed, in speaking of a "nation," it is impossible, in our conceptions, to separate the land from the people, or the people from the land. If the people were removed from the land, they could not properly be considered as a "nation;" nor could the term "nation" be properly applied to a tract of country without an inhabitant . . .

The author, although highly sensible of the importance of precise, specific definitions, in all polemic disquisitions, often confounds the terms nation and government, and uses them as convertible terms; whereas, there are not two terms in the English language of more distinct and separate meaning. The difference between a part and a whole. Government may be defined to be, a corporation consisting of one or more persons, invested with the exercise of all rightful political power, over a nation, and is a constituent part of such nation. Governments have been derived either from force, fraud or compact. Those derived from force and fraud, have been said, to have their origin in the immediate gift of God, to the respective Governors, without any intermediate right, or invention of the people. Those derived from compact, have their origin in the people, as the rightful source of all political power through the gift of God to them in their original native character. The people being then the original sovereign owners of all power derived from the gift of God to them in their native State, they by written compacts, have granted out certain portions thereof, to governments in their corporate character, to be exercised for the benefit of the people in their original character. The Constitutions of the several States and of the United States, afford the first examples of the formation of governments of this description, and of course, they are of recent origin. This discovery has heretofore been thought to promise much for improving and meliorating the polit-

ical condition of man; and the first experiments under it, were thought to have been successful, even beyond the most sanguine hope, or expectation of the most sanguine admirers of this invention; but lamentable to be told, the writer thinks this great American invention, so much wanted by all mankind, and so much cherished and beloved by the American people, is already strangled in its infancy by the untaught, unthinking, unwise, visionary, ambitious, political fashionables.

If then, by the term "nation," the author merely meant that a nation consisted of a certain extent of country within prescribed limits for the purpose of government, and the inhabitants of that country amalgamated in one conception, it is admitted, in that sense; that "a nation is an unity," *E Pluribus Unum* — but then this amalgamation must be made up of its different integral units composing the whole, with all the properties rightfully belonging to each, whether these units consist of States, governments, or individuals. In this sense, the author's great fundamental principle would not answer his purpose. He, therefore, proceeds to explain the sense in which he uses the term, and in which sense alone, can it be made to answer his purpose. Thus — "It" (a nation) "possesses a unity of rights, a unity of interests, and a unity of possessions." This also may be true, if it be confined to the lawful rights, interests and possessions of a nation in its national character, as, for instance, the rights, interests, and possessions of the unsold lands belonging to the nation of the United States, as contradistinguished from the rights of the individual members thereof; whether sovereign States, State Governments, or individuals: but if in this unity, is intended to be comprehended all the rights, &c. of the integral units composing this nation, whether States, Governments, or individuals, then it is not true. It then becomes a principle involving the most unfounded, despotic, and preposterous results. Yet it is in this sense only, in which the unity of a nation can be made to answer the author's object: in developing his frightful elementary principles of political economy. What can the author mean, by an unity of rights, &c. belonging to a nation, unless it be all rights natural and derivative? He makes no distinction; and must, therefore, be understood to include the whole. It is a matter of some surprise to the writer, that political economists, have not heretofore made some attempts to draw more precisely the line of discrimination between these two great descriptions of rights. The writer does not now propose to make the attempt; but he will sketch out a few of the first description, which, he thinks, will be sufficient abundantly to shew the preposterous absurdity of a national unity of all rights, natural and derivative. The right to labor—the right to make bread —and the right to eat it, it is presumed, will be admitted to be natural rights. Man is absolute sovereign over these rights, in his individual native character, and in that character, he exercises them at his pleasure. Suppose in this amalgamation of rights, he could and would give them up to the nation for the purpose of forming its quality of unity; how could it be exercised by a nation in this quality of unity? Could this unity eat bread for an individual, and digest it after eating it? The notion is absurd and preposterous. The right of marriage is a natural right. Could a nation in its quality of unity execute this right? If so, the writer calls upon the author for the modus operandi in either case. When a man becomes a member of a nation, he does not abandon these rights, but he retains them with him to be executed in his individual original character, in his associated State? These are simple, but important rights; more important than the whole tribe of conventional rights put together; for upon their exercise depend the very existence and continuation of the human species. These and innumerable other natural rights, precious as numberless, belong to individual man, whether in a natural or associated State, to be exercised by him in his individual character as original sovereign owner. Without descending into a more minute illustration at this time, the writer thinks this view will demonstrate the absurdity and folly of an amalgamation of all rights natural and conventional, individual and corporate, as the foundation of this magic quality of national unity. Every individual after becoming a member of a nation, retains to himself all that portion of his natural rights, which, in free governments, is not ceded by his voluntary consent, and in despotic ones, which is not compulsively taken from his by the government. Even in the most despotic European Government, the writer thinks, there are some rights reserved to each individual member, to be exercised in his original, native character,

if not in the avowed theory of such governments, certainly in the practical administration of them. This is one respect, in which the writer thinks, the author's notions of the extent of governmental powers over individual rights, would not be avowed by the most depotic Government in Europe. This point will be more particularly explained hereafter. The author's principle, strips the individual members of government of all rights, and usurps the whole for the nation in its united character, to be exercised by the government of that nation in its corporate character. Not a vestige of right is to be executed by the individual member in his original native character. On the contrary, the writer contends, that each individual member retains to himself his most important natural rights. That he is absolute sovereign over these retained rights to be exercised by himself at his own pleasure; and that no government can rightfully control him in the exercise of these retained rights. This is the practice, whatever be the theory of governments, one and indivisible, when acting under the claims of sovereign unlimited powers; but it appears now to be disavowed by the disciples of the new school, in their application of the Government of the United States, although limited in its powers by a specific charter . . .

The States also, thus become despoiled of all rights, whilst the Government of "this Union," one and indivisible, becomes possessed of all rights, interests and possessions in absolute sovereignty. Now when it is considered, according to the author's hypothesis, that this national unity is to be controlled and directed by legislators who are made God's vicegerents upon the earth for that purpose, and consist of good for nothing fellows, a "mass of stupidity and ignorance," unrestrained by any other influence than the laws by which God governs the world; can the imagination conceive of a more frightful form of government, held forth to the American people by this admired and lauded disciple of the new political school? What invention or device, could more effectually abrogate every restraining principle in the Constitution of the United States? What more vauntingly defies and insults the fundamental laws of every American political institution? . . .

It was on this ground that States and State Governments now to be annihilated become essential ingredients in our beautiful system of fundamental laws; and above all, from the difference in the great principles of labour, established in different sections of the territory, upon which, the community in each, depends for its subsistence, its prosperity, and its happiness. In estimating these views of this part of the subject, it should be primarily observed and should never be forgotten; that none of these differences in sectional pursuits and interests grow out of the natural relations of different occupations in society. They are all created by the artificial intermeddling of the Government. It is impossible to find any difference in the natural relations of the slave-holding and the non-slave-holding States, nor in the different occupations of their inhabitants respectively. The cotton planter of the South raises an article which is indispensable to the prosperity of the manufacturer of the East, whilst he wants the manufactured article in return.

In the natural operation of their different sectional pursuits, they become reciprocally beneficial to each other, and no difference of interests is seen to exist between them; but the moment the government intermeddles with these occupations, and artificially takes from the cotton planter a certain portion of the annual proceeds of his labour, and gives it to the Eastern manufacturer, then commences the difference of interests between these two sectional occupations. This difference of interests consists in precisely the quantum of the produce of the labour of the one, compulsively taken by Government and given to the other. The interest of the one is to increase, of the other to lessen, the quantum of labour. Let nothing be taken from the one and given to the other, and all difference of interests instantly vanishes, and reciprocity of interest, becomes instantly restored. The one condition being the natural and rightful relation of these two occupations; the other, the wrongful artificial relation created by the Government. Different occupations in society, and still more, if such occupations be sectional, afford the most fruitful means of Governments, of creating artificial differences of interests in society; and through such artificial differences of establishing and confirming their own despotism. The most detestable acts of the most detestable tyrants have often derived their pestilential

influence from this condition of society. They play off the interest of one occupation against another; and thus make all dependent upon them, for the favors they capriciously deal out to each. The Tariff law, is the most illustrative example of the truth of this doctrine . . .

Without giving further attention at this time, to the prefatory preparations of the author for the great object of his work, the writer will proceed at once to his chapter on "protecting duties." This subject appears to be the git of the whole work; and it seems to have been written principally with the view of proving the right of the General Government to lay duties for the sole object of protecting domestic manufactures. From the circumstances attending the publication, it may fairly be presumed to have been written, at the request and under the influence of the manufacturing interest . . . and . . . it would appear evident, that the principles avowed in this work, form the basis of the right to pass the Tariff bill, and have been received as orthodox, by the supporters of that law, and by the disciples of the new political school—the present political fashionables. This sect of politicians, now constitute the dominant party in the practical Government, as the writer believes; and, therefore, these principles deserve to be profoundly considered and well understood by the whole American people . . .

Hear the author, in the next place, in relation to the right of the Government to take private property for the public good, "They seem to suppose, that the right of property is absolute in the individual; and that every one has a right to sell to whom he pleases, and to buy of whom he pleases, &c. This is a manifest error." Again, 'The public right to property is superior to the private right of the individual owner. Hence the right of the public to take any man's property from him, whenever it becomes necessary for the public good."—Extract from the sixth amendment of the Constitution of the United States: "Nor (shall any person,) be deprived of life, liberty, or property, without due process of law: nor shall private property be taken for public uses, without just compensation." These great fundamental principles, are asserted in every State Constitution in the Union, in which the subject is expressly mentioned, and where it is not, it is implied: and the

Constitution, in every case, is bottomed upon it. It would be a waste of time and of words, to resort to arguments to show, the preposterous errors of the author, upon these all-important points, when these high obligatory sanctions, are presented in direct contradiction of them. Yet it is upon these most abominable, heretical errors, that the author has bottomed the right of the Government of "this Union," to pass the tariff law, for the protection of domestic manufactures. This law the author admits, was intended to take, and in fact, does take property from one man and give it to another without just compensation. The author, nevertheless, justifies all this, from the potent, bewitching influence of his enchanted notion of national unity . . .

Fellow-citizens! look at these cabalistical phrases—look at the powers usurped under cover of them—look at the despotic character of these powers—then turn to your Constitutions—examine well all your own fundamental laws; and see if one of these powers be granted to the practical Government of the United States. If not, is it not your first duty? Is it not your first interest to recur to these fundamental principles; to tear from the practical Government, all usurpations not having their only legitimate santion; to correct its destructive abberrations; and thus to restore to your fundamental laws, their pristine wisdom, purity and energy; and to yourselves, all your violated rights.

SUGGESTIONS FOR FURTHER READING

Lee Benson, *The Concept of Jacksonian Democracy*, Atheneum, New York, 1961.

Richard H. Brown, "The Missouri Crisis, Slavery and the Politics of Jacksonianism," *South Atlantic Quarterly*, **65** (1966).

Stuart Bruchey, *The Roots of American Economic Growth, 1607–1861*, Harper & Row, New York, 1965.

William N. Chambers and Walter Dean Burnham (eds.), *The American Party System*, Oxford University Press, New York, 1967.

William W. Freehling, *Prelude to Civil War*, Harper & Row, New York, 1966.

David Grimsted, "Rioting in its Jacksonian Setting," *American Historical Review*, 77 (1972).

Bray Hammond, "Jackson, Biddle and the Bank of the United States," *Journal of Economic History*, 7 (1947)

Oscar and Mary Handlin, *Commonwealth, 1774–1861*, Harvard University Press, Cambridge, 1969.

Louis Hartz, *The Liberal Tradition in America*, Harcourt, Brace & World, New York, 1955.

F. K. Henrich, "The Development of American Laissez Faire," *Journal of Economic History*, 3 (Supplement, 1943).

Sidney Mead, *The Lively Experiment*, Harper & Row, New York, 1963.

Marvin Meyers, *The Jacksonian Persuasion*, Vintage, New York, 1957.

Richard Niebuhr, *The Kingdom of God in America*, Harper & Row, New York, 1959.

David Potter, *People of Plenty*, University of Chicago Press, Chicago, 1954.

Robert V. Remini, *Martin Van Buren and the Making of the Democratic Party*, W. W. Norton, New York, 1959.

Arthur Schlesinger, Jr., *The Age of Jackson*, Little, Brown, Boston, 1946.

George R. Taylor, *The Transportation Revolution, 1815–1860*, Harper & Row, New York, 1951.

John W. Ward, *Andrew Jackson: Symbol for an Age*, Oxford University Press, New York, 1955.

Bernard Weisberger, *They Gathered at the River*, Quadrangle, Chicago, 1959.

AMERICAN GROWTH AND THE REFORM IMPULSE

Chapter 8   1829-1850

The pressures within American society in the middle years of the 19th century began to cause visible cracks in the liberal consensus and fissures in the political structure. Even expansion and abundance created problems. With churches reduced to mere voluntary organizations and the federal government hemmed in by the assertion of states' rights, no institution in American life existed to protect the vulnerable. The growing complexity of the American economy was creating money power with no check. Prosperity was promoting materialistic values which affronted the spiritual and intellectual sensibilities of many. The forceful drive of the South for new territory precipitated a war with Mexico and raised new fears about the spread of slavery while a sharp increase in the rate of immigration caused many native-born Americans to worry about the future ethnic composition of the nation.

Sectionalism had become a marked feature of American politics during the early decades of the 19th century when the states of the South, Northeast, and West became highly conscious of their different interests. The federalism established by the Constitution sought to guard such local interests of member states while providing for effective national government. Any one state was in a minority position in relation to the whole, but the operating assumption was that the states would be able to protect vital interests by forming alliances with other states to ward off legislation unfavorable to their most important concerns. This working arrangement is destroyed, however, when a single issue overrides all others and produces a permanent majority of states against a minority. Then no amount of participation in the process of initiating and deliberating on legislation can compensate for the inevitable failure when the votes are counted. The position of a permanent minority in a political process in which decisions are made by the majority is one of impotence.

Madison, writing in *The Federalist Papers*, had suggested that there would be many different groupings in the extended republic of the United States, and that this fact would cause constantly changing majorities of farmers, of Methodists, of enthusiastic democrats, of commercial interests, of German descendents, depending upon the legislation under consideration. Diversity, it was hoped, would prevent the formation of a permanent minority and majority. In the years before the Civil War, however, the interests which the Southern leaders held in common came to dominate the interests some Southerners might share with some Northerners or Westerners. The specific demands of the slave economy and the need to protect slavery from hostile legislation became the overriding consideration of Southern statesmen who fortified themselves behind a radical states' rights doctrine.

Three events took place in 1831 which gave a decisive turn to the issue of slavery in the United States. William Lloyd Garrison began publishing the *Liberator.* Nat Turner led his famous Virginia slave insurrection which resulted in some 150 deaths and twenty executions, and Southern legislators began passing laws severely restricting the circulation of anti-slavery literature in their states. The Georgia State Senate, for instance, offered a $500 reward for the arrest and conviction of *The Liberator's* publisher. A thoroughly aroused South was prepared to defend slavery from outside propaganda at almost any cost. After 1831, a kind of cotton curtain was drawn behind which no man, woman, or child could

safely discuss the pros and cons of slavery. A solid South was in the making, and the Mason-Dixon line, originally a simple colonial boundary, became the political border between two diverging societies within the American nation.

As the founding of *The Liberator* indicated, the North's long silence on the South's peculiar institution had come to an end. With slavery abolished in much of Latin America, its continued existence in the United States elicited widespread criticism. A small group of Americans was now ready to take up the cause of abolition with total dedication. They based their campaign upon appeals to the individual conscience and in doing so pushed to the fore one of the unresolved conflicts of American ideology. Can the majority confer justice upon its decisions or are there immutable standards of right and wrong which alone can make legal rules moral? In a country where majority vote decided so many things, it was difficult not to believe that the voting process conferred rightfulness upon the majority's decisions. The issue of slavery drove home the dilemma between conscience and law with particular forcefulness, because Southerners relied upon the Constitution to protect their state laws, and abolitionists urged men to flout all laws which supported slavery. Two important components of American political thought were in obvious conflict — majority rule and the belief in higher law. The defenders of slavery spoke of the union, the Constitution, and the rule of law, while the abolitionists told their fellow Americans that civil disobedience was necessary when law offended the dictates of conscience. Both the Constitution's protection of state institutions and the majority's decision-making power were being challenged.

Economically, America was also undergoing a fundamental restructuring. By 1840 the middle Atlantic and New England states had the essential requirements for industrialization: a large home market, machinery, capital, an abundance of labor, men with managerial skills, and river, road, and canal transportation. With a population of seventeen million, the United States was large enough to stimulate sustained investments in manufacturing. A growing urban population was creating new demands for western foodstuffs. In actual and potential wealth, the North and West were displacing the South, whose cotton exports had long been the driving force in American expansion. While the South continued to send the bulk of her cotton crop outside the country to England, the North and West were drawing together through a new reciprocity of needs. The shift to an economy based upon industrial capitalism had begun. America continued to export raw materials, but the development of her own industries freed the country from dependence upon foreign manufactured goods. The switch from a commercial to an industrial base had opened up the possibility of real economic self-sufficiency.

Unprecedented population growth throughout the western world also had a profound impact upon the United States. In good times, the European economies could support their growing population, but a bad harvest or trade depression could push thousands of Europeans to the edge of starvation. When this happened, America's opportunities beckoned. Changes in the English Poor Laws and political repression on the Continent enhanced the appeal of America. The push-pull of immigration motives went into full operation in the 1840's, when immigrants began arriving at the rate of 1000 a day. Economically, the United States could absorb these new people, but socially they presented painful problems. The substantial increase in the proportion of alien to native-born Americans made the presence of foreigners very obvious.

The process of assimilating the new arrivals was further complicated by the fact that many of them were Roman Catholics. With all its religious variety, America had a distinctly Protestant bias. The many different Protestant denominations had made religious toleration and disestablishment a practical necessity, but America's religious liberty — usually expressed in universal terms — actually operated within the Protestant fold. Protestant social ethics supported the anti-authoritarian cast of the American mind. They complemented the American ideal of the independent

individual competent to make his own choices. Such American virtues as hard work, individual initiative, and plain living were cultural by-products of Protestantism. The Catholic Church spoke to different human needs and emphasized different qualities, and it was in references to these values, rather than to specific doctrinal differences, that native-born Americans took alarm at the increased Catholic immigration.

To some the very core of national identity was being challenged. Foreign paupers given to celebrating the Sabbath with beer-drinking picnics and professing humble obedience to a faraway pope were threatening the moral fiber, sober habits, and political independence of Americans. The number of American voters who feared unrestricted immigration was sufficient to make nativism a potent political force. A new national political party — the Know-Nothings, or American party — emerged with programs for limiting immigration and disenfranchising aliens. The actual practice of the Catholic religion was protected by the Constitution, but outside the purview of the first amendment, Catholics were reviled, discriminated against, and sometimes even violently assaulted in what one historian has grimly labelled "the Protestant Crusade."

Immigration had other social complications. As Southerners were quick to point out, the North was not without its share of human misery. The factory system fed by the flood of newcomers had developed without government regulation, leaving vulnerable members of society — women, children, and foreigners — unprotected. The strong tide of egalitarianism had washed away the last vestiges of political inequality at the very time that developments in the American economy were creating new concentrations of wealth. As Americans were to discover, it was difficult to have true political equality when economic power was controlled by the wealthy few.

This same decade witnessed the first labor organizations which formed and dissolved in response to successes, failures, and shifts in the business cycle. The laboring class had a large number of foreigners. Immigrants from the British Isles had no language barrier to overcome in their new home, so they were able to participate in public life immediately. Having a much keener sense of the exploitative possibilities of a fully industrialized society like that of England, they introduced a radical strain into the American labor movement. None of the early labor organizations, however, was long-lasting. Mainly composed of skilled laborers, the unions had aims which were ill-defined, ranging from "bread and butter" demands to broad social goals like penal reform and public education. Although workers' associations were more common in the 1840's, the appeal of personal ambition and social mobility acted as a constant check to their growth. Their importance in these decades lay not so much in their tangible achievements as in their capacity to frighten Americans who were being simultaneously threatened by foreign immigration and the problems of industrialization.

These changes in American society also called into question the basis of American nationhood. America's political ideals could and did supply a sense of national identity to a country marked by diversity. In the absence of common national origins, Americans could feel themselves to be American by virtue of their commitment to the principles of the Declaration of Independence, but anti-Catholic and antialien sentiments undermined this basis of unity. Influential native born Americans began pulling back from an open-ended national creed. They accepted in its place an explanation of the country's free institutions in terms of its English background. In this view, America owed its political freedom and economic productivity to the fact that the founding colonists were Anglo-Saxon and Protestant. Southerners gravitated to this explanation of American liberties because they agreed with its implicit denial of the equality of man, always an embarrassing concept to slave-holders, but the promotion of Anglo-Saxon virtues went on throughout the country and unhappily was fostered by some of the most vocal churchmen.

The assertion of Anglo-Saxon Protestant superiority was congenial to the foreign policy pursued by America in the 1840's. Southerners, trying to get out of their restricted corner of the United States, had moved into Mexico with their slaves. Americans in Texas, soon a majority of this underpopulated Mexican province, successfully fought off Mexican authority and declared Texas independent. Several American presidents tried to buy the area, but were disdainfully rejected by Mexico's president. Finally, Congress passed a joint resolution which annexed Texas. Mexico was unwilling to consider annexation as anything but a euphemism for theft, and the two neighbors went to war. The idea of ethnic superiority helped to explain why the United States had a peculiar destiny to spread political enlightenment, religious freedom, and productive agriculture across the North American continent. The fact that an underdeveloped, politically weak, and racially mixed Catholic population lay in the path of American expansion made the new Americanism of superior ancestry particularly useful as the justification of a war with Mexico. The older tradition of identifying American nationalism with lofty political principles was far from dead, however. The Mexican War was vigorously criticized as a betrayal of the founding ideals of the United States. Supporters of a new peace movement protested the use of war to gain territory for America, and the abolitionists attacked it as evidence of the power of the slavocracy, as they began calling the men who led the Southern states. The difficulty in defining American nationalism was mirrored in the confusion which the boundless opportunity, rapid growth, and unrestrained individual freedom had created in the America of the 1840's.

There were positive forces working in American society, as well. The 1840's witnessed a remarkable outpouring of human sympathy and set in motion hundreds of humanitarian causes. This philanthropy was fundamentally ameliorative and utopian. Most churches and charitable organizations were concerned with relieving suffering rather than with reforming the system which had caused the misery. Appeals for helping those in need were in uneasy tension with assertions that all was well. Any attack upon private property or suggestion of restricting individual freedom in favor of broader community goals was condemned as radical. Still a minority of reformers gifted with the intellectual independence to probe for the root cause of slavery, slums, and the increasing alienation of man in modern society did emerge in New England. Closely associated with the Transcendentalists, these writers and philosophers used their talents and prestige to focus American attention upon sore spots in the society. More importantly, they infused into public life aesthetic and moral perceptions which America's material well-being was obscuring. At the same time these social critics and philanthropists shared in the country's common cultural perceptions. They believed that society's problems could best be solved through persuasion and education, and they insisted upon the primacy of the individual. Dogged in their faith in voluntary action, they also reasserted that the true identity of America lay in moral rather than material qualities.

These cross-currents of thought contained in embryo almost every public issue debated in the closing years of the century. In the 1840's, however, the tensions caused by immigration, industrialization, and territorial expansion were mitigated by American abundance. For the overwhelming majority of Americans, the promise of the future still came in the shape of a cornucopia. Popular government, free enterprise — even the annexation of Texas — seemed justified by the use Americans made of them. Only the issue of slavery was made worse, instead of better, by growth and prosperity. In this fact lies one of the explanations of the Civil War.

Although there were always a few opponents of slavery beating on the door to the American conscience, the antislavery movement begun with such promise in the Revolutionary period had slowly lost its steam. The remarkable growth in the world cotton market had extinguished the shallow hopes that slavery would wither away; the Missouri Compromise of 1820, while promoting a full-scale Congressional debate on the extension of slavery, had settled the most pressing questions about the Louisiana Purchase territory. Congress had even passed a resolution refusing to receive any more memorials against slavery. But the period of quiescence did not last long, and in the late 1820's the stirrings of a new, militant abolitionist movement became noticeable. In part a response to the successful English campaign to abolish slavery in their colonies of the Caribbean, the American abolitionist movement drew upon the moral enthusiasm of the early 19th century. The religious revivals of the previous decades, the faith in the goodness of the free individual, the exuberant hopes for a voluntary reform of society's ills all prepared the ground for the spread of abolitionist sentiment among Americans in the 1830's. At the same time prosperity and the many opportunities to indulge private ambitions created a barrier to any program which threatened to disturb domestic tranquility. The abolitionists made gains, but as they became more strident in their denunciations of American tolerance to slavery, they became the objects of violent hostility.

More than any other person, William Lloyd Garrison (1805–1879) brought to an end the public silence on the slave question. Founder of the militant American Antislavery Society, Garrison introduced a radical spirit into the campaign. His total commitment to abolitionism appeared as a kind of fanaticism to Northerners and Southerners, but his great strength lay in the uncompromising position he took. Where earlier efforts to send American Negroes to an African colony had temporized on the moral aspects of slavery, Garrison preached that it was the zenith of evil. To tolerate slavery, he insisted, was far worse than disavowing the Constitution or fomenting dissension. In

the Fourth-of-July speech from which the first reading in this section is taken, Garrison appealed to the ideals of the American Declaration of Independence. However, late in the 1840's and 1850's, when the Constitution was used to shore up the slaveholder's rights, Garrison did not hesitate to invoke a higher law in condemnation of man-made legislation. Three years after this speech, Garrison began his famous abolitionist journal, *The Liberator*, and the abolitionist movement began in full force.

Unlike those who made up the antislavery movement of the revolutionary period, many abolitionists accepted — even sought — the participation of blacks. Nor were they hesitant about appealing to the slaves themselves where this was possible. Abolitionists opened their houses to runaway slaves as stations in the underground railroad to Canada. Their willingness to accept blacks socially earned them derision even in the North, but it also confronted white Americans with the implications of their denial of this human fellowship. One of the most remarkable of the black abolitionists was David Walker (1785–1830), whose father was a slave and whose mother was a free Negro. His *Appeal*, from which the second reading is taken, was widely circulated.

In the 1830's, Southern opinion — at least that opinion vocalized by Southern officials — shifted from an uneasy acceptance of slaveholding as a temporarily necessary evil to a bold justification of slavery as a social good. Those Southerners who had been youths during the formation of the United States had retained much of the revolutionary attitude of disapproval, but their sons disavowed antislavery sentiment altogether. When an active abolitionist movement began in the North, Southern lawmakers were prepared to fight back with the full force of the state power in their hands. Abolitionist literature could not be sent through the mail and the circulation of abolitionist propaganda to slaves was made a crime punishable by death. The primordial loyalties of race unified Southern sentiments, suppressing the real differences that divided the powerful Southern slaveholders from the overwhelming majority of rather poor Southern farmers. In the last reading, Governor George McDuffie (1790–1851) summons the South Carolina legislature to protect the state from the menace of abolitionism, touching in his rhetoric most of the themes that would become central to Southern thought in the next three decades.

William Lloyd Garrison: Fourth-of-July address (1829)

Fifty-three years ago, the Fourth of July was a proud day for our country. It clearly and accurately defined the rights of man; it made no vulgar alterations in the established usages of society; it presented a revelation adapted to the common sense of mankind; it vindicated the omnipotence of public opinion over the machinery of kingly government; it shook, as with the voice of a great earthquake, thrones which were seemingly propped up with Atlantean pillars; it gave an impulse to the heart of the world, which yet thrills to its extremities.

It may be profitable to inquire, whether the piety which founded, and the patriotism which achieved our liberties, remain unimpaired in principle, undiminished in devotion. Possibly our Samson is sleeping in the lap of Delilah, with his locks shorn and his strength departed. Possibly his enemies have put out his eyes, and bound him with fetters of brass, and compelled him to grind in the prison-house; and if, in his rage and blindness, he find the pillars of the fabric, woe to those for whose sport he is led forth! . . .

We are a vain people, and our love of praise is inordinate. We imagine, and are annually taught to believe, that the republic is immortal; that its flight, like a strong angel's, has been perpetually upward, till it has soared above the impurities of earth, and beyond the remotest star; and, having attained perfection, is forever out of the reach of circumstance and change. An earthquake may rock all Europe, and ingulph empires at a stroke; but it cannot raise an inch of republican territory, nor disturb the composure of a platter on our shelves. The ocean may gather up its forces for

a second deluge, and overtop the tallest mountains; but our ark will float securely when the world is drowned. The storm may thicken around us; but a smile from the goddess of Liberty will disperse the gloom, and build a rainbow wherever she turns her eye. We shall remain 'till the heavens be no more.'

It is this fatal delusion, which so terrifies men of reflection and foresight; which makes the Christian shudder at the prospect before us, and the Patriot weep in despair; which, unless the mercy of God interpose, seals the doom of our country . . .

I know that this may be viewed as the phantasm of a disordered imagination. I know, too, it is easy to persuade ourselves that we shall escape those maladies, which have destroyed other nations. But, how closely soever a republic may resemble the human body in its liability to disease and death, the instance is not on record, where a people expired on account of excessive watchfulness over their own health, or of any premature apprehension of decay; and there is no national epitaph which says, 'they were well, they wished to be better, they took physic, and died.'

I speak not as a partisan or an opponent of any man or measures, when I say, that our politics are rotten to the core. We boast of our freedom, who go shackled to the polls, year after year, by tens, and hundreds, and thousands! We talk of free agency, who are the veriest machines — the merest automata — in the hands of unprincipled jugglers! We prate of integrity, and virtue, and independence, who sell our birthright for office, and who, nine times in ten, do not get Esau's bargain — no, not even a mess of pottage! Is it republicanism to say, that the majority can do no wrong? Then I am not a republican. Is it aristocracy to say, that the people sometimes shamefully abuse their high trust? Then I am an aristocrat. Rely upon it, the republic does not bear a charmed life: our prescriptions, administered through the medium of the ballot-box — the mouth of the political body — may kill or cure, according to the nature of the disease, and our wisdom in applying the remedy . . .

But there is another evil, which, if we had to contend against nothing else, should make us quake for the issue. It is a gangrene preying upon our vitals — an earthquake rumbling under our feet — a mine accumulating materials for a national catastrophe. It

Wendell Phillips Garrison (ed.), *William Lloyd Garrison, The Story of His Life Told by His Children*, The Century company, New York, 1885, I, 44–61.

should make this a day of fasting and prayer, not of boisterous merriment and idle pageantry — a day of great lamentation, not of congratulatory joy. It should spike every cannon, and haul down every banner. Our garb should be sackcloth — our heads bowed in the dust — our supplications, for the pardon and assistance of Heaven . . .

I stand up here in a more solemn court, to assist in a far greater cause; not to impeach the character of one man, but of a whole people — not to recover the sum of a hundred thousand dollars, but to obtain the liberation of two millions of wretched, degraded beings, who are pining in hopeless bondage — over whose sufferings scarcely an eye weeps, or a heart melts, or a tongue pleads either to God or man. I regret that a better advocate had not been found, to enchain your attention, and to warm your blood. Whatever fallacy, however, may appear in the argument, there is no flaw in the indictment; what the speaker lacks, the cause will supply.

Sirs, I am not come to tell you that slavery is a curse, debasing in its effect, cruel in its operation, fatal in its continuance. The day and the occasion require no such revelation. I do not claim the discovery as my own, 'that all men are born equal,' and that among their inalienable rights are 'life, liberty, and the pursuit of happiness.' Were I addressing any other than a free and Christian assembly, the enforcement of this truth might be pertinent. Neither do I intend to analyze the horrors of slavery for your inspection, nor to freeze your blood with authentic recitals of savage cruelty. Nor will time allow me to explore even a furlong of that immense wilderness of suffering, which remains unsubdued in our land. I take it for granted that the existence of these evils is acknowledged, if not rightly understood. My object is to define and enforce our duty, as Christians and Philanthropists . . .

I assume, as distinct and defensible propositions,

I. That the slaves of this country, whether we consider their moral, intellectual or social condition, are pre-eminently entitled to the prayers, and sympathies, and charities of the American people; and that their claims for redress are as strong as those of any Americans could be, in a similar condition.

II. That, as the free States — by which I mean non-slaveholding States — are constitutionally involved in the guilt of slavery, by adhering to a national compact that sanctions it; and in the danger, by liability to be called upon for aid in case of insurrection; they have the right to remonstrate against its continuance, and it is their duty to assist in its overthrow.

III. That no justificative plea for the perpetuity of slavery can be found in the condition of its victims; and no barrier against our righteous interference, in the laws which authorize the buying, selling and possessing of slaves, nor in the hazard of a collision with slaveholders.

IV. That education and freedom will elevate our colored population to a rank with the whites — making them useful, intelligent and peaceable citizens.

In the first place, it will be readily admitted, that it is the duty of every nation primarily to administer relief to its own necessities, to cure its own maladies, to instruct its own children, and to watch over its own interests. He is 'worse than an infidel,' who neglects his own household, and squanders his earnings upon strangers; and the policy of that nation is unwise, which seeks to proselyte other portions of the globe at the expense of its safety and happiness. Let me not be misunderstood. My benevolence is neither contracted nor selfish. I pity that man whose heart is not larger than a whole continent. I despise the littleness of that patriotism which blusters only for its own rights, and, stretched to its utmost dimensions, scarcely covers its native territory; which adopts as its creed, the right to act independently, even to the verge of licentiousness, without restraint, and to tyrannize wherever it can with impunity. This sort of patriotism is common. I suspect the reality, and deny the productiveness of that piety, which confines its operations to a particular spot — if that spot be less than the whole earth; nor scoops out, in every direction, new channels for the waters of life. Christian charity, while it 'begins at home,' goes abroad in search of misery . . . But I mean to say, that, while we are aiding and instructing foreigners, we ought not to forget our own degraded countrymen; that neither duty nor honesty requires us to defraud ourselves, that we may enrich others.

The condition of the slaves, in a religious point of view, is deplorable, entitling them to a higher consideration, on our part, than any other race; higher than the Turks or Chinese, for they have the privileges of instruction; higher than the Pagans, for they are not dwellers in a gospel land; higher than our red men of the forest, for we do not bind them with gyves, nor treat them as chattels.

And here let me ask, what has Christianity done, by direct effort, for our slave population? Comparatively nothing. She has explored the isles of the ocean for objects of commiseration; but, amazing stupidity! she can gaze without emotion on a multitude of miserable beings at home, large enough to constitute a nation of freemen, whom tyranny has heathenized by law. In her public services, they are seldom remembered, and in her private donations they are forgotten. From one end of the country to the other, her charitable societies form golden links of benevolence, and scatter their contributions like rain-drops over a parched heath; but they bring no sustenance to the perishing slave. The blood of souls is upon her garments, yet she heeds not the stain. The clankings of the prisoner's chains strike upon her ear, but they cannot penetrate her heart.

I have said, that the claims of the slaves for redress are as strong as those of any Americans could be, in a similar condition. Does any man deny the position? The proof, then, is found in the fact, that a very large proportion of our colored population were born on our soil, and are therefore entitled to all the privileges of American citizens. This is their country by birth, not by adoption. Their children possess the same inherent and unalienable rights as ours; and it is a crime of the blackest dye to load them with fetters.

Every Fourth of July, our Declaration of Independence is produced, with a sublime indignation, to set forth the tyranny of the mother country, and to challenge the admiration of the world. But what a pitiful detail of grievances does this document present, in comparison with the wrongs which our slaves endure! In the one case, it is hardly the plucking of a hair from the head; in the other, it is the crushing of a live body on the wheel; the stings of the wasp contrasted with the tortures of the inquisition. Before God, I must say, that such a glaring contradiction, as exists between our creed and practice, the annals of six thousand years cannot parallel. In view of it, I am ashamed of my country.

I am sick of our unmeaning declamation in praise of liberty and equality; of our hypocritical cant about the unalienable rights of man. I could not, for my right hand, stand up before a European assembly, and exult that I am an American citizen, and denounce the usurpations of a kingly government as wicked and unjust; or, should I make the attempt, the recollection of my country's barbarity and despotism would blister my lips, and cover my cheeks with burning blushes of shame . . .

Let us suppose that endurance has passed its bounds, and that the slaves, goaded to desperation by cruelty of their oppressors, have girded on the armor of vengeance. Let us endeavor to imagine the appeal which they would publish to the world, in extenuation of their revolt. The preamble might be taken from our own Declaration of Independence, with a few slight alterations. Then what a detail of wrongs would follow! Speaking at first from the shores of Africa, and changing their situation with the course of events, they would say:

'They, (the American people,) arrogantly styling themselves the champions of freedom, for a long course of years have been guilty of the most cruel and protracted tyranny. They have invaded our territories, depopulated our villages, and kindled among us the flames of an exterminating war. They have wedged us into the holds of their 'floating hells,' with suffocating compactness, and without distinction of age or sex— allowing us neither to inhale the invigorating air of heaven, nor to witness the cheering light of the sun, neither wholesome food nor change of raiment—by which treatment thousands have expired under the most horrible sufferings. They have brought us to a free and Christian land, (so called,) and sold us in their market-places like cattle—even in the proud Capital of their Union, and within sight of their legislative halls, where Tyranny struts in the semblance of Liberty. They have cruelly torn the wife from her husband, the mother from her daughter, and children from their parents, and sold them into perpetual exile. They have confined us in loathsome cells and secret prisons—driven us in large droves from State to State, beneath a burning sky, half naked, and heavily manacled—nay, retaken and sold many, who had by years of toil obtained their liberation.

They have compelled us 'to till their ground, to carry them, to fan them when they sleep, and tremble when they wake,' and rewarded us only with stripes, and hunger, and nakedness. They have lacerated our bodies with whips, and brands, and knives, for the most innocent and trifling offences, and often solely to gratify their malignant propensities; nor do they esteem it a crime worthy of death to murder us at will. Nor have they deprived us merely of our liberties. They would destroy our souls, by endeavoring to deprive us of the means of instruction—of a knowledge of God, and Jesus Christ, and the Holy Spirit, and a way of salvation: at the same time, they have taxed the whole country (our own labor among other things) to instruct and enlighten those who are at a great remove from them, whom they never fettered nor maimed, whose condition is not so dark or pitiable as our own. They have —'

But why need I proceed? My powers of description are inadequate to the task. A greater than Jefferson would fail. Only the pen of the recording angel can declare their manifold wrongs and sufferings; and the revelation will not be made till the day of judgment.

We say, that the disabilities imposed upon our fathers, by the mother country, furnished just cause for rebellion; that their removal was paramount to every other consideration; and that the slaughter of our oppressors was a justifiable act; for we should resist unto blood to save our liberties. Suppose that to-morrow should bring us tidings that the slaves at the South had revolted, en masse, and were spreading devastation and death among the white population. Should we celebrate their achievements in song, and justify their terrible excesses? And why not, if our creed be right? Their wrongs are unspeakably grievous, and liberty is the birthright of every man.

We say, that France was justified in assisting our fathers to maintain their independence; and that, as a nation, we owe her our liveliest gratitude for her timely interference. Suppose, in case of a revolt, that she, or some other European power, should furnish our slaves with guns and ammunition, and pour her troops into our land. Would it be treacherous or cruel? Why, according to our revolutionary credenda? The argument, tremendous as it is, is against us!

We say, that the imprisonment of an inconsiderable number of our seamen, by Great Britain, authorized the late war; and we boast of our promptitude to redress their wrongs. More than a million of native-born citizens are at this moment enduring the galling yoke of slavery. Who cries for justice? None. "But they are blacks!" True, and they are also men; and, moreover, they are Americans by birth.

If it be said, (which assertion is false,) that the present race are beyond recovery; then I reply, in the language of a warm-hearted philanthropist, "Let us make no more slaves . . ."

It may be objected, that the laws of the slave States form insurmountable barriers to any interference on our part.

Answer. I grant that we have not the right, and I trust not the disposition, to use coercive measures. But do these laws hinder our prayers, or obstruct the flow of of our sympathies? Cannot our charities alleviate the condition of the slave, and perhaps break his fetters? Can we not operate upon public sentiment, (the lever that can move the moral world,) by way of remonstrance, advice, or entreaty? Is Christianity so powerful, that she can tame the red men of our forests, and abolish the Burman caste, and overthrow the gods of Paganism, and liberate lands over which the darkness of Superstition has lain for ages; and yet so weak, in her own dwelling-place, that she can make no impression upon her civil code? Can she contend sucessfully with cannibals, and yet be conquered by her own children?

Suppose that, by a miracle, the slaves should suddenly become white. Would you shut your eyes upon their sufferings, and calmly talk of constitutional limitations? No; your voice would peal in the ears of the taskmasters like deep thunder; you would carry the Constitution by force, if it could not be taken by treaty; patriotic assemblies would congregate at the corner of every street; the old Cradle of Liberty would rock to a deeper tone than ever echoed therein at British aggression; the pulpit would acquire new and unusual eloquence from our holy religion. The argument, that these white slaves are degraded, would not then obtain. You would say, it is enough that they are white, and in bondage, and they ought immediately to be set free. You would multiply your schools of instruction, and your temples of worship, and rely upon them for security.

But the plea is prevalent, that any interference by the free States, however benevolent or cautious it might be, would only irritate and inflame the jealousies of the South, and retard the cause of emancipation.

If any man believes that slavery can be abolished without a struggle with the worst passions of human nature, quietly, harmoniously, he cherishes a delusion. It can never be done, unless the age of miracles return. No; we must expect a collision, full of sharp asperities and bitterness. We shall have to contend with the insolence, and pride, and selfishness, of many a heartless being. But these can be easily conquered by meekness, and perseverance, and prayer.

It is often despondingly said, that the evil of slavery is beyond our control. Dreadful conclusion, that puts the seal of death upon our country's existence! If we cannot conquer the monster in his infancy, while his cartilages are tender and his limbs powerless, how shall we escape his wrath when he goes forth a gigantic cannibal, seeking whom he may devour? If we cannot safely unloose two millions of slaves now, how shall we bind upwards of Twenty millions at the close of the present century? But there is no cause for despair. We have seen how readily, and with what ease, that horrid gorgon, Intemperance, has been checked in its ravages. Let us take courage. Moral influence, when in vigorous exercise, is irresistible. It has an immortal essence. It can no more be trod out of existence by the iron foot of time, or by the ponderous march of iniquity, than matter can be annihilated. It may disappear for a time; but it lives in some shape or other, in some place or other, and will rise with renovated strength. Let us, then, be up and doing. In the simple and stirring language of the stout-hearted Lundy, 'all the friends of the cause must go to work, keep to work, hold on, and never give up.' ...

And since so much is to be done for our country; since so many prejudices are to be dispelled, obstacles vanquished, interests secured, blessings obtained; since the cause of emancipation must progress heavily, and meet with much unhallowed opposition, why delay the work? There must be a beginning, and now

is a propitious time—perhaps the last opportunity that will be granted us by a long-suffering God. No temporising, lukewarm measures will avail aught. We must put our shoulder to the wheel, and heave with our united strength. Let us not look coldly on, and see our southern brethren contending single-handed against an all-powerful foe—faint, weary, borne down to the earth. We are all alike guilty. Slavery is strictly a national sin. New-England money has been expended in buying human flesh; New-England ships have been freighted with sable victims; New-England men have assisted in forging the fetters of those who groan in bondage.

I call upon the ambassadors of Christ every where to make known this proclamation: 'Thus saith the Lord God of the Africans, Let this people go, that they may serve me.' I ask them to 'proclaim liberty to the captives, and the opening of the prison to them that are bound'—to light up a flame of philanthropy, that shall burn till all Africa be redeemed from the night of moral death, and the song of deliverance be heard throughout her borders.

I call upon the churches of the living God to lead in this great enterprise. If the soul be immortal, priceless, save it from redeemless woe. Let them combine their energies, and systematize their plans, for the rescue of suffering humanity. Let them pour out their supplications to heaven in behalf of the slave. Prayer is omnipotent: its breath can melt adamantine rocks—its touch can break the stoutest chains. Let anti-slavery charity-boxes stand uppermost among those for missionary, tract and educational purposes. On this subject, Christians have been asleep; let them shake off their slumbers, and arm for the holy contest.

I call upon our New-England women to form charitable associations to relieve the degraded of their sex. As yet, an appeal to their sympathies was never made in vain. They outstrip us in every benevolent race. Females are doing much for the cause at the South; let their example be imitated, and their exertions surpassed, at the North.

I call upon the great body of newspaper editors to keep this subject constantly before their readers; to sound the trumpet of alarm, and to plead eloquently for the rights of man. They must give the tone to public sentiment. One press may ignite twenty; a city may warm a State; a State may impart a generous heat to a whole country.

I call upon the American people to enfranchise a spot, over which they hold complete sovereignty; to cleanse that worse than Augean stable, the District of Columbia, from its foul impurities. I conjure them to select those as Representatives, who are not too ignorant to know, too blind to see, nor too timid to perform their duty.

I will say, finally, that I tremble for the republic while slavery exists therein. If I look up to God for success, no smile of mercy or forgiveness dispels the gloom of futurity; if to our resources, they are daily diminishing; if to all history, our destruction is not only possible, but almost certain. Why should we slumber at this momentous crisis? If our hearts were dead to every throb of humanity; if it were lawful to oppress, where power is ample; still, if we had any regard for our safety and happiness, we should strive to crush the Vampyre which is feeding upon our life-blood . . .

David Walker: An appeal to the Coloured citizens of the world (1830)

My dearly beloved Brethren and Fellow Citizens.

Having travelled over a considerable portion of these United States, and having, in the course of my travels, taken the most accurate observations of things as they exist—the result of my observations has warranted the full and unshaken conviction, that we, (coloured people of these United States,) are the most degraded, wretched, and abject set of beings that ever lived since the world began; and I pray God that none like us ever may live again until time shall be no more. They tell us of the Israelites in Egypt, the Helots in Sparta, and of the Roman Slaves, which last were made up from almost every nation under heaven, whose sufferings under those ancient and heathen nations, were, in comparison with ours, under this enlightened and Christian nation, no more than a cypher — or, in other words, those heathen nations of antiquity, had but little more among them

than the name and form of slavery; while wretchedness and endless miseries were reserved, apparently in a vial, to be poured out upon our fathers, ourselves and our children, by Christian Americans!

These positions I shall endeavour, by the help of the Lord, to demonstrate in the course of this Appeal, to the satisfaction of the most incredulous mind—and may God Almighty, who is the Father of our Lord Jesus Christ, open your hearts to understand and believe the truth . . .

I am fully aware, in making this appeal to my much afflicted and suffering brethren, that I shall not only be assailed by those whose greatest earthly desires are, to keep us in abject ignorance and wretchedness, and who are of the firm conviction that Heaven has designed us and our children to be slaves and beasts of burden to them and their children. I say, I do not only expect to be held up to the public as an ignorant, impudent and restless disturber of the public peace, by such avaricious creatures, as well as a mover of insubordination—and perhaps put in prison or to death, for giving a superficial exposition of our miseries, and exposing tyrants. But I am persuaded, that many of my brethren, particularly those who are ignorantly in league with slave-holders or tyrants, who acquire their daily bread by the blood and sweat of their more ignorant brethren—and not a few of those too, who are too ignorant to see an inch beyond their noses, will rise up and call me cursed—Yea, the jealous ones among us will perhaps use more abject subtlety, by affirming that this work is not worth perusing, that we are well situated, and there is no use in trying to better our condition, for we cannot. I will ask one question here.—Can our condition be any worse?—Can it be more mean and abject? If there are any changes, will they not be for the better, though they may appear for the worst at first? Can they get us any lower? . . .

I appeal to Heaven for my motive in writing—who knows that my object is, if possible, to awaken in the breasts of my afflicted, degraded and slumbering brethren, a spirit of inquiry and investigation respecting our miseries and wretchedness in this Republican Land of Liberty!. . .

Has Mr. Jefferson declared to the world that we are inferior to the whites both in the endowments of our bodies and of minds? It is indeed surprising,

Walker's Appeal in Four Articles, Boston, 1830, pp. 3–5, 12–22, 24–25, 30–35.

that a man of such great learning, combined with such excellent natural parts, should speak so of a set of men in chains. I do not know what to compare it to, unless, like putting one wild deer in an iron cage, where it will be secured, and hold another by the side of the same, then let it go, and expect the one in the cage to run as fast as the one at liberty. So far, my brethren, were the Egyptians from heaping these insults upon their slaves, that Pharoah's daughter took Moses, a son of Israel for her own . . .

O! that the coloured people were long since of Moses' excellent disposition, instead of courting favour with, and telling news and lies to our natural enemies, against each other—aiding them to keep their hellish chains of slavery upon us. Would we not long before this time, have been respectable men, instead of such wretched victims of oppression as we are? Would they be able to drag our mothers, our fathers, our wives, our children and ourselves, around the world in chains and hand-cuffs as they do, to dig up gold and silver for them and theirs? This question, my brethren, I leave for you to digest; and may God Almighty force it home to your hearts. Remember that unless you are united, keeping your tongues within your teeth, you will be afraid to trust your secrets to each other, and thus perpetuate our miseries under the Christians! . . .

Never make an attempt to gain our freedom or natural right, from under our cruel oppressors and murderers, until you see your way clear—when that hour arrives and you move, be not afraid or dismayed; for be you assured that Jesus Christ the King of heaven and of earth who is the God of justice and of armies, will surely go before you. And those enemies who have for hundreds of years stolen our rights, and kept us ignorant of Him and His divine worship, he will remove. Millions of whom, are this day, so ignorant and avaricious, that they cannot conceive how God can have an attribute of justice, and show mercy to us because it pleased Him to make us black—which colour, Mr. Jefferson calls unfortunate! As though we are not as thankful to our God, for having made us as it pleased himself, as they, (the whites,) are for having made them white. They think because they hold us in their infernal chains of slavery, that we wish to be white, or of their color—but they are

dreadfully deceived—we wish to be just as it pleased our Creator to have made us, and no avaricious and unmerciful wretches, have any business to make slaves of, or hold us in slavery. How would they like for us to make slaves of, and hold them in cruel slavery, and murder them as they do us?—But is Mr. Jefferson's assertions true? viz. "that it is unfortunate for us that our Creator has been pleased to make us black." We will not take his say so, for the fact. The world will have an opportunity to see whether it is unfortunate for us, that our Creator has made us darker than the whites . . .

I saw a paragraph, a few years since, in a South Carolina paper, which, speaking of the barbarity of the Turks, it said: "The Turks are the most barbarous people in the world—they treat the Greeks more like brutes than human beings." And in the same paper was an advertisement, which said: Eight well built Virginia and Maryland Negro fellows and four wenches will positively be sold this day, to the highest bidder!" And what astonished me still more was, to see in this same humane paper! the cuts of three men, with clubs and budgets on their backs, and an advertisement offering a considerable sum of money for their apprehension and delivery. I declare, it is really so amusing to hear the Southerners and Westerners of this country talk about barbarity, that it is positively, enough to make a man smile . . .

Can Christian Americans deny these barbarous cruelties? Have you not, Americans, having subjected us under you, added to these miseries, by insulting us in telling us to our face, because we are helpless, that we are not of the human family? I ask you, O! Americans, I ask you, in the name of the Lord, can you deny these charges? Some perhaps may deny, by saying, that they never thought or said that we were not men. But do not actions speak louder than words?—have they not made provisions for the Greeks and Irish? Nations who have never done the least thing for them, while we, who have enriched their country with our blood and tears—have dug up gold and silver for them and their children, from generation to generation, and are in more miseries than any other people under heaven, are not seen, but by comparatively, a handful of the American people? . . .

I have been for years troubling the pages of

historians, to find out what our fathers have done to the white Christians of America, to merit such condign punishment as they have inflicted on them, and do continue to inflict on us their children. But I must aver, that my researches have hitherto been to no effect. I have therefore, come to the immoveable conclusion, that they (Americans) have, and do continue to punish us for nothing else, but for enriching them and their country. For I cannot conceive of any thing else. Nor will I ever believe otherwise, until the Lord shall convince me.

The world knows, that slavery as it existed among the Romans, (which was the primary cause of their destruction) was, comparatively speaking, no more than a cypher, when compared with ours under the Americans. Indeed I should not have noticed the Roman slaves, had not the very learned and penetrating Mr. Jefferson said, "when a master was murdered, all his slaves in the same house, or within hearing, were condemned to death."—Here let me ask Mr. Jefferson, (but he is gone to answer at the bar of God, for the deeds done in his body while living,) I therefore ask the whole American people, had I not rather die, or be put to death, than to be a slave to any tyrant, who takes not only my own, but my wife and children's lives by the inches? Yea, would I meet death with avidity far! far! ! in preference to such servile submission to the murderous hands of tyrants. Mr. Jefferson's very severe remarks on us have been so extensively argued upon by men whose attainments in literature, I shall never be able to reach, that I would not have meddled with it, were it not to solicit each of my brethren, who has the spirit of a man, to buy a copy of Mr. Jefferson's "Notes on Virginia," and put it in the hand of his son. For let no one of us suppose that the refutations which have been written by our white friends are enough—they are whites—we are blacks. We, and the world wish to see the charges of Mr. Jefferson refuted by the blacks themselves, according to their chance; for we must remember that what the whites have written respecting this subject, is other men's labours, and did not emanate from the blacks. I know well, that there are some talents and learning among the coloured people of this country, which we have not a chance to develop, in consequence of oppression; but our oppression

ought not to hinder us from acquiring all we can. For we will have a chance to develop them by and by. God will not suffer us, always to be oppressed. Our sufferings will come to an end, in spite of all the Americans this side of eternity. Then we will want all the learning and talents among ourselves, and perhaps more, to govern ourselves.—"Every dog must have its day," the American's is coming to an end.

But let us review Mr. Jefferson's remarks respecting us some further. Comparing our miserable fathers, with the learned philosophers of Greece, he says: "Yet notwithstanding these and other discouraging circumstances among the Romans, their slaves were often their rarest artists. They excelled too, in science, insomuch as to be usually employed as tutors to their master's children; Epictetus, Terence and Phaedrus, were slaves,—but they were of the race of whites. It is not their condition then, but nature, which has produced the distinction." See this, my brethren! ! Do you believe that this assertion is swallowed by millions of the whites? Do you know that Mr. Jefferson was one of as great characters as ever lived among the whites? See his writings for the world, and public labours for the United States of America. Do you believe that the assertions of such a man, will pass away into oblivion unobserved by this people and the world? If you do you are much mistaken—See how the American people treat us—have we souls in our bodies? Are we men who have any spirits at all? I know that there are many swell-bellied fellows among us, whose greatest object is to fill their stomachs. Such I do not mean—I am after those who know and feel, that we are men, as well as other people; to them, I say, that unless we try to refute Mr. Jefferson's arguments respecting us, we will only establish them.

But the slaves among the Romans. Every body who has read history, knows, that as soon as a slave among the Romans obtained his freedom, he could rise to the greatest eminence in the State, and there was no law instituted to hinder a slave from buying his freedom. Have not the Americans instituted laws to hinder us from obtaining our freedom? Do any deny this charge? Read the laws of Virginia, North Carolina, &c. Further: have not the Americans instituted laws to prohibit a man of colour from obtaining and holding any office whatever, under the government of the United States of America? Now, Mr. Jefferson tells us, that our condition is not so hard, as the slaves were under the Romans!

It is time for me to bring this article to a close. But before I close it, I must observe to my brethren that at the close of the first Revolution in this country, with Great Britain, there were but thirteen States in the Union, now there are twenty-four, most of which are slave-holding States, and the whites are dragging us around in chains and in handcuffs, to their new States and Territories to work their mines and farms, to enrich them and their children — and millions of them believing firmly that we being a little darker than they, were made by our Creator to be an inheritance to them and their children for ever — the same as a parcel of *brutes*.

Are we men! ! — I ask you, O my brethren! are we men? Did our Creator make us to be slaves to dust and ashes like ourselves? Are they not dying worms as well as we? Have they not to make their appearance before the tribunal of Heaven, to answer for the deeds done in the body, as well as we? Have we any other Master but Jesus Christ alone? Is he not their Master as well as ours? — What right then, have we to obey and call any other Master, but Himself? How we could be so submissive to a gang of men, whom we cannot tell whether they are as good as ourselves or not, I never could conceive. However, this is shut up with the Lord, and we cannot precisely tell — but I declare, we judge men by their works.

The whites have always been an unjust, jealous, unmerciful, avaricious and blood-thirsty set of beings, always seeking after power and authority. — We view them all over the confederacy of Greece, where they were first known to be any thing, (in consequence of education) we see them there, cutting each other's throats — trying to subject each other to wretchedness and misery — to effect which, they used all kinds of deceitful, unfair, and unmerciful means. We view them next in Rome, where the spirit of tyranny and deceit raged still higher. We view them in Gaul, Spain, and in Britain. — In fine, we view them all over Europe, together with what were scattered about in Asia and Africa, as heathens, and we see them acting more like devils than accountable men. But some may ask, did

not the blacks of Africa, and the mulattoes of Asia, go on in the same way as did the whites of Europe. I answer, no — they never were half so avaricious, deceitful and unmerciful as the whites, according to their knowledge.

But we will leave the whites or Europeans as heathens, and take a view of them as Christians, in which capacity we see them as cruel, if not more so than ever. In fact, take them as a body, they are ten times more cruel, avaricious and unmerciful than ever they were; for while they were heathens, they were bad enough it is true, but it is positively a fact that they were not quite so audacious as to go and take vessel loads of men, women and children, and in cold blood, and through devilishness, throw them into the sea, and murder them in all kind of ways. While they were heathens, they were too ignorant for such barbarity. But being Christians, enlightened and sensible, they are completely prepared for such hellish cruelties . . .

Ignorance, my brethren, is a mist, low down into the very dark and almost impenetrable abyss in which, our fathers for many centuries have been plunged. The Christians, and enlightened of Europe, and some of Asia, seeing the ignorance and consequent degradation of our fathers, instead of trying to enlighten them, by teaching them that religion and light with which God had blessed them, they have plunged them into wretchedness ten thousand times more intolerable, than if they had left them entirely to the Lord, and to add to their miseries, deep down into which they have plunged them tell them, that they are an inferior and distinct race of beings, which they will be glad enough to recall and swallow by and by. Fortune and misfortune, two inseparable companions, lay rolled up in the wheel of events, which have from the creation of the world, and will continue to take place among men until God shall dash worlds together . . .

Ignorance and treachery one against the other — a grovelling servile and abject submission to the lash of tyrants, we see plainly, my brethren, are not the natural elements of the blacks, as the Americans try to make us believe; but these are misfortunes which God has suffered our fathers to be enveloped in for many ages, no doubt in consequence of their disobedience to their Maker, and which do, indeed, reign at this time among

us, almost to the destruction of all other principles:
for I must truly say, that ignorance, the mother of
treachery and deceit, gnaws into our very vitals. Ignorance, as it now exits among us, produces a state of
things, Oh my Lord! too horrible to present to the
world. Any man who is curious to see the full force
of ignorance developed among the coloured people of
the United States of America, has only to go into the
southern and western states of this confederacy, where,
if he is not a tyrant, but has the feelings of a human
being, who can feel for a fellow creature, he may see
enough to make his very heart bleed! He may see
there, a son take his mother, who bore almost the
pains of death to give him birth, and by the command
of a tyrant, strip her as naked as she came into the
world, and apply the cow-hide to her, until she falls a
victim to death in the road! He may see a husband
take his dear wife, not unfrequently in a pregnant
state, and perhaps far advanced, and beat her for an
unmerciful wretch, until his infant falls a lifeless lump
at her feet! Can the Americans escape God Almighty?
If they do, can he be to us a God of Justice? God is
just, and I know it — for he has convinced me to my
satisfaction — I cannot doubt him. My observer may
see fathers beating their sons, mothers their daughters,
and children their parents, all to pacify the passions of
unrelenting tyrants. He may also, see them telling
news and lies, making mischief one upon another.
These are some of the productions of ignorance, which
he will see practised among my dear brethren, who are
held in unjust slavery and wretchedness, by avaricious
and unmerciful tyrants, to whom, and their hellish
deeds, I would suffer my life to be taken before I
would submit . . .

Now, I ask you, had you not rather be killed than
to be a slave to a tyrant, who takes the life of your
mother, wife, and dear little children? Look upon
your mother, wife and children, and answer God
Almighty; and believe this, that it is no more harm for
you to kill a man, who is trying to kill you, than it is
for you to take a drink of water when thirsty; in fact,
the man who will stand still and let another murder
him, is worse than an infidel, and, if he has common
sense, ought not to be pitied . . . Oh! coloured people
of these United States, I ask you, in the name of that
God who made us, have we, in consequence of oppression, nearly lost the spirit of man, and, in no very trifling degree, adopted that of brutes? Do you answer,
no? — I ask you, then, what set of men can you point
me to, in all the world, who are so abjectly employed
by their oppressors, as we are by our natural enemies?
How can, Oh! how can those enemies but say that we
and our children are not of the human family, but were
made by our Creator to be an inheritance to them and
theirs for ever? How can the slaveholders but say that
they can bribe the best coloured person in the country,
to sell his brethren for a trifling sum of money, and
take that atrocity to confirm them in their avaricious
opinion, that we were made to be slaves to them and
their children? How could Mr. Jefferson but say, "I
advance it therefore as a suspicion only, that the blacks,
whether originally a distinct race, or made distinct by
time and circumstances, are inferior to the whites in
the endowments both of body and mind?" — "It," says
he, "is not against experience to suppose, that different
species of the same genius, or varieties of the same
species, may possess different qualifications." . . . He
goes on further, and says: "This unfortunate difference
of colour, and perhaps of faculty, is a powerful obstacle
to the emancipation of these people. Many of their
advocates, while they wish to vindicate the liberty of
human nature are anxious also to preserve its dignity
and beauty. Some of these, embarrassed by the question, 'What further is to be done with them?' join
themselves in opposition with those who are actuated
by sordid avarice only." Now I ask you candidly, my
suffering brethren in time, who are candidates for the
eternal worlds, how could Mr. Jefferson but have given
the world these remarks respecting us, when we are so
submissive to them, and so much servile deceit prevail
among ourselves . . .

Men of colour, who are also of sense, for you particularly is my appeal designed. Our more ignorant
brethren are not able to penetrate its value. I call upon
you therefore to cast your eyes upon the wretchedness
of your brethren, and to do your utmost to enlighten
them — *go to work and enlighten your brethren!* . . .

There is a great work for you to do, as trifling as
some of you may think of it. You have to prove to the
Americans and the world, that we are *men*, and not
brutes, as we have been represented, and by millions
treated . . .

Governor George McDuffie: Message on the slavery question to the South Carolina Legislature (1835)

. . . Since your last adjournment, the public mind, throughout the slave-holding states, has been intensely, indignantly and justly excited by the wanton, officious and incendiary proceedings of certain societies and persons in some of the non-slaveholding states, who have been actively employed in attempting to circulate among us pamphlets, papers and pictorial representations of the most offensive and inflammatory character, and eminently calculated to seduce our slaves from their fidelity, and excite them to insurrection and massacre. These wicked monsters and deluded fanatics, overlooking the numerous objects in their own vicinity, who have a moral, if not a legal claim upon their charitable regard, run abroad, in the expansion of their hypocritical benevolence, muffled up in the saintly mantle of Christian meekness, to fulfil the fiend-like errand of mingling the blood of the master and the slave, to whose fate they are equally indifferent, with the smouldering ruins of our peaceful dwellings. No principle of human action so utterly baffles all human calculation as that species of fanatical enthusiasm, which is made of envy and ambition, assuming the guise of religious zeal, and acting upon the known prejudices, religious or political, of an ignorant multitude. Under the influence of this species of voluntary madness, nothing is sacred that stands in the way of its purposes. Like all other religious impostures, it has power to consecrate every act, however atrocious, and every person, however covered with "multiplying villanies," that may promote its diabolical ends, or worship at its infernal altars. By its unholy creed, murder itself becomes a labor of love and charity, and the felon renegado, who flies from the justice of his country, finds not only a refuge, but becomes a sainted minister, in the sanctuary of its temple. No error can be more mischievous, than to underrate the danger of such a principle, and no policy can be more fatal than to neglect it, from a contempt for the supposed insignificance of its agents. The experience of both France and Great Britain fearfully instruct us, from what small and contemptible beginnings, this

Journal of the General Assembly of the State of South Carolina for the Year 1835, 1836

ami des noirs philanthropy may rise to a gigantic power too mighty to be resisted by all the influence and energy of the government; in the one case, shrouding a wealthy and flourishing island in the blood of its white inhabitants; in the other, literally driving the ministry, by means of an instructed parliament, to perpetrate that act of suicidal legislation, and colonial oppression, the emancipation of slaves in the British West Indies. It may be not unaptly compared to the element of fire, of which, a neglected spark, amongst combustible materials, which a timely stamp of the foot might have extinguished forever, speedily swells into a sweeping torrent of fiery desolation, which no human power can arrest or control. In the opinion of the intelligent West India planters, it is because the local authorities, from a sense of false security neglected to hang up the first of these political missionaries that made their appearance on the British Islands, that they are doomed to barrenness and desertion, and to be the wretched abodes of indolent and profligate blacks, exhibiting, in their squalid poverty, gross immorality and slavish subjection to an iron despotism of British bayonets, the fatal mockery of all the promised blessings of emancipation.

Under these circumstances, and in this critical conjuncture of our affairs, the solemn and responsible duty devolves on the legislature, of "taking care that the republic receive no detriment."

The crime which these foreign incendiaries have committed against the peace of the State, is one of the very highest grade known to human laws. It not only strikes at the very existence of society, but seeks to accomplish the catastrophe, by the most horrible means, celebrating the obsequies of the State in a saturnial carnival of blood and murder, and while brutally violating all the charities of life, and desecrating the very altars of religion, impiously calling upon Heaven to sanction these abominations. It is my deliberate opinion, that the laws of every community should punish this species of interference by death without benefit of clergy, regarding the authors of it as "enemies of the human race." Nothing could be more appropriate than for South Carolina to set this example in the present crisis, and I trust the Legislature will not adjourn till it discharges this high duty of patriotism.

It cannot be disguised, however, that any laws which may be enacted by the authority of this State, however adequate to punish and repress offences committed within its limits, will be wholly insufficient to meet the exigencies of the present conjuncture. If we go no farther than this, we had as well do nothing.

The outrages against the peace and safety of the State are perpetrated in other communities, which hold and exercise sovereign and exclusive jurisdiction over all persons and things within their territorial limits. It is within these limits, protected from responsibility to our laws by the sovereignty of the States in which they reside, that the authors of all this mischief, securely concoct their schemes, plant their batteries, and hurl their fiery missiles among us, aimed at that mighty magazine of combustible matter, the explosion of which would lay the State in ruins.

It will, therefore, become our imperious duty, recurring to those great principles of international law, which still exist in all their primitive force amongst the sovereign States of this confederacy, to demand of our sovereign associates the condign punishment of those enemies of our peace, who avail themselves of the sanctuaries of their respective jurisdictions, to carry on schemes of incendiary hostility against the institutions, the safety, and the existence of the State. In performing this high duty, to which we are constrained by the great law of self-preservation, let us approach to our co-states with all the fraternal mildness which becomes us as members of the same family of confederated republics, and at the same time with that firmness and decision, which becomes a sovereign State, while maintaining her dearest interests and most sacred rights.

For the institution of domestic slavery we hold ourselves responsible only to God, and it is utterly incompatible with the dignity and the safety of the State, to permit any foreign authority to question our right to maintain it. It may nevertheless be appropriate, as a voluntary token of our respect for the opinions of our confederate brethren, to present some views to their consideration on this subject, calculated to disabuse their minds of false opinions and pernicious prejudices.

No human institution, in my opinion, is more manifestly consistent with the will of God, than domestic slavery, and no one of his ordinances is written in more legible characters than that which consigns the African race to this condition, as more conducive to their own happiness, than any other of which they are susceptible. Whether we consult the sacred Scriptures, or the lights of nature and reason, we shall find these truths as abundantly apparent, as if written with a sunbeam in the heavens. Under both the Jewish and Christian dispensations of our religion, domestic slavery existed with the unequivocal sanction of its prophets, its apostles and finally its great Author. The patriarchs themselves, those chosen instruments of God, were slave-holders. In fact the divine sanction of this institution is so plainly written that "he who runs may read" it, and those over-righteous pretenders and Pharisees, who affect to be scandalized by its existence among us, would do well to inquire how much more nearly they walk in the ways of Godliness, than did Abraham, Isaac and Jacob. That the African negro is destined by Providence to occupy this condition of servile dependence, is not less manifest. It is marked on the face, stamped on the skin, and evinced by the intellectual inferiority and natural improvidence of this race. They have all the qualities that fit them for slaves, and not one of those that would fit them to be freemen. They are utterly unqualified not only for rational freedom, but for self-government of any kind. They are, in all respects, physical, moral, and political, inferior to millions of the human race, who have for consecutive ages, dragged out a wretched existence under a grinding political despotism, and who are doomed to this hopeless condition by the very qualities which unfit them for a better. It is utterly astonishing that any enlightened American, after contemplating all the manifold forms in which even the white race of mankind are doomed to slavery and oppression, should suppose it possible to reclaim the African race from their destiny. The capacity to enjoy freedom is an attribute not to be communicated by human power. It is an endowment of God, and one of the rarest which it has pleased his inscrutable wisdom to bestow upon the nations of the earth. It is conferred as the reward of merit, and only upon those who are qualified to enjoy it. Until the "Ethiopian can change his skin," it will be in vain to attempt, by any human power, to make freemen of those whom God has doomed to be slaves, by all their attributes.

Let not, therefore, the misguided and designing

intermeddlers who seek to destroy our peace, imagine that they are serving the cause of God by practically arraigning the decrees of his Providence. Indeed it would scarcely excite surprise, if with the impious audacity of those who projected the tower of Babel, they should attempt to scale the battlements of Heaven, and remonstrate with the God of wisdom for having put the mark of Cain and the curse of Ham upon the African race, instead of the European.

If the benevolent friends of the black race would compare the condition of that portion of them which we hold in servitude, with that which still remains in Africa totally unblessed by the lights of civilization or Christianity, and groaning under a savage despotism, as utterly destitute of hope as of happiness, they would be able to form some tolerable estimate, of what our blacks have lost by slavery in America, and what they have gained by freedom in Africa. Greatly as their condition has been improved, by their subjection to an enlightened and Christian people, (the only mode under heaven by which it could have been accomplished,) they are yet wholly unprepared for any thing like a rational system of self-government. Emancipation would be a positive curse, depriving them of a guardianship essential to their happiness, and they may well say in the language of the Spanish proverb, "Save us from our friends and we will take care of our enemies." If emancipated, where would they live and what would be their condition? The idea of their remaining among us is utterly visionary. Amalgamation is abhorrent to every sentiment of nature; and if they remain as a separate caste, whether endowed with equal privileges or not, they will become our masters or we must resume the mastery over them. This state of political amalgamation and conflict, which the Abolitionists evidently aim to produce, would be the most horrible condition imaginable, and would furnish Dante or Milton with the type for another chapter illustrating the horrors of the infernal regions. The only disposition, therefore, that could be made of our emancipated slaves would be their transportation to Africa, to exterminate the natives or be exterminated by them; contingencies, either of which may well serve to illustrate the wisdom, if not the philanthropy of these superserviceable madmen, who in the name of humanity would desolate the fairest region of the earth and destroy the most perfect system of social and political happiness, that ever has existed.

It is perfectly evident that the destiny of the Negro race is, either the worst possible form of political slavery, or else domestic servitude as it exists in the slave-holding States. The advantage of domestic slavery over the most favorable condition of political slavery, does not admit of a question. It is the obvious interest of the master, not less than his duty, to provide comfortable food and clothing for his slaves; and whatever false and exaggerated stories may be propagated by mercenary travellers, who make a trade of exchanging calumny for hospitality, the peasantry and operatives of no country in the world are better provided for, in these respects, than the slaves of our country. In the single empire of Great Britain, the most free and enlightened nation in Europe, there are more wretched paupers and half starving operatives, than there are Negro slaves in the United States. In all respects, the comforts of our slaves are greatly superior to those of the English operatives, or the Irish and continental peasantry, to say nothing of the millions of paupers crowded together in those loathsome receptacles of starving humanity, the public poor-houses. Besides the hardships of incessant toil, too much almost for human nature to endure, and the sufferings of actual want, driving them almost to despair, these miserable creatures are perpetually annoyed by the most distressing cares for the future condition of themselves and their children.

From this excess of labor, this actual want, and these distressing cares, our slaves are entirely exempted. They habitually labor from two to four hours a day less than the operatives in other countries, and it has been truly remarked, by some writer, that a negro cannot be made to injure himself by excessive labor. It may be safely affirmed that they eat as much wholesome and substantial food in one day, as English operatives or Irish peasants eat in two. And as it regards concern for the future, their condition may well be envied even by their masters. There is not upon the face of the earth, any class of people, high or low, so perfectly free from care and anxiety. They know that their masters will provide for them, under all circumstances, and that in the extremity of old age, instead of being driven to beggary or to seek public charity in a poor-house, they will be comfortably accommodated and kindly treated among their relatives and associates.

Cato, the elder, has been regarded as a model of Roman virtue, and yet he is said to have sold his super-annuated slaves to avoid the expense of maintaining them. The citizens of this State may not aspire to rival the virtue of the Romans, but it may be safely affirmed, that they would doom to execration the master who should imitate the inhuman example of the Roman paragon. The government of our slaves is strictly patriarchal, and produces those mutual feelings of kindness which result from a constant interchange of good offices, and which can only exist in a system of domestic or patriarchal slavery. They are entirely unknown either in a state of political slavery, or in that form of domestic servitude which exists in all other communities.

In a word, our slaves are cheerful, contented and happy, much beyond the general condition of the human race, except where those foreign intruders and fatal ministers of mischief, the emancipationists, like their arch-prototype in the Garden of Eden, and actuated by no less envy, have tempted them to aspire above the condition to which they have been assigned in the order of Providence.

Nor can it be admitted, as some of our statesmen have affirmed, in a mischievous and misguided spirit of sickly sentimentality, that our system of domestic slavery is a curse to the white population — a moral and political evil, much to be deplored, but incapable of being eradicated. Let the tree be judged by its fruit. More than half a century ago, one of the most enlightened statesmen who ever illustrated the parliamentary annals of Great Britain, looking into political causes, with an eye of profound philosophy, ascribed the high and indomitable spirit of liberty which distinguished the Southern Colonies, to the existence of domestic slavery; referring to the example of the free states of antiquity as a confirmation of his theory. Since those colonies have become independent States, they have amply sustained the glory of their primitive character. There is no coloring of national vanity in the assertion, which impartial history will ratify, that the principles of rational liberty are not less thoroughly understood, and have been more vigilantly, resolutely and effectively defended against all the encroachments of power, by the slave-holding States, than by any other members of the confederacy. In which of our

great political conflicts is it, that they have not been found arrayed against every form of usurpation, and fighting under the flag of liberty? Indeed it is a fact of historical notoriety, that those great Whig principles of liberty, by which government is restrained within constitutional limits, have had their origin, and for a long time have had their abiding place, in the slave-holding States.

Reason and philosophy can easily explain what experience so clearly testifies. If we look into the elements of which all political communities are composed, it will be found that servitude, in some form, is one of the essential constituents. No community ever has existed without it, and we may confidently assert, none ever will. In the very nature of things there must be classes of persons to discharge all the different offices of society, from the highest to the lowest. Some of those offices are regarded as degrading, though they must and will be performed. Hence those manifold forms of dependent servitude which produce a sense of superiority in the masters or employers, and of inferiority on the part of the servants. Where these offices are performed by members of the political community, a dangerous element is introduced into the body politic. Hence the alarming tendency to violate the rights of property by agrarian legislation, which is beginning to be manifest in the older States, where universal suffrage prevails without domestic slavery, a tendency that will increase in the progress of society with the increasing inequality of wealth. No government is worthy of the name that does not protect the rights of property, and no enlightened people will long submit to such a mockery. Hence it is that in older countries, different political orders are established to effect this indispensable object, and it will be fortunate for the non-slaveholding States, if they are not in less than a quarter of a century, driven to the adoption of a similar institution, or to take refuge from robbery and anarchy under a military despotism. But where the menial offices and dependent employments of society are performed by domestic slaves, a class well defined by their color and entirely separated from the political body, the rights of property are perfectly secure, without the establishment of artificial barriers. In a word, the institution of domestic slavery supersedes the necessity of an order of nobility, and all the other appendages of a hereditary system of government. If our slaves were emancipated, and admitted, bleached or unbleached, to an equal participation in our political privileges, what a commentary should we furnish upon the doctrines of the emancipationists, and what a revolting spectacle of republican equality should we exhibit to the mockery of the world! No rational man would consent to live in such a state of society, if he could find a refuge in any other.

Domestic slavery, therefore, instead of being a political evil, is the corner-stone of our republican edifice. No patriot who justly estimates our privileges will tolerate the idea of emancipation, at any period, however remote, or on any conditions of pecuniary advantage, however favorable. I would as soon open a negotiation for selling the liberty of the State at once, as for making any stipulations for the ultimate emancipation of our slaves. So deep is my conviction on this subject, that if I were doomed to die immediately after recording these sentiments, I could say in all sincerity and under all the sanctions of Christianity and patriotism, "God forbid that my descendants, in the remotest generations, should live in any other than a community having the institution of domestic slavery, as it existed among the patriarchs of the primitive Church and in all the free states of antiquity."

If the Legislature should concur in these general views of this important element of our political and social system, our confederates should be distinctly informed, in any communications we may have occasion to make to them, that in claiming to be exempted from all foreign interference, we can recognize no distinction between ultimate and immediate emancipation.

It becomes necessary, in order to ascertain the extent of our danger, and the measures of precaution necessary to guard against it, that we examine into the real motives and ultimate purposes of the Abolition Societies and their prominent agents. To justify their officious and gratuitous interference in our domestic affairs, — the most insulting and insolent outrage which can be offered to a community — they profess to hold themselves responsible for the pretended sin of our domestic slavery, because forsooth, they tolerate its existence among us. If they are at all responsible for the sin of slavery, whatever that may be, it is not because they tolerate it now, but because their

ancestors were the agents and authors of its original introduction. These ancestors sold ours the slaves and warranted the title, and it would be a much more becoming labor of filial piety for their descendants to pray for their souls, if they are Protestants, and buy masses to redeem them from purgatory, if they are Catholics, than to assail their warranty and slander their memory by denouncing them as "man-stealers and murderers." But this voluntary and gratuitous assumption of responsibility, in imitation of a recent and high example in our history, but imperfectly conceals a lurking principle of danger, which deserves to be examined and exposed. What is there to make the people of New York or Massachusetts responsible for slavery in South Carolina, any more than the people of Great Britain? To assume that the people of those States are responsible for the continuance of this institution, is distinctly to assume that they have a right to abolish it. And whatever enforced disclaimers they may make, their efforts would be worse than unprofitable on any other hypothesis. The folly of attempting to convert the slave-holders to voluntary emancipation, by a course of slander and denunciation, is too great to be ascribed even to fanaticism itself. They do not, indeed, disguise the fact that their principal object is to operate on public opinion in the non-slaveholding States. And to what purpose? They cannot suppose that the opinion of those States, however unanimous, can break the chains of slavery by some moral magic. The whole tenor of their conduct and temper of their discussions clearly demonstrate that their object is to bring the slave-holding States into universal odium, and the public opinion of the non-slaveholding to the point of emancipating our slaves by federal legislation, without the consent of their owners. Disguise it as they may, "to this complexion it must come at last."

It is in this aspect of the subject, that it challenges our grave and solemn consideration. It behooves us then, in my opinion, to demand, respectfully, of each and every one of the slave-holding States:

1. A formal and solemn disclaimer, by its Legislature, of the existence of any rightful power, either in such State or the United States, in Congress assembled, to interfere in any manner, whatever, with the institution of domestic slavery in South Carolina.

2.   The immediate passage of penal laws by such Legislature, denouncing against the incendiaries of whom we complain, such punishments as will speedily and forever suppress their machinations against our peace and safety. Though the right to emancipate our slaves by coercive legislation has been very generally disclaimed by popular assemblages in the non-slaveholding States, it is nevertheless important that each of those States should give this disclaimer and the authentic and authoritative form of a legislative declaration, to be preserved as a permanent record for our future security. Our right to demand of those States the enactment of laws for the punishment of those enemies of our peace, who avail themselves of the sanctuary of their sovereign jurisdiction to wage a war of extermination against us, is founded on one of the most salutary and conservative principles of international law. Every State is under the most sacred obligations, not only to abstain from all such interference with the institutions of another as is calculated to disturb its tranquillity or endanger its safety; but to prevent its citizens or subjects from such interference, either by inflicting condign punishment itself, or by delivering them up to the justice of the offending community. As between separate and independent nations, the refusal of a State to punish these offensive proceedings against another, by its citizens or subjects, makes the State so refused an accomplice in the outrage, and furnishes a just cause of war. These principles of international law are universally admitted, and none have been more sacredly observed by just and enlightened nations. The obligations of the non-slaveholding States to punish and repress the proceedings of their citizens against our domestic institutions and tranquillity are greatly increased, both by the nature of those proceedings and the fraternal relation which subsists between the States of this confederacy. For no outrage against any community can be greater than to stir up the elements of servile insurrection, and no obligation to repress it can be more sacred than that which adds to the sanctions of international law, the solemn guarantee of a constitutional compact, which is at once the bond and the condition of our union. The liberal, enlightened and magnanimous conduct of the people in many portions of the non-slaveholding States forbids us to anticipate a refusal on the part of those States to fulfil these high obligations of national faith and duty. And we have the less reason to look forward to this inauspicious result, from considering the necessary consequences which would follow, to the people of those States, and of the whole commercial world, from the general emancipation of our slaves. These consequences may be presented, as an irresistible appeal, to every rational philanthropist in Europe or America. It is clearly demonstrable that the production of cotton depends not so much on soil and climate, as on the existence of domestic slavery. In the relaxing latitudes where it grows, not one half the quantity would be produced but for the existence of this institution, and every practical planter will concur in the opinion, that if all the slaves in these States were now emancipated, the American crop would be reduced the very next year from 1,100,000 to 600,000 bales. No great skill in political economy will be required to estimate how enormously the price of cotton would be increased by this change, and no one who will consider how largely this staple contributes to the wealth of manufacturing nations, and to the necessaries and comforts of the poorer classes all over the world, can fail to perceive the disastrous effects of so great a reduction in the quantity, and so great an enhancement in the price of it. In Great Britain, France and the United States, the catastrophe would be overwhelming, and it is not extravagant to say, that for little more than two millions of negro slaves, cut loose from their tranquil moorings, and set adrift upon the untried ocean, of at least a doubtful experiment, ten millions of poor white people would be reduced to destitution, pauperism and starvation. An anxious desire to avoid the last sad alternative of an injured community prompts this final appeal to the interests and enlightened philanthropy of our Confederate States. And we cannot permit ourselves to believe, that our just demands, thus supported by every consideration of humanity and duty, will be rejected by States, who are united to us by so many social and political ties, and who have so deep an interest in the preservation of that union . . .

In the 1830's the predominantly Protestant culture of America was threatened by a large immigration of Irish and German Catholics. Although the Constitution protected religious freedom, a good many native Americans believed that the Catholic religion was incompatible with free political institutions. The common influences which had acted upon all American Protestants during the preceding half century had produced a very similar religious outlook based upon free choice, voluntary support, and what was assumed to be the heart of the Christian message. Tolerance among these different Protestant denominations was easy, but this cohesion from similar convictions was challenged by the arrival of the Catholics who claimed a strong tie to the historic Christian church and brought with them very different religious attitudes. Priests, bishops, convents, and parochial schools followed, and the latent anti-Catholicism in America flared up, causing some ugly incidents of mob violence, including the burning of a convent in Charlestown, Massachusetts. At the political level, alarmed citizens — a good many of them ardent Protestants — began a campaign for restricting immigration. The new nativist drive to check the flow of aliens drew strength from the anti-Catholic propaganda as well as from a more diffused dislike of foreigners in general. Prominent in this campaign was Samuel Finley Breese Morse (1791–1872), the celebrated inventor of the telegraph. The first reading in this section comes from Morse's *Imminent Dangers to the Free Institutions of the United States Through Foreign Immigration,* a widely circulated pamphlet in which Morse explained how European governments hostile to the United States were sending their subjects to America to undermine her free institutions.

With the arrival of learned churchmen, the Catholics in America found spokesmen to defend the practice of the Catholic faith from the abuse spewed out in hundreds of nativist tracts. Particularly effective as a Catholic apologist was Archbishop John Hughes. A sharp and perceptive observer of American political life, Hughes was quick to spot the unexamined assumptions of American culture. Naturally combative, he rarely let an egregious example of Protestant smugness escape challenge. In the last two readings, Archbishop Hughes and Michigan's popular army hero, Lewis Cass (1782–1866), exchange views on the meaning of liberty of conscience. Hughes began the exchange when he wrote a letter to a New York newspaper condemning a recent public meeting which had been called to protest the imprisonment of the Madiai, a Protestant couple who had been arrested in the Italian state of Tuscany for proselyting among the Tuscans. After criticizing the anti-Catholic tenor of the Madiai protest meeting, Hughes discussed Senator Cass's program to secure religious freedom for traveling Americans when they were in foreign countries. Cass, who was the Democratic candidate for president in 1848, represented the true American faith in the free individual. Growing up a part of that democratic culture which Tocqueville so astutely described, he failed to see what Hughes found so distressing — the fact that American religious tolerance was based upon a shared set of convictions rather than a willingness to tolerate genuinely different opinions.

Samuel F. B. Morse: Imminent dangers to the free institutions of the United States through foreign immigration* (1835)

The great question regarding Foreigners, and a change in our Naturalization laws, is a National question, and at this time a very serious one. It is therefore with deep regret that I perceive an attempt made by both parties, (however to be expected,) to turn the just National excitement on this subject each to the account of their own party. The question, Whether Foreigners shall be subjected to a new law of naturalization? which grave circumstances have recently made it necessary to examine, is one entirely separate at present from party politics, as parties are now constituted, and is capable of being decided solely on its own merits . . .

---

*pp. 1, 6–13, 24–25.

The danger to which I would call attention is not imaginary. It is a danger arising from a new position of the social elements in the onward march of the world to liberty. The great struggle for some years has till now been principally confined to Europe. But we cannot exclude, if we would, the influence of foreign movements upon our own political institutions, in the great contest between liberty and despotism. It is an ignorance unaccountable in the conductors of the press at this moment, not to know, and a neglect of duty unpardonable, not to guard the people against the dangers resulting from this source. To deny the danger, is to shut one's eyes. It stares us in the face. And to seek to allay the salutary alarm arising from a demonstration of its actual presence among us, by attributing this alarm to any but the right cause, is worse than folly, it is madness, it is flinging away our liberties, not only without a struggle, but without the slightest concern, at the first appearance of the enemy . . .

Our country, in the position it has given to foreigners who have made it their home, has pursued a course in relation to them, totally different from that of any other country in the world. This course, while it is liberal without example, subjects our institutions to peculiar dangers. In all other countries the foreigner, to whatever privileges he may be entitled by becoming a subject, can never be placed in a situation to be politically dangerous, for he has no share in the government of the country; even in England, he has no political influence, for even after naturalization an alien cannot become a member of the House of Commons, or of the Privy Council, or hold offices or grants under the Crown.

In the other countries of Europe, the right of naturalization in each particular case, belongs to the Executive branch of government. It is so in France, in Bavaria, and all the German States. In France, indeed, a residence of 10 years gives to the alien all the rights of a citizen, even that of becoming a member of the Chambers of Deputies, but the limited suffrage in that country operates as a check on any abuse of this privilege.

This country on the contrary opens to the foreigner, without other check than an oath, that he has resided five years in the country, a direct influence on its political affairs.

This country, therefore, stands alone, without guide from the example of any other; and I am to show in the sequel some of the peculiar dangers to which our situation in this respect exposes us. But the better to comprehend these dangers, let me briefly trace the prominent steps in European politics which connect the past with the present.

Europe has been generally at rest from war for some 10 years past. The activity of mind which had so long been engaged in war, in military schemes of offence and defence in the field, was, at the general pacification of the world, to be transferred to the Cabinet, and turned to the cultivation of the arts of peace. It was at this period of a General Peace, that a Holy Alliance of the Monarchs of Europe was formed. The Sovereigns professed to be guided by the maxims of religion, and with holy motives seemed solicitous only for the peace of the world. But they have long since betrayed that their plans of tranquillity were to be intimately connected with the preservation of their own arbitrary power, and the destruction of popular liberty every where. Whatever militated against this power, or favoured this liberty, was to be crushed. To this single end has been directed all the diplomatic talent of Europe for years. The "General Peace" was, and still is, the ever ready plea in excuse for every new act of oppression at home, or of interference abroad. The mental elements, however, set in motion remotely by the Protestant Reformation, but more strongly agitated by the American Revolution, are yet working among the people of these governments to give the Tyrants of the earth uneasiness . . .

Can the example of Democratic liberty which this country shows, produce no uneasiness to monarchs? Does not every day bring fresh intelligence of the influence of American Democracy directly in England, France, Spain, Portugal, and Belgium, and indirectly in all the other European countries? And is there no danger of a re-action from Europe? Have we no interest in these changing aspects of European politics? The writer believes, that since the time of the American Revolution, which gave the principles of Democratic liberty a home, those principles have never been in greater jeopardy than at the present moment. To his reasons for thus believing, he invites the unimpassioned investigation of every American citizen. If there is danger, let it arouse to defence. If it is a false alarm, let such explanations be given of most suspicious appearances as shall safely allay it. It is no party question, and the attempt to make it one, should be at once suspected. It concerns all of every party.

There is danger of re-action from Europe; and it is the part of common prudence to look for it, and to provide against it. The great political truth has recently been promulged at the capital of one of the principal courts of Europe, Vienna, and by one of the profoundest scholars of Germany, the great truth, clearly and unanswerably proved, that the political revolutions to which European governments have been so long subjected, from the popular desires for liberty, are the natural effects of the Protestant Reformation. That Protestantism favours Republicanism, while Popery as naturally supports Monarchical power. In these lectures, delivered . . . for the purpose of strengthening the cause of absolute power, . . . there is a most important allusion to this country; and as it demonstrates one of the principal connecting points between European and American politics, and is the key to many of the mysterious doings that are in operation against American institutions under our own eyes, let Americans treasure it well in their memories. This is the passage: — "The great Nursery of these destructive principles, (the principles of Democracy,) the Great Revolutionary school for France and the rest of Europe, is North America!" Yes, (I address Democratic Americans,) the influence of this Republican government, of your democratic system, is vitally felt by Austria. She confesses it. It is proscribed by the Austrian Cabinet. This country is designated directly to all her people, and to her allied despots, as the great plague spot of the world, the poisoned foundation whence flow all the deadly evils which threaten their own existence. Is there nothing intended by this language of Austria? The words of Despots are few, but they are full of meaning. If action, indeed, did not follow their speeches, they might be safely indulged in their harmless proscriptions. But this is not the case. — Austria has followed out her words into actions. Is it wonderful after such an avowal in regard to America, that she

should do something to rid herself and the world of such a tremendous evil? Does not her own existence in truth depend upon destroying our example? Would it not be worth all the treasures of wealth that she could collect, if they could but purchase this great good? But how shall she attack us? She cannot send her armies, they would be useless. She has told us by the mouth of her Counsellor of Legation, that Popery, while it is the natural antagonist to Protestantism, is opposed in its whole character to Republican liberty, and is the promoter and supporter of arbitrary power. How fitted then is Popery for her purpose! This she can send without alarming our fears, or, at least, only the fears of those "miserable," "intolerant fanatics," and "pious bigots," who affect to see danger to the liberties of the country in the mere introduction of a religious system opposed to their own, and whose cry of danger, be it ever so loud, will only be regarded as the result of "sectarian fear," and the plot ridiculed as a "quixotic dream." But is there any thing so irrational, in such a scheme? Is it not the most natural and obvious act for Austria to do, with her views of the influence of Popery upon the form of government, its influence to pull down Republicanism, and build up Monarchy; I say, is it not her most obvious act to send Popery to this country if it is not here, or give it a fresh and vigorous impulse if it is already here? At any rate she is doing it. She has set herself to work with all her activity to disseminate throughout the country the Popish religion. Immediately after the delivery of Schlegel's lectures, which was in the year 1828, a great society was formed in the Austrian capital, in Vienna, in 1829. The late Emperor, and Prince Metternich, and the Crown Prince, (now Emperor,) and all the civil and ecclesiastical officers of the empire, with the princes of Savoy and Piedmont, uniting in it, and calling it after the name of a canonized King, St. Leopold. This society is formed for a great and express purpose. It has all the officers of government interested in it, from the Emperor down to the humblest in the Empire; and what is this purpose? Why, that "of promoting the greater activity Catholic missions in America;" these are the words of their own reports. Yes; these Foreign despots are suddenly stirred up to combine and promote the greater activity of Popery in this country;

and this, too, just after they had been convinced of the truth, or, more properly speaking, had their memories quickened with it, that Popery is utterly opposed to Republican liberty. These are the facts in the case. Americans, explain them in your own way. If any choose to stretch their charity so far as to believe that these crowned gentlemen have combined in this Society solely for religious purposes; that they have organized a Society to collect moneys to be spent in this country, and have sent Jesuits as their almoners, and ship-loads of Roman Catholic emigrants, and for the sole purpose of converting us to the religion of Popery, and without any political design, credat Judaeus Apella, non ego.

I have shown that a Society, (the "St. Leopold Foundation") is organized in a Foreign Absolute government, having its central direction in the capital of that government at Vienna, under the patronage of the Emperor of Austria, and the other Despotic Rulers,—a Society for the purpose of spreading Popery in this country. Of this fact there is no doubt . . .

And is such an extensive combination in foreign countries for the avowed purpose of operating in this country, (no matter for what purpose,) so trivial an affair, that we may safely dismiss it with a sneer? Have these foreign Rulers so much sympathy with our system of government, that we may trust them safely to meddle with it, in any way? Are they so impotent in combination as to excite in us no alarm? May they send money, and agents, and a system of government wholly at variance with our own, and spread it through all our borders with impunity from our search, because it is nick-named Religion? There was a time when American sensibilities were quick on the subject of foreign interference. What has recently deadened them?

Let us examine the operations of this Austrian Society, for it is hard at work all around us; yes, here in this country, from one end to the other, at our very doors, in this city. From a machinery of such a character and power, we shall doubtless be able to see already some effect. With its head-quarters at Vienna, under the immediate direction and inspection of Metternich, the well-known great managing general of the diplomacy of Europe, it makes itself already felt through the republic. Its emissaries are here.

And who are these emissaries? They are Jesuits. This society of men, after exerting their tyranny for upwards of 200 years, at length became so formidable to the world, threatening the entire subversion of all social order, that even the Pope, whose devoted subjects they are, and must be, by the vow of their society, was compelled to dissolve them. They had not been suppressed, however, for 50 years, before the waning influence of Popery and Despotism required their useful labours, to resist the spreading light of Democratic liberty, and the Pope, (Pius VII,) simultaneously with the formation of the Holy Alliance, revived the order of the Jesuits in all their power. From their vow of "unqualified submission to the Sovereign Pontiff," they have been appropriately called the Pope's body guard. It should be known, that Austrian influence elected the present Pope; his body guard are therefore at the service of Austria, and these are the soldiers that the Leopold Society has sent to this country, and they are agents of this society, to execute its designs, whatever these designs may be. And do Americans need to be told what Jesuits are? If any are ignorant, let them inform themselves of their history without delay; no time is to be lost: their workings are before you in every day's events: they are a secret society, a sort of Masonic order, with superadded features of most revolting odiousness, and a thousand times more dangerous. They are not confined to one class in society; they are not merely priests, or priests of one religious creed, they are merchants, and lawyers, and editors, and men of any profession, and no profession, having no outward badge, (in this country,) by which to be recognised; they are about in all your society. They can assume any character, that of angels of light, or ministers of darkness, to accomplish their one great end, the service upon which they are sent, whatever that service may be. "They are all educated men, prepared, and sworn to start at any moment, in any direction, and for any service, commanded by the general of their order, bound to no family, community, or country, by the ordinary ties which bind men; and sold for life to the cause of the Roman Pontiff."

These are the men at this moment ordered to America. And can they do nothing, Americans, to

derange the free workings of your democratic institutions? Can they not, and do they not fan the slightest
embers of discontent into a flame, those thousand
little differences which must perpetually occur in
any society, into riot, and quell its excess among
their own people as it suits their policy and the
establishment of their own control? Yes, they can be
the aggressors, and contrive to be the aggrieved. They
can do the mischief, and manage to be publicly
lauded for their praiseworthy forbearance and their
suffering patience. They can persecute, and turn
away the popular indignation, ever roused by the cry
of persecution from themselves, and make it fall upon
their victim. They can control the press in a thousand
secret ways. They can write under the signature of
"Whig," to-day, and if it suits their turn, "Tory,"
to-morrow. They can be Democrat to-day, and
Aristocrat to-morrow. They can out-American
Americans in admiration of American institutions to-
day, and "condemn them as unfit for any people"
to-morrow. These are the men that Austria has sent
here, that she supplies with money, with whom she
keeps up an active correspondence, and whose officers
(the Bishops) are passing back and forth between
Europe and America, doubtless to impart that information orally which would not be so safe committed to
writing.

Is there no danger to the Democracy of the
country from such formidable foes arrayed against it.
Is Metternich its friend? Is the Pope its friend? Are
his official documents now daily put forth, Democratic
in their character?

O there is no danger to the Democracy; for those
most devoted to the Pope, the Roman Catholics,
especially the Irish Catholics, are all on the side of
Democracy. Yes; to be sure they are on the side of
Democracy. They are just where I should look for
them. Judas Iscariot joined with the true disciples.
Jesuits are not fools. They would not startle our
slumbering fears, by bolting out their monarchical
designs directly in our teeth, and by joining the opposing ranks, except so far as to cover their designs.
This is a Democratic country, and the Democratic
party is and ever must be the strongest party, unless
ruined by traitors and Jesuits in the camp? Yes; it is
in the ranks of Democracy I should expect to find

them, and for no good purpose be assured. Every
measure of Democratic policy in the least exciting will
be pushed to ultraism, so soon as it is introduced for
discussion. Let every real Democrat guard against
this common Jesuitical artifice of tyrants, an artifice
which there is much evidence to believe is practising
against them at this moment, an artifice which if
not heeded will surely be the ruin of Democracy: it
is founded on the well-known principle that "extremes
meet." The writer has seen it pass under his own
eyes in Europe, in more than one instance . . .

That Jesuits are at work upon the passions of the
American community, managing in various ways to
gain control, must be evident to all. They who have
learned from history the general mode of proceeding
of this crafty set of men, could easily infer that they
were here, even were it not otherwise confirmed by
unquestionable evidence in their correspondence with
their foreign masters in Austria. There are some, perhaps, who are under the impression that the order of
Jesuits is a purely religious Society for the dissemina-
tion of the Roman Catholic religion; and therefore
comes within the protection of our laws, and must
be tolerated. There cannot be a greater mistake. It
was from the beginning a political organization, an
absolute Monarchy masked by religion. It has been
aptly styled "tyranny by religion." . . .

And here let me make the passing remark, that
there has been a great deal of mawkish sensitiveness
on the subject of introducing any thing concerning
religion into political discussions. This sensitiveness,
as it is not merely foolish, arising from ignorance of
the true line which separates political and theological
matters, but also exposes the political interests of
the country to manifest danger, I am glad to see is
giving way to a proper feeling on the subject. Church
and State must be for ever separated, but it is the
height of folly to suppose, that in political discussions,
Religion especially, the political character of any and
every religious creed may not be publicly discussed.
The absurdity of such a position is too manifest to
dwell a moment upon it. And in considering the
materials in our society adapted to the purposes of
hostile attack upon our Institutions, we must of
necessity notice the Roman Catholic religion. It
is this form of religion that is most implicated in

the conspiracy against our liberties. It is in this sect that the Jesuits are organized. It is this sect that is proclaimed by one of its own most brilliant and profound literary men to be hostile in its very nature to republican liberty; and it is the active extension of this sect that Austria is endeavouring to promote throughout this Republic. And Americans will not be cowed into silence by the cries of persecution, intolerance, bigotry, fanaticism, and such puerile catchwords, perpetually uttered against those who speak or write ever so calmly against the dangers of Popery. I can say, once for all, that no such outcry weighs a feather with me, nor does it weigh a feather with the mass of the American people. They have good sense enough to discriminate, especially in a subject of such vital importance to their safety, between words and things. I am not tenacious of words, except for convenience sake, the better to be understood, but if detestation of Jesuitism and tyranny, whether in a civil or ecclesiastical shape, is in future to be called intolerance, be it so; only let it be generally understood, and I will then glory in intolerance. When that which is now esteemed virtue, is to be known by general consent only by the name vice, why I will not be singular, but glory in vice, since the word is used to embody the essential qualities of virtue. I will just add, that those who are so fond of employing these epithets, forget that by so constantly, loosely, and indiscriminately using them, they cease to convey any emotions but those of disgust towards those who use them.

To return to the subject; it is in the Roman Catholic ranks that we are principally to look for the materials to be employed by the Jesuits, and in what condition do we find this sect at present in our country? We find it spreading itself into every nook and corner of the land; churches, chapels, colleges, nunneries and convents, are springing up as if by magic every where; an activity hitherto unknown among the Roman Catholics pervades all their ranks, and yet whence the means for all these efforts? Except here and there funds or favours collected from an inconsistent Protestant, (so called probably because born in a Protestant country, who is flattered or wheedled by some Jesuit artifice to give his aid to their cause,) the greatest part of the pecuniary means for all these

works are from abroad. They are the contributions of his Majesty the Emperor of Austria, of Prince Metternich, of the late Charles X., and the other Despots combined in the Leopold Society. And who are the members of the Roman Catholic communion? What proportion are natives of this land, nurtured under our own institutions, and well versed in the nature of American liberty? Is it not notorious that the greater part are Foreigners from the various Catholic countries of Europe. Emigration has of late years been specially promoted among this class of Foreigners, and they have been in the proportion of three to one of all other emigrants arriving on our shores; they are from Ireland, Germany, Poland, and Belgium. From the period of the formation of the Leopold Society, Catholic emigration increased in an amazing degree . . .

Facts like these I have enumerated might be multiplied, but these are the most important, and quite sufficient to make every American settle the question with himself, whether there is, or is not, danger to the country from the present state of our Naturalization Laws. I have stated what I believe to be facts. If they are not facts, they will easily be disproved, and I most sincerely hope they will be disproved. If they are facts, and my inferences from them are wrong, I can be shown where I have erred, and an inference more rational, and more probable, involving less, or perhaps no, danger to the country, can be deduced from them, which deduction, when I see it, I will most cheerfully accept, as a full explanation of these most suspicious doings of Foreign Powers.

I have spoken in these numbers freely of a particular religious sect, the Roman Catholics, because from the nature of the case it was unavoidable; because the foreign political conspiracy is identified with that creed. With the religious tenets properly so called, of the Roman Catholic, I have not meddled. If foreign powers, hostile to the principles of this government, have combined to spread any religious creed, no matter of what denomination, that creed does by that very act become a subject of political interest to all citizens, and must and will be thoroughly scrutinized. We are compelled to examine it. We have no choice about it. If instead of combining to spread with the greatest activity the Catholic Religion throughout our country, the Monarchs of Europe had united to spread Presbyterianism, or Methodism, I presume, there are few who would not see at once the propriety and the necessity of looking most narrowly at the political bearings of the peculiar principles of these Sects, or of any other Protestant Sects; and members of any Protestant Sects too, would be the last to complain of the examination. I know not why the Roman Catholics in this land of scrutiny are to plead exclusive exemption from the same trial . . . The arbitrary governments of Europe, — those governments who keep the people in the most abject obedience at the point of the bayonet, with Austria at their head, have combined to attack us in every vulnerable point that the nation exposes to their assault. They are impelled by self-preservation to attempt our destruction, — they must destroy democracy. It is with them a case of life and death, — they must succeed or perish. If they do not overthrow American liberty, American liberty will overthrow their despotism. They know this fact well. They have declared it. They are acting in accordance with their convictions, and declarations, and they are acting wisely. They have already sent their chains, and oh! to our shame be it spoken, are fastening them upon a sleeping victim. Americans, you are marked for their prey, not by foreign bayonets, but by weapons surer of effecting the conquest of liberty than all the munitions of physical combat in the military or naval storehouses of Europe. Will you not awake to the apprehension of the reality and extent of your danger? Will you be longer deceived by the pensioned Jesuits, who having surrounded your press, are now using it all over the country to stifle the cries of danger, and lull your fears by attributing your alarm to a false cause. Up! up! I beseech you. Awake! To your posts! Let the tocsin sound from Maine to Louisiana. Fly to protect the vulnerable places of your Constitution and Laws. Place your guards; you will need them, and quickly too. — And first, shut your gates. Shut the open gates. The very first step of safety is here. It is the beginning of defence. Your enemies, in the guise of friends, by thousands, are at this moment rushing in to your ruin through the open portals of naturalization. Stop them, or you are lost, irrevocably lost. The first battle is here at the gates. Concentrate here . . .

Archbishop John Hughes: Letters on the Madiai (1854)

. . . Connected with the case of the Madiai, a new national policy has been broached in the Senate of the United States, by no less distinguished a Senator than General Cass. This policy, with which the gentlemen at Metropolitan Hall appeared to be very familiar, purports to be a vindication of the rights of conscience, to be secured to all American citizens in whatever countries they may choose to travel or sojourn. The ground on which this policy is advanced is, that in this country strangers of every nation are allowed to exercise their religion as their conscience may dictate, and therefore in all other countries Americans have the right to claim and exercise a similar privilege. It is hardly necessary for me to observe that freedom of conscience which is here contended for is inviolable in its very nature and essence. To say that any man or any nation has either physical or moral power to destroy freedom of conscience, is to give utterance to a patent absurdity. Conscience without freedom is not conscience, but for this very reason the freedom of conscience is beyond the reach of man's power. God has provided in the human soul a fortress to which it can retreat, and from which it can hurl defiance against all invaders. I presume, therefore, that there is a confusion of ideas in the minds of those who with General Cass plead eloquently for that which requires no pleading, namely, freedom of conscience. That is universal, — that is indestructible, — that is inviolable. They must be understood to mean liberty of external action according to conscience, which is quite a different thing. This external liberty of action according to conscience in all countries is regulated, to a certain extent, by the enactment of positive laws. In some countries the range is wider, in others more restricted; but it is limited in all, not even excepting the United States. The liberty of conscience which is recognized and applauded in Connecticut will not be tolerated (on certain subjects) in South Carolina or in Alabama. The Mormons have been obliged to seek retirement in

Letter of Archbishop Hughes on the Madiai; Speech of the Hon. Lewis Cass, on Religious Freedom Abroad; Letter of Archbishop Hughes, in Reply to General Cass, and in Self-vindication, J. Murphy & Co., Baltimore, 1854.

Deseret, in order to enjoy what they call liberty of conscience, and the liberty they there enjoy would not be allowed them under the toleration of the laws of New York. Is it expected, then, in the project of General Cass, that they too shall have the privilege of exercising liberty of conscience in their peregrinations among foreign States?

Again, the assumption of General Cass is a fallacy. He assumes that the freedom of religion in this country is a boon conceded by Protestant liberality to all the inhabitants of the land. This is not so. It is a privilege which was won by the good swords of Catholics and Protestants in the battles for national independence. It is a common right, therefore, and is not to be regarded as a concession from one denomination to the other. This arrangement, in regard to liberty of conscience, suited the policy of the country, and was absolutely indispensable after the Revolutionary war. Does General Cass mean to say, that because it suited us all other nations must adopt it, whether it suits them or not? As well might England say, that because it suited her finances to admit free trade, she will insist upon it that all other nations shall do the same. General Cass knows as well as any man living, that until this country becomes vastly stronger, and foreign States much weaker than they are, all pleadings on this subject will be treated as driveling by foreign States. Oh, if you have a mind to arrange the constitutions and laws of European States by the power of armies and navies, that, indeed, is another matter. But the United States will expose themselves to ridicule if they drag such a question into their diplomatic intercourse with foreign governments.

It is a recognized principle in this country, that every sovereign and independent nation has the right to adopt its own constitution and laws. The constitution and laws of a country are but the aggregate of general principles applicable to the peculiar situation, protection and welfare of the citizens or subjects of which it is composed. They may be regarded as the public and permanent expression of the aggregate conscience of that State. Thus, without going out of our own country, Massachusetts has one form of public conscience, Louisiana has another. Does Mr. Cass mean to say that an abolitionist from Boston, under plea of liberty of conscience, still has the right to talk in New Orleans, and preach, and harangue, and write, and publish on the subject of slavery as he might choose to do in Faneuil Hall? If not, I would say with all respect, that the policy in regard to this subject which General Cass advocates in the Senate, is calculated to have no practical effect either at home or abroad, except to stir up sectarian animosities against his Catholic fellow citizens; and this is hardly worthy of his patriotic services, advanced age or accumulated honors.

Indeed, I am quite persuaded that the country has lowered itself in dignity if it be true, as the newspapers have stated, that the President, through Secretary Everett, has become a petitioner side by side with Lord Roden, and taken his place of expectation and hope in the ante-chamber of the Grand Duke of Tuscany. The supreme government of this country ought not to stoop to an investigation, however sacred may be the occasion, of a political trial in the petty States of Italy. In doing so, it exposes itself to humiliation and rebuke without redress. The Grand Duke can easily ask Mr. Secretary Everett certain questions about the liberty of conscience in this country, which the latter would find himself exceedingly puzzled to answer. If the Grand Duke or his Minister should ask Mr. Everett whether liberty of conscience is recognized in the United States as unlimited — the same in one State as in another — the Secretary will have to reply, "No." If the same interrogator should ask Mr. Everett what became of the helpless female inmates of a certain Convent in Charlestown, near Boston, who were driven out without accusation, or trial, or condemnation before any civil tribunal, expelled from their peaceful home in the depths of night, their house and furniture committed to the flames — can Mr. Everett tell what happened to them afterwards? Again the Secretary would have to answer, "No." Did the State of Massachusetts make any compensation to those persons for the destruction of their property or the violation of their rights? Mr. Everett would have to answer, "No." Is the State of Massachusetts bound to protect the individual rights of its citizens? Mr. Everett would have to answer "Yes," (in theory,) — in practice (in this case, at least), "No." How then, it might further be asked, do you pretend that liberty of conscience is extended to all the citizens of the United States? Is there any practical difference between the social intolerance which prevails in your country where there are so many religions, and the legal intolerance of our dominions where there is but one? It seems to me that the Secretary of the United States, who has it not in his power to give different answers to questions such as these, rather exposes himself and his native State, if not his country, by going all the way to Florence to plead for liberty of conscience, whilst such violations of its rights have been perpetrated, and left unrecompensed at his own door. Other violations of liberty of conscience in different parts of the country are by no means rare in our history. They occurred in Philadelphia, where churches and convents were burned to ashes by the intolerance of the mob. There is this, however, to be said in extenuation — that, at least, if the civil authorities of Pennsylvania did not protect its citizens from these outrages, it allowed compensation for the damage done to their property. I fear much that social intolerance is not to be ascribed so much to the principles of any religion, as to the diseased moral nature which is the common inheritance of us all. The evidence of this can be discovered no less in the United States than elsewhere. There is among us a superabundance of social and domestic intolerance, in despite of those laws of religious freedom of which we are so ready to boast, but which, unfortunately, have no power to protect the object of that intolerance. Is it rare that poor servants are driven out from their employment because they will not, against their conscience, join the domestic religion "of State" which the family has made exclusive? Is it unusual to hear of men disinheriting their own offspring for no cause except that of practising their acknowledged rights of conscience? These are matters with which we are made too familiar, notwithstanding our boasted rights and liberty of conscience.

I have offered these remarks not in any spirit of controversy, but in the spirit of peace and of truth. There are moments when every citizen, who feels that he can say something promotive of the welfare of his countrymen, and of advantage to his country, is authorized to give public utterance to his sentiments, how humble soever he may be. With such a feeling I offer the foregoing reflections to the consideration of my fellow-citizens for what they are worth — no more.

Hon. Lewis Cass: *Religious freedom abroad (1854)*

Mr. Cass said: Mr. President: — Agreeably to the notice I gave some time since, I shall now trouble the Senate with some remarks in support of the motion to refer the excellent report, made by Mr. Underwood at the last session of Congress, on the subject of the claim of American citizens to be protected in the freedom of religious worship abroad, to the Committee on Foreign Relations.

When this matter was first under consideration, I did not suppose a single man in the country could be found who would deny the principle involved in the application, or question the propriety of some kind of interference to assert and maintain it. It was no sectarian movement. It sought, not merely to protect a Catholic in a Protestant country, a Protestant in a Catholic country, a Jew in a Christian country, but an American in all countries. I earnestly advocate the proper action of the Government, not less in favor of our brethren of the Hebrew faith, than in favor of their Christian fellow-citizens. The descendant of the Patriarchs, and the believer in Jesus Christ, are entitled to the same protection. Jew or Gentile, all are equal in this land of law and liberty; and as the former suffers most from illiberal persecution, his case is entitled to the most commiseration, and sure am I, that public sentiment would strongly reprove any attempt to create a distinction between them. And the protection demanded is not a claim inconsistent with the just laws of man, but one to secure to all our people the inalienable right of worshipping God agreeably to the dictates of their own conscience, and while yielding obedience to local legislation within the legitimate sphere of its operation . . . In the document, to which I shall refer, my course in this matter is criticised, if not arraigned and condemned, with that tone of confident superiority in the discussion which ought rarely to be assumed in polemical controversy. That document is in the form of a letter, addressed by Archbishop Hughes to the editor of the New York Freeman's Journal, and is, in fact, a review of the proceedings of the Senate at its last session, in relation to this question of the religious freedom of American citizens in foreign countries . . .

He begins by observing that the "heading of this

communication suggests the matter it proposes to discuss." That matter involves the true question of religious freedom, and the proceedings of which its assertion had given rise in this body as well as elsewhere, and the object is to prove that we were all wrong, and that the claim on behalf of American citizens "to exercise their religion as their conscience may dictate," is in fact the result of a "confusion of ideas," for that the freedom of conscience which is here contended for is inviolable in its very essence, because conscience is not within the reach of legislation, and therefore always free, whatever external force may be brought to bear upon the body itself. — The question thus resolves itself into the power of thinking, which is all a man can claim as a right; for beyond this is the province of the law-maker, who, "to a certain extent" — to what extent we are not told — may regulate religious actions of men by the enactment of positive laws. A position I deny emphatically, as I do the statement that such laws exist in this country. I deny that any human Legislature can rightfully interfere with acts of religious worship, I mean true religious worship, not impious pretensions founded in fanaticism or hypocrisy, and at war with the well-being of society, or that the statute-books of the different States of this Union are disgraced by such presumption . . .

The Archbishop calls the performance of this duty a new national policy broached by me. I am entitled to no such honor. The history of his country should have told him that it was a part of our policy when I was an infant, as I shall show by and by, introduced by great names, and recorded in the diplomatic annals of the Republic.

As to the alleged sectarian bearing, I disclaim and deny it emphatically. Archbishop Hughes, though he does not directly charge me with such a design, seems to intimate it, as a conclusion, either from the remarks I made, or from the course I pursued; and strange indeed is this deduction drawn from the premises he lays down. He says:

"Thus, without going out of our own country, Massachusetts has one form of public conscience, Louisiana another. Does Mr. Cass mean to say that an Abolitionist from Boston, under the plea of liberty of conscience, has the right to talk in New Orleans, and preach, and harangue, and write and publish, on the subject of slavery, as he might choose to do in Faneuil Hall? If not, I would say with all respect, that the policy in regard to this subject which General Cass advocates in the Senate, is calculated to have no practical effect either at home or abroad, except to stir up sectarian animosities against his Catholic fellow-citizens, and this is hardly worthy of his patriotic services, advanced age, or accumulated honors."

No, sir, I do not say so. I do not say that an Abolitionist from Boston, or from any other place, has the right to preach his doctrine to the slaves of the South. I say he has no such right thus, in effect, to strike at the very existence of society; and, by an act like that, he exposes himself to the punishment which the local laws have provided for so heinous an offence. And the error of this analogical reasoning is in the assumption that to preach abolitionism to a slave population is the mere exercise of a right of conscience, as inviolable in principle as the right to worship God freely and peacefully. That hypocrites might claim this exemption for the consequences of their acts is not to be wondered at in this day of strange things; but that a learned and highly esteemed prelate, speaking *ex cathedra* to the American people, should assume the same immunity for acts like this, caused by the wanton excesses of an ill-regulated or ill-instructed conscience, or justified by mere pretexts where there is no conscience at all — for no human tribunal can determine the honesty or dishonesty of such a pretension with the worship of the Creator, equally dictated by reason and by revelation — is to me one of those truths only to be learned by actual observation, and which are almost stranger than fiction. As I shall have occasion to advert more fully to this pretension, which practically denies all the rights of conscience, in consequence of the abuses to which their exercise may lead, I shall here pursue the subject no further.

But I cannot pass over without a remark the observation of Archbishop Hughes respecting the tendency of the proposed measure "to stir up sectarian animosities against our Catholic fellow-citizens." This measure has no connection with religious sects. It seeks to elevate no one, to depress no one. The resolution proposed makes not the slightest allusion to any religious denomination; nor do I suppose there is one Senator, intending to vote for it, who will be influenced by any such consideration.

There are Protestant as well as Catholic countries where the true principles of religious freedom are denied; and there are Catholic as well as Protestant Countries where they are freely enjoyed; and their recognition everywhere will be an inestimable benefit to all our citizens whom the accidents of life may require to leave their own country.

For myself, sir, it seems hardly worth while to disclaim all intention to stir up sectarian animosities, or to try to bring reproach upon the Catholic religion. The whole course of my life redeems me from such a charge. That man does not live who ever heard me utter one disrespectful word against that great branch of the Christian church, or against its priests or its professors.

I have lived a great portion of my life, both at home and abroad, surrounded by its members, and I have always done justice to the learning, and piety, and exemplary conduct of the clergy, and to the salutary influence of its principles upon the laity of that church. I do not intend to be led from the path before me — that of defending a great principle — into other inquiries, unless so far as may be necessary to correct erroneous impressions respecting the true ground I occupy. I seek to know neither sectarians nor schismatics in the performance of such a duty . . .

The worship of God, the relations between man and his Creator, constitute the noblest province of this freedom, as these are the highest duties man is called upon to perform. Many a powerful intellect has been brought to bear upon the problem of reconciling the greatest liberty of conscience with the salutary restraints of society; and no one can deny that a palpable boundary, at all times clear and distinct, if not absolutely incompatible, with the condition of humanity, is a discovery in the science of political morals yet to be made. But Archbishop Hughes, with a courage which all may applaud, however his discretion may be doubted, or his success denied, marches up to this question, and with a single stroke of his controversial sword cuts this worse than Gordian knot, which has so long baffled the mental efforts of all his predecessors in

this field of intellectual inquiry. He claims for human governments the right — how limited he does not tell us — to regulate the duties most closely connected with the religious opinions of their people; but while maintaining this thesis, he seems unwilling or unprepared to maintain its necessary corollary, that of a power over the human conscience, by drawing a distinction between that great moral faculty and the exercise of its dictates, thus leaving it a mere abstract sentiment . . .

This "national policy" is destined soon to be an established and a successful one, founded as it is upon the inalienable rights of man; and even if it were "new" in practice, as it is not, it is old in principle, and it comes to do its work at an age of the world when other considerations besides those of antiquity enter into the determination of grave questions affecting the welfare of mankind. It is but yesterday, as it were, that the "new" policy of "throwing off Governments destructive of the ends for which they are instituted," was announced in our Declaration of Independence; but young as it is, it already commands the assent of every liberal mind through the world, and ere long will become one of the great practical truths in all political systems.

The Archbishop assumes that this policy is pressed here on the ground that, as foreigners are allowed the exercise of their religion in this country, therefore in all other countries Americans have the right to claim and exercise a similar privilege.

Mr. President, this is too narrow a foundation for this great claim of religious immunity. It rests on no example, but on the everlasting decree of the Creator. We do not undertake to say to any other Government that American citizens ought to enjoy the rights of religious worship within your jurisdiction because your subjects enjoy them in our country, but we say these are rights which belong to man everywhere; and we can ask you as a matter of comity to permit their enjoyment, with the more freedom, because every one, citizen or foreigner, in our country, is allowed to worship God in his own way.

The motive of the Archbishop in the promulgation of this moral theorem is not, at first, very obvious. Where it does not degenerate into a mere dispute about words, and assumes to be a psychological truth, it is at war with the common sentiment of mankind. To assert that the human conscience is free to fulfil its appropriate functions, whatever external force may be applied to its corporeal tenement, is to ask our assent to a proposition contradicted by universal experience. There is no profession however sacred, no position however elevated, no knowledge however extensive, no intellect however profound, which can give plausibility even to such an assumption — doctrine I will not call it — so utterly irreconcilable with the very instincts of our nature. For almost six thousand years the world has been groping in darkness, according to Archbishop Hughes, mistaking what is meant by the liberty of conscience, which, instead of ever being menaced by human authority, is entirely beyond its reach, and needs no defence, because it is exposed to no danger. According to this self-protecting theory, a man at the stake, with the fires burning around him, enjoys full liberty of conscience, because this resolves itself into the possession of the power of thinking, which is indestructible while life endures. That inward judge which decides between right and wrong is equally undisturbed by the presence of physical torture, and by the advent of impending death.

What degree of force — of physical trial, rather — will obscure the moral judgment, is, perhaps, a question of bodily endurance as much as of mental fortitude. Archbishop Hughes, in his highly figurative language, has provided a "fortress to which the conscience can retreat, and from which it can hurl defiance against all invaders." This metaphor will hardly stand the test of critical scrutiny, and is out of place in a grave moral investigation . . .

But to pass from these speculations to practical inquiry. I desire to ask Archbishop Hughes what object he had in view in this effort to show that the human conscience is always free, whatever may be the external circumstances with which it may be surrounded, and that it is therefore absurd to fear its thraldom or to endeavor to guard against it? There is but one assignable reason for the assumption of this postulate, both physical and ethical in its character, and that is, an unwillingness to claim for any Government the naked right to interfere with, and to restrain or destroy the freedom of conscience. I do not believe that Archbishop Hughes would advocate such a doctrine,

so understanding it; and certainly to do so would be a bold experiment upon the feelings of this country, which would be sure to be frowned down by public indignation. The difficulty of the position in which the Archbishop was placed resulted, on the one hand, from the opinion entertained by him that human lawmakers have the right to legislate upon questions of religious worship, and on the other from a conviction that freedom of conscience is not within the pale of human authority; and the dilemma caused by these conflicting principles is to be avoided by reducing freedom of conscience to a mere operation of the mind, leaving it in its fortress, but leaving also to the tender mercies of the municipal magistrate the power to control and direct its dictates by all the terrible punishments which persecution has devised and faith endured. The grasp is upon the shadow, while the substance escapes. — And the universal sentiment, that he alone is free who is free from violence, is rebuked as a patent absurdity, originating in a confusion of ideas, which the Archbishop kindly undertakes to make clear.

But, after all, the learned writer will find that it required no new Galileo to explore the human intellect, in order to discover and announce that the mind of man is beyond the direct jurisdiction of earthly laws. It is to measure the knowledge of the world by a low standard indeed to suppose that this obvious truth had so long escaped its penetration. In fact, it was as well known on the day of the Exodus from Eden, as it now is, even with the benefit of the distinguished prelate's labors.

But at best, according to the Archbishop's own showing, this branch of the inquiry degenerates into a verbal disquisition. The world chooses to call the freedom of external action the freedom of conscience, which he considers little better than an absurdity. Be it so; but this leaves the question just where it found it. A change of nomenclature does not change the object, which is to protect the conscience of man from human legislation, by denying to it jurisdiction over those duties which conscience dictates. And this is the very proposition to which Archbishop Hughes finally comes, and fights against most manfully . . .

What is this liberty of conscience, thus inviolable, and the denial of which is so sternly rebuked? Not Archbishop Hughes' power of thinking — for no man in his senses ever denied that; but it is "freedom from compulsion" — these are the words of the author — without which this moral agent, inviolable as it should be, is violated, "to the disgrace of human nature." . . .

The principle advanced by Archbishop Hughes, and the illustrations in support of it, are sadly inconsistent with each other. But, adhering to the former and rejecting the latter, he maintains that freedom of conscience is beyond the reach of human legislation, but the external action which the world considers, and justly, as the true freedom of conscience, may be the rightful object of control; and while the former is shut up in his fortress, the latter may be dealt with at the pleasure of the ruler. I cannot ascertain, from a careful perusal of Archbishop Hughes' remarks, what practical limitation, if any, there is to the exercise of this power; for he says, "this external liberty of action in all countries is regulated, to a certain extent, by the enactment of positive laws. In some countries the range is wider, in others more restricted, but it is limited in all, not excepting the United States."

The human conscience embraces in its operations a vast field of duty, the extent of which it is not necessary, for any purpose I have in view, to examine. I am dealing with a practical question — with the freedom of religious worship — one of the branches of the rights of conscience. Whatever illustrations the subject may receive from other considerations, these are but accessory, and I design to restrict my investigation to the freedom of religious worship — to the relations, as I have said between a man and his Maker. The object of our proposed action is to procure for American citizens abroad immunity from local laws, so far as these interfere with the liberty of worshipping God. With respect to other conscientious scruples in the affairs of life, by which men may be placed in opposition to municipal laws, as the subject is not now in my way, I shall not turn aside to seek it. Prudent Governments should avoid as far as may be, the adoption of measures revolting to the moral sense of their people.

But, sir, I say, as I said on a former occasion, I am no believer in what has been falsely called the higher law; for it should be called the lower law, or rather no law at all, as the principle involved in it would be destructive of all law, leaving every man free from the obligations of legal obedience who should declare he had conscientious scruples respecting sub-

mission. — And I say, also, that if a man is required by law to do what he thinks he ought not to do, the only course by which he can reconcile his faith and his duty, is to sit still and suffer as a martyr, instead of resisting as a criminal; unless, indeed, the oppressive acts result in revolution. That was the doctrine and the practice of the Apostles. And he who believes that any other is consistent with the maintenance of social order for a single day, in the face of the hallucinations of the human intellect, or of the pretexts of human hypocrisy, has yet to learn the very first rudiments of the nature of man. But the inquiry I am making is into the rights of rulers, not into the duty of the ruled. And this brings me to the true point, whether Governments may rightfully control, at their will, the religious opinions of their citizens; and I mean, by controlling them, the just authority to punish all who disobey their mandates . . . This discussion turns upon the claim of Governments to control the religious freedom of their people by prohibiting the exercise of any religion but the dominant one established by the State, or by requiring all within their jurisdiction to conform to it. I am aware of the apologies for this monstrous usurpation, which are to be found in some of the European elementary writers. They do not weigh one feather with me, not enough to justify even a consideration of their views — arguments there are none. Their day has gone by, and contempt is the only feeling excited in the breast of an American by such sentiments as the following, the type of their class, advanced with all due gravity by a celebrated, perhaps the most celebrated writer upon natural law:

"There is nothing on earth more august and sacred than a sovereign; and why should God, who calls him by his providence to watch over the safety and happiness of a whole nation, deprive him of the direction of the most powerful spring (religion) that actuates mankind?" . . .

It is not every vagary of the imagination, nor every ebullition of feeling, nor every impulse of the passions, however honest the motives may be, which can lay claim to the rights of conscience. That great moral faculty is an improving one, and should be improved and instructed by all the means within our reach; and he who neglects that duty will have much to answer for. It is no excuse, by the laws of God or man, that he who, in a state of security, commits a crime, believes he was called upon to do it. Certainly, were such a doctrine established, there would be little security for society, for immunity from punishment would be sure to lead to the relaxation of moral perception, and to the accommodation of the conscience to any temptations which might present themselves. Every man is responsible for the use of this endowment, as he is responsible for every other gift which God has bestowed upon him . . .

Undoubtedly here is room for abuse and oppression as there must be, more or less, in all human institutions; but it is inseparable, in the very nature of things, from the position of the parties, governors, and governed. And in this very circumstance is found one of the great blessings of free institutions, which neither sacrifice the protection of the community nor of individuals, but endeavor to preserve the just rights of both; while the constant efforts of irresponsible power, and of governments not depending on the will of the people, are to circumscribe personal freedom, and to rule over the mind as well as the body. Let not, therefore, Archbishop Hughes deduce the right to claim exemption from any and all laws from the position that there are some laws which carry with them no moral obligation, and which the human lawmaker has no right to pass. The attempt is equally illogical and unreasonable. The true object of human governments is to protect man in a state of society; and in the execution of the duty thus devolved upon them there must necessarily be various modifications of systems, operating in different parts of the globe, and much latitude of discretion in their administration. Still, in an inquiry into the just rights of these governments, not into their practical working, it is vain to tell us what they have assumed to do; for they have assumed to do much, and have done much, for which there was neither authority nor justification.

The reference, therefore, to our country, to Connecticut and South Carolina, even if the facts bore upon the discussion, would be merely to furnish examples of bad legislation, leaving untouched the question of right. But I deny that religious worship is the subject of American legislation. There is no part of our country, not a solitary nook, from these marble Halls, where the representatives of the American States and people assemble to do the will of their sovereign, to the remotest log cabin, upon the very verge of civilization, where a man may not freely and lawfully worship God, unrestrained by any law, local or Federal. I make this assertion without the fear of contradiction. In Connecticut, in South Carolina, in Oregon, and everywhere else, any man may perform his religious services to his Creator without the slightest fear of interruption or punishment. But there are other considerations connected with this subject and necessary to its full development, in order to prevent a confusion of ideas, which I am surprised to find have escaped the penetration of so practiced a logician and sagacious an observer as Archbishop Hughes. It is obvious, on the slightest reflection, that in the practical operations of governments, cases may rise in which it may be difficult to ascertain distinctly where just authority ends and usurpation begins. Like many other questions in life, the extremes may be obvious; though the intermediate shades of difference may not be well defined. It is perfectly clear that no Legislature can rightfully touch a man because he reads his Bible, or falls on his knees to pray, or performs any other act of worship compatible with the peace and healthful condition of society; and equally clear is it that he who, pretending to worship God, commits acts inconsistent with social order, by whatever vagary impelled, whether the result of distempered intellect, or of hypocritical cunning, seeking profit or distinction from human credulity, can claim no exemption from the just consequences of his own acts . . .

Even our own country at this very moment exhibits a humiliating spectacle, in an association of men, degrading the name of Christians by appropriating it to themselves, and openly professing and practicing doctrines irreconcilable with an orderly condition of society, and which hold out the reward of lust to strengthen the conviction and conversion of its followers. Examples of this mental obliquity — monomania very often, for it cannot be doubted that many who embrace such tenets are honest in their allegiance to them — might be multiplied indefinitely, were the task a necessary or profitable one. But it is neither, and these illustrations of the general principle are enough for my purpose. Now in all such cases, the civil magistrate may rightfully interfere and provide punishments not for acts of religious worship, but for crimes, before which the peace of society would disappear. But as I have said, between the extreme boundaries there is a debatable land, where doubts may arise, and where just allowance should be made for the imperfection of the human judgment . . .

I must confess my astonishment that the learned and able prelate thus deals with the great principle of religious freedom, reducing it to the level of those questions of mere expediency which may well be decided one way to-day and another to-morrow, as the circumstances that control them change from time to time. I do not mean to say that because the arrangement suited us, therefore it suits and should be adopted by all other nations — I mean to say, it suits all nations, and all time as a law of right, implanted by the Divine Lawgiver in the human breast, and whoever violates it, be the guilty party prince or people or priest, will in vain seek to avoid the just consequence of presumptuous intolerance.

The Archbishop then proceeds to say:

"It is a recognized principle in this country, that every sovereign and independent nation has the right to adopt its own Constitution and laws. The Constitution and laws of a country are but the aggregate of general principles, applicable to the peculiar situation, protection, and welfare of the citizens or subjects of which it is composed. They may be regarded as the public and permanent expression of the aggregate conscience of that State."

It is certainly not to be controverted, that the principle here asserted, that independent States have a right to adopt their own Constitution and laws, is fully recognized in this country, and, indeed, I suppose, at least theoretically, everywhere else, unless, indeed, where the divine right to reign leaves no other right but that of obedience.

But I must again bring to the notice of the Archbishop that this investigation does not touch forms of government, nor their powers as political communities. It has a much higher aim; and that is, to ascertain their moral right to control the consciences of their people, by prescribing their mode of faith, and the manner in which they shall worship God. With respect to the "aggregate of general principles applicable to the peculiar situation, protection, and welfare

of citizens;" though I must confess my ideas are much confused as to what this means, yet, from my glimmering of it, I have only to say, that such considerations are lighter than the small dust of the balance in a moral inquiry as important as this. Segregate or aggregate what principles you may, the great principle remains inviolable, rising superior to all other considerations, that man has a right to worship God unrestrained by human laws. There is no situation, protection, nor welfare, which can rightfully interfere with this duty; or, rather, there is no situation in which it is not the best protection, promoting the greatest welfare of mankind.

As to the "aggregate conscience" of a State, I neither comprehend distinctly its meaning nor its application . . .

It is carrying figurative language to the very verge of mysticism to employ it thus loosely as an element in a search after truth. And this "aggregate conscience of a State" is made up, not of the consciences of those who obey its government, and ought to direct it, but of its own Constitution and laws, which form the expression of "the aggregate of the general principles applicable to the peculiar situation, protection, and welfare of its citizens," &c. That is, in other words, the administration of every Government expresses the aggregate conscience of the State it rules. Well, this is an easy, if not a satisfactory, way to dispose of this grave question of public morality. It comes to this: that the aggregate conscience of France is permanently expressed by its Constitution and laws, that is, at present, by the rules of Louis Napoleon; of Turkey, by the successor of the Prophet; of Russia, by the Czar; and so on to the end of the chapter of Governments, good and bad. I said I did not comprehend the application of this doctrine, were it even true, and I do not. But so able a controversialist as Archbishop Hughes did not advance it without design; and the only bearing I can discover which it was to have, is to offset this "aggregate conscience" against the consciences of individuals, this moral faculty of Massachusetts, which has one form, and of Louisiana, which has another, thus giving the right of final judgment and control in all cases to this abstract national faculty, and practically justifying the most revolting tyranny because the law is the expression of the public conscience, and the public conscience is the foundation of the law . . .

For myself, sir, I have not the least design to undertake the task of pointing out the errors into which Archbishop Hughes has fallen in relation to this topic. I desire, however, to say I do not doubt but that acts of social intolerance like those he alludes to, and justly censures, may have occured in this country; but I trust and believe they are rare, and I know they are not chargeable to any particular denomination, but may happen as well to members of the Catholic faith as to those of the various sects of Protestants. And I know still more, that they are less likely to happen in this country than in any other under Heaven, from the very nature of our social condition, and of our political organization, which are hostile to sectarian prejudices, and insure their being visited by public condemnation . . .

The past is a pledge for the future. Within the memory of the present generation the abuses of ages seemed to possess an impregnable fortress, occupying its position in the midst of Christianity and civilization, and overlooking and overawing both. But one after another its outworks have fallen before the efforts of truth, and ere long the citadel itself will be leveled to the ground. And are the representatives of the American people to lay their hands on their mouths, and their mouths in the dust, to look on and see the persecutions and oppressions to which their countrymen are exposed abroad, and not even express their demands? And all from an affectation of national decorum, national squeamishness, it should be called, which is so tender to the presumption of others as to sacrifice our own true rights and honor. I trust no such humiliation is in store for us.

Archbishop John Hughes: *Reply to General Cass, and self-vindication (1854)*

. . . The honorable senator has represented me as attempting to balance accounts between this country and the Grand Little Duchy of Tuscany. This was not fair. I made no accusations against this country. I merely suggested that civil governments, our own included, are sometimes unable to escape difficulties such as have sent the Madiai from Florence, according to law, and driven unprotected ladies from their dove-

cot in Charlestown, in Massachusetts, against law, into common banishment. General Cass thinks that inasmuch as the banishment of the Madiai was according to law, in Tuscany, and that of the Ursulines against law and by violence, the comparison is wonderfull against Tuscany and in our favor. I believe directly the reverse. The laws of Tuscany had made known to all parties beforehand, that the establishment of domestic conventicles for the purpose of proselytizing the subjects of the Grand Duchy from the established religion, would be visited with the judicial decisions of the established courts, and would be followed on conviction of parties with the penalties which the law had in such case provided. Here there was at least fair notice given beforehand. The commonwealth of Massachusetts, on the other side, had proclaimed to all the inhabitants of the land, that property, reputation, and life would be safe under the shield of her sovereign protection, unless in the case that all or either should be forfeited according to law and justice applicable to the case. The Madiai of Florence had not been deceived by the laws of the country under which they lived. The nuns of Charlestown, in regard to the laws of the country in which they had confided, were deceived. The latter, without having incurred even a reproach, much less an impeachment, or trial by jury, or judicial sentence consequent on such trial, were driven from their own home in violation of law, their property destroyed, the very graves of their departed sisters desecrated. What then? "Oh," says General Cass, "that was a mob." My answer is, "So much the worse for his side of the comparison." The State of Massachusetts ought not to have allowed those ladies to spend their money in building a house, and confiding their safety and property to the high promise of its sovereign protection, if the State of Massachusetts felt itself incapable of protecting them. But although in any country in the world it may happen, as it has happened in nearly all, that a mob may have violated the laws, still, when order is restored, such sovereign State having pledged itself to protect personal rights, ought to be prepared to make such puny reparations as would be possible with a view to vindicate its own character of sovereignty. Massachusetts has neither protected, nor has she compensated. General Cass thinks that reparation should have been made. This shows the benevolence of his heart. But the outrage has been on record in the public annals of the country and of the world for the last twenty years, and even General Cass had never before betrayed, so far as I am aware, the secret of his kind sympathies to the poor ladies of Charlestown. Neither has any of the great men of Massachusetts, so far as has come to my knowledge, expressed publicly such sympathy for them. Mr. Everett, or his great predecessor, Mr. Webster, since the burning of the Convent at Charlestown, has hardly been able to find himself in a locality from which it would be possible to look on the Bunker Hill monument, without having at the same time within the range of his vision the black walls and the ruins of Mount Benedict. I have a vague recollection that Mr. Everett did, on one occasion, many years ago, refer to the subject in language of regret; but if I am not mistaken in my memory, he alleged on that occasion that by false zeal the convent had been raised, and by false zeal it had been destroyed, — thereby ignoring all distinction between acts loyally and honestly done in faith of protection from the sovereignty of the State, and acts done in violation of the State's laws and contempt of its authority . . .

The Senator from Michigan maintains the supremacy of individual conscience; but he nullifies that supremacy according to his definition of conscience, by limiting the right to follow its dictates, and subjecting that right to the prohibition of law, human or divine. Now if the conscience of the individual is supreme, and the law of the land of any country is supreme also, which supremacy shall give way to the other? These are the premises laid down by General Cass; but, unfortunately, he has left the conclusions to be drawn from them, respectively to destroy or annihilate each other. His idea of conscience is not that it is a superior and indestructible, independent, moral faculty in the human soul, enabling every man to distinguish and choose between what seems to him good and evil; but that conscience gives right to the individual to act out or manifest in words or deeds its interior dictates. On the other hand, he arms the civil authorities of all countries with the acknowledged right to control outward actions; so that, by confounding outward actions with conscience itself, he betrays and hands over that sacred principle to be judged of and controlled by magistrates and civil governments.

His first ebullition in favor of conscience is the proclamation that his purpose is "not merely to protect a Catholic in a Protestant country, a Protestant in a Catholic country, a Jew in a Christian country, but an American in all countries." General Cass professes to speak and act in regard to this subject on the ground of principle. Principle is neither Catholic, nor Protestant, nor Jewish, nor Christian — at least in the sense in which it has been employed by him. Principle, if any thing, is universal. And since General Cass has attributed to what he calls an American, something like a special prerogative, he ought to show some grounds why an American, here classified under the head of religious denominations, should have any special or exceptional preference. Four religious denominations are mentioned, namely: Catholic, Protestant, Jew, and Christian. This nomenclature General Cass may explain. Its terms, theologically considered, are, at least, intelligible. But when he comes to rank an American as a representative of a fifth sect, I really do not understand what he means.

If an American, as such, has a right to protection in all countries, why not also a European, an Asiatic, or an African? It seems, according to him, that religious denominations, in general, should be treated, by condescension, with kindness in all countries; but when a man professes the American religion, which General Cass has not explained, such a man has a preeminent right to special protection everywhere; that wherever he appears in foreign lands, the sovereignty of the State, in regard to all questions appertaining to religion, must fall back the moment he proclaims himself an American. And it shall be understood that when he arrives on the shore of such country, with a full measure of American atmosphere, American sunbeams, and American religion according to Mr. Cass, sufficient for his consumption during the period of his passage through or sojourning within that country, he shall have the right to say and do what he thinks proper, provided always it be according to the dictates of his conscience.

If this doctrine can obtain, several consequences which Mr. Cass had tried to guard against in other parts of his speech must necessarily follow. Every nation has the real or supposed element of sovereignty within itself. But if the rights of conscience are

supreme, and an American is to be protected everywhere in acting out its dictates, then the sovereignty of
such nation must give way to the sovereignty of his
conscience. When then? Two sovereignties are
immediately in conflict. Which shall yield to the other?
If the sovereignty of the State must give way to the
sovereignty of the individual, provided that individual
be an American, then let foreign sovereign States hide
their diminished heads, for it is obvious that two
rivals sovereignties cannot both prevail in the same
State.

There is no difference between General Cass's
conception of conscience as a moral faculty and mine.
He, however, betrays the right and liberty of conscience, as I understand it, by identifying this moral
faculty with the outward actions which are supposed
to manifest its dictates from within. No civil government that ever existed has, or ever had, either the
right or the power, physical or moral, to coerce or
extinguish man's conscience. It is beyond the reach
of government. They might as well attempt to pass
laws regulating the exercise of memory as regulating
the decisions of man's conscience. This freedom of
conscience, however, General Cass has identified with
outward action; and on the other hand, by recognizing
the rights of civil government to control the outward
actions of men, he has betrayed conscience into the
hands of the magistrate. All human law has for objects
either persons, or things, or acts, and beyond these
human legislation cannot go. Conscience, according
to my distinction, does not come within the reach of
law, but as understood and represented by General
Cass, he hands it over into the domain of civil government, and confounds it with things over which that
government has acknowledged rights and legitimate
power of interference. I am bound, therefore, to
vindicate the liberty of conscience in reply to the
dangerous doctrines of General Cass . . .

General Cass has not taken the pains to distinguish
the whole office of conscience. It may be expressed
in brief words. The whole duty of man is to "avoid
evil and to do good." Now, although evil and good
are relative terms, and not judged of at all times and
in all places by the same standard, nevertheless,
conscience is the faculty whereby the distinction is
made. A thing may seem morally evil to a man. He

cannot do it, without sinning, offending God and offending his own conscience. Another thing may appear
good, and there is no obligation on him to do it, even
though his conscience approve, unless the circumstances
warrant its performance . . .

Hence, if any Protestant, American or not, who,
travelling or sojourning in a Catholic State, should be
called upon by the civil power to make a declaration
or to do an act which his conscience condemns, he
cannot comply. Let us suppose him to be required
to swear that he believes in the Pope's supremacy.
Being a Protestant, his conscience will oblige him to
refuse. And if, in consequence of this refusal, physical torture be applied, one of two things will happen,
— he will suffer the torture and be loyal to conscience,
or he will betray conscience by swearing to a lie. If any
thing of this kind should be attempted in a Catholic
country, or any act required which any American's
conscience condemns, General Cass will find me ready
to vote for the employment of the American army
and navy to punish that nation which would impiously
dare to commit so unlawful an outrage. Not because
the man's conscience had been violated, for that is
impossible, but because the law of such country would
have gone beyond the boundaries of all human law,
since these relate not to the faculties of the human soul,
but to outward persons, things, and acts. And as the
person here supposed would have done no act bringing
him under the law, his right of person would have
been violated, and it would become lawful for his
country to inflict condign punishment on the nation
or parties so violating it.

But whilst no civil government or power on earth
has a right to require that a man shall do a sinful or
immoral act, it does not by any means follow that
governments are bound to permit a man to act out-
wardly what his conscience tells him is good. In the one
case his conscience decides for himself alone. In the
other case its dictates would prompt him to decide
for others, by doing what he supposes good, whether
it be suitable for others or not. Here civil governments have a right to come in and say, "Let us see
about that." They have a right also to refer to their
laws as a rule for personal conduct. If the individual
still imagines that his conscience requires him to do
some act forbidden by the law, but yet highly

praiseworthy in his estimation, he can make the experiment, but he must abide the consequences.

But in General Cass's view of conscience there is no distinction, or but a fallacious one, between conscience acting for the individual, forbidding him to do an evil act, and conscience dictating to him to do good, or what he may think good, without regard to others, wherever he may find himself. If this principle were carried out, I fear that strange exhibitions of individual zeal would become very frequent. If the supposed American should happen to be a Mormon, he will have a right to carry out the dictates of his conscience in all countries. If he should happen to be a Millerite, visiting Rome, it shall be his privilege to pitch his tent in front of St. Peter's church, then and there, under the protection of General Cass's doctrine, to speak and act according to the dictates of his conscience. He will undertake to prove that the end of the world is at hand. And by applying "figures, which never lie," to the Book of Daniel and of Revelations, and elucidating the subject still more by exhibiting appropriate drawings of the big horn and the little horns, with various references to the number of the beast, descriptive of Anti-christ, — prove clearly that his doctrine is right. In the mean time it might happen that this supposed Antichrist, the Pope, would be looking down from some window of the Vatican, unable to interfere, lest his Government should be understood as violating the rights of American conscience as shadowed forth by General Cass.

I am not unmindful that General Cass has ascribed very high powers, and, in my judgment, extravagant powers to human governments, in a supposed right of theirs to judge what is conscience and what is not. And in this he betrays again the faculty of conscience as understood by me. "It is not," he says, "every vagary of the imagination, nor every ebullition of feeling, nor every impulse of the passions, however honest the motive may be, which can lay claim to the rights of conscience." Again, "The human legislator has the right to separate presumptions or unfounded pretensions, at war with the just constitution of society, from conscientious dictates properly regulated and operating within their just sphere." Here General Cass takes away from individual conscience the very rights which he had claimed for it elsewhere; and he refers to the legislator, because he is a legislator, to determine whether a doctrine held by the conscience of a man is to be regarded as a vagary of the imagination, or is consistent with the just constitution of society. In other parts, his position is that there is no lord or judge of a man's conscience, but God and the man himself. However, I find such mutual contradiction in the phrases of General Cass, as he touches now on one topic and now another, that it may become necessary for me hereafter to examine his speech more in specific detail . . .

This letter is already too long, and I hope I may be pardoned if I make a few general remarks bearing more or less directly on the circumstances which directed it. The first remark is, that in this country at least, no man is oppressed, in consequence of his religious belief, so long as he submits legally to the constitution and laws by which it is governed. And yet, I regret to say, that many of our citizens are hardly satisfied with this equal and common privilege, unless there be furnished them, from time to time, occasions on which they may give vent to that lamentable intolerance which lurks in human nature every where, no less than in human governments in Europe, Asia, Africa, and America. How tame would be the proceedings of such meetings as that, for purposes of sympathy with the Madiai, or those of our anniversary week, were it not for the vent which they furnish for the denunciation of Pope and Popery. There is not, and there ought not to be, opposition to or complaint of these proceedings. The Catholics of the United States are accustomed to such. Many respectable Protestants are rather offended by them. But on the whole, this is a country of free speech and free writing, and it is better to bear with the abuse of either than that any legislation be employed to prevent it. In the mean time, we of the clergy are obliged occasionally to travel abroad — sometimes because we have not received a suitable call at home; and sometimes feeble health, by bronchitis especially, compels us to seek the benefit of foreign climates. Still wherever we go we must never forget the object of our vacation, which is to do good. And thus, forgetting the difference between restraints on the outward development of individual conscience in other countries, and the unbounded freedom in this respect which we enjoy at home, we are liable in a mistaken zeal, but always with the best intentions, to get into little difficulties with the police of foreign cities or states. What will be the consequence, if, according to General Cass's project, we shall have a quasi right, under the high sanction of the Congress of the United States, to hand on to the buttons of our Foreign Ministers, and pull them right and left into the little dogmatical squabbles in which we may have contrived to get ourselves involved? . . .

For my own part, I think that as we have no established religion at home — which in our circumstances I regard as a great benefit — so it might be as well for us to deal with other nations prudently and modestly, just as we find them, until, little by little, influenced by our beautiful example, they shall be induced to imitate it. The Congress of the United States are too well qualified to discharge the duties for which they were elected, to require the slightest suggestion from any private citizen as to the course they should pursue in regard to the matter which General Cass has brought before them. He has suggested to his fellow-senators that I pronounced their course all wrong. This was a mistake. I spoke of him alone, and of no other member of Congress.

If I may be allowed to express an opinion, as an humble citizen, conscious of loyalty to the Constitution, obedience to the laws, respect for and benevolence towards all my fellow-citizens, without distinction of creed, to give expression to my own sentiments, I should sum them up, not as regards this special topic, but as regards the general policy of the country, in a very few words. I would say that whilst the power, almost pre-potency, of the United States is admitted and acknowledged wherever I have traveled in Europe, there is still a prevalent idea abroad that this greatness is rather detracted from by a certain tone of self-complacency and of contemptuous reference towards other States. They say that we are too great to stand in need of boasting; that we are too powerful and too rich to be under the necessity of acquiring a right to property by fraudulent means. I do not pretend to judge how far these imputations are correct, but for my own part I would say, that the honor and dignity of this great free nation are likely to be best and most permanently sustained by adhering to a

principle which is ascribed to as true an American as ever lived, namely — We ask for nothing that is not strictly right, and will submit to nothing that is wrong.

The revolutionary movements which had swept the western world at the end of the 18th century had stimulated an interest in the problems of ordinary people and raised hopes that poverty, ignorance, disease, oppression, and exploitation might be eliminated. Indeed, the entire theory of progress which had so profoundly impressed itself upon the modern mind was predicated upon the assumption that human suffering was the result of specific and remediable causes. Hopes for reform unleased a flood of human energy in the early decades of the 19th century as men and women embarked upon programs to rehabilitate criminals, protect orphaned children, raise living standards, educate the masses, improve the status of women, evangelize non-Christians, abolish slavery, and end war.

While organized efforts were being made to liberate the poor from their oppression of mind and body, the tremendous growth of industry was disrupting the social patterns of every Western nation. The problems of the lower classes loomed larger than ever. The United States, although still predominantly agricultural, felt the effect of the new industrial economy as well. The growth of manufacturing in the northern cities increased the number of urban workers and stimulated an interest in working class movements. Most American reformers believed that the problem of the urban poor could be solved through education and charity, but a few intellectuals became interested in the new socialist ideas coming out of France, Germany, and England. The first reading in this section is taken from an article by Orestes Brownson (1803–1876), a New England clergyman and publisher. Brownson, writing in his own *Brownson's Quarterly Review*, analyzed the vulnerability of American working people from the perspective of current European socialist thought. Even though he later repudiated his radical indictment of the middle class, his writings were circulated during the 1840 presidential campaign to embarrass the Democratic Party.

Far more compatible with the American ethos was the campaign to establish free schools. Even here, however, the idea of public education involved a con-

flict in American values. It took taxes from some people to pay for the education of other people's children and increased the powers of the government as the educating agent. On the other hand, the very notion of a society of equals leading their lives without the interference of authoritarian institutions carried with it the need to start each person off with equal social skills. As a practical matter, universal public education spread as all men — rich and poor — got the vote, but it required vigorous champions to secure the necessary legislation. The second reading comes from a speech by Horace Mann (1796–1859), who had created a nationwide interest in public education. During his years of lobbying and public speaking, Mann had been forced to analyze what in American culture created an opposition to so benign an idea as free schools. Although public education has since been widely accepted, the conflict between social welfare and individual responsibility which he described in his *Report* continued to influence efforts to develop public programs in the areas of health, higher education, and family care.

A peculiarly American addition to 19th century humanitarian thought came from a group of writers, teachers, and clergymen who were called Transcendentalists. The Transcendentalists were interested in personal moral reform, particularly the regeneration of feeling, sensibility, charity, and conscience. Characteristically American in their faith in the voluntary efforts of the free individual, the Transcendentalists rejected the stern Calvinistic ethos of New England's Puritan founders as well as the crass materialism of their own day. Their most ambitious program was initiated by a Unitarian minister, George Ripley (1802–1880). With a group of like-minded people, Ripley purchased Brook Farm, nine miles west of Boston, and established a cooperative farm where he and some twenty others lived for five years. The third reading, taken from their *Articles of Agreement*, sets forth the goals of the Brook Farm associates. The fourth reading is from the preamble to the Brook Farm Constitution.

The last reading, from the diary of Nathaniel Hawthorne (1804–1864), affords a different glimpse of

Ripley's social experiment. Hawthorne, not yet a famous novelist in 1842, spent a year at Brook Farm largely to escape the boredom of his job in the Boston customhouse. His reactions to Transcendental farming offer an amusing insight into the varieties of American individualism.

The reform movements covered in this section laid bare the contradictions in American attitudes toward society and progress. The liberal philosophy which undergirt most institutions in the United States assumed that every person, if protected in his individual rights, could prosper without special social attention. At the same time the stimulation of philanthropy and humanitarian sympathies implied a responsibility between man and man. A similar confusion lay in the proofs Americans used. While agreeing that spiritual values took precedence over material ones, Americans were apt to justify a whole range of personal and national activities in terms of their tangible results in productivity or power. So, too, America's high moral purpose was more often asserted than defined. Having ignored philosophical systems and rejected the authority of any institution to articulate values, Americans held their ideals in an uneasy tension which only the crisis of the 1860's would uncover.

Orestes Brownson: *The laboring classes (1840)*

The middle class is always a firm champion of equality, when it concerns humbling a class above it; but it is its inveterate foe, when it concerns elevating a class below it. Manfully have the British Commoners struggled against the old feudal aristocracy, and so successfully that they now constitute the dominant power in the state. To their struggles against the throne and the nobility is the English nation indebted for the liberty it so loudly boasts, and which, during the last half of the last century, so enraptured the friends of Humanity throughout Europe.

But this class has done nothing for the laboring population, the real *proletarii*. It has humbled the aristocracy; it has raised itself to dominion, and it is now conservative, — conservative in fact, whether it call itself Whig or Radical . . .

No one can observe the signs of the times with

much care, without perceiving that a crisis as to the relation of wealth and labor is approaching. It is useless to shut our eyes to the fact, and like the ostrich fancy ourselves secure because we have so concealed our heads that we see not the danger. We or our children will have to meet this crisis. The old war between the Kind and the Barons is well nigh ended, and so is that between the Barons and the Merchants and Manufacturers, — landed capital and commercial capital. The business man has become the peer of my Lord. And now commences the new struggle between the operative and his employer, between wealth and labor. Every day does this struggle extend further and wax stronger and fiercer; what or when the end will be God only knows.

In this coming contest there is a deeper question at issue than is commonly imagined; a question which is but remotely touched in your controversies about United States Banks and Sub Treasuries, chartered Banking and free Banking, free trade and corporations, although these controversies may be paving the way for it to come up. We have discovered no presentiment of it in any king's or queen's speech, nor in any president's message. It is embraced in no popular political creed of the day, whether christened Whig or Tory, *Juste-milieu* or Democratic. No popular senator, or deputy, or peer seems to have any glimpse of it; but it is working in the hearts of the million, is struggling to shape itself, and one day it will be uttered, and in thunder tones. Well will it be for him, who, on that day, shall be found ready to answer it.

What we would ask is, throughout the Christian world, the actual condition of the laboring classes, viewed simply and exclusively in their capacity of laborers? They constitute at least a moiety of the human race. We exclude the nobility, we exclude also the middle class, and include only actual laborers, who are laborers and not proprietors, owners of none of the funds of production, neither houses, shops, nor lands, nor implements of labor, being therefore solely dependent on their hands . . .

Now we will not so belie our acquaintance with political economy, as to allege that these alone perform all that is necessary to the production of wealth. We are not ignorant of the fact, that the merchant, who is literally the common carrier and exchange dealer, performs a useful service, and is therefore entitled to a portion of the proceeds of labor. But make all necessary deductions on his account, and then ask what portion of the remainder is retained, either in kind or in its equivalent, in the hands of the original producer, the workingman? All over the world this fact stares us in the face, the workingman is poor and depressed, while a large portion of the non-workingmen, in the sense we now use the term, are wealthy. It may be laid down as a general rule, with but few exceptions, that men are rewarded in an inverse ratio to the amount of actual service they perform. Under every government on earth the largest salaries are annexed to those offices, which demand of their incumbents the least amount of actual labor either mental or manual. And this is in perfect harmony with the whole system of repartition of the fruits of industry, which obtains in every department of society. Now here is the system which prevails, and here is its result. The whole class of simple laborers are poor, and in general unable to procure anything beyond the bare necessaries of life.

In regard to labor two systems obtain; one that of slave labor, the other that of free labor. Of the two, the first is, in our judgment, except so far as the feelings are concerned, decidedly the least oppressive. If the slave has never been a free man, we think, as a general rule, his sufferings are less than those of the free laborer at wages. As to actual freedom one has just about as much as the other. The laborer at wages has all the disadvantages of freedom and none of its blessings, while the slave, if denied the blessings, is freed from the disadvantages. We are no advocates of slavery, we are as heartily opposed to it as any modern abolitionist can be; but we say frankly that, if there must always be a laboring population distinct from proprietors and employers, we regard the slave system as decidedly preferable to the system at wages. It is no pleasant thing to go days without food, to lie idle for weeks, seeking work and finding none, to rise in the morning with a wife and children you love, and know not where to procure them a breakfast, and to see constantly before you no brighter prospect than the almshouse. Yet these are no unfrequent incidents in the lives of our laboring population. Even in seasons of general prosperity, when there was only the ordinary cry of "hard times," we have seen hundreds of people in a not very populous village, in a wealthy portion of our common country, suffering for the want of the necessaries of life, willing to work, and yet finding no work to do. Many and many is the application of a poor man for work, merely for his food, we have seen rejected. These things are little thought of, for the applicants are poor; they fill no conspicuous place in society, and they have no biographers. But their wrongs are chronicled in heaven. It is said there is no want in this country. There may be less than in some other countries. But death by actual starvation in this country is, we apprehend, no uncommon occurrence. The sufferings of a quiet, unassuming but useful class of females in our cities, in general sempstresses, too proud to beg or to apply to the alms-house, are not easily told. They are industrious; they do all that they can find to do; but yet the little there is for them to do, and the miserable pittance they receive for it, is hardly sufficient to keep soul and body together. And yet there is a man who employs them to make shirts, trousers, &c., and grows rich on their labors. He is one of our respectable citizens, perhaps is praised in the newspapers for his liberal donations to some charitable institution. He passes among us as a pattern of morality, and is honored as a worthy Christian. And why should he not be, since our Christian community is made up of such as he, and since our clergy would not dare question his piety, lest they should incur the reproach of infidelity, and lose their standing, and their salaries? Nay, since our clergy are raised up, educated, fashioned, and sustained by such as he? Not a few of our churches rest on Mammon for their foundation. The basement is a trader's shop.

We pass through our manufacturing villages, most of them appear neat and flourishing. The operatives are well dressed, and we are told, well paid. They are said to be healthy, contented, and happy. This is the fair side of the picture; the side exhibited to distinguished visitors. There is a dark side, moral as well as physical. Of the common operatives, few, if any, by their wages, acquire a competence . . . The great mass wear out their health, spirits, and morals, without becoming one whit better off than when they commenced labor. The bills of mortality in these factory villages are not striking, we admit, for the poor girls when they can toil no longer go home to die. The average life, working life we mean, of the girls that come to Lowell, for instance, from Maine, New Hampshire, and Vermont, we have been assured, is only about three years. What becomes of them then? Few of them ever marry; fewer still ever return to their native places with reputations unimpaired. "She has worked in a Factory," is almost enough to damn to infamy the most worthy and virtuous girl. We know no sadder sight on earth than one of our factory villages presents, when the bell at break of day, or at the hour of breakfast, or dinner, calls out its hundreds or thousands of operatives. We stand and look at these hard working men and women hurrying in all directions, and ask ourselves, where go the proceeds of their labors? The man who employs them, and for whom they are toiling as so many slaves, is one of our city nabobs, revelling in luxury; or he is a member of our legislature, enacting laws to put money in his own pocket; or he is a member of Congress, contending for a high Tariff to tax the poor for the benefit of the rich; or in these times he is shedding crocodile tears over the deplorable condition of the poor laborer, while he docks his wages twenty-five per cent.; building miniature log cabins, shouting Harrison and "hard cider." And this man too would fain pass for a Christian and a republican. He shouts for liberty, stickles for equality, and is horrified at a Southern planter who keeps slaves.

One thing is certain; that of the amount actually produced by the operative, he retains a less proportion than it costs the master to feed, clothe, and lodge his slave. Wages is a cunning device of the devil, for the benefit of tender consciences, who would retain all the advantages of the slave system, without the expense, trouble, and odium of being slave-holders . . .

Now, what is the prospect of those who fall under the operation of this system? We ask, is there a reasonable chance that any considerable portion of the present generation of laborers, shall ever become owners of a sufficient portion of the funds of production, to be able to sustain themselves by laboring on their own capital, that is, as independent laborers? We need not ask this question, for everybody knows there is not. Well, is the condition of a laborer at wages the best that the great mass of the working people ought to be able to aspire to? Is it a condition, — nay can it be made a condition, — with which a man should be satis-

fied; in which he should be contented to live and die?

In our own country this condition has existed under its most favorable aspects, and has been made as good as it can be. It has reached all the excellence of which it is susceptible. It is now not improving but growing worse. The actual condition of the workingman to-day, viewed in all its bearings, is not so good as it was fifty years ago. If we have not been altogether misinformed, fifty years ago, health and industrious habits, constituted no mean stock in trade, and with them almost any man might aspire to competence and independence. But it is so no longer. The wilderness has receded, and already the new lands are beyond the reach of the mere laborer, and the employer has him at his mercy. If the present relation subsist, we see nothing better for him in reserve than what he now possesses, but something altogether worse.

We are not ignorant of the fact that men born poor become wealthy, and that men born to wealth become poor; but this fact does not necessarily diminish the numbers of the poor, nor augment the numbers of the rich. The relative numbers of the two classes remain, or may remain, the same. But be this as it may; one fact is certain, no man born poor has ever, by his wages, as a simple operative, risen to the class of the wealthy. Rich he may have become, but it has not been by his own manual labor. He has in some way contrived to tax for his benefit the labor of others. He may have accumulated a few dollars which he has placed at usury, or invested in trade; or he may, as a master workman, obtain a premium on his journeymen; or he may have from a clerk passed to a partner, or from a workman to an overseer. The simple market wages for ordinary labor, has never been adequate to raise him from poverty to wealth. This fact is decisive of the whole controversy, and proves that the system of wages must be supplanted by some other system, or else one half of the human race must forever be the virtual slaves of the other.

Now the great work for this age and the coming, is to raise up the laborer, and to realize in our own social arrangements and in the actual condition of all men, that equality between man and man, which God has established between the rights of one and those of another. In other words, our business is to emancipate the proletaries, as the past has emancipated the

slaves. This is our work. There must be no class of
our fellow men doomed to toil through life as mere
workmen at wages. If wages are tolerated it must be,
in the case of the individual operative, only under such
conditions that by the time he is of a proper age to
settle in life, he shall have accumulated enough to be
an independent laborer on his own capital, — on his
own farm or in his own shop. Here is our work. How
is it to be done?

Reformers in general answer this question, or
what they deem its equivalent, in a manner which we
cannot but regard as very unsatisfactory. They would
have all men wise, good, and happy; but in order to
make them so, they tell us that we want not external
changes, but internal; and therefore instead of declaim-
ing against society and seeking to disturb existing social arrangements, we should confine ourselves to the
individual reason and conscience; seek merely to lead
the individual to repentance, and to reformation of
life; make the individual a practical, a truly religious
man, and all evils will either disappear, or be sanctified
to the spiritual growth of the soul.

This is doubtless a capital theory, and has the
advantage that kings, hierarchies, nobilities, — in a
word, all who fatten on the toil and blood of their
fellows, will feel no difficulty in supporting it . . .

For our part, we yield to none in our reverence
for science and religion; but we confess that we look
not for the regeneration of the race from priests and
pedagogues. They have had a fair trial. They cannot
construct the temple of God. They cannot conceive
its plan, and they know not how to build. They daub
with untempered mortar, and the walls they erect
tumble down if so much as a fox attempt to go up
thereon. [In a word they always league with the people's masters, and seek to reform without disturbing
the social arrangements which render reform necessary.] They would change the consequents without
changing the antecedents, secure to men the rewards
of holiness, while they continue their allegiance to the
devil. We have no faith in priests and pedagogues.
They merely cry peace, peace, and that too when there
is no peace, and can be none.

We admit the importance of what Dr. Channing
in his lectures on the subject we are treating recom-
mends as "self-culture." Self-culture is a good thing,
but it cannot abolish inequality, nor restore men to
their rights. As a means of quickening moral and intellectual energy, exalting the sentiments, and preparing
the laborer to contend manfully for his rights, we admit
its importance, and insist as strenuously as any one
on making it as universal as possible; but as constituting
in itself a remedy for the vices of the social state, we
have no faith in it. As a means it is well, as the end
it is nothing.

The truth is, the evil we have pointed out is not
merely individual in its character. It is not, in the
case of any single individual, of any one man's procuring, nor can the efforts of any one man, directed
solely to his own moral and religious perfection, do
aught to remove it. What is purely individual in its
nature, efforts of individuals to perfect themselves,
may remove. But the evil we speak of is inherent in
all our social arrangements, and cannot be cured without a radical change of those arrangements. Could we
convert all men to Christianity in both theory and
practice, as held by the most enlightened sect of
Christians among us, the evils of the social state
would remain untouched. Continue our present
system of trade, and all its present evil consequences
will follow, whether it be carried on by your best men
or your worst. Put your best men, your wisest, most
moral, and most religious men, at the head of your
paper money banks, and the evils of the present banking system will remain scarcely diminished. The only
way to get rid of its evils is to change the system, not
its managers. The evils of slavery do not result from
the personal characters of slave masters. They are
inseparable from the system, let who will be masters.
Make all moral and intellectual energy which exists
in our country, indeed throughout Christendom, and
which would, if rightly directed, transform this wilderness world into a blooming paradise of God, is now by
the pseudo-gospel, which is preached, rendered wholly
inefficient, by being wasted on that which, even if
effected, would leave all the crying evils of the times
untouched. Under the influence of the Church, our
efforts are not directed to the reorganization of
society, to the introduction of equality between
man and man, to the removal of the corruptions of
the rich, and the wretchedness of the poor. We think
only of saving our own souls, as if a man must not

put himself so out of the case, as to be willing to be damned before he can be saved. Paul was willing to be accursed from Christ, to save his brethren from the vengeance which hung over him. But nevertheless we think only of saving our own souls; or if perchance our benevolence is awakened, and we think it desirable to labor for the salvation of others, it is merely to save them from imaginary sins and the tortures of an imaginary hell. The redemption of the world is understood to mean simply the restoration of mankind to the favor of God in the world to come. Their redemption from the evils of inequality, of factitious distinctions, and iniquitous social institutions, counts for nothing in the eyes of the Church. And this is its condemnation.

We cannot proceed a single step, with the least safety, in the great work of elevating the laboring classes, without the exaltation of sentiment, the generous sympathy and the moral courage which Christianity alone is fitted to produce or quicken. But it is lamentable to see how, by means of the mistakes of the Church, the moral courage, the generous sympathy, the exaltation of sentiment, Christianity does actually produce or quicken, is perverted, and made efficient only in producing evil, or hindering the growth of good. Here is wherefore, it is necessary on the one hand to condemn in the most pointed terms the Christianity of the Church, and to bring out on the other hand in all its clearness, brilliancy, and glory the Christianity of Christ ...

Now the evils of which we have complained are of a social nature. That is, they have their root in the constitution of society as it is, and they have attained to their present growth by means of social influences, the action of government, of laws, and of systems and institutions upheld by society, and of which individuals are the slaves. This being the case, it is evident that they are to be removed only by the action of society, that is, by government, for the action of society is government.

But what shall government do? Its first doing must be an undoing. There has been thus far quite too much government, as well as government of the wrong kind. The first act of government we want, is a still further limitation of itself. It must begin by circumscribing within narrower limits its powers.

And then it must proceed to repeal all laws which bear against the laboring classes, and then to enact such laws as are necessary to enable them to maintain their equality. We have no faith in those systems of elevating the working classes, which propose to elevate them without calling in the aid of the government. We must have government, and legislation expressly directed to this end.

But again what legislation do we want so far as this country is concerned? We want first the legislation which shall free the government, whether State or Federal, from the control of the Banks. The Banks represent the interest of the employer, and therefore of necessity interests adverse to those of the employed; that is, they represent the interests of the business community in opposition to the laboring community. So long as the government remains under the control of the Banks, so long it must be in the hands of the natural enemies of the laboring classes, and may be made, nay, will be made, an instrument of depressing them yet lower ...

Following the distruction of the Banks, must come that of all monopolies, of all privilege. There are many of these. We cannot specify them all; we therefore select only one, the greatest of them all, the privilege which some have of being born rich while others are born poor. It will be seen at onee that we allude to the hereditary descent of property, an anomaly in our American system, which must be removed, or the system itself will be destroyed. We cannot now go into a discussion of this subject, but we promise to resume it at our earliest opportunity. We only say now, that as we have abolished hereditary monarchy and hereditary nobility, we must complete the work by abolishing hereditary property. A man shall have all he honestly acquires, so long as he himself belongs to the world in which he acquires it. But his power over his property must cease with his life, and his property must then become the property of the state, to be disposed of by some equitable law for the use of the generation which takes his place. Here is the principle without any of its details, and this is the grand legislative measure to which we look forward. We see no means of elevating the laboring classes which can be effectual without this. And is this a measure to be easily carried? Not at all. It will cost infinitely more than it cost to abolish either hereditary monarchy or hereditary nobility. It is a great measure, and startling. The rich, the business community, will never voluntarily consent to it, and we think we know too much of human nature to believe that it will ever be effected peaceably. It will be effected only by the strong arm of physical force.

It will come, if it ever come at all, only at the conclusion of war, the like of which the world as yet has never witnessed, and from which, however inevitable it may seem to the eye of philosophy, the heart of Humanity recoils with horror.

We are not ready for this measure yet. There is much previous work to be done, and we should be the last to bring it before the legislature. The time, however, has come for its free and full discussion. It must be canvassed in the public mind, and society prepared for acting on it. No doubt they who broach it, and especially they who support it, will experience a due share of contumely and abuse. They will be regarded by the part of the community they oppose, or may be thought to oppose, as "graceless varlets," against whom every man of substance should set his face. But this is not, after all, a thing to disturb a wise man, nor to deter a true man from telling his whole thought. He who is worthy of the name of man, speaks what he honestly believes the interests of his race demand, and seldom disquiets himself about what may be the consequences to himself. Men have, for what they believed the cause of God or man, endured the dungeon, the scaffold, the stake, the cross, and they can do it again, if need be. This subject must be freely, boldly, and fully discussed, whatever may be the fate of those who discuss it.

Horace Mann: The ground of the free school system (1846)

The Pilgrim Fathers amid all their privations and dangers conceived the magnificent idea, not only of a universal, but of a free education for the whole people. To find the time and the means to reduce this grand conception to practice, they stinted themselves, amid all their poverty, to a still scantier pit-

Old South Leaflet No. 109, Directors of the Old South Work, Boston, 1903, pp. 1-16.

tance; amid all their toils, they imposed upon themselves still more burdensome labors; and, amid all their perils, they braved still greater dangers. Two divine ideas filled their great hearts, — their duty to God and to posterity. For the one they built the church, for the other they opened the school. Religion and knowledge, — two atributes of the same glorious and eternal truth, and that truth the only one on which immortal or mortal happiness can be securely founded! . . .

In later times, and since the achievement of American independence, the universal and ever-repeated argument in favor of free schools has been that the general intelligence which they are capable of diffusing, and which can be imparted by no other human instrumentality, is indispensable to the continuance of a republican government. This argument, it is obvious, assumes, as a postulatum, the superiority of a republican over all other forms of government; and, as a people, we religiously believe in the soundness both of the assumption and of the argument founded upon it. But, if this be all, then a sincere monarchist, or a defender of arbitrary power, or a believer in the divine right of kings, would oppose free schools for the identical reasons we offer in their behalf . . .

Again, the expediency of free schools is sometimes advocated on grounds of political economy. An educated people is always a more industrious and productive people. Intelligence is a primary ingredient in the wealth of nations . . . The moralist, too, takes up the argument of the economist. He demonstrates that vice and crime are not only prodigals and spendthrifts of their own, but defrauders and plunderers of the means of others, that they would seize upon all the gains of honest industry and exhaust the bounties of Heaven itself without satiating their rapacity; and that often in the history of the world whole generations might have been trained to industry and virtue by the wealth which one enemy to his race has destroyed.

And yet, notwithstanding these views have been presented a thousand times with irrefutable logic, and with a divine eloquence of truth which it would seem that nothing but combined stolidity and depravity could resist, there is not at the present time, with the exception of the States of New England

and a few small communities elsewhere, a country or a state in Christendom which maintains a system of free schools for the education of its children . . .

I believe that this amazing dereliction from duty, especially in our own country, originates more in the false notions which men entertain respecting the nature of their right to property than in any thing else. In the district school meeting, in the town meeting, in legislative halls, everywhere, the advocates for a more generous education could carry their respective audiences with them in behalf of increased privileges for our children, were it not instinctively foreseen that increased privileges must be followed by increased taxation. Against this obstacle, argument falls dead. The rich man who has no children declares that the exaction of a contribution from him to educate the children of his neighbor is an invasion of his rights of property. The man who has reared and educated a family of children denounces it as a double tax when he is called upon to assist in educating the children of others also; or, if he has reared his own children without educating them, he thinks it peculiarly oppressive to be obliged to do for others what he refrained from doing even for himself. Another, having children, but disdaining to educate them with the common mass, withdraws them from the public school, puts them under what he calls "selecter influences," and then thinks it a grievance to be obliged to support a school which he contemns. Or, if these different parties so far yield to the force of traditionary sentiment and usage, and to the public opinion around them, as to consent to do something for the cause, they soom reach the limit of expense at which their admitted obligation or their alleged charity terminates.

It seems not irrelevant, therefore, in this connection, and for the purpose of strengthening the foundation on which our free-school system reposes, to inquire into the nature of a man's right to the proper property he possesses, and to satisfy ourselves respecting the question whether any man has such an indefeasible title to his estates or such an absolute ownership of them as renders it unjust in the government to assess upon him his share of the expenses of educating the children of the community up to such a point as the nature of the institutions under which

he lives, and the well-being of society, require.

I believe in the existence of a great, immortal, immutable principle of natural law, or natural ethics,— a principle antecedent to all human institutions, and incapable of being abrogated by any ordinance of man,— a principle of divine origin, clearly legible in the ways of Providence as those ways are manifested in the order of nature and in the history of the race, which proves the absolute right to an education of every human being that comes into the world, and which, of course, proves the correlative duty of every government to see that the means of that education are provided for all.

In regard to the application of this principle of natural law,—that is, in regard to the extent of the education to be provided for all at the public expense,—some differences of opinion may fairly exist under different political organizations; but, under our republican government, it seems clear that the minimum of this education can never be less than such as is sufficient to qualify each citizen for the civil and social duties he will be called to discharge, — such an education as teaches the individual the great laws of bodily health, as qualifies for the fulfilment of parental duties, as is indispensable for the civil functions of a witness or a juror, as is necessary for the voter in municipal and in national affairs, and, finally, as is requisite for the faithful and conscientious discharge of all those duties which devolve upon the inheritor of a portion of the sovereignty of this great republic . . .

To any one who looks beyond the mere surface of things, it is obvious that the primary and natural elements or ingredients of all property consist in the riches of the soil, in the treasures of the sea, in the light and warmth of the sun, in the fertilizing clouds and streams and dews, in the winds, and in the chemical and vegetative agencies of Nature. In the majority of cases, all that we call property, all that makes up the valuation or inventory of a nation's capital, was prepared at the creation, and was laid up of old in the capacious storehouses of Nature. For every unit that a man earns by his own toil or skill, he receives hundreds and thousands, without cost and without recompense, from the all-bountiful Giver. A proud mortal, standing in the midst of his luxuriant wheat-fields or cotton-plantations, may arrogantly call them his own; yet what barren wastes would they be, did not Heaven send down upon them its dews and its rains, its warmth and its light, and sustain, for their growth and ripening, the grateful vicissitude of the seasons! It is said that from eighty to ninety per cent of the very substance of some of the great staples of agriculture are not taken from the earth, but are absorbed from the air; so that these productions may more properly be called fruits of the atmosphere than of the soil. Who prepares this elemental wealth? Who scatters it, like a sower, through all the regions of the atmosphere, and sends the richly freighted winds, as His messengers, to bear to each leaf in the forest, and to each blade in the cultivated field, the nourishment which their infinitely varied needs demand? Aided by machinery, a single manufacturer performs the labor of hundreds of men. Yet what could he accomplish without the weight of the waters which God causes ceaselessly to flow, or without those gigantic forces which he has given to steam? And how would the commerce of the world be carried on, were it not for those great laws of Nature — of electricity, of condensation, and of rarefaction — that give birth to the winds, which, in conformity to the will of Heaven and not in obedience to any power of man, forever traverse the earth, and offer themselves as an unchartered medium for interchanging the products of all the zones? These few references show how vast a proportion of all the wealth which men presumptuously call their own, because they claim to have earned it, is poured into their lap, unasked and unthanked for, by the Being so infinitely gracious in his physical as well as in his moral bestowments.

But for whose subsistence and benefit were these exhaustless treasuries of wealth created? Surely not for any one man, nor for any one generation, but for the subsistence and benefit of the whole race from the beginning to the end of time. They were not created for Adam alone, nor for Noah alone, nor for the first discoverers or colonists who may have found or have peopled any part of the earth's ample domain. No. They were created for the race collectively, but to be possessed and enjoyed in succession as the generations, one after another, should come into existence, — equal rights, with a successive enjoyment of them. If we consider the earth and the fulness thereof as one great habitation or domain, then each

generation, subject to certain modifications for the encouragement of industry and frugality, — which modifications it is not necessary here to specify, — has only a life-lease in them. There are certain reasonable regulations, indeed, in regard to the outgoing and the incoming tenants, — regulations which allow to the outgoing generations a brief control over their property after they are called upon to leave it, and which also allow the incoming generations to anticipate a little their full right of possession. But, subject to these regulations, nature ordains a perpetual entail and transfer from one generation to another of all property in the great, substantive, enduring element of wealth, — in the soil, in metals and minerals, in precious stones, and in more precious coal and iron and granite, in the waters and winds and sun; and no one man, nor any one generation of men, has any such title to or ownership in these ingredients and substantials of all wealth that his right is evaded when a portion of them is taken for the benefit of posterity.

This great principle of natural law may be illustrated by a reference to some of the unstable elements, in regard to which each individual's right of property is strongly qualified in relation to his contemporaries, even while he has the acknowledged right of possession. Take the streams of water or the wind, for an example. A stream, as it descends from its sources to its mouth, is successively the property of all those through whose land it passes. My neighbor who lives above me owned it yesterday, while it was passing through his lands: I own it to-day, while it is descending through mine; and the contiguous proprietor below will own it to-morrow, while it is flowing through his, as it passes onward to the next. But the rights of these successive owners are not absolute and unqualified. They are limited by the rights of those who are entitled to the subsequent possession and use. While a stream is passing through my lands, I may not corrupt it, so that it shall be offensive or valueless to the adjoining proprietor below. I may not stop it in its downward course, nor divert it into any other direction, so that it shall leave this channel dry. I may lawfully use it for various purposes — for agriculture, as in irrigating lands or watering cattle; for manufactures, as in turning wheels, etc.; — but, in all my uses of it, I must pay regard to the rights of my neighbors lower down . . .

Is not the inference irresistible, then, that no man, by whatever means he may have come into possession of his property, has any natural right, any more than he has a moral one, to hold it, or to dispose of it, irrespective of the needs and claims of those who, in the august processions of the generations, are to be his successors on the stage of existence? Holding his rights subject to their rights, he is bound not to impair the value of their inheritance either by commission or by omission.

Generation after generation proceeds from the creative energy of God. Each one stops for a brief period upon the earth, resting, as it were, only for a night, like migratory birds upon their passage, and then leaving it forever to others whose existence is as transitory as its own; and the migratory flocks of water-fowl which sweep across our latitudes in their passage to another clime have as good a right to make a perpetual appropriation to their own use of the lands over which they fly as any one generation has to arrogate perpetual dominion and sovereignty, for its own purposes, over that portion of the earth which it is its fortune to occupy during the brief period of its temporal existence.

Another consideration bearing upon this arrogant doctrine of absolute ownership or sovereignty has hardly less force than the one just expounded. We have seen how insignificant a portion of any man's possessions he can claim in any proper and just sense to have earned, and that, in regard to all the residue, he is only taking his turn in the use of a bounty bestowed in common, by the Giver of all, upon his ancestors, upon himself, and upon his posterity, — a line of indefinite length, in which he is but a point. But this is not the only deduction to be made from his assumed rights. The present wealth of the world has an additional element in it. Much of all that is capable of being earned by man has been earned by our predecessors, and has come down to us in a solid and enduring form. We have not erected all the houses in which we live, nor constructed all the roads on which we travel, nor built all the ships in which we carry on our commerce with the world. We have not reclaimed from the wilderness all the fields whose harvests we now reap; and, if we had no precious

metals or stones or pearls but such as we ourselves had dug from the mines or brought up from the bottom of the ocean, our coffers and our caskets would be empty indeed. But, even if this were not so, whence came all the arts and sciences, the discoveries and the inventions, without which, and without a common right to which, the valuation of the property of a whole nation would scarcely equal the inventory of a single man, — without which, indeed, we should now be in a state of barbarism? Whence came a knowledge of agriculture, without which we should have so little to reap? or a knowledge of astronomy, without which we could not traverse the oceans? or a knowledge of chemistry and mechanical philosophy, without which the arts and trades could not exist? Most of all this was found out by those who have gone before us; and some of it has come down to us from a remote antiquity. Surely, all these boons and blessings belong as much to posterity as to ourselves. They have not descended to us to be arrested and consumed here or to be sequestrated from the ages to come. Cato and Archimedes, and Kepler and Newton, and Franklin and Arkwright and Fulton, and all the bright host of benefactors to science and art, did not make or bequeath their discoveries or inventons to benefit any one generation, but to increase the common enjoyments of mankind to the end of time. So of all the great lawgivers and moralists who have improved the civil institutions of the state, who have made it dangerous to be wicked, or, far better than this, have made it hateful to be so. Resourses developed and property acquired after all these ages of preparation, after all these facilities and securities, accrue, not to the benefit of the possessor only, but to that of the next and of all succeeding generations.

Surely, these considerations limit still more extensively that absoluteness of ownership which is so often claimed by the possessors of wealth.

But sometimes the rich farmer, the opulent manufacturer, or the capitalist, when sorely pressed with his natural and moral obligation to contribute a portion of his means for the education of the young, replies, — either in form or in spirit, — "My lands, my machinery, my gold, and my silver are mine: may I not do what I will with my own?" There is one supposable case, and only one, where this argument would have plausibility. If it were made by an isolated, solitary being, — a being having no relations to a community around him, having no ancestors to whom he had been indebted for ninety-nine parts in every hundred of all he possesses, and expecting to leave no posterity after him, — it might not be easy to answer it . . .

The society of which we necessarily constitute a part must be preserved; and, in order to preserve it, we must not look merely to what one individual or one family needs, but to what the whole community needs, not merely to what one generation needs, but to the wants of a succession of generations. To draw conclusions without considering these facts is to leave out the most important part of the premises.

A powerfully corroborating fact remains untouched. Though the earth and the beneficent capabilities with which it is endued belong in common to the race, yet we find that previous and present possessors have laid their hands upon the whole of it, — have left no part of it unclaimed and unappropriated. They have circumnavigated the glove; they have drawn lines across every habitable portion of it, and have partitioned amongst themselves not only its whole area or superficial contents, but have claimed it down to the centre and up to the concave, — a great inverted pyramid for each proprietor, — so that not an unclaimed rood is left, either in the caverns below or in the aerial spaces above, where a new adventurer upon existence can take unresisted possession. They have entered into a solemn compact with each other for the mutual defence of their respective allotments. They have created legislators and judges and executive officers, who denounce and inflict penalties even to the taking of life; and they have organized armed bands to repel aggression upon their claims. Indeed, so grasping and rapacious have mankind been in this particular, that they have taken more than they could use, more than they could perambulate and survey, more than they could see from the top of the masthead or from the highest peak of the mountain. There was some limit to their physical power of taking possession, but none to the exorbitancy of their desires. Like robbers, who divide their spoils before they know whether they shall find a victim, men

have claimed a continent while still doubtful of its existence, and spread out their title from ocean to ocean before their most adventurous pioneers had ever seen a shore of the realms they coveted. The whole planet, then, having been appropriated, — there being no waste or open lands from which the new generations may be supplied as they come into existence, — have not those generations the strongest conceivable claim upon the present occupants for that which is indispensable to their well-being? . . .

The claim of a child, then, to a portion of pre-existent property, begins with the first breath he draws. The new-born infant must have sustenance and shelter and care. If the natural parents are removed or parental ability fails, in a word, if parents either cannot or will not supply the infant's wants, — then society at large — the government having assumed to itself the ultimate control of all property — is bound to step in and fill the parent's place. To deny this to any child would be equivalent to a sentence of death, a capital execution of the innocent, — at which every soul shudders. It would be a more cruel form of infanticide than any which is practised in China or in Africa.

But to preserve the animal life of a child only, and there to stop, would be, not the bestowment of a blessing or the performance of a duty, but the infliction of a fearful curse. A child has interests far higher than those of mere physical existence. Better that the wants of the natural life should be disregarded than that the higher interests of the character should be neglected. If a child has any claim to bread to keep him from perishing, he has a far higher claim to knowledge to preserve him from error and its fearful retinue of calamities. If a child has any claim to shelter to protect him from the destroying elements, he has a far higher claim to be rescued from the infamy and perdition of vice and crime.

All moralists agree, nay, all moralists maintain, that a man is as responsible for his omissions as for his commissions; that he is as guilty of the wrong which he could have prevented, but did not, as for that which his own hand has perpetrated. They, then, who knowingly withhold sustenance from a new-born child, and he dies, are guilty of infanticide. And, by the same reasoning, they who refuse to enlighten the intellect of the rising generation are guilty of degrading the human race. They who refuse to train up children in the way they should go are training up incendiaries and madmen to destroy property and life, and to invade and pollute the sanctuaries of society. In a word, if the mind is as real and substantive a part of human existence as the body, then mental attributes, during the periods of infancy and childhood, demand provision at least as imperatively as bodily appetites. The time when these respective obligations attach corresponds with the periods when the nurture, whether physical or mental, is needed. As the right of sustenance is of equal date with birth, so the right of intellectual and moral training begins at least as early as when children are ordinarily sent to school. At that time, then, by the irrepealable law of Nature, every child succeeds to so much more of the property of the community as is necessary for his education. He is to receive this, not in the form of lands, or of gold and silver, but in the form of knowledge and a training to good habits. This is one of the steps in the transfer of property from a present to a succeeding generation. Human sagacity may be at fault in fixing the amount of property to be transferred or the time when the transfer should be made to a dollar or to an hour; but certainly, in a republican government, the obligation of the predecessors, and the right of the successors, extend to and embrace the means of such an amount of education as will prepare each individual to perform all the duties which devolve upon him as a man and a citizen. It may go farther than this point: certainly, it cannot fall short of it.

Under our political organization the places and the processes where this transfer is to be provided for, and its amount determined, are the district-school meeting, the town-meeting, legislative halls, and conventions for establishing or revising the fundamental laws of the State. If it be not done there, society is false to its high trusts; and any community, whether national or state, that ventures to organize a government, or to administer a government already organized, without making provision for the free education of all its children, dares the certain vengeance of Heaven; and in the squalid forms of poverty and destitution, in the scourges of violence and misrule, in the heart-destroying corruptions of licentiousness and debauchery,

and in political profligacy and legalized perfidy, in all the blended and mutually aggravated crimes of civilization and barbarism, will be sure to feel the terrible retributions of its delinquency.

I bring my argument on this point, then, to a close; and I present a test of its validity, which, as it seems to me, defies denial or evasion.

In obedience to the laws of God and to the laws of all civilized communities, society is bound to protect the natural life of children; and this natural life cannot be protected without the appropriation and use of a portion of the property which society possess. We prohibit infanticide under penalty of death. We practise a refinement in this particular. The life of an infant is inviolable, even before he is born; and he who feloniously takes it, even before birth, is as subject to the extreme penalty of the law as though he had struck down manhood in its vigor, or taken away a mother by violence from the sanctuary of home where she blesses her offspring. But why preserve the natural life of a child, why preserve unborn embryos of life, if we do not intend to watch over and to protect them, and to expand their subsequent existence into usefulness and happiness? As individuals, or as an organized community, we have no natural right, we can derive no authority or countenance from reason, we can cite no attribute or purpose of the divine nature, for giving birth to any human being, and then inflicting upon that being the curse of ignorance, of poverty, and of vice, with all their attendant calamities. We are brought, then, to this startling but inevitable alternative, — the natural life of an infant should be extinguished as soon as it is born, or the means should be provided to save that life from being a curse to its possessor; and, therefore, every State is morally bound to enact a code of laws legalizing and enforcing infanticide or a code of laws establishing free schools . . .

Brook Farm Associates: Articles of Agreement and Association between the members of the Institute for Agriculture and Education (1842)

In order more effectually to promote the great purposes of human culture; to establish the external rela-

John T. Codman, *Brook Farm: Historic and Personal Memoirs*, Arena, Boston, 1894, pp. 11–15.

tions of life on a basis of wisdom and purity; to apply the principles of justice and love to our social organization in accordance with the laws of Divine Providence; to substitute a system of brotherly cooperation for one of selfish competition; to secure to our children, and to those who may be entrusted to our care, the benefits of the highest physical, intellectual and moral education in the present state of human knowledge, the resources at our command will permit; to institute an attractive, efficient and productive system of industry; to prevent the exercise of worldly anxiety by the competent supply of our necessary wants; to diminish the desire of excessive accumulation by making the acquisition of individual property subservient to upright and disinterested uses; to guarantee to each other the means of physical support and of spiritual progress, and thus to impart a greater freedom, simplicity, truthfulness, refinement and moral dignity to our mode of life, —

We, the undersigned, do unite in a Voluntary Association, to wit: —

Article 1. The name and style of the Association shall be "(The Brook Farm) Institute of Agriculture and Education." All persons who shall hold one or more shares in the stock of the Association, and shall sign the articles of agreement, or who shall hereafter be admitted by the pleasure of the Association, shall be members thereof.

Art. 2. No religious test shall ever be required of any member of the Association; no authority assumed over individual freedom of opinion by the Association, nor by any member over another; nor shall anyone be held accountable to the Association except for such acts as violate rights of the members, and the essential principles on which the Association is founded; and in such cases the relation of any member may be suspended, or discontinued, at the pleasure of the Association.

Art. 3. The members of this Association shall own and manage such real and personal estate, in joint stock proprietorship, as may, from time to time, be agreed on, and establish such branches of industry as may be deemed expedient and desirable.

Art. 4. The Association shall provide such employment for all of its members as shall be adapted to their capacities, habits and tastes, and each member shall select and perform such operation of labor, whether corporal or mental, as he shall deem best suited to his own endowments, and the benefit of the Association.

Art. 5. The members of this Association shall be paid for all labor performed under its direction and for its advantage, at a fixed and equal rate, both for men and women. This rate shall not exceed one dollar per day, nor shall more than ten hours in the day be paid for as a day's labor.

Art. 6. The Association shall furnish to all its members, their children and family dependents, house-rent, fuel, food and clothing, and all other comforts and advantages possible, at the actual cost, as nearly as the same can be ascertained; but no charge shall be made for education, medical or nursing attendance, or the use of the library, public rooms or baths to the members; nor shall any charge be paid for food, rent or fuel by those deprived of labor by sickness, nor for food of children under ten years of age, nor for anything on members over seventy years of age, unless at the special request of the individual by whom the charges are paid, or unless the credits in his favor exceed, or equal, the amount of such charges.

Art. 7. All labor performed for the Association shall be duly credited, and all articles furnished shall be charged, and a full settlement made with every member once every year.

Art. 8. Every child over ten years of age shall be charged for food, clothing, and articles furnished at cost, and shall be credited for his labor, not exceeding fifty cents per day, and on the completion of his education in the Association at the age of twenty, shall be entitled to a certificate of stock, to the amount of credits in his favor, and may be admitted a member of the Association.

Art. 9. Every share-holder in the joint-stock proprietorship of the Association, shall be paid on such stock, at the rate of five per cent, annually.

Art. 10. The net profits of the Association remaining in the treasury after the payments of all demands for interest on stock, labor performed, and necessary repairs, and improvements, shall be divided into a number of shares corresponding with the number of days' labor, and every member shall be entitled to one share for every day's labor performed by him.

Art. 11.   All payments may be made in certificates of stock at the option of the Association; but in any case of need, to be decided by himself, every member may be permitted to draw on the funds of the treasury to an amount not exceeding the credits in his favor.

Art. 12.   The Association shall hold an annual meeting for the choice of officers, and such other necessary business as shall come before them.

Art. 13.   The officers of the Association shall be twelve directors, divided into four departments, as follows: first, General Direction; second, Direction of Agriculture; third, Direction of Education; fourth, Direction of Finance; consisting of three persons each, provided that the same persons may be a member of each Direction at the pleasure of the Association.

Art. 14.   The Chairman of the General Direction shall be presiding officer in the Association, and together with the Direction of Finance, shall constitute a Board of Trustees, by whom the property of the Association shall be managed.

Art. 15.   The General Direction shall oversee and manage the affairs of the Association so that every department shall be carried on in an orderly and efficient manner.   Each department shall be under the general supervision of its own Direction, which shall select, and, in accordance with the General Direction, shall appoint, all such overseers, directors and agents, as shall be necessary to the complete and systematic organization of the department, and shall have full authority to appoint such persons to these stations as they shall judge best qualified for the same.

Art. 16.   No Directors shall be deemed to possess any rank superior to the other members of the Association, nor shall be chosen in reference to any other consideration than their capacity to serve the Association; nor shall they be paid for their official service except at the rate of one dollar for ten hours in a day, actually employed in official duties.

Art. 17.   The Association may, from time to time, adopt such rules and regulations, not inconsistent with the spirit and purpose of the Articles of Agreement, as shall be found expedient and necessary.

George Ripley, Minot Pratt, Charles A. Dana: Preamble to the Constitution of the Brook Farm Association (1844)

All persons who are not familiar with the purposes of Association, will understand from this document that we propose a radical and universal reform rather than to redress any particular wrong, or to remove the sufferings of any single class of human beings. We do this in the light of universal principles in which all differences, whether of religion, or politics, or philosophy, are reconciled, and the dearest and most private hope of every man has the promise of fulfilment. Herein, let it be understood, we would remove nothing that is truly beautiful or venerable; we reverence the religious sentiment in all its forms, the family and whatever else has its foundation either in human nature or Divine Providence. The work we are engaged in is not destruction, but true conservation; it is not a mere resolution, but, as we are assured, a necessary step in the progress which no one can be blind enough to think has yet reached its limit.

We believe that humanity, trained by these long centuries of suffering and struggle, led on by so many saints and heroes and sages, is at length prepared to enter into that universal order toward which it has perpetually moved. Thus we recognize the worth of the whole past, and of every doctrine and institution it has bequeathed us; thus also we perceive that the present has its own high mission, and we shall only say what is beginning to be seen by all sincere thinkers, when we declare that the imperative duty of this time and this country, nay, more, that its only salvation and the salvation of civilized countries, lies in the reorganization of society according to the unchanging laws of human nature, and of universal harmony.

We look, then, to the generous and helpful of all classes for sympathy, for encouragement and for actual aid; not to ourselves only, but to all who are engaged in this great work. And whatever may be the result of any special efforts, we can never doubt that the object we have in view will be finally attained; that human life shall yet be developed, not in discord and misery, but in harmony and joy, and that the perfected earth shall at last bear on her bosom a race of men worthy of the name.

Nathaniel Hawthorne: The American Notebooks* (1840–1841)

March 15th. — I pray that in one year more I may find some way of escaping from this unblest Custom House; for it is a very grievous thraldom. I do detest all offices, — all, at least, that are held on a political tenure. And I want nothing to do with politicians. Their hearts wither away and die out of their bodies. Their consciences are turned to india-rubber, or to some substance as black as that, and which will stretch as much. One thing, if no more, I have gained by my custom house experience, — to know a politician. It is a knowledge which no previous thought or power of sympathy could have taught me, because the animal, or the machine rather, is not a nature.

March 23d. — I do think that it is the doom laid upon me, of murdering so many of the brightest hours of the day at the Custom House, that makes such havoc with my wits, for here I am again trying to write worthily, . . . yet with a sense as if all the noblest part of man had been left out of my composition, or had decayed out of it since my nature was given to my own keeping . . . Never comes any bird of Paradise into that dismal region. A salt or even a coal ship is ten million times preferable; for there the sky is above me, and the fresh breeze around me, and my thoughts, having hardly anything to do with my occupation, are as free as air.

Nevertheless, you are not to fancy that the above paragraph gives a correct idea of my mental and spiritual state . . . It is only once in a while that the image and desire of a better and happier life makes me feel the iron of my chain; for, after all, a human spirit may find no insufficiency of food fit for it, even in the Custom House. And, with such materials as these, I do think and feel and learn things that are worth knowing, and which I should not know unless I had learned them there, so that the present portion of my life shall not be quite left out of the sum of my real existences . . . It is good for me, on many accounts, that my life has had this passage in it. I know much more than I did a year ago. I have a stronger sense of power to act as a man among men. I have gained worldly wisdom, and wisdom also that is not altogether of this world. And, when I quit this earthly cavern where I am now buried, nothing will cling to me that ought to be left behind. Men will not perceive, I trust, by my look, or the tenor of my thoughts and feelings, that I have been a custom house officer.

April 7th. — It appears to me to have been the most uncomfortable day that ever was inflicted on poor mortals . . . Besides the bleak, unkindly air, I have been plagued by two sets of coal-shovellers at the same time, and have been obliged to keep two separate tallies simultaneously. But I was conscious that all this was merely a vision and a fantasy, and that, in reality, I was not half frozen by the bitter blast, nor tormented by those grimy coal-heavers, but that I was basking quietly in the sunshine of eternity . . . Any sort of bodily and earthly torment may serve to make us sensible that we have a soul that is not within the jurisdiction of such shadowy demons, — it separates the immortal within us from the mortal. But the wind has blown my brains into such confusion that I cannot philosophize now.

April 19th. . . . What a beautiful day was yesterday! My spirit rebelled against being confined in my darksome dungeon at the Custom House. It seemed a sin, — a murder of the joyful young day, — a quenching of the sunshine. Nevertheless, there I was kept a prisoner till it was too late to fling myself on a gentle wind, and be blown away into the country. . . When I shall be again free, I will enjoy all things with the fresh simplicity of a child of five years old. I shall grow young again, made all over anew. I will go forth and stand in a summer shower, and all the worldly dust that has collected on me shall be washed away at once, and my heart will be like a bank of fresh flowers for the weary to rest upon . . .

6 P.M. — I went out to walk about an hour ago, and found it very pleasant, though there was a somewhat cool wind. I went round and across the Common, and stood on the highest point of it, where I could see miles and miles into the country. Blessed be God for this green tract, and the view of which it affords,

---

*pp. 216–19, 226–37.

whereby we poor citizens may be put in mind, sometimes, that all his earth is not composed of blocks of brick houses, and of stone or wooden pavements. Blessed be God for the sky, too, though the smoke of the city may somewhat change its aspect, — but still it is better than if each street were covered over with a roof. There were a good many people walking on the mall, — mechanics apparently, and shopkeepers' clerks, with their wives; and boys were rolling on the grass, and I would have liked to lie down and roll too . . .

April 30th. . . . I arose this morning feeling more elastic than I have throughout the winter; for the breathing of the ocean air has wrought a very beneficial effect. . . What a beautiful, most beautiful afternoon this has been! It was a real happiness to live. If I had been merely a vegetable, — a hawthorn-bush, for instance, — I must have been happy in such an air and sunshine; but, having a mind and a soul, . . . I enjoyed somewhat more than mere vegetable happiness . . . The footsteps of May can be traced upon the islands in the harbor, and I have been watching the tints of green upon them gradually deepening, till now they are almost as beautiful as they ever can be . . .

Articulate words are a harsh clamor and dissonance. When man arrives at his highest perfection, he will again be dumb! for I suppose he was dumb at the Creation, and must go round an entire circle in order to return to that blessed state.

Brook Farm, Oak Hill, April 13th, 1841. Here I am in a polar Paradise! I know not how to interpret this aspect of nature, — whether it be of good or evil omen to our enterprise. But I reflect that the Plymouth pilgrims arrived in the midst of storm, and stepped ashore upon mountain snow-drifts; and, nevertheless, they prospered, and became a great people, — and doubtless it will be the same with us. I laud my stars, however, that you will not have your first impressions of (perhaps) our future home from such a day as this . . . Through faith, I persist in believing that Spring and Summer will come in their due season; but the unregenerated man shivers within me, and suggests a doubt whether I may not have wandered within the precincts of the Arctic Circle, and chosen my heritage among everlasting snows . . . Provide

yourself with a good stock of furs, and, if you can obtain the skin of a polar bear, you will find it a very suitable summer dress for this region . . .

I have not yet taken my first lesson in agriculture, except that I went to see our cows foddered, yesterday afternoon. We have eight of our own; and the number is now increased by a transcendental heifer belonging to Miss Margaret Fuller. She is very fractious, I believe, and apt to kick over the milk-pail . . . I intend to convert myself into a milkmaid this evening, but I pray Heaven that Mr. Ripley may be moved to assign me the kindliest cow in the herd, otherwise I shall perform my duty with fear and trembling.

I like my brethren in affliction very well; and, could you see us sitting round our table at meal-times, before the great kitchen fire, you would call it a cheerful sight. Mrs. B —— is a most comfortable woman to behold. She looks as if her ample person were stuffed full of tenderness, — indeed, as if she were all one great, kind heart . . .

April 14th, 10 A.M. . . . I did not milk the cows last night, because Mr. Ripley was afraid to trust them to my hands, or me to their horns, I know not which. But this morning I have done wonders. Before breakfast, I went out to the barn and began to chop hay for the cattle, and with such "righteous vehemence," as Mr. Ripley says, did I labor, that in the space of ten minutes I broke the machine. Then I brought wood and replenished the fires; and finally went down to breakfast, and ate up a huge mound of buckwheat cakes. After breakfast, Mr. Ripley put a four-pronged instrument into my hands, which he gave me to understand was called a pitchfork; and he and Mr. Farley being armed with similar weapons, we all three commenced a gallant attack upon a heap of manure. This office being concluded, and I having purified myself, I sit down to finish this letter . . .

Miss Fuller's cow hooks the other cows, and has made herself ruler of the herd, and behaves in a very tyrannical manner . . . I shall make an excellent husbandman, — I feel the original Adam reviving within me.

April 16th . . . Since I last wrote, there has been an addition to our community of four gentlemen in sables, who promise to be among our most useful and respectable members. They arrived yesterday about noon. Mr. Ripley had proposed to them to join us, no longer ago than that very morning. I had some conversation with them in the afternoon, and was glad to hear them express much satisfaction with their new abode and all the arrangements. They do not appear to be very communicative, however, — or perhaps it may be merely an external reserve, like my own, to shield their delicacy. Several of their prominent characteristics, as well as their black attire, lead me to believe that they are members of the clerical profession; but I have not yet ascertained from their own lips what has been the nature of their past lives. I trust to have much pleasure in their society, and, sooner or later, that we shall all of us derive great strength from our intercourse with them. I cannot too highly applaud the readiness with which these four gentlemen in black have thrown aside all the fopperies and flummeries which have their origin in a false state of society. When I last saw them, they looked as heroically regardless of the stains and soils incident to our profession as I did when I emerged from the gold-mine . . .

I have milked a cow! ! ! . . . The herd has rebelled against the usurpation of Miss Fuller's heifer; and, whenever they are turned out of the barn, she is compelled to take refuge under our protection. So much did she impede my labors by keeping close to me, that I found it necessary to give her two or three gentle pats with a shovel; but still she preferred to trust herself to my tender mercies, rather than venture among the horns of the herd. She is not an amiable cow; but she has a very intelligent face, and seems to be of a reflective cast of character. I doubt not that she will soon perceive the expediency of being on good terms with the rest of the sisterhood.

I have not yet been twenty yards from our house and barn; but I begin to perceive that this is a beautiful place. The scenery is of a mild and placid character, with nothing bold in its aspect; but I think its beauties will grow upon us, and make us love it the more, the longer we live here. There is a brook, so near the house that we shall be able to hear its ripple in the summer evenings, . . . but, for agricultural purposes, it has been made to flow in a straight and rectangular fashion, which does it infinite damage as a picturesque

object . . .

April 22d . . . What an abominable hand do I scribble! but I have been chopping wood, and turning a grindstone all the forenoon; and such occupations are likely to disturb the equilibrium of the muscles and sinews. It is an endless surprise to me how much work there is to be done in the world; but, thank God, I am able to do my share of it, — and my ability increases daily. What a great, broad-shouldered, elephantine personage I shall become by and by! . . .

I milked two cows this morning, and would send you some of the milk, only that it is mingled with that which was drawn forth by Mr. Dismal View and the rest of the brethren.

April 28th. . . . I was caught by a cold during my visit to Boston. It has not affected my whole frame, but took entire possession of my head, as being the weakest and most vulnerable part. Never did anybody sneeze with such vehemence and frequency; and my poor brain has been in a thick fog; or, rather, it seemed as if my head were stuffed with coarse wool. . . . Sometimes I wanted to wrench it off, and give it a great kick, like a football.

This annoyance has made me endure the bad weather with even less than ordinary patience; and my faith was so far exhausted that, when they told me yesterday that the sun was setting clear, I would not even turn my eyes towards the west. But this morning I am made all over anew, and have no greater remnant of my cold than will serve as an excuse for doing no work to-day . . .

The family has been dismal and dolorous throughout the storm. The night before last, William Allen was stung by a wasp on the eyelid; whereupon the whole side of his face swelled to an enormous magnitude, so that, at the breakfast-table, one half of him looked like a blind giant (the eye being closed), and the other half had such a sorrowful and ludicrous aspect that I was constrained to laugh out of sheer pity. The same day, a colony of wasps was discovered in my chamber, where they had remained throughout the winter, and were now just bestirring themselves, doubtless with the intention of stinging me from head to foot . . . A similar discovery was made in Mr. Farley's room. In short, we seem to have taken up our abode in a wasps' nest. Thus you see a rural life is not one of unbroken quiet and serenity.

If the middle of the day prove warm and pleasant, I promise myself to take a walk . . . I have taken one walk with Mr. Farley; and I could not have believed that there was such seclusion at so short a distance from a great city. Many spots seem hardly to have been visited for ages, — not since John Eliot preached to the Indians here. If we were to travel a thousand miles, we could not escape the world more completely than we can here . . .

I read no newspapers, and hardly remember who is President, and feel as if I had no more concern with what other people trouble themselves about than if I dwelt in another planet.

May 1st. . . . Every day of my life makes me feel more and more how seldom a fact is accurately stated; how, almost invariably, when a story has passed through the mind of a third person, it becomes, so far as regards the impression that it makes in further repetitions, little better than a falsehood, and this, too, though the narrator be the most truthseeking person in existence. How marvellous the tendency is! . . . Is truth a fantasy which we are to pursue forever and never grasp? . . .

My cold has almost entirely departed. Were it a sunny day, I should consider myself quite fit for labors out of doors; but as the ground is so damp, and the atmosphere so chill, and the sky so sullen, I intend to keep myself on the sick-list this one day longer, more especially as I wish to read Carlyle on Heroes . . .

There has been but one flower found in this vicinity, — and that was an anemone, a poor, pale, shivering little flower, that had crept under a stone-wall for shelter. Mr. Farley found it, while taking a walk with me. . . . This is May-Day! Alas, what a difference between the ideal and the real!

May 4th. . . . My cold no longer troubles me, and all the morning I have been at work under the clear, blue sky, on a hill-side. Sometimes it almost seemed as if I were at work in the sky itself, though the material in which I wrought was the ore from our gold-mine. Nevertheless, there is nothing so unseemly and disagreeable in this sort of toil as you could think. It defiles the hands, indeed, but not the soul. This gold ore is a pure and wholesome substance,

else our mother Nature would not devour it so readily, and derive so much nourishment from it, and return such a rich abundance of good grain and roots in requital of it.

The farm is growing very beautiful now, — not that we yet see anything of the peas and potatoes which we have planted; but the grass blushes green on the slopes and hollows. I wrote that word "blush" almost unconsciously; so we will let it go as an inspired utterance. When I go forth afield, . . . I look beneath the stone-walls, where the verdure is richest, in hopes that a little company of violets, or some solitary bud, prophetic of the summer, may be there . . . But not a wild-flower have I yet found. One of the boys gathered some yellow cowslips last Sunday; but I am well content not to have found them, for they are not precisely what I should like to send to you, though they deserve honor and praise, because they come to us when no others will. We have our parlor here dressed in evergreen as at Christmas. That beautiful little flower-vase . . . stands on Mr. Ripley's studytable, at which I am now writing. It contains some daffodils and some willow-blossoms. I brought it here rather than keep it in my chamber, because I never sit there, and it gives me pleasant emotions to look round and be surprised —for it is often a surprise, though I well know that it is there . . .

I do not believe that I should be patient here if I were not engaged in a righteous and heaven-blessed way of life. When I was in the Custom House and then at Salem I was not half so patient . . .

We had some tableaux last evening, the principal characters being sustained by Mr. Farley and Miss Ellen Slade. They went off very well . . .

I fear it is time for me — sod-compelling as I am — to take the field again.

May 11th. . . . This morning I arose at milking time in good trim for work; and we have been employed partly in an Augean labor of clearing out a wood-shed, and partly in carting loads of oak. This afternoon I hope to have something to do in the field, for these jobs about the house are not at all to my taste.

Ausust 12th. . . . I am very well, and not at all weary, for yesterday's rain gave us a holiday; and, moreover, the labors of the farm are not so pressing as they have been. And, joyful thought! in a little more than a fortnight I shall be free from my bondage, — ... free to enjoy Nature, — free to think and feel! ... Even my Custom House experience was not such a thraldom and weariness; my mind and heart were free. Oh, labor is the curse of the world and nobody can meddle with it without becoming proportionably brutified! Is it a praiseworthy matter that I have spent five golden months in providing food for cows and horses? It is not so.

August 18th. — I am very well, only somewhat tired with walking half a dozen miles immediately after breakfast, and raking hay ever since. We shall quite finish haying this week, and then there will be no more very hard or constant labor during the one other week that I shall remain a slave.

August 22d. ... I had an indispensable engagement in the bean-field, whither, indeed, I was glad to betake myself, in order to escape a parting scene with — . He was quite out of his wits the night before, and I sat up with him till long past midnight. The farm is pleasanter now that he is gone; for his unappeasable wretchedness threw a gloom over everything ... Since I last wrote, we have done haying, and the remainder of my bondage will probably be light. It will be a long time, however, before I shall know how to make a good use of leisure, either as regards enjoyment or literary occupation ...

It is extremely doubtful whether Mr. Ripley will succeed in locating his community on this farm. He can bring Mr. E —— to no terms, and the more they talk about the matter, the further they appear to be from a settlement ... Whatever may be my gifts, I have not hitherto shown a single one that may avail to gather gold. I confess that I have strong hopes of good from this arrangement with M ——; but when I look at the scanty avails of my past literary efforts, I do not feel authorized to expect much from the future ...Whatever is to be done must be done by my own undivided strength. I shall not remain here through the winter, unless with an absolute certainty that there will be a house ready for us in the spring. Otherwise, I shall return to Boston, — still, however, considering myself an associate of the community, so that we may take advantage of any more favorable aspect of affairs. How much depends on these little books! Methinks if anything could draw out my whole strength, it would be the motives that now press upon me. Yet, after all, I must keep these considerations out of my mind, because an external pressure always disturbs instead of assisting me.

Salem, September 3rd. ... But really I should judge it to be twenty years since I left Brook Farm; and I take this to be one proof that my life there was an unnatural and unsuitable, and therefore an unreal, one. It already looks like a dream behind me. The real Me was never an associate of the community; there has been a spectral Appearance there, sounding the horn at daybreak, and milking the cows, and hoeing potatoes, and raking hay, toiling in the sun, and doing me the honor to assume my name. But this spectre was not myself. Nevertheless, it is somewhat remarkable that my hands have, during the past summer, grown very brown and rough, insomuch that many people persist in believing that I, after all, was the aforesaid spectral horn-sounder, cow-milker, potato-hoer, and hay-raker. But such people do not know a reality from a shadow. Enough of nonsense.

Americans were enormously proud of their accomplishments in taming the virgin wilderness. In the early decades of the 19th century, pioneers had moved into the richest, most fertile land on the entire continent. A steady foreign demand for foodstuffs had hastened the transformation of this frontier into prosperous agricultural communities. Farming families — the typical Americans in most people's eyes — had turned the Mohawk, Ohio, and Mississippi Valleys into bountiful bread baskets. Americans surely knew how to make the land fruitful and without considering too much the unusual resources they had been given, they developed a highly flattering self-image. By contrast, the arid, sun-parched Southern lands stretching west of the Mississippi reflected poorly upon the Mexican occupants. Thus many Americans, when confronted with the opportunity to take Texas and California and the vast domain in between in the settlement of the Mexican war, were ready to justify these conquests on grounds that Americans would make the land more productive.

John O'Sullivan (1813–1895), who edited the *United States Magazine and Democratic Review* from which the first reading is taken, consistently gave expression to this point of view. Credited with coining the phrase, "manifest destiny," O'Sullivan never tired of extolling the genius of American democracy in the columns of his magazine. O'Sullivan's enthusiasm for America's special greatness showed how these sentiments could be a cohesive force, for he was an Irish immigrant. Nativists tended to emphasize the concepts of ethnic, Anglo-Saxon superiority, although the emotional and inspirational context in which these predictions and justifications were set made them far too vague for a rigorous intellectual investigation. Indeed, their appeal was to people already susceptible to the themes and anxious to believe that a democracy of hard-working, God-fearing, free people could do no wrong.

President James K. Polk had been elected in 1844 on an "annex Texas" platform, but when annexation led to the outbreak of hostilities with Mexico, many Americans became disenchanted with manifest destiny through conquest. Glib justifications of the war like those in O'Sullivan's *Democratic Review* did not go down at all well in New England, where people were much more inclined to suspect the intentions of Southern slaveholders who had moved into Texas. The Massachusetts legislature even conducted an investigation into the origins of the war and decided that it had been provoked by Americans. Worse yet, the ill-gotten gains of the war, they decided, would benefit only those who wished to add more slave states to the Union. While many Northerners were ready to believe that the war was the result of a Southern conspiracy, one of New England's most outstanding men, Henry David Thoreau (1817–1862), viewed it as an indictment of all Americans, New Englanders as well as Southerners. Explaining his reasons for going to jail rather than pay his taxes, Thoreau explored the whole question of law and conscience in his *Essay on Civil Disobedience*, which is the second reading in this section. No less an individualist than the most ambitious entrepreneur, Thoreau attempted to ground social morality on the concept of private moral duty.

John O'Sullivan: Annexation (1845)

It is time now for opposition to the Annexation of Texas to cease, all further agitation of the waters of bitterness and strife, at least in connexion with this question, — even though it may perhaps be required of us as a necessary condition of the freedom of our institutions, that we must live on for ever in a state of unpausing struggle and excitement upon some subject of party division or other. But, in regard to Texas, enough has now been given to Party. It is time for the common duty of Patriotism to the Country to succeed; — or if this claim will not be recognized, it is at least time for common sense to acquiesce with decent grace in the inevitable and the irrevocable.

Texas is now ours. Already, before these words are written, her Convention has undoubtedly ratified the acceptance, by her Congress, of our proffered

United States Magazine and Democratic Review, **17** (1845), 5–10.

invitation into the Union; and made the requisite
changes in her already republican form of constitution
to adopt it to its future federal relations. Her star and
her stripe may already be said to have taken their
place in the glorious blazon of our common nationality; and the sweep of our eagle's wing already includes
within its circuit the wide extent of her fair and fertile
land. She is no longer to us a mere geographical space
— a certain combination of coast, plain, mountain,
valley, forest and stream. She is no longer to us a
mere country on the map. She comes within the dear
and sacred designation of Our Country; no longer a
pays, she is a part of *la patrie*; and that which is at
once a sentiment and a virtue, Patriotism, already begins to thrill for her too within the national heart . . .
The next session of Congress will see the representatives of the new young State in their places in both our
halls of national legislation, side by side with those of
the old Thirteen. Let their reception into "the family"
be frank, kindly, and cheerful, as befits such an occasion, as comports not less with our own self-respect
than patriotic duty towards them. Ill betide those
foul birds that delight to 'file their own nest, and disgust the ear with perpetual discord of ill-omened
croak.

Why, were other reasoning wanting, in favor of
now elevating this question of the reception of Texas
into the Union, out of the lower region of our past
party dissensions, up to its proper level of a high and
broad nationality, it surely is to be found, found abundantly, in the manner in which other nations have
undertaken to intrude themselves into it, between us
and the proper parties to the case, in a spirit of hostile
interference against us, for the avowed object of thwart-
ing our policy and hampering our power, limiting our
greatness and checking the fulfilment of our manifest
destiny to overspread the continent allotted by Providence for the free development of our yearly multiplying millions. This we have seen done by England, our
old rival and enemy; and by France, strangely coupled
with her against us, under the influence of the Angli-
cism strongly tinging the policy of her present prime
minister, Guizot. The zealous activity with which this
effort to defeat us was pushed by the representatives
of those governments, together with the character of
intrigue accompanying it, fully constituted that case

of foreign interference, which Mr. Clay himself declared should, and would unite us all in maintaining the
common cause of our country against the foreigner and
the foe. We are only astonished that this effect has not
been more fully and strongly produced, and that the
burst of indignation against this unauthorized, insolent
and hostile interference against us, has not been more
general even among the party before opposed to Annexation, and has not rallied the national spirit and national
pride unanimously upon that policy . . .

It is wholly untrue, and unjust to ourselves, the
pretence that the Annexation has been a measure of
spoliation, unrightful and unrighteous — of military
conquest under forms of peace and law — of territorial
aggrandizement at the expense of justice, and justice
due by a double sanctity to the weak. This view of the
question is wholly unfounded, and has been before so
amply refuted in these pages, as well as in a thousand
other modes, that we shall not again dwell upon it.
The independence of Texas was complete and absolute.
It was an independence, not only in fact but of right.
No obligation of duty towards Mexico tended in the
least degree to restrain our right to effect the desired
recovery of the fair province once our own — whatever
motives of policy might have prompted a more deferential consideration of her feelings and her pride, as
involved in the question. If Texas became peopled
with an American population, it was by no contrivance
of our government, but on the express invitation of
that of Mexico herself; accompanied with such guaranties of State independence, and the maintenance of a
federal system analogous to our own, as constituted a
compact fully justifying the strongest measures of redress on the part of those afterwards deceived in this
guaranty, and sought to be enslaved under the yoke
imposed by its violation. She was released, rightfully
and absolutely released, from all Mexican allegiance, or
duty of cohesion to the Mexican political body, by the
acts and fault of Mexico herself, and Mexico alone.
There never was a clearer case. It was not revolution;
it was resistance to revolution; and resistance under
such circumstances as left independence the necessary
resulting state, caused by the abandonment of those
with whom her former federal association had existed.
What then can be more preposterous than all this
clamor by Mexico and the Mexican interest, against

Annexation, as a violation of any rights of hers, any duties of ours?

We would not be understood as approving in all its features the expediency or propriety of the mode in which the measure, rightful and wise as it is in itself, has been carried into effect. Its history has been a sad tissue of diplomatic blundering. How much better it might have been managed — how much more smoothly, satisfactorily and successfully! Instead of our present relations with Mexico — instead of the serious risks which have been run, and those plausibilities of opprobrium which we have had to combat, not without great difficulty, nor with entire success — instead of the difficulties which now throng the path to a satisfactory settlement of all our unsettled questions with Mexico — Texas might, by a more judicious and conciliatory diplomacy, have been as securely in the Union as she is now — her boundaries defined — California probably ours — and Mexico and ourselves united by closer ties than ever; of mutual friendship, and mutual support in resistance to the intrusion of European interference in the affairs of the American republics. All this might have been, we little doubt, already secured, had counsels less violent, less rude, less one-sided, less eager in precipitation from motives widely foreign to the national question, presided over the earlier stages of its history. We cannot too deeply regret the mismanagement which has disfigured the history of this question; and especially the neglect of the means which would have been so easy, of satisfying even the unreasonable pretensions, and the excited pride and passion of Mexico . . .

Nor is there any just foundation for the charge that Annexation is a great pro-slavery measure — calculated to increase and perpetuate that institution. Slavery had nothing to do with it. Opinions were and are greatly divided, both at the North and South, as to the influence to be exerted by it on Slavery and the Slave States. That it will tend to facilitate and hasten the disappearance of Slavery from all the northern tier of the present Slave States, cannot surely admit of serious question. The greater value in Texas of the slave labor now employed in those States, must soon produce the effect of draining off that labor southwardly, by the same unvarying law that bids water descend the slope that invites it. Every new Slave State in Texas will

make at least one Free State from among those in which that institution now exists — to say nothing of those portions of Texas on which slavery cannot spring and grow — to say nothing of the far more rapid growth of new States in the free West and Northwest, as these fine regions are overspread by the emigration fast flowing over them from Europe, as well as from the Northern and Eastern States of the Union as it exists. On the other hand, it is undeniably much gained for the cause of the eventual voluntary abolition of slavery, that it should have been thus drained off towards the only outlet which appeared to furnish much probability of the ultimate disappearance of the negro race from our borders. The Spanish-Indian-American populations of Mexico, Central America and South America, afford the only receptacle capable of absorbing that race whenever we shall be prepared to slough it off — to emancipate it from slavery, and (simultaneously necessary) to remove it from the midst of our own. Themselves already of mixed and confused blood, and free from the "prejudices" which among us so insuperably forbid the social amalgamation which can alone elevate the Negro race out of a virtually servile degradation even though legally free, the regions occupied by those populations must strongly attract the black race in that direction; and as soon as the destined hour of emancipation shall arrive, will relieve the question of one of its worst difficulties, if not absolutely the greatest.

No — Mr. Clay was right when he declared that Annexation was a question with which slavery had nothing to do. The country which was the subject of Annexation in this case, from its geographical position and relations, happens to be — or rather the portion of it now actually settled, happens to be — a slave country. But a similar process might have taken place in proximity to a different section of our Union; and indeed there is a great deal of Annexation yet to take place, within the life of the present generation, along the whole line of our northern border. Texas has been absorbed into the Union in the inevitable fulfilment of the general law which is rolling our population westward; the connexion of which with that ratio of growth in population which is destined within a hundred years to swell our numbers to the enormous population of two hundred and fifty millions (if not more), is too evident to leave us in doubt of the manifest design of

Providence in regard to the occupation of this continent. It was disintegrated from Mexico in the natural course of events, by a process perfectly legitimate on its own part, blameless on ours; and in which all the censures due to wrong, perfidy and folly, rest on Mexico alone. And possessed as it was by a population which was in truth but a colonial detachment from our own, and which was still bound by myriad ties of the very heart-strings to its old relations, domestic and political, their incorporation into the Union was not only inevitable, but the most natural, right and proper thing in the world — and it is only astonishing that there should be any among ourselves to say it nay.

In respect to the institution of slavery itself, we have not designed, in what has been said above, to express any judgment of its merits or demerits, pro or con. National in its character and aims, this Review abstains from the discussion of a topic pregnant with embarrassment and danger — intricate and double-sided — exciting and embittering — and necessarily excluded from a work circulating equally in the South as in the North. It is unquestionably one of the most difficult of the various social problems which at the present day so deeply agitate the thoughts of the civilized world. Is the negro race, or is it not, of equal attributes and capacities with our own? Can they, on a large scale, coexist side by side in the same country on a footing of civil and social equality with the white race? In a free competition of labor with the latter, will they or will they not be ground down to a degradation and misery worse than slavery? When we view the condition of the operative masses of the population in England and other European countries, and feel all the difficulties of the great problem, of the distribution of the fruits of production between capital, skill and labor, can our confidence be undoubting that in the present condition of society, the conferring of sudden freedom upon our negro race would be a boon to be grateful for? Is it certain that competitive wages are very much better, for a race so situated, than guaranteed support and protection? Until a still deeper problem shall have been solved than that of slavery, the slavery of an inferior to a superior race — a relation reciprocal in certain important duties and obligations — is it certain that the cause of true wisdom and philanthropy is not rather, for the present, to aim to meliorate that institution as it exists, to guard against its abuses, to mitigate its evils, to modify it when it may contravene sacred principles and rights of humanity, by prohibiting the separation of families, excessive severities, subjection to the licentiousness of mastership, &c? Great as may be its present evils, is it certain that we would not plunge the unhappy Helot race which has been entailed upon us, into still greater ones, by surrendering their fate into the rash hands of those fanatic zealots of a single idea, who claim to be their special friends and champions? Many of the most ardent social reformers of the present day are looking towards the idea of Associated Industry as containing the germ of such a regeneration of society as will relieve its masses from the hideous weight of evil which now depresses and degrades them to a condition which these reformers often describe as no improvement upon any form of legal slavery — is it certain, then, that the institution in question — as a mode of society, as a relation between the two races, and between capital and labor, — does not contain some dim undeveloped germ of that very principle of reform thus aimed at, out of which proceeds some compensation at least for its other evils, making it the duty of true reform to cultivate and develop the good, and remove the evils? . . .

With no friendship for slavery, though unprepared to excommunicate to eternal damnation, with bell, book, and candle, those who are, we see nothing in the bearing of the Annexation of Texas on that institution to awaken a doubt of the wisdom of that measure, or a compunction for the humble part contributed by us towards its consummation.

California will, probably, next fall away from the loose adhesion which, in such a country as Mexico, holds a remote province in a slight equivocal kind of dependence on the metropolis. Imbecile and distracted, Mexico never can exert any real governmental authority over such a country. The impotence of the one and the distance of the other, must make the relation one of virtual independence; unless, by stunting the province of all natural growth, and forbidding that immigration which can alone develop its capabilities and fulfil the purposes of its creation, tyranny may retain a military dominion which is no government in the legitimate sense of the term. In the case of California this is now impossible. The Anglo-Saxon foot is already on its borders. Already the advance guard of the irresistible army of Anglo-Saxon emigration has begun to pour down upon it, armed with the plough and the rifle, and marking its trail with schools and colleges, courts and representative halls, mills and meeting-houses. A population will soon be in actual occupation of California, over which it will be idle for Mexico to dream of dominion. They will necessarily become independent. All this without agency of our government, without responsibility of our people — in the natural flow of events, the spontaneous working of principles, and the adaptation of the tendencies and wants of the human race to the elemental circumstances in the midst of which they find themselves placed. And they will have a right to independence — to self-government — to the possession of the homes conquered from the wilderness by their own labors and dangers, sufferings and sacrifices — a better and a truer right than the artificial title of sovereignty in Mexico a thousand miles distant, inheriting from Spain a title good only against those who have none better. Their right to independence will be the natural right of self-government belonging to any community strong enough to maintain it — distinct in position, origin and character, and free from any mutual obligations of membership of a common political body, binding it to others by the duty of loyalty and compact of public faith. This will be their title to independence; and by this title, there can be no doubt that the population now fast streaming down upon California will both assert and maintain that independence. Whether they will then attach themselves to our Union or not, is not to be predicted with any certainty. Unless the projected rail-road across the continent to the Pacific be carried into effect, perhaps they may not; though even in that case, the day is not distant when the Empires of the Atlantic and Pacific would again flow together into one, as soon as their inland border should approach each other. But that great work, colossal as appears the plan on its first suggestion, cannot remain long unbuilt. Its necessity for this very purpose of binding and holding together in its iron clasp our fast settling Pacific region with that of the Mississippi valley — the natural facility of the route — the ease with which any amount of labor for the construction can be drawn in from the overcrowded populations of Europe, to be paid in the lands made valuable by the progress of the work itself — and its immense utility to the commerce of the world with the whole eastern coast of Asia, alone almost sufficient for the support of such a road — these considerations give assurance that the day cannot be distant which shall witness the conveyance of the representatives from Oregon and California to Washington within less time than a few years ago was devoted to a similar journey by those from Ohio; while the magnetic telegraph will enable the editors of the "San Francisco Union," the "Astoria Evening Post," or the "Nootka Morning News" to set up in type the first half of the President's Inaugural, before the echoes of the latter half shall have died away beneath the lofty porch of the Capitol, as spoken from his lips.

Away, then, with all idle French talk of balances of power on the American Continent. There is no growth in Spanish America! Whatever progress of population there may be in the British Canadas, is only for their own early severance of their present colonial relation to the little island three thousand miles across the Atlantic; soon to be followed by Annexation, and destined to swell the still accumulating momentum of our progress. And whosoever may hold the balance, though they should cast into the opposite scale all the bayonets and cannon, not only of France and England, but of Europe entire, how would it kick the beam against the simple solid weight of the two hundred and fifty, or three hundred millions — and American millions — destined to gather beneath the flutter of the stripes and stars, in the fast hastening year of the Lord 1945!

Henry David Thoreau: *Essay on Civil Disobedience (1847)*

I heartily accept the motto, "That government is best which governs least;" and I should like to see it acted up to more rapidly and systematically. Carried out, it finally amounts to this, which also I believe, — "That government is best which governs not at all;" and when men are prepared for it, that will be the kind of government which they will have. Government is at best but

The Writings of Henry David Thoreau, Houghton Mifflin, New York, 1906, VI, 356–87.

an expedient; but most governments are usually, and all governments are sometimes, inexpedient. The objections which have been brought against a standing army, and they are many and weighty, and deserve to prevail, may also at last be brought against a standing government. The standing army is only an arm of the standing government. The government itself, which is only the mode which the people have chosen to execute their will, is equally liable to be abused and perverted before the people can act through it. Witness the present Mexican war, the work of comparatively a few individuals using the standing government as their tool; for, in the outset, the people would not have consented to this measure.

This American government, — what is it but a tradition, though a recent one, endeavoring to transmit itself unimpaired to posterity, but each instant losing some of its integrity? It has not the vitality and force of a single living man; for a single man can bend it to his will. It is a sort of wooden gun to the people themselves. But it is not the less necessary for this; for the people must have some complicated machinery or other, and hear its din, to satisfy that idea of government which they have. Governments show thus how successfully men can be imposed on, even impose on themselves, for their own advantage. It is excellent, we must all allow. Yet this government never of itself furthered any enterprise, but by the alacrity with which it got out of its way. *It* does not keep the country free. *It* does not settle the West. *It* does not educate. The character inherent in the American people has done all that has been accomplished; and it would have done somewhat more, if the government had not sometimes got in its way. For government is an expedient by which men would fain succeed in letting one another alone; and, as has been said, when it is most expedient, the governed are most let alone by it. Trade and commerce, if they were not made of india-rubber, would never manage to bounce over the obstacles which legislators are continually putting in their way; and, if one were to judge these men wholly by the effects of their actions and not partly by their intentions, they would deserve to be classed and punished with those mischievous persons who put obstructions on the railroads.

But, to speak practically and as a citizen, unlike those who call themselves no-government men, I ask for, not at once no government, but at once a better government. Let every man make known what kind of government would command his respect, and that will be one step toward obtaining it.

After all, the practical reason why, when the power is once in the hands of the people, a majority are permitted, and for a long period continue, to rule is not because they are most likely to be in the right, nor because this seems fairest to the minority, but because they are physically the strongest. But a government in which the majority rule in all cases cannot be based on justice, even as far as men understand it. Can there not be a government in which majorities do not virtually decide right and wrong, but conscience? — in which majorities decide only those questions to which the rule of expediency is applicable? Must the citizen ever for a moment, or in the least degree, resign his conscience to the legislator? Why has every man a conscience, then? I think that we should be men first, and subjects afterward. It is not desirable to cultivate a respect for the law, so much as for the right. The only obligation which I have a right to assume is to do at any time what I think right. It is truly enough said that a corporation has no conscience; but a corporation of conscientious men is a corporation with a conscience. Law never made men a whit more just; and, by means of their respect for it, even the well-disposed are daily made the agents of injustice. A common and natural result of an undue respect for law is, that you may see a file of soldiers, colonel, captain, corporal, privates, powder-monkeys, and all, marching in admirable order over hill and dale to the wars, against their wills, ay, against their common sense and consciences, which makes it very steep marching indeed, and produces a palpitation of the heart. They have no doubt that it is a damnable business in which they are concerned; they are all peaceably inclined. Now, what are they? Men at all? or small movable forts and magazines, at the service of some unscrupulous man in power? . . .

The mass of men serve the state thus, not as men mainly, but as machines, with their bodies. They are the standing army, and the militia, jailers, constables, *posse comitatus*, etc. In most cases there is no free exercise whatever of the judgment or of the moral sense; but they put themselves on a level with wood and earth and stones; and wooden men can perhaps be manufactured that will serve the purpose as well. Such command no more respect than men of straw or a lump of dirt. They have the same sort of worth only as horses and dogs. Yet such as these even are commonly esteemed good citizens. Others — as most legislators, politicians, lawyers, ministers, and office-holders — serve the state chiefly with their heads; and, as they rarely make any moral distinctions, they are as likely to serve the devil, without intending it, as God. A very few — as heroes, patriots, martyrs, reformers in the great sense, and *men* — serve the state with their consciences also, and so necessarily resist it for the most part; and they are commonly treated as enemies by it . . .

He who gives himself entirely to his fellow-men appears to them useless and selfish; but he who gives himself partially to them is pronounced a benefactor and philanthropist.

How does it become a man to behave toward this American government to-day? I answer, that he cannot without disgrace be associated with it. I cannot for an instant recognize that political organization as my government which is the slave's government also.

All men recognize the right of revolution; that is, the right to refuse allegiance to, and to resist, the government, when its tyranny or its inefficiency are great and unendurable. But almost all say that such is not the case now. But such was the case, they think, in the Revolution of '75. If one were to tell me that this was a bad government because it taxed certain foreign commodities brought to its ports, it is most probable that I should not make an ado about it, for I can do without them. All machines have their friction; and possibly this does enough good to counterbalance the evil. At any rate, it is a great evil to make a stir about it. But when the friction comes to have its machine, and oppression and robbery are organized, I say, let us not have such a machine any longer. In other words, when a sixth of the population of a nation which has undertaken to be the refuge of liberty are slaves, and a whole country is unjustly overrun and conquered by a foreign army, and subjected to military law, I think that it is not too soon for honest men to rebel and revolutionize. What makes this duty the more urgent is the fact that the country so overrun is not our own,

but ours is the invading army.

Paley, a common authority with many on moral questions, in his chapter on the "Duty of Submission to Civil Government," resolves all civil obligation into expediency; and he proceeds to say that "so long as the interest of the whole society requires it, that is, so long as the established government cannot be resisted or changed without public inconveniency, it is the will of God . . . that the established government be obeyed, — and no longer. This principle being admitted, the justice of every particular case of resistance is reduced to a computation of the quantity of the danger and grievance on the one side, and of the probability and expense of redressing it on the other." Of this, he says, every man shall judge for himself. But Paley appears never to have contemplated those cases to which the rule of expediency does not apply, in which a people, as well as an individual, must do justice, cost what it may. If I have unjustly wrested a plank from a drowning man, I must restore it to him though I drown myself. This, according to Paley, would be inconvenient. But he that would save his life, in such a case, shall lose it. This people must cease to hold slaves, and to make war on Mexico, though it cost them their existence as a people . . .

Practically speaking, the opponents to a reform in Massachusetts are not a hundred thousand politicians at the South, but a hundred thousand merchants and farmers here, who are more interested in commerce and agriculture than they are in humanity, and are not prepared to do justice to the slave and to Mexico, cost what it may. I quarrel not with far-off foes, but with those who, near at home, cooperate with, and do the bidding of, those far away, and without whom the latter would be harmless. We are accustomed to say, that the mass of men are unprepared; but improvement is slow, because the few are not materially wiser or better than the many. It is not so important that many should be as good as you, as that there be some absolute goodness somewhere; for that will leaven the whole lump. There are thousands who are in opinion opposed to slavery and to the war, who yet in effect do nothing to put an end to them; who, esteeming themselves children of Washington and Franklin, sit down with their hands in their pockets, and say that they know not what to do, and do nothing; who even postpone the question of freedom to the question of free trade, and quietly read the prices-current along with the latest advices from Mexico, after dinner, and, it may be, fall asleep over them both. What is the price-current of an honest man and patriot to-day? They hesitate, and they regret, and sometimes they petition; but they do nothing in earnest and with effect. They will wait, well disposed, for others to remedy the evil, that they may no longer have it to regret. At most, they give only a cheap vote, and a feeble countenance and God-speed, to the right, as it goes by them. There are nine hundred and ninety-nine patrons of virtue to one virtuous man. But it is easier to deal with the real possessor of a thing than with the temporary guardian of it.

All voting is a sort of gaming, like checkers or backgammon, with a slight moral tinge to it, a playing with right and wrong, with moral questions; and betting naturally accompanies it. The character of the voters is not staked. I cast my vote, perchance, as I think right; but I am not vitally concerned that that right should prevail. I am willing to leave it to the majority. Its obligation, therefore, never exceeds that of expediency. Even voting for the right is doing nothing for it. It is only expressing to men feebly your desire that it should prevail. A wise man will not leave the right to the mercy of chance, nor wish it to prevail through the power of the majority. There is but little virtue in the action of masses of men. When the majority shall at length vote for the abolition of slavery, it will be because they are indifferent to slavery, or because there is but little slavery left to be abolished by their vote. They will then be the only slaves. Only his vote can hasten the abolition of slavery who asserts his own freedom by his vote.

I hear of a convention to be held at Baltimore, or elsewhere, for the selection of a candidate for the Presidency, made up chiefly of editors, and men who are politicians by profession; but I think, what is it to any independent, intelligent, and respectable man what decision they may come to? Shall we not have the advantage of his wisdom and honesty, nevertheless? Can we not count upon some independent votes? Are there not many individuals in the country who do not attend conventions? But no: I find that the respectable man, so called, has immediately

drifted from his position, and despairs of his country, when his country has more reason to despair of him. He forthwith adopts one of the candidates thus selected as the only available one, thus proving that he is himself available for any purposes of the demagogue. His vote is of no more worth than that of any unprincipled foreigner or hireling native, who may have been bought. O for a man who is a *man*, and, as my neighbor says, has a bone in his back which you cannot pass your hand through! Our statistics are at fault: the population has been returned too large. How many *men* are there to a square thousand miles in this country? Hardly one. Does not America offer any inducement for men to settle here? The American has dwindled into an Odd Fellow, — one who may be known by the development of his organ of gregariousness, and a manifest lack of intellect and cheerful self-reliance; whose first and chief concern, on coming into the world, is to see that the almshouses are in good repair; and, before yet he has lawfully donned the virile garb, to collect a fund for the support of the widows and orphans that may be; who, in short, ventures to live only by the aid of the Mutual Insurance company, which has promised to bury him decently.

It is not a man's duty, as a matter of course, to devote himself to the eradication of any, even the most enormous, wrong; he may still properly have other concerns to engage him; but it is his duty, at least, to wash his hands of it, and, if he gives it no thought longer, not to give it practically his support. If I devote myself to other pursuits and contemplations, I must first see, at least, that I do not pursue them sitting upon another man's shoulders. I must get off him first, that he may pursue his contemplations too. See what gross inconsistency is tolerated. I have heard some of my townsmen say, "I should like to have them order me out to help put down an insurrection of the slaves, or to march to Mexico; — see if I would go;" and yet these very men have each, directly by their allegiance, and so indirectly, at least, by their money, furnished a substitute. The soldier is applauded who refuses to serve in an unjust war by those who do not refuse to sustain the unjust government which makes the war; is applauded by those whose own act and authority he disregards and sets at naught; as if the state were penitent to that degree that it hired one to scourge it while it sinned, but not to that degree that it left off sinning for a moment. Thus, under the name of Order and Civil Government, we are all made at last to pay homage to and support our own meanness. After the first blush of sin comes its indifference; and from immoral it becomes, as it were, unmoral, and not quite unnecessary to that life which we have made.

The broadest and most prevalent error requires the most disinterested virtue to sustain it. The slight reproach to which the virtue of patriotism is commonly liable, the noble are most likely to incur. Those who, while they disapprove of the character and measures of a government, yield to it their allegiance and support are undoubtedly its most conscientious supporters, and so frequently the most serious obstacles to reform. Some are petitioning the State to dissolve the Union, to disregard the requisitions of the President. Why do they not dissolve it themselves, — the union between themselves and the State, — and refuse to pay their quota into its treasury? Do not they stand in the same relation to the State that the State does to the Union? And have not the same reasons prevented the State from resisting the Union which have prevented them from resisting the State?

How can a man be satisfied to entertain an opinion merely, and enjoy it? Is there any enjoyment in it, if his opinion is that he is aggrieved? If you are cheated out of a single dollar by your neighbor, you do not rest satisfied with knowing that you are cheated, or with saying that you are cheated, or even with petitioning him to pay you your due; but you take effectual steps at once to obtain the full amount, and see that you are never cheated again. Action from principle, the perception and the performance of right, changes things and relations; it is essentially revolutionary, and does not consist wholly with anything which was. It not only divides States and churches, it divides families; ay, it divides the individual, separating the diabolical in him from the divine.

Unjust laws exist: shall we be content to obey them, or shall we endeavor to amend them, and obey them until we have succeeded, or shall we transgress them at once? Men generally, under such a government as this, think that they ought to wait

until they have persuaded the majority to alter them. They think that, if they should resist, the remedy would be worse than the evil. But it is the fault of the government itself that the remedy is worse than the evil. *It* makes it worse. Why is it not more apt to anticipate and provide for reform? Why does it not cherish its wise minority? Why does it cry and resist before it is hurt? Why does it not encourage its citizens to be on the alert to point out its faults, and do better than it would have them? Why does it always crucify Christ, and excommunicate Copernicus and Luther, and pronounce Washington and Franklin rebels?

One would think, that a deliberate and practical denial of its authority was the only offence never contemplated by government; else, why has it not assigned its definite, its suitable and proportionate, penalty? If a man who has no property refuses but once to earn nine shillings for the State, he is put in prison for a period unlimited by any law that I know, and determined only by the discretion of those who placed him there; but if he should steal ninety times nine shillings from the State, he is soon permitted to go at large again.

If the injustice is part of the necessary friction of the machine of government, let it go, let it go: perchance it will wear smooth, — certainly the machine will wear out. If the injustice has a spring, or a pulley, or a rope, or a crank, exclusively for itself, then perhaps you may consider whether the remedy will not be worse than the evil; but if it is of such a nature that it requires you to be the agent of injustice to another, then, I say, break the law. Let your life be a counter-friction to stop the machine. What I have to do is to see, at any rate, that I do not lend myself to the wrong which I condemn.

As for adopting the ways which the State has provided for remedying the evil, I know not of such ways. They take too much time, and a man's life will be gone. I have other affairs to attend to. I came into this world, not chiefly to make this a good place to live in, but to live in it, be it good or bad. A man has not everything to do, but something; and because he cannot do everything, it is not necessary that he should do something wrong. It is not my business to be petitioning the Governor or the Legislature any more than it is theirs to petition me; and if they should not hear my petition, what should I do then? But in this case the State has provided no way: its very Constitution is the evil. This may seem to be harsh and stubborn and unconciliatory; but it is to treat with the utmost kindness and consideration the only spirit that can appreciate or deserves it. So is all change for the better, like birth and death, which convulse the body.

I do not hesitate to say, that those who call themselves Abolitionists should at once effectually withdraw their support, both in person and property, from the government of Massachusetts, and not wait till they constitute a majority of one, before they suffer the right to prevail through them. I think that it is enough if they have God on their side, without waiting for that other one. Moreover, any man more right than his neighbors constitutes a majority of one already.

I meet this American government, or its representative, the State government, directly, and face to face, once a year — no more — in the person of its tax-gatherer; this is the only mode in which a man situated as I am necessarily meets it; and it then says distinctly, Recognize me; and the simplest, the most effectual, and, in the present posture of affairs, the indispensablest mode of treating with it on this head, of expressing your little satisfaction with and love for it, is to deny it then. My civil neighbor, the tax-gatherer, is the very man I have to deal with, — for it is, after all, with men and not with parchment that I quarrel, — and he has voluntarily chosen to be an agent of the government. How shall he ever know well what he is and does as an officer of the government, or as a man, until he is obliged to consider whether he shall treat me, his neighbor, for whom he has respect, as a neighbor and well-disposed man, or as a maniac and disturber of the peace, and see if he can get over this obstruction to his neighborliness without a ruder and more impetuous thought or speech corresponding with his action. I know this well, that if one thousand, if one hundred, if ten men whom I could name, — if ten honest men only, — ay, if *one* honest man, in this State of Massachusetts, ceasing to hold slaves, were actually to withdraw from this copartnership, and be locked up in the county jail therefor, it would be the

abolition of slavery in America. For it matters not how small the beginning may seem to be: what is once well done is done forever. But we love better to talk about it: that we say is our mission. Reform keeps many scores of newspapers in its service, but not one man. If my esteemed neighbor, the State's ambassador, who will devote his days to the settlement of the question of human rights in the Council Chamber, instead of being threatened with the prisons of Carolina, were to sit down the prisoner of Massachusetts, that State which is so anxious to foist the sin of slavery upon her sister, — though at present she can discover only an act of inhospitality to be the ground of a quarrel with her, — the legislature would not wholly waive the subject the following winter.

Under a government which imprisons any unjustly, the true place for a just man is also a prison. The proper place to-day, the only place which Massachusetts has provided for her freer and less desponding spirits, is in her prisons, to be put out and locked out of the State by her own act, as they have already put themselves out by their principles. It is there that the fugitive slave, and the Mexican prisoner on parole, and the Indian come to plead the wrongs of his race should find them; on that separate, but more free and honorable, ground, where the State places those who are not with her, but against her, — the only house in a slave State in which a free man can abide with honor. If any think that their influence would be lost there, and their voices no longer afflict the ear of the State, that they would not be as an enemy within its walls, they do not know by how much truth is stronger than error, nor how much more eloquently and effectively he can combat injustice who has experienced a little in his own person. Cast your whole vote, not a strip of paper merely, but your whole influence. A minority is powerless while it conforms to the majority; it is not even a minority then; but it is irresistible when it clogs by its whole weight. If the alternative is to keep all just men in prison, or give up war and slavery, the State will not hesitate which to choose. If a thousand men were not to pay their tax-bills this year, that would not be a violent and bloody measure, as it would be to pay them, and enable the State to commit violence and shed innocent blood. This is, in fact, the definition of a peaceable revolution, if any such is possible. If the tax-gatherer, or any other public officer, asks me, as one has done, "But what shall I do?" my answer is, "If you really wish to do anything, resign your office." When the subject has refused allegiance, and the officer has resigned his office, then the revolution is accomplished. But even suppose blood should flow. Is there not a sort of blood shed when the conscience is wounded? Through this wound a man's real manhood and immorality flow out, and he bleeds to an everlasting death. I see this blood flowing now. I have contemplated the imprisonment of the offender, rather than the seizure of his goods, — though both will serve the same purpose, — because they who assert the purest right, and consequently are most dangerous to a corrupt State, commonly have not spent much time in accumulating property. To such the State renders comparatively small service, and a slight tax is wont to appear exorbitant, particularly if they are obliged to earn it by special labor with their hands. If there were one who lived wholly without the use of money, the State itself would hesitate to demand it of him. But the rich man — not to make any invidious comparison — is always sold to the institution which makes him rich. Absolutely speaking, the more money, the less virtue; for money comes between a man and his objects, and obtains them for him; and it was certainly no great virtue to obtain it. It puts to rest many questions which he would otherwise be taxed to answer; while the only new question which it puts is the hard but superfluous one, how to spend it. Thus his moral ground is taken from under his feet. The opportunities of living are diminished in proportion as what are called the "means" are increased. The best thing a man can do for his culture when he is rich is to endeavor to carry out those schemes which he entertained when he was poor . . .

When I converse with the freest of my neighbors, I perceive that, whatever they may say about the magnitude and seriousness of the question, and their regard for the public tranquillity, the long and the short of the matter is, that they cannot spare the protection of the existing government, and they dread the consequences to their property and families of disobedience to it. For my own part, I should not like to think that I ever rely on the protection of the State. But, if I deny the authority of the State when it presents its taxbill, it will

soon take and waste all my property, and so harass me and my children without end. This is hard. This makes it impossible for a man to live honestly, and at the same time comfortably, in outward respects. It will not be worth the while to accumulate property; that would be sure to go again. You must hire or squat somewhere, and raise but a small crop, and eat that soon. You must live within yourself, and depend upon yourself always tucked up and ready for a start, and not have many affairs . . .

I have paid no poll-tax for six years. I was put into a jail once on this account, for one night; and, as I stood considering the walls of solid stone, two or three feet thick, the door of wood and iron, a foot thick, and the iron grating which strained the light, I could not help being struck with the foolishness of that institution which treated me as if I were mere flesh and blood and bones, to be locked up. I wondered that it should have concluded at length that this was the best use it could put me to, and had never thought to avail itself of my services in some way. I saw that, if there was a wall of stone between me and my townsmen, there was a still more difficult one to climb or break through before they could get to be as free as I was. I did not for a moment feel confined, and the walls seemed a great waste of stone and mortar. I felt as if I alone of all my townsmen had paid my tax. They plainly did not know how to treat me, but behaved like persons who are under-bred. In every threat and in every compliment there was a blunder; for they thought that my chief desire was to stand the other side of that stone wall. I could not but smile to see how industriously they locked the door on my meditations, which followed them out again without let or hindrance, and they were really all that was dangerous. As they could not reach me, they had resolved to punish my body; just as boys, if they cannot come at some person against whom they have a spite, will abuse his dog. I saw that the State was half-witted, that it was timid as a lone woman with her silver spoons, and that it did not know its friends from its foes, and I lost all my remaining respect for it, and pitied it.

Thus the State never intentionally confronts a man's sense, intellectual or moral, but only his body, his senses. It is not armed with superior wit or honesty, but with superior physical strength. I was not born to be forced. I will breathe after my own fashion. Let us see who is the strongest. What force has a multitude? They only can force me who obey a higher law than I. They force me to become like themselves. I do not hear of *men* being forced to live this way or that by masses of men. What sort of life were that to live? When I meet a government which says to me, "Your money or your life," why should I be in haste to give it my money? It may be in a great strait, and not know what to do: I cannot help that. It must help itself; do as I do. It is not worth the while to snivel about it. I am not responsible for the successful working of the machinery of society. I am not the son of the engineer. I perceive that, when an acorn and a chestnut fall side by side, the one does not remain inert to make way for the other, but both obey their own laws, and spring and grow and flourish as best they can, till one, perchance, over-shadows and destroys the other. If a plant cannot live according to its nature, it dies; and so a man.

The night in prison was novel and interesting enough. The prisoners in their shirt-sleeves were en-joying a chat and the evening air in the doorway, when I entered. But the jailer said, "Come, boys, it is time to lock up;" and so they dispersed, and I heard the sound of their steps returning into the hollow apart-ments. My roommate was introduced to me by the jailer as "a first-rate fellow and clever man." When the door was locked, he showed me where to hang my hat, and how he managed matters there. The rooms were whitewashed once a month; and this one, at least, was the whitest, most simply furnished, and probably the neatest apartment in the town. He naturally wanted to know where I came from, and what brought me there; and, when I had told him, I asked him in my turn how he came there, presuming him to be an honest man, of course; and, as the world goes, I believe he was. "Why," said he, "they accuse me of burning a barn; but I never did it." As near as I could discover, he had probable gone to bed in a barn when drunk, and smoked his pipe there; and so a barn was burnt. He had the reputation of being a clever man, had been there some three months waiting for his trial to come on, and would have to wait as much longer; but he was quite domesticated and contented, since he got his board for nothing, and thought that he was well treated.

He occupied one window, and I the other; and I saw that if one stayed there long, his principal business would be to look out the window. I had soon read all the tracts that were left there, and examined where former prisoners had broken out, and where a grate had been sawed off, and heard the history of the various occupants of that room; for I found that even here there was a history and a gossip which never circulated beyond the walls of the jail. Probably this is the only house in the town where verses are composed, which are afterward printed in a circular form, but not published. I was shown quite a long list of verses which were composed by some young men who had been detected in an attempt to escape, who avenged themselves by singing them.

I pumped my fellow-prisoner as dry as I could, for fear I should never see him again; but at length he showed me which was my bed, and left me to blow out the lamp.

It was like traveling into a far country, such as I had never expected to behold, to lie there for one night. It seemed to me that I never had heard the town clock strike before, nor the evening sounds of the village; for we slept with the windows open, which were inside the grating. It was to see my native village in the light of the Middle Ages, and our Concord was turned into a Rhine stream, and visions of knights and castles passed before me. They were the voices of old burghers that I heard in the streets. I was an in-voluntary spectator and auditor of whatever was done and said in the kitchen of the adjacent village inn, — a wholly new and rare experience to me. It was a closer view of my native town. I was fairly inside of it. I never had seen its institutions before. This is one of its peculiar institutions; for it is a shire town. I began to comprehend what its inhabitants were about.

In the morning, our breakfasts were put through the hole in the door, in small oblong-square tin pans, made to fit, and holding a pint of chocolate, with brown bread, and an iron spoon. When they called for the vessels again, I was green enough to return what bread I had left; but my comrade seized it, and said that I should lay that up for lunch or dinner.

Soon after he was let out to work at haying in a neighboring field, whither he went every day, and would
not be back till noon; so he bade me good-day, saying
that he doubted if he should see me again.

When I came out of prison, — for some one interfered, and paid that tax, — I did not perceive that
great changes had taken place on the common, such
as he observed who went in a youth and emerged a
tottering and gray-headed man; and yet a change had
to my eyes come over the scene, — the town, and
State, and country, — greater than any that mere time
could effect. I saw yet more distinctly the State in
which I lived. I saw to what extent the people among
whom I lived could be trusted as good neighbors and
friends; that their friendship was for summer weather
only; that they did not greatly propose to do right;
that they were a distinct race from me by their prejudices and superstitions, as the Chinamen and Malays
are; that in their sacrifices to humanity they ran no
risks, not even to their property; that after all they
were not so noble but they treated the thief as he had
treated them, and hoped, by a certain outward observance and a few prayers, and by walking in a particular straight though useless path from time to time,
to save their souls. This may be to judge my neighbors
harshly; for I believe that many of them are not aware
that they have such an institution as the jail in their
village.

It was formerly the custom in our village, when
a poor debtor came out of jail, for his acquaintances
to salute him, looking through their fingers, which
were crossed to represent the grating of a jail window,
"How do ye do?" My neighbors did not thus salute
me, but first looked at me, and then at one another,
as if I had returned from a long journey. I was put
into jail as I was going to the shoemaker's to get a
shoe which was mended. When I was let out the next
morning, I proceeded to finish my errand, and, having
put on my mended shoe, joined a huckleberry party,
who were impatient to put themselves under my conduct; and in half an hour, — for the horse was soon
tackled, — was in the midst of a huckleberry field, on
one of our highest hills, two miles off, and then the
State was nowhere to be seen.

This is the whole history of "My Prisons."

I have never declined paying the highway tax, because I am as desirous of being a good neighbor as I am
of being a bad subject; and as for supporting schools, I
am doing my part to educate my fellow-countrymen
now. It is for no particular item in the tax-bill that I
refuse to pay it. I simply wish to refuse allegiance to
the State, to withdraw and stand aloof from it effectually. I do not care to trace the course of my dollar,
if I could, till it buys a man or a musket to shoot one
with, — the dollar is innocent, — but I am concerned to
trace the effects of my allegiance. In fact, I quietly
declare war with the State, after my fashion, though I
will still make what use and get what advantage of her
I can, as is usual in such cases.

If others pay the tax which is demanded of me,
from a sympathy with the state, they do but what
they have already done in their own case, or rather
they abet injustice to a greater extent than the State
requires. If they pay the tax from a mistaken interest
in the individual taxed, to save his property, or prevent
his going to jail, it is because they have not considered
wisely how far they let their private feelings interfere
with the public good.

This, then, is my position at present. But one
cannot be too much on his guard in such a case, lest
his action be biased by obstinacy or an undue regard
for the opinions of men. Let him see that he does
only what belongs to himself and to the hour.

I think sometimes, Why, this people mean well,
they are only ignorant; they would do better if they
knew how: why give your neighbors this pain to treat
you as they are not inclined to? But I think again,
This is no reason why I should do as they do, or permit
others to suffer much greater pain of a different kind.
Again, I sometimes say to myself, When many millions
of men, without heat, without ill will, without personal feeling of any kind, demand of you a few
shillings only, without the possibility, such is their
constitution, of retracting or altering their present
demand, and without the possibility, on your side,
of appeal to any other millions, why expose yourself to this overwhelming brute force? You do not
resist cold and hunger, the winds and the waves,
thus obstinately; you quietly submit to a thousand
similar necessities. You do not put your head into
the fire. But just in proportion as I regard this as
not wholly a brute force, but partly a human force,

and consider that I have relations to those millions as to so many millions of men, and not of mere brute or inanimate things, I see that appeal is possible, first and instantaneously, from them to the Maker of them, and, secondly, from them to themselves. But if I put my head deliberately into the fire, there is no appeal to fire or to the Maker of fire, and I have only myself to blame. If I could convince myself that I have any right to be satisfied with men as they are, and to treat them accordingly, and not according, in some respects, to my requisitions and expectations of what they and I ought to be, then, like a good Mussulman and fatalist, I should endeavor to be satisfied with things as they are, and say it is the will of God. And, above all, there is this difference between resisting this and a purely brute or natural force, that I can resist this with some effect; but I cannot expect, like Orpheus, to change the nature of the rocks and trees and beasts.

I do not wish to quarrel with any man or nation. I do not wish to split hairs, to make fine distinctions, or set myself up as better than my neighbors. I seek rather, I may say, even an excuse for conforming to the laws of the land. I am but too ready to conform to them. Indeed, I have reason to suspect myself on this head; and each year, as the tax-gatherer comes round, I find myself disposed to review the acts and position of the general and State governments, and the spirit of the people, to discover a pretext for conformity ... I believe that the State will soon be able to take all my work of this sort out of my hands, and then I shall be no better a patriot than my fellow-countrymen. Seen from a lower point of view, the Constitution, with all its faults, is very good; the law and the courts are very respectable; even this State and this American government are, in many respects, very admirable, and rare things, to be thankful for, such as a great many have described them; but seen from a point of view a little higher, they are what I have described them; seen from a higher still, and the highest, who shall say what they are, or that they are worth looking at or thinking of at all?

However, the government does not concern me much, and I shall bestow the fewest possible thoughts on it. It is not many moments that I live under a government, even in this world. If a man is thought-free,

fancy-free, imagination-free, that which *is not* never for a long time appearing *to be* to him, unwise rulers or reformers cannot fatally interrupt him.

I know that most men think differently from myself; but those whose lives are by profession devoted to the study of these or kindred subjects content me as little as any. Statesmen and legislators, standing so completely within the institution, never distinctly and nakedly behold it. They speak of moving society, but have no resting-place without it. They may be men of a certain experience and discrimination, and have no doubt invented ingenious and even useful systems, for which we sincerely thank them; but all their wit and usefulness lie within certain not very wide limits. They are wont to forget that the world is not governed by policy and expediency ... The lawyer's truth is not Truth, but consistency or a consistent expediency. Truth is always in harmony with herself, and is not concerned chiefly to reveal the justice that may consist with wrong-doing ...

They who know of no purer sources of truth, who have traced up its stream no higher, stand, and wisely stand, by the Bible and the Constitution, and drink at it there with reverence and humility; but they who behold where it comes trickling into this lake or that pool, gird up their loins once more, and continue their pilgrimage toward its fountain-head.

No man with a genius for legislation has appeared in America. They are rare in the history of the world. There are orators, politicians, and eloquent men, by the thousand; but the speaker has not yet opened his mouth to speak who is capable of settling the much-vexed questions of the day. We love eloquence for its own sake, and not for any truth which it may utter, or any heroism it may inspire. Our legislators have not yet learned the comparative value of free trade and of freedom, of union, and of rectitude, to a nation. They have no genius or talent for comparatively humble questions of taxation and finance, commerce and manufactures and agriculture. If we were left solely to the wordy wit of legislators in Congress for our guidance, uncorrected by the seasonable experience and the effectual complaints of the people, America would not long retain her rank among the nations. For eighteen hundred years, though perchance I have no right to say it, the New Testament has been written; yet where is the legislator who has wisdom and practical talent enough to avail himself of the light which it sheds on the science of legislation?

The authority of government, even such as I am willing to submit to, — for I will cheerfully obey those who know and can do better than I, and in many things even those who neither know nor can do so well, — is still an impure one: to be strictly just, it must have the sanction and consent of the governed. It can have no pure right over my person and property but what I concede to it. The progress from an absolute to a limited monarchy, from a limited monarchy to a democracy, is a progress toward a true respect for the individual. Even the Chinese philosopher was wise enough to regard the individual as the basis of the empire. Is a democracy, such as we know it, the last improvement possible in government? Is it not possible to take a step further towards recognizing and organizing the rights of man? There will never be a really free and enlightened State until the State comes to recognize the individual as a higher and independent power, from which all its own power and authority are derived, and treats him accordingly. I please myself with imagining a State at last which can afford to be just to all men, and to treat the individual with respect as a neighbor; which even would not think it inconsistent with its own repose if a few were to live aloof from it, not meddling with it, nor embraced by it, who fulfilled all the duties of neighbors and fellowmen. A State which bore this kind of fruit, and suffered it to drop off as fast as it ripened, would prepare the way for a still more perfect and glorious State, which also I have imagined, but not yet anywhere seen.

SUGGESTIONS FOR FURTHER READING

Ray A. Billington, *The Protestant Crusade*, Quadrangle, Chicago, 1964.

Jesse T. Carpenter, *The South as a Conscious Minority, 1789-1861*, Peter Smith, Magnolia, Massachusetts, 1930.

Merle Curti, *The American Peace Crusade*, Duke University Press, Durham, N. C., 1929.

David Brion Davis, "Some Themes of Counter Subversion: An Analysis of Anti-Masonic, Anti-Catholic, and Anti-Mormon Literature," *Mississippi Valley Historical Review* (1960).

Martin Duberman, ed., *The Anti-Slavery Vanguard*, Princeton University Press, Princeton, 1965.

Clement Eaton, *The Freedom of Thought Struggle in the Old South*, Harper, New York 1964.

Marcus Lee Hansen, *The Atlantic Migration*, Peter Smith, Magnolia, Massachusetts, 1941.

Martin E. Marty, *Righteous Empire*, Dial Press, New York, 1970.

Russel B. Nye, "The Search for the Individual: 1750-1850," *The Centennial Review*, 5 (1961).

Julius W. Pratt, "The Ideology of American Expansion," in Avery Craven (ed.), *Essays in Honor of William E. Dodd*, 1935.

Timothy Smith, *Revivalism and Social Reform in Mid-Nineteenth Century America*, Abingdon Press, New York, 1957.

Alice Felt Tyler, *Freedom's Ferment*, Harper, New York, 1944.

Albert K. Weinberg, *Manifest Destiny*, Quadrangle, Chicago, 1963.

THE AMERICAN EXPERIENCE AND THE CIVIL WAR

Chapter 9   1850-1861

From 1850 until the outbreak of the Civil War the American people, relying upon familiar assumptions about the citizen and society, struggled to resolve the issues that divided them. In the process they brought out into the open tensions which had existed from the beginning of the American experience. The liberal commitment to limited government and maximum individual freedom, the federal balance between state power and national union, the boundless optimism floating on a broad material base, the faith that America stood for high moral purpose — all came under increasing pressure in the years leading up to the Civil War. On a less exalted plane, competitive economic interests, sectional rivalries, and contending definitions of American nationalism cried out for an authority competent to decide among them. It was just this kind of an overarching authority, however, which had been rejected. Americans were truly at a crossroads at midcentury. Could they continue to allow the South to strengthen its sectional position and hope to create a strong nation? Could they leave individualism unchecked and preserve even the semblance of a society of ordered freedom and justice for all? Could they indulge their dreams of high moral purpose and keep a fifth of the population enslaved? Could they find a means to resolve these problems and keep intact their faith in natural laws which automatically harmonized the activities of free individuals?

413

At the center of the crisis of the 1850's was slavery, but the precipitating cause was the necessity to decide when and upon what terms the territories acquired through the Mexican War were to be integrated into the Union. Such decisions had become increasingly difficult to make. Each time Congress had to legislate on the formation of territories and the admission of new states, fundamental issues were unavoidably raised. The nature of the federal compact and the powers of Congress were subjected to a new scrutiny. Establishing territorial units meant planning the future of new states and arousing the expectations and fears of the entire nation. Particularly was this the case in legislating on slavery in the new territories. Most Northerners were willing to concede that the South had inherited the problem of slavery and that no easy solutions for its elimination existed, but new additions to the national domain were free of such an ugly encumbrance and might through legislation be made permanently so. The question of slavery and the territorial acquisitions of the war was raised first in 1846 when Congressman David Wilmot proposed an amendment to a military appropriations bill to bar slavery from any land which might be acquired from Mexico. Antislavery Northerners, already suspicious of the South's enthusiastic support of the war, made the Wilmot Proviso a vehicle for their protests, adding it to congressional bills whenever possible. In this they had the support of the antislavery farmers of the West. Most of these Westerners had little sympathy for black people, but they hated and feared the spread of slavery and made "free soil" the rallying cry for all who looked to the expansion of self-supporting white families across the western plains. For the South, Wilmot's Proviso was evidence of what they had long feared, that West and North would join forces and use their numerical strength in Congress to raise permanent obstructions to Southern interests.

The Treaty of Guadaloupe–Hildago had added a vast domain to the United States, including California with a population large enough for immediate admission to the union. The ensuing congressional controversy over slavery and the new territories dominated all other national concerns and revealed just how much public opinion had changed since the Missouri Compromise of 1820.

After four years of furious debate, a series of measures were passed which broke the Congressional impasse. A compromise in name only, the laws of 1850 led to more bitterness. Both sides considered their concessions greater than their gains. California was admitted to the union as a free state, but the rest of the new territory was organized without any exclusion of slavery. The detested domestic slave trade was abolished in the District of Columbia, but in return for this concession to antislavery sentiment, the South was given a rigorous new fugitive slave law which enabled slaveholders to reclaim black men alleged to be runaway slaves through federal commissioners. Without trials, jury decisions, or the testimony of the accused runaways, men and women were sent back to servitude in the South in what seemed like a flagrant rejection of the most elemental principles of justice.

Probably no other piece of legislation stirred up so much antagonism to the South. In New England mobs forced federal officers to free recaptured slaves, and in one instance a New York Grand Jury actually indicted a federal marshal with kidnapping! Because the fugitive slave law had been duly passed by the United States Congress, it posed again the conflict between conscience and law. Many previously indifferent Northerners became receptive to antislavery literature, while the abolitionists themselves boldly disavowed congress and the Constitution. Even though they failed to infect the majority of Northerners with their sympathy for the black man, the abolitionists were able to convince most people of the absolute necessity of fixing on the means for the eventual extinction of slavery.

After 1854, the spread of slavery became the crux of the issue. Northerners were willing to let the South solve its own problems as long as slavery was not introduced into the territories. For the South such a concession was unthinkable, for it amounted to an acquiescence in the Northern condemnation of Southern institutions. Compromise might have resolved the conflict during the 1850's had the public debates not taken on an increasingly moral tone. Political leaders found it difficult to discuss slavery in terms of pragmatic adjustment and practical accommodations, for people began to feel uncomfortable mingling appeals to expediency with denunciations of injustice. This was no less true in the South than outside it. For both Northerners and Southerners, the questions involved were fundamental, moral, and virtually irreconcilable.

A crucial development in the estrangement of North and South was the emergence of the Republican party, which put up its first presidential candidate in 1856. All of the enemies of the South poured into this new party — the Western farmers who were determined to exclude slavery from the new territories, the Northern capitalists who wanted legislation to stimulate American growth, those abolitionists who looked to the federal government to check the power of the slavocracy, and the anti-immigrant nativists who put their faith in a strong nationalistic spirit. The Republican party gave political muscle to the opponents of the South, and having no representation in the South had nothing to lose from opposing Southern interests. The Democratic party struggled on as a national party, trying desperately to neutralize the slave issue, but Democratic leaders also found themselves swimming against a new and powerful tide of nationalism which found political expression in programs for strengthening the powers of the federal government.

The Southern campaign to check the growth of national government had found a supporting echo in the rest of the country in the 1830's, when Jackson blocked the renewal of the bank and vetoed a succession of bills for federal building projects. After 1840 the South's interest in limiting federal power remained the same, while outside the South, changing conditions predisposed an increasing number of voters to favor the kinds of programs that Jackson had attacked. Earlier, Americans had been able to do almost everything they wanted to do themselves or through their state governments, but as the American economy became more integrated, federal government action was not so easily dispensed with. Forces were at work making Americans more

national in their thinking and more willing to expand the powers of the federal government. By mid-19th century, America's economy of many individualistic producers and merchants was giving way to more complex commercial and industrial enterprises. Economic progress could be promoted through tariff protection of home industries, through fiscal policies and federal aid to railroad builders. The internal market in which Americans bought and sold farm and factory products was becoming more important than foreign trade. Northern industrialists and Western farmers needed the powers and the purse of government to stimulate and facilitate economic growth. Not since Alexander Hamilton introduced his programs had there been so much interest in the contributions of government as there was in the 1850's. With California now in the union, ambitious plans were developed for a transcontinental railroad. State boundaries, particularly for those states without colonial histories, were becoming far less important than the common identity as citizens of a United States which stretched from the Atlantic to the Pacific. The self-conscious sectional pride of the South was at odds with the yearning for national unity now beginning to stir in Westerners and Northerners. Americans outside the South moved tentatively towards political and economic centralization, but Southerners claimed a local autonomy as strong as that of the pre-Constitution period.

Northerners and Southerners entrenched themselves behind unassailable positions. While racial prejudice knew no Mason-Dixon line, people in the North became convinced that slavery was a national curse and must end. Southerners dependent upon a slave economy and unwilling to concede the immorality of an institution which formed the very backbone of their society were equally determined to force other Americans to admit that there was nothing in law, morality, or the U. S. Constitution which forbade their use of slaves. The liberal philosophy which vested the free individual with society's only moral authority was silent about moral conflicts between individuals or groups of individuals, and the natural laws which were supposed to harmonize the random and private activities of millions of individual members of society had ceased to operate. The political art of persuasion and compromise which Americans had developed to near perfection failed when a new political party emerged with no necessity to placate the South. There was still the law, but increasingly Americans appealed to two different legal authorities — the South to the Constitution with its protection of local state laws, and the North to the majority with its fundamental right to sovereign power in a popular government. Minorities, it was true, were guaranteed certain inalienable rights according to American political philosophy, but who was to decide whether the enslaving of a human being defined by state law as property constituted an inalienable right? When the Republican party succeeded in electing its first president, Abraham Lincoln, the alternatives had narrowed considerably. They consisted of the South's right to secede or to submit to a hostile national government, and the North's right to use force to maintain the union or to acquiesce in Southern secession. Lincoln would not allow the peaceful dissolution of the union, and the Civil War began.

Beneath the terrible years of bloodshed, destruction, and civil discord there remained fundamental questions about the American experience. Could the Constitution be so construed as to prevent the majority from legislating in areas of vital concern to them? Was the United States to be a great national republic or a loosely confederated group of distinctive states? And at a more profound level, do people free from authoritarian institutions possess sufficient virtue and wisdom to govern themselves justly? American culture was built upon the conviction that they did, but the Civil War resolved only the first two questions. By force of arms the Northern interpretation of the Constitution was preserved, and the majority's right to decide for the whole nation was won on the battlefield. Henceforth, the balance between state and federal power would be tipped decisively in favor of the national government. The other question — the liberal faith in popular government — is still being asked and still being tested. Because it is a profound question about man and society

it brings American culture in touch with the eternal concerns of human history, a truth which Lincoln expressed in the Gettysburg Address:

> It is for us the living, rather, to be dedicated here to the unfinished work which they who fought here have thus far so nobly advanced . . . that this nation, under God, shall have a new birth of freedom — and that government of the people, by the people, for the people, shall not perish from the earth.

Public attitudes had changed decisively since 1820, when the Missouri Compromise was passed. When Congress began discussing the question of slavery and the Mexican territories in 1846, a significant number of Northerners condemned any congressional acquiescence in the spread of slavery. The abolitionists had succeeded in quickening the conscience of many, and important interest groups — Northern industrialists and Western free soil farmers — felt threatened by the power of the great cotton magnates. The typical American citizen was completely out of touch with Southern sentiments. David Wilmot's campaign to keep slavery out of all the new territory appealed to these groups which were willing to let slavery slowly wither away in the South, but were determined to stop its spread. The defeat of Wilmot's Proviso came at the hands of Congress itself, the representatives and senators who felt the urgency for some accommodation of both the Northern and the Southern positions. They were able to patch together a compromise in 1850, but the compromisers themselves were reviled for their efforts. The abolitionists and intellectuals of New England felt that they had been betrayed by Massachusetts' great senator, Daniel Webster — who unleashed all his forensic skill to get the new fugitive slave law passed — while Kentucky's senator, Henry Clay, the architect of the compromise, was denounced throughout the South for his concessions to antislavery sentiment.

War was averted, but not continued conflict over slavery. Suspicions of Southern intentions spread among moderate Northerners, and talk of secession was tolerated openly in the South. Up until the Mexican territory debates, the South had been far from solid in its political loyalties. Both the Whig and the Democratic parties were well represented in the South, but every agitation of the slavery question weakened the ties between Northern and Southern Whigs, Northern and Southern Democrats. The idea of a Southern party uniting all the defenders of Southern institutions gained ground when Southern leaders of the national parties failed to hold their Northern colleagues to a hands-off position on Southern interests.

The readings in this section detail the opposing positions. David Wilmot (1814–1868), the Pennsylvania Democrat who started the furor, explains his amendment for restricting slavery in a speech before the House of Representatives, while the Southern position is set forth by the future president of the Confederacy, Jefferson Davis (1808–1889), during the senate debates over the Compromise of 1850. The final selection is from Charles Francis Adams (1807–1886), son and grandson of the Adams presidents and himself a distinguished diplomat. In naming his speech "What Makes Slavery a Question of National Concern?" Adams struck a theme which sound and sober Northerners could no longer avoid.

David Wilmot: Speech on the amendment restricting slavery (1847)

Mr. Wilmot . . . What do we ask? We demand justice and right. If this were a question of compromise, I would yield much. Were it a question of this character I would go as far as any man. But it is no question for compromise or concession. It is a question of naked and abstract right; and, in the language of my colleague from the Erie district, (Mr. Thompson,) sooner shall this right shoulder be drawn from its socket, than I will yield one jot or tittle of the ground upon which I stand. No concession, sir, no compromise. What, I repeat, do we ask? That free territory shall remain free. We demand the neutrality of this Government upon the question of slavery. Is there any complexion of Abolitionism in this, sir? I have stood up at home, and battled, time and again, against the Abolitionists of the North. I have assailed them publicly, upon all occasions, when it was proper to do so. I have met them in their own meetings, and face to face combatted them. Any efforts, sir, that may be made, here or elsewhere, to give an abolition character to this movement, cannot, so far as my district

Speech of Mr. Wilmot of Pennsylvania, on his amendment restricting slavery from territory hereafter acquired, delivered in the House of Representatives of the United States, February 8, 1847, Washington, 1847, pp. 2–5.

and my people are concerned, have the least effect. Any efforts made to give to me the character of an Abolitionist, will fall harmless when they reach my constituents. They know me upon this question. They know me distinctly upon all questions of public interest. My opinions have ever been proclaimed without reserve, and adhered to without change, or the shadow of turning. I stand by the Constitution upon this question. I adhere to its letter and its spirit. I would never invade one single right of the South. So far from it, I stand ready at all times and upon all occasions, as do nearly the entire North, to sustain the institutions of the South as they exist. When the day of trial comes, as many, many southern men fear it may come, we stand ready, with our money and our blood, to rush to the rescue. When that day comes, sir, the North will stand shoulder to shoulder with their brethren of the South. We stand by the Constitution and all its compromises.

But, sir, the issue now presented is not, whether slavery shall exist unmolested where it now is, but whether it shall be carried to new and distant regions, now free, where the foot-print of a slave cannot be found. This, sir, is the issue. Upon it I take my stand, and from it I cannot be frightened or driven by idle charges of Abolitionism. I ask not that slavery be abolished. I demand that this Government preserve the integrity of *free* territory against the aggressions of slavery — against its wrongful usurpations. Sir, I was in favor of the annexation of Texas. I supported it with my whole influence and strength. I was willing to take Texas as she was. I sought not to change the character of her institutions. Slavery existed in Texas — planted there, it is true, in defiance of law; still it existed. It gave character to the country. True, it was held out to the North, that at least two of the five States to be formed out of Texas would be free. Yet, sir, the whole of Texas has been given up to slavery. The Democracy of the North, almost to a man, went for annexation. Yes, sir, here was an Empire larger than France given up to slavery. Shall farther concessions be made by the North? Shall we give up free territory, the inheritance of free labor? Must we yield this also? Never, sir, never, until we ourselves are fit to be slaves . . .

But, sir, we are told, that the joint blood and treasure of the whole country being expended in this acqui-

sition, therefore it should be divided, and slavery allowed to take its share. Sir, the South has her share already — the instalment for slavery was paid in advance. We are fighting this war for Texas and for the South. I affirm it — every intelligent man knows it — Texas is the primary cause of this war. For this, sir, northern treasure is being exhausted, and northern blood poured out upon the plains of Mexico. We are fighting this war cheerfully, not reluctantly — cheerfully fighting this war for Texas; and yet we seek not to change the character of her institutions. Slavery is there, there let it remain. Sir, the whole history of this question, is a history of concessions on the part of the North. The money of the North was expended in the purchase of Louisiana, two-thirds of which was given up to slavery. Again, in the purchase of Florida, did slavery gain new acquisitions. Slavery acquired an Empire in the annexation of Texas. Three slave States have been admitted out of the Louisiana purchase. The slave State of Florida has been received into the Union . . . Now, sir, we are told that California is ours — that New Mexico is ours — won by the valor of our arms. They are free. Shall they remain free? Shall these fair provinces be the inheritance and homes of the white labor of freemen, or the black labor of slaves? This, sir, is the issue — this the question . . . All we ask is, that their character be preserved. They are now free. It is a general principle of the law of Nations, that in conquered or acquired territories, all laws therein existing, not inconsistent with its new allegiance, shall remain in force until altered or repealed. This law prohibits slavery in California, and in New Mexico. But the South contend, that in their emigration to this free territory they have the right to take and hold slaves, the same as other property. Unless the Amendment I have offered be adopted, or other early legislation is had upon this subject, they will do so. Indeed they, unitedly, as one man, have declared their right and purpose so to do, and the work has already begun. Slavery follows in the rear of our armies. Shall the war power of our Government be exerted to produce such a result? Shall this government depart from its neutrality on this question, and lend its power and influence to plant slavery in these territories? There is no question of abolition here, sir. Shall the South be permitted, by aggression, by invasion of the right, by subduing free territory and planting slavery upon it, to wrest these provinces from northern free-men, and turn them to the accomplishment of their own sectional purposes and schemes? This is the question. Men of the North answer. Shall it be so? Shall we of the North submit to it? If we do, we are coward slaves, and deserve to have the manacles fastened upon our own limbs.

Sir, it has been objected to this measure that it was brought forward at an untimely period. An attempt has been made to cast both ridicule and reproach upon it. It is said that we are already quarrelling about territory which does not belong to us; that it will be in time to agitate this question when the country shall be acquired. Sir, I affirm that now is the time, and the only time. To hesitate at such a crisis is to surrender the whole ground; to falter is to betray . . .

Already, sir, on the route of travel between Missouri and New Mexico slaves are found, who are being removed thither. Slavery is there, sir — there, in defiance of law. Slavery does not wait for all the forms of annexation to be consummated. It is on the move, sir. It is in New Mexico. It is in Oregon. Yes, sir, it is in Oregon; and this day, in that distant territory of the Union, does the lash of the Missouri master drive his negro slaves to the field of labor. We passed but a few days ago through this House a Bill for the establishment of a territorial government in Oregon, in which we excluded slavery from that territory. The slavery restriction has been struck out from that Bill by the Senate committee, a majority of whom are southern men, and a clause inserted establishing slavery. Yet, sir, in the face of all of these facts, we are told that our action is premature, untimely. "Wait," says my colleague, (Mr. McClean,) "until we get the skin of the lion, before we dispute about his hide." Sir, we have the skin, and slavery is already grappling for it. I invoke my colleague to the rescue. I repeat it, sir, now is the time, and the only time. Southern men declare that they desire this question settled now. Neither party should be deceived. The North ought not to be betrayed under the idea held out, that slavery cannot, or will not, exist there. Let not the South be deceived. Let no prospect be held out to her that this war is to result in strengthening and extending this institution. Now, sir, is the time, and the honest time, to meet this question . . .

Jefferson Davis: Senate speech on slavery in the Territories (1850)

. . . A large part of the non-slaveholding States have declared war against the institution of slavery. They have announced that it shall not be extended, and with that annunciation have coupled the declaration that it is a stain upon the Republic–that it is a moral blot which should be obliterated. Now, sir, can any one believe, does any one hope, that the southern States in this Confederacy will continue, as in times gone by, to support the Union, to bear its burdens, in peace and in war, in a degree disproportioned to their numbers, if that very Government is to be arrayed in hostility against an institution so interwoven with its interests, its domestic peace, and all its social relations, that it cannot be disturbed without causing their overthrow? This Government is the agent of all of the States; can it be expected of any of them that they will consent to be bound by its acts, when that agent announces the settled purpose in the exercise of its power to overthrow that which it was its duty to uphold? That obligation ceases whenever such a construction shall be placed upon its power by the Federal Government. The essential purpose for which the grant was made being disregarded, the means given for defence being perverted to assault, State allegiance thenceforward resumes its right to demand the service, the whole service, of all its citizens.

The claim is set up for the Federal Government not only to restrict slavery from entering the Territories, but to abolish slavery in the District of Columbia, to abolish it in the arsenals and dockyards, to withdraw from it the protection of the American flag wherever it is found upon the high seas; in fact, to strip it of every protection it derives from Government. All this under the pretext that property in slaves is local in its nature, and derives its existence from municipal law. Slavery existed before the formation of this Union. It derived from the Constitution that recognition which it would not have enjoyed without the confederation. If the

Dunbar Rowland (ed.), *Jefferson Davis, Constitutionalist: His Letters, Papers and Speeches,* printed for the Mississippi State Department of Archives and History, Jackson, Mississippi, 1923, I, 266–69, 296–98. Used by permission of the Department.

States had not united together, there would have been no obligation on adjoining States to regard any species of property unknown to themselves. But it was one of the compromises of the Constitution that the slave property in the southern States should be recognized as property throughout the United States. It was so recognized in the obligation to restore fugitives – recognized in the power to tax them as persons – recognized in their representation in the halls of Congress. As a property recognized by the Constitution, and held in a portion of the States, the Federal Government is bound to admit it into all the Territories, and to give it such protection as other private property receives . . .

It becomes us, it becomes you – all who seek to preserve this Union, and to render it perpetual – to ask, why is this power claimed? Why is its exercise sought? Why is this resolution to obstruct the extension of slavery into the Territories introduced? It must be for the purpose of political power; it can have no other rational object. Every one must understand that, whatever be the evil of slavery, it is not increased by its diffusion. Every one familiar with it knows that it is in proportion to its sparseness that it becomes less objectionable. Wherever there is an immediate connection between the master and slave, whatever there is of harshness in the system is diminished. Then it preserves the domestic character, and strictly patriarchal relation. It is only when the slaves are assembled in large numbers, on plantations, and are removed from the interested, the kind, the affectionate care of the master, that it ever can partake of that cruelty which is made the great charge against it by those who know nothing of it, and which, I will passingly say, probably exists to a smaller extent than in any other relation of labor to capital. It is, then, for the purpose of political power; and can those who, in violation of constitutional rights, seek and acquire political power, which, in progress of time, will give them the ability to change the Constitution of the United States, be supposed just then to be seized with a feeling of magnanimity and justice, which will prevent them from using the power which they thus corruptly sought and obtained? . . .

I believe, Mr. President, it is essential that neither section should have such power in Congress as would render them able to trample upon the rights of the other section of this Union. It would be a blessing, an essential means to preserve the Confederacy, that in one branch of Congress the North and in the other the South should have a majority of representation. Ours is but a limited agency. We have but few powers, and those are of a general nature; and, if legislation was restricted and balanced in the mode I have suggested, Congress would never be able to encroach upon their rights and institutions of any portion of the Union, nor could its acts ever meet with resistance from any part of it. The reverse being the case, who knows how soon the time may come when men will rise in arms to oppose the laws of Congress? Whenever you take from the people of this country the confidence that this is their Government, that it reflects their will, that it looks to their interests, the foundation upon which it was laid is destroyed, and the fabric falls to the ground. More emphatically in this than in any other – though it was said by the great Emperor of Europe to be true of all – does this Government depend upon the consent of the people . . .

I claim, sir, that slavery being property in the United States, and so recognized by the Constitution, a slaveholder has the right to go with that property into any part of the United States where some sovereign power has not forbidden it. I deny sir, that this Government has the sovereign power to prohibit it from the Territories. I deny that any territorial community, being a dependence of the United States, has that power, or can prohibit it, and therefore my claim presented is this, that the slaveholder has a right to go with his slave into any portion of these United States, except in a State where the fundamental law has forbidden it. I know, sir, that the popular doctrine obtains, that every community has that power; and I was sorry to hear the Senator from Kentucky, in some portion of his speech, assent to it, though in others he did oppose it. Who constitute the communities which are to exercise sovereign rights over the Territories? Those who, in the race for newly-acquired regions, may first get there. By what right sir, do they claim to exercise it? The Territories belong to the United States, and by the States only can sovereignty be alienated. . . . The General Government has, as agent, to dispose of the public lands, the power necessary to execute that trust. How far this extends it may not be very easy by fixed standard to determine, but it is easy to perceive that this cannot give sovereignty, or any other than the subordinate functions of government. . .

Mr. President, in all the controversy which has arisen about the validity and extent of the Mexican law, no species of property has ever been denied the right to enter the territory we have acquired, except slaves. Why is this? What is there in the character of that property which excludes it from the general benefit of the principles applied to all other property? It is true that gentlemen have asserted that this is local, and depends upon the laws of the States in which it exists; that is was established by municipal regulations. But gentlemen must understand that this slave property, like all other, is not the creation of statute, it is regulated by law like other tenures and relations of society, but like other property, must have existed before laws were passed concerning it; like other property, resulted from the dominion of mind over matter, and, more distinctly than most other species of property, is traced back to the remotest period of antiquity. Following up the stream of time, as far as history will guide us, we find there, in the earliest stage of society, slavery existing, and legislated upon as an established institution . . .

We at the South are an agricultural people, and we require an extended territory. Slave labor is a wasteful labor, and it therefore requires a still more extended territory than would the same pursuits if they could be prosecuted by the more economical labor of white men. We have a right, in fairness and justice, to expect from our brethren of the North, that they shall not attempt, in consideration of our agricultural interests — if that alone be considered — to restrict the territory of the South. We have a right to claim that our territory shall increase with our population, and the statistics show that the natural increase of our population is as great as that of any part of the United States. Take out the accession from foreign immigration, and compare the increase of population in the northern States and the southern States, and the latter will be found a fraction greater. With this increase of population we must require increased territory; and it is but just, and fair, and honest that it should be accorded to us without any restriction or reservation. . . We claim that it is the duty of the Government to protect every species of property — that the Government has no right to discriminate between one species of property and another.

It is equally bound to protect on the high seas the slave in the vessel as the hull of the vessel itself; and it is equally bound to protect slave property, if wrecked on a foreign coast, against a hostile assertion of foreign power, as it would be the wreck of the vessel itself. And to this error — for so I must consider it — this confounding of sovereign and delegated authority, is to be attributed the claim which is set up, of power to abolish slavery, as derived from the exclusive legislation granted to the Government in this District. This construction of the word "exclusive" would render it synonymous with the word "unlimited." That exclusive legislation was necessary for the protection of the seat of government will be readily conceded. It was essential to the Government to have exclusive legislation, so that no other authority might interfere with its functions. But unlimited legislation surely is not required, and I say it could not have been granted by the Constitution; nay, more, I hold that the grant of exclusive legislation does not necessarily extend to the full power permissible under the Constitution of the United States, that there are restrictions, and broad distinctions, growing out of the vested rights and interests of others — in this case not merely of the ceding States, but of all the States of the Union. . .

Charles Francis Adams: "What makes slavery a question of national concern?" (1855)

. . . What makes the slave-question of national concern in America? How is it to be treated on the part of the people of the free states? To the examination of these do I propose with your leave to devote the present evening.

In order to aid in the explanation of this matter, let me, first of all, begin logically by laying my premises. Domestic slavery is established in at least fifteen out of thirty-one of the states of this Union. This fact is beyond dispute. The number of human beings held in slavery now exceeds three millions of souls, being more than the sum of the whole of the population of the thirteen original states at the breaking out of the Revolutionary War, eighty years ago. This fact will scarcely be denied. Now, if these two postulates are conceded to me, it follows, that, by pushing the calculation of

Little Brown, Boston, 1855, pp. 4–9, 18–22, 27–28, 43–45.

increase — which is found correct for the eighty years that are past — to the eighty years that are to come, without permitting the introduction of any unusual or extraordinary causes to accelerate or retard the natural progress of population, we arrive at the conclusion that the number of slaves may then exceed the whole of the population of all descriptions now embraced within the limits of the thirty-one states, — that is, five or six and twenty millions of souls, or thereabouts (for, to my immediate purpose, precise accuracy in numbers is not material).

Now, without going into any more distant futurity, let us stop to think of twenty-six millions of men, women, and children, held as slaves in the heart of a nation composed of a number of communities, separate for certain purposes, but indissolubly united for others. Can it be maintained for a moment, that, in the prospect of an experiment like this, without example among modern nations, the unavoidable relations of all of us to such an agglomerating mass are not a fit and legitimate subject of anxious consideration, no matter where we may be geographically situated? . . . Is it true that the increase in the Union of a prodigious number of human beings kept in slavery, without education or morals, without discretion or responsibility, no matter how bounded by conventional lines, is going to produce effects upon the character, the interests, the moral and material concerns, of only one portion of that Union? I think this question cannot be conscientiously answered in the affirmative, even upon the general view, much less when I consider that the men most deeply interested, and most directly affected by their relations to this mass, — those, I mean, who hold the slaves, — are likewise men whose public action has a bearing as direct upon the decision of all national questions in which we are involved for good or for evil, as our own. . .

If, then, I am asked the question, What makes the slave-question of national concern in America? I answer at once, and with perfect confidence, *Overpowering necessity.* It has been quite usual among a large class of citizens, whose prejudices I cannot despise (for they are honestly held), to charge individuals with wantonly and maliciously, and for their own selfish ends, exciting this controversy. This impression has the same source which I have already pointed out. But slavery is here. It is not a stationary matter. It goes on developing itself, more and more, from day to day. This is a free country. If gentlemen who pride themselves for their practical talent choose to shut their eyes, and then say they do not see the progress of slavery, — if, because they do not thus see it, they expect that everybody else should follow their example, — I ask, is this course deserving to be called practical? Is it not quite as visionary as any thing they lay to the account of the men they call fanatical? How long can such voluntary blindness be expected to last? . . .

When the Saviour of the race described himself as the sower who went out to sow, he predicted the fate of much of his seed, — that some would fall by the wayside, some on rocks, some on thorns; but yet that a portion would reach congenial soil, from which, sooner or later, would spring up plants to yield fruit, perhaps a hundred-fold. This truth has now received a verification of two thousand years . . .

Up to the hour of his advent, the full relation of man to his fellows had never been clearly recognized in the moral systems of the most refined and civilized nations. The right of the strongest, established by the universal custom, hardened itself into law, susceptible of mitigation according to the circumstances of the weak. War acknowledged no rule for the victor but his pleasure. If he spared the life of his fallen enemy, he could do so from natural generosity, or he might be tempted to it by baser motives. He could bargain it away for a price in money, or in personal service for months or years, for life, or for the lives of unborn generations. Hence sprung slavery. Hence came the subjection of the feeble throughout the world, and the establishment of habits and customs which justified the wrong by weaving into the framework of government the authority which prescription makes. Suddenly, in the obscurity of Judea, an inspired voice summoned the race to a more exalted conception of mutual obligation: "All things whatsoever ye would that men should do to you, do ye even so to them; for this is the law and the prophets." It was compelling the law of love to others to keep pace with the most selfish tendencies of the human heart. The seed seemed for the moment to have fallen upon stony ground; but it was not so. The voice was heard through all the din of arms. It appealed to the generous and noble impulses of man; and it did not appeal in vain. Echo caught the sound, and the chains of the slave rattled until they snapped asunder. Emancipation then began, seeking for its natural home the altar of every Christian church. And thus it went on, ever enlarging the sphere of its exercise, until checked by the cupidity of the European, who found, in the diversity at once of color and of religious belief, an excuse for listening to the promptings of his baser nature. An African or an Indian, because he was not white, and knew nothing of Christianity, was therefore not within the purview of the precept which enjoins love to man: hence he might be turned into a slave. Such was the logic of a generation corrupted by the discovery of American gold. So far did this reasoning extend, that it recorded itself in the statute-book, even of puritan Massachusetts, which swerved alike from its devotion to liberty and the cause of God, by provisions for perpetuating the exclusion of the African race from the benefits of the Christian faith. Time brought with it better feelings, and a new generation redeemed the dishonor by striking at its very source in the African slave-trade. The instance is encouraging to us, who trust in the ever-living force of truth upon the conscience of future generations. It shows that, like the grains which for thousands of years have remained inert in the bosoms of withered corpses, nothing is necessary but to transfer it from dead to living hands to find it once more reviving with the unimpaired energies of youth . . . kept too busy in establishing the rights to which they were entitled as freemen out of the borders of the slave-states, to have time, even had they felt the wish, to make an inroad upon them. They had been brought up in the belief, that liberty, in America at least, if nowhere else, meant something. They had heard, on every Fourth of July, a chorus of eulogists dilating upon the ineffable excellence of those axioms engrafted upon the declaration of our national independence by the hand of the great apostle of modern democracy, Thomas Jefferson. If the slave-owners find themselves now somewhat embarrassed by the docility of these scholars in mastering the lesson their representative taught them, they must comfort themselves with the remembrance of the triumphs their state once obtained in the Union through the popular confidence in him which his championship of these maxims alone had inspired. The maxims, when he introduced them into the creed of the nation, were certainly in advance of the sentiments entertained by the majority of the people for whom they were spoken . . . It was in *their* name, and not in the name of the colonies, that certain truths were put forth as self-evident. It was in *their* name announced that "all men are created equal; that they are endowed by their Creator with certain unalienable rights; that among these are life, *liberty,* and the pursuit of happiness." Yet doubtless one half of the representatives who set their names to the paper, as well as a great number of those in whose lips these words were placed, were at the moment depriving, both of their liberty and of the pursuit of happiness, a large number of men constituting a part of the great whole in whose behalf that independence was declared. The truths were in reality in advance of the age. Once more the sower had gone out to sow; but this time it was in the political field. Some of his seed fell on the rocks, some on thorns which choked it; but some was lucky enough to fall on good ground, and bear fruit immediately. Honest and single-hearted patriots picked it up, in good faith, at the time, saved it, and transmitted it to their descendants. Opinion became so fixed that not many have been since found bold enough publicly to resist it. And when the hour struck in which a few men and women, for an attempt to express their devotion to these truths, were treated like malefactors, and, as disturbers of the public peace, menaced with punishment, those were not wanting in America who felt that an occasion had happened to test their fidelity and their courage . . .

The present generation has designated these men under the odious names of fanatics, incendiaries, and traitors. But the calmer judgment of history will declare that a more self-sacrificing, disinterested, patriotic band are not to be found in the annals of mankind. I say this the more readily that I can claim no personal share in the praise. I was then among the number convinced, that time, which was daily increasing the preponderance of the free states, would bring with it a remedial public sentiment, without the need of agitation; and I shared the delusion of the majority, that discussion would rouse more obstacles than it could remove. The heroic few, who saw more clearly into the depth of the evil, understood, that time, instead of approximating the freedom of the slave, threatened to fasten fetters upon themselves. They felt that the slave-power, from the very constitution of its nature necessarily aggressive in its spirit, had in silence succeeded in intrenching itself firmly in the government of the nation, and that abstaining from resistance was only giving new means for perpetuating its sway. In the face of a combination such as the country never before had witnessed, — with the press, the politicians, the merchants, the lawyers, the church, the government, and its army of dependants of every sort, and, lastly, with the popular prejudices against the slaves because they were black, all united against them to protect slavery; with everything to lose, and little to gain to themselves, from their determination, — these few calmly began the struggle. They were forthwith abused, traduced, vilified, denounced. The batteries of a press little scrupulous in the use of poisoned weapons, especially against those not shielded by the world's regard, were opened in all their fury upon them. They were calumniated, persecuted in their business, hunted down. A price was set upon their heads. Some were mobbed, their property destroyed or burned, and one at least was shot . . .

What makes slavery of national concern in America? I say that it is the unavoidable consequence of the presence of a power, which, as it steadily and surely increases, deranges more and more the natural operation of a republican government, and from which there can be no escape but by a resolute and persevering system of counteraction. Thus far, that system has been almost entirely negative in its character, confined to the strict limits of self-defence and self-restoration. I dwell upon this point the more, that such pains have been taken to create an opposite impression upon the public mind. The slave-owners have been held up as objects of sympathy for the persecutions they have undergone, at the very time that they have been straining every nerve to convert the federal government into an engine to extend and confirm the power they have gained over the free states . . . It remains to me only to append a few suggestions relative to the other question which I submitted, How is this defence to be conducted for the future by the people who have felt it their duty to enlist in it?

To arrive at an accurate answer, it is indispensable, first of all, to take a calm survey of the disposition and the strength of the opposing forces in the field. It must be conceded, that the slave-power is now in undisputed possession of the official strongholds in the general government. It directs the Executive and the Legislative departments, and holds in reserve the federal Judiciary as a last resort. This slave-power consists, in fact, of about three hundred and fifty thousand active men, spreading over a large territorial surface, commanding the political resources of fifteen states directly, and, through their connections, materially affecting those of five or six more. These persons, and all their numerous friends and dependents, in and out of the slave-holding region, are held together in interest by a common bond, in the sum of two thousand millions of dollars worth of what they consider property. For the sake of protecting this against the prevailing tendencies of the age, and the effect of public sentiment created by a large body of their own countrymen, it is impossible that they should escape adopting a system of policy agressive upon the rights of freemen. They become, in their action, to all intents and purposes, men of one idea. This idea necessarily includes the extension of their own power, whether they are sensible of its influence in that direction or not. They throw into the public councils their allotted portion of representatives, all equally pledged to be faithful to it, whatever they may think upon other subjects. The unity of policy thus secured for all the time spreads its influence far beyond the limits of its own circle . . .

Am I asked what I desire to see done? The answer is plain. I would have the people do no injury to the slaveholder, rob him of none of his rest, nor harm a hair of his head, or of any of those who are dear to him. But I would have them do all that is possible to deprive him of the power of harm to the country or to them. To this end, it seems indispensable that he be dislodged from the strongholds in the federal government. Neither he, nor any one that he will select, should be made President of the United States, or be placed in any other situation of responsibility in which he could avail aught to prevent an entire reversal of the policy which has, for a long time back, been prompted to promote his peculiar interests. Instead of perpetuating and extending slavery, every effort should be directed to the great object of releasing the general government from all responsibility for it or connection with it. The word should not be seen in the statute-book. The thing should not be known where the national flag waves over national territory. The seat of government should not be dishonored by its presence. The free states should be secure from its encroachments. And upon no consideration whatever should any extension of the slave-power in the councils of the Union, by the introduction of new states subject to its influence, be permitted . . .

At the same time that Eli Whitney developed a machine that could extract the seeds from common short staple cotton, English textile manufacturers perfected a process for making cotton cloth using only power-driven machinery. Thus in 1793 a type of cotton that could be grown throughout the South was suddenly in great demand. Cotton replaced the crops of the colonial period, and the plantation system of the Tidewater areas was rapidly introduced into the Southern hinterland, carrying with it a population of black slaves. In succeeding decades cotton became the chief American export. Cotton paid for the food grown in the North; cotton attracted the capital and credit of European investors. The great magnates of Southern agriculture were certain that without cotton the whole economy would stagnate. Since it had become axiomatic that cotton could only be profitably produced by slave labor organized by white plantation owners, Southerners argued that Northern capitalists would never permit abolitionist sentiment to destroy the most profitable crop in the country. The most thorough exploration of this theme came from a Southern writer, David Christy (1802–1867?), whose book, *Cotton is King,* supplied a whole generation of Southern editors and politicians with arguments for the indispensability of cotton to America's well-being. The first reading in this section is taken from Christy's work and shows how he inferred the permanence of slavery from the extent of Southern exports. What eluded Christy, as it did many other contemporaries, was the fact that America was turning from a dependence upon world customers to an economy based upon home consumption of American agricultural and manufactured products.

The only serious challenge to Christy's theories came from another Southerner, Hinton Rowan Helper (1829–1909). Helper, observing the Southern economy from the vantage point of a poor farmer of North Carolina, was convinced that Southern institutions were disastrous for all but a few large slaveholders. He poured over the same 1850 census statistics that Christy had used and came up with a comparison of Northern and Southern economic growth which was highly unfavourable to the slave states. Helper wrote *The Im-*

pending Crisis to alert poor white Southerners to the blight slavery was. In the South his book was banned, but it was enormously popular in the North where much of the Southern self-image had long been accepted.

David Christy: Cotton is King (1855)

The institution of Slavery, at this moment, gives indications of a vitality that was never anticipated by its friends or foes. Its enemies often supposed it about ready to expire, from the wounds they had inflicted, when in truth it had taken two steps in advance; while they had taken twice the number in an opposite direction. In each successive conflict, its assailants have been weakened, while its dominion has been extended.

This has arisen from causes too generally overlooked. Slavery is not an isolated system, but is so mingled with the business of the world, that it derives facilities from the most innocent transactions. Capital and labor, in Europe and America, are largely employed in the manufacture of cotton. These goods, to a great extent, may be seen freighting every vessel, from Christian nations, that traverses the seas of the globe; and filling the warehouses and shelves of the merchants, over two-thirds of the world. By the industry, skill, and enterprise, employed in the manufacture of cotton, mankind are better clothed; their comfort better promoted; general industry more highly stimulated; commerce more widely extended; and civilization more rapidly advanced, than in any preceding age.

To the superficial observer, all the agencies, based upon the manufacture and sale of cotton, seem to be legitimately engaged in promoting human happiness; and he, doubtless, feels like invoking Heaven's choicest blessings upon them. When he sees the stockholders in the cotton corporations receiving their dividends, the operatives their wages, the merchants their profits, and civilized people everywhere clothed comfortably in cottons, he can not refrain from explaining: "The lines

Cincinnati, Ohio, 1855, pp. 36–43, 54–55, 104–06, 110–12, 116–17, 122–23, 180–87.

have fallen unto them in pleasant places; yea, they have a goodly heritage!"

But turn a moment to the source whence the raw cotton, the basis of these operations, is obtained, and observe the aspect of things in that direction. When the statistics on the subject are examined, it appears that nearly all the cotton consumed in the Christian world, is the product of the Slave labor of the United States. It is this monopoly that has given Slavery its commercial value; and, while this monopoly is retained, the institution will continue to extend itself wherever it can find room to spread. He who looks for any other result, must expect that nations, which, for centuries, have waged war to extend their commerce, will now abandon their means of aggrandizement, and bankrupt themselves, to force the abolition of American Slavery!

This is not all. The economical value of Slavery as an agency for supplying the means of extending manufactures and commerce, has long been understood by statesmen. The discovery of the power of steam, and the inventions in machinery, for preparing and manufacturing cotton, revealed the important fact, that a single Island, having the monopoly secured to itself, could supply the world with clothing. Great Britain attempted to gain this monopoly; and, to prevent other countries from rivaling her, she long prohibited all emigration of skillful mechanics from the kingdom, as well as all exports of machinery. As country after country was opened to her commerce, the markets for her manufactures were extended, and the demand for the raw material increased. The benefits of this enlarged commerce of the world, were not confined to a single nation, but mutually enjoyed by all. As each had products to sell, peculiar to itself, the advantages often gained by one, were no detriment to the others. The principal articles demanded by this increasing commerce, have been coffee, sugar, and cotton–in the production of which Slave labor has greatly predominated. Since the enlargement of manufactures, cotton has entered more extensively into commerce than coffee and sugar, though the demand for all three has advanced with the greatest rapidity. England could only become a great commercial nation, through the agency of her manufactures. She was the best supplied, of all the nations, with the necessary capital, skill, labor, and fuel, to extend her commerce by this means. But, for the raw material, to supply her manufactories, she was dependent upon other countries. The planters of the United States were the most favorably situated for the cultivation of cotton, and attempted to monopolize the markets for the staple. This led to a fusion of interests between them and the manufacturers of Great Britain; and to the invention of notions, in political economy, that would, so far as adopted, promote the interests of this coalition. With the advantages possessed by the English manufacturers, "Free Trade" would render all other nations subservient to their interests; and, so far as their operations should be increased, just so far would the demand for American cotton be extended. The details of the success of the parties to this combination, and the opposition they have had to encounter, are left to be noticed more fully hereafter. To the cotton planters, the copartnership has been eminently advantageous.

How far the other agricultural interests of the United States are promoted, by extending the cultivation of cotton, may be inferred from the Census returns of 1850, . . . Of cotton and tobacco, we export more than two-thirds of the amount produced; while of other products, of the agriculturists, less than the one-forty-sixth part is exported. Foreign nations, generally, can grow their provisions, but can not grow their tobacco and cotton. Our surplus provisions, not exported, go to the villages, towns, and cities, to feed the mechanics, manufacturers, merchants, professional men, and others; or to the cotton and sugar districts of the South, to feed the planters and their slaves. The increase of mechanics and manufacturers at the North, and the expansion of Slavery at the South, therefore, augment the markets for provisions, and promote the prosperity of the farmer. As the mechanical population increases, the implements of husbandry, and articles of furniture, are multiplied, so that both farmer and planter can be supplied with them on easier terms. As foreign nations open their markets to cotton fabrics, increased demands, for the raw material, are made. As new grazing and grain-growing States are developed, and teem with their surplus productions, the mechanic is benefited, and the planter, relieved from food-raising, can employ his slaves more extensively upon cotton. It is thus that our exports are increased; our foreign commerce advanced; the home markets of the mechanic and farmer extended, and the wealth of the nation promoted. It is thus, also, that the Free labor of the country finds remunerating markets for its products — though at the expense of serving as an efficient auxiliary in the extension of Slavery! . . .

But this subject demands a still closer scrutiny, as to its past connections with national politics, in order that the causes of the failure of Abolitionism to arrest the progress of Slavery, as well as the present relations of the institution to the politics of the country, may fully appear.

Slave labor has seldom been made profitable where it has been wholly employed in grazing and grain growing; but it becomes remunerative in proportion as the planters can devote their attention to cotton, sugar, rice, or tobacco. To render Southern Slavery profitable in the highest degree, therefore, the slaves must be employed upon some one of these articles, and be sustained by a supply of food and draught animals from Northern agriculturists; and, before the planter's supplies are complete, to these must be added cotton gins, implements of husbandry, furniture, and tools, from Northern mechanics. This is a point of the utmost moment, and must be considered more at length.

It has long been a vital question to the success of the Slaveholder, to know how he could render the labor of his slaves the most profitable. The grain growing States had to emancipate their slaves, to rid themselves of a profitless system. The cotton growing States, ever after the invention of the cotton gin, had found the production of that staple, highly remunerative. The logical conclusion, from these different results, was, that the less provisions, and the more cotton grown by the planter, the greater would be his profits. Markets for the surplus products of the farmer of the North, were equally as important to him as the supply of provisions was to the planter. But the planter, to be eminently successful, must purchase his supplies, at the lowest possible prices; while the farmer, to secure his prosperity, must sell his products at the highest possible rates. Few, indeed, can be so ill informed, as not to know, that these two topics, for many years, were involved in the "Free Trade" and "Protective Tariff" doctrines, and afforded the materiel of the political contests between the North and the South — between free labor and slave labor . . .

The results of the contest, in relation to Protection and Free Trade, have been more or less favorable to all parties. This has been an effect, in part, of the changeable character of our legislation; and, in part, of the occurrence of events over which politicians had no control. The manufacturing States, while protection lasted, succeeded in placing their establishments upon a comparatively permanent basis; and, by engaging largely in the manufacture of cottons, as well as woolens, have rendered home manufactures, practically, very advantageous to the South. Our cotton factories, in 1850, consumed as much cotton as those of Great Britain did in 1831; thus affording indications, that, by proper encouragement, they may be multiplied so as to consume the whole crop of the country. The cotton and woolen factories, in 1850, employed over 130,000 work hands, and had $102,619,581 of capital invested in them. They thus afford an important market to the farmer, and, at the same time, have become an equally important auxiliary to the planter. They may yet afford him the only market for his cotton.

The cotton planting States, toward the close of the contest, found themselves rapidly accumulating strength, and approximating the accomplishment of the grand object at which they aimed — the monopoly of the cotton markets of the world. This success was due, not so much to any triumph over the North — to any prostration of our manufacturing interests — as to the general policy of other nations. All rivalry to the American planters, in the West Indies, was removed by emancipation; as, under freedom, the cultivation of cotton was nearly abandoned. Mehemet Ali had become imbecile, and the indolent Egyptians neglected its culture. The South Americans, after achieving their independence, were more readily enlisted in military forays, than in the art of agriculture, and they produced little cotton for export . . . While the cultivation of cotton was thus stationary or retrograding, everywhere outside of the United States, England and the Continent were rapidly increasing their consumption of the article, which they nearly doubled from 1835 to 1845; so that the demand for the raw material called loudly for its increased production. Our planters gathered a rich harvest of profits by these events . . .

The West, which had long looked to the East for a market, had its attention now turned to the South, as the most certain and convenient mart for the sale of its products — the Planters affording to the Farmers, the markets they had in vain sought from the Manufacturers. In the meantime steamboat navigation was acquiring perfection on the Western rivers — the great natural outlets for Western products — and became a means of communication between the Northwest and the Southwest, as well as with the trade and commerce of the Atlantic cities. This gave an impulse to industry and enterprise, west of the Alleghanies, unparalleled in the history of the country. While, then, the bounds of Slave labor were extending from Virginia, the Carolinas, and Georgia, westward, over Tennessee, Alabama, Mississippi, and Arkansas, the area of Free labor was enlarging, with equal rapidity, in the Northwest, throughout Ohio, Indiana, Illinois, and Michigan. Thus within these Provision and Cotton regions, were the forests cleared away, or the prairies broken up, simultaneously, by these old antagonistic forces, opponents no longer, but harmonized by the fusion of their interests — the connecting link between them being the steamboat. Thus, also, was a tripartite alliance formed, by which the Western Farmer, the Southern Planter, and the English Manufacturer, became united in a common bond of interest — the whole giving their support to the doctrines of Free Trade . . .

The competition for Western products enhanced their price, and stimulated their more extended cultivation. This required an enlargement of the markets; and the extension of Slavery became essential to Western prosperity.

We have not reached the end of the alliance between the Western Farmer and Southern Planter. The emigration which has been filling Iowa and Minnesota, and is now rolling like a flood into Kansas and Nebraska, is but a repetition of what has occurred in the other Western States and Territories . . .

And should the Anti-Slavery voters succeed in gaining the political ascendency in these Territories, and bring them as free States triumphantly into the Union; what can they do, but turn in, as all the rest of the Western States have done, and help to feed slaves, or those who manufacture or who sell the products of the labor of slaves. There is no other resource left, either to them or ourselves, without an entire change in almost every branch of business and of domestic econo-

my. Look at your bills of dry-goods for the year, and what do they contain? At least three-fourths of the amount are French, English, or American cotton fabrics, woven from Slave-labor cotton. Look at your bills for groceries, and what do they contain? Coffee, sugar, molasses, rice — from Brazil, Cuba, Louisiana, Carolina; while only a mere fraction of them are from Free-labor countries. As now employed, our dry-goods merchants and grocers constitute an immense army of agents for the sale of fabrics and products, coming directly or indirectly, from the hand of the slave; and all the remaining portion of the people, free colored, as well as white, are exerting themselves, according to their various capacities, to gain the means of purchasing the greatest possible amount of these commodities. Nor can the country, at present, by any possibility, pay for the amount of foreign goods consumed, but by the labor of the slaves of the planting States. This cannot be doubted for a moment . . .

From this view of the subject, it appears that Slavery is not a self-sustaining system, independently remunerative; but that it attains its importance to the nation and to the world, by standing as an agency, intermediate between the grain-growing States and foreign commerce. As the distillers of the West transformed the surplus grain into whisky, that it might bear transport, so Slavery takes the products of the North and metamorphoses them into cotton, that they may bear export.

It seems, indeed, when the whole of the facts brought to view are considered, that American Slavery, though of little force unaided, yet, properly sustained, is the great central power, or energizing influence, not only of nearly all the industrial interests of our own country, but also of those of Great Britain and much of the Continent; and that, if stricken from existence, the whole of these interests, with the advancing civilization of the age, would receive a shock that must retard their progress for years to come.

This is no exaggerated picture of the present imposing power of Slavery. It is literally true . . .

The reason can now be clearly comprehended, why Abolitionists have had so little moral power over the conscience of the Slaveholder. Their practice has been inconsistent with their precepts; or, at least, their conduct has been liable to this construction. Nor do we perceive how they can exert a more potent influence, in the future, unless their energies are directed to efforts such as will relieve them from a position so inconsistent with their professions, as that of constantly purchasing products which they, themselves, declare to be the fruits of robbery. While, therefore, things remain as they are, with the world so largely dependent upon Slave labor, how can it be otherwise, than that the system will continue to flourish? And while its products are used by all classes, of every sentiment, and country, nearly, how can the Slaveholder be brought to see anything, in the practice of the world, to alarm his conscience, and make him cringe, before his fellow-men, as a guilty robber?

As the monopoly of the culture of Cotton, imparts to Slavery its economical value, the system will continue as long as this monopoly is maintained. Slave-Labor products have now become necessities of human life, to the extent of more than half the commercial articles supplied to the Christian world. Even Free labor, itself, is made largely subservient to Slavery, and vitally interested in its perpetuation and extension.

Can this condition of things be changed? It may be reasonably doubted, whether anything efficient can be speedily accomplished: not because there is lack of territory where freemen may be employed in tropical cultivation; not because intelligent free-labor is less productive than slave-labor; but because freemen, whose constitutions are adapted to tropical climates, will not avail themselves of the opportunity offered for commencing such an enterprise.

King Cotton cares not whether he employs slaves or freemen. It is the *cotton*, not the *slaves*, upon which his throne is based. Let freemen do his work as well, and he will not object to the change . . .

King Cotton is a profound statesman, and knows what measures will best sustain his throne. He is an acute mental philosopher, acquainted with the secret springs of human action, and accurately perceives who will best promote his aims. He has no evidence that colored men can grow his cotton, but in the capacity of slaves. It is his policy, therefore, to defeat all schemes of emancipation. To do this, he stirs up such agitations as lure his enemies into measures that will do him no injury. The venal politician is always at his call, and assumes the form of saint or sinner, as the service may

demand. Nor does he overlook the enthusiast, engaged in Quixotic endeavors for the relief of suffering humanity, but influences him to advocate measures which tend to tighten, instead of loosing the bands of Slavery . . .

Hinton Rowan Helper: *The impending crisis of the South (1857)*

It is not our intention in this chapter to enter into an elaborate ethnographical essay, to establish peculiarities of difference, mental, moral, and physical, in the great family of man. Neither is it our design to launch into a philosophical disquisition on the laws and principles of light and darkness, with a view of educing any additional evidence of the fact, that as a general rule, the rays of the sun are more fructifying and congenial than the shades of night. Nor yet is it our purpose, by writing a formal treatise on ethics, to draw a broad line of distinction between right and wrong, to point out the propriety of morality and its advantages over immorality, nor to waste time in pressing a universally admitted truism — that virtue is preferable to vice. Self-evident truths require no argumentative demonstration.

What we mean to do is simply this: to take a survey of the relative position and importance of the several states of this confederacy, from the adoption of the national compact; and when, of two sections of the country starting under the same auspices, and with **equal** natural advantages, we find the one rising to a degree of almost unexampled power and eminence, and the other sinking into a state of comparative imbecility and obscurity, it is our determination to trace out the causes which have led to the elevation of the former, and the depression of the latter, and to use our most earnest and honest endeavors to utterly extirpate whatever opposes the progress and prosperity of any portion of the union . . .

As a true hearted southerner, whose ancestors have resided in North Carolina between one and two hundred years, and as one who would rather have his native clime excel than be excelled, we feel constrained to confess that we are deeply abashed and chagrined at the disclosures of the comparison thus instituted. At the

Burdick Brothers, New York, 1857, pp. 11-13, 16-27, 40-44. 54-55, 80-84.

time of the adoption of the Constitution, in 1789, we commenced an even race with the North. All things considered, if either the North or the South had the advantage, it was the latter. In proof of this, let us introduce a few statistics, beginning with the states of New York and Virginia.

In 1790, when the first census was taken, New York contained 340,120 inhabitants; at the same time the population of Virginia was 748,308, being more than twice the number of New York. Just sixty years afterward, as we learn from the census of 1859, New York had a population of 3,097,394; while that of Virginia was only 1,421,661, being less than half the number of New York! In 1791, the exports of New York amounted to $2,505,465; the exports of Virginia amounted to $3,130,865. In 1852, the exports of New York amounted to $87,484,456; the exports of Virginia, during the same year, amounted to only $2,724,657. In 1790, the imports of New York and Virginia were about equal; in 1853, the imports of New York amounted to the enormous sum of $178,270,999; while those of Virginia, for the same period, amounted to the pitiful sum of only $399,004. In 1850, the products of manufactures, mining and the mechanic arts in New York amounted to only $29,705,387. At the taking of the last census, the value of real and personal property in Virginia, including negroes, was $391,646,438; that of New York, exclusive of any monetary valuation of human beings, was $1,080,309,216 . . .

In 1790, Massachusetts contained 378,717 inhabitants; in the same year North Carolina contained 393,751; in 1850, the population of Massachusetts was 994,514, all freemen; while that of North Carolina was only 869,039, of whom 288,548 were slaves . . .

In 1850, the products of manufactures, mining and mechanic arts in Massachusetts, amounted to $151,137,-145; those of North Carolina, to only $9,111,245. In 1856, the products of these industrial pursuits in Massachusetts had increased to something over $288,000,000, a sum more than twice the value of the entire cotton crop of all the Southern States! In 1850, the cash value of all the farms, farming implements and machinery in Massachusetts, was $112,285,931; the value of the same in North Carolina, in the same year, was only $71,823,-298 . . . In 1856, the real and personal estate assessed in the City of Boston amounted in valuation to within

a fraction of $250,000,000, showing conclusively that so far as dollars and cents are concerned, that single city could buy the whole State of North Carolina . . . In 1850, there were in Massachusetts 1,861 native white and free colored persons over twenty years of age who could not read and write; in the same year, the same class of persons in North Carolina numbered 80,083; while her 288,548 slaves were, by legislative enactments, kept in a state of absolute ignorance and unconditional subordination . . .

An old gentleman, now residing in Charleston, told us, but a few months since, that he had a distinct recollection of the time when Charleston imported foreign fabrics for the Philadelphia trade, and when, on a certain occasion, his mother went into a store on Market-street to select a silk dress for herself, the merchant, unable to please her fancy, persuaded her to postpone the selection for a few days, or until the arrival of a new stock of superb styles and fashions which he had recently purchased in the metropolis of South Carolina . . . In 1760, as we learn from Mr. Benton's "Thirty Years' View," the foreign imports into Charleston were $2,662,-000; in 1855, they amounted to only $1,750,000! . . .

As shown by the census report of 1850, which was prepared under the superintendence of a native of South Carolina, who certainly will not be suspected of injustice to his own section of the country, the Southern states, the cash value of all the farms, farming implements, and machinery in Pennsylvania, was $422,598,-640; the value of the same in South Carolina, in the same year, was only $86,518,038. From a compendium of the same census, we learn that the value of all the real and personal property in Pennsylvania, actual property, no slaves, amounted to $729,144,998; the value of the same in South Carolina, including the estimated — we were about to say fictitious — value of 384,925 negroes, amounted to only $288,257,694 . . .

The incontrovertible facts we have thus far presented are, we think, amply sufficient, both in number and magnitude, to bring conviction to the mind of every candid reader, that there is something wrong, socially, politically and morally wrong, in the policy under which the South has so long loitered and languished. Else, how is it that the North, under the operations of a policy directly the opposite of ours, has surpassed us in almost everything great and good, and left us standing before the world, an object of merited reprehension and derision?

For one, we are heartily ashamed of the inexcusable weakness, inertia and dilapidation everywhere so manifest throughout our native section; but the blame properly attaches itself to an usurping minority of the people, and we are determined that it shall rest where it belongs . . .

It is a fact well known to every intelligent Southerner that we are compelled to go to the North for almost every article of utility and adornment, from matches, shoepegs and paintings up to cotton-mills, steamships and statuary; that we have no foreign trade, no princely merchants, nor respectable artists; that, in comparison with the free states, we contribute nothing to the literature, polite arts and inventions of the age; that, for want of profitable employment at home, large numbers of our native population find themselves necessitated to emigrate to the West, whilst the free states retain not only the larger proportion of those born within their own limits, but induce, annually, hundreds of thousands of foreigners to settle and remain amongst them; that almost everything produced at the North meets with ready sale, while, at the same time, there is no demand, even among our own citizens, for the productions of Southern industry; that, owing to the absence of a proper system of business amongst us, the North becomes, in one way or another, the proprietor and dispenser of all our floating wealth, and that we are dependent on Northern capitalists for the means necessary to build our railroads, canals and other public improvements; that if we want to visit a foreign country, even though it may lie directly South of us, we find no convenient way of getting there except by taking passage through a Northern port; and that nearly all the profits arising from the exchange of commodities, from insurance and shipping offices, and from the thousand and one industrial pursuits of the country, accrue to the North, and are there invested in the erection of those magnificent cities and stupendous works of art which dazzle the eyes of the South, and attest the superiority of free institutions!

The North is the Mecca of our merchants, and to it they must and do make two pilgrimages per annum — one in the spring and one in the fall. All our commercial, mechanical, manufactural, and literary supplies come from there. We want Bibles, brooms, buckets and books, and we go to the North; we want pens, ink, paper, wafers and envelopes, and we go to the North; we want shoes, hats, handkerchiefs, umbrellas and pocket knives, and we go to the North, we want furniture, crockery, glassware and pianos, and we go to the North; we want toys, primers, school books, fashionable apparel, machinery, medicines, tombstones, and a thousand other things, and we go to the North for them all. Instead of keeping our money in circulation at home, by patronizing our own mechanics, manufacturers, and laborers, we send it all away to the North, and there it remains; it never falls into our hands again.

In one way or another we are more or less subservient to the North every day of our lives. In infancy we are swaddled in Northern muslin; in childhood we are humored with Northern gewgaws; in youth we are instructed out of Northern books; at the age of maturity we sow our "wild oats" on Northern soil; in middle-life we exhaust our wealth, energies and talents in the dishonorable vocation of entailing our dependence on our children and on our children's children, and, to the neglect of our own interests and the interests of those around us, in giving aid and succor to every department of Northern power; in the decline of life we remedy our eye-sight with Northern spectacles, and support our infirmities with Northern canes; in old age we are drugged with Northern physic; and, finally, when we die, our inanimate bodies, shrouded in Northern cambric, are stretched upon the bier, borne to the grave in a Northern carriage, entombed with a Northern space, and memorized with a Northern slab!

But it can hardly be necessary to say more in illustration of this unmanly and unnational dependence, which is so glaring that it cannot fail to be apparent to even the most careless and superficial observer. All the world sees, or ought to see, that in a commercial, mechanical, manufactural, financial, and literary point of view, we are as helpless as babes; that, in comparison with the Free States, our agricultural resources have been greatly exaggerated, misunderstood and mismanaged; and that, instead of cultivating among ourselves a wise policy of mutual assistance and co-operation with respect to individuals, and of self-reliance with respect to the South at large, instead of giving countenance and encouragement to the industrial enterprises projected in our midst, and instead of building up, aggrandizing and beautifying our own States, cities and towns, we have been spending our substance at the North, and are daily augmenting and strengthening the very power which now has us so completely under its thumb . . .

Our repugnance to the institution of slavery, springs from no one-sided idea, or sickly sentimentality. We have not been hasty in making up our mind on the subject; we have jumped at no conclusions; we have acted with perfect calmness and deliberation; we have carefully considered, and examined the reasons for and against the institution, and have also taken into account the probable consequences of our decision. The more we investigate the matter, the deeper becomes the conviction that we are right; and with this to impel and sustain us, we pursue our labor with love, with hope, and with constantly renewing vigor . . .

Though neither a prophet nor the son of a prophet, our vision is sufficiently penetrative to divine the future so far as to be able to see that the "peculiar institution" has but a short, and, as heretofore, inglorious existence before it. Time, the righter of every wrong, is ripening events for the desired consummation of our labors and the fulfillment of our cherished hopes. Each revolving year brings nearer the inevitable crisis. The sooner it comes the better; may heaven, through our humble efforts, hasten its advent.

The first and most sacred duty of every Southerner, who has the honor and the interest of his country at heart, is to declare himself an unqualified and uncompromising abolitionist. No conditional or half-way declaration will avail; no mere threatening demonstration will succeed. With those who desire to be instrumental in bringing about the triumph of liberty over slavery, there should be neither evasion, vacillation, nor equivocation . . .

In making up these tables we have two objects in view; the first is to open the eyes of the non-slaveholders of the South, to the system of deception, that has so long been practiced upon them, and the second is to show slaveholders themselves — we have reference only to those who are not too perverse, or ignorant, to perceive naked truths — that free labor is far more respectable, profitable, and productive, than slave labor. In the South, unfortunately, no kind of labor is either free or respectable. Every white man who is under the necessity of earning his bread, by the sweat of his brow, or by manual labor, in any capacity, no matter how unassuming in deportment, or exemplary in morals, is treated as if he was a loathsome beast, and shunned with the utmost disdain. His soul may be the very seat of honor and integrity, yet without slaves — himself a slave — he is accounted as nobody, and would be deemed intolerably presumptuous, if he dared to open his mouth, even so wide as to give faint utterance to a three-lettered monosyllable, like yea or nay, in the presence of an august knight of the whip and the lash.

There are few Southerners who will not be astonished at the disclosures of these statistical comparisons, between the free and the slave States. That the astonishment of the more intelligent and patriotic non-slaveholders will be mingled with indignation, is no more than we anticipate. We confess our own surprise, and deep chagrin, at the result of our investigations. Until we examined into the matter, we thought and hoped the South was really ahead of the North in one particular, that of agriculture; but our thoughts have been changed, and our hopes frustrated, for instead of finding ourselves the possessors of a single advantage, we behold our dear native South stripped of every laurel, and sinking deeper and deeper in the depths of poverty and shame; while, at the same time, we see the North, our successful rival, extracting and absorbing the few elements of wealth yet remaining amongst us, and rising higher and higher in the scale of fame, fortune, and invulnerable power. Thus our disappointment gives way to a feeling of intense mortification, and our soul involuntarily, but justly, we believe, cries out for retribution against the treacherous, slave-driving legislators, who have so basely and unpatriotically neglected the interests of their poor white constituents and bargained away the rights of posterity. Notwithstanding the fact that the white non-slaveholders of the South, are in the majority, as five to one, they have never yet had any part or lot in framing the laws under which they live. There is no legislation except for the benefit of slavery, and slaveholders. As a general rule, poor white persons are regarded with less esteem and attention than negroes, and though the condition of the latter is wretched beyond description, vast numbers of the former are infinitely worse off. A cunningly devised mockery of freedom is guaranteed to them, and that is all. To all intents and purposes they are disfranchised, and outlawed, and the only privilege extended to them, is a shallow and circumscribed participation in the political movements that usher slaveholders into office.

We have not breathed away seven and twenty years in the South, without becoming acquainted with the demagogical manoeuverings of the oligarchy. Their intrigues and tricks of legerdemain are as familiar to us as household words; in vain might the world be ransacked for a more precious junto of flatterers and cajolers. It is amusing to ignorance, amazing to credulity, and insulting to intelligence, to hear them in their blattering efforts to mystify and pervert the sacred principles of liberty, and turn the curse of slavery into a blessing. To the illiterate poor whites — made poor and ignorant by the system of slavery — they hold out the idea that slavery is the very bulwark of our liberties, and the foundation of American independence! For hours at a time, day after day, will they expatiate upon the inexpressible beauties and excellencies of this great, free and independent nation; and finally with the most extravagant gesticulations and rhetorical flourishes conclude their nonsensical ravings, by attributing all the glory and prosperity of the country, from Maine to Texas, and from Georgia to California, to the "invaluable institutions of the South!" With what patience we could command, we have frequently listened to the incoherent and truth-murdering declamations of these champions of slavery, and, in the absence of a more politic method of giving vent to our disgust and indignation, have involuntarily bit our lips into blisters.

The lords of the lash are not only absolute masters of the blacks, who are bought and sold, and driven about like so many cattle, but they are also the oracles and arbiters of all non-slaveholding whites, whose freedom is merely nominal, and whose unparalleled illiteracy and degradation is purposely and fiendishly perpetuated. How little the "poor white trash, " the great majority of the Southern people, know of the real condition of the country is, indeed, sadly astonishing. The truth is, they know nothing of public measures, and little of private affairs, except what their imperious masters, the slave-drivers, condescend to tell, and that is but precious little, and even that little, always garbled and one-sided, is never told except in public harangues; for the haughty cavaliers of shackles and handcuffs will not degrade themselves by holding private converse with those who have neither dimes nor hereditary rights in human flesh . . .

The value of cotton to the South, to the North, to the nation, and to the world, has been so grossly exaggerated, and so extensive have been the evils which have resulted in consequence of the extraordinary misrepresentations concerning it, that we should feel constrained to reproach ourself for remissness of duty, if we failed to make an attempt to explode the popular error . . . So hyperbolically has the importance of cotton been magnified by certain pro-slavery politicians of the South, that the person who would give credence to all their fustian and bombast, would be under the necessity of believing that the very existence of almost everything, in the heaven above, in the earth beneath, and in the water under the earth, depended on it. The truth is, however, that the cotton crop is of but little value to the South. New England and Old England, by their superior enterprise and sagcity, turn it chiefly to their own advantage. It is carried in their ships, spun in their factories, woven in their looms, insured in their offices, returned again in their own vessels, and, with double freight and cost of manufacturing added, purchased by the South at a high premium. Of all the parties engaged or interested in its transportation and manufacture, the South is the only one that does not make a profit. Nor does she, as a general thing, make a profit by producing it . . .

In wilfully traducing and decrying everything North of Mason and Dixon's line, and in excessively magnifying the importance of everything South of it, the oligarchy have, in the eyes of all liberal and intelligent men, only made an exhibition of their uncommon folly and dishonesty. For a long time, it is true, they have succeeded in deceiving the people, in keeping them humbled in the murky sloughs of poverty and ignorance, and in instilling into their untutored minds passions and prejudices expressly calculated to strengthen and protect the accursed institution of slavery; but, thanks to heaven, their inglorious reign is fast drawing to a close; with irresistible brilliancy, and in spite of the interdict of tyrants, light from the pure fountain of knowledge is now streaming over the dark places of our land, and, ere long — mark our words — there will ascend from Delaware, and from Texas, and from all the intermediate States, a huzza for Freedom and for Equal Rights, that will utterly confound the friends of despotism, set at defiance the authority of usurpers, and carry consternation to the heart of every slavery-propagandist.

To undeceive the people of the South, to bring them to a knowledge of the inferior and disreputable position which they occupy as a component part of the Union, and to give prominence and popularity to those plans which, if adopted, will elevate us to an equality, socially, morally, intellectually, industrially, politically, and financially, with the most flourishing and refined nation in the world, and, if possible, to place us in the van of even that, is the object of this work. Slaveholders, either from ignorance or from a wilful disposition to propagate error, contend that the South has nothing to be ashamed of, that slavery has proved a blessing to her, and that her superiority over the North in an agricultural point of view makes amends for all her shortcomings in other respects. On the other hand, we contend that many years of continual blushing and severe penance would not suffice to cancel or annul the shame and disgrace that justly attaches to the South in consequence of slavery — the direst evil that e'er befell the land — that the South bears nothing like even a respectable approximation to the North in navigation, commerce, or manufactures, and that, contrary to the opinion entertained by ninety-nine hundredths of her people, she is far behind the free States in the only thing of which she has ever dared to boast — agriculture . . .

Facts truly astounding are disclosed in the two last tables, and we could heartily wish that every intelligent American would commit them to memory. The total value of all the real and personal property of the free States, with an area of only 612,597 square miles, is one billion one hundred and sixty-six million eighty-one thousand three hundred and seventy-one dollars greater than the total value of all the real and personal property, including the price of 3,204,313 negroes, of the slave States, which have an area of 851,508 square miles! But extraordinary as this difference is in favor of the North, it is much less than the true amount. On the authority of Southrons themselves, it is demonstrable beyond the possibility of refutation that the intrinsic value of all the property in the free States is more than three times greater than the intrinsic value of all the property in the slave States . . .

True Wealth of the Free States, ... $4,102,172,108
True Wealth of the Slave States, ... <u>1,336,090,737</u>

Balance in favor of the Free States, . . $2,766,081,371

There, friends of the South and of the North, you have the conclusion of the whole matter. Liberty and slavery are before you; choose which you will have; as for us, in the memorable language of the immortal Henry, we say, "give us liberty, or give us death!" In the great struggle for wealth that has been going on between the two rival systems of free and slave labor, the balance above exhibits the net profits of the former. The struggle on the one side has been calm, laudable, and eminently successful; on the other, it has been attended by tumult, unutterable cruelties and disgraceful failure. We have given the slave drivers every conceivable opportunity to vindicate their domestic policy, but for them to do it is a moral impossibility.

Less than three-quarters of a century ago — say in 1789, for that was about the average time of the abolition of slavery in the Northern States — the South, with advantages in soil, climate, rivers, harbors, minerals, forests, and, indeed, almost every other natural resource, began an even race with the North in all the important pursuits of life; and now, in the brief space of scarce three score years and ten, we find her completely distanced, enervated, dejected and dishonored. Slavedrivers are the sole authors of her disgrace; as they have sown so let them reap . . .

While Congress was deciding the specific issues involved in slavery extension and states rights, a tug-o-war was going on between the opponents and defenders of American slavery. Each side wooed the uncommitted public with editorials, articles, sociological studies, novels, plays, poetry, and endless speech making. The most successful piece of Northern propaganda was Harriet Beecher Stowe's *Uncle Tom's Cabin*. An effective novelist, Mrs. Stowe (1811–1896) took the slavery debate out of the realm of angry political discourse and put it into a form that appealed to those Americans indifferent to constitutional law and economic theories. White Northerners could identify with the novel's black characters who struggled to save their humanity in the inhumane context of Southern slavery. An immediate hit as a magazine serial, *Uncle Tom's Cabin* became a best-selling book and a hit play. The first selection in this section is taken from the opening chapters of *Uncle Tom's Cabin.*

Although Northern antislavery literature could not circulate freely in the South, Southern apologists still felt the sting of Northern critics and recognized the importance of getting their side of the slavery story before the Northern public. They also wished to bolster the loyalty of any Southerners who might be wavering under the fire of antislavery tracts. Dozens of Southern rebuttals to *Uncle Tom's Cabin* were published, and the second reading presents a review of the novel by George Frederick Holmes (1820–1897), a prominent Southern writer, lecturer, and professor. The need to defend the South's institutions turned other Southern writers into very astute critics of Northern society. George Fitzhugh (1806–1888), a Virginia lawyer, undertook to defend slavery by describing what he called the failure of free society. Although Fitzhugh's endorsment of slavery rested upon two shaky assumptions — the inferiority of the black race and the custodial kindness of slaveholders — his analysis of Northern society was brilliant. In fact, the *Sociology for the South,* from which the last reading in this section is taken, represents one of the few American efforts to examine the assumptions upon which liberal ideals are based.

Harriet Beecher Stowe: Uncle Tom's Cabin (1852)

Late in the afternoon of a chilly day in February, two gentlemen were sitting alone over their wine, in a well-furnished dining parlor, in the town of P——, in Kentucky. There were no servants present, and the gentlemen, with chairs closely approaching, seemed to be discussing some subject with great earnestness.

For convenience sake, we have said, hitherto, two gentlemen. One of the parties, however, when critically examined, did not seem, strictly speaking, to come under the species. He was a short, thick set man, with coarse, commonplace features, and that swaggering air of pretension which marks a low man who is trying to elbow his way upward in the world. He was much overdressed, in a gaudy vest of many colors, a blue neckerchief, bedropped gayly with yellow spots, and arranged with a flaunting tie, quite in keeping with the general air of the man. His hands, large and coarse, were plentifully bedecked with rings; and he wore a heavy gold watchchain, with a bundle of seals, of portentous size and a great variety of colors, attached to it — which, in the ardor of conversation, he was in the habit of flourishing and jingling with evident satisfaction. His conversation was in free and easy defiance of Murray's Grammar, and was garnished at convenient intervals with various profane expressions, which not even the desire to be graphic in our account shall induce us to transcribe.

His companion, Mr. Shelby, had the appearance of a gentleman; and the arrangements of the house, and the general air of the housekeeping, indicated easy, and even opulent circumstances. As we before stated, the two were in the midst of an earnest conversation.

"That is the way I should arrange the matter," said Mr. Shelby.

"I can't make trade that way — I positively can't, Mr. Shelby," said the other, holding up a glass of wine between his eye and the light.

"Why, the fact is, Haley, Tom is an uncommon fellow; he is certainly worth the sum anywhere — steady, honest, and capable, manages my whole farm like a clock."

John P. Jewett, 1852

"You mean honest, as niggers go." said Haley, helping himself to a glass of brandy.

"No; I mean, really, Tom is a good, steady, sensible, pious fellow. He got religion at a camp-meeting, four years ago; and I believe he really did get it. I've trusted him, since then, with everything I have — money, house, horses — and let him come and go round the country: and I always found him true and square in everything."

"Some folks don't believe there is pious niggers, Shelby," said Haley, with a candid flourish of his hand, "but I do, I had a fellow, now, in this yer last lot I took to Orleans — 't was as good as a meetin', now, really, to hear that critter pray; and he was quite gentle and quiet like. He fetched me a good sum, too, for I bought him cheap of a man that was 'bliged to sell out; so I realized six hundred on him. Yes, I consider religion a valeyable thing in a nigger, when it's the genuine article, and no mistake."

"Well, Tom's got the real article, if ever a fellow had," rejoined the other. "Why, last fall, I let him go to Cincinnati alone, to do business for me, and bring home five hundred dollars. 'Tom,' says I to him, 'I trust you, because I think you're a Christian — I know you wouldn't cheat,' Tom comes back, sure enough; I knew he would. Some low fellows, they say, said to him — 'Tom, why don't you make tracks for Canada?' 'Ah, master trusted me, and I couldn't' — they told me about it. I am sorry to part with Tom, I must say. You ought to let him cover the whole balance of the debt; and you would, Haley, if you had any conscience."

"Well, I've got just as much conscience as any man in business can afford to keep — just as little, you know, to swear by, as't were," said the trader, jocularly; "and, then, I'm ready to do anything in reason to 'blige friends: but this yer, you see, is a leetle too hard on a fellow — a leetle too hard." The trader sighed contemplatively, and poured out some more brandy.

"Well, then, Haley, how will you trade?" said, Mr. Shelby, after an uneasy interval of silence.

"Well, haven't you a boy or gal that you could throw in with Tom?"

"Hum! — none that I could well spare; to tell the truth, it's only hard necessity makes me willing to sell at all. I don't like parting with any of my hands, that's a fact."

Here the door opened, and a small quadroon boy, between four and five years of age, entered the room. There was something in his appearance remarkably beautiful and engaging. His black hair, fine as floss silk, hung in glossy curls about his round, dimpled face, while a pair of large dark eyes, full of fire and softness, looked out from beneath the rich, long lashes, as he peered curiously into the apartment. A gay robe of scarlet and yellow plaid, carefully made and neatly fitted, set off to advantage the dark and rich style of his beauty; and a certain comic air of assurance, blended with bashfulness, showed that he had been not unused to being petted and noticed by his master.

"Hulloa, Jim Crow!" said Mr. Shelby, whistling, and snapping a bunch of raisins toward him, "pick that up, now!"

The child scampered, with all his little strength, after the prize, while his master laughed.

"Come here, Jim Crow," said he. The child came up, and the master patted the curly head, and chucked him under the chin.

"Now, Jim, show this gentleman how you can dance and sing." The boy commenced one of those wild, grotesque songs common among the negroes, in a rich, clear voice, accompanying his singing with many comic evolutions of the hands, feet, and whole body, all in perfect time to the music.

"Bravo!" said Haley, throwing him a quarter of an orange.

"Now, Jim, walk like old Uncle Cudjoe, when he has the rheumatism," said his master.

Instantly the flexible limbs of the child assumed the appearance of deformity and distortion, as, with his back humped up, and his master's stick in his hand, he hobbled about the room, his childish face drawn into a doleful pucker, and spitting from right to left, in imitation of an old man.

Both gentlemen laughed uproariously . . .

At this moment the door was pushed gently open, and a young quadroon woman, apparently about twenty-five, entered the room.

There needed only a glance from the child to her, to identify her as its mother. There was the same rich, full, dark eye, with its long lashes; the same ripples of silky black hair. The brown of her complexion gave way on the cheek to a perceptible flush, which deepened as she saw the gaze of the strange man fixed upon her in bold and undisguised admiration. Her dress was of the neatest possible fit, and set off to advantage her finely molded shape; a delicately formed hand and a trim foot and ankle were items of appearance that did not escape the quick eye of the trader, well used to run up at a glance the points of a fine female article.

"Well, Eliza?" said her master, as she stopped and looked hesitatingly at him.

"I was looking for Harry, please, sir;" and the boy bounded toward her, showing his spoils, which he had gathered in the skirt of his robe.

"Well, take him away, then," said Mr. Shelby; and hastily she withdrew, carrying the child on her arm.

"By Jupiter," said the trader, turning to him in admiration, "there's an article, now! You might make your fortune on that ar gal in Orleans, any day. I've seen over a thousand, in my day, paid down for gals not a bit handsomer."

"I don't want to make my fortune on her," said Mr. Shelby, dryly; and, seeking to turn the conversation, he uncorked a bottle of fresh wine, and asked his companion's opinion of it.

"Capital, sir — first chop!" said the trader; then turning and slapping his hand familiarly on Shelby's shoulder, he added:

"Come, how will you trade about the gal? what shall I say for her — what'll you take?"

"Mr. Haley, she is not to be sold," said Shelby. "My wife would not part with her for her weight in gold."

"Ay, ay! women always say such things, cause they ha'nt no sort of calculation. Just show 'em how many watches, feathers, and trinkets, one's weight in gold would buy, and that alters the case, I reckon."

"I tell you, Haley, this must not be spoken of; I say no, and I mean no," said Shelby, decidedly.

"Well, you'll let me have the boy, though," said the trader; "you must own I've come down pretty handsomely for him."

"What on earth can you want with the child?" said Shelby.

"Why, I've got a friend that's going into this yer branch of the business — wants to buy up handsome boys to raise for the market. Fancy articles entirely —

sell for waiters, and so on, to rich 'uns, that can pay for handsome 'uns. It sets off one of yer great places — a real handsome boy to open door, wait, and tend. They fetch a good sum: and this little devil is such a comical, musical concern, he's just the article."

"I would rather not sell him," said Mr. Shelby, thoughtfully; "the fact is, sir, I'm a humane man, and I hate to take the boy from his mother, sir."

"O, you do? La! yes — something of that ar natur. I understand, perfectly. It is mighty onpleasant getting on with women, sometimes. I al'ays hates these yer screechin', screamin' times. They are might onpleasant; but, as I manages business, I generally avoids 'em, sir. Now, what if you get the girl off for a day, or a week, or so; then the thing's done quietly — all over before she comes home. Your wife might get her some earrings, or a new gown, or some such truck, to make up with her."

"I'm afraid not."

"Lor' bless ye, yes! These critters ain't like white folks, you know; they gets over things, only manage right. Now, they say," said Haley, assuming a candid and confidential air, "that this kind o' trade is hardening to the feelings; but I never found it so. Fact is, I never could do things up the way some fellers manage the business. I've seen 'em as would pull a woman's child out of her arms, and set him up to sell, and she screechin' like mad all the time; very bad policy — damages the article — makes 'em quite unfit for service sometimes. I knew a real handsome gal once, in Orleans, as was entirely ruined by this sort o' handling. The fellow that was trading for her didn't want her baby; and she was one of your real high sort, when her blood was up. I tell you, she squeezed up her child in her arms, and talked, and went on real awful. It kinder makes my blood run cold to think on't; and when they carried off the child, and locked her up, she jest went ravin' mad, and died in a week. Clear waste, sir, of a thousand dollars, just for want of management — there's where 't is. It's always best to do the humane thing, sir; that's been my experience." And the trader leaned back in his chair, and folded his arms, with an air of virtuous decision, apparently considering himself a second Wilberforce.

The subject appeared to interest the gentleman deeply, for while Mr. Shelby was thoughtfully peeling an orange; Haley broke out afresh, with becoming diffidence, but as if actually driven by the force of truth to say a few words more.

"It don't look well, now, for a feller to be praisin' himself; but I say it jest because it's the truth. I believe I'm reckoned to bring in about the finest droves of niggers that is brought in — at least, I've been told so; if I have once, I reckon I have a hundred times — all in good case — fat and likely, and I lose as few as any man in the business. And I lays it all to my management, sir; and humanity, sir, I may say, is the great pillar of my management." . . .

"Well, call up this evening, between six and seven, and you shall have my answer," said Mr. Shelby, and the trader bowed himself out of the apartment.

"I'd like to have been able to kick the fellow down the steps," said he to himself, as he saw the door fairly closed, "with his impudent assurance; but he knows how much he has me at advantage. If anybody had ever said to me that I should sell Tom down south to one of those rascally traders, I should have said, 'Is thy servant a dog, that he should do this thing?' And now it must come for ought I see. And Eliza's child, too! I know that I shall have some fuss with wife about that; and, for that matter, about Tom, too. So much for being in debt — heigho! The fellow sees his advantage, and means to push it."

Perhaps the mildest form of the system of slavery is to be seen in the State of Kentucky. The general prevalence of agricultural pursuits of a quiet and gradual nature, not requiring those periodic seasons of hurry and pressure that are called for in the business of more southern districts, makes the task of the negro a more healthful and reasonable one; while the master, content with a more gradual style of acquisition, has not those temptations to hardheartedness which always overcome frail human nature when the prospect of sudden and rapid gain is weighed in the balance, with no heavier counterpoise than the interests of the helpless and unprotected.

Whoever visits some estates there and witnesses the good-humored indulgence of some masters and mistresses, and the affectionate loyalty of some slaves, might be tempted to dream the off-fabled poetic legend of a patriarchal institution, and all that; but over and above the scene there broods a portentous shadow —

the shadow of *law*. So long as the law considers all these human beings, with beating hearts and living affections, only as so many *things* belonging to a master — so long as the failure, or misfortune, or imprudence, or death of the kindest owner may cause them any day to exchange a life of kind protection and indulgence for one of hopeless misery and toil — so long it is impossible to make anything beautiful or desirable in the best regulated administration of slavery.

Mr. Shelby was a fair average kind of man, good-natured and kindly, and disposed to easy indulgence of those around him, and there had never been a lack of anything which might contribute to the physical comfort of the negroes on his estate. He had, however, speculated largely and quite loosely; had involved himself deeply, and his notes to a large amount had come into the hands of Haley; and this small piece of information is the key to the preceding conversation.

Now, it had so happened that, in approaching the door Eliza had caught enough of the conversation to know that a trader was making offers to her master for somebody.

She would gladly have stopped at the door to listen, as she came out; but her mistress just then calling, she was obliged to hasten away.

Still she thought she heard the trader make an offer for her boy; could she be mistaken? Her heart swelled and throbbed, and she involuntarily strained him so tight that the little fellow looked up into her face in astonishment.

"Eliza, girl, what ails you to-day?" said her mistress, when Eliza had upset the wash-pitcher, knocked down the work-stand, and finally was abstractedly offering her mistress a long night-gown in place of the silk dress she had ordered her to bring from the wardrobe.

Eliza started. "O, missis!" she said, raising her eyes; then, bursting into tears she sat down in a chair, and began sobbing.

"Why, Eliza my child! what ails you?" said her mistress.

"O! missis, missis," said Eliza, "there's been a trader talking with master in the parlor! I heard him."

"Well, silly child, suppose there has."

"O, missis, *do* you suppose mas'r would sell my Harry?" And the poor creature threw herself into a chair, and sobbed convulsively.

"Sell him! No, you foolish girl. You know your master never deals with those southern traders, and never means to sell any of his servants, as long as they behave well. Why, you silly child, who do you think would want to buy your Harry? Do you think all the world are set on him as you are, you goosie? Come, cheer up, and hook my dress. There now, put my back hair up, in that pretty braid you learned the other day, and don't go listening at doors any more."

"Well, but, missis, you never would give your consent — to — to —"

"Nonsense child! to be sure, I shouldn't. What do you talk so for? I would as soon have one of my own children sold. But, really, Eliza, you are getting altogether too proud of that little fellow. A man can't put his nose into the door, but you think he must be coming to buy him."

Reassured by her mistress' confident tone, Eliza proceeded nimbly and adroitly with her toilet, laughing at her own fears, as she proceeded.

Mrs. Shelby was a woman of a high class, both intellectually and morally. To that natural magnanimity and generosity of mind which one often marks as characteristic of the women of Kentucky, she added high moral and religious sensibility and principle, carried out with great energy and ability into practical results. Her husband, who made no professions to any particular religious character, nevertheless reverenced and respected the consistency of her's and stood, perhaps, a little in awe of her opinion. Certain it was that he gave her unlimited scope in all her benevolent efforts for the comfort, instruction, and improvement of her servants, though he never took any decided part in them himself . . .

The heaviest load on his mind, after his conversation with the trader, lay in the foreseen necessity of breaking to his wife the arrangement contemplated — meeting the importunities and opposition which he knew he should have reason to encounter.

Mrs. Shelby, being entirely ignorant of her husband's embarrassments, and knowing only the general kindliness of his temper, had been quite sincere in the entire incredulity with which she had met Eliza's suspicions. In fact, she dismissed the matter from her mind, without a second thought; and being occupied in preparations for an evening visit, it passed out of her

thoughts entirely . . .

Mr. and Mrs. Shelby had retired to their apartment for the night. He was lounging in a large easy chair, looking over some letters that had come in the afternoon mail, and she was standing before her mirror, brushing out the complicated braids and curls in which Eliza had arranged her hair; for, noticing her pale cheeks and haggard eyes, she had excused her attendance that night, and ordered her to bed. The employment, naturally enough, suggested her conversation with the girl in the morning; and, turning to her husband, she said carelessly, —

"By the by, Arthur, who was that low-bred fellow that you lugged in to our dinner-table to-day?"

"Haley is his name," said Shelby, turning himself rather uneasily in his chair, and continuing with his eyes fixed on a letter.

"Haley! Who is he, and what may be his business here, pray?"

"Well, he's a man that I transacted some business with, last time I was at Natchez," said Mr. Shelby.

"And he presumed on it to make himself quite at home, and call and dine here, ay?"

"Why, I invited him; I had some accounts with him," said Shelby.

"Is he a negro-trader?" said Mrs. Shelby, noticing a certain embarrassment in her husband's manner.

"Why, my dear, what put that into your head?" said Shelby, looking up.

"Nothing, — only Eliza came in here after dinner, in a great worry, crying and taking on, and said you were talking with a trader, and that she heard him make an offer for her boy, — the ridiculous little goose!"

"She did, hey?" said Mr. Shelby, returning to his paper, which he seemed for a few moments quite intent upon, not perceiving that he was holding it bottom upwards.

"It will have to come out," said he, mentally; "as well now as ever."

"I told Eliza," said Mrs. Shelby, as she continued brushing her hair, "that she was a little fool for her pains, and that you never had anything to do with that sort of persons. Of course, I knew you never meant to sell any of our people, — least of all, to such a fellow."

"Well, Emily," said her husband, "so I have always felt and said; but the fact is that my business lies so that I cannot get on without. I shall have to sell some of my hands."

"To that creature? Impossible! Mr. Shelby, you cannot be serious."

"I'm sorry to say that I am," said Mr. Shelby. I've agreed to sell Tom."

"What! our Tom? — that good, faithful creature! — been your faithful servant from a boy! Oh, Mr. Shelby! — and you have promised him his freedom, too, — you and I have spoken to him a hundred times of it. Well, I can believe anything now, — I can believe now that you could sell little Harry, poor Eliza's only child!" said Mrs. Shelby, in a tone between grief and indignation.

"Well, since you must know all, it is so. I have agreed to sell Tom and Harry both; and I don't know why I am to be rated, as if I were a monster, for doing what every one does every day."

"But why, of all others, choose these?" said Mrs. Shelby. "Why sell them, of all on the place, if you must sell at all?"

"Because they will bring the highest sum of any, — that's why. I could choose another, if you say so. The fellow made me a high bid on Eliza, if that would suit you any better," said Mr. Shelby.

"The wretch!" said Mrs. Shelby, vehemently.

"Well, I didn't listen to it, a moment — out of regard to your feelings, I wouldn't; — so give me some credit."

"My dear," said Mrs. Shelby, recollecting herself, "forgive me. I have been hasty. I was surprised, and entirely unprepared for this; — but surely you will allow me to intercede for these poor creatures. Tom is a noble-hearted, faithful fellow, if he is black. I do believe, Mr. Shelby, that if he were put to it, he would lay down his life for you."

"I know it, — I dare say; — but what's the use of all this? — I can't help myself."

"Why not make a pecuniary sacrifice? I'm willing to bear my part of the inconvenience. Oh, Mr. Shelby, I have tried — tried most faithfully, as a Christian woman should — to do my duty to these poor, simple, dependent creatures. I have cared for them, instructed them, watched over them, and known all their little cares and joys, for years; and how can I ever hold up my head again among them, if, for the sake of a little

paltry gain, we sell such a faithful, excellent, confiding creature as poor Tom, and tear from him in a moment all we have taught him to love and value? I have taught them the duties of the family, of parent and child, and husband and wife; and how can I bear to have this open acknowledgment that we care for no tie, no duty, no relation, however sacred, compared with money? I have talked with Eliza about her boy, — her duty to him as a Christian mother, to watch over him, pray for him, and bring him up in a Christian way; and now what can I say, if you tear him away, and sell him, soul and body, to a profane, unprincipled man, just to save a little money? I have told her that one soul is worth more than all the money in the world; and how will she believe me when she sees us turn round and sell her child? — sell him, perhaps, to certain ruin of body and soul!"

"I'm sorry you feel so about it, Emily, — indeed I am," said Mr. Shelby; "and I respect your feelings, too, though I don't pretend to share them to their full extent; but I tell you now, solemnly, it's of no use, — I can't help myself. I didn't mean to tell you this, Emily; but in plain words, there is no choice between selling these two and selling everything. Either they must go, or all must. Haley has come into possession of a mortgage, which, if I don't clear off with him directly, will take everything before it. I've raked, and scraped, and borrowed, and all but begged, — and the price of these two was needed to make up the balance, and I had to give them up. Haley fancied the child; he agreed to settle the matter that way and no other. I was in his power, and *had* to do it. If you feel so to have them sold, would it be any better to have *all* sold?"

Mrs. Shelby stood like one stricken. Finally, turning to her toilet, she rested her face in her hands, and gave a sort of groan.

"This is God's curse on slavery! — a bitter, bitter, most accursed thing! — a curse to the master and a curse to the slave! I was a fool to think I could make anything good out of such a deadly evil. It is a sin to hold a slave under laws like ours, — I always felt it was, — I always thought so when I was a girl, — I thought so still more after I joined the church; but I thought I could gild it over, — I thought, by kindness, and care, and instruction, I could make the condition of mine better than freedom, — fool that I was!"

"Why, wife, you are getting to be an abolitionist, quite."

"Abolitionist! if they knew all I know about slavery they might talk! We don't need them to tell us; you know I never thought that slavery was right, — never felt willing to own slaves."

"Well, therein you differ from many wise and pious men," said Mr. Shelby. "You remember Mr. B's sermon, the other Sunday?"

"I don't want to hear such sermons; I never wish to hear Mr. B. in our church again. Ministers can't help the evil, perhaps, — can't cure it, any more than we can, — but defend it! — it always went against my common sense. And I think you didn't think much of that sermon either."

"Well," said Shelby, "I must say these ministers sometimes carry matters further than we poor sinners would exactly dare to do . . . But now, my dear, I trust you see the necessity of the thing; and you see that I have done the very best that circumstances would allow."

"Oh yes, yes!" said Mrs. Shelby, hurriedly and abstractedly fingering her gold watch, — "I haven't any jewelry of any amount," she added, thoughtfully; "but would not this watch do something? — it was an expensive one when it was bought. If I could only at least save Eliza's child, I would sacrifice anything I have."

"I'm sorry, very sorry, Emily," said Mr. Shelby, "I'm sorry this takes hold of you so; but it will do no good. The fact is, Emily, the thing's done; the bills of sale are already signed, and in Haley's hands; and you must be thankful it is no worse. That man has had it in his power to ruin us all, — and now he is fairly off. If you knew the man as I do, you'd think that we had had a narrow escape."

"Is he so hard, then?"

"Why, not a cruel man, exactly, but a man of leather, — a man alive to nothing but trade and profit, — cool, and unhesitating, and unrelenting, as death and the grave. He'd sell his own mother at a good percentage, — not wishing the old woman any harm, either."

"And this wretch owns that good, faithful Tom, and Eliza's child!"

"Well, my dear, the fact is that this goes rather hard with me; it's a thing I hate to think of. Haley wants to drive matters, and take possession to-morrow. I'm going to get out my horse bright and early, and be off. I can't see Tom, that's a fact; and you had better arrange a drive somewhere, and carry Eliza off. Let the thing be done when she is out of sight."

"No, no," said Mrs. Shelby; "I'll be in no sense accomplice or help in this cruel business. I'll go and see poor old Tom, God help him, in his distress! They shall see, at any rate, that their mistress can feel for and with them. As to Eliza, I dare not think about it. The Lord forgive us! What have we done, that this cruel necessity should come on us?"

There was one listener to this conversation whom Mr. and Mrs. Shelby little suspected.

Communicating with their apartment was a large closet, opening by a door into the outer passage. When Mrs. Shelby had dismissed Eliza for the night her feverish and excited mind had suggested the idea of this closet; and she had hidden herself there, and with her ear pressed close against the crack of the door, had lost not a word of the conversation.

When the voices died into silence, she rose and crept stealthily away. Pale, shivering, with rigid features and compressed lips, she looked an entirely altered being from the soft and timid creature she had been hitherto. She moved cautiously along the entry, paused one moment at her mistress's door and raised her hands in mute appeal to Heaven, and then turned and glided into her own room. It was a quiet, neat apartment, on the same floor with her mistress. There was the pleasant sunny window, where she had often sat singing at her sewing; there, a little case of books, and various little fancy articles, ranged by them, the gifts of Christmas holidays; there was her simple wardrobe in the closet and in the drawers: — here was, in short, her home; and, on the whole, a happy one it had been to her. But there, on the bed, lay her slumbering boy, his long curls falling negligently around his unconscious face, his rosy mouth half open, his little fat hands thrown out over the bedclothes, and a smile spread like a sunbeam over his whole face.

"Poor boy! poor fellow!" said Eliza; "they have sold you! but your mother will save you yet!"

No tear dropped over that pillow; in such straits as these the heart has no tears to give, — it drops only blood, bleeding itself away in silence. She took a piece of paper and a pencil, and wrote hastily, —

"Oh, Missis! dear Missis! don't think me ungrateful, — don't think hard of me, any way, — I heard all you and master said to-night. I am going to try to save my boy, — you will not blame me! God bless and reward you for all your kindness!"

Hastily folding and directing this, she went to a drawer and made up a little package of clothing for her boy, which she tied with a handkerchief firmly round her waist; and, so fond is a mother's remembrance, that, even in the terrors of that hour, she did not forget to put in the little package one or two of his favorite toys, reserving a gayly painted parrot to amuse him when she should be called on to awaken him. It was some trouble to arouse the little sleeper; but, after some effort, he sat up, and was playing with his bird, while his mother was putting on her bonnet and shawl.

"Where are you going, mother?" said he, as she drew near the bed, with his little coat and cap.

His mother drew near, and looked so earnestly into his eyes, that he at once divined that something unusual was the matter.

"Hush, Harry," she said; "mustn't speak loud, or they will hear us. A wicked man was coming to take little Harry away from his mother, and carry him 'way off in the dark; but mother won't let him, — she's going to put on her little boy's cap and coat, and run off with him, so the ugly man can't catch him."

Saying these words, she had tied and buttoned on the child's simple outfit, and, taking him in her arms, she whispered to him to be very still; and, opening a door in her room which led into the outer veranda, she glided noiselessly out . . .

George Frederick Holmes: Review of Uncle Tom's Cabin (1852)

Assuredly, there is no necessity to convince the slave owners, or the residents in the Southern States, that the condition of society, the status of the slave, the incidents and accidents of slavery, the practices or even the rights of masters, are exhibited in a false light, and are falsely stated in Uncle Tom's Cabin; and that, by whatever jugglery or sorcery the result is obtained, the picture, with all its ostensible desire of truthful delineation, is distorted and discolored, and presents at one time a caricature, at another a total misrepresentation of things amongst us. It is not to Southern men that it is necessary to address any argument on a topic like this. They are already aware of the grossness of the slander by their own observation and experience. No,

the tribunal to which our defence must be addressed, is the public sentiment of the North and of Europe. In both latitudes, the case is already prejudged and decided against us; in both, popular ignorance and popular fanaticism, and a servile press have predetermined the question. The special circumstances of the condition of society in both have led to the complete extinguishment of slavery, *co nomine;* and what was dictated by pecuniary interest, and achieved by folly or accident, is believed to furnish the immutable canon for the action of all communities, and to constitute the valid criterion of a higher law . . .

In this manner, we may understand both the cause of the thousands of copies of Uncle Tom's Cabin, which have been sold at the North and in England, and also the extreme difficulty, not to say absolute impossibility, of securing a dispassionate hearing for our defence, or of introducing the antidote where the poison has spread. There is no obduracy so impracticable — no deafness so incurable — as that Pharisaical self sanctification and half-conscious hypocrisy, which gilds its own deliberate delusions with the false colors of an extravagant morality, and denounces all dissent from its own fanatical prejudices, as callous vice and irremediable sin. The whole phalanx of Abolition literature, in all its phases and degrees, is fully imbued with this self-righteous spirit; and its influence, under all forms — in fiction and in song — in sermon and in essay — in political harangue as in newspaper twaddle — is completely turned against us: and an aggregation of hostile tendencies is brought to bear upon us so as to deny to our complaints, our recriminations, or our apologies, either consideration or respect. The potency of literature, in this age of the world, when it embraces all manifestations of public or individual thought and feeling, and permeates, in streams, more or less diluted, all classes of society, can scarcely be misapprehended . . .

It is a natural and inevitable consequence of this silly and fatal indifference to the high claims of a native and domestic literature, that the South is now left at the mercy of every witling and scribbler who panders to immediate profit or passing popularity, by harping on a string in unison with the prevailing fanaticism. It is a necessary result of the same long continued im-

Southern Literary Messenger XVIII 18 (1852), pp. 721–31.

prudence, that no defence can be heard, no refutation of vile slander regarded in the courts of literature, which comes from a land whose literary claims have been disparaged and crushed by its own blind recklessness and meanness. In Uncle Tom's Cabin, there is certainly neither extraordinary genius nor remarkable strength; the attack is unquestionably a weak one: there is only that semblance of genius which springs from intense fanaticism and an earnest purpose; and that plausibility which is due to concentrated energy and a narrow one-sided exposition of human afflictions . . .

We will concede for the nonce, the general truth of the facts alleged, and will maintain that notwithstanding this concession, the culpability of the work, its fallacy and its falsehood remain the same. In the one case, the false conclusions are erected upon the basis of false assertions; in the other, we overlook the untruth of the statements, and find that they are deliberately employed for the insinuation of untrue and calumnious impressions. We will suppose, then, that such enormities as are recounted in Uncle Tom's Cabin, do occur at the South: that George Harris and Eliza his wife, with that seraphic little mulatto, their child, have, in truth, their prototypes among our slaves, and that the brutal treatment of the former by his owner, might find its parallel in actual life. We will endeavor to imagine the reality of the murder of Prue, and the probability of the virtues, misfortunes and martyrdom of Uncle Tom — and, still heavier tax upon our credulity, we will suppose the angelical mission of that shrewish Yankee maiden, Miss Ophelia, for the conversion of hopeless niggers, and the redemption of Ebo, to have been a fact: — and, yet, notwithstanding all this, and it is tough, indeed, to swallow, we will maintain the doctrines of the book to be most pernicious, the representation given to be most erroneous, the impression designed to be produced to be most criminal and false, and the iniquity of the scandalous production to be entitled to unmitigated censure and reprobation. We will not even limit our concession so far as might be requisite to bring the delineation within any reasonable approximation of the truth: we will not insist that the incidents conceded must be regarded as exceptional cases: for it is perceived in Uncle Tom's Cabin, that to admit them to be exceptions, would be to change, entirely, the character of the argument, and destroy

its validity . . . We will concede all the facts stated in the work: all that we will not concede, is the significance attributed to them, and their relevancy for the purpose for which they are employed. And, having granted all this, we still believe that we can offer an ample vindication of the South, and justify the severest censure of this inflamatory and seditious production.

We cannot, however, pass to what may be regarded as the argument of the work, without noting that the hero and heroine of the tale — the tawny Apollo and Venus, with the interesting yellow Cupid, on whom so large a portion of the plot is concentrated — belong exactly to that particular shade of tainted blood, when the laws of many of the Southern States, if not of all, would recognize them as free. George and Eliza Harris, as represented, have a larger proportion of white blood in their veins, than is compatible with the continuance of the servile condition. The jurisprudence of those very communities which are vilified for their imaginary mistreatment of this elegant pair, is not savage enough to retain them in bondage. It would only have been necessary for them to exhibit their radiant countenances, their soft, glossy hair, and curling ringlets, and prove the superabundance of their Caucasian blood in any of our courts of justice, to be assured of obtaining their free papers. If the work was intended for an exposition of the enormities incident to slavery, and for a protestation in favor of the injured and down-trodden African race, is it not a singular dishonesty of procedure to assume as types of this class, those who are rather degraded specimens of the white blood, than in any sense, representatives of the African, and who do not, legitimately, by the laws of the South, belong to the class intended to be redeemed by the exhibition of their sufferings, but more properly to the tribe of the alleged oppressors. Into such inconsistencies is malice betrayed, when it aims at producing false impressions, and is utterly unscrupulous in the employment of any means which seem calculated to heighten the false effect desired.

But leaving this exceedingly vulnerable characteristic of Uncle Tom's Cabin, the argument of the work — for there is an argument even in excessive dramatic pictures designed to produce given effect, as well as in successive syllogisms assigned to establish a special conclusion: — the argument of the work is, in plain and precise terms, that any organization of society — any social institution, which can by possibility result in such instances of individual misery, or generate such examples of individual cruelty as are exhibited in this fiction, must be criminal in itself, a violation of all the laws of Nature and of God, and ought to be universally condemned, and consequently immediately abolished. Unhappily, in all the replies to Uncle Tom's Cabin which have hitherto been attempted under the form of corresponding fiction, usually, we are sorry to say, by weak and incompetent persons, it has not been recognized with sufficient distinctness that the whole strength of the attack, as the whole gist of the argument, lies in this thesis. The formal rejoinders have consequently been directed to the wrong point: the real question has been mistaken; and the formal issue never joined . . .

The true and sufficient reply to this proposition is a very brief one. It is simply this, that the position is absolutely fatal to all human society — to all social organization, civilized or savage, whatever. It strikes at the very essence and existence of all community among men, it lays bare and roots up all the foundations of law, order and government. It is the very evangel of insubordination, sedition, and anarchy, and is promulgated in support of a cause worthy of the total ruin which it is calculated to produce. Pandemonium itself would be a paradise compared with what all society would become, if this apparently simple and plausible position were tenable, and action were accordingly regulated by it. Ate herself, hot from hell, could not produce more mischievous or incurable disorder than this little thesis, on which the whole insinuated argument of Uncle Tom's Cabin is founded, if this dogma were once generally or cordially received. In all periods of history — under all forms of government — under all the shifting phases of the social condition of man, instances of misery and barbarity equal to any depicted in this atrocious fiction, have been of constant recurrence, and, whatever changes may hereafter take place, unless the nature of man be also changed, they must continually recur until the very end of time. In thousands of instances, of almost daily occurrence, the affliction or the crime has sprung as directly from existing laws, manners, and institutions, as in the examples erroneously charged to the score of slavery in Un-

cle Tom's Cabin. But in all of them the real causes have been the innate frailties of humanity, the play of fortuitous circumstances, the native wickedness of particular individuals, and the inability of human wisdom or legislation to repress crime without incidentally ministering to occasional vices. If there be any latent truth in the dogma enforced by the nefarious calumnies of Uncle Tom's Cabin, it furnishes a stronger argument against all other departments of social organization than it does against slavery, as the records of our courts of justice and the inmates of our penitentiaries would testify. There is no felon who might not divest himself of his load of guilt, and extricate his neck from the halter, if such an argument was entitled to one moment's weight or consideration. In the complicated web of trials, difficulties and temptations, with which Providence in its wisdom has thought proper to intertwine the threads of human existence, an unbroken career of happiness or prosperity is not to be found. Every heart has its own sorrows, — every condition as every class its own perils and afflictions, and every individual his own bitter calamities to bewail. The very aptitude of this life for that state of probation which it was designed to be, depends upon the alternation and juxtaposition of weakness and virtue, of joy and misery, of gratifications and trials, of blessings and misfortunes, of adversity and prosperity. These varying shadows of our earthly career are due partly to the accidents by which we are surrounded, partly to the temper and conduct of our own hearts, but more than all to the concurrent or conflicting action of the members of the community among which our lot has been cast. The virtues of our neighbors may aid or encourage us, but their vices or their crimes may crush our hopes, ruin our fortunes, and entail irretrievable woe on our children as well as on ourselves. From this discord of fate it is our stern duty to educe the elements of our own career: beset with temptations, menaced by vicious intrigue, cheered by high examples or consoling counsel, but ever at the mercy of fortune, we must pursue our rough journey through the thorny paths of a world of trial. We cannot invent an Elysium or reclaim a Paradise: we can only turn to the utmost possible good and diverse conditions which encompass us around on all sides. It is only the insane hope of a frivolous and dreamy philanthropy to expect or wish that this order and variety of sublunary changes should be altered; as it is only the malignant hate of a splenetic and frenzied fanaticism which would venture to charge upon a particular institution, as its peculiar and characteristic vice, the common incidents of humanity in all times and under all its phases.

It is no distinctive feature of the servile condition that individual members of the class should suffer most poignantly in consequence of the crimes, the sins, the follies, or the thoughtlessness of others; — that children should be torn from their parents, husbands separated from their wives, and fathers rudely snatched away from their families. The same results, with concomitant infamy, are daily produced by the operation of all penal laws, and the same anguish and distress are thereby inflicted upon the helpless and innocent, yet such laws remain and must remain upon our statute books for the security and conservation of any social organization at all. The ordinary play of human interests, of human duties, of human necessities, and even of human ambition — unnoticed and commonplace as it may be conceived to be, produces scenes more terrible and agony more poignant and heart-rending than any attributed to slavery in Uncle Tom's Cabin. The temptations of worldly advancement, the hopes of temporary success, the lures of pecuniary gain, in every civilized or barbarous community throughout the world — in the deserts of Sahara as amid the snows of Greenland — in the streets of Boston and Lowell as in those of London, Manchester, and Paris, may and do exhibit a longer register of sadder results than even a treacherous imagination, or fiction on the hunt for falsehood has been able to rake up from the fraudulent annals of slavery in the present work. There is scarccly one revolution of a wheel in a Northern or European cottonmill, which does not, in its immediate or remote effects, entail more misery on the poor and the suffering than all the incidents of servile misery gathered in the present work from the most suspicious and disreputable sources. The annual balance sheet of a Northern millionaire symbolizes infinitely greater agony and distress in the labouring or destitute classes than even the foul martyrdom of Uncle Tom. Are the laws of debtor and creditor — and the processes by which gain is squeezed from the life-blood of the indigent, more gentle; — or the hard, grasping, demoniac avarice of a yankee trader more

merciful than the atrocious heart of the fiendish yankee, Simon Legree? Was the famine in Ireland productive of no calamities which might furnish a parallel to the scenes in Uncle Tom's Cabin? We would hazard even the assertion that the Australian emigration from Great Britain, and the Californian migration in our country — both impelled by the mere hope of sudden and extraordinary gains, have been attended with crimes and vices, sorrows, calamities and distresses far surpassing the imaginary ills of the slaves whose fictitious woes are so hypocritically bemoaned. But such are the incidents of life, and we would neither denounce nor revolutionize society, because such consequences were inseparable from its continuance.

It should be observed that the whole tenor of this pathetic tale derives most of its significance and colouring from a distorted representation or a false conception of the sentiments and feelings of the slave. It presupposes an identity of sensibilities between the races of the free and the negroes, whose cause it pretends to advocate. It takes advantage of this presumption, so unsuspiciously credited where slavery is unknown, to arouse sympathies for what might be grievous misery to the white man, but is none to the indifferently tempered black. Every man adapts himself and his feelings more or less to the circumstances of his condition: without this wise provision of nature life would be intolerable to most of us. Every race in like manner becomes habituated to the peculiar accidents of its particular class; even the Paria may be happy. Thus what would be insupportable to one race, or one order of society, constitutes no portion of the wretchedness of another . . .

The proposition, then, which may be regarded as embodying the peculiar essence of Uncle Tom's Cabin, is a palpable fallacy, and inconsistent with all social organization. Granting, therefore, all that could be asked by our adversaries, it fails to furnish any proof whatever of either the iniquity or the enormity of slavery. If it was capable of proving anything at all, it would prove a great deal too much. It would demonstrate that all order, law, government, society was a flagrant and unjustifiable violation of the rights, and mockery of the feelings of man and ought to be abated as a public nuisance . . . The fundamental position, then, of these dangerous and dirty little volumes is a deadly blow to all the interests and duties of humanity, and is utterly impotent to show any inherent vice in the institution of slavery which does not also appertain to all other institutions whatever. But we will not be content to rest here: we will go a good bow-shot beyond this refutation, though under no necessity to do so: and we maintain that the distinguishing characteristic of slavery is its tendency to produce effects exactly opposite to those laid to its charge: to diminish the amount of individual misery in the servile classes: to mitigate and alleviate all the ordinary sorrows of life: to protect the slaves against want as well as against material and mental suffering: to prevent the separation and dispersion of families; and to shield them from the frauds, the crimes, and the casualties of others, whether masters or fellow-slaves, in a more eminent degree than is attainable under any other organization of society, where slavery does not prevail. This is but a small portion of the peculiar advantages to the slaves themselves resulting from the institution of slavery, but these suffice for the present, and furnish a most overwhelming refutation of the philanthropic twaddle of this and similar publications.

Notwithstanding the furious and ill-omened outcry which has been made in recent years against the continuance of slavery, the communities where it prevails exhibit the only existing instance of a modern civilized society in which the interests of the labourer and the employer of labour are absolutely identical, and in which the reciprocal sympathies of both are assured. The consequence is that both interest and inclination, the desire of profit and the sense or sentiment of duty concur to render the slave-owner considerate and kind toward the slave. So general is the feeling, so habitual the consciousness of this intimate harmony of the interests and duties of both, that it has formed an efficient public sentiment at the South which brands with utter reprobation the slaveholder who is either negligent of his slaves or harsh in his treatment of them. It goes even further than this; it makes every man at the South the protector of the slave against injury by whomsoever offered, thus establishing an efficient and voluntary police, of which everyone is a member, for the defence of the slave against either force, fraud, or outrage. Such habitual regard for the rights of a subordinate class generates in its members a kindliness of

feeling and a deference of bearing to the slave-holder in general, which no severity could produce and no rigor maintain. It is this intercommunion of good offices and good will, of interests and obligations, which renders the realities of slavery at the South so entirely different from what they are imagined to be by those who have no intimate familiarity with its operation. Hence, too, in great measure it is, that, except where inveterate idleness or vice compels a sale, or the changes of fortune, or the casualties of life, break up an establishment, families are rarely dispersed, but are held together without being liable to those never-ending separations which are of daily occurrence with the labouring or other classes elsewhere. Even where the misfortunes of the owner necessitates a sale, if the negroes enjoy a respectable character, there is every probability that they will never be removed from the district in which they have lived, but will either be bought with the place on which they have worked, be transferred en masse to some neighboring locality, or scattered about within easy distances of each other in the same vicinity.

It is true that the continued agitation of the slavery question, and the nefarious practices of the abolitionists, which are so cordially eulogised in Uncle Tom's Cabin, have in some degree modified the relations between master and slave in those frontier settlements which border on the Ohio river, and have rendered imperative a harsher intercourse and more rigid management, than prevails where the feelings and principles of the negroes are not tampered with by incendiary missionaries. This is but one of the melancholy fruits of that philanthropical fanaticism, which injures by every movement which it makes those whom it pretends so sympathetically to serve . . .

If then all the facts alleged in Uncle Tom's Cabin, and entering into the composition of the pitiful tale, be conceded, they furnish no evidence whatever against the propriety or expediency of slavery. But, if the facts be false, what might have been error and delusion in the former case, becomes deliberate fraud and malignant slander. If they were true, we might pity the ignorance which had suffered itself to be perverted to crime by its ill-disposed credulity. If they are false, we must execrate the infamous virulence which fanatically employs falsehoods to breed dissension. If they were true, but did not legitimately minister to the purpose for which they were introduced, we could not pardon the folly, the presumption, and the unchristian spirit, which used them to fan the flames of discord, and to stir up the embers of civil war. If they are false, the diabolical hate which presided over the composition of the work, and clothed itself in the tempting hues of tender charity and melting philanthropy, for the surer accomplishment of its infernal aims, stands revealed in all its naked deformity, seared with the brand of infamy, and blackened with the deep damnation of its guilt. It is Satan starting up from his disguise, in the monstrous proportions and with the fiendish visage of the prince of hell, at the presence of the angels of heaven, and the touch of the spear of truth. That the facts as stated and as intended to be received are false, we solemnly aver — and for the confirmation of this averment we confidently appeal to every resident in the South, who has dispassionately reflected upon his own experience and observation — whether he be slaveowner or not: — whether he be native, yankee immigrant, or foreigner. That the isolated statements may accidentally be true *sub modo*, we will not utterly deny: the range of fiction is wide but the miracles of reality far surpass it: but that they are true under the colouring with which they are depicted we do absolutely gainsay . . .

We dismiss Uncle Tom's Cabin with the conviction and declaration that every holier purpose of our nature is misguided, every charitable sympathy betrayed, every loftier sentiment polluted, every moral purpose wrenched to wrong, and every patriotic feeling outraged, by its criminal prostitution of the high functions of the imagination to the pernicious intrigues of sectional animosity, and to the petty calumnies of wilful slander.

George Fitzhugh: Sociology for the South (1854)

Free Trade

Political economy is the science of free society. Its theory and its history alike establish this position. Its fundamental maxims, *Laissez-faire* and *"Pas trop gouverner,"* are at war with all kinds of slavery, for they

Richmond, Virginia, 1854, pp. 7–11, 22–26, 29–37, 86, 94–95, 175–83.

in fact assert that individuals and peoples prosper most when governed least. It is not, therefore, wonderful that such a science should not have been believed or inculcated whilst slavery was universal. Roman and Greek masters, feudal lords and Catholic priests, if conscientious, must have deemed such maxims false and heritical, or if unconscientious, would find in their self-interest sufficient reasons to prevent their propagation. Accordingly we find no such maxims current, no such science existing, until slavery and serfdom were extinct and Catholicism maimed and crippled, in the countries that gave them birth . . . After the abolition of feudalism and Catholicism, an immense amount of unfettered talent, genius, industry and capital, was brought into the field of free competition. The immediate result was, that all those who possessed either of those advantages prospered as they had never prospered before, and rose in social position and intelligence. At the same time, and from the same causes, the aggregate wealth of society, and probably its aggregate intelligence, were rapidly increased. Such was no doubt part of the effects of unfettering the limbs, and minds and consciences of men. It was the only part of those effects that scholars and philosophers saw or heeded. Here was something new under the sun, which refuted and rebuked the wisdom of Solomon. Up to this time, one-half of mankind had been little better than chattels belonging to the other half. A central power, with branches radiating throughout the civilized world, had trammeled men's consciences, dictated their religious faith, and prescribed the forms and modes of worship. All this was done away with, and the new world just started into existence was certainly making rapid progress and seemed to the ordinary observer to be very happy. About such a world, nothing was to be found in books. Its social, its industrial and its moral phenomena, seemed to be as beautiful as they were novel. They needed, however, description, classification and arrangement. Men's social relations and moral duties were quite different under a system of universal liberty and equality of rights, from what they had been in a state of subordination and dependence on the one side, and of power, authority and protection on the other. The reciprocal duties and obligations of master and slave, of lord and vassal, of priest and layman, to each other, were altogether unlike those that should be practiced between the free and equal citizens of regenerated society. Men needed a moral guide, a new philosophy of ethics; for neither the sages of the Gentiles, nor the Apostles of Christianity, had foreseen or provided for the great light which was now to burst upon the world. . .

A philosophy that should guide and direct industry was equally needed with a philosophy of morals. The occasion found and made the man. For writing a one-sided philosophy, no man was better fitted than Adam Smith. He possessed extraordinary powers of abstraction, analysis and generalization. He was absent, secluded and unobservant. He saw only that prosperous and progressive portion of society whom liberty or free competition benefitted, and mistook its effects on them for its effects on the world. He had probably never heard the old English adage, "Every man for himself, and Devil take the hindmost." This saying comprehends the whole philosophy, moral and economical, of the "Wealth of Nations." . . .

Adam Smith's philosophy is simple and comprehensive, *(teres et rotundus.)* Its leading and almost its only doctrine is, that individual well-being and social and national wealth and prosperity will be best promoted by each man's eagerly pursuing his own selfish welfare unfettered and unrestricted by legal regulations, or governmental prohibitions, farther than such regulations may be necessary to prevent positive crime. That some qualifications of this doctrine will not be found in his book, we shall not deny; but this is his system . . . Its authors never seem to be aware that they are writing an ethical as well as an economical code; yet it is probable that no writings, since the promulgation of the Christian dispensation, have exercised so controlling an influence on human conduct as the writings of these authors. The morality which they teach is one of simple and unadulterated selfishness. The public good, the welfare of society, the prosperity of one's neighbors, is, according to them, best promoted by each man's looking solely to the advancement of his own pecuniary interests. They maintain that national wealth, happiness and prosperity being but the aggregate of individual wealth, happiness and prosperity, if each man pursues exclusively his own selfish good, he is doing the most he can to promote the general good. They seem to forget that men eager in the pursuit of wealth are never satisfied with the fair earnings of

their own bodily labor, but find their wits and cunning employed in overreaching others much more profitable than their hands. *Laissez-faire*, free competition begets a war of the wits, which these economists encourage, quite as destructive to the weak, simple and guileless, as the war of the sword . . .

It begets another war in the bosom of society still more terrible than this. It arrays capital against labor. Every man is taught by political economy that it is meritorious to make the best bargains one can. In all old countries, labor is superabundant, employers less numerous than laborers; yet all the laborers must live by the wages they receive from the capitalists. The capitalist cheapens their wages; they compete with and underbid each other, for employed they must be on any terms. This war of the rich with the poor and the poor with one another, is the morality which political economy inculcates. It is the only morality, save the Bible, recognized or acknowledged in free society, and is far more efficacious in directing worldly men's conduct than the Bible, for that teaches self-denial, not self-indulgence and aggrandizement. This process of underbidding each other by the poor, which universal liberty necessarily brings about, has well been compared by the author of Alton Locke to the prisoners in the Black Hole of Calcutta strangling one another. A beautiful system of ethics this, that places all mankind in antagonistic positions, and puts all society at war. What can such a war result in but the oppression and ultimate extermination of the weak? In such society the astute capitalist, who is very skilful and cunning, gets the advantage of every one with whom he competes or deals; the sensible man with moderate means gets the advantage of most with whom he has business, but the mass of the simple and poor are outwitted and cheated by everybody.

Woman fares worst when thrown into this warfare of competition. The delicacy of her sex and her nature prevents her exercising those coarse arts which men do in the vulgar and promiscuous jostle of life, and she is reduced to the necessity of getting less than half price for her work. To the eternal disgrace of human nature, the men who employ her value themselves on the Adam Smith principle for their virtuous and sensible conduct. "Labor is worth what it will bring; they have given the poor woman more than any one else would, or she would not have taken the work." Yet she and her children are starving, and the employer is growing rich by giving her half what her work is worth. Thus does free competition, the creature of free society, throw the whole burden of the social fabric on the poor, the weak and ignorant. They produce every thing and enjoy nothing. They are "the muzzled ox that treadeth out the straw."

In free society none but the selfish virtues are in repute, because none other help a man in the race of competition. In such society virtue loses all her loveliness, because of her selfish aims. Good men and bad men have the same end in view: self-promotion, self-elevation. The good man is prudent, cautious, and cunning of fence; he knows well, the arts (the virtues, if you please) which enable him to advance his fortunes at the expense of those with whom he deals; he does not "cut too deep"; he does not cheat and swindle, he only makes good bargains and excellent profits. He gets more subjects by this course; everybody comes to him to be bled. He bides his time; takes advantage of the follies, the improvidence and vices of others, and makes his fortune out of the follies and weaknesses of his fellow-men. The bad man is rash, hasty, unskilful and impolite. He is equally selfish, but not half so prudent and cunning. Selfishness is almost the only motive of human conduct in free society, where every man is taught that it is his first duty to change and better his pecuniary situation.

The first principles of the science of political economy inculcate separate, individual action, and are calculated to prevent that association of labor without which nothing great can be achieved; for man isolated and individualized is the most helpless of animals. We think this error of the economists proceeded from their adopting Locke's theory of the social contract. We believe no heresy in moral science has been more pregnant of mischief than this theory of Locke. It lies at the bottom of all moral speculations, and if false, must infect with falsehood all theories built on it. Some animals are by nature gregarious and associative. Of this class are men, ants and bees. An isolated man is almost as helpless and ridiculous as a bee setting up for himself. Man is born a member of society, and does not form society. Nature, as in the cases of bees and ants, has it ready formed for him. He and society are

congenital. Society is the being — he one of the members of that being. He has no rights whatever, as opposed to the interests of society; and that society may very properly make any use of him that will redound to the public good. Whatever rights he has are subordinate to the good of the whole; and he has never ceded rights to it, for he was born its slave, and had no rights to cede . . .

A maxim well calculated not only to retard the progress of civilization, but to occasion its retrogression, has grown out of the science of political economy. "The world is too much governed," has become quite an axiom with many politicians. Now the need of law and government is just in proportion to man's wealth and enlightenment. Barbarians and savages need and will submit to but few and simple laws, and little of government. The love of personal liberty and freedom from all restraint, are distinguishing traits of wild men and wild beasts. Our Anglo-Saxon ancestors loved personal liberty because they were barbarians, but they did not love it half so much as North American Indians or Bengal tigers, because they were not half so savage. As civilization advances, liberty recedes: and it is fortunate for man that he loses his love of liberty just as fast as he becomes more moral and intellectual. The wealthy, virtuous and religious citizens of large towns enjoy less of liberty than any other persons whatever, and yet they are the most useful and rationally happy of all mankind. The best governed countries, and those which have prospered most, have always been distinguished for the number and stringency of their laws. Good men obey superior authority, the laws of God, of morality, and of their country; bad men love liberty and violate them. It would be difficult very often for the most ingenious casuist to distinguish between sin and liberty; for virtue consists in the performance of duty, and the obedience to that law or power that imposes duty, whilst sin is but the violation of duty and disobedience to such law and power . . .

All men concur in the opinion that some government is necessary. Even the political economist would punish murder, theft, robbery, gross swindling, &c.; but they encourage men to compete with and slowly undermine and destroy one another by means quite as effective as those they forbid. We have heard a distinguished member of this school object to negro slavery, because the protection it afforded to an inferior race would perpetuate that race, which, if left free to compete with the whites, must be starved out in a few generations. Members of Congress, of the Young American party, boast that the Anglo-Saxon race is manifestly destined to eat out all other races, as the wire-grass destroys and takes the place of other grasses. Nay, they allege this competitive process is going on throughout all nature; the weak are everywhere devouring the strong; the hardier plants and animals destroying the weaker, and the superior races of man exterminating the inferior. They would challenge our admiration for this war of nature, by which they say Providence is perfecting its own work — getting rid of what is weak and indifferent, and preserving only what is strong and hardy. We see the war, but not the improvement. This competitive, destructive system has been going on from the earliest records of history; and yet the plants, the animals, and the men of to-day are not superior to those of four thousand years ago. To restrict this destructive, competitive propensity, man was endowed with reason, and enabled to pass laws to protect the weak against the strong. To encourage it, is to encourage the strong to oppress the weak, and to violate the primary object of all government. It is strange it should have entered the head of any philosopher to set the weak, who are the majority of mankind, to competing, contending and fighting with the strong, in order to improve their condition.

Hobbes maintains that "a state of nature is a state of war." This is untrue of a state of nature, because men are naturally associative; but it is true of a civilized state of universal liberty, and free competition, such as Hobbes saw around him, and which no doubt suggested his theory. The wants of man and his history alike prove that slavery has always been part of his social organization. A less degree of subjection is inadequate for the government and protection of great numbers of human beings . . .

Negro Slavery

It has been the practice in all countries and in all ages, in some degree, to accommodate the amount and character of government control to the wants, intelligence, and moral capacities of the nations or individuals to be governed. A highly moral and intellectual people, like the free citizens of ancient Athens, are best governed by a democracy. For a less moral and intellectual one, a limited and constitutional monarchy will answer. For a people either very ignorant or very wicked, nothing short of military despotism will suffice. So among individuals, the most moral and well-informed members of society require no other government than law. They are capable of reading and understanding the law, and have sufficient self-control and virtuous disposition to obey it. Children cannot be governed by mere law; first, because they do not understand it, and secondly, because they are so much under the influence of impulse, passion and appetite, that they want sufficient self-control to be deterred or governed by the distant and doubtful penalties of the law. They must be constantly controlled by parents or guardians, whose will and orders shall stand in the place of law for them. Very wicked men must be put into penitentiaries; lunatics into asylums, and the most wild of them into straight jackets, just as the most wicked of the sane are manacled with irons; and idiots must have committees to govern and take care of them. Now, it is clear the Athenian democracy would not suit a negro nation, nor will the government of mere law suffice for the individual negro. He is but a grown up child, and must be governed as a child, not as a lunatic or criminal. The master occupies towards him the place of parent or guardian. We shall not dwell on this view, for no one will differ with us who thinks as we do of the negro's capacity, and we might argue till dooms-day, in vain, with those who have a high opinion of the negro's moral and intellectual capacity . . .

The negro is improvident; will not lay up in summer for the wants of winter; will not accumulate in youth for the exigencies of age. He would become an insufferable burden to society. Society has the right to prevent this, and can only do so by subjecting him to domestic slavery. We would remind those who deprecate and sympathize with negro slavery, that his slavery here relieves him from a far more cruel slavery in Africa, or from idolatry and cannibalism, and every brutal vice and crime that can disgrace humanity; and that it christianizes, protects, supports and civilizes him; that it governs him far better than free laborers at the North are governed. There, wife-murder has become a mere holiday pastime; and where so many wives are murdered, almost all must be brutally treated . . . Our negroes are not only better off as to physical comfort than free laborers, but their moral condition is better . . .

The kind of slavery is adapted to the men enslaved. Wives and apprentices are slaves; not in theory only, but often in fact. Children are slaves to their parents, guardians and teachers. Imprisoned culprits are slaves. Lunatics and idiots are slaves also. Three-fourths of free society are slaves, no better treated, when their wants and capacities are estimated, than negro slaves. The masters in free society, or slave society, if they perform properly their duties, have more cares and less liberty than the slaves themselves. "In the sweat of thy face shalt thou earn thy bread!" made all men slaves, and such all *good* men continue to be.

Negro slavery would be changed immediately to some form of peonage, serfdom or villienage, if the negroes were sufficiently intelligent and provident to manage a farm. No one would have the labor and trouble of management, if his negroes would pay in hires and rents one-half what free tenants pay in rent in Europe. Every negro in the South would be soon liberated, if he would take liberty on the terms that white tenants hold it. The fact that he cannot enjoy liberty on such terms, seems conclusive that he is only fit to be a slave . . .

We deem this peculiar question of negro slavery of very little importance. The issue is made throughout the world on the general subject of slavery in the abstract. The argument has commenced. One set of ideas will govern and control after awhile the civilized world. Slavery will every where be abolished, or every where be re-instituted. We think the opponents of practical, existing slavery, are estopped by their own admission; nay, that unconsciously, as socialists, they are the defenders and propagandists of slavery, and have furnished the only sound arguments on which its defence and justification can be rested. We have introduced the subject of negro slavery to afford us a better opportunity to disclaim the purpose of reducing the white man any where to the condition of negro slaves here. It would be very unwise and unscientific to govern white men as you would negroes. Every shade and variety of slavery has existed in the world. In some cases there has been much of legal regulation, much restraint of the master's authority; in others, none at all. The character of slavery necessary to protect the

whites in Europe should be much milder than negro slavery, for slavery is only needed to protect the white man, whilst it is more necessary for the government of the negro even than for his protection. But even negro slavery should not be outlawed. We might and should have laws in Virginia, as in Louisiana, to make the master subject to presentment by the grand jury and to punishment, for any inhuman or improper treatment or neglect of his slave.

We abhor the doctrine of the "Types of Mankind;" first, because it is at war with scripture, which teaches us that the whole human race is descended from a common parentage; and, secondly, because it encourages and incites brutal masters to treat negroes, not as weak, ignorant and dependent brethren, but as wicked beasts, without the pale of humanity. The Southerner is the negro's friend, his only friend. Let no intermeddling abolitionist, no refined philosophy, dissolve this friendship . . .

Declaration of Independence and Virginia Bill of Rights

The human mind became extremely presumptuous, and undertook to form governments on exact philosophical principles, just as men make clocks, watches or mills. They confounded the moral with the physical world, and this was not strange, because they had begun to doubt whether there was any other than a physical world. Society seemed to them a thing whose movement and action could be controlled with as much certainty as the motion of a spinning wheel, provided it was organized on proper principles. It would have been less presumptuous in them to have attempted to have made a tree, for a tree is not half so complex as a society of human beings, each of whom is fearfully and wonderfully compounded of soul and body, and whose aggregate, society, is still more complex and difficult of comprehension than its individual members. Trees grow and man may lop, trim, train and cultivate them, and thus hasten their growth, and improve their size, beauty and fruitfulness. Laws, institutions, societies, and governments grow, and men may aid their growth, improve their strength and beauty, and lop off their deformities and excrescences, by punishing crime and rewarding virtue. When society has worked long enough, under the hand of God and nature, man observing its operations, may discover its laws and constitution . . .

The abstractions contained in the various instruments on which we professed, but professed falsely, to found our governments, did no harm, because, until abolition arose, they remained a dead letter. Now, and not till now, these abstractions have become matters of serious practical importance, and we propose to give some of them a candid, but fearless examination. We find these words in the preamble and Declaration of Independence,

"We hold these truths to be self-evident, that all men are created equal; that they are endowed by their Creator with certain inalienable rights, that among them, are life, liberty, and the pursuit of happiness; that to secure these rights governments are instituted among men, deriving their just powers from the consent of the governed; that whenever any form of government becomes destructive of these ends it is the right of the people to alter or abolish it, and to institute a new government, laying its foundations on such principles, and organizing its powers in such form, as to them shall seem most likely to effect their safety and happiness."

It is, we believe, conceded on all hands, that men are not born physically, morally or intellectually equal, – some are males, some females, some from birth, large, strong and healthy, others weak, small and sickly – some are naturally amiable, others prone to all kinds of wickednesses – some brave, others timid. Their natural inequalities beget inequalities of rights. The weak in mind or body require guidance, support and protection; they must obey and work for those who protect and guide them – they have a natural right to guardians, committees, teachers or masters. Nature has made them slaves; all that law and government can do, is to regulate, modify and mitigate their slavery. In the absence of legally instituted slavery, their condition would be worse under that natural slavery of the weak to the strong, the foolish to the wise and cunning. The wise and virtuous, the brave, the stong in mind and body, are by nature born to command and protect, and law but follows nature in making them rulers, legislators, judges, captains, husbands, guardians, committees and masters. The naturally depraved class, those born prone to crime, are our brethren too; they are entitled to education, to reli-

gious instruction, to all the means and appliances proper to correct their evil propensities, and all their failings; they have a right to be sent to the penitentiary, – for there, if they do not reform, they cannot at least disturb society. Our feelings, and our consciences teach us, that nothing but necessity can justify taking human life.

We are but stringing together truisms, which every body knows as well as ourselves, and yet if men are created unequal in all these respects, what truth or what meaning is there in the passage under consideration? Men are not created or born equal, and circumstances, and education, and association, tend to increase and aggravate inequalities among them, from generation to generation. Generally, the rich associate and intermarry with each other, the poor do the same; the ignorant rarely associate with or intermarry with the learned, and all society shuns contact with the criminal, even to the third and fourth generations.

Men are not "born entitled to equal rights!" It would be far nearer the truth to say, "that some were born with saddles on their backs, and others booted and spurred to ride them," – and the riding does them good. They need the reins, the bit and the spur. No two men by nature are exactly equal or exactly alike. No institutions can prevent the few from acquiring rule and ascendency over the many. Liberty and free competition invite and encourage the attempt of the strong to master the weak; and insure their success.

"Life and liberty" are not "inalienable;" they have been sold in all countries, and in all ages, and must be sold so long as human nature lasts. It is an inexpedient and unwise, and often unmerciful restraint, on a man's liberty of action, to deny him the right to sell himself when starving, and again to buy himself when fortune smiles. Most countries of antiquity, and some, like China at the present day, allowed such sale and purchase. The great object of government is to restrict, control and punish man "in the pursuit of happiness." All crimes are committed in its pursuit. Under the free or competitive system, most men's happiness consists in destroying the happiness of other people. This, then, is no inalienable right.

The author of the Declaration may have, and probably did mean, that all men were created with an equal title to property. Carry out such a doctrine, and it would subvert every government on earth.

In practice, in all ages, and in all countries, men had sold their liberty either for short periods, for life, or hereditarily; that is, both their own liberty and that of their children after them. The laws of all countries have, in various forms and degrees, in all times recognised and regulated this right to *alien* or sell liberty. The soldiers and sailors of the revolution had aliened both liberty and life, the wives in all America had aliened their liberty, so had the apprentices and wards at the very moment this verbose, newborn, false and unmeaning preamble was written.

Mr. Jefferson was an enthusiastic speculative philosopher; Franklin was wise, cunning and judicious; he made no objection to the Declaration, as prepared by Mr. Jefferson, because, probably, he saw it would suit the occasion and supposed it would be harmless for the future. But even Franklin was too much of a physical philosopher, too utilitarian and material in his doctrines, to be relied on in matters of morals or government. We may fairly conclude, that liberty is alienable, that there is a natural right to alien it, first, because the laws and institutions of all countries have recognized and regulated its alienation; and secondly, because we cannot conceive of a civilized society, in which there were no wives, no wards, no apprentices, no sailors and no soldiers; and none of these could there be in a country that practically carried out the doctrine, that liberty is inalienable.

The soldier who meets death at the cannon's mouth, does so because he has aliened both life and liberty. Nay, more, he has aliened the pursuit of happiness, else he might desert on the eve of battle, and pursue happiness in some more promising quarter than the cannon's mouth. If the pursuit of happiness be inalienable, men should not be punished for crime, for all crimes are notoriously committed in the pursuit of happiness. If these abstractions have some hidden and cabalistic meaning, which none but the initiated can comprehend, then the Declaration should have been accompanied with a translation, and a commentary to fit it for common use, — as it stands, it deserves the tumid yet appropriate epithets which Major Lee somewhere applies to the writings of Mr. Jefferson, it is, "exhuberantly false, and arborescently fallacious."

Nothing can be found in all history more unphil-

osophical, more presumptuous, more characteristic of the infidel philosophy of the 18th century, than the language that follows that of which we have been treating. How any observant man, however unread, should have come to the conclusion, that society and government were such plastic, man-created things, that starting on certain general principles, he might frame them successfully as he pleased, we are at a loss to conceive. But infidelity is blind and foolish, and infidelity then prevailed. Lay your foundations of government on what principles you please, organize its powers in what form you choose, and you cannot foresee the results. You can only tell what laws, institutions and governments will effect, when you apply them to the same race or nation under the same circumstances in which they have already been tried. But philosophy then was in the chrysalis state. She has since deluged the world with blood, crime and pauperism. She has had full sway, and has inflicted much misery, and done no good. The world is beginning to be satisfied, that it is much safer and better, to look to the past, to trust to experience, to follow nature, than to be guided by the ignis fatuus of *a priori* speculations of closet philosophers. If all men had been created equal, all would have been competitors, rivals, and enemies. Subordination, difference of caste and classes, difference of sex, age and slavery beget peace and good will.

We were only justified in declaring our independence, because we were sufficiently wise, numerous and strong to govern ourselves, and too distant and distinct from England to be well governed by her.

Moses and Confucius, Solon, Lycurgus and English Alfred, were Reformers, Revisors of the Code. They, too, were philosophers, but too profound to mistake the province of philosophy and attempt to usurp that of nature. They did not frame government on abstract principles, they indulged in no *a priori* reasoning; but simply lopped off what was bad, and retained, modified and simplified what was good in existing institutions . . .

Although the bundle of congressional compromises passed in 1850 failed to still the agitation over slavery, these measures did decide the immediate issues, and public debates returned to general, less threatening discussions of the future. The respite for Congress and the country did not last for long, however, for again the question of admitting new states into the union precipitated a crisis. This time some Northerners, anxious to speed the development of a transcontinental railroad, proposed organizing the area west of the Mississippi River into territories preparatory for statehood. Southern leaders whose parity in the Senate had been unbalanced by the admission of free California, refused to cooperate unless they could hope for the creation of future slave states. The area involved, however, was part of the old Louisiana Purchase and came under the 1820 Missouri Compromise legislation banning the introduction of slavery into territories organized north of the line 36° 30′.

To end this impasse, Stephen Douglas (1813–1861), a popular Illinois Democrat, sponsored the Kansas-Nebraska Act which created two new territories and repealed the old restriction on the introduction of slavery. In place of this restriction, Douglas offered the principle of popular sovereignty which left the decision to the settlers themselves when they drafted their state constitution. The choice was thus deferred until the territory involved was ready to apply for admission into the union. In the meantime slave-owners could carry their slaves into the new territories. Douglas' compromise measure appealed to a good many Americans. Westerners approved its implicit endorsement of self-determination and popular vote. Southerners, although by no means interested in promoting majoritarian decisions, were happy because it repealed the hated ban on slavery in the territories, and most Americans not profoundly moved by the moral questions involved were happy to find an antiseptic device like vote counting to resolve the conflict. In actuality, the Kansas-Nebraska Act opened up Kansas to a mad scramble. Slave-holders and free-soilers poured into the new territory bent on dominating each other in

the determination of Kansas's future status. The territory became Bleeding Kansas, with recurring violence to remind the deeply divided nation what was involved in removing the restraints to the endless extension of slavery.

Having unsettled a standing rule of thirty years, Congress opened up the whole question of federal restrictions on slavery. Southern slaveholders now claimed an absolute constitutional protection of their slave property while antislavery forces maintained that slavery violated the fundamental principles of American government. The debate went right to the heart of American government. Expressed from the Southern point of view the question was "Does the Constitution permit the majority to interfere with the institutions of a particular state?" For Northerners the question was whether the Constitution could prevent the majority from abolishing an institution which seemed flagrantly at odds with American principles. Did the minority have a constitutional means of protecting its local laws? Did the majority have the power to decide for the nation as a whole?

In 1857, the Supreme Court had a chance to rule on this issue in the case of Dred Scott, a slave who claimed his freedom on the grounds that his master had carried him into the free state of Illinois as well as into the Louisiana Territory where slavery had been outlawed by the Missouri Compromise. Scott's case involved the separate questions of his freedom, his right as a citizen to sue, and the constitutional power of Congress to outlaw slavery in the territories. All three decisions were favorable to the South. Chief Justice Roger B. Taney (1777–1864) who delivered the opinion for the court declared slaves to be like any other form of property and hence subject to constitutional protection. Congress' prior exclusion of slavery in the territories was declared unconstitutional. Scott's right to sue was denied as was his claim to freedom. In effect, Taney denied that the revolutionary heritage was ever meant to apply to black Americans, but like so many other Southern triumphs, the Dred Scott decision was purchased at the price of further alarming significant numbers of Northerners.

Again the country was thrown into furious debates. Within each section there was conflict about the proper course to take. Proponents of the popular sovereignty principle were challenged by those who insisted upon restricting slavery to its present limits. In Illinois, Stephen Douglas was running as the state Democratic party's candidate for the United States Senate, opposing the Republican's choice, Abraham Lincoln (1809–1865). Since both men were planning campaign tours of the state, they arranged a series of consecutive debates in order to give the voters a chance to hear them defend their positions on the most important questions they would confront as Senators. Douglas was already in the national limelight as the author of the Kansas-Nebraska Act, and Lincoln attracted a nationwide audience with his articulate exposition of the Republican party's position. The Illinois state legislature sent Douglas to the Senate, but Lincoln won the national reputation which carried him to the White House three years later.

The readings in this section begin with Chief Justice Taney's decision in the Dred Scott case, followed by Lincoln's analysis of the Taney decision. Lincoln's acceptance speech to his nomination as the Illinois Republicans' candidate for the Senate in 1858 is the fourth reading. The last selection presents Douglas' and Lincoln's last joint debate. Responding in part to Taney's decision, they developed two different Northern answers to the Southern problem, each appealing to powerful strains in the American consciousness.

Dred Scott v. Sandford (1857)

Mr. Chief Justice Taney delivered the opinion of the Court . . .

The question is simply this: can a negro, whose ancestors were imported into this country and sold as slaves, become a member of the political community formed and brought into existence by the Constitution of the United States, and as such become entitled to all the rights, and privileges, and immunities, guaranteed by that instrument to the citizen? One of which rights is the privilege of suing in a Court of the

19 Howard 393

United States in the cases specified in the Constitution.

It will be observed, that the plea applies to that class of persons only whose ancestors were Negroes of the African race and imported into this country, and sold and held as slaves. The only matter in issue before the Court, therefore, is, whether the descendants of such slaves, when they shall be emancipated, or who are born of parents who had become free before their birth, are citizens of a State, in the sense in which the word 'citizen' is used in the Constitution of the United States . . .

The words 'people of the United States' and 'citizens' are synonymous terms, and mean the same thing. They both describe the political body who, according to our republican institutions, form the sovereignty, and who hold the power and conduct the government through their representatives. They are what we familiarly call the 'sovereign people,' and every citizen is one of this people, and a constituent member of this sovereignty. The question before us is, whether the class of persons described in the plea in abatement compose a portion of this people, and are constituent members of this sovereignty? We think they are not, and that they are not included, and were not intended to be included, under the word 'citizens' in the Constitution, and can therefore claim none of the rights and privileges which that instrument provides for and secures to citizens of the United States.

On the contrary, they were at that time considered as a subordinate and inferior class of beings, who had been subjugated by the dominant race, and, whether emancipated or not, yet remained subject to their authority, and had no rights or privileges but such as those who held the power and the government might choose to grant them.

It is not the province of the Court to decide upon the justice or injustice, the policy or impolicy, of these laws. The decision of that question belonged to the political or law-making power; to those who formed the sovereignty and framed the Constitution. The duty of the Court is, to interpret the instrument they have framed, with the best lights we can obtain on the subject, and to administer it as we find it, according to its true intent and meaning when it was adopted.

In discussing this question, we must not confound the rights of citizenship which a State may confer within its own limits, and the rights of citizenship as a member of the Union. It does not by any means follow, because he has all the rights and privileges of a citizen of a State, that he must be a citizen of the United States. He may have all of the rights and privileges of the citizen of a State, and yet not be entitled to the rights and privileges of a citizen in any other State. For, previous to the adoption of the Constitution of the United States, every State had the undoubted right to confer on whomsoever it pleased the character of citizen, and to endow him with all its rights. But this character of course was confined to the boundaries of the State, and gave him no rights or privileges in other States beyond those secured to him by the laws of nations and the comity of States. Nor have the several States surrendered the power of conferring these rights and privileges by adopting the Constitution of the United States. Each State may still confer them upon an alien or any one it thinks proper, or upon any class or description of persons; yet he would not be a citizen in the sense in which that word is used in the Constitution of the United States nor entitled to sue as such in one of its courts, nor to the privileges and immunities of a citizen in the other States. The rights which he would acquire would be restricted to the State which gave them . . .

It is very clear, therefore, that no State, can by any act or law of its own, passed since the adoption of the Constitution, introduce a new member into the political community created by the Constitution of the United States. It cannot make him a member of this community by making him a member of its own. And for the same reason it cannot introduce any person, or description of persons, who were not intended to be embraced in this new political family, which the Constitution brought into existence, but were intended to be excluded from it.

The question then arises, whether the provisions of the Constitution, in relation to the personal rights and privileges to which the citizen of a State should be entitled, embraced the negro African race, at that time in this country, or who might afterwards be imported, who had then or should afterwards be made free in any State; and to put it in the power of a single State to make him a citizen of the United States and endue him with the full rights of citizenship in every other State without their consent? Does the Constitution of the United States act upon him whenever he shall be made free under the laws of a State, and raised there to the rank of a citizen, and immediately clothe him with all the privileges of a citizen in every other State, and in its own courts?

The Court thinks that the affirmative of these propositions cannot be maintained. And if it cannot, the plaintiff in error could not be a citizen of the State of Missouri, within the meaning of the Constitution of the United States, and consequently, was not entitled to sue in its courts.

It is true, every person, and every class and description of persons, who were at the time of the adoption of the Constitution recognized as citizens in the several States, became also citizens of this new political body; but none other; it was formed by them, and for them and their posterity, but for no one else. And the personal rights and privileges guaranteed to citizens of this new sovereignty were intended to embrace those only who were then members of the several state communities, or who should afterwards by birthright or otherwise become members, according to the provision of the Constitution, and the principles on which it was founded. It was the union of those who were at that time members of distinct and separate political communities into one political family, whose power, for certain specified purposes, was to extend over the whole territory of the United States. And it gave to each citizen rights and privileges outside of his State which he did not before possess, and placed him in every other State upon a perfect equality with its own citizens as to rights of persons and rights of property; it made him a citizen of the United States.

It becomes necessary, therefore, to determine who were citizens of the several States when the Constitution was adopted. And in order to do this, we must recur to the governments and institutions of the thirteen colonies, when they separated from Great Britain and formed new sovereignties, and took their places in the family of independent nations. We must inquire who, at that time, were recognized as the people or citizens of a State, whose rights and liberties had been outraged by the English government; and who declared their independence, and assumed the powers of government to defend their rights by force of arms.

In the opinion of the Court, the legislation and histories of the time, and the language used in the Declaration of Independence show, that neither the class of persons who had been imported as slaves, nor their descendants, whether they had become free or not, were then acknowledged as a part of the people, nor intended to be included in the general words used in that memorable instrument.

It is difficult at this day to realize the state of public opinion in relation to that unfortunate race, which prevailed in the civilized and enlightened portions of the world at the time of the Declaration of Independence, and when the Constitution of the United States was framed and adopted. But the public history of every European nation displays it in a manner too plain to be mistaken.

They had for more than a century before been regarded as beings of an inferior order, and altogether unfit to associate with the white race, either in social or political relations; and so far inferior, that they had no rights which the white man was bound to respect; and that the negro might justly and lawfully be reduced to slavery for his benefit. He was bought and sold, and treated as an ordinary article of merchandise and traffic, whenever a profit could be made by it. This opinion was at that time fixed and universal in the civilized portion of the white race. It was regarded as an axiom in morals as well as in politics, which no one thought of disputing, or supposed to be open to dispute; and men in every grade and position of society daily and habitually acted upon it in their private pursuits, as well as in matters of public concern, without doubting for a moment the correctness of this opinion.

And in no nation was this opinion more firmly fixed or more uniformly acted upon than by the English government and English people. They not only seized them on the coast of Africa, and sold them or held them in slavery for their own use; but they took them, as ordinary articles of merchandise to every country where they could make a profit on them, and were far more extensively engaged in this commerce than any other nation in the world.

The opinion thus entertained and acted upon in England was naturally impressed upon the colonies they founded on this side of the Atlantic. And, accordingly, a negro of the African race was regarded by them as an article of property, and held and bought and sold as such, in every one of the thirteen colonies which united in the Declaration of Independence, and afterwards formed the Constitution of the United States. The slaves were more or less numerous in the different colonies, as slave labor was found more or less profitable. But no one seems to have doubted the correctness of the prevailing opinion of the time.

The legislation of the different colonies furnishes positive and indisputable proof of this fact . . .

The language of the Declaration of Independence is equally conclusive:

It begins by declaring that, 'when in the course of human events it becomes necessary for one people to dissolve the political bands which have connected them with another, and to assume among the powers of the earth the separate and equal station to which the laws of nature and nature's God entitle them, a decent respect for the opinions of mankind requires that they should declare the causes which impel them to the separation.'

It then proceeded to say: 'we hold these truths to be self-evident, that all men are created equal; that they are endowed by their Creator with certain inalienable rights; that among them is life, liberty and the pursuit of happiness; that to secure these rights governments are instituted, deriving their just powers from the consent of the governed.'

The general words above quoted would seem to embrace the whole human family, and if they were used in a similar instrument at this day would be so understood. But it is too clear for dispute, that the enslaved African race were not intended to be included, and formed no part of the people who framed and adopted this declaration; for if the language, as understood in that day, would embrace them, the conduct of the distinguished men who framed the Declaration of Independence would have been utterly and flagrantly inconsistent with the principles they asserted; and instead of the sympathy of mankind, to which they so confidently appealed, they would have deserved and received universal rebuke and reprobation . . .

The legislation of the States therefore shows, in a manner not to be mistaken, the inferior and subject condition of that race at the time the Constitution was adopted, and long afterwards, throughout the thirteen States by which that instrument was framed; and it is hardly consistent with the respect due to these States, to suppose that they regarded at that time, as fellow-citizens and members of the sovereignty, a class of beings whom they had thus stigmatized; whom, as we are bound, out of respect to the State sovereignties, to assume they had deemed it just and necessary thus to stigmatize, and upon whom they had impressed such deep and enduring marks of inferiority and degradation; or, that when they met in convention to form the Constitution, they looked upon them as a portion of their constituents, or designed to include them in the provisions so carefully inserted for the security and protection of the liberties and rights of their citizens. It cannot be supposed that they intended to secure to them rights, and privileges, and rank, in the new political body throughout the Union, which every one of them denied within the limits of its own dominion. More especially it cannot be believed that the large slaveholding States regarded them as included in the word 'citizens,' or would have consented to a Constitution which might compel them to receive them in that character from another State. For if they were so received, and entitled to the privileges and immunities of citizens, it would exempt them from the operation of the special laws and from the police regulations which they considered to be necessary for their own safety. It would give to persons of the negro race, who were recognized as citizens in any one State of the Union, the right to enter every other State whenever they pleased, singly or in companies, without pass or passport, and without obstruction, to sojourn there as long as they pleased, to go where they pleased at every hour of the day or night without molestation, unless they committed some violation of law for which a white man would be punished; and it would give them the full liberty of speech in public and private upon all subjects upon which its own citizens might speak; to hold public meetings upon political affairs, and to keep and carry arms wherever they went. And all of this would be done in the face of the subject race of the same color, both free and slaves, and inevitably producing discontent and insubordination among them, and endangering the peace and safety of the State . . .

No one, we presume, supposes that any change in public opinion or feeling in relation to this unfortunate race, in the civilized nations of Europe or in this country, should induce the courts to give to the words of the Constitution a more liberal construction in their favor than they were intended to bear when the instrument was framed and adopted. Such an argument would be altogether inadmissible in any tribunal called on to interpret it. If any of its provisions are deemed unjust, there is a mode prescribed in the instrument itself by which it may be amended; but while it remains unaltered, it must be construed now as it was understood at the time of its adoption. It is not only the same in words but the same in meaning, and delegates the same power to the government and reserves and secures the same rights and privileges to the citizen; and as long as it continues to exist in its present form, it speaks not only with the same words, but with the same meaning and intent with which it spoke when it came from the hands of its framers, and was voted on and adopted by the people of the United States. Any other rule of construction would abrogate the judicial character of this Court, and make it the mere reflex of the popular opinion or passion of the day. This Court was not created by the Constitution for such purposes. Higher and graver trusts have been confided to it, and it must not falter in the path of duty.

What the construction was at that time, we think can hardly admit of doubt. We have the language of the Declaration of Independence and of the Articles of Confederation, in addition to the plain words of the Constitution itself; we have the legislation of the different States, before, about the time, and since, the Constitution was adopted; we have the legislation of Congress, from the time of its adoption to a recent period; and we have the constant and uniform action to the executive department, all concurring together, and leading to the same result. And if anything in relation to the construction of the Constitution can be regarded as settled, it is that which we now give to the word 'citizen' and the word 'people.'

And upon a full and careful consideration of the subject, the Court is of opinion, that, upon the facts stated in the plea in abatement, Dred Scott was not a citizen of Missouri within the meaning of the Constitution of the United States, and not entitled as such to sue in its courts; and, consequently, that the Circuit Court has no jurisdiction of the case, and that the judgment on the plea in abatement is erroneous . . .

We proceed, therefore, to inquire whether the facts relied on by the plaintiff entitled him to his freedom . . .

In considering this part of the controversy, two questions arise:

1. Was he, together with his family, free in Missouri by reason of the stay in the territory of the United States hereinbefore mentioned?

And 2. If they were not, is Scott himself free by reason of his removal to Rock Island, in the State of Illinois, as stated in the above admissions?

We proceed to examine the first question.

The Act of Congress, upon which the plaintiff relies, declares that slavery and involuntary servitude, except as a punishment for crime, shall be forever prohibited in all that part of the territory ceded by France, under the name of Louisiana, which lies north of thirty-six degrees thirty minutes north latitude, and not included within the limits of Missouri. And the difficulty which meets us at the threshold of this part of the inquiry is, whether Congress was authorized to pass this law under any of the powers granted to it by the Constitution; for if the authority is not given by that instrument, it is the duty of this Court to declare it void and inoperative, and incapable of conferring freedom upon any one who is held as a slave under the laws of any one of the States.

The counsel for the plaintiff has laid much stress upon that article in the Constitution which confers on Congress the power 'to dispose of and make all needful rules and regulations respecting the territory or other property belonging to the United States;' but in the judgment of the Court, that provision has no bearing on the present controversy, and the power there given, whatever it may be, is confined, and was intended to be confined, to the territory which at that time belonged to, or was claimed by, the United States, and was within their boundaries as settled by the treaty with Great Britain, and can have no influence upon a territory afterwards acquired from a foreign government . . .

At the time when the territory in question was obtained by cession from France, it contained no population fit to be associated together and admitted as a State; and it therefore was absolutely necessary to hold possession of it, as a territory belonging to the United States, until it was settled and inhabited by a civilized community capable of self-government, and in a condition to be admitted on equal terms with the other States as a member of the Union. But, as we have before said, it was acquired by the general government, as the representative and trustee of the people of the United States, and it must therefore be held in that character for their common and equal benefit; for it was the people of the several States, acting through their agent and representative, the Federal Government, who in fact acquired the territory in question, and the government holds it for their common use until it shall be associated with the other states as a member of the Union.

But until that time arrives, it is undoubtedly necessary that some government should be established, in order to organize society, and to protect the inhabitants in their persons and property; and as people of the United States could act in this matter only through the government which represented them, and through which they spoke and acted when the territory was obtained, it was not only within the scope of its powers, but it was its duty to pass such laws and establish such a government as would enable those by whose authority they acted to reap the advantages anticipated from its acquisition, and to gather there a population which would enable it to assume the position to which it was destined among the States of the Union . . .

Now, as we have already said in an earlier part of this opinion, upon a different point, the right of property in a slave is distinctly expressed and affirmed in the Constitution. The right to traffic in it, like an ordinary article of merchandise and property, was guaranteed to the citizens of the United States, in every State that might desire it, for twenty years. And the government in express terms is pledged to protect it in all future time, if the slave escapes from his owner. This is done in plain words — too plain to be misunderstood. And no word can be found in the Constitution which gives Congress a greater power over slave property, or which entitles property of that kind to less protection than property of any other description. The only power conferred is the power coupled with the duty of guarding and protecting the owner in his rights.

Upon these considerations, it is the opinion of the Court that the Act of Congress which prohibited a citizen from holding and owning property of this kind in the territory of the United States north of the line therein mentioned, is not warranted by the Constitution, and is therefore void; and that neither Dred Scott himself, nor any of his family, were made free by being carried into this territory; even if they had been carried there by the owner, with the intention of becoming a permanent resident.

We have so far examined the case, as it stands under the Constitution of the United States, and the power thereby delegated to the Federal Government.

But there is another point in the case which depends on State power and State law. And it is contended, on the part of the plaintiff, that he is made free by being taken to Rock Island, in the State of Illinois, independently of his residence in the territory of the United States; and being so made free he was not again reduced to a state of slavery by being brought back to Missouri.

Our notice of this part of the case will be very brief; for the principle on which it depends was decided in this Court, upon much consideration, in the case of Strader et al. v. Graham, reported in 10th Howard, 82. In that case, the slaves had been taken from Kentucky to Ohio, with the consent of the owner, and afterwards brought back to Kentucky. And this Court held that their status or condition, as free or slave, depended upon the laws of Kentucky, when they were brought back into that State, and not of Ohio; and that this Court had no jurisdiction to revise the judgement of a State court upon its own laws.

Upon the whole, therefore, it is the judgment of this Court, that it appears by the records before us that the plaintiff in error is not a citizen of Missouri, in the sense in which that word is used in the Constitution; and that the Circuit Court of the United States, for that reason, had no jurisdiction in the case, and could give no judgment in it. Its judgment for the defendant must consequently, be reversed, and a mandate issued, directing the suit to be dismissed for want of jurisdiction.

Abraham Lincoln: Springfield speech (1857)

Judicial decisions have two uses — first, to absolutely determine the case decided; and secondly, to indicate to the public how other similar cases will be decided when they arise. For the latter use, they are called "precedents" and "authorities."

We believe as much as Judge Douglas (perhaps more) in obedience to, and respect for, the judicial department of government. We think its decisions on constitutional questions, when fully settled, should control not only the particular cases decided, but the general policy of the country, subject to be disturbed only by amendments of the Constitution as provided in that instrument itself. More than this would be revolution. But we think the Dred Scott decision is erroneous. We know the court that made it has often overruled its own decisions, and we shall do what we can to have it to overrule this. We offer no resistance to it.

Judicial decisions are of greater or less authority as precedents according to circumstances. That this should be so accords both with common sense and the customary understanding of the legal profession.

If this important decision had been made by the unanimous concurrence of the judges, and without any apparent partizan bias, and in accordance with legal public expectation and with the steady practice of the departments throughout our history, and had been in no part based on assumed historical facts which are not really true; or, if wanting in some of these, it had been before the court more than once, and had there been affirmed and reaffirmed through a course of years, it then might be, perhaps would be, factious, nay, even revolutionary, not to acquiesce in it as a precedent.

But when, as is true, we find it wanting in all these claims to the public confidence, it is not resistance, it is not factious, it is not even disrespectful, to treat it as not having yet quite established a settled doctrine for the country . . .

John G. Nicolay and John Hay (eds.), *The Complete Works of Abraham Lincoln,* F. D. Tandy, New York, 1905, IV, 320–39; V, 1–3, 13–14.

I have said, in substance, that the Dred Scott decision was in part based on assumed historical facts which were not really true, and I ought not to leave the subject without giving some reasons for saying this; I therefore give an instance or two, which I think fully sustains me. Chief Justice Taney, in delivering the opinion of the majority of the court, insists at great length that negroes were no part of the people who made, or for whom was made, the Declaration of Independence, or the Constitution of the United States.

On the contrary, Judge Curtis, in his dissenting opinion, shows that in five of the then thirteen States—to-wit, New Hampshire, Massachusetts, New York, New Jersey, and North Carolina — free negroes were voters, and in proportion to their numbers had the same part in making the Constitution that the white people had. He shows this with so much particularity as to leave no doubt of its truth; and as a sort of conclusion on that point, holds the following language:

The Constitution was ordained and established by the people of the United States, through the action, in each State, of those persons who were qualified by its laws to act thereon in behalf of themselves and all other citizens of the State. In some of the States, as we have seen, colored persons were among those qualified by law to act on the subject. These colored persons were not only included in the body of "the people of the United States" by whom the Constitution was ordained and established; but in at least five of the States they had the power to act, and doubtless did act, by their suffrages, upon the question of its adoption.

Again, Chief Justice Taney says:

It is difficult at this day to realize the state of public opinion, in relation to that unfortunate race, which prevailed in the civilized and enlightened portions of the world at the time of the Declaration of Independence, and when the Constitution of the United States was framed and adopted.

And again, after quoting from the Declaration, he says:

The general words above quoted would seem to include the whole human family, and if they were used in a similar instrument at this day, would be so understood.

In these the Chief Justice does not directly assert, but plainly assumes, as a fact, that the public estimate of the black man is more favorable now than it was in the days of the Revolution. This assumption is a mistake. In some trifling particulars the condition of that race has been ameliorated; but as a whole, in this country, the change between then and now is decidedly the other way; and their ultimate destiny has never appeared so hopeless as in the last three or four years. In two of the five States — New Jesery and North Carolina — that then gave the free negro the right of voting, the right has since been taken away, and in a third — New York — it has been greatly abridged; while it has not been extended, so far as I know, to a single additional State, though the number of the States has more than doubled. In those days, as I understand, masters could, at their own pleasure, emancipate their slaves; but since then such legal restraints have been made upon emancipation as to amount almost to prohibition. In those days legislatures held the unquestioned power to abolish slavery in their respective States, but now it is becoming quite fashionable for the State constitutions to withhold that power from the legislatures. In those days, by common consent, the spread of the black man's bondage to the new countries was prohibited, but now Congress decides that it will not continue the prohibition, and the Supreme Court decides that it could not if it would. In those days our Declaration of Independence was held sacred by all, and thought to include all; but now, to aid in making the bondage of the negro universal and eternal, it is assailed and sneered at and construed, and hawked at and torn, till, if its framers could rise from their graves, they could not at all recognize it. All the powers of earth seem rapidly combining against him. Mammon is after him, ambition follows, philosophy follows, and the theology of the day is fast joining the cry. They have him in his prison-house; they have searched his person, and left no prying instrument with him. One after another they have closed the heavy iron doors upon him; and now they have him, as it were, bolted in with a lock of a hundred keys, which can never be unlocked without the concurrence of every key — the keys in the hands of a hundred different men, and they scattered to a hundred different and distant places; and they stand musing as to what invention, in all the dominions of mind and matter, can be produced to make the impossibility of his escape more complete than it is.

It is grossly incorrect to say or assume that the public estimate of the negro is more favorable now than it was at the origin of the government . . .

There is a natural disgust in the minds of nearly all white people at the idea of an indiscriminate amalgamation of the white and black races; and Judge Douglas evidently is basing his chief hope upon the chances of his being able to appropriate the benefit of this disgust to himself. If he can, by much drumming and repeating, fasten the odium of that idea upon his adversaries, he thinks he can struggle through the storm. He therefore clings to this hope, as a drowning man to the last plank. He makes an occasion for lugging it in from the opposition of the Dred Scott decision. He finds the Republicans insisting that the Declaration of Independence includes all men, black as well as white, and forthwith he boldly denies that it includes negroes at all, and proceeds to argue gravely that all who contend it does do so only because they want to vote, and eat, and sleep, and marry with negroes! He will have it that they cannot be consistent else. Now I protest against the counterfeit logic which concludes that, because I do not want a black woman for a slave I must necessarily want her for a wife. I need not have her for either. I can just leave her alone. In some respects she certainly is not my equal; but in her natural right to eat the bread she earns with her own hands without asking leave of any one else, she is my equal, and the equal of all others.

Chief Justice Taney, in his opinion in the Dred Scott case, admits that the language of the Declaration is broad enough to include the whole human family, but he and Judge Douglas argue that the authors of that instrument did not intend to include negroes, by the fact that they did not at once actually place them on an equality with the whites. Now this grave argument comes to just nothing at all, by the other fact that they did not at once, or ever afterward, actually place all white people on an equality with one another. And this is the staple argument of both the chief justice and the senator for doing this obvious violence to the plain, unmistakable language of the Declaration.

I think the authors of that notable instrument intended to include all men, but they did not intend to declare all men equal in all respects. They did not mean to say all were equal in color, size, intellect, moral developments, or social capacity. They defined with tolerable distinctness in what respects they did consider all men created equal — equal with "certain inalienable rights, among which are life, liberty, and the pursuit of happiness." This they said, and this they meant. They did not mean to assert the obvious untruth that all were then actually enjoying that equality, nor yet that they were about to confer it immediately upon them. In fact, they had no power to confer such a boon. They meant simply to declare the right, so that enforcement of it might follow as fast as circumstances should permit.

They meant to set up a standard maxim for free society, which should be familiar to all, and revered by all; constantly looked to, constantly labored for, and even though never perfectly attained, constantly approximated, and thereby constantly spreading and deepening its influence and augmenting the happiness and value of life to all people of all colors everywhere. The assertion that "all men are created equal" was of no practical use in effecting our separation from Great Britain; and it was placed in the Declaration not for that, but for future use. Its authors meant it to be — as, thank God, it is now proving itself — a stumbling-block to all those who in after times might seek to turn a free people back into the hateful paths of despotism. They knew the proneness of prosperity to breed tyrants, and they meant when such should reappear in this fair land and commence their vocation, they should find left for them at least one hard nut to crack.

I have now briefly expressed my view of the meaning and object of that part of the Declaration of Independence which declares that "all men are created equal."

Now let us hear Judge Douglas's view of the same subject, as I find it in the printed report of his late speech. Here it is:

No man can vindicate the character, motives, and conduct of the signers of the Declaration of Independence, except upon the hypothesis that they referred to the white race alone, and not to the African, when they declared all men to have been created equal; that they were speaking of British subjects on this continent being equal to British subjects born and residing in Great Britain; that they were entitled to the same alienable rights, and among them were enumerated life, liberty, and the pursuit of happiness. The Declaration was adopted for the purpose of justifying the colonists in the eyes of the civilized world in withdrawing their allegiance from the British crown, and dissolving their connection with the mother country.

My good friends, read that carefully over some leisure hour, and ponder well upon it; see what a mere wreck — mangled ruin — it makes of our once glorious Declaration.

"They were speaking of British subjects on this continent being equal to British subjects born and residing in Great Britain!" Why, according to this, not only negroes but white people outside of Great Britain and America were not spoken of in that instrument. The English, Irish, and Scotch, along with white Americans, were included, to be sure, but the French, Germans, and other white people of the world are all gone to pot along with the judge's inferior races!

I had thought the Declaration promised something better than the condition of British subjects; but no, it only meant that we should be equal to them in their own oppressed and unequal condition. According to that, it gave no promise that, having kicked off the king and lords of Great Britain, we should not at once be saddled with a king and lords of our own.

I had thought the Declaration contemplated the progressive improvement in the condition of all men everywhere; but no, it merely "was adopted for the purpose of justifying the colonists in the eyes of the civilized world in withdrawing their allegiance from the British crown, and dissolving their connection with the mother country." Why, that object having been effected some eighty years ago, the Declaration is of no practical use now — mere rubbish — old wadding left to rot on the battle-field after the victory is won.

And now I appeal to all — to Democrats as well as others — are you really willing that the Declaration shall thus be frittered away? — thus left no more, at most, than an interesting memorial of the dead past? — thus shorn of its vitality and practical value, and left without the germ or even the suggestion of the individual rights of man in it?

But Judge Douglas is especially horrified at the thought of the mixing of blood by the white and black races. Agreed for once — a thousand times agreed.

There are white men enough to marry all the white women, and black men enough to marry all the black women; and so let them be married. On this point we fully agree with the judge, and when he shall show that his policy is better adapted to prevent amalgamation than ours, we shall drop ours and adopt his. Let us see. In 1850 there were in the United States 405,751 mulattos. Very few of these are the offspring of whites and free blacks; nearly all have sprung from black slaves and white masters . . .

I have said that the separation of the races is the only perfect preventive of amalgamation. I have no right to say all the members of the Republican party are in favor of this, nor to say that as a party they are in favor of it. There is nothing in their platform directly on the subject. But I can say a very large proportion of its members are for it, and that the chief plank in their platform — opposition to the spread of slavery — is most favorable to that separation.

Such separation, if ever effected at all, must be effected by colonization; and no political party, as such, is now doing anything directly for colonization . . .

How differently the respective courses of the Democratic and Republican parties incidentally bear on the question of forming a will — a public sentiment — for colonization, is easy to see. The Republicans inculcate, with whatever of ability they can, that the negro is a man, that his bondage is cruelly wrong, and that the field of his oppression ought not to be enlarged. The Democrats deny his manhood; deny, or dwarf to insignificance, the wrong of his bondage; so far as possible, crush all sympathy for him, and cultivate and excite hatred and disgust against him; compliment themselves as Union-savers for doing so; and call the indefinite outspreading of his bondage "a sacred right of self-government."

The plainest print cannot be read through a gold eagle; and it will be ever hard to find many men who will send a slave to Liberia, and pay his passage, while they can send him to a new country — Kansas, for instance — and sell him for fifteen hundred dollars, and the rise.

*Abraham Lincoln: Springfield acceptance speech
(1858)*

Mr. President and Gentlemen of the Convention:

If we could first know where we are, and whither
we are tending, we could better judge what to do, and
how to do it. We are now far into the fifth year since
a policy was initiated with the avowed object and
confident promise of putting an end to slavery agitation. Under the operation of that policy, that agitation
has not only not ceased but has constantly augmented.
In my opinion, it will not cease until a crisis shall have
been reached and passed. "A house divided against itself cannot stand." I believe this government cannot
endure permanently half slave and half free. I do not
expect the Union to be dissolved — I do not expect
the house to fall — but I do expect it will cease to be
divided. It will become all one thing, or all the other.
Either the opponents of slavery will arrest the further
spread of it, and place it where the public mind shall
rest in the belief that it is in the course of ultimate extinction; or its advocates will push it forward till it
shall become alike lawful in all the States, old as well
as new, North as well as South.

Have we no tendency to the latter condition?

Let any one who doubts carefully contemplate
that now almost complete legal combination — piece
of machinery, so to speak — compounded of the
Nebraska doctrine and the Dred Scott decision. Let
him consider not only what work the machinery is
adapted to do, and how well adapted; but also let him
study the history of the construction, and trace, if he
can, or rather fail, if he can, to trace the evidences of
design and concert of action among its chief archi-
tects, from the beginning.

The new year of 1854 found slavery excluded
from more than half the States by State constitutions,
and from most of the national territory by congressional prohibition. Four days later commenced the
struggle which ended in repealing that congressional
prohibition. This opened all the national territory to
slavery, and was the first point gained.

But, so far, Congress only had acted; and an in-
dorsement by the people, real or apparent, was indispensable to save the point already gained and give
chance for more.

This necessity had not been overlooked, but had
been provided for, as well as might be, in the notable
argument of "squatter sovereignty," otherwise called
"sacred right of self-government," which latter phrase,
though expressive of the only rightful basis of any government, was so perverted in this attempted use of it
as to amount to just this: That if any one man choose
to enslave another, no third man shall be allowed to
object. That argument was incorporated into the
Nebraska bill itself, in the language which follows: "It
being the true intent and meaning of this act not to
legislate slavery into any Territory or State, nor to exclude it therefrom; but to leave the people thereof perfectly free to form and regulate their domestic institutions in their own way, subject only to the Constitution
of the United States." Then opened the roar of loose
declamation in favor of "squatter sovereignty" and
"sacred right of self-government." "But," said opposition members, "let us amend the bill so as to expressly
declare that the people of the Territory may exclude
slavery." "Not we," said the friends of the measure;
and down they voted the amendment . . .

Judge Douglas, if not a dead lion for this work, is
at least a caged and toothless one. How can he oppose
the advances of slavery? He don't care anything about
it. His avowed mission is impressing the "public heart"
to care nothing about it. A leading Douglas Democratic
newspaper thinks Douglas's superior talent will be needed to resist the revival of the African slave-trade. Does
Douglas believe an effort to revive that trade is approaching? He has not said so. Does he really think
so? But if it is, how can he resist it? For years he has
labored to prove it a sacred right of white men to take
negro slaves into the new Territories. Can he possibly
show that it is less a sacred right to buy them where
they can be bought cheapest? And unquestionably
they can be bought cheaper in Africa than in Virginia.
He has done all in his power to reduce the whole question of slavery to one of a mere right of property; and
as such, how can he oppose the foreign slave-trade?
How can he refuse that trade in that "property" shall
be "perfectly free," unless he does it as a protection to
the home production? And as the home producers
will probably not ask the protection, he will be wholly
without a ground of opposition.

Senator Douglas holds, we know, that a man may
rightfully be wiser to-day than he was yesterday — that

he may rightfully change when he finds himself wrong. But can we, for that reason, run ahead, and infer that he will make any particular change of which he, himself, has given no intimation? Can we safely base our action upon any such vague inference? Now, as ever, I wish not to misrepresent Judge Douglas's position, question his motives, or do aught that can be personally offensive to him. Whenever, if ever, he and we can come together on principle so that our great cause may have assistance from his great ability, I hope to have interposed no adventitious obstacle. But clearly, he is not now with us — he does not pretend to be — he does not promise ever to be . . .

Stephen A. Douglas and Abraham Lincoln: Joint debate at Alton (1858)

Senator Douglas' Speech

Ladies and Gentlemen: — It is now nearly four months since the canvass between Mr. Lincoln and myself commenced. On the 16th of June the Republican Convention assembled at Springfield and nominated Mr. Lincoln as their candidate for the United States Senate, and he, on that occasion, delivered a speech in which he laid down what he understood to be the Republican creed, and the platform on which he proposed to stand during the contest.

The principal points in that speech of Mr. Lincoln's were: First, that this Government could not endure permanently divided into Free and Slave States, as our fathers made it; that they must all become Free or all become Slave; all become one thing, or all become the other, — otherwise this Union could not continue to exist. I give you his opinions almost in the identical language he used. His second proposition was a crusade against the Supreme Court of the United States because of the Dred Scott decision, urging as an especial reason for his opposition to that decision that it deprived the negroes of the rights and benefits of that clause in the Constitution of the United States which guarantees to the citizens of each State all the rights, privileges, and immunities of the citizens of the several States.

On the 10th of July I returned home, and delivered a speech to the people of Chicago, in which I an-

nounced it to be my purpose to appeal to the people of Illinois to sustain the course I had pursued in Congress . . . On the next day, the 11th of July, Mr. Lincoln replied to me at Chicago, explaining at some length and reaffirming the positions which he had taken in his Springfield speech. In that Chicago speech he even went further than he had before, and uttered sentiments in regard to the negro being on an equality with the white man. He adopted in support of this position the argument which Lovejoy and Codding and other Abolition lecturers had made familiar in the northern and central portions of the State; to wit, that the Declaration of Independence having declared all men free and equal, by divine law, also that negro equality was an inalienable right, of which they could not be deprived. He insisted, in that speech, that the Declaration of Independence included the negro in the clause asserting that all men were created equal, and went so far as to say that if one man was allowed to take the position that it did not include the negro, others might take the position that it did not include other men. He said that all these distinctions between this man and that man, this race and the other race, must be discarded, and we must all stand by the Declaration of Independence, declaring that all men were created equal.

The issue thus being made up between Mr. Lincoln and myself on three points, we went before the people of the State, analyzed them, and pointed out what I believed to be the radical errors contained in them. First, in regard to his doctrine that this Government was in violation of the law of God, which says that a house divided against itself cannot stand, I repudiated it as a slander upon the immortal framers of our Constitution. I then said, I have often repeated, and now again assert, that in my opinion our Government can endure forever, divided into Free and Slave States as our fathers made it, — each State having the right to prohibit, abolish, or sustain slavery, just as it pleases.

This Government was made upon the great basis of the sovereignty of the States, the right of each State to regulate its own domestic institutions to suit itself; and that right was conferred with the understanding and expectation that inasmuch as each locality had separate interests, each locality must have different and distinct local and domestic institutions, corre-

---

Political Debates between Hon. Abraham Lincoln and Hon. Stephen A. Douglas, Follett, Foster, Columbus, Ohio, 1860.

sponding to its wants and interests. Our fathers knew when they made the Government that the laws and institutions which were well adapted to the Green Mountains of Vermont were unsuited to the rice plantations of South Carolina. They knew then, as well as we know now, that the laws and institutions which would be well adapted to the beautiful prairies of Illinois would not be suited to the mining regions of California. They knew that in a Republic as broad as this, having such a variety of soil, climate, and interest, there must necessarily be a corresponding variety of local laws, — the policy and institutions of each State adapted to its condition and wants. For this reason this Union was established on the right of each State to do as it pleased on the question of slavery, and every other question; and the various States were not allowed to complain of, much less interfere with, the policy of their neighbors.

Suppose the doctrine advocated by Mr. Lincoln and the Abolitionists of this day had prevailed when the Constitution was made, what would have been the result? Imagine for a moment that Mr. Lincoln had been a member of the Convention that framed the Constitution of the United States, and that when its members were about to sign that wonderful document, he had arisen in that Convention as he did at Springfield this summer, and, addressing himself to the President, had said, "A house divided against itself cannot stand; this Government, divided into Free and Slave States cannot endure, they must all be Free or all be Slave; they must all be one thing, or all the other, — otherwise, it is a violation of the law of God, and cannot continue to exist;" — suppose Mr. Lincoln had convinced that body of sages that that doctrine was sound, what would have been the result? Remember that the Union was then composed of thirteen States, twelve of which were slaveholding, and one free. Do you think that the one Free State would have outvoted the twelve slaveholding States, and thus have secured the abolition of slavery? On the other hand, would not the twelve slaveholding States have outvoted the one Free State, and thus have fastened slavery, by a constitutional provision, on every foot of the American Republic forever?

You see that if this Abolition doctrine of Mr. Lincoln had prevailed when the Government was made, it would have established slavery as a permanent institution in all the States, whether they wanted it or not; and the question for us to determine in Illinois now, as one of the Free States, is whether or not we are willing, having become the majority section, to enforce a doctrine on the minority which we would have resisted with our hearts' blood had it been attempted on us when we were in a minority. How has the South lost her power as the majority section in this Union, and how have the Free States gained it, except under the operation of that principle which declares the right of the people of each State and each Territory to form and regulate their domestic institutions in their own way? It was under that principle that slavery was abolished in New Hampshire, Rhode Island, Connecticut, New York, New Jersey, and Pennsylvania; it was under that principle that one half of the slaveholding States became free; it was under that principle that the number of Free States increased until, from being one out of twelve States, we have grown to be the majority of States of the whole Union, with the power to control the House of Representatives and Senate, and the power, consequently, to elect a President by Northern votes, without the aid of a Southern State . . .

After having pressed these arguments home on Mr. Lincoln for seven weeks, publishing a number of my speeches, we met at Ottawa in joint discussion, and he then began to crawfish a little, and let himself down. I there propounded certain questions to him. Amongst others, I asked him whether he would vote for the admission of any more Slave States, in the event the people wanted them . . . I will show you what his answer was. After saying that he was not pledged to the Republican doctrine of "no more Slave States," he declared:

"I state to you very frankly, that I should be exceedingly sorry ever to be put in the position of having to pass upon that question. I should be exceedingly glad to know that there would never be another Slave State admitted into this Union."

Here permit me to remark, that I do not think the people will ever force him into a position against his will. He went on to say:

"But I must add, in regard to this, that if slavery shall be kept out of the Territory during the Territorial existence of any one given Territory, and then the people should, having a fair chance and clear field, when they come to adopt a constitution, if they should do the extraordinary thing of adopting a slave constitution uninfluenced by the actual presence of the institution among them, I see no alternative, if we own the country, but we must admit it into the Union."

That answer Mr. Lincoln supposed would satisfy the Old Line Whigs, composed of Kentuckians and Virginians, down in the southern part of the State. Now, what does it amount to? I desired to know whether he would vote to allow Kansas to come into the Union with slavery or not, as her people desired . . . Why can he not say whether he is willing to allow the people of each State to have slavery or not as they please, and to come into the Union, when they have the requisite population, as a Slave or a Free State as they decide? I have no trouble in answering the question. I have said everywhere, and now repeat it to you, that if the people of Kansas want a Slave State they have a right, under the Constitution of the United States, to form such a State, and I will let them come into the Union with slavery or without, as they determine. If the people of any other Territory desire slavery, let them have it. If they do not want it, let them prohibit it. It is their business, not mine. It is none of our business in Illinois whether Kansas is a Free State or a Slave State. It is none of your business in Missouri whether Kansas shall adopt slavery or reject it. It is the business of her people, and none of yours. The people of Kansas have as much right to decide that question for themselves as you have in Missouri to decide it for yourselves, or we in Illinois to decide it for ourselves.

I hold that there is no power on earth, under our system of government, which has the right to force a constitution upon an unwilling people. Suppose that there had been a majority of ten to one in favor of slavery in Kansas, and suppose there had been an Abolition President and an Abolition Administration, and by some means the Abolitionists succeeded in forcing an Abolition Constitution on those slaveholding people, would the people of the South have submitted to that act for one instant? Well, if you of the South would not have submitted to it a day, how can you, as fair, honorable, and honest men, insist on putting a slave constitution on a people who desire a Free State? Your safety and ours depends upon both

of us acting in good faith, and living up to that great principle which asserts the right of every people to form and regulate their domestic institutions to suit themselves, subject only to the Constitution of the United States . . .

I hold it is a violation of the fundamental principles of this Government to throw the weight of Federal power into the scale, either in favor of the Free or the Slave States. Equality among all the States of this Union is a fundamental principle in our political system. We have no more right to throw the weight of the Federal Government into the scale in favor of the slaveholding than the Free States, and least of all should our friends in the South consent for a moment that Congress should withhold its powers either way when they know that there is a majority against them in both Houses of Congress . . .

My friends, there never was a time when it was as important for the Democratic party, for all national men, to rally and stand together, as it is to-day. We find all sectional men giving up past differences and uniting on the one question of slavery; and when we find sectional men thus uniting, we should unite to resist them and their treasonable designs. Such was the case in 1850, when Clay left the quiet and peace of his home, and again entered upon public life to quell agitation and restore peace to a distracted Union. Then we Democrats, with Cass at our head, welcomed Henry Clay, whom the whole nation regarded as having been preserved by God for the times. He became our leader in that great fight, and we rallied around him the same as the Whigs rallied around Old Hickory in 1832 to put down nullification.

Thus you see that whilst Whigs and Democrats fought fearlessly in old times about banks, the tariff, distribution, the specie circular, and the sub-treasury, all united as a band of brothers when the peace, harmony, or integrity of the Union was imperiled. It was so in 1850, when Abolitionism had even so far divided this country, North and South, as to endanger the peace of the Union; Whigs and Democrats united in establishing the Compromise Measures of that year, and restoring tranquility and good feeling. These measures passed on the joint action of the two parties. They rested on the great principle that the people of each State and each Territory should be left perfectly free to form and regulate their domestic institutions to suit themselves. You Whigs and we Democrats justified them in that principle. In 1854, when it became necessary to organize the Territories of Kansas and Nebraska, I brought forward the bill on the same principle. In the Kansas-Nebraska bill you find it delcared to be the true intent and meaning of the Act not to legislate slavery into any State or Territory, nor to exclude it therefrom, but to leave the people thereof perfectly free to form and regulate their domestic institutions in their own way. I stand on that same platform in 1858 that I did in 1850, 1854, and 1856 . . .

The whole South is rallying to the support of the doctrine that if the people of a Territory want slavery, they have a right to have it, and if they do not want it, that no power on earth can force it upon them. I hold that there is no principle on earth more sacred to all the friends of freedom than that which says that no institution, no law, no constitution, should be forced on an unwilling people contrary to their wishes; and I assert that the Kansas and Nebraska bill contains that principle. It is the great principle contained in that bill. It is the principle on which James Buchanan was made President. Without that principle, he never would have been made President of the United States. I will never violate or abandon that doctrine, if I have to stand alone. I have resisted the blandishments and threats of power on the one side, and seduction on the other, and have stood immovably for that principle, fighting for it when assailed by Northern mobs, or threatened by Southern hostility. I have defended it against the North and the South, and I will defend it against whoever assails it, and I will follow it wherever its logical conclusions lead me. I say to you that there is but one hope, one safety for this country, and that is to stand immovably by that principle which declares the right of each State and each Territory to decide these questions for themselves. This Government was founded on that principle, and must be administered in the same sense in which it was founded.

But the Abolition party really think that under the Declaration of Independence the negro is equal to the white man, and that negro equality is an inalienable right conferred by the Almighty, and hence that all human laws in violation of it are null and void. With such men it is no use for me to argue. I hold that

the signers of the Declaration of Independence had no reference to negroes at all when they declared all men to be created equal. They did not mean negroes, nor the savage Indians, nor the Fiji Islanders, nor any other barbarous race. They were speaking of white men. They alluded to men of European birth and European descent, – to white men, and to none others, – when they declared that doctrine. I hold that this Government was established on the white basis. It was established by white men for the benefit of white men and their posterity forever, and should be administered by white men, and none others.

But it does not follow, by any means, that merely because the negro is not a citizen, and merely because he is not our equal, that, therefore, he should be a slave. On the contrary, it does follow that we ought to extend to the negro race, and to all other dependent races, all the rights, all the privileges, and all the immunities which they can exercise consistently with the safety of society. Humanity requires that we should give them all these privileges; Christianity commands that we should extend those privileges to them. The question then arises, What are those privileges, and what is the nature and extent of them? My answer is, that that is a question which each State must answer for itself. We in Illinois have decided it for ourselves. We tried slavery, kept it up for twelve years, and finding that it was not profitable, we abolished it for that reason, and became a Free State. We adopted in its stead the policy that a negro in this State shall not be a slave and shall not be a citizen. We have a right to adopt that policy. For my part, I think it is a wise and sound policy for us . . .

Why can we not thus have peace? Why should we thus allow a sectional party to agitate this country, to array the North against the South, and convert us into enemies instead of friends, merely that a few ambitious men may ride into power on a sectional hobby? How long is it since these ambitious Northern men wished for a sectional organization? Did any one of them dream of a sectional party as long as the North was the weaker section and the South the stronger? Then all were opposed to sectional parties; but the moment the North obtained the majority in the House and Senate by the admission of California, and could elect a President without the aid of Southern votes, that moment ambitious Northern men formed a scheme to excite the North against the South, and make the people be governed in their votes by geographical lines, thinking that the North, being the stronger section, would out-vote the South, and consequently they, the leaders, would ride into office on a sectional hobby . . .

Mr. Lincoln's Reply

I have stated upon former occasions, and I may as well state again, what I understand to be the real issue in this controversy between Judge Douglas and myself. On the point of my wanting to make war between the Free and the Slave States, there has been no issue be-tween us. So, too, when he assumes that I am in favor of introducing a perfect social and political equality between the white and black races. These are false issues, upon which Judge Douglas has tried to force the controversy. There is no foundation in truth for the charge that I maintain either of these propositions. The real issue in this controversy — the one pressing upon every mind — is the sentiment on the part of one class that looks upon the institution of slavery as a wrong, and of another class that does not look upon it as a wrong.

The sentiment that contemplates the institution of slavery in this country as a wrong is the sentiment of the Republican party. It is the sentiment around which all their actions, all their arguments, circle, from which all their propositions radiate. They look upon it as being a moral, social, and political wrong; and while they contemplate it as such, they neverthe-less have due regard for its actual existence among us, and the difficulties of getting rid of it in any satisfac-tory way, and to all the constitutional obligations thrown about it. Yet, having a due regard for these, they desire a policy in regard to it that looks to its not creating any more danger. They insist that it should, as far as may be, be treated as a wrong; and one of the methods of treating it as a wrong is to make provision that it shall grow no larger. They also desire a policy that looks to a peaceful end of slavery at some time, as being wrong.

These are the views they entertain in regard to it as I understand them; and all their sentiments, all their arguments and propositions, are brought within this range. I have said, and I repeat it here, that if there be a man amongst us who does not think that the institu-tion of slavery is wrong in any one of the aspects of which I have spoken, he is misplaced, and ought not to be with us. And if there be a man amongst us who is so impatient of it as a wrong as to disregard its actual presence among us and the difficulty of getting rid of it suddenly in a satisfactory way, and to disregard the constitutional obligations thrown about it, that man is misplaced if he is on our platform. We disclaim sympathy with him in practical action. He is not placed properly with us.

On this subject of treating it as a wrong, and limiting its spread, let me say a word. Has anything ever threatened the existence of this Union save and except this very institution of slavery? What is it that we hold most dear amongst us? Our own liberty and prosperity. What has ever threatened our liberty and prosperity, save and except this institution of slavery? If this is true, how do you propose to improve the condition of things by enlarging slavery, — by spread-ing it out and making it bigger? You may have a wen or cancer upon your person, and not be able to cut it out, lest you bleed to death; but surely it is no way to cure it, to engraft it and spread it over your whole body. That is no proper way of treating what you regard a wrong. You see this peaceful way of dealing with it as a wrong, — restricting the spread of it, and not allowing it to go into new countries where it has not already existed. That is the peaceful way, the old-fashioned way, the way in which the fathers them-selves set us the example.

On the other hand, I have said there is a senti-ment which treats it as *not* being wrong. That is the Democratic sentiment of this day. I do not mean to say that every man who stands within that range positively asserts that it is right. That class will in-clude all who positively assert that it is right, and all who, like Judge Douglas, treat it as indifferent and do not say it is either right or wrong. These two classes of men fall within the general class of those who do not look upon it as a wrong. And if there be among you anybody who supposes that he, as a Democrat, can consider himself "as much opposed to slavery as anybody," I would like to reason with him. You never treat it as a wrong . . .

The Democratic policy in regard to that institution will not tolerate the merest breath, the slightest hint, of the least degree of wrong about it.

Try it by some of Judge Douglas's arguments. He says he "don't care whether it is voted up or voted down" in the Territories. I do not care myself, in dealing with that expression, whether it is intended to be expressive of his individual sentiments on the subject, or only of the national policy he desires to have established. It is alike valuable for my purpose. Any man can say that, who does not see anything wrong in slavery; but no man can logically say it who does see a wrong in it, because no man can logically say he don't care whether a wrong is voted up or voted down. He may say he don't care whether an indifferent thing is voted up or down; but he must logically have a choice between a right thing and a wrong thing. He contends that whatever community wants slaves has a right to have them. So they have, if it is not a wrong. But if it is a wrong, he cannot say people have a right to do wrong. He says that upon the score of equality, slaves should be allowed to go into a new Territory, like other property. This is strictly logical if there is no difference between it and other property. If it and other property are equal, his argument is entirely logical. But if you insist that one is wrong and the other right, there is no use to institute a comparison between right and wrong. You may turn over everything in the Democratic policy from beginning to end, whether in the shape it takes on the statute book, in the shape it takes in the Dred Scott decision, in the shape it takes in conversation, or the shape it takes in short maxim-like arguments, — it everywhere carefully excludes the idea that there is anything wrong in it.

That is the real issue. That is the issue that will continue in this country when these poor tongues of Judge Douglas and myself shall be silent. It is the eternal struggle between these two principles — right and wrong — throughout the world. They are the two principles that have stood face to face from the beginning of time, and will ever continue to struggle. The one is the common right of humanity, and the other the "divine right of kings." It is the same principle in whatever shape it develops itself. It is the same spirit that says, "You work and toil and earn bread, and I'll eat it." No matter in what shape it comes, whether from the mouth of a king who seeks to bestride the people of his own nation and live by the fruit of their labor, or from one race of men as an apology for enslaving another race, it is the same tyrannical principle.

I was glad to express my gratitude at Quincy, and I re-express it here to Judge Douglas, — that he looks to no end of the institution of slavery. That will help the people to see where the struggle really is. It will hereafter place with us all men who really do wish the wrong may have an end. And whenever we can get rid of the fog which obscures the real question, when we can get Judge Douglas and his friends to avow a policy looking to its perpetuation, — we can get them out from among the class of men and bring them to the side of those who treat it as a wrong. Then there will soon be an end of it, and that end will be its "ultimate extinction."

The Lincoln-Douglas debates were actually a preview of the presidential campaign of 1860 when Lincoln and Douglas were the two Northern candidates. The rift between North and South had grown sufficiently great by that time that the parties themselves were divided along sectional lines. The North's superior population won Lincoln the office, but none of the four candidates got a majority, and Lincoln failed to carry a single Southern state. Between his November election and the March inauguration, eight of the eleven states of the future Southern Confederacy had seceded from the union.

The secession crisis went right to the heart of the American faith in individual rights and voluntary solutions. Confronted by the South's determination to break up the union, many people fell back upon the only arbiter they recognized in society — individual choice. Southern secessionist theory was actually an elaboration of this same conviction. Only in this case the individual was the state which had voluntarily joined the union and could as freely leave. For the past thirty years, Southerners had expounded the belief that the Constitution was a compact of the states rather than the creation of the American people as a whole, and while most Northerners felt that the majority should rule within the union, their commitment to free choice lent support to the Southern position that states could secede from the union. It is not surprising then that many people were willing to see the seceding states depart in peace.

Lincoln's victory in November of 1860 had prompted the Southern states to secede from the Union, but he himself had said nothing about his intentions toward the South during the months which elapsed between his election and his March inauguration. Finally, in his inaugural address, Lincoln explained to a waiting nation what he believed to be his duties as President in this crisis of the union.

Masked often by the American politicians' art of compromise was the fact that within any society the power to make decisions must lodge somewhere. Lincoln was willing to recognize this truth. He was also committed to the preservation of the union. In a carefully reasoned argument, he moved from this affirmation of the union to an explanation of who with within the union must be the final arbiter. The first reading of this section presents the South Carolina Secession Ordinance with its explication of the Southern view of the nature of the federal union. The second reading comes from a *New York Tribune* editorial by Horace Greeley (1811–1872), and the readings close with Lincoln's First Inaugural, a document of enduring relevance to the American people.

South Carolina's Ordinance of Secession (1860)

We, the People of the State of South Carolina, in Convention assembled, do declare and ordain, and it is hereby declared and ordained.

That the Ordinance adopted by us in Convention, on the twenty-third day of May, in the year of our Lord one thousand seven hundred and eighty-eight, whereby the Constitution of the United States of America was ratified, and also, all Acts and parts of Acts of the General Assembly of this State, ratifying amendments of the said Constitution, are hereby repealed; and that the union now subsisting between South Carolina and other States, under the name of "The United States of America," is hereby dissolved.

Declaration of the immediate causes which induce and justify the secession of South Carolina from the Federal Union.

The People of the State of South Carolina, in Convention assembled, on the 26th day of April, A.D., 1852, declared that the frequent violations of the Constitution of the United States, by the Federal Government, and its encroachments upon the reserved rights of the States, fully justified this State in then withdrawing from the Federal Union; but in deference to the opinions and wishes of the other slaveholding States, she forbore at that time to exercise this right. Since

---

Declaration of the immediate causes which induce and justify the secession of South Carolina from the federal union, Evans and Cogswell, Charleston, 1860.

that time, these encroachments have continued to increase, and further forbearance ceases to be a virtue.

And now the State of South Carolina having resumed her separate and equal place among nations, deems it due to herself, to the remaining United States of America, and to the nations of the world, that she should declare the immediate causes which have led to this act.

In the year 1765, that portion of the British Empire embracing Great Britain, undertook to make laws for the government of that portion composed of the thirteen American Colonies. A struggle for the right of self-government ensued, which resulted, on the 4th July, 1776, in a Declaration, by the Colonies, "that they are, and of right ought to be, *Free and independent states*; and that, as free and independent States, they have full power to levy war, conclude peace, contract alliances, establish commerce, and to do all other acts and things which independent States may of right do."

They further solemnly declared that whenever any "form of government becomes destructive of the ends for which it was established, it is the right of the people to alter or abolish it, and to institute a new government." Deeming the Government of Great Britain to have become destructive of these ends, they declared that the Colonies "are absolved from all allegiance to the British Crown, and that all political connection between them and the State of Great Britain is, and ought to be, totally dissolved."

In pursuance of this Declaration of Independence, each of the thirteen States proceeded to exercise its separate sovereignty; adopted for itself a Constitution, and appointed officers for the administration of government in all its departments — Legislative, Executive and Judicial. For purposes of defence, they united their arms and their counsels; and, in 1778, they entered into a League known as the Articles of Confederation, whereby they agreed to entrust the administration of their external relations to a common agent, known as the Congress of the United States, expressly declaring, in the first article, "that each State retains its sovereignty, freedom and independence, and every power, jurisdiction and right which is not, by this Confederation, expressly delegated to the United States in Congress assembled.

Under this Confederation the War of the Revolution was carried on, and on the 3d September, 1783, the contest ended, and a definitive Treaty was signed by Great Britain, in which she acknowledged the Independence of the Colonies in the following terms:

"Article 1. — His Britannic Majesty acknowledges the said United States, viz: New Hampshire, Massachusetts Bay, Rhode Island and Providence Plantations, Connecticut, New York, New Jersey, Pennsylvania, Delaware, Maryland, Virginia, North Carolina, South Carolina and Georgia, to be *free, sovereign and independent states;* that he treats with them as such; and for himself, his heirs and successors, relinquishes all claims to the government, propriety and territorial rights of the same and every part thereof."

Thus were established the two great principles asserted by the Colonies, namely: the right of a State to govern itself; and the right of a people to abolish a Government when it becomes destructive of the ends for which it was instituted. And concurrent with the establishment of these principles, was the fact, that each Colony became and was recognized by the mother country as a *free, sovereign and independent state.*

In 1787, Deputies were appointed by the States to revise the Articles of Confederation, and on 17th September, 1787, these Deputies recommended, for the adoption of the States, the Articles of Union, known as the Constitution of the United States.

The parties to whom this Constitution was submitted, were the several sovereign States; they were to agree or disagree, and when nine of them agreed, the compact was to take effect among those concurring; and the General Government, as the common agent, was then to be invested with their authority.

If only nine of the thirteen States had concurred, the other four would have remained as they were — separate sovereign States, independent of any of the provisions of the Constitution. In fact, two of the States did not accede to the Constitution until long after it had gone into operation among the other eleven; and during that interval, they each exercised the functions of an independent nation.

By this Constitution, certain duties were imposed upon the several States, and the exercise of certain of their powers was restrained, which necessarily implied their continued existence as sovereign States. But, to remove all doubt, an amendment was added, which declared that the powers not delegated to the United States by the Constitution, nor prohibited by it to the States, are reserved to the States, respectively, or to the people. On 23d May, 1788, South Carolina, by a Convention of her people, passed an Ordinance assenting to this Constitution, and afterwards altered her own Constitution, to conform herself to the obligations she had undertaken.

Thus was established, by compact between the States, a Government, with defined objects and powers, limited to the express words of the grant. This limitation left the whole remaining mass of power subject to the clause reserving it to the States or to the people, and rendered unnecessary any specification of reserved rights.

We hold that the Government thus established is subject to the two great principles asserted in the Declaration of Independence; and we hold further, that the mode of its formation subjects it to a third fundamental principle, namely: the law of compact. We maintain that in every compact between two or more parties, the obligation is mutual; that the failure of one of the contracting parties to perform a material part of the agreement, entirely releases the obligation of the other; and that where no arbiter is provided, each party is remitted to his own judgment to determine the fact of failure, with all its consequences.

In the present case, that fact is established with certainty. We assert, that fourteen of the States have deliberately refused for years past to fulfil their constitional obligations, and we refer to their own Statutes for the proof.

The Constitution of the United States, in its 4th Article, provides as follows:

"No person held to service or labor in one State, under the laws thereof, escaping into another, shall, in consequence of any law or regulation therein, be discharged from such service or labor, but shall be delivered up, on claim of the party to whom such service or labor may be due."

This stipulation was so material to the compact, that without it that compact would not have been made. The greater number of the contracting parties held slaves, and they had previously evinced their estimate of the value of such a stipulation by making it a condition in the Ordinance for the government of the territory ceded by Virginia, which now composes the States north of the Ohio river.

The same article of the Constitution stipulates also for rendition by the several States of fugitives from justice from the other States.

The General Government, as the common agent, passed laws to carry into effect these stipulations of the States. For many years these laws were executed. But an increasing hostility on the part of the non-slaveholding States to the Institution of Slavery has led to a disregard to their obligations, and the laws of the General Government have ceased to effect the objects of the Constitution. The States of Maine, New Hampshire, Vermont, Massachusetts, Connecticut, Rhode Island, New York, Pennsylvania, Illinois, Indiana, Michigan, Wisconsin and Iowa, have enacted laws which either nullify the Acts of Congress or render useless any attempt to execute them. In many of these States the fugitive is discharged from the service or labor claimed, and in none of them has the State Government complied with the stipulation made in the Constitution. The State of New Jersey, at an early day, passed a law in conformity with her constitional obligation; but the current of anti-slavery feeling has led her more recently to enact laws which render inoperative the remedies provided by her own law and by the laws of Congress. In the State of New York even the right of transit for a slave has been denied by her tribunals; and the States of Ohio and Iowa have refused to surrender to justice fugitives charged with murder, and with inciting servile insurrection in the State of Virginia. Thus the constitutional compact has been deliberately broken and disregarded by the non-slaveholding States, and the consequence follows that South Carolina is released from her obligation.

The ends for which this Constitution was framed are declared by itself to be "to form a more perfect union, establish justice, insure domestic tranquility, provide for the common defence, promote the general welfare, and secure the blessings of liberty to ourselves and our posterity."

These ends it endeavored to accomplish by a Federal Government, in which each State was recognized as an equal, and had separate control over its own institutions. The right of property in slaves was recognized by giving to free persons distinct political rights, by giving them the right to represent, and burthening them with direct taxes for three-fifths of their slaves; by authorizing the importation of slaves for twenty years; and by stipulating for the rendition of fugitives from labor.

We affirm that these ends for which this Government was instituted have been defeated, and the Government itself has been made destructive of them by the action of the nonslaveholding States. Those States have assumed the right of deciding upon the propriety of our domestic institutions; and have denied the rights of property established in fifteen of the States and recognized by the Constitution; they have denounced as sinful the institution of Slavery; they have permitted the open establishment among them of societies, whose avowed object is to disturb the peace and to eloign the property of the citizens of other States. They have encouraged and assisted thousands of our slaves to leave their homes; and those who remain, have been incited by emissaries, books and pictures to servile insurrection.

For twenty-five years this agitation has been steadily increasing, until it has now secured to its aid the power of the Common Government. Observing the *forms* of the Constitution, a sectional party has found within that article establishing the Executive Department, the means of subverting the Constitution itself. A geographical line has been drawn across the Union, and all the States north of that line have united in the election of a man to the high office of President of the United States whose opinions and purposes are hostile to slavery. He is to be entrusted with the administration of the Common Government, because he has declared that that "Government cannot endure permanently half slave, half free," and that the public mind must rest in the belief that Slavery is in the course of ultimate extinction.

This sectional combination for the subversion of the Constitution, has been aided in some of the States by elevating to citizenship, persons, who, by the Supreme Law of the land, are incapable of becoming citizens; and their votes have been used to inaugurate a new policy, hostile to the South, and destructive of its peace and safety.

On the 4th March next, this party will take possession of the Government. It has announced, that the South shall be excluded from the common Territory; that the Judicial Tribunals shall be made sectional, and that a war must be waged against slavery until it shall cease throughout the United States.

The Guaranties of the Constitution will then no longer exist; the equal rights of the States will be lost. The slaveholding States will no longer have the power of self-government, or self-protection, and the Federal Government will have become their enemy.

Sectional interest and animosity will deepen the irritation, and all hope of remedy is rendered vain, by the fact that public opinion at the North has invested a great political error with the sanctions of a more erroneous religious belief.

We, therefore, the people of South Carolina, by our delegates, in Convention assembled, appealing to the Supreme Judge of the world for the rectitude of our intentions, have solemnly declared that the Union heretofore existing between this State and the other States of North America, is dissolved, and that the State of South Carolina has resumed her position among the nations of the world, as a separate and independent State; with full power to levy war, conclude peace, contract alliances, establish commerce, and to do all other acts and things which independent States may of right do. —

Horace Greeley: *The right of Secession (1860)*

The Albany Evening Journal courteously controverts our views on the subject of Secession. Here is the gist of its argument:

" 'Seven or eight States' have 'pretty unanimously made up their minds' to leave the Union. Mr. Buchanan, in reply, says that 'ours is a Government of popular opinion,' and hence, if States rebel, there is no power residing either with the Executive or in Congress, to resist or punish. Why, then, is not this the end of the controversy? Those 'seven or eight States' are going out. The Government remonstrates, but acquiesces. And The Tribune regards it 'unwise to undertake to resist such Secession by Federal force.'

"If an individual, or 'a single State,' commits

A. Oakley Hall, *Horace Greeley Decently Dissected*, Ross and Tourey, New York, 1862, pp. 34–35.

treason, the same act in two or more individuals or two or more States is alike treasonable. And how is treason against the Federal Government to be resisted, except by 'Federal force'?

"Precisely the same question was involved in the South Carolina Secession of 1833. But neither President Jackson, nor Congress, nor the people took this view of it. The President issued a Proclamation declaring Secession treason. Congress passed a Force Law; and South Carolina, instead of 'madly shooting from its sphere,' returned, if not to her senses, back into line."

Does the Journal mean to say that if all the States and their people should become tired of the Union, it would be treason on their part to seek its dissolution?

We have repeatedly asked those who dissent from our view of this matter to tell us frankly whether they do or do not assent to Mr. Jefferson's statement in the Declaration of Independence that governments "derive their just powers from the consent of the governed; and that whenever any form of government becomes destructive of these ends; it is the right of the people to alter or abolish it, and to institute a new government," &c., &c. We do heartily accept this doctrine, believing it intrinsically sound, beneficent, and one that, universally accepted, is calculated to prevent the shedding of seas of human blood. *And if it justified the secession from the British Empire of three millions of colonists in 1776, we do not see why it would not justify the secession of five millions of Southrons from the federal union in 1861.* If we are mistaken on this point, why does not some one attempt to show wherein and why? For our own part, while we deny the right of slaveholders to hold slaves against the will of the latter, we cannot see how twenty millions of people can rightfully hold ten, or even five, in a detested union with them, by military force.

Of course, we understand that the principle of Jefferson, like any other broad generalization, may be pushed to extreme and baleful consequences. We can see why Governor's Island should not be at liberty to secede from the State and Nation and allow herself to be covered with French and British batteries commanding and threatening our city. There is hardly a great principle which may not be thus "run into the ground." But if seven or eight contiguous States shall present themselves authentically at Washington, saying, "We hate the Federal Union; we have withdrawn from it; we give you the choice between acquiescing in our secession and arranging amicably all incidental questions on the one hand, and attempting to subdue us on the other" — we could not stand up for coercion, for subjugation, for we do not think it would be just. We hold the right of Self-Government sacred, even when invoked in behalf of those who deny it to others. So much for the question of Principle.

Now as to the matter of Policy:

South Carolina will certainly secede. Several other Cotton States will probably follow her example. The Border States are evidently reluctant to do likewise. South Carolina has grossly insulted them by her dictatorial, reckless course. What she expects and desires is a clash of arms with the Federal Government, which will at once commend her to the sympathy and co-operation of every slave State, and to the sympathy (at least) of the pro-slavery minority in the free States. It is not difficult to see that this would speedily work a political revolution, which would restore to slavery all, and more than all, it has lost by the canvass of 1860. We want to obviate this. We would expose the seceders to odium as disunionists, not commend them to pity as the gallant though mistaken upholders of the rights of their section in an unequal military conflict.

We fully realize that the dilemma of the incoming Administration will be a critical one. It must endeavor to uphold and enforce the laws, as well against rebellious slaveholders as fugitive slaves. The new President must fulfill the obligations assumed in his inauguration oath, no matter how shamefully his predecessor may have defied them. We fear that Southern madness may precipitate a bloody collision that all must deplore. But if ever "seven or eight States" send agents to Washington to say, "We want to get out of the Union," we shall feel constrained by our devotion to Human Liberty to say, Let them go! And we do not see how we could take the other side without coming in direct conflict with those

Rights of Man which we hold paramount to all political arrangements, however convenient and advantageous.

Abraham Lincoln: First inaugural address (1861)

Fellow citizens of the United States:

In compliance with a custom as old as the government itself, I appear before you to address you briefly, and to take, in your presence, the oath prescribed by the Constitution of the United States, to be taken by the President "before he enters on the execution of his office."

I do not consider it necessary, at present, for me to discuss those matters of administration about which there is no special anxiety, or excitement.

Apprehension seems to exist among the people of the Southern States, that by the accession of a Republican Administration, their property, and their peace, and personal security, are to be endangered. There has never been any reasonable cause for such apprehension. Indeed, the most ample evidence to the contrary has all the while existed, and been open to their inspection. It is found in nearly all the published speeches of him who now addresses you. I do but quote from one of those speeches when I declare that "I have no purpose, directly or indirectly, to interfere with the institution of slavery in the States where it exists. I believe I have no lawful right to do so, and I have no inclination to do so." Those who nominated and elected me did so with full knowledge that I had made this, and many similar declarations, and had never recanted them. And more than this, they placed in the platform, for my acceptance, and as a law to themselves, and to me, the clear and emphatic resolution which I now read:

"*Resolved*, That the maintenance inviolate of the rights of the States, and especially the right of each State to order and control its own domestic institutions according to its own judgment exclusively, is essential to that balance of power on which the perfection and endurance of our political fabric depend; and we denounce the lawless invasion by armed force

of the soil of any State or Territory, no matter under what pretext, as among the gravest of crimes."

I now reiterate these sentiments: and in doing so, I only press upon the public attention the most conclusive evidence of which the case is susceptible, that the property, peace and security of no section are to be in anywise endangered by the now incoming Administration. I add too, that all the protection which, consistently with the Constitution and the laws, can be given, will be cheerfully given to all the States when lawfully demanded, for whatever cause — as cheerfully to one section, as to another.

There is much controversy about the delivering up of fugitives from service or labor. The clause I now read is as plainly written in the Constitution as any other of its provisions:

"No person held to service or labor in one State, under the laws thereof, escaping into another, shall, in consequence of any law or regulation therein, be discharged from such service or labor, but shall be delivered up on claim of the party to whom such service or labor may be due."

It is scarcely questioned that this provision was intended by those who made it, for the reclaiming of what we call fugitive slaves; and the intention of the law-giver is the law. All members of Congress swear their support to the whole Constitution — to this provision as much as to any other. To the proposition, then, that slaves whose cases come within the terms of this clause, "shall be delivered up," their oaths are unanimous. Now, if they would make the effort in good temper, could they not, with nearly equal unanimity, frame and pass a law, by means of which to keep good that unanimous oath?

There is some difference of opinion whether this clause should be enforced by national or by state authority; but surely that difference is not a very material one. If the slave is to be surrendered, it can be of but little consequence to him, or to others, by which authority it is done. And should any one, in any case, be content that his oath shall go unkept, on a merely unsubstantial controversy, as to how it shall be kept?

Again, in any law upon this subject, ought not all the safeguards of liberty known in civilized and humane jurisprudence to be introduced, so that a free man be

James D. Richardson (ed.), *A Compilation of the Messages and Papers of the Presidents*, 1789–1897, Government Printing Office, Washington, 1896–99, VI, 3–11.

not, in any case, surrendered as a slave? And might it not be well, at the same time, to provide by law for the enforcement of that clause in the Constitution which guarranties that "The citizens of each State shall be entitled to all privileges and immunities of citizens in the several States?"

I take the official oath to-day, with no mental reservations, and with no purpose to construe the Constitution or laws, by any hypercritical rules. And while I do not choose now to specify particular acts of Congress as proper to be enforced, I do suggest, that it will be much safer for all, both in official and private stations, to conform to, and abide by, all those acts which stand unrepealed, than to violate any of them, trusting to find impunity in having them held to be unconstitutional.

It is seventy-two years since the first inauguration of a President under our national Constitution. During that period fifteen different and greatly distinguished citizens, have, in succession, administered the executive branch of the government. They have conducted it through many perils; and, generally, with great success. Yet, with all this scope for precedent, I now enter upon the same task for the brief constitutional term of four years, under great and peculiar difficulty. A disruption of the Federal Union heretofore only menaced, is now formidably attempted.

I hold, that in contemplation of universal law, and of the Constitution, the Union of these States is perpetual. Perpetuity is implied, if not expressed, in the fundamental law of all national governments. It is safe to assert that no government proper, ever had a provision in its organic law for its own termination. Continue to execute all the express provisions of our national Constitution, and the Union will endure forever — it being impossible to destroy it, except by some action not provided for in the instrument itself.

Again, if the United States be not a government proper, but an association of States in the nature of contract merely, can it, as a contract, be peaceably unmade, by less than all the parties who made it? One party to a contract may violate it — break it, so to speak; but does it not require all to lawfully rescind it?

Descending from these general principles, we find the proposition that, in legal contemplation, the Union is perpetual, confirmed by the history of the Union itself. The Union is much older than the Constitution. It was formed in fact, by the Articles of Association in 1774. It was matured and continued by the Declaration of Independence in 1776. It was further matured and the faith of all the then thirteen States expressly plighted and engaged that it should be perpetual, by the Articles of Confederation in 1778. And finally, in 1787, one of the declared objects for ordaining and establishing the Constitution, was "to form a more perfect union."

But if destruction of the Union, by one, or by a part only, of the States, be lawfully possible, the Union is less perfect that before the Constitution, having lost the vital element of perpetuity.

It follows from these views that no State, upon its own mere motion, can lawfully get out of the Union, — that resolves and ordinances to that effect are legally void; and that acts of violence, within any State or States, against the authority of the United States, are insurrectionary or revolutionary, according to circumstances.

I therefore consider that, in view of the Constitution and the laws, the Union is unbroken; and, to the extent of my ability, I shall take care, as the Constitution itself expressly enjoins upon me, that the laws of the Union be faithfully executed in all the States. Doing this I deem to be only a simple duty on my part; and I shall perform it, so far as practicable, unless my rightful masters, the American people, shall withhold the requisite means, or, in some authoritative manner, direct the contrary. I trust this will not be regarded as a menace, but only as the declared purpose of the Union that it will constitutionally defend, and maintain itself.

In doing this there needs to be no bloodshed or violence; and there shall be none, unless it be forced upon the national authority. The power confided to me, will be used to hold, occupy, and possess the property, and places belonging to the government, and to collect the duties and imposts; but beyond what may be necessary for these objects, there will be no invasion — no using of force against, or among the people anywhere. Where hostility to the United States, in any interior locality, shall be so great and so universal, as to prevent competent resident citizens from holding the Federal offices, there will be no attempt to force obnoxious strangers among the people for that object. While the strict legal right may exist in the government to enforce the exercise of these offices, the attempt to do so would be so irritating, and so nearly impracticable with all, that I deem it better to forego, for the time, the uses of such offices.

The mails, unless repelled, will continue to be furnished in all parts of the Union. So far as possible, the people everywhere shall have that sense of perfect security which is most favorable to calm thought and reflection. The course here indicated will be followed, unless current events, and experience, shall show a modification, or change, to be proper; and in every case and exigency, my best discretion will be exercised, according to circumstances actually existing, and with a view and a hope of a peaceful solution of the national troubles, and the restoration of fraternal sympathies and affections.

That there are persons in one section, or another who seek to destroy the Union at all events, and are glad of any pretext to do it, I will neither affirm or deny; but if there be such, I need address no word to them. To those, however, who really love the Union, may I not speak?

Before entering upon so grave a matter as the destruction of our national fabric, with all its benefits, its memories, and its hopes, would it not be wise to ascertain precisely why we do it? Will you hazard so desperate a step, while there is any possibility that any portion of the ills you fly from, have no real existence? Will you, while the certain ills you fly to, are greater than all the real ones you fly from? Will you risk the commission of so fearful a mistake?

All profess to be content in the Union, if all constitutional rights can be maintained. Is it true, then, that any right, plainly written in the Constitution, has been denied? I think not. Happily the human mind is so constituted, that no party can reach to the audacity of doing this. Think, if you can, of a single instance in which a plainly written provision of the Constitution has ever been denied. If, by the mere force of numbers, a majority should deprive a minority of any clearly written constitutional right, it might, in a moral point of view, justify revolution — certainly would, if such right were a vital one. But such is not our case. All the vital rights of minorities, and of individuals, are so plainly assured to them, by affirmations and negations, guarranties and prohibitions, in the Constitution, that controversies never arise concerning them. But no organic law can ever be framed with a provision specifically applicable to every question which may occur in practical administration. No foresight can anticipate, nor any document of reasonable length contain express provisions for all possible questions. Shall fugitives from labor be surrendered by national or by State authority? The Constitution does not expressly say. *May* Congress prohibit slavery in the territories? The Constitution does not expressly say. *Must* Congress protect slavery in the territories? The Constitution does not expressly say.

From questions of this class spring all our constitutional controversies, and we divide upon them into majorities and minorities. If the minority will not acquiesce, the majority must, or the government must cease. There is no other alternative; for continuing the government, is acquiescence on one side or the other. If a minority, in such case, will secede rather than acquiesce, they make a precedent which, in turn, will divide and ruin them; for a minority of their own will secede from them, whenever a majority refuses to be controlled by such minority. For instance, why may not any portion of a new confederacy, a year or two hence, arbitrarily secede again, precisely as portions of the present Union now claim to secede from it. All who cherish disunion sentiments, are now being educated to the exact temper of doing this. Is there such perfect identity of interests among the States to compose a new Union, as to produce harmony only, and prevent renewed secession?

Plainly, the central idea of secession, is the essence of anarchy. A majority, held in restraint by constitutional checks, and limitations, and always changing easily, with deliberate changes of popular opinions and sentiments, is the only true sovereign of a free people. Whoever rejects it, does, of necessity, fly to anarchy or to despotism. Unanimity is impossible; the rule of a minority, as a permanent arrangement, is wholly inadmissable; so that, rejecting the majority principle, anarchy, or despotism in some form, is all that is left ... Physically speaking, we cannot separate. We cannot remove our respective sections from each other, nor build an impassable wall between them. A husband

and wife may be divorced, and go out of the presence, and beyond the reach of each other; but the different parts of our country cannot do this. They cannot but remain face to face; and intercourse, either amicable or hostile, must continue between them. Is it possible then to make that intercourse more advantageous, or more satisfactory, after separation than before? Can aliens make treaties easier than friends can make laws? Can treaties be more faithfully enforced between aliens, than laws can among friends? Suppose you go to war, you cannot fight always; and when, after much loss on both sides, and no gain on either, you cease fighting, the identical old questions, as to terms of intercourse, are again upon you.

This country, with its institutions, belongs to the people who inhabit it. Whenever they shall grow weary of the existing government, they can exercise their constitutional right of amending it, or their revolutionary right to dismember, or overthrow it. I can not be ignorant of the fact that many worthy, and patriotic citizens are desirous of having the national constitution amended. While I make no recommendation of amendments, I fully recognize the rightful authority of the people over the whole subject, to be exercised in either of the modes prescribed in the instrument itself; and I should, under existing circumstances, favor, rather than oppose, a fair oppertunity being afforded the people to act upon it . . .

The Chief Magistrate derives all his authority from the people, and they have conferred none upon him to fix terms for the separation of the States. The people themselves can do this also if they choose; but the executive, as such, has nothing to do with it. His duty is to administer the present government, as it came to his hands, and to transmit it, unimpaired by him, to his successor.

Why should there not be a patient confidence in the ultimate justice of the people? Is there any better, or equal hope, in the world? In our present differences, is either party without faith of being in the right? If the Almighty Ruler of nations, with his eternal truth and justice, be on your side of the North, or on yours of the South, that truth, and that justice, will surely

prevail, by the judgment of this great tribunal, the American people.

By the frame of the government under which we live, this same people have wisely given their public servants but little power for mischief; and have, with equal wisdom, provided for the return of that little to their own hands at very short intervals.

While the people retain their virtue, and vigilence, no administration, by any extreme of wickedness or folly, can very seriously injure the government, in the short space of four years.

My countrymen, one and all, think calmly and well, upon this whole subject. Nothing valuable can be lost by taking time. If there be an object to hurry any of you, in hot haste, to a step which you would never take deliberately, that object will be frustrated by taking time; but no good object can be frustrated by it. Such of you as are now dissatisfied, still have the old Constitution unimpaired, and, on the sensitive point, the laws of your own framing under it; while the new administration will have no immediate power, if it would, to change either. If it were admitted that you who are dissatisfied, hold the right side in the dispute, there still is no single good reason for precipitate action. Intelligence, patriotism, Christianity, and a firm reliance on Him, who has never yet forsaken this favored land, are still competent to adjust, in the best way, all our present difficulty.

In *your* hands, my dissatisfied fellow countrymen, and not in *mine*, is the momentous issue of civil war. The government will not assail *you*. You can have no conflict, without being yourselves the aggressors. You have no oath registered in Heaven to destroy the government, while I shall have the most solemn one to "preserve, protect and defend" it.

I am loth to close. We are not enemies, but friends. We must not be enemies. Though passion may have strained, it must not break our bonds of affection. The mystic chords of memory, stretching from every battle-field, and patriot grave, to every living heart and hearthstone, all over this broad land, will yet swell the chorus of the Union, when again touched, as surely they will be, by the better angels of our nature.

SUGGESTIONS FOR FURTHER READING

Arthur Bestor, "The American Civil War as a Constitutional Crisis," *American Historical Review*, **69** (1963).

W. J. Cash, *The Mind of the South*, Vintage, New York, 1941.

David Brion Davis, *The Problem of Slavery in Western Culture*, Cornell University Press, Ithaca, 1966.

David Herbert Donald, *Lincoln Reconsidered*, Knopf, New York, 1956.

Allan Nevins, "The Constitution, Slavery and the Territories," *The Gaspar Bacon Lectures on the Constitution of the United States, 1940–1950*, Boston University Press, Boston, 1953.

Phillip S. Paludan, "The American Civil War Considered as a Crisis in Law and Order," *American Historical Review*, **77** (1972).

Charles G. Sellers, Jr. (ed.), *The Southerner as an American*, E. P. Dutton, New York, 1960.

Kenneth M. Stampp, "The Historian and Southern Negro Slavery," *American Historical Review*, **57** (1952).

William R. Taylor, *Cavalier and Yankee*, Harper & Row, New York, 1961.